Windows 7

THE MISSING MANUAL

*The book that
should have been
in the box*®

Windows 7

David Pogue

POGUE PRESS™
O'REILLY®

Beijing • Cambridge • Farnham • Köln • Sebastopol • Taipei • Tokyo

Windows 7: The Missing Manual
by David Pogue

Published by O'Reilly Media, Inc., 1005 Gravenstein Highway North, Sebastopol, CA 95472.

O'Reilly Media books may be purchased for educational, business, or sales promotional use. Online editions are also available for most titles: *safari.oreilly. com.* For more information, contact our corporate/institutional sales department: 800-998-9938 or *corporate@oreilly.com.*

March 2010:   First Edition.

ISBN: 978-0-596-80639-2

[03/10]

Table of Contents

The Missing Credits

About the Author

 David Pogue (author) is the weekly tech columnist for *The New York Times*, Emmy-winning correspondent for *CBS News Sunday Morning*, weekly CNBC contributor, and the creator of the Missing Manual series. He's the author or coauthor of over 50 books, including 26 in this series, six in the *For Dummies* line (including *Macs, Magic, Opera,* and *Classical Music*), two novels, and *The World According to Twitter*. In his other life, David is a former Broadway show conductor, a magician, and a funny public speaker. He lives in Connecticut with his wife and three awesome children.

Links to his columns and funny weekly videos await at *www.davidpogue.com*. He welcomes feedback about his books by email at *david@pogueman.com*.

About the Creative Team

Julie Van Keuren (copy editor, indexer) is a freelance editor, writer, and desktop publisher who runs her "little media empire" from her home in Billings, Montana. In her spare time she enjoys swimming, biking, running, and (hey, why not?) triathlons. She and her husband, M.H., have two sons, Dexter and Michael. Email: *little_media@ yahoo.com*.

Brian Jepson (technical editor, updater of the sections on remote desktop, domains, Registry, and installation) is a senior editor for O'Reilly Media. He cowrote *Mac OS X for Unix Geeks* and has written or edited a number of other tech books. He's the cofounder of Providence Geeks and serves as an all-around geek for AS220, a nonprofit, unjuried, and uncensored arts center in Providence, Rhode Island. Email: *bjepson@oreilly.com*.

Phil Simpson (design and layout) works out of his office in Southbury, Connecticut, where he has had his graphic design business since 1982. He is experienced in many facets of graphic design, including corporate identity/branding, publication design, and corporate and medical communications. Email: *pmsimpson@earthlink.net*.

Acknowledgments

The Missing Manual series is a joint venture between the dream team introduced on these pages and O'Reilly Media. I'm grateful to all of them, and also to a few people who did massive favors for this book. They include Microsoft's Greg Chiemingo, who helped dig up answers to the tweakiest Windows 7 questions; HP and Toshiba for loaning me multitouch PCs to test; O'Reilly's Peter Meyers, Joe Wikert and Chris Nelson, who accommodated my nightmarish schedule like gentlemen; and proofreaders Kellee Katagi, Diana D'Abruzzo, and Jennifer Carney.

In previous editions of this book, I relied on the talents of several guest authors; some of their prose and expertise lives on in this edition. They include author/columnist/teacher/consultant Joli Ballew (Tablet PC and Media Center chapters); author/speaker/Microsoft Certified Trainer C.A. Callahan (Control Panel chapter); and prolific author/newspaper writer Preston Gralla (security, backup and maintenance chapters).

Similarly, in this edition, I was grateful for the assistance of John Pierce, who expertly updated the previous edition's coverage of peripherals, laptops, and printing/faxing. Adam Ornstein scoured the Web to compile every known Windows 7 keyboard shortcut for Appendix D.

Finally, a special nod of thanks to my squadron of meticulous, expert volunteer beta readers, who responded to my invitation via Twitter: Torsten Lyngaas, Betsy Hunter, Ryan Yi, Pathum Karunaratne, Luka Sucic, Henry Koren, Henry Braithwaite, Jesse McCulloch, Scott Winkler, Geroge M. Sun, Chris Smolen, Carlos Rodriguez, Bill Vetter, and Andreas Kleutgens. They're the superstars of crowdsourcing.

Thanks to David Rogelberg for believing in the idea, and above all, to Jennifer, Kelly, Tia, and Jeffrey, who make these books—and everything else—possible.

—David Pogue

The Missing Manual Series

Missing Manual books are superbly written guides to computer products that don't come with printed manuals (which is just about all of them). Each book features a handcrafted index; cross-references to specific page numbers (not just "See Chapter 14"); and RepKover, a detached-spine binding that lets the book lie perfectly flat without the assistance of weights or cinder blocks. Recent and upcoming titles include:

Access 2007: The Missing Manual by Matthew MacDonald

CSS: The Missing Manual by David Sawyer McFarland

Creating Web Sites: The Missing Manual by Matthew MacDonald

Dreamweaver CS4: The Missing Manual by David Sawyer McFarland

eBay: The Missing Manual by Nancy Conner

Excel 2007: The Missing Manual by Matthew MacDonald

Facebook: The Missing Manual by E.A. Vander Veer

FileMaker Pro 10: The Missing Manual by Geoff Coffey and Susan Prosser

Flash CS4: The Missing Manual by Chris Grover

Google Apps: The Missing Manual by Nancy Conner

Google SketchUp: The Missing Manual by Chris Grover

The Internet: The Missing Manual by David Pogue and J.D. Biersdorfer *iMovie '09 & iDVD: The Missing Manual* by David Pogue

iPhone: The Missing Manual, 3rd Edition by David Pogue

iPhoto '09: The Missing Manual by David Pogue

iPod: The Missing Manual, 8th Edition by J.D. Biersdorfer

JavaScript: The Missing Manual by David Sawyer McFarland

Mac OS X Snow Leopard: The Missing Manual by David Pogue

Microsoft Project 2007: The Missing Manual by Bonnie Biafore

Netbooks: The Missing Manual by J.D. Biersdorfer

Office 2007: The Missing Manual by Chris Grover, Matthew MacDonald, and E.A. Vander Veer

Office 2008 for Macintosh: The Missing Manual by Jim Elferdink

Palm Pre: The Missing Manual by Ed Baig

PCs: The Missing Manual by Andy Rathbone

Photoshop CS5: The Missing Manual by Lesa Snider

Photoshop Elements 8 for Windows: The Missing Manual by Barbara Brundage

Photoshop Elements 8 for Mac: The Missing Manual by Barbara Brundage

PowerPoint 2007: The Missing Manual by E.A. Vander Veer

Premiere Elements 8: The Missing Manual by Chris Grover

QuickBase: The Missing Manual by Nancy Conner

QuickBooks 2010: The Missing Manual by Bonnie Biafore

Quicken 2009: The Missing Manual by Bonnie Biafore

Switching to the Mac: The Missing Manual, Snow Leopard Edition by David Pogue

Wikipedia: The Missing Manual by John Broughton

Windows Vista: The Missing Manual by David Pogue

Windows Vista for Starters: The Missing Manual by David Pogue

Word 2007: The Missing Manual by Chris Grover

Living Green: The Missing Manual by Nancy Conner

Your Brain: The Missing Manual by Matthew MacDonald

Buying a Home: The Missing Manual by Nancy Conner

Your Money: The Missing Manual by J.D. Roth

Your Body: The Missing Manual by Matthew MacDonald

Introduction

It must be a great time to work at Microsoft. For the first time in years, the people who work on Windows can hold their heads high in public.

Windows 7 is the best-reviewed, best-loved, and, well, *best* version of Windows ever. Maybe part of the positive reception is because of Win7's contrast to Windows Vista, which was almost universally despised. Maybe Microsoft saw that it was losing market-share ground to Mac OS X and Linux and maybe even Google and, its back to the wall, did some of its best work.

But whatever the reason, Windows 7 is a hit.

It's technically an evolution of Windows Vista, so Windows 7 maintains all the stuff that was good about Vista: stability, security, just enough animation and eye candy to keep things interesting. "Blue screen of death" jokes have almost completely disappeared from the Internet.

Yet Windows 7 fixes what everybody hated about Vista:

- **Speed.** In *PC Magazine's* tests, Windows 7 was 12 to 14 percent faster than Vista. It's especially brisk when starting up, going to sleep, and waking from sleep. A lot of other things have between tweaked for speed, too, like noticing USB gadgets you've plugged in.

- **Hardware requirements.** PCs have steadily grown faster and more powerful since Vista's debut in 2007, but the hardware requirements for Windows 7 are exactly the same. Even those $300 netbooks manage to run Windows 7 without bogging down.

- **Intrusiveness.** Windows Vista used to freak out, with full-screen, show-stopping warning boxes that required your password to continue, at every potential security threat. But Win7 leaves you in peace far more often. In fact, 10 categories of warnings now pile up quietly in a single, unified new control panel called the Action Center, and don't interrupt you at all.

If You're Coming from Windows XP

If you're coming to Windows 7 from Windows Vista, you'll probably land with all guns blazing. Most of the layout, techniques, and functions are very similar.

If you're coming straight to Windows 7 from Windows XP, though, you might feel as though you came home from college to find that your parents turned your old bedroom into a home office. Where is everything? A lot went on while you were away.

This book will treat you, the XP veteran, very well; you'll find frequent references to the major departures from XP. But here's a heads-up to some of the biggest changes:

Security. You could fill several books with information about the security enhancements Microsoft has made to Windows. A lot of them are so technical, they'd make your eyes glaze over, but here's a sampling.

User Account Control is a dialog box that pops up whenever you try to install a program or adjust a PC-wide setting, requesting that you type your password. It means that viruses can no longer make changes to your system without your knowing about it. You'll see one of these dialog boxes, and if you aren't the one trying to make the change, you'll click Cancel instead of Continue. Windows Defender protects your PC from spyware (downloads from the Internet that, unbeknownst to you, send information back to their creators or hijack your Web browser).

A cosmetic overhaul. Thanks to a new design scheme called Aero, window edges are translucent; menus and windows fade away when closed; the taskbar shows actual thumbnail images of the open documents, not just their names; all the icons have been redesigned with a clean, 3-D look and greater resolution; and so on.

(Not everyone gets to enjoy these Aero features. Some PCs are too slow to handle all this graphics processing; on those machines, the transparency and taskbar features are missing.)

The Start menu is a better-organized, two-column affair; that awful XP business of superimposing the All Programs menu on top of the two other columns is long gone.

New programs and features. Lots of new or upgraded software programs and features debuted in Vista. For example:

Instant Search. With one keystroke (the 🎝 key), you open the Start menu's new Search box. It searches your entire PC for the search phrase you type—even inside files that have different names.

New apps. Check out the Snipping Tool (for capturing patches of the screen as graphics, for use in illustrating computer books) and Windows Fax and Scan, one-stop shopping for scanning and faxing. Speech Recognition lets you dictate email and documents, and even control Windows itself, all by voice.

Laptop goodies. You'll find folder synchronization with another computer, more powerful battery-control settings, and a central Mobility Center that governs all laptop features in one place.

New Explorer features. Explorer windows can now have information panels and controls on all four edges, including the Navigation pane (left); task toolbar (top); Preview pane (right); and Details pane (bottom). The new address bar, which displays the path you've taken to burrow into the folder you're now inspecting, is loaded with doodads and clickable spots that make navigation far easier.

All of this is covered in this book, of course—but may this list prepare you for some of the post-XP shocks you're in for.

Microsoft added a few choice new features, not the usual list of several hundred. This time around, the master plan wasn't "Triple the length of the feature list," as usual at Microsoft. Instead, it was "Polish and fix what we've already got."

The formula worked. New color schemes make the whole thing feel lighter and less daunting. New fonts make everything cleaner and sharper. There's a new design consistency, too, featuring plain-English, lowercase, one-click toolbar commands for the things you're most likely to want to do at the moment ("Burn," "New folder," "Share," and so on).

What's New

That's not to say that Microsoft didn't add any new features at all in Win7. Here are some of the highlights:

- **New taskbar.** The taskbar, the traditional row of buttons at the bottom of the screen (representing your open programs), has been given the most radical overhaul in years. Now it resembles the Dock on the Mac: It holds the icons for open programs *and* icons you've dragged there for quick access.

  If you point to a program's icon, Triscuit-sized miniatures of its windows pop up. You can either click one, to bring that window forward, or you can just run your cursor across them; as you do so, the corresponding full-size windows flash to the fore. All of this means easier navigation in a screen awash with window clutter.

- **Jump lists.** Another taskbar feature. When you right-click a taskbar icon, you get a new, specialized list of shortcuts called a jump list. It maintains a list of that program's most recently or frequently opened documents, and offers a few other important program-related commands too.

- **New window treatments.** Now Windows does more for windows. You can drag a window's edge against the top or side edge of your screen to make it fill the whole screen or half of it. You can give a window a little shake with the mouse to minimize all *other* windows when you need a quick look at your desktop. The Show Desktop button has been reborn as a sliver at the right end of the taskbar—a one-click shortcut for hiding all windows instantly.

- **A new folder concept: Libraries.** *Libraries* are like meta-folders: They display the contents of up to 50 *other* folders, which may be scattered all over your system or even all over your network.

  Libraries make it easy to keep project files together, to back them up en masse, or to share them with other PCs on the network.

- **Effortless networking.** Windows has always been good at networking computers together—but Microsoft has never been especially good at making that easy for the average non-techie. That all changes with Windows 7's HomeGroups feature.

  You just enter a one-time password on each machine in your house. Once that's done, each computer can see the photos, music, printers, and documents on all the other ones. At no time do you have to mess with accounts, permissions, or passwords. Obviously, homegroups aren't ideal for government agencies or NASA—but if it's just you and a couple of family members, the convenience of sharing your printers and music collections may well be more important than big-deal security barriers.

- **Wild music sharing.** Windows Media Player lets you listen to the music from one PC while seated at another one—across the room, across the network, or even across the Internet.

- **Better plug-and-play.** Microsoft's little driver slave drivers were busy during the three-year gestation of Windows 7. Thousands more gadgets now work automatically when you plug them in, without your having to worry about drivers or software installation. The new Device Stage window even shows a picture of the camera/phone/printer/scanner you've just plugged in, describes it for you, and offers links to its most useful functions.

- **Multitouch.** Does the world really want multitouch laptops and desktop PCs that work like an iPhone? It's too soon to tell, but Microsoft is ready for the new wave of multitouch screens. Windows 7 recognizes the basic two-finger "gestures": pinching and zooming (to shrink or enlarge a photo or a Web page), rotating (for a photo), dragging a finger (to scroll), and so on.

Other new-and-improved items lurk around every corner; among other improvements, somebody with a degree in English has swept through every corner and rewritten buttons, links, and dialog boxes for better clarity.

Note: Microsoft has taken a bunch of stuff away, too. Most of it is complicated clutter, introduced in Vista, that nobody wound up using. The not-so-dearly departed features include Stacking in desktop windows, the Quick Launch toolbar, the Sidebar, and Offline Favorites.

If you're among the few, the proud, who actually used these features, don't despair; this book proposes replacements for all of them.

The Bummers

Windows 7 is pretty great, but it's not all sunshine and bunnies. You should know up front that you're in for a few rude surprises:

Upgrading from Windows XP

Upgrading your current PC from Vista is easy. But upgrading from Windows XP involves a clean install—moving all your programs and files off the hard drive, installing Windows 7, and then copying everything back on again.

Clearly, Microsoft hopes that XP holdouts won't even bother, that they'll just get Windows 7 preinstalled on a new PC.

The Matrix of Windows versions lives on

You thought Windows XP was bad, with its two different versions (Home and Pro)?

Like Windows Vista, Windows 7 comes in a raft of different versions, each with a different set of features at a different price.

Microsoft says each version is perfectly attuned to a different kind of customer, as though each edition had been somehow conceived differently. In fact, though, the main thing that distinguishes the editions is the suite of programs that comes with each one.

Each main heading in this book bears a handy cheat sheet, like this:

Home Premium • Professional • Enterprise • Ultimate

This line lets you know at a glance whether or not that feature discussion applies to you.

Meanwhile, if a description of this or that feature makes you salivate, fear not. Microsoft is delighted to let you upgrade your copy of Windows 7 to a more expensive edition, essentially "unlocking" features for a fee. See page 268 for details.

Here, for the record, is what they are:

- **Starter.** This stripped-down version of Windows 7 is what you'll probably get preinstalled on a netbook (that is, a lightweight, inexpensive laptop that doesn't have a CD/DVD drive).

  The Starter edition lacks Aero (the suite of animations, window-manipulation gestures, pop-up taskbar thumbnails, and other eye candy); Windows Media Center; DVD playback; streaming of music and video to or from other computers; the ability to connect a second monitor; XP Mode for accommodating older programs; and a 64-bit edition. The Starter version also doesn't let you change your desktop picture or your visual design scheme, or switch accounts without logging off.

  Sounds like a lot of missing stuff. But the truth is, none of those things diminish the things you'd want to do on a netbook: emailing, surfing the Web, writing, working with photos, and so on.

Note: Perhaps surprisingly, Starter doesn't actually save you any hard drive space. Every copy of Windows 7 is actually a complete Ultimate edition on the hard drive—but with features turned off. That's how Microsoft is able to pull off the instant-upgrade feature known as the Anytime Upgrade. Choose its name from the Start menu, pay a few bucks at a Web site, and presto: Your PC has just acquired one of the fancier editions of Windows 7.

- **Home Basic.** In the Vista days, the Home Basic edition was the cheapest and most bare-bones edition sold in the U.S. But not anymore. Oh, it's still the cheapest and most bare-bones—but now it's sold only in third-world countries.

- **Home Premium.** This is the one you're most likely to get when you, a normal person, buy a single PC. It's the mainstream consumer edition.

- **Professional.** Has all the features of Home Premium, but adds Presentation Mode (shuts off anything that might interrupt during PowerPoint slideshows); the ability to join a corporate network; the Encrypting File System (lets you encode certain files or folders for security); XP Mode; and location-aware printing.

(This was called the Business edition in the Vista days.)

Note: In the Vista days, the Home editions offered some features that the corporate editions lacked, and vice versa. Now, each more expensive edition includes all the features of the previous one. No more must corporate drones have to miss out on the joy of Windows Media Center.

• **Enterprise, Ultimate.** Same version, just sold different ways. (Enterprise is sold directly to corporations; Ultimate is sold in stores.) Has everything Professional has, plus it can run in multiple languages at once, has even more fancy networking features, can run Unix programs, and can use a feature called BitLocker to encrypt your hard drive for total security.

Note: As an Ultimate owner, you no longer get access to a special suite of free bonus goodies exclusive to your version, as you did in the Vista days.

• **N and K editions.** These are special editions sold in Europe and Korea, respectively, to comply with antitrust laws there. They're identical to the Home Premium, Professional, and Ultimate editions—but they have Windows Media Player and DVD Maker stripped out. (You can download those missing free apps at any time, so what was the point? What a waste of everyone's time!)

To make matters even more complicated, each version except Starter is available in both 32-bit or 64-bit flavors (see page 263 for what this means). Good luck figuring out why some cool Windows 7 feature isn't on your PC.

Missing Apps

Out of fear of antitrust headaches, Microsoft has stripped Windows 7 of a bunch of programs that usually come with mainstream operating systems. Believe it or not, Windows 7 doesn't come with a calendar, an address book, photo management, video editing, instant messaging, or even email!

That's not to say that Microsoft is leaving you without these programs entirely; they're available in a single, free, downloadable suite called Windows Live Essentials. One click and you're done—not a big deal. (The company you buy your PC from may even preinstall them.)

But you may be confused at first, especially if you upgrade your Vista machine to Windows 7—the installer actually *deletes* your copies of Windows Mail, Movie Maker, Calendar, Contacts, and Photo Gallery! (Mercifully, it preserves your data.)

Windows still has some long-standing frustrations, too. It's still copy-protected, it still offers way too many ways to get to a certain feature, it still requires antivirus software. And it's still an enormous, seething, vast hunk of 50 million lines of computer code that must appeal equally well to a third-grader and a NASA systems analyst; sooner or later, everybody runs into parts of it they could do without.

On the other hand, it's still Windows in a good way, too. It's still the 800-pound gorilla of the computer world, so it's compatible with the world's largest catalog of programs, games, and add-on gadgets.

About This Book

Despite the many improvements in Windows over the years, one feature hasn't improved a bit: Microsoft's documentation. In fact, Windows 7 comes with no printed user guide at all. To learn about the thousands of pieces of software that make up this operating system, you're expected to read the online help screens.

Unfortunately, as you'll quickly discover, these help screens are tersely written, offer very little technical depth, and lack examples. You can't even mark your place, underline, or read them in the bathroom. Some of the help screens are actually on Microsoft's Web site; you can't see them without an Internet connection. Too bad if you're on a plane somewhere with your laptop.

The purpose of this book, then, is to serve as the manual that should have accompanied Windows. In these pages, you'll find step-by-step instructions for using almost every Windows feature, including those you may not even have understood, let alone mastered.

System Requirements for Your Brain

Windows 7: The Missing Manual is designed to accommodate readers at every technical level (except system administrators, who will be happier with a very different sort of book).

The primary discussions are written for advanced-beginner or intermediate PC users. But if you're a first-time Windows user, special sidebar articles called "Up To Speed" provide the introductory information you need to understand the topic at hand. If you're an advanced PC user, on the other hand, keep your eye out for similar shaded boxes called "Power Users' Clinic." They offer more technical tips, tricks, and shortcuts for the veteran PC fan.

About the Outline

This book is divided into seven parts, each containing several chapters:

- Part 1, **The Desktop,** covers everything you see on the screen when you turn on a Windows 7 computer: icons, windows, menus, scroll bars, the taskbar, the Recycle Bin, shortcuts, the Start menu, shortcut menus, and so on. It also covers the system-wide, instantaneous Search feature.

- Part 2, **Windows 7 Software,** is dedicated to the proposition that an operating system is little more than a launch pad for *programs*. Chapter 6 describes how to work with applications and documents in Windows—how to launch them, switch among them, swap data between them, use them to create and open files, and so on—and how to use the microprograms called *gadgets*.

This part also offers an item-by-item discussion of the individual software nuggets that make up this operating system. These include not just the items in your Control Panel, but also the long list of free programs that Microsoft threw in: Windows Media Player, WordPad, Speech Recognition, and so on.

- Part 3, **Windows Online**, covers all the special Internet-related features of Windows, including setting up your Internet account, Windows Live Mail (for email), Internet Explorer 8 (for Web browsing), and so on. The massive Chapter 10 also covers Windows's dozens of Internet fortification features: the firewall, anti-spyware software, parental controls, and on and on.

- Part 4, **Pictures, Music, & TV**, takes you into multimedia land. Here are chapters that cover the Windows Live Photo Gallery picture editing and organizing program; Media Player 12 (music playback); and Media Center (TV recording and playback).

- Part 5, **Hardware and Peripherals**, describes the operating system's relationship with equipment you can attach to your PC—scanners, cameras, disks, printers, and so on. Special chapters describe faxing, fonts, laptops, and tablet PC touch-screen machines.

- Part 6, **PC Health,** explores Windows 7's greatly beefed-up backup and troubleshooting tools. It also describes some advanced hard drive formatting tricks and offers tips for making your PC run faster and better.

- Part 7, **Networking & Homegroups,** is for the millions of households and offices that contain more than one PC. If you work at home or in a small office, these chapters show you how to build your own network; if you work in a corporation where some highly paid professional network geek is on hand to do the troubleshooting, these chapters show you how to exploit Windows's considerable networking prowess. File sharing, accounts and passwords, and the new HomeGroups insta-networking feature are here, too.

At the end of the book, four appendixes provide a guide to installing or upgrading to Windows 7, an introduction to editing the Registry, a master list of Windows keyboard shortcuts, and the "Where'd It Go?" Dictionary, which lists every feature Microsoft moved or deleted on the way to Windows 7.

About→These→Arrows

Throughout this book, and throughout the Missing Manual series, you'll find sentences like this: "Open the Start→Computer→Local Disk (C:)→Windows folder." That's shorthand for a much longer instruction that directs you to open three nested icons in sequence, like this: "Click the Start menu to open it. Click Computer in the Start menu. Inside the Computer window is a disk icon labeled Local Disk (C:); double-click it to open it. Inside *that* window is yet *another* icon called Windows. Double-click to open it, too."

Similarly, this kind of arrow shorthand helps to simplify the business of choosing commands in menus. "Choose Start→Control Panel" means to open the Start menu, and then click the Control Panel command in it. Figure I-1 shows the story.

Figure I-1:
In this book, arrow notations help to simplify folder and menu instructions. For example, "Choose Start→ Control Panel→ AutoPlay" is a more compact way of saying, "Click the Start button. When the Start menu opens, point to Control Panel; without clicking, now slide to the right onto AutoPlay," as shown here.

The Very Basics

To get the most out of Windows with the least frustration, it helps to be familiar with the following concepts and terms. If you're new to Windows, be prepared to encounter these words and phrases over and over again—in the built-in Windows help, in computer magazines, and in this book.

Windows Defined

Windows is an *operating system,* the software that controls your computer. It's designed to serve you in several ways:

- **It's a launching bay.** At its heart, Windows is a home base, a remote-control clicker that lets you call up the various software programs (applications) you use to do work or kill time. When you get right down to it, applications are the real reason you bought a PC.

Windows 7 is a well-stocked software pantry unto itself; for example, it comes with such basic programs as a Web browser, a simple word processor, and a calculator. And a suite of games, too. (Chapter 7 covers all these freebie programs.)

If you were stranded on a desert island, the built-in Windows programs could suffice for everyday operations. But if you're like most people, sooner or later, you'll buy and install more software. That's one of the luxuries of using Windows: You can choose from a staggering number of add-on programs. Whether you're a left-handed beekeeper or a German-speaking nun, some company somewhere is selling Windows software designed just for you, its target audience.

- **It's a file cabinet.** Every application on your machine, as well as every document you create, is represented on the screen by an *icon,* a little picture that symbolizes the underlying file or container. You can organize these icons into onscreen file folders. You can make backups (safety copies) by dragging file icons onto a flash drive or blank CD, or send files to people by email. You can also trash icons you no longer need by dragging them onto the Recycle Bin icon.

- **It's your equipment headquarters.** What you can actually see of Windows is only the tip of the iceberg. An enormous chunk of Windows is behind-the-scenes plumbing that controls the various functions of your computer—its modem, screen, keyboard, printer, and so on.

The Right Mouse Button is King

One of the most important features of Windows isn't on the screen—it's in your hand. The standard mouse or trackpad has two mouse buttons. You use the left one to click buttons, highlight text, and drag things around on the screen.

When you click the right button, however, a *shortcut menu* appears onscreen, like the one shown at left in Figure I-3. Get into the habit of *right-clicking* things—icons, folders, disks, text inside a paragraph, buttons on your menu bar, pictures on a Web page, and so on. The commands that appear on the shortcut menu will make you much more productive and lead you to discover handy functions you never knew existed.

This is a big deal: Microsoft's research suggests that nearly 75 percent of Windows users don't use the right mouse button and therefore miss hundreds of timesaving shortcuts. Part of the rationale behind Windows 7's redesign is putting these functions out in the open. Even so, many more shortcuts remain hidden under your right mouse button.

Tip: Microsoft doesn't discriminate against left-handers…much. You can swap the functions of the right and left mouse buttons easily enough.

Choose Start→Control Panel. Click "Classic view." Open the Mouse icon. When the Mouse Properties dialog box opens, click the Buttons tab, and then turn on "Switch primary and secondary buttons." Then click OK. Windows now assumes that you want to use the left mouse button as the one that produces shortcut menus.

Wizards = Interviews

A *wizard* is a series of screens that walk you through the task you're trying to complete. Wizards make configuration and installation tasks easier by breaking them down into smaller, more easily digested steps. Figure I-2 offers an example.

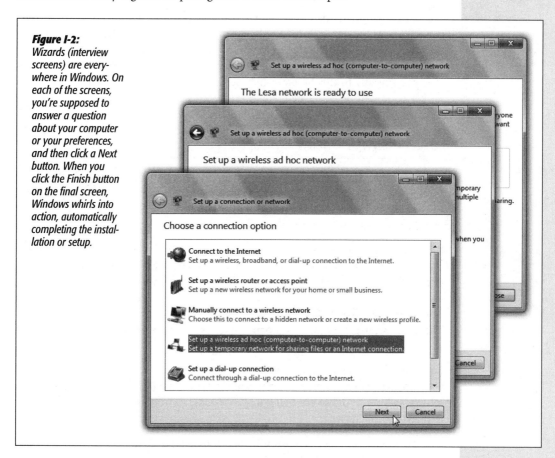

Figure I-2:
Wizards (interview screens) are everywhere in Windows. On each of the screens, you're supposed to answer a question about your computer or your preferences, and then click a Next button. When you click the Finish button on the final screen, Windows whirls into action, automatically completing the installation or setup.

There's More Than One Way to Do Everything

No matter what setting you want to adjust, no matter what program you want to open, Microsoft has provided five or six different ways to do it. For example, here are the various ways to delete a file: Press the Delete key; choose File→Delete; drag the file icon onto the Recycle Bin; or right-click the filename, and then choose Delete from the shortcut menu.

Pessimists grumble that there are too many paths to every destination, making it much more difficult to learn Windows. Optimists point out that this abundance of approaches means that almost everyone will find, and settle on, a satisfying method for each task. Whenever you find a task irksome, remember that you have other options.

You Can Use the Keyboard for Everything

In earlier versions of Windows, underlined letters appeared in the names of menus and dialog boxes. These underlines were clues for people who found it faster to do something by pressing keys than by using the mouse.

The underlines are hidden in Windows 7, at least in disk and folder windows. (They may still appear in your individual software programs.) If you miss them, you can make them reappear by pressing the Alt key, Tab key, or an arrow key whenever the menu bar is visible. (When you're operating menus, you can release the Alt key immediately after pressing it.) In this book, in help screens, and in computer magazines, you'll see key combinations indicated like this: Alt+S (or Alt+ whatever the letter key is).

Note: In some Windows programs, in fact, the entire menu bar is gone until you press Alt (or F10). That includes everyday Explorer windows.

Once the underlines are visible, you can open a menu by pressing the underlined letter (F for the File menu, for example). Once the menu is open, press the underlined letter key that corresponds to the menu command you want. Or press Esc to close the menu without doing anything. (In Windows, the Esc key always means *cancel* or *stop*.)

If choosing a menu command opens a dialog box, you can trigger its options by pressing Alt along with the underlined letters. (Within dialog boxes, you can't press and release Alt; you have to hold it down while typing the underlined letter.)

The Start Menu is Fastest

The fastest way to almost anything in Windows 7 is the Search box at the bottom of the Start menu.

For example, to open Outlook, you can open the Start menu and type *outlook*. To get to the password-changing screen, you can type *password*. To adjust your network settings, *network*. And so on. *Display. Speakers. Keyboard. BitLocker. Excel. Photo Gallery. Firefox.* Whatever.

Each time, Windows does an uncanny job of figuring out what you want and highlighting it in the results list in the Start menu, usually right at the top.

Here's the thing, though: You don't need the mouse to open the Start menu. You can just tap the 🏁 key.

You also don't need to type the whole thing. If you want the Sticky Notes program, *sti* is usually all you have to type. In other words, without ever lifting your hands from the keyboard, you can hit 🏁, type *sti*, and hit Enter—and you've opened Sticky Notes. Really, really fast.

Now, there is almost always a manual, mouse-clickable way to get at the same function in Windows—in fact, there are usually about six of them. Here, for example, is how you might open the Device Manager, a window that lists all the components of your PC. First, the mouse way:

1. **Open the Start menu. In the right-side column, click Control Panel.**

   The Control Panel opens, teeming with options.

2. **Click "Hardware and Sound."**

   Now a second Control Panel screen appears, filled with options having to do with external gadgets.

3. **Click Device Manager.**

   The Device Manager dialog box opens.

OK then. Here, by contrast, is how you'd get to exactly the same place using the Start menu method:

1. **Press ⊞ to open the Start menu. Type enough of *device manager* to make Device Manger appear highlighted in the results list; press Enter.**

   The Device Manager appears. One step instead of three.

Now, you're forgiven for exclaiming, "What!? Get to things by typing? I thought the whole idea behind the Windows revolution was to eliminate the DOS-age practice of typing commands!"

Well, not exactly. Typing has always offered a faster, more efficient way to getting places and doing things—what everyone hated was the *memorizing* of commands to type.

UP TO SPEED

Scrolling: The Missing Manual

These days, PC monitors are bigger than ever—but so are the Web pages and documents they display.

Scroll bars, of course, are the strips that may appear at the right side and/or bottom of a window. The scroll bar signals you that the window isn't big enough to reveal all of its contents.

Click the arrows at each end of a scroll bar to move slowly through the window, or drag the rectangular handle (the thumb) to move faster. (The position of the thumb in the scroll bar reflects your relative position in the entire window or document.) You can quickly move to a specific part of the window by holding the mouse button down on the scroll bar where you want the thumb to be. The scroll bar rapidly scrolls to the desired location and then stops.

Scrolling is such a frequently needed skill, though, that all kinds of other scrolling gadgets have cropped up.

Your mouse probably has a little wheel on the top. You can scroll in most programs just by turning the wheel with your finger, even if your cursor is nowhere near the scroll bar. You can turbo-scroll by dragging the mouse upward or downward while keeping the wheel pressed down inside the window.

Laptops often have some kind of scrolling gizmo, too. Maybe you have an actual roller, or maybe the trackpad offers drag-here-to-scroll strips on the right side and across the bottom.

And if you have one of the new breed of touchscreen computers, of course, you can scroll just by dragging around with a finger (or two fingers, on multitouch screens).

Of course, keyboard addicts should note that you can scroll without using the mouse at all. Press the Page Up or Page Down keys to scroll the window by one window-full, or use the ↑ or ↓ keys keys to scroll one line at a time.

But the Start menu requires no memorization; that's the beauty of it. You can be vague. You can take a guess. And almost every time, the Start menu knows what you want, and offers it in the list.

For that reason, this book almost always provides the most direct route to a certain program or function: the one that involves the Start menu's Search box. There's always a longer, slower, mousier alternative, but hey: This book is plenty fat already, and those rainforests aren't getting any bigger.

About Shift+Clicking

Here's another bit of shorthand you'll find in this book (and others): instructions to *Shift+click* something. That means you should hold down the Shift key, and then click before releasing the key. If you understand that much, the meaning of instructions like "Ctrl+click" and "Alt+click" should be clear.

You Could Spend a Lifetime Changing Properties

You can't write an operating system that's all things to all people, but Microsoft has certainly tried. You can change almost every aspect of the way Windows looks and works. You can replace the gray backdrop of the screen (the *wallpaper*) with your favorite photograph, change the typeface used for the names of your icons, or set up a particular program to launch automatically every time you turn on the PC.

When you want to change some *general* behavior of your PC, like how it connects to the Internet, how soon the screen goes black to save power, or how quickly a letter repeats when you hold down a key, you use the Control Panel window (described in Chapter 8).

Many other times, however, you may want to adjust the settings of only one particular element of the machine, such as the hard drive, the Recycle Bin, or a particular application. In those cases, simply right-click the corresponding icon. In the resulting shortcut menu, you'll often find a command called Properties. When you click it, a

---

UP TO SPEED

The Service Pack Story

Microsoft dribbles out a steady stream of Windows bug fixes, touchups, driver updates, and security patches. If you have Windows Update turned on (page 662), then you get them all automatically, or nearly so, as they're released.

Microsoft also periodically gathers up all of these little touchups into a much bigger, all-in-one, free update called a Service Pack.

Service Packs show up maybe once a year, or even less. Each one contains hundreds of tiny adjustments and tweaks,

nearly all of them invisible to you. They're under-the-hood changes, mostly for the sake of security and compatibility. Copying files might be a little bit faster in some situations, a frustrating feature might be addressed, drivers might be updated, and so on.

Should you install Windows 7 SP1 when, inevitably, it comes along? Probably. You gain a lot of invisible security and compatibility improvements; on balance, it's progress.

---

dialog box appears, containing settings or information about that object, as shown in Figure I-3, right.

Tip: As a shortcut to the Properties command, just highlight an icon and then press Alt+Enter.

It's also worth getting to know how to operate *tabbed dialog boxes,* like the one shown in Figure I-3. These are windows that contain so many options, Microsoft has had to split them up into separate panels, or *tabs.* To reveal a new set of options, just click a different tab (called General, Tools, Hardware, Sharing, Security, Previous Versions, and Quota in Figure I-3). These tabs are designed to resemble the tabs at the top of file folders.

Tip: You can switch tabs without using the mouse by pressing Ctrl+Tab (to "click" the next tab to the right) or Ctrl+Shift+Tab (for the previous tab).

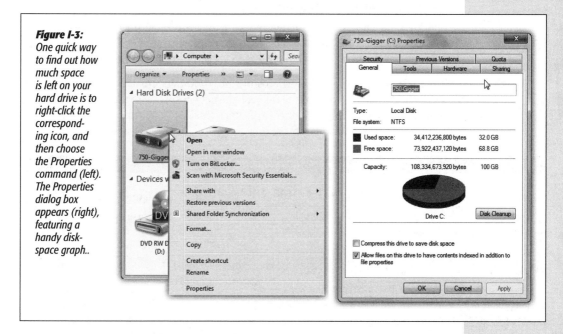

Figure I-3:
One quick way to find out how much space is left on your hard drive is to right-click the corresponding icon, and then choose the Properties command (left). The Properties dialog box appears (right), featuring a handy disk-space graph..

Every Piece of Hardware Requires Software

When computer geeks talk about their *drivers,* they're not talking about their chauffeurs (unless they're Bill Gates); they're talking about the controlling software required by every hardware component of a PC.

The driver is the translator between your PC's brain and the equipment attached to it: mouse, keyboard, screen, DVD drive, scanner, digital camera, palmtop, and so on. Without the correct driver software, the corresponding piece of equipment doesn't work at all.

When you buy one of these gadgets, you receive a CD containing the driver software. If the included driver software works fine, then you're all set. If your gadget acts up, however, remember that equipment manufacturers regularly release improved (read: less buggy) versions of these software chunks. (You generally find such updates on the manufacturers' Web sites.)

Fortunately, Windows 7 comes with drivers for over 15,000 components, saving you the trouble of scavenging for them on a disk or on the Internet. Most popular gizmos from brand-name companies work automatically when you plug them in—no CD installation required (Chapter 18).

It's Not Meant to Be Overwhelming

Windows has an absolutely staggering array of features. You can burrow six levels down, dialog box through dialog box, and never come to the end of it. There are enough programs, commands, and help screens to keep you studying the rest of your life.

It's crucial to remember that Microsoft's programmers created Windows in modules—the digital-photography team here, the networking team there—with different audiences in mind. The idea, of course, was to make sure that no subset of potential customers would find a feature lacking.

GEM IN THE ROUGH

Not Your Father's Keyboard

Keyboards built especially for using Windows contain some extra keys on the bottom row:

On the left, between the Ctrl and Alt keys, you may find a key bearing the Windows logo (⊞). No, this isn't just a tiny Microsoft advertising moment; you can press this key to open the Start menu without having to use the mouse. (On desktop PCs, the Windows key is usually on the bottom row; on laptops, it's sometimes at the top of the keyboard.)

On the right, you may find a duplicate ⊞ key, as well as a key whose icon depicts a tiny menu, complete with a microscopic cursor pointing to a command. Press this key to simulate a right-click at the current location of your cursor.

Even better, the ⊞ key offers a number of useful functions when you press it in conjunction with other keys. For a complete list, see Appendix D, the Master Windows 7 Keystroke List. But here are a few important ones to get you started:

⊞ opens the Start menu.

⊞+**number key** opens the corresponding icon on the taskbar, left to right (⊞+1, ⊞+2, etc.).

⊞+**D** hides or shows all your application windows (ideal for jumping to the desktop for a bit of housekeeping).

⊞+**E** opens an Explorer window.

⊞+**F** opens the Search window.

⊞+**L** locks your screen. Everything you were working on is hidden by the login screen; your password is required to get past it.

⊞+**Tab** cycles through all open windows using the three-dimensional Flip 3D feature.

But if *you* don't have a digital camera, a network, or whatever, there's absolutely nothing wrong with ignoring everything you encounter on the screen that isn't relevant to your setup and work routine. Not even Microsoft's CEO uses every single feature of Windows.

About MissingManuals.com

To get the most out of this book, visit *www.missingmanuals.com*. Click the "Missing CD-ROM" link—and then this book's title—to reveal a neat, organized, chapter-by-chapter list of the shareware and freeware mentioned in this book.

The Web site also offers corrections and updates to the book. (To see them, click the book's title, and then click View/Submit Errata.) In fact, please submit such corrections and updates yourself! In an effort to keep the book as up to date and accurate as possible, each time O'Reilly prints more copies of this book, I'll make any confirmed corrections you've suggested. I'll also note such changes on the Web site so that you can mark important corrections into your own copy of the book, if you like.

Part One:
The Windows 7 Desktop

1

Getting Started, Desktop, & Start Menu

Microsoft wants to make one thing perfectly clear: Compared with Windows XP, Windows 7 isn't just a whole new ball game—it's practically a different sport. It's different on the surface, under the hood, and everywhere in between. (It's so different, in fact, that this book includes an appendix called "Where'd It Go?" which lets you look up a familiar Windows landmark and figure out where Microsoft stuck it in Windows 7.)

If you're moving to Windows 7 from Vista, well, your new world won't be *quite* as much of a shock. But the landscape still has shifted quite a bit.

Either way, it's hard to predict exactly what you'll see at the fateful moment when the Windows 7 screen first lights up on your monitor. You may see a big welcome screen bearing the logo of Dell or whomever; it may be the Windows 7 Setup Wizard (Appendix A); or it may be the *login* screen, where you're asked to sign in by clicking your name in a list. (Skip to page 737 for details on logging in.)

The best place to start, though, might be the shining majesty of the Getting Started window shown in Figure 1-1. If it doesn't open automatically, choose Start→Getting Started.

Getting Started
All Versions

Getting Started is supposed to be an antidote to the moment of dizzy disorientation you'd otherwise feel the first time you fired up Windows 7. It's basically a window full of links to useful places in the Windows empire. What's confusing is that just clicking one of these promising-looking buttons ("Back up your files"? Hey, yeah!) doesn't actually do anything except change the billboard in the top part of the window. You have to *double-click* to open up the control panel or program you need to make changes.

Figure 1-1:
Getting Started offers links to various useful corners of the operating system. Most are designed to help you set up a new PC. (Click once to read a description, and then double-click to open the link.)

Here are a few highlights:

- **Go online to find out what's new in Windows 7.** Sure enough: Takes you to a Web page describing the new features.

- **Use a homegroup to share with other computers in your home.** One of Microsoft's most important promises is that it's finally simple to set up a home network if you have more than one PC. By all means, double-click here to get started, but have Chapter 26 in front of you.

- **Back up your files.** Fires up the Backup and Restore Center, which is described on page 688.

- **Personalize Windows.** Sure, sure, eventually you'll be plotting rocket trajectories and mapping the genome—but let's not kid ourselves. The first order of business is decorating: choosing your screen saver, replacing the desktop background (wallpaper), choosing a different cursor shape, adjusting your monitor resolution, and so on. Double-click here to open the appropriate control panel.

- **Choose when to be notified about changes to your computer.** Windows 7 has tamed one of Vista's most ornery features: User Account Control (otherwise known as "the infuriating nag box that pops up every time I make a change, asking, 'Are you sure?' 'Are you sure?'"). However, UAC still gets in your face from time to time. Double-click here to open the User Account Control settings so you can tone it down.

- **Add new users to your computer.** If you're the lord of the manor, the sole user of this computer, then you can ignore this little item. But if you and other family members, students, or workers *share* this computer, you'll want to consult Chapter 23 about how to set up a separate *account* (name, password, and working environment) for each person.

- **Transfer files and settings from another computer.** This program, now called Windows Easy Transfer, is a beefed-up version of the old Files and Settings Transfer Wizard. Its purpose is to transfer files and settings from an older PC, and it's described on page 830.

- **Go online to get Windows Live Essentials.** Weird as it may seem, Windows 7 is the first mainstream operating system in recent memory to arrive *completely stripped down.* It comes with no email program, no photo or video editing app, no chat program, no calendar or address book. (In fact, if you upgraded from Vista, you'll discover that the Windows 7 installer has actually *deleted* the Microsoft apps you used to have for these purposes! Big whoops!)

  There's actually a good reason (well, OK, a dumb reason) for Microsoft's decision: Its lawyers were attempting to protect the company from more antitrust lawsuits. Whatever. The point is that if you want these standard, free programs, then you have to download them yourself by clicking this link. Details are at the beginning of Chapter 7.

Note: You may not have to do this manual downloading. Some PC companies, like Dell, preinstall these apps when they sell you a new PC.

- **Change the size of the text on your screen.** Over-40-year-olds, you know who you are. Now, with one click, you can make *all* text in *all* programs 25 or 50 percent larger, thanks to this handy option.

To get rid of the Getting Started window, click its Close box—or press Alt+F4, the universal Windows keystroke for "close this window."

The Windows Desktop—Now with Aero!

Home Premium • Professional • Enterprise • Ultimate

Once you've recovered from the excitement of Getting Started, you get your first glimpse of the full Windows 7 desktop (Figure 1-2). If you'd rather not go through life staring at the Windows logo, then by all means choose one of the much more attractive Windows 7 desktop pictures, as described in Chapter 4.

All the usual Windows landmarks are here—the Start menu, the taskbar, and the Recycle Bin—but they've been given an extreme makeover, especially if you're used to Windows XP.

What you're seeing is the latest face of Windows, known to fans as *Aero*. (It supposedly stands for Authentic, Energetic, Reflective, and Open, but you can't help suspecting that somebody at Microsoft retrofitted those words to fit the initials.) It debuted in Windows Vista, and it's been refined in Windows 7.

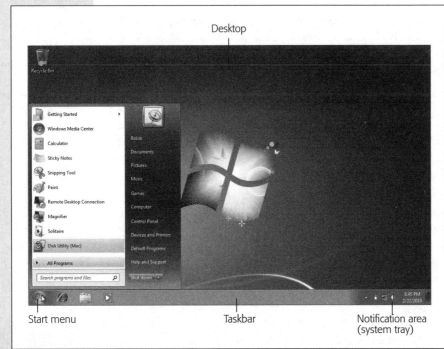

Desktop

Start menu   Taskbar   Notification area
                                                         (system tray)

Figure 1-2:
There are some gorgeous new desktop pictures in Windows 7– Microsoft evidently endured one Teletubbies joke too many during the Windows XP era–although the factory-installed wallpaper isn't among them.

See page 179 for details on choosing a better-looking background.

NOSTALGIA CORNER

Restoring the Desktop Icons

The Windows 7 desktop is awfully pretty–but awfully barren. If you're a longtime Windows veteran, you may miss the handy desktop icons that once provided quick access to important locations on your PC, like My Computer, My Documents, My Network Places, and Control Panel.

You can still get to these locations (they're listed in your Start menu), but opening them requires two mouse clicks–an egregious expenditure of caloric effort.

However, it's easy enough to put these icons back on the desktop. To do so, right-click a blank spot on the desktop;

from the shortcut menu, choose Personalize. (This option isn't available in the Starter edition of Windows 7.)

Now the Personalization dialog box appears. In the Tasks pane on the left side, click "Change desktop icons." In the resulting dialog box, checkboxes for common desktop icons now await your summons: Computer, Network, Recycle Bin, Control Panel, and User's Files (that is, your Personal folder–see page 33).

Turn on the ones you'd like to install to the desktop and then click OK. Your old favorite icons are now back where they once belonged.

If you're into this kind of thing, here's the complete list of what makes Aero, Aero:

- The edges of windows are thicker than they were in the XP days (for easier targeting with your mouse). Parts of the Start menu and window edges are transparent. Windows and dialog boxes cast subtle shadows on the background, as though they're floating.

- A new, bigger, more modern font is used for menus and labels.

- When you point to a window button without clicking, the button "lights up." The Minimize and Maximize buttons glow blue; the Close button glows red.

- The *default* button in a dialog box—the one Microsoft thinks you really want, like Save or Print—pulses gently, using fading color intensity to draw your eye.

- Little animations liven up the works, especially when you minimize, maximize, or close a window.

Aero isn't just looks, either—it also includes a couple of features, like Flip 3D and live taskbar icons. You can read about these two useful features in Chapter 2.

UP TO SPEED

The Windows Experience Index

Quick—which computer is better, an AMD Turion 64 ML-34 processor at 1.80 gigahertz but only 512 megs of RAM, or a Core Duo 2.0 gigahertz with 1 gig of RAM but only a Radeon Xpress 200M graphics card?

If you know the answer offhand, you shouldn't be reading a book about Windows; you should be writing your own darned book.

The point is, of course, that today's Windows is extremely demanding. It craves horsepower, speed, and memory. But Microsoft doesn't really expect the average person, or even the average IT manager, to know at a glance whether a particular PC is up to the Windows 7 challenge.

That's why Windows analyzes the guts of your computer and boils the results down to a single numerical rating, on a scale of 1 to 7.9 To find out yours, open the Start menu; start typing the word *experience* until you see "Check the Windows Experience Index" in the results list. Click that link. On the resulting screen, click "Rate this computer." (Or if you've just installed new components into your PC, thereby making the

index out of date, click Refresh Now.) After a minute or so, you'll see your PC's horsepower scores.

The final score is the lowest of any of the subscores. For example, if your memory, hard drive, and graphics all get scores over 4, but your processor's score is only 3.1, then your overall score is 3.1, which makes it easy to spot the bottleneck.

A score of 7.9 is the best; it means you'll be able to run all of Windows's features well and fast. You need a score of at least 4 to play and edit high-definition video. A 3 is the minimum for running Aero (page 23). A 1 is the worst; Windows will be dog slow unless you turn off some of the eye-candy features, as described on page 173.

True, finding out that the computer you bought last year for $2,800 is now worth only a measly 2 on the performance scale could deal your ego quite a bruise.

Fortunately, Microsoft also offers the Windows 7 Upgrade Advisor (page 268). This free program reveals your PC's report card *before* you install Windows 7, so at least you can avoid getting a rude surprise.

The Aero design may not actually be Authentic or whatever, but it does look clean and modern. You see it, however, *only* if you have a fairly fast, modern PC. Basically, you need a Windows Experience Index score of 3 or higher (page 25), meaning a good amount of memory and a recent graphics card.

Tip: If you're not seeing the Aero goodies, and your Experience Index score indicates that you should, let the new Windows 7 Aero troubleshooter help you figure out why. Open the Start menu. Into the Search box, type *aero*. Click "Find and fix problems with transparency and other visual effects." Click Next to walk through the wizard. It will check things like your video memory, your Desktop Windows Manager (DWM) service, your screen's color settings, your chosen visual theme, your power settings, and so on. After this analysis, Windows tries to fix whatever was wrong.

Furthermore, the Aero features are not available in the Starter edition of Windows 7.

If you don't have Aero, you can still enjoy most of Windows 7's features—just without the transparencies, animations, and other eye candy. The pictures in this book still match the buttons and text you see on the screen, but without so much decoration around the edges.

Nobody ever said Microsoft's specialty was making things simple.

The Start Menu
All Versions

Windows is composed of 50 million lines of computer code, scattered across your hard drive in thousands of files. The vast majority of them are support files, there for behind-the-scenes use by Windows and your applications—they're not for you. They may as well bear a sticker reading, "No user-serviceable parts inside."

That's why the Start menu is so important (Figure 1-3). It lists every *useful* piece of software on your computer, including commands, programs, and files. Just about everything you do on your PC begins—or can begin—with your Start menu.

In Windows 7, as you've probably noticed, the *word* "Start" doesn't actually appear on the Start menu, as it did for years; now the Start menu is just a round, backlit, glass pebble with a Windows logo behind it. But it's still called the Start menu, and it's still the gateway to everything on the PC.

If you're the type who bills by the hour, you can open the Start menu (Figure 1-3) by clicking it with the mouse. If you feel that life's too short, however, open it by tapping the ▉ key on the keyboard instead. (If your antique, kerosene-operated keyboard has no ▉ key, pressing Ctrl+Esc does the same thing.)

Tip: To find out what something is—something in your Start menu (right side), All Programs menu, or indeed anywhere on your desktop—point to it with your cursor without clicking. A tinted, rectangular tooltip bar appears, containing a text description. (If the tooltip doesn't appear, it might be that the window you're pointing to isn't the *active* window on your desktop. Click the window and then try again.)

Anatomy of the Start Menu

The Start menu is split down the middle into two columns:

- **Left side (white).** At the top, above the thin divider line, is the *pinned items list*, which is yours to modify; it lists programs, folders, documents, and anything else you want to open quickly. This list never changes unless you change it.

  (If you don't see a divider line, then you have a brand-spankin'-fresh Windows 7 installation, and you haven't put anything *into* the pinned list yet.)

  Below the fine line is the standard Windows *most frequently used programs list*. This list is computed automatically by Windows and may change from day to day.

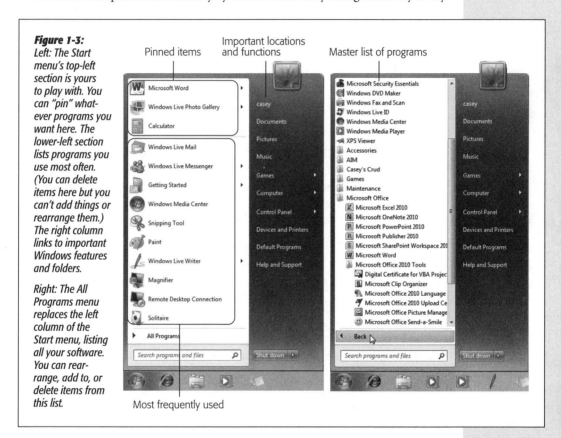

Figure 1-3:
Left: The Start menu's top-left section is yours to play with. You can "pin" whatever programs you want here. The lower-left section lists programs you use most often. (You can delete items here but you can't add things or rearrange them.) The right column links to important Windows features and folders.

Right: The All Programs menu replaces the left column of the Start menu, listing all your software. You can rearrange, add to, or delete items from this list.

Pinned items

Important locations and functions

Master list of programs

Most frequently used

Tip: You can, if you wish, ask Windows *not* to display a list of the programs you've used most recently. You might want to do that if, for example, it would be best that your boss or your spouse didn't know what you've been up to.

If that's your situation, then right-click the Start button; from the shortcut menu, choose Properties. In the resulting dialog box, turn off "Store and display recently opened programs in the Start menu." (While you're here, if you're especially paranoid, you can also turn off "Store and display recently opened items in the Start menu and the taskbar"—a reference to the jump lists feature described on page 51.) Click OK.

When you next inspect the Start menu, you'll be happy to see that the lower-left quadrant, where the recently used programs are usually listed, is creepily blank.

If you see a submenu arrow (▸) next to a program's name in the Start menu, congrats. You've just found a *jump list,* a new Windows 7 feature that gives you quick access to documents you've opened recently. See page 51 for details on creating, deleting, and working with jump lists.

At the very bottom is the All Programs list described below, plus the all-important Search box, which gets a whole chapter to itself (Chapter 3).

- **Right side (dark).** In general, the right side of the Start menu is devoted to listing important *places* on the computer: folders like Documents, Pictures, and Music; or special windows like Network, Control Panel, and Computer.

   At the bottom is the Shut Down button, which turns the PC off. The ▸ button next to it offers several variations of "off," like "Log off," Lock (for when you're about to wander away for coffee, so that a password is required to re-enter), Restart, Sleep, and Hibernate.

Tip: After many years, the "My" prefix finally disappeared from all the important folders of your PC in Windows Vista (My Pictures, My Music, My Documents, My Computer, and so on). Maybe Microsoft was tired of all the lawsuits from Fisher-Price.

In Windows 7, "My" may be gone from the *libraries* containing those file types. But within your own Personal folder, there they are again: My Pictures, My Music...! Page 143 explains why, but in the meantime, you're not stuck with "My." You can rename these special icons just as you would any other icon (page 145). Call it "My Computer," call it "Your Computer," call it "Jar Jar Binks"—makes no difference to Windows.

Keyboard Navigation

You can navigate and control the Start menu in either of two ways:

Use the arrow keys

Once the Start menu is open, you can use the arrow keys to "walk" up and down the menu. For example, press ↑ to enter the left-hand column from the bottom. Or press → to enter the right-hand column.

Either way, once you've highlighted something in either column, you can press the ← or → keys to hop to the opposite side of the menu; press the ↑ or ↓ keys to highlight other commands in the column (even the Shut Down button); or type the first initial of something's name to highlight it. (If there's more than one command that starts with, say, W, press *W* repeatedly to cycle through them.)

Once you've highlighted something, you can press Enter to "click" it (open it), or tap the ![windows] key or Esc to close the Start menu and forget the whole thing.

Use the Search box

This thing is *awesome.* The instant you pop open the Start menu, your insertion point blinks in the new Start Search box at the bottom of the menu (Figure 1-4). That's your cue that you can begin typing the name of whatever you want to open.

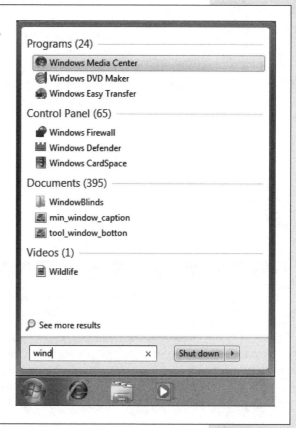

Figure 1-4:
As you type, Windows winnows down the list of found items, letter by letter. (You don't have to type the full search term and then press Enter.) If the list of results is too long to fit the Start menu, click "See more results" below the list. In any case, Windows highlights the first item in the results. If that's what you want to open, press Enter. If not, you can click what you want to open, or use the arrow keys to walk down the list and then press Enter to open something.

The instant you start to type, you trigger Windows's very fast, whole-computer search function. This search can find files, folders, programs, email messages, address book entries, calendar appointments, pictures, movies, PDF documents, music files, Web bookmarks, and Microsoft Office documents, among other things. It also finds anything *in* the Start menu, making it a very quick way to pull up something without having to click through a bunch of submenus.

You can read the meaty details about search in Chapter 3.

The All Programs List
All Versions

When you click All Programs at the bottom of the Start menu, you're shown an important list indeed: the master catalog of every program on your computer. You can jump directly to your word processor, calendar, or favorite game, for example, just by choosing its name from the Start→All Programs menu.

Clearly, Microsoft has abandoned the superimposed-menus effect of Windows XP. Rather than covering up the regularly scheduled Start menu, the All Programs list *replaces* it (or at least the left-side column of it).

You can restore the original left-side column by clicking Back (at the bottom of the list) or pressing the Esc key.

Tip: When the Start menu is open, you can open the All Programs menu in a number of ways: by clicking the phrase "All Programs," by pointing to it and keeping the mouse still for a moment, or by pressing the ↑ key (to highlight All Programs) and then tapping the Enter key, the → key, or the space bar. Just for keyboard fanatics: Once the programs list is open, you can also choose anything in it without involving the mouse. Just type the first letter of a program or folder name, or press the ↑ and ↓ keys, to highlight the item you want. Then press Enter to seal the deal.

Folders
As you'll quickly discover, the All Programs list doesn't list just programs. It also houses a number of *folders*.

NOSTALGIA CORNER

Restoring the Traditional Folder Listings

Some of the commands that populated the Start menus of previous Windows versions no longer appear in the Start menu of Windows 7. Microsoft is trying to make Windows look less overwhelming.

But if you miss some of the old folders—Favorites, Printers, and the Run command, for example—it's easy enough to put them back.

Right-click the Start menu. From the shortcut menu, choose Properties. Now the Taskbar and Start Menu Properties dialog box appears; click the Customize button.

In the scrolling list, you'll find checkboxes and buttons that hide or show all kinds of things that can appear in the right column of the Start menu: Computer, Connect To, Control Panel, Default Programs, Documents, Favorites, Games, Help, Music, Network, Pictures, Printers, Run, Search, and System Administrative Tools (a set of utilities described in Chapter 20).

Click OK twice to return to the desktop and try out your changes.

Software-company folders

Some of them bear the names of software you've installed; you might see a folder called, for example, PowerSoft or Logitech. These generally contain programs, uninstallers, instruction manuals, and other related junk.

Tip: Submenus, also known as cascading menus, have been largely eliminated from the Start menu. Instead, when you open something that contains *other* things—like a folder listed in the Start menu—you see its contents listed beneath, indented slightly, as shown in Figure 1-3. Click the folder name again to collapse the sublisting.

Keyboard freaks should note that you can also open a highlighted folder in the list by pressing the Enter key (or the → key). Close the folder by pressing Enter again (or the ← key).

Program-group folders

Another set of folders is designed to trim down the Programs menu by consolidating related programs, like Games, Accessories (little single-purpose programs), and Maintenance. Everything in these folders is described in Chapter 7.

The Startup folder

This folder contains programs that open automatically every time you start Windows. This can be a very useful feature. For instance, if you check your email every morning, you may as well save yourself a few mouse clicks by putting your email program into the Startup folder. If you spend all day long word processing, you may as well put Microsoft Word in there.

In fact, although few PC users suspect it, what you put into the Startup folder doesn't have to be an application. It can just as well be a *document* you consult every day. It can even be a folder or disk icon whose window you'd like to find open and waiting each time you turn on the PC. (The Documents folder is a natural example.)

Of course, you may be interested in the Startup folder for a different reason: to *stop* some program from launching itself. This is a particularly common syndrome if somebody else set up your PC. Some program seems to launch itself, unbidden, every time you turn the machine on.

Tip: All kinds of programs dump components into this folder. Over time, they can begin to slow down your computer. If you're having trouble determining the purpose of one startup program or another, visit this Web page, which provides a comprehensive list of every startup software nugget known, with instructions for turning off each one: *http://www.sysinfo.org/startupinfo.html.*

Fortunately, it's easy to either add or remove items from the Startup folder:

- **Deleting something. With the Startup folder's listing visible in the All Programs menu, right-click whatever you want to delete. From the shortcut menu, choose Delete. Click** Yes to send the icon to the Recycle Bin.

  Enjoy your newfound freedom from self-launching software.

• **Adding something.** With the All Programs list open, right-click the Startup folder and, from the shortcut menu, choose Open. You've just opened the Startup folder itself.

Once its window is open, navigate to the disk, folder, **program**, or document icon you want to add. (Navigating to your files and folders is described in the following chapters.)

Using the right mouse button, drag the icon directly into the Startup window, as shown in Figure 1-5. When you release the button, a shortcut menu appears; from the shortcut menu, choose **Create Shortcuts Here.**

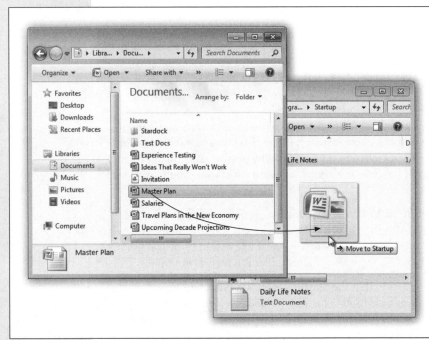

Figure 1-5:
It's easy to add a program or document icon to your Startup folder so that it launches automatically every time you turn on the computer. Here, a document from the Documents library is being added. You may also want to add a shortcut for the Documents library itself, which ensures that its window will be open and ready each time the computer starts up.

Return to the Old Start Menu

The fancily redesigned Start menu has its charms, including its translucent look. But as we all know, change can be stressful.

In Windows Vista, you could return to the organization and design of the old, single-column Start menu. (It was an option in the Start menu Properties dialog box.) But it's gone in

Windows 7. Microsoft seems to be saying, "Come on, now, people. Seriously. Let's move on."

If you're among the Windows 2000 crowd who genuinely preferred the old arrangement, the free CSMenuLanucher program can do the job for you. It's available from this book's "Missing CD" page at *www.missingmanuals.com.*

Close any windows you've opened. From now on, each time you turn on or restart your computer, the program, file, disk, or folder you dragged will open by itself.

Start Menu: The Right Side

All Versions

As noted earlier, the left-hand Start menu column, the white column, is your launcher for program, files, and folders you use a lot. The right side, the dark column, contains links to important functions and places. Here's a whirlwind tour of these options, from top to bottom.

Start→[Your Name]: The Personal Folder

As the box on this page makes clear, Windows keeps *all* your stuff—your files, folders, email, pictures, music, bookmarks, even settings and preferences—in one handy, central location: your *Personal folder*. This folder bears your name, or whatever account name you typed when you installed Windows 7.

As described in Chapter 23, everyone with an account on your PC has a Personal folder.

FREQUENTLY ASKED QUESTION

Secrets of the Personal Folder

Why did Microsoft bury my files in a folder three levels deep?

Because Windows has been designed for *computer sharing.* It's ideal for any situation where family members, students, or workers share the same PC.

Each person who uses the computer will turn on the machine to find his own separate desktop picture, set of files, Web bookmarks, font collection, and preference settings. (You'll find much more about this feature in Chapter 23.)

Like it or not, Windows considers you one of these people. If you're the only one who uses this PC, fine—simply ignore the sharing features. But in its little software head, Windows still considers you an account holder, and stands ready to accommodate any others who should come along.

In any case, now you should see the importance of the Users folder in the main hard drive window. Inside are folders—the Personal folders—named for the people who use this PC. In general, nobody is allowed to touch what's inside anybody else's folder.

If you're the sole proprietor of the machine, of course, there's only one Personal folder in the Users folder—named for you. (You can ignore the Public folder, which is described on page 774.)

This is only the first of many examples in which Windows imposes a fairly rigid folder structure. Still, the approach has its advantages. By keeping such tight control over which files go where, Windows 7 keeps itself pure—and very, very stable. (Other operating systems known for their stability, including Mac OS X, work the same way.)

Furthermore, keeping all your stuff in a single folder makes it very easy for you to back up your work. It also makes life easier when you try to connect to your machine from elsewhere in the office (over the network) or elsewhere in the world (over the Internet), as described in Chapters 26 and 27.

Technically, your Personal folder lurks inside the C:→Users folder. But that's a lot of burrowing when you just want a view of your entire empire. That's why your Personal folder is also listed here, at the top of the Start menu's right-side column. Choose this listing to open the folder that you'll eventually fill with new folders, organize, back up, and so on.

Start→Documents

This command opens up your Documents folder, a very important folder indeed. It's designed to store just about all the work you do on your PC—everything except music, pictures, and videos, which get folders of their own.

Of course, you're welcome to file your documents *anywhere* on the hard drive, but most programs propose depositing newly created documents into the Documents folder. That principle makes navigation easy. You never have to wonder where you filed something, since all your stuff is sitting right there in Documents.

Note: The Documents folder actually sits in the Computer→Local Disk (C:)→Users→*[Your Name]* folder.

If you study that path carefully, it should become clear that what's in Documents when *you* log in (page 737) isn't the same thing other people will see when *they* log in. That is, each account holder (Chapter 23) has a different Documents folder, whose contents switch according to who's logged in.

Start→Pictures, Music

Microsoft assumes (correctly) that most people these days use their home computers for managing digital photos and music collections. As you can probably guess, the Pictures and Music folders are intended to house them—and these Start menu commands are quick ways to open them.

In fact, whatever software came with your digital camera or MP3 player probably dumps your photos into, and sucks your music files out of, these folders automatically. You'll find much more on these topics in Chapters 14 and 15.

Start→Games

This item opens the Games folder, where Microsoft has stashed 11 computer games for your procrastination pleasure. (You get only six in the Starter edition of Windows 7.)

Note: The first time you open the Games folder, a message pops up to ask if you want to use the recommended update and folder settings. If so, Windows will notify you when updates to your games are available; auto-download rating and genre details about your games; and, in certain folder views, show when you last played a game.

Start→Computer

The Computer command is the trunk lid, the doorway to every single shred of software on your machine. When you choose this command, a window opens to reveal icons that represent each disk drive (or drive partition) in your machine, as shown in Figure 1-6.

For example, by double-clicking your hard drive icon and then the various folders on it, you can eventually see the icons for every single file and folder on your computer.

Start→Control Panel

This command opens an extremely important window: the Control Panel, which houses more than 50 mini-programs that you'll use to change almost every important setting on your PC. It's so important, in fact, that it gets a chapter of its own (Chapter 8).

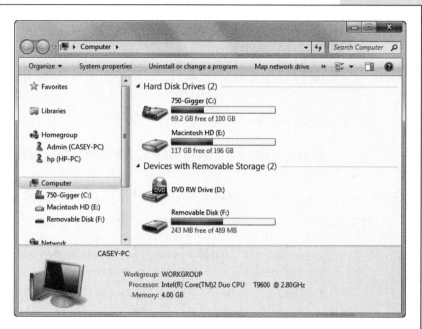

Figure 1-6:
The Computer window lists your PC's drives—hard drives, CD drives, USB flash drives, and so on; you may see networked drives listed here, too. This computer has two hard drives, a USB flash drive, and a CD-ROM drive. (If there's a disk in the CD drive, you see its name, not just its drive letter.) When you select a disk icon, the Details pane (if visible) shows its capacity and amount of free space (bottom).

Start→Devices and Printers

Yes, kids, it's a direct link to the Devices and Printers pane of the Control Panel, where you can fiddle with the settings for various gadgets (cameras, cellphones, headsets, scanners, fax machines, printers, monitors, mice, and so on). Details in Chapter 18.

Start→Default Programs

This command is a shortcut to the Default Programs control panel. It has two functions:

- To let you specify which program (not necessarily Microsoft's) you want to use as your Web browser, email program, instant-messaging program, Java module, and music player—choices offered by Microsoft to placate the U.S. Justice Department. Details are on page 319.

- To specify which program opens when you double-click a certain kind of document. For example, if you double-click a JPEG graphic, do you want it to open in Picasa or Windows Photo Gallery? Details on page 319.

Note: Grizzled, longtime Windows veterans may want to note that this file-association function used to be called File Types, and it was in the Folder Options window.

Start→Help and Support
All Versions

Choosing Start→Help and Support opens the Windows Help and Support Center window (Chapter 5).

Tip: Once again, speed fans have an alternative to using the mouse—just press the F1 key to open the Help window. (If that doesn't work, some other program may have Windows's focus. Try it again after clicking the desktop.)

Start→Shut down (Sleep, Restart, Log Off...)
All Versions

What should you do with your PC when you're finished using it for the moment?

Millions of people shut their PCs off, but they shouldn't; it's a colossal waste of time on both ends. When you shut down, you have to wait for all your programs to close—and then the next morning, you have to reopen everything, reposition your windows, and get everything back the way you had it.

You shouldn't just leave your computer *on* all the time, either. That's a massive waste of electricity, a security risk, and a black mark for the environment.

What you *should* do is put your PC to sleep. The Sleep command, along with Shut down, Restart, and other relevant options, appears in the "Shut down" pop-up menu at the lower-right corner of the Start menu.

Click the ▶ to see these commands. As shown in Figure 1-7, these are the options for finishing your work session:

FREQUENTLY ASKED QUESTION

Start→Stop

Could someone explain why all the variations of "Shut down" are in a menu called Start?

The Name-the-Button Committee at Microsoft probably thought you'd interpret Start to mean "Start here to get something accomplished."

But you wouldn't be the first person to find it illogical to click Start when you want to stop. Microsoft probably should have named the button "Menu," saving all of us a lot of confusion.

- **"Switch user."** This command refers to Windows's *accounts* feature, in which each person who uses this PC gets to see her own desktop picture, email account, files, and so on. (See Chapter 23.)

  When you choose "Switch user," somebody else can log into the computer with her own name and password—to do a quick calendar or email check, for example. But whatever *you* had running remains open behind the scenes. After the interloper is finished, you can log in again to find all your open programs and documents exactly as you left them.

Note: In Windows XP, there was a Fast User Switching on/off switch. Nowadays, there's no off switch; Fast User Switching is in effect full time.

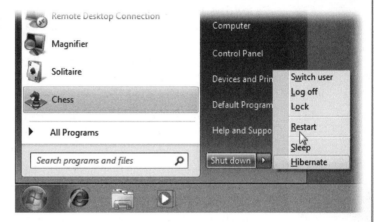

Figure 1-7:
How do you want to stop working today?

Microsoft offers you six different ways. It's all about choice.

- **"Log off."** If you click "Log off," Windows closes all your open programs and documents (giving you an opportunity to save any unsaved documents first). It then presents a new Welcome screen (page 766) so that the next person can sign in.

- **Lock.** This command locks your computer—in essence, it throws a sheet of inch-thick steel over everything you were doing, hiding your screen from view. This is an ideal way to protect your PC from nosy people who happen to wander by your desk while you're away getting coffee or lunch.

  All they'll find on your monitor is the standard Logon screen. They (and even you) will have to enter your account password to get past it (page 766).

Tip: You can trigger this button entirely from the keyboard. Hit these keys, in sequence: ⊞, → (twice), letter O. (The underlined letter in the word Lock lets you know that O is the shortcut key.)

- **Restart.** This command quits all open programs, and then quits and restarts Windows again automatically. The computer doesn't actually turn off. (You might do this to "refresh" your computer when you notice that it's responding sluggishly, for example.)

- **Sleep.** In the olden days, Windows offered a command called Standby. This special state of PC consciousness reduced the amount of electricity the computer used, putting it in suspended animation until you used the mouse or keyboard to begin working again. Whatever programs or documents you were working on remained in memory.

When using a laptop on battery power, Standby was a real boon. When the flight attendant handed over your microwaved chicken teriyaki, you could take a break without closing all your programs or shutting down the computer.

Unfortunately, there were two big problems with Standby, especially for laptops. First, the PC still drew a trickle of power this way. If you didn't use your laptop for a few days, the battery would silently go dead—and everything you had open and unsaved would be lost forever. Second, drivers or programs sometimes interfered with Standby, so your laptop remained on even though it was closed inside your carrying case. Your plane would land on the opposite coast, you'd pull out the laptop for the big meeting, and you'd discover that (a) the thing was roasting hot, and (b) the battery was dead.

The command is now called Sleep, and it doesn't present those problems anymore. First, drivers and applications are no longer allowed to interrupt the Sleep process. No more Hot Laptop Syndrome.

Second, the instant you put the computer to sleep, Windows quietly transfers a copy of everything in memory into an invisible file on the hard drive. But it still keeps everything alive in memory—the battery provides a tiny trickle of power—in case you return to the laptop (or desktop) and want to dive back into work.

If you do return soon, the next startup is lightning-fast. Everything reappears on the screen faster than you can say, "Redmond, Washington."

If you *don't* return shortly, then Windows eventually cuts power, abandoning what it had memorized in RAM. (You control when this happens using the advanced power plan settings described in Chapter 8.) Now your computer is using no power at all; it's in *hibernate* mode.

Fortunately, Windows still has the hard drive copy of your work environment. So *now* when you tap a key to wake the computer, you may have to wait 30 seconds or so—not as fast as 2 seconds, but certainly better than the 5 minutes it would take to start up, reopen all your programs, reposition your document windows, and so on.

The bottom line: When you're done working for the moment—or for the day—put your computer to Sleep instead of shutting it down. You save power, you save time, and you risk no data loss.

You can send a laptop to Sleep just by closing the lid. On any kind of computer, you can trigger Sleep by choosing Start→Sleep or by pushing the PC's power button, if you've set it up that way (see page 40).

Tip: You can also trigger Sleep entirely from the keyboard by pressing ⊞, then → twice, then S.

- **Hibernate.** Hibernate mode is a lot like Sleep, except that it *doesn't* offer a period during which the computer will wake up instantly. Hibernate equals the *second* phase of Sleep mode, in which your working world is saved to the hard drive. Waking the computer from Hibernate takes about 30 seconds.

Tip: You can configure your computer to sleep or hibernate automatically after a period of inactivity, or to require a password to bring it out of hibernation. See page 329 for details.

- **Shut down.** This is what most people would call "really, really off." When you shut down your PC, Windows quits all open programs, offers you the opportunity to save any unsaved documents, exits Windows, and turns off the computer.

   Truth is, there's almost no reason to shut down your PC anymore. Sleep is almost always better all the way around.

   The only exceptions have to do with hardware installation. Anytime you have to open up the PC to make a change (installing memory, hard drives, sound or video cards), or connect something external that doesn't just use a USB or FireWire (1394) port, you should shut the thing down first.

Tip: Once again, it's worth noting that you can trigger any of these commands entirely from the keyboard; save your mouse for Photoshop.

Hit the ⊞ key to open the Start menu. Then hit the → key twice to open the menu shown in Figure 1-7. At this point, you can type the underlined letter of the command you want: *L* for "Log off," *S* for Sleep, and so on.

Three Triggers for Sleep/Shut Down—and How to Change Them

You now know how to trigger the Shut down command using the mouse (Start→Shut down) or by pressing a keyboard sequence. But there are even faster ways.

If you have a laptop, just close the lid. If you have a desktop PC, just press its power button (⏻).

In all these cases, though—menu, lid, power button—*you* can decide whether the computer shuts down, goes to sleep, hibernates, or just ignores you. That's really important, because Microsoft's proposed responses aren't always the best ones. For example, "Shut down" is what's listed at the bottom of the Start menu, but Sleep is what you'll probably want more often.

Here's how to change the factory setting when you open the Start menu, close the lid, or hit the power button:

- **Change what the Start menu's Shut down command says.** Right-click the Start menu. From the shortcut menu, choose Properties. On the Start Menu tab of the resulting dialog box, use the "Power button action" pop-up menu. You can choose

Switch user, Log off, Lock, Restart, Sleep, Hibernate, or Shut down—whichever you'd like to see listed at the bottom of the Start menu, where it started out saying "Shut down" (see Figure 1-8).

Figure 1-8:
In this dialog box (left), you can change what it says at the bottom of the Start menu (right). For most people, the best option is Sleep—not Shut down.

- **Change what happens when you close the lid.** Open the Start menu. In the Search box, start typing *power options* until you see "Change what closing the lid does" in the search results. Click that link. In the resulting dialog box, you can choose any of the usual options (Sleep, Restart, Hibernate, and so on) for "When I close the lid." In fact, you can even choose this setting independently for when the laptop is plugged in and when it's running on battery, although Sleep is really the best choice in both cases.

- **Change what happens when you press the power button.** Open the Start menu. In the Search box, start typing *power options* until you see "Change what the power buttons do" in the search results. Click that link. In the resulting dialog box, you can choose any of the usual options (Sleep, Restart, Hibernate, and so on) for "When I press the power button." (You can also specify what happens "When I press the sleep button," except that your PC probably doesn't *have* a sleep button.)

Commands That No Longer Appear

If you're coming from an earlier version of Windows, you may wonder what became of a few useful Start menu commands, like Recent Items, Connect To, Network, and Run. Turns out they're gone, but not forgotten; you can restore them, if you like, as described next.

Customizing the Start Menu

All Versions

It's possible to live a long and happy life without ever tampering with the Start menu. In fact, for many people, the idea of fiddling with it comes dangerously close to nerd territory.

Still, Start-menu customizing got a big boost in Windows 7, so you may as well sniff around to see what Microsoft offers. Besides, knowing how to manipulate the Start menu listings provides an interesting glimpse into the way Windows works, and tweaking it can pay off in efficiency down the road.

Note: Thanks to the User Accounts feature described in Chapter 23, any changes you make to the Start menu apply only to *you.* Each person with an account on this PC has an independent, customized Start menu.

Start Menu Settings

Microsoft offers a fascinating set of customization options for the Start menu. It's hard to tell whether these options were selected by a scientific usability study or by a dartboard, but you're likely to find something that suits you.

To view and change the basic options, right-click the Start menu; from the shortcut menu, choose Properties. Now the Taskbar and Start Menu Properties dialog box opens (Figure 1-9, top). When you click Customize, you see the dialog box shown at bottom in Figure 1-9. Here you're offered an assortment of Start-menu tweaks, neatly listed in alphabetical order; they affect the Start menu in some fairly simple yet profound ways.

The hide/show switches for things in the Start menu

Most of the checkboxes in·this scrolling list are on/off switches for things that appear on the *right side* of the Start menu: Games, Music, Computer, Control Panel, your Personal folder, Pictures, and so on. If you never use some of these things, then for heaven's sake turn them off; you'll reduce clutter and eliminate that nagging feeling that you're not using all of Windows's features.

Also in this list, though, are checkboxes for items Microsoft *didn't* put in the Start menu but that you, the oddball fringe case, can put there if you like. Here's what they are:

- **Connect To.** This command opens the "Connect to a network" dialog box, a simple list of all the dial-up, VPN (virtual private networking), and wireless networks your computer can "see" at the moment. The thing is, in Windows 7, there are easier ways to see the networks around you (see Chapter 9).

- **Downloads.** For decades, novice computer users have been baffled: They download something from the Web but then can't find where it went. Now you'll know. Out of the box, Internet Explorer puts your downloaded files into the Downloads folder (which is inside your Personal folder). It makes sense to add this item to your Start menu so you have quick access to it.

- **Favorites menu.** The Favorites menu is a list of your favorite Web sites—the same ones you've bookmarked using Internet Explorer (page 409). If you turn on this item, you can use the Start menu to launch Internet Explorer and travel directly to the selected site. (Of course, jump lists, described later in this chapter, provide a similar feature.)

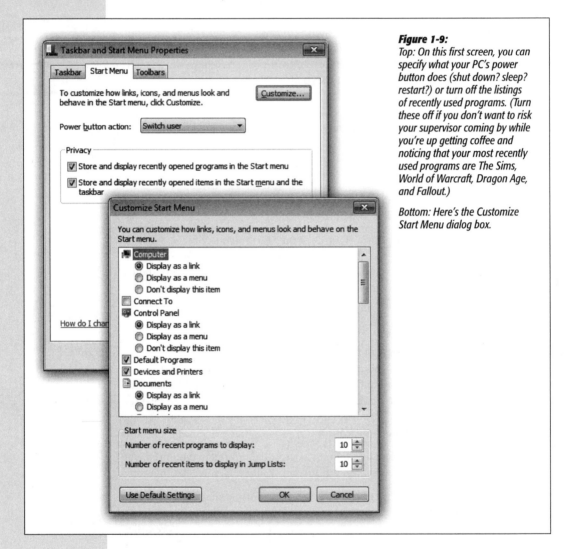

Figure 1-9:
Top: On this first screen, you can specify what your PC's power button does (shut down? sleep? restart?) or turn off the listings of recently used programs. (Turn these off if you don't want to risk your supervisor coming by while you're up getting coffee and noticing that your most recently used programs are The Sims, World of Warcraft, Dragon Age, and Fallout.)

Bottom: Here's the Customize Start Menu dialog box.

- **Homegroup.** This item adds a direct link to a list of the Windows 7 PCs on your home network, as described on page 775. Of course, since there's a link to them in the Navigation pane of every Explorer window, having it in the Start menu isn't especially critical.

- **Network.** There's no Network item in the Start menu, because you can see all available networked computers right there at the left side of every Explorer window. Details on networking are in Chapters 23, 24, 25, and 26.

- **Recorded TV.** You'd have no reason to use this unless your computer came equipped with a TV tuner, meaning that it's a *Media Center PC* (described on page 547). This item is a link to the TV shows you've recorded on your PC.

- **Recent Items.** The Recent Items command is a little redundant. The left side of the Start menu lists the most recently used *programs,* and jump lists (page 51) list your most recently used *documents.* But if you're a fan of Recent Items from previous Windows versions, here you go.

- **Run command.** The Run command is a power-user tool that's actually pretty cool. It gets a writeup of its own at the end of this chapter; for now, note that you don't really need to put it in the Start menu to enjoy it. Just press ⊞+R whenever you want to run something.

- **System administrative tools.** This one is a folder of techie diagnostic tools like Performance Monitor, Task Scheduler, and Windows Memory Diagnostic. They're described later in this book, and they're way over the heads of most people who don't do PCs for a living.

  If you *are* in the market for this sort of tool, the options here let you install a link to these tools either (a) in the All Programs menu, or (b) both there and in the right side of the Start menu.

- **Videos.** Do you want a link to your Movies folder to appear in the Start menu, just as Music and Pictures do? If so, knock yourself out.

A note about "Display as menu"

Take a look at the options for **Computer, Control Panel, Documents, Downloads, Games, Music, Personal folder, Pictures, Recorded TV, System administrative tools, Videos.** Beneath each of these headings, you'll find three options:

- **Display as a link.** In other words, "list in my Start menu the usual way."

FREQUENTLY ASKED QUESTION

Opening the Control Panel Window When You Can't

OK, I'm with you—I turned on "Display as a menu" for the Control Panel, so now I can open any Control Panel program directly from my Start menu. Trouble is, now I can't open the Control Panel window itself! Nothing happens when I click the Start→Control Panel command. How do I open the Control Panel window?

Ah, there's a troublemaker in every class.

Open the Start menu and then *right-click* Control Panel. Choose Open from the shortcut menu. You're back in business.

• **Display as a menu.** This option is extremely useful. It means that instead of simply listing the name of a folder, your Start menu sprouts a submenu listing the *contents* of that folder, as shown on the right in Figure 1-10.

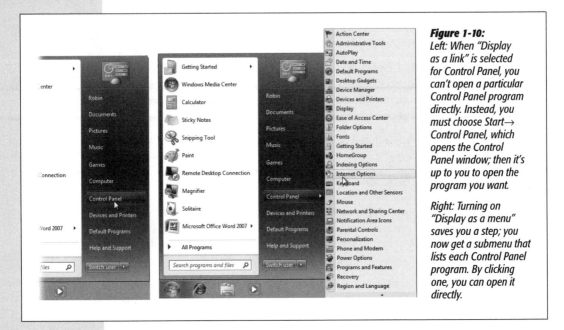

Figure 1-10:
Left: When "Display as a link" is selected for Control Panel, you can't open a particular Control Panel program directly. Instead, you must choose Start→ Control Panel, which opens the Control Panel window; then it's up to you to open the program you want.

Right: Turning on "Display as a menu" saves you a step; you now get a submenu that lists each Control Panel program. By clicking one, you can open it directly.

• **Don't display this item.** This option, of course, removes the folder from your Start menu altogether. That's a good point to remember if you ever sit down at your PC and discover that, for example, the Control Panel appears to have disappeared.

More options for the Start menu

A few of the checkboxes in the list aren't on/off switches for Start menu *items,* but rather checkboxes that control the Start menu's *behavior.* For example:

• **Enable context menus and dragging and dropping.** There's not much reason to turn off this checkbox; after all, it has two benefits. First, it lets you customize your Start menu simply by dragging icons onto it, as described in the next section. Second, it lets you right-click Start-menu items, which produces a useful shortcut menu containing commands like Rename and Remove from This List. (If this checkbox is turned off, then right-clicking Start menu items has no effect.)

• **Highlight newly installed programs.** Whenever you (or some techie in the building) installs a new program into the Start menu, it shows up with colored highlighting for a few days. The idea, of course, is to grab your attention and make you aware of your expanded software suite. If you could do without this kind of reminder, then just turn off this checkbox.

• **Open submenus when I pause on them with the mouse pointer.** When this checkbox is turned on, you don't actually have to click a submenu to view its options.

- **Search other files and libraries.** These options govern the Start menu's Search command. "Search with public folders" means "search the Public folder on my computer." (You can read more about this folder on page 774.)

  The third option here is "Don't search." If you select this, the Search command won't search *files and documents* at all. Seems like that would greatly diminish the usefulness of Search. But this could be a speedy arrangement if you use Search for opening programs and nothing else. (That assumes, of course, that you leave "Search programs and Control Panel" turned on, as described next.)

- **Search programs and Control Panel.** Suppose you *never* want the Search command to pull up the names of programs and Control Panel items—you want it to find *only* files, pictures, documents, and so on. In that case, turn off this box.

Note: This option is the inverse of "Search other files and libraries." If you turn off both of these options, then the Start menu's Search box will never find anything, ever. (To prevent that, select one of the two search options under "Search other files and libraries, and/or turn on "Search programs and Control Panel.")

- **Sort All Programs menu by name.** Yep, here it is, the feature that the world's compulsives have been waiting for: a self-alphabetizing All Programs list. (All right, that was uncalled for; truth is, having the list in A-to-Z order can make life easier for just about anyone.)

Note: If you turn off this option, you can always make the All Programs list snap into alphabetical order on your command, as described in the tip on page 47.

- **Use large icons.** You don't need a book to explain *this* one. This option affects the little icon that appears next to each Start menu item's name (in the left column—either the regular Start menu or the All Programs list). Bigger icons are pretty, and on today's high-resolution monitors, they may rescue your Start-menu items from disappearing completely. On the other hand, on smaller monitors, large icons may limit the number of items the list can hold.

Below the scrolling list

Below the massive list of checkboxes, two additional controls await in the Customize dialog box:

- **Number of recent programs to display.** The number here refers to the lower-left column of the Start menu, the one that lists programs you've used most recently. By increasing this number, you make the Start menu taller—but you ensure that more of your favorite programs are listed and ready to launch. If this item is dimmed, it's because you've turned off "Store and display recently opened items in the Start menu and the taskbar" (page 53).

- **Number of recent items to display in Jump lists.** For details on jump lists, see page 51. If this control is dimmed, it's because you turned off "Store and display recently opened items in the Start menu and the taskbar" (page 53).

Add Your Own Icons to the Start Menu

Usually, when you install a new program, its installer inserts the program's name and icon in your Start→All Programs menu. There may be times, however, when you want to add something to the Start menu yourself, such as a folder, document, or even a disk.

The "free" sections of the Start menu

In the following pages, you'll read several references to the "free" portions of the Start menu. These are the two areas that you, the lowly human, are allowed to modify freely—adding, removing, renaming, or sorting as you see fit:

- **The top-left section of the Start menu.** This little area lists what Microsoft calls *pinned* programs and files—things you use often enough that you want a fairly permanent list of them at your fingertips.

- **The All Programs menu.** This, of course, is the master list of programs (and anything else—documents, folders, disks—you want to see listed).

These two areas are highlighted back in Figure 1-3.

In other words, most of the following techniques don't work in the *right* column, nor the lower-*left* quadrant of the Start menu, where Windows lists your most recently used programs.

Microsoft wouldn't be Microsoft if it didn't provide at least 437 different ways to do this job. Here are two of the world's favorites:

Method 1: Drag an icon directly

1. **Locate the icon you want to add to your Start menu.**

   It can be a program (see the box on page 30), a document, a folder you frequently access, one of the programs in your Control Panel's folder, or even your hard drive or DVD-drive icon. (Adding disks and folders to the Start menu is especially handy, because it lets you dive directly into their contents without having to drill down through the Computer window.)

Tip: Adding an application name to your All Programs menu requires that you find the program *file*, as described on page 141. To do so, either use the Search command (Chapter 3), or just dig around for it in any Explorer window. You can find your program files in the Computer→Local Disk (C:)→Program Files folder.

---

2. **Drag it directly onto the Start button.**

   If you release the mouse now, Windows adds the icon's name to the bottom of the "pinned items" list (Figure 1-11, right). You're now welcome to drag it up or down within this list.

   But if you *keep the mouse button pressed* as you drag onto the Start button, the Start menu itself opens. As long as the button is still pressed, you can drag the new icon wherever you want among the items listed in the top-left section of the menu (Figure 1-11, left).

Note: If this drag-and-dropping business doesn't seem to work, it's because you've turned off "Enable drag-ging and dropping," as described in the previous section. And if Windows *doesn't* let you drag it anywhere you like, it's because you've turned on "Sort All Programs menu by name," also described earlier.

In fact, as long as you haven't stopped pressing the mouse button, you can even drag your icon onto the words "All Programs." Your programs list opens, and you can deposit whatever you're dragging anywhere in *that* menu.

Tip: If "Sort All Programs menu by name" is *not* turned on, your All Programs list may gradually become something of a mess.

If you want to restore some order to it—specifically, alphabetical—then right-click anywhere on the open All Programs menu and choose Sort by Name from the shortcut menu. (This command doesn't appear if "Sort All Programs menu by name" is already turned on.)

Figure 1-11:
Left: You can add something to the top of your Start menu by dragging it onto the Start button to open the Start menu, and then dragging it into position. (You can also drag it onto the All Programs link and then anywhere in that list.)

Right: When you release the mouse, the item is happily ensconced where you dropped it. Remember, too, that you're free to drag anything up or down in the "free" areas: the circled area shown here, and the All Programs list. (One exception: when alphabetical sorting is on.)

Method 2: Use the Start menu folders

Windows builds the All Programs menu by consulting two critical folders:

- **Local Disk (C:)→ProgramData→Microsoft→Windows→Start Menu→Programs folder.** This folder contains shortcuts for programs that are available to everybody who has an account on your machine (Chapter 23).

- **Local Disk (C:)→Users→[your name]→AppData→Roaming→Microsoft→Windows→Start Menu→Programs folder.** This invisible folder stashes shortcuts for the programs you have added to the Start menu—and they appear only when *you* have logged into the machine.

Therefore, instead of the fancy drag-and-drop scheme described above, you may prefer to fine-tune your Start menu the low-tech way.

Unfortunately, these folders are normally hidden. Fortunately, you don't really care; there's a quick shortcut to opening them, as described in Figure 1-12. Then, once you've opened the relevant Programs folder, you can add shortcut icons there, remove them, or rename them. Whatever changes you make are reflected in your All Programs menu.

Removing Icons from the Start Menu

When it comes time to prune an overgrown Start menu, there are two different sets of instructions, depending on which section of the Start menu needs purging.

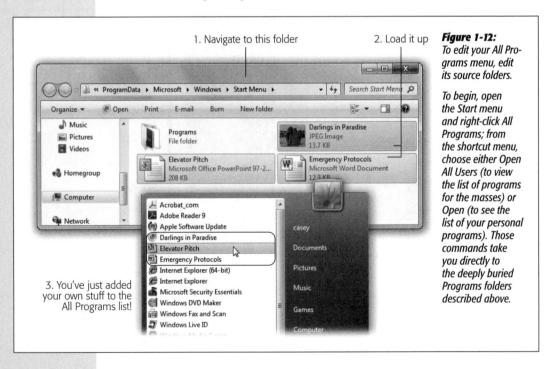

Figure 1-12:
To edit your All Programs menu, edit its source folders.

To begin, open the Start menu and right-click All Programs; from the shortcut menu, choose either Open All Users (to view the list of programs for the masses) or Open (to see the list of your personal programs). Those commands take you directly to the deeply buried Programs folders described above.

- **The left-side column, the All Programs list, and jump lists.** Right-click the item you've targeted for extinction, and then, from the shortcut menu, choose either "Remove from this list" or "Delete."

  In both cases, you're only deleting the *shortcut* on the menu. You're not actually deleting any software.

- **The right-side column.** Open the Properties→Customize dialog box for the Start menu (page 30), and then turn off the checkboxes for all the items you want expunged.

Tip: You can spawn instant shortcuts (page 160) of anything in the left-hand column of the Start menu by *dragging* them off the menu—onto the desktop, for example. That's a handy tactic if you want a desktop icon for something you use often, so you don't even have to open the Start menu to get at it.

Renaming Start-Menu Items

Although few people realize it, you can rename anything in the Start menu's left side (or in the top half of the right side—like Pictures, Music, or Documents). Open the Start menu, right-click the item you want to rename, and choose Rename from the shortcut menu. The command sprouts a little editing box. Type the new name and then press Enter.

Reorganizing the Start Menu

To change the order of listings in the "free" portions of the Start menu, including the All Programs list, just drag the items up and down the lists as you see fit. As you drag, a black line appears to show you the resulting location of your dragging action. Release the mouse when the black line is where you want the relocated icon to appear.

Tip: If you change your mind while you're dragging, press the Esc key to leave everything as it was.

You can drag program names from the lower-left section of the Start menu, too—but only into one of the "free" areas.

Tip: A reminder: If you can't seem to drag program names around in the All Programs list, it's probably because you've told Windows to auto-alphabetize this list (page 47).

Add folders to hold submenus

As noted earlier, some items in the All Programs list are actually folders. For example, clicking Games reveals a submenu of the games that come with Windows (see Figure 1-13).

It's worthwhile to know that you can create All Programs menu folders of your own and stock them with whatever icons you like. For instance, you may want to create a folder for CD-ROM games, eliminating those items from a too-long All Programs menu.

To add a folder to the All Programs menu, follow these steps:

---

1. **Open the Start menu. Right-click the All Programs command. From the shortcut menu, choose Open.**

   You're about to create subfolders that will show up only when *you* are logged on. (If you want to make a change that affects *everybody* with an account on this computer, then choose Open All Users from the shortcut menu instead.)

   In any case, the Start Menu Explorer window appears.

Figure 1-13:
Some All Programs menu items have sub-menu folders and sub-submenu folders. As you move through the layers, you're performing an action known as "drilling down." This phrase shows up a lot in manuals and computer books—for example, "Drill down to the Calculator to crunch a few quick numbers."

2. **Open the Programs folder.**

   Its contents are arrayed before you, as shown in Figure 1-14.

3. **In the window toolbar, click "New folder."**

   Or, if your right mouse button hasn't been getting enough exercise, right-click a blank spot in the window, and then choose New→Folder from the shortcut menu. (Or just press Shift+Ctrl+N.)

4. **When the new folder appears, type a folder name and then press Enter.**

   Close the window, if you like.

Tip: You can even create folders *within* folders in your Start→All Programs menu. Just double-click to open any of the existing folders in the Programs folder, and then repeat from step 3.

Your new folder appears in the folders list of the Start→All Programs menu, already sorted into alphabetical order.

Now you can put your favorite file, folder, disk, or application icons *into* this new folder. To do so, drag an icon onto the Start→All Programs menu, and then, without releasing the mouse, onto the All Programs link, and then into the new folder/submenu you created.

Figure 1-14:
Notice that some of the items in Programs have folder icons; these are the folders that will become submenus in the Start menu.

Jump Lists
All Versions

There's one more bit of Start-menu customization left. It's one of the stars of Windows 7, a new feature called *jump lists*.

They're handy submenus that list frequently or recently opened files in each of your programs. For example, the jump list for Internet Explorer shows the Web sites you visit most often; the jump list for Windows Media Player shows songs you've played a lot lately.

The point, of course, is that you can *re*open a file just by clicking its name. Jump lists can save you time when you want to resume work on something you had open recently but you're not in the mood to burrow through folders to find its icon.

Often, jump lists also include shortcut-menu-ish commands, like New Message (for an email program), Play/Pause (for a jukebox program), or Close All Windows (just about any program). As Microsoft puts it, it's like having a separate Start menu for *every single program.*

Interestingly enough, the same jump lists appear both in the Start menu and in your taskbar (Figure 1-15).

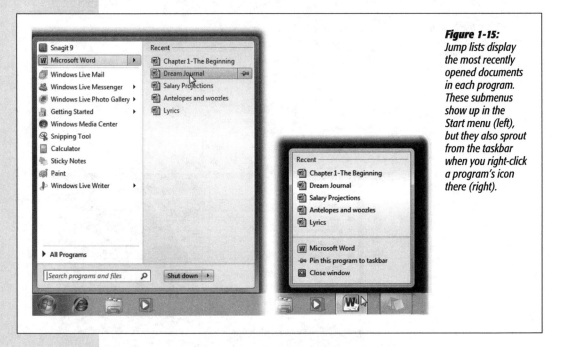

Figure 1-15:
Jump lists display the most recently opened documents in each program. These submenus show up in the Start menu (left), but they also sprout from the taskbar when you right-click a program's icon there (right).

You have several ways to make jump lists appear:

• **In the Start menu.** A ▸ button next to a program's name in the Start menu means a jump list awaits. (In general, a program sprouts a jump list automatically if you've used it to open or play files.)

To open the jump list, either click the ▸ or just point to the program's name without clicking. The submenu opens automatically after about half a second.

Note: If no jump lists ever appear, it's probably because you've turned this feature off. To turn it back on, right-click the Start menu. From the shortcut menu, choose Properties. Turn on "Store and display recently opened items in the Start menu and the taskbar." (Yes, that's the on/off switch for jump lists.) Click OK.

And if the submenu doesn't pop open by itself when you point without clicking, you've probably turned that feature off, too. To turn it back on, right-click the Start menu. From the shortcut menu, choose Properties. Click Customize. Turn on "Open submenus when I pause on them with the mouse pointer." Click OK.

- **On the taskbar.** The nearly identical jump list appears when you right-click a program's icon on your taskbar (page 101).

  Actually, there's a second, secret way to make the jump list appear: Swipe upward from the program's icon. (That is, give the mouse a flick upward while you're clicking.)

  This technique isn't such a huge benefit when you're using a mouse or trackpad. But if you're using a touchscreen computer, where right-clicking can be a little hard to figure out, you'll be glad to have this alternative.

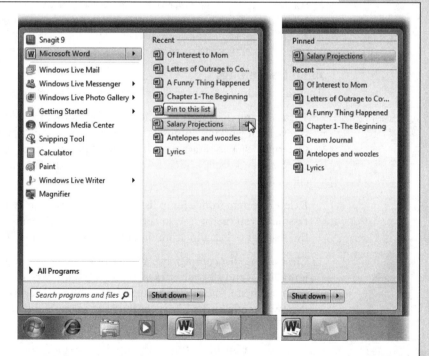

Figure 1-16:
Suppose there's a document you refer to a lot, and you don't want it to vanish from its program's jump list. Just point to its name without clicking, and then click the pushpin icon (left). Now there's a new section in the jump list called Pinned, where that document will remain undisturbed until you unpin it by clicking the pushpin again (right).

Pinning

In general, jump lists maintain themselves. Windows decides which files you've opened or played most recently or most frequently and builds the jump lists accordingly. New document listings appear, older ones vanish, all without your help.

You can, however, *pin* an item to a program's jump list so it *doesn't* disappear. It's out of Windows's clutches, at least until you *un*pin it. Figure 1-16 shows the technique.

Jump List Caveats

Jump lists are great and all, but you should be aware of a few things:

- They don't know when you've deleted a document or moved it to another folder or disk; they continue to list the file even after it's gone. In that event, clicking the document's listing produces only an error message. And you're offered the chance to delete the listing (referred to as "this shortcut" in the error message) so you don't confuse yourself again the next time.

- Some people consider jump lists a privacy risk, since they reveal everything you've been up to recently to whatever spouse or buddy happens to wander by. (You know who you are.)

  In that case, you can turn off jump lists, or just the incriminating items, as described next.

Tip: Of course, even if you turn off jump lists, there's another easy way to open a document you've recently worked on—from within the program you used to create it. Many programs maintain a list of recent documents in the File menu.

Jump List Settings

There are all kinds of ways to whip jump lists into submission. For example:

- **Turn off jump lists.** If the whole idea of Windows (or your boss) tracking what you've been working on upsets you, you can turn this feature off entirely. To do that, right-click the Start menu. From the shortcut menu, choose Properties. Turn off "Store and display recently opened items in the Start menu and taskbar" and click OK.

- **Delete one item from a jump list.** For privacy, for security, or out of utter embarrassment, you may not want some file or Web site's name to show up in a jump list. Just right-click and, from the shortcut menu, choose "Remove from this list."

- **Clear a jump list completely.** At other times, you may want to wipe out *all* your jump lists—and all your tracks. To do that, right-click the Start menu. From the shortcut menu, choose Properties. Turn off the checkbox that says "Store and display recently opened items in the Start menu and taskbar" (that's the master on/off switch for jump lists). Click Apply; you've just erased all the jump lists.

  If you didn't intend to turn off jump lists for good, though, turn the "Store and display" checkbox back on again before clicking OK. Your jump lists are now ready to start memorizing *new* items.

- **Change the number of documents in the list.** Ordinarily, jump lists track the 10 most recent (or most frequently used) items, but you can goose that number up or down. To do that, right-click the Start menu. From the shortcut menu, choose Properties. Click Customize. Adjust the "Number of recent items to display in Jump Lists" item at the bottom of the dialog box, and then click OK.

Tip: Jump-list items are draggable. For example, suppose you're composing an email message, and you want to attach your latest book outline. If it's in your Start menu, in a jump list, you can drag the document's icon directly from the jump list into your email message to attach it. Cool.

The Run Command
All Versions

The Start menu in a fresh installation of Win7 doesn't include the Run command. But power users and über-geeks may well want to put it back in the Start menu, following the instructions on page 30. (Or don't bother. Whenever you want the Run command, you can just press ⊞+R, or type *run* into the Start menu's Search box and then hit Enter.)

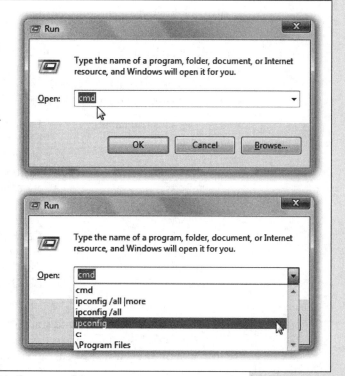

Figure 1-17:
Top: The last Run command you entered appears automatically in the Open text box. You can use the drop-down list to see a list of commands you've previously entered.

Bottom: The Run command knows the names of all your folders and also remembers the last few commands you typed here. As you go, you're shown the best match for the characters you're typing. When the name of the folder you're trying to open appears in the list, click it to prevent having to type the rest of the entry.

The Run command gets you to a *command line,* as shown in Figure 1-17. A command line is a text-based method of performing a task. You type a command, click OK, and something happens as a result.

Note: The command line in the Run dialog box is primarily for *opening* things. Windows 7 also comes with a program called Command Prompt that offers a far more complete environment—not just for opening things, but for controlling and manipulating them. Power users can type long sequences of commands and symbols in Command Prompt.

Working at the command line is becoming a lost art in the world of Windows, because most people prefer to issue commands by choosing from menus using the mouse. However, some old-timers still love the command line, and even mouse-lovers encounter situations when a typed command is the *only* way to do something.

If you're a PC veteran, your head probably teems with neat Run commands you've picked up over the years. If you're new to this idea, however, the following are a few of the useful and timesaving functions you can perform with the Run dialog box.

Open a Program

For example, you can use the Run command as a program launcher. Just type any program's *program filename* in the Open text box and then press Enter. For both pros and novices, it's frequently faster to launch a program this way than to click the Start→All Programs menu with the mouse.

Unfortunately, the program filename isn't the same as its plain-English name; it's a cryptic, abbreviated version. For example, if you want to open Microsoft Word, you must type *winword*. That's the actual name of the Word program icon as it sits in your Computer→Local Disk (C:)→Program Files→Microsoft Office→Office folder. Some other common program filenames are here:

Program's real name	Program's familiar name
iexplore	Internet Explorer
explorer	Windows Explorer
write	WordPad
msworks	Microsoft Works
msimn	Mail
wmplayer	Windows Media Player
control	Classic Control Panel
regedit	Registry Editor
cleanmgr	Disk Cleanup
defrag	Disk Defragmenter
calc	Calculator

To discover the real filename of a certain program, open Computer→Local Disk (C:)→Program Files. Inspect the folders there; with the window in Details view, you'll be able to spot the icons whose type is "application."

Note: True, the Start Search box at the bottom of the Start menu offers another way to find and open any program without taking your hands off the keyboard. But the Run method is more precise, and may require less effort because you're not typing the *entire* program name.

In fact, keyboard lovers, get this: You can perform this entire application-launching stunt without using the mouse at all. Just follow these steps in rapid succession:

1. **Press ⊞+R.**

   That's the keyboard shortcut for the Run command, whose dialog box now opens.

2. **Type the program file's name in the Open box.**

   If you've typed the name before, just type a couple of letters; Windows fills in the rest of the name automatically.

3. **Press Enter.**

   Windows opens the requested program instantly. Keystrokes: 4; Mouse: 0.

Open Any Program or Document

Using the Run dialog box is handy for opening favorite applications, because it requires so few keystrokes. But you can also use the Run dialog box to open *any* file on the computer.

The trick here is to type in the entire *path* of the program or document you want. (See the box on page 58 if you're new to the idea of file paths.) For example, to open the family budget spreadsheet that's in Harold's Documents folder, you might type *C:\Users\Harold\Documents\familybudget.xls*.

Of course, you probably wouldn't *actually* have to type all that, since the AutoComplete pop-up menu offers to complete each folder name as you start to type it.

Tip: Typing the path in this way is also useful for opening applications that don't appear in the Start→All Programs menu. (If a program doesn't appear there, you must type its entire *pathname*—or click Browse to hunt for its icon yourself.)

For example, some advanced Windows utilities (including the *Registry Editor,* an advanced diagnostic program) are accessible only through the command line. You also need to use the Run command to open some older command-line programs that don't come with a listing in the All Programs menu.

Open a Drive Window

When you click Computer in your Start menu, you see that Windows assigns a letter of the alphabet to each disk drive attached to your machine—the hard drive, the DVD drive, the floppy drive, and so on. The floppy drive is A:, the hard drive is usually C:, and so on. (There hasn't been a B: drive since the demise of the two-floppy computer.)

By typing a drive letter followed by a colon (for example, *C:*) into the Run box and pressing Enter, you make a window pop open, showing what's on that drive.

Open a Folder Window

You can also use the Run dialog box to open the window for any folder on your machine. To do so, type a backslash followed by the name of a folder (Figure 1-17, bottom of screen). You might type, for example, the first few letters of *Program Files* to see your complete software collection.

Note: The Run command assumes you're opening a folder on Drive C. If you want to open a folder on a different drive, add the drive letter and a colon before the name of the folder (for example, *D:\data*).

If you're on a network, you can even open a folder that's sitting on another computer on the network. To do so, type *two* backslashes, the computer's name, and then the shared folder's name. For instance, to access a shared folder called Budgets on a computer named Admin, enter *admin\budgets*. (See Chapter 26 for more on sharing folders over the network.)

It might make you feel extra proficient to know that you've just used the *Universal Naming Convention,* or UNC, for the shared folder. The UNC is simply the two-backslash, computer name\folder name format (for example: *ComputerName\foldername*).

Tip: In any of these cases, if you don't remember the precise name of a file or folder you want to open in the Run dialog box, then click the Browse button to display the Browse dialog box, as shown in Figure 1-17, bottom.

Connect to a Web Page

You can jump directly to a specific Web page by typing its Web address (URL)—such as *http://www.bigcompany.com*—into the Run dialog box and then pressing Enter. You don't even have to open your Web browser first.

Once again, you may not have to type very much; the drop-down list in the Run dialog box lists every URL you've previously entered. Simply click one (or press the ↓ key to highlight the one you want, and then press Enter) to go to that site.

The Path to Enlightenment about Paths

Windows is too busy to think of a particular file as "that family album program in the Program Files folder, which is in the Programs folder on the C drive." Instead, it uses shorthand to specify each icon's location on your hard drive—a series of disk and folder names separated by backslashes, like this: *C:\program files\pbsoftware\beekeeperpro.exe.*

This kind of location code is that icon's *path.* (Capitalization doesn't matter, even though you may see capital letters in Microsoft's examples.)

You'll encounter file paths when using several important Windows features. The Run dialog box described in this section is one. The address bar at the top of every Explorer window is another, although Microsoft has made addresses easier to read by displaying triangle separators in the address bar instead of slashes. (That is, you now see Users ▸ Casey instead of Users\Casey.)

Try not to be confused by the fact that Web addresses use forward slashes (/) instead of backslashes (\)!

Explorer, Windows, & the Taskbar

W indows got its name from the rectangles on the screen—the windows—
where all your computer activity takes place. You look at a Web page in a
window, type into a window, read email in a window, and look at lists of
files in a window. But as you create more files, stash them in more folders, and open
more programs, it's easy to wind up paralyzed before a screen awash with cluttered,
overlapping rectangles.

Fortunately, Windows has always offered icons, buttons, and other inventions to help
you keep these windows under control—and Windows 7 positively crawls with them.

Universal Window Controls

All Versions

As Figure 2-1 shows, a lot has changed in windows since the Windows of a few years
ago. If you're feeling disoriented, firmly grasp a nearby stationary object and read
the following breakdown.

Here are the controls that appear on almost every window, whether in an application
or in Explorer:

- **Title bar.** It's really not much of a title bar anymore, since the window's *title only*
rarely appears here (Figure 2-1). But this big, fat top strip is still a giant handle
you can use to drag a window around.

Tip: The title bar offers two great shortcuts for maximizing a window, making it expand to fill your entire screen exactly as though you had clicked the Maximize button described below. Shortcut 1: Double-click the title bar. (Double-click it again to restore the window to its original size.) Shortcut 2: Drag the title bar up against the top of your monitor. That maximizing shortcut is new in Windows 7.

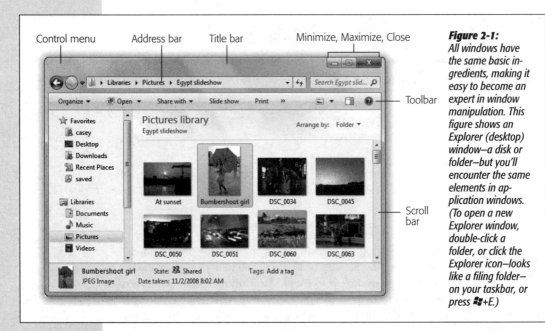

Control menu   Address bar   Title bar   Minimize, Maximize, Close

Toolbar

Scroll bar

Figure 2-1:
All windows have the same basic in-gredients, making it easy to become an expert in window manipulation. This figure shows an Explorer (desktop) window—a disk or folder—but you'll encounter the same elements in application windows. (To open a new Explorer window, double-click a folder, or click the Explorer icon—looks like a filing folder—on your taskbar, or press ⊞+E.)

- **Window edges.** You can reshape a window by dragging any edge except the top. Position your cursor over any border until it turns into a double-headed arrow. Then drag inward or outward to make the window smaller or bigger. (To resize a full-screen window, click the "restore down" button first.)

Tip: You can resize a window in two dimensions at once by dragging one of its corners. Sometimes a dotted triangle appears at the lower-right corner, sometimes not; in either case, all *four* corners work the same way.

On most computers, window edges are also transparent, revealing a slightly blurry image of what's underneath. (That's the Aero effect at work; see page 25.) Truth be told, being able to see what's underneath the edges of your window (sort of) doesn't really offer any particular productivity advantage. Sure does look cool, though.

- **Minimize, Maximize, [restore down].** These three window-control buttons, at the top of every Windows window, cycle a window among its three modes—minimized, maximized, and restored, as described on page the following pages.

- **Close button.** Click the ⊠ button to close the window. *Keyboard shortcut:* Press Alt+F4.

Tip: Isn't it cool how the Minimize, Maximize, and Close buttons "light up" when your cursor passes over them? (At least they do if you've got Aero, as described in Chapter 1.)

Actually, that's not just a gimmick; it's a cue that lets you know when the button is clickable. You might not otherwise realize, for example, that you can close, minimize, or maximize a *background* window without first bringing it forward. But when the background window's Close box beams bright red, you know.

- **Scroll bar.** A scroll bar appears on the right side or bottom of the window if the window isn't large enough to show all its contents.

- **Control menu.** In Windows XP and earlier versions, there was a tiny icon in the upper-left corner of every Explorer window. It was a menu of commands for sizing, moving, and closing the window.

  In Windows 7, the Control menu is *invisible*. But if you click where it's supposed to be, the menu opens. It's clearly intended for use only by the initiated who pass on the secret from generation to generation.

  One of the Control menu's commands is Move. It turns your cursor into a four-headed arrow; at this point, you can move the window by dragging *any* part of it, even the middle. Why bother, since you can always just drag the top edge of a window to move it? Because sometimes, windows get dragged *past* the top of your screen. You can hit Alt+space to open the Control menu, type *M* to trigger the Move command, and then move the window by pressing the arrow keys (or by dragging *any* visible portion). When the window is where you want it, hit Enter to "let go," or the Esc key to return the window to its original position.

Tip: You can double-click the Control menu spot to close a window.

Sizing, Moving, and Closing Windows

A Windows window can cycle among three altered states.

Maximized

A maximized window is one that fills the screen, edge to edge, so you can't see anything behind it. It gets that way when you do one of these things:

- Click its Maximize button (identified in Figure 2-1).

- Double-click the title bar.

- Drag the window up against the top of the screen. (That's a new technique in Windows 7, as described below.)

- Press ⊞+↑. (That's also new in Windows 7, and it's awesome.)

- Press Alt+space, then X. (That's the clumsy *old* key sequence.)

Maximizing the window is an ideal arrangement when you're surfing the Web or working on a document for hours at a stretch, since the largest possible window means the least possible scrolling.

Once you've maximized a window, you can restore it to its usual, free-floating state in any of these ways:

- Drag the window away from the top edge of the screen.

- Double-click the title bar.

- Click the Restore Down button (▣). (The Maximize button looks like that only when the window is, in fact, maximized.)

- Press ⊞+↓. (New in Windows 7.)

Tip: If the window *isn't* maximized, this keystroke minimizes it instead.

- Press Alt+space, then R.

Minimized

When you click a window's *Minimize* button (▬), the window gets out of your way. It shrinks down into the form of a button on your taskbar, at the bottom of the screen. Minimizing a window is a great tactic when you want to see what's behind it. *Keyboard shortcut:* ⊞+↓.

You can bring the window back, of course (that'd kind of be a bummer otherwise). Point to the taskbar button that represents that window's *program.* For example, if you minimized an Explorer (desktop) window, point to the Explorer icon.

If Aero is working (page 23), the program's button sprouts handy thumbnail miniatures of the minimized windows when you point to it without clicking. Click a window's thumbnail to restore it to full size. (You can read more about this trick later in this chapter.)

If you're in a non-Aero mode, the program's button sprouts the *names* of the minimized windows. Click the window name you want to bring it back again.

Tip: In Windows 7, there's a cool twist on minimizing, described in the following section, called Aero Shake.

Restored

A *restored* window is neither maximized nor minimized; it's a loose cannon, floating around on your screen as an independent rectangle. Because its edges aren't attached to the walls of your monitor, you can make it any size you like by dragging its borders.

Moving a Window

Moving a window is easy—just drag the big, fat top edge.

Closing a Window

Microsoft wants to make absolutely sure you're never without some method of closing a window. It offers at least nine ways to do it:

- Click the Close button (the ⊠ in the upper-right corner).

Tip: If you've managed to open more than one window, Shift-click that button to close *all* of them.

- Press Alt+F4. (This one's worth memorizing. You'll use it everywhere in Windows.)
- Double-click the window's upper-left corner.
- Click the invisible Control menu in the upper-left corner, and then choose Close from the menu.
- Right-click the window's taskbar button (see page 105), and then choose Close from the shortcut menu.
- Point to a taskbar button without clicking; if you have Aero working (page 23), thumbnail images of its windows appear. Point to a thumbnail; an ⊠ button appears in its upper-right corner. Click it.
- Right-click the window's title bar (top edge), and choose Close from the shortcut menu.
- In an Explorer window, choose Organize→Close. In many other programs, you can choose File→Close.
- Quit the program you're using, log off, or shut down the PC.

Be careful. In many programs, including Internet Explorer, closing the window also quits the program entirely.

Tip: If you see *two* ⊠ buttons in the upper-right corner of your screen, then you're probably using a program like Microsoft Excel. It's what Microsoft calls an MDI, or *multiple document interface* program. It gives you a window within a window. The outer window represents the application itself; the inner one represents the particular *document* you're working on.

If you want to close one document before working on another, be careful to click the *inner* Close button. If you click the outer one, you'll exit the entire application.

Layering Windows

When you have multiple windows open on your screen, only one window is *active*, which affects how it works:

- It's in the foreground, *in front* of all other windows.
- It's the window that "hears" your keystrokes and mouse clicks.
- Its Close button is red. (Background windows' Close buttons are transparent or window-colored, at least until you point to them.)

As you would assume, clicking a background window brings it to the front.

Tip: And pressing Alt+Esc sends an active window to the *back.* Bet you didn't know that one!

And what if it's so far back that you can't even see it? That's where Windows's window-management tools come in; read on.

Tip: For quick access to the desktop, clear the screen by clicking Show Desktop—the skinny rectangle at the far right end of the taskbar—or by pressing ⊞+D. Pressing that keystroke again brings all the windows back to the screen exactly as they were.

New Window Tricks in Windows 7

Home Premium • Professional • Enterprise • Ultimate

There are a few new shortcuts in Windows 7, expressly designed for managing windows. Most of them involve some clever *mouse gestures*—special dragging techniques. Thanks to those mouse movements and the slick animations you get in response, goofing around with your windows may become the new Solitaire.

Aero Snap

Microsoft applies that name—Aero Snap—to a set of expando-window tricks.

Note: Despite the word Aero in the name, the Snap features work in the Home Basic and Starter editions of Windows 7, too.

Here's the rundown:

- **Maximize a window** by dragging its title bar against the top edge of your monitor.
- **Restore a maximized window** by dragging its title bar *down* from the top of the screen.
- **Make a full-height, half-width window** by dragging it against one side of your screen.

Tip: Actually, it's faster to use the new keyboard shortcuts: ⊞+← to snap the window against the left side, or ⊞+→ to snap it against the right. To move the window back again, either hit the same keystroke a couple more times (it cycles left, right, and original spot, over and over), or use the ⊞ key with the opposite arrow key.

And if you have more than one monitor, add the Shift key to move the frontmost window to the next monitor, left or right.

And why would you bother? Well, a full-height, half-width window is ideal for reading an article, for example. You wouldn't want your eyes to keep scanning the text all the way across the football field of your screen; and you wouldn't want to spend a lot of fussy energy trying to make the window tall enough to read without scrolling a lot. This gesture sets things up for you with one quick drag.

But this half-screen-width trick is even more useful when you apply it to *two* windows, as shown in Figure 2-2. Now it's simple to compare two windows' contents, or to move or copy stuff between them.

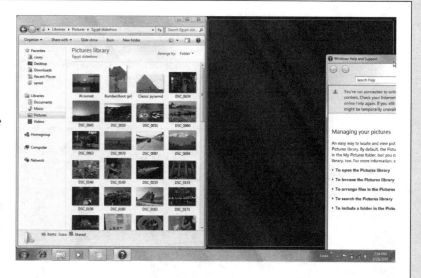

Figure 2-2:
Parking two windows side by side is a convenient preparation for copying information between them or comparing their contents— and it's super-easy in Windows 7. Just drag the first window against the right or left side of your screen; then drag the second window against the opposite side (shown here in progress on the right). Each one gracefully snaps to the full height of your monitor, but only half its width.

• **Make a window the full height of the screen.** This trick never got much love from Microsoft's marketing team, probably because it's a little harder to describe. But it can be very useful.

NOSTALGIA CORNER

Turn Off All the Snapping and Shaking

It's cool how Windows now makes a window snap against the top or side of your screen. Right? I mean, it is better than before, right?

It's perfectly OK to answer, "I don't think so. It's driving me crazy. I don't want my operating system manipulating my windows on its own."

In that case, you can turn off the snapping and shaking features. Open the Start menu. Type enough of the word

shaking until you see "Turn off automatic window arrangement." Click it.

You've just opened the "Make the mouse easier to use" control panel. At the bottom, turn on "Prevent windows from being automatically arranged when moved to the edge of the screen," and then click OK.

From now on, windows move only when and where you move them. (Shaking a window's title bar doesn't hide other windows now, either.)

It's not the same as the previous trick; this one doesn't affect the *width* of the window. It does, however, make the window exactly as tall as your screen, sort of like *half*-maximizing it; see Figure 2-3.

Tip: There's a new keyboard shortcut for this new feature: Shift+⊞+↑ to create the full-height effect, and (of course) Shift+⊞+↓ to restore the window's original height.

To restore the window to its original dimensions, drag its top or bottom edge away from the edge of your screen.

Note: These new window-morphing tricks make a good complement to the traditional "Cascade windows," "Show windows stacked," and "Show windows side by side" commands that appear when you right-click an empty spot on the taskbar.

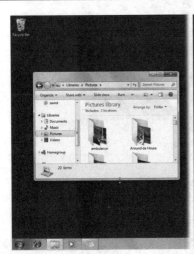

Figure 2-3:
The before-and-after effect of the full-screen-height feature of Aero Snap. To make this work, grab the bottom edge of your window (left) and drag it down to the bottom edge of your screen. The window snaps only vertically, but maintains its width and horizontal position (right).

Aero Shake

If you've become fond of minimizing windows—and why not?—then you'll love this one. If you give your window's title bar a rapid back-and-forth *shake*, you minimize all *other* windows. The one you shook stays right where it was (Figure 2-4).

Tip: Aero Shake makes a very snazzy YouTube demo video, but it's not actually the easiest way to isolate one window. If the window you want to focus on is already the frontmost window, you can just press ⊞+Home key to achieve the same effect. Press that combo a second time to restore all the minimized windows.

Handily enough, you can bring all the hidden windows back again, just by giving the hero window another title-bar shake.

Note: Dialog boxes (for example, boxes with OK and Cancel buttons) aren't affected by this Aero Shake thing—only full-blown windows.

Figure 2-4:
Top: OK, this is the state of your screen. You want to have a look at your desktop—but oy, what a cluttered mess!

Bottom: So you give this window's title bar a little shake—at least a couple of horizontal or vertical back-and-forths—and boom! All other windows are minimized to the taskbar, so you can see what you're doing. Give the title bar a second shake to bring the hidden windows back again.

The Show Desktop Button

Believe it or not, that bizarre little reflective-looking stick of Trident in the lower-right corner of your screen—at the right end of your taskbar—is actually a button. It's the old Show Desktop button (Figure 2-5), now moved to a new location.

It has two functions:

- **Point to it without clicking** to make all windows completely transparent, leaving behind only their outlines. (Holding down ▦+Space bar does the same thing.)

  This technique is primarily useful when (a) you want an easier look at your Windows *gadgets* (page 234), or (b) you want to show people how cool Windows 7 is.

Note: This point-without-clicking thing works only if your PC can handle Aero (page 23) and if you've selected an Aero theme (page 178).

- **Click it** to make all windows and dialog boxes disappear *completely*, so you can do some work on your desktop. They're not minimized—they don't shrink down into the taskbar—they're just gone. Click the Show Desktop button a second time to bring them back from invisible-land.

Tip: Once again, there's a less flashy, but more efficient keyboard trick that achieves the same effect. Next time you want to minimize all windows, revealing your entire desktop, press ▦+M (which you can think of as M for "Minimize all"). Add the Shift key (Shift+▦+M) to bring them all back.

Figure 2-5:
There was a Show Desktop button in previous versions of Windows, but it's never been a vertical column at the right end of the taskbar before (inset). If you find yourself triggering it accidentally, you can turn the feature off. Right-click the taskbar; from the shortcut menu, choose Properties; turn off the "Use Aero Peek to preview the desktop" checkbox, and click OK.

Windows Flip (Alt+Tab)

All Versions

In its day, the concept of overlapping windows on the screen was brilliant, innovative, and extremely effective. In that era before digital cameras, MP3 files, and the Web, managing your windows was easy this way; after all, you had only about three of them.

These days, however, managing all the open windows in all your programs can be like herding cats. Off you go, burrowing through the microscopic pop-up menus of your taskbar buttons, trying to find the window you want. And heaven help you if you need to duck back to the desktop—to find a newly downloaded file, for example, or to eject a disk. You have to fight your way through 50,000 other windows on your way to the bottom of the "deck."

Windows 7 offers the same window-shuffling tricks that were available in previous editions:

- **Use the taskbar.** Clicking a button on the taskbar (page 101) makes the corresponding program pop to the front, along with any of its floating toolbars, palettes, and so on.

- **Click the window.** You can also bring any window forward by clicking any visible part of it.

- **Alt+Tab.** For years, this keyboard shortcut has offered a quick way to bring a different window to the front without using the mouse. If you press Tab while holding down the Alt key, a floating palette displays the icons of all running programs, as shown at the top in Figure 2-6. Each time you press Tab again (still keeping the Alt key down), you highlight the next icon; when you release the keys, the highlighted program jumps to the front, as though in a high-tech game of duck-duck-goose.

  This feature has been gorgeous-ized, as shown in Figure 2-6; if Aero is working, then all windows turn into invisible outlines except the one you've currently tabbed

Figure 2-6:
Alt+Tab highlights successive icons; add Shift to move backward. (Add the Ctrl key to lock the display, so you don't have to keep Alt down. Tab to the icon you want; then press the space bar or Enter.)

to (in Figure 2-6, it's the Sticky Notes program). Alt+Tab has been renamed, too; it's now called Windows Flip.

> **Tip:** If you just *tap* Alt+Tab without *holding down* the Alt key, you get an effect that's often even more useful: You jump back and forth between the *last two* windows you've had open. It's great when, for example, you're copying sections of a Web page into a Word document.

Windows Flip 3D

Home Premium • Professional • Enterprise • Ultimate

If your PC can run Aero (page 23), Microsoft has something much slicker for this purpose: Flip 3D, a sort of holographic alternative to the Alt+Tab trick.

The concept is delicious. With the press of a keystroke, Windows shrinks *all windows in all programs* so that they all fit on the screen (Figure 2-7), stacked like the exploded view of a deck of cards. You flip through them to find the one you want, and you're there. It's fast, efficient, animated, and a lot of fun.

> **Tip:** You even see, among the other 3-D "cards," a picture of the desktop itself. If you choose it, Windows minimizes all open windows and takes you to the desktop for quick access to whatever is there.

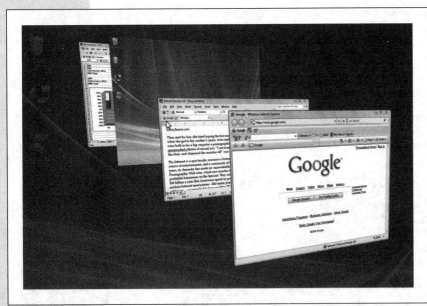

Figure 2-7:
These window miniatures aren't snapshots; they're "live." That is, if anything is changing inside a window (a movie is playing, for example), you'll see it right on the 3-D miniature.

By the way: Don't miss the cool slow-motion trick described in Appendix B..

Here's how you use it, in slow motion. First, press ⊞+Tab. If you keep your thumb on the ⊞ key, you see something like Figure 2-7.

At this point, you can shuffle through the "deck" of windows using either of these techniques:

- Tap the Tab key repeatedly. (Add the Shift key to move backward through the stack.)

- Turn your mouse's scroll wheel toward you. (Roll it away to move backward.)

When the window you want is in front, release the key. The 3-D stack vanishes, and the lucky window appears before you at full size.

Flip 3D Without Holding Down Keys

That Flip 3D thing is very cool, but do you really want to exhaust yourself by keeping your thumb pressed on that ⊞ key? Surely you'll wind up with the painful condition known as Nerd's Thumb.

Fortunately, you can also use Flip 3D without holding down keys. You can trigger it using these methods:

- Add the Ctrl key to the usual keystroke. That is, press ⊞+Ctrl+Tab. This time, you don't have to *keep* any keys pressed.

- Press the Flip 3D *key* on your keyboard, if it has one.

Any of these tactics triggers the 3-D floating-windows effect shown in Figure 2-7. At this point, you can use the arrow keys or your mouse's scroll wheel to flip through the open windows *without* having to hold down any keys. When you see the one you want, press the Esc key to choose it and bring it to the front.

Explorer Window Controls
All Versions

When you're working at the desktop—that is, opening Explorer folder windows— you'll find a few additional controls dotting the edges. They're quite a bit different from the controls of Windows XP and its predecessors.

Address Bar

In a Web browser, the address bar is where you type the addresses of the Web sites you want to visit. In an Explorer window, the address bar is more of a "bread-crumbs bar" (a shoutout to Hansel and Gretel fans). That is, it now shows the path you've taken—folders you burrowed through—to arrive where you are now (Figure 2-8).

There are three especially cool things about this address bar:

- **It's much easier to read.** Those ▸ little ▸ triangles are clearer separators of folder names than the older\slash\notation. And instead of drive letters like C:, you see the drive *names*.

Tip: If the succession of nested folders' names is too long to fit the window, then a tiny « icon appears at the left end of the address. Click it to reveal a pop-up menu showing, from last to first, the other folders you've had to burrow through to get here.

(Below the divider line, you see, for your convenience, the names of all the folders on your desktop.)

• **It's clickable.** You can click any breadcrumb to open the corresponding folder. For example, if you're viewing the Casey ▸ Pictures ▸ Halloween folder, you can click the *word* Pictures to backtrack to the Pictures folder.

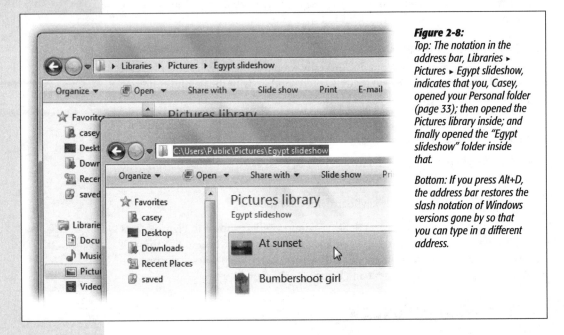

Figure 2-8:
Top: The notation in the address bar, Libraries ▸ Pictures ▸ Egypt slideshow, indicates that you, Casey, opened your Personal folder (page 33); then opened the Pictures library inside; and finally opened the "Egypt slideshow" folder inside that.

Bottom: If you press Alt+D, the address bar restores the slash notation of Windows versions gone by so that you can type in a different address.

• **You can still edit it.** The address bar of old was still a powerful tool, because you could type in a folder address directly (using the slash notation).

Actually, you still can. You can "open" the address bar for editing in any of four different ways: (1) Press Alt+D. (2) Click the tiny icon to the left of the address. (3) Click any blank spot. (4) Right-click anywhere in the address; from the shortcut menu, choose Edit Address.

In each case, the address bar changes to reveal the old-style slash notation, ready for editing (Figure 2-8, bottom).

Tip: After you've had a good look, press Esc to restore the ▸ notation.

Components of the address bar

On top of all that, the address bar houses a few additional doodads that make it easy for you to jump around on your hard drive (Figure 2-9):

• **Back (←), Forward (→).** Just as in a Web browser, the Back button opens whatever window you opened just before this one. Once you've used the Back button, you can then use the Forward button to return to the window where you started. *Keyboard shortcuts:* Alt+←, Alt+→.

- **Recent pages list.** Click the ▾ to the left of the address bar to see a list of folders you've had open recently; it's like a multilevel Back button.

- **Recent folders list.** Click the ▾ at the *right* end of the address bar to see a pop-up menu listing addresses you've recently typed.

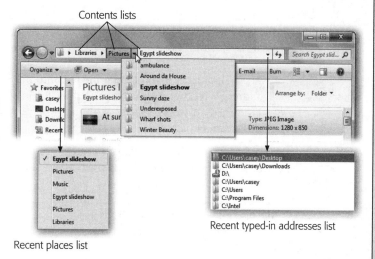

Figure 2-9:
The address bar is crawling with useful controls and clickable gizmos. It may take you awhile to appreciate the difference between the little ▾ to the left of the address bar and the one to its right, though. The left-side one shows a list of folders you've had open recently; the right-side one shows addresses you've explicitly typed (and not passed through by clicking).

Contents lists

Recent places list

Recent typed-in addresses list

- **Contents list.** This one takes some explaining, but for efficiency nuts, it's a gift from the gods.

  It turns out that the little ▸ next to each bread crumb (folder name) is actually a pop-up menu. Click it to see what's *in* the folder name to its left.

  How is this useful? Suppose you're viewing the contents of the USA ▸ Florida ▸ Miami folder, but you decide that the file you're looking for is actually in the USA ▸ California folder. Do you have to click the Back button, retracing your steps to the USA folder, only to then walk back down a different branch of the folder tree? No, you don't. You just click the ▸ that's next to the USA folder's name and choose California from the list.

- **Refresh (↻).** If you suspect that the window contents aren't up to date (for example, that maybe somebody has just dropped something new into it from across the network), click this button, or press F5, to make Windows update the display.

- **Search box.** Type a search phrase into this box to find what you're looking for *within this window.* Page 130 has the details.

What to type into the address bar

When you click the tiny folder icon at the left end of the address bar (or press Alt+D), the triangle ▸ notation changes to the slash\notation, meaning that you can edit the address. At this point, the address bar is like the little opening in the glass divider that lets you speak to your New York cab driver; you tell it where you want to go. Here's what you can type there (press Enter afterward):

- **A Web address.** You can leave off the *http://* portion. Just type the body of the Web address, such as *www.sony.com*, into this strip. When you press Enter (or click the → button, called the Go button), Internet Explorer opens to the Web page you specified.

Tip: If you press Ctrl+Enter instead of just Enter, you can surround whatever you've just typed into the address bar with *http://www.* and *.com*. See Chapter 11 for even more address shortcuts along these lines.

- **A search phrase.** If you type some text into this strip that isn't obviously a Web address, Windows assumes you're telling it, "Go online and search for this phrase." From here, it works exactly as though you've used the Internet search feature described on page 403.

- **A folder name.** You can also type one of several important folder names into this strip, such as *Computer, Documents, Music,* and so on. When you press Enter, that particular folder window opens.

Tip: This window has AutoComplete. That is, if you type *pi* and then press Tab, the address bar will complete the word *Pictures* for you. (If it guesses wrong, press Tab again.)

- **A program or path name.** In this regard, the address bar works just like the Run command (page 55).

In each case, as soon as you begin to type, a pop-up list of recently visited Web sites, files, or folders appears below the address bar. Windows is trying to save you some

---

NOSTALGIA CORNER

Would You Like to See the Menu Bar?

You may have noticed already that there's something dramatically different about the menu bar (File, Edit, View, and so on): It's gone. Microsoft decided you'd rather have a little extra space to see your icons.

Fortunately, you can bring it back, in three ways.

Temporarily. Press the Alt key or the F10 key. Presto! The traditional menu bar reappears. You even get to see the classic one-letter underlines that tell you what letter keys you can type to operate the menus without the mouse.

Permanently, all windows. On the task toolbar, choose Organize→Layout→"Menu bar." The traditional menu

bar appears, right above the task toolbar. There it will stay forever, in all Explorer windows, at least until you turn it off using the same command.

Permanently, all windows (alternate method). Here's another trick that achieves the same thing. Open Folder Options. (Do that by typing *folder op* into the Start menu's Search box, or by choosing Organize→"Folder and search options" in any Explorer window.)

In the resulting dialog box, click the View tab. Turn on "Always show menus," and then click OK.

typing. If you see what you're looking for, click it with the mouse, or press the ↓ key to highlight the one you want and then press Enter.

The Task Toolbar

See the colored strip that appears just below the address bar? That's the *task toolbar*. It's something like a menu bar, in that some of the words on it (like Organize) are menus. But it's also like the task pane of Windows XP, in that its buttons are different in different windows. In a folder that contains pictures, you see buttons here like "Slide show" and "Share with"; in a folder that contains music files, the buttons might say "Play all" and "Burn."

Later in this chapter, you'll meet some of the individual commands in this toolbar.

Note: You can't hide the task toolbar.

Optional Window Panes
All Versions

Most Explorer windows have some basic informational stuff across the top: the address bar and the task toolbar, at the very least.

But that's just the beginning. As shown in Figure 2-10, the Organize menu on the task toolbar lets you hide or show as many as four *other* strips of information. Turning them all on at once may make your windows feel a bit claustrophobic, but at least you'll know absolutely everything there is to know about your files and folders.

The trick is to choose a pane name from the Organize→Layout command, as shown in Figure 2-10. Here are the options you'll find there.

Tip: You can adjust the size of any pane by dragging the dividing line that separates it from the main window. (You know you've got the right spot when your cursor turns into a double-headed arrow.)

Details Pane

This strip appears at the *bottom* of the window, and it can be extremely useful. It reveals all kinds of information about whatever icon you've clicked in the main part of the window: its size, date, type, and so on. Some examples:

- For a music file, the Details pane reveals the song's duration, band and album names, genre, the star rating you've provided, and so on.

- For a disk icon, you get statistics about its formatting scheme, capacity, and how much of it is full.

- For a Microsoft Office document, you see when it was created and modified, how many pages it has, who wrote it, and so on.

- If *nothing* is selected, you get information about the open window itself: namely, how many items are in it.

• If you select several icons at once, this pane shows you the sum of their file sizes—a great feature when you're burning a CD, for example, and don't want to exceed the 650 MB limit. You also see the *range* of dates when they were created and modified.

What's especially intriguing is that you can *edit* many of these details, as described on page 87.

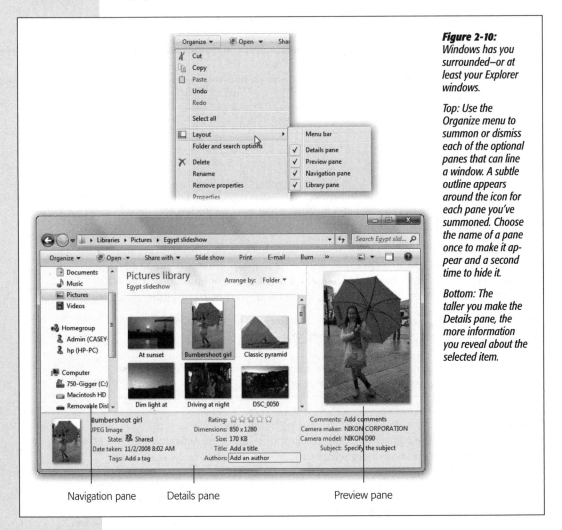

Figure 2-10:
Windows has you surrounded–or at least your Explorer windows.

Top: Use the Organize menu to summon or dismiss each of the optional panes that can line a window. A subtle outline appears around the icon for each pane you've summoned. Choose the name of a pane once to make it appear and a second time to hide it.

Bottom: The taller you make the Details pane, the more information you reveal about the selected item.

Navigation pane   Details pane   Preview pane

Preview Pane

The Preview pane appears at the *right* side of the window. That's right: You can now have information strips that wrap *all four sides* of a window.

Anyway, the Preview pane can be handy when you're examining common file types like pictures, text files, RTF files, sounds, and movies. As you click each icon, you see a magnified thumbnail version of what's actually *in* that document. As Figure 2-11 demonstrates, a controller lets you play sounds and movies right there in the Explorer window, without having to fire up Windows Media Player. (Cool.)

Tip: You don't have to fuss with the Organize→Layout command to make the Preview pane appear and disappear. Instead, you can just click the Preview icon identified in Figure 2-11. That's new in Windows 7.

Figure 2-11:
In many windows, the Preview pane can get in the way, because it shrinks the window space without giving you much useful information. But when you're browsing movies or sound files, it's awesome; it lets you play the music or the movie right in place, right in the window, without having to open up a playback program.

Now, the Preview pane isn't omniscient; right out of the box, Windows can't display the contents of oddball document types like, say, sheet-music documents or 3-D modeling files. But as you install new programs, the Preview pane can get smarter. Install Office, for example, and it can display Office files' contents; install Adobe Acrobat, and it can show you PDF files. Whether or not the Preview pane recognizes a certain document type depends on the effort expended by the programmers who wrote its program (that is, whether they wrote *preview handlers* for their document types).

Navigation Pane

The Navigation pane is the helpful folder map at the left side of an Explorer window. It's come a long way, baby, since the folder hierarchy of Windows XP, and even since the Navigation pane of Windows Vista. Today, it's something like a master map of your computer, with a special focus on the places and things you might want to visit most often.

Favorite Links list

At the top of the Navigation pane, there's a collapsible list of Favorites. These aren't Web-browser bookmarks, even though Microsoft uses the same term for those. Instead, these are *places* to which you want quick access. Mostly, that means folders or disks, but saved searches and libraries are eligible, too (both are described later in this chapter).

Since this pane will be waiting in every Explorer window you open, taking the time to install your favorite folders here can save you a lot of repetitive folder-burrowing. One click on a folder name opens the corresponding window. For example, click the Pictures icon to view the contents of your Pictures folder in the main part of the window (Figure 2-12).

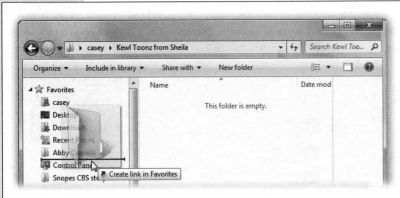

Figure 2-12:
The Navigation pane makes navigation very quick, because you can jump back and forth between distant corners of your PC with a single click. Folder and disk icons here work just like normal ones. You can drag a document onto a folder icon to file it there, for example.

Out of the box, this list offers icons for your desktop and your Downloads folder (which is actually inside your Personal folder), plus a Recent Places link that reveals all the folders and Control Panel items you've opened recently.

Tip: If you click the word Favorites itself, you open the Favorites window, where the shortcuts for all your Favorites are stored. Now you have a quick way to add, delete, or rename the items in your favorite links all at once.

The beauty of this parking lot for containers is that it's so easy to set up with *your* favorite places. For example:

• **Remove** an icon by dragging it out of the window entirely and onto the Recycle Bin icon; it vanishes from the list. Or right-click it and, from the shortcut menu, choose Remove. (Of course, you haven't actually removed anything from your *PC*; you've just unhitched its alias from the Navigation pane.)

Tip: If you delete one of the starter icons (Desktop, Downloads, Recent Places) and later wish you had it back, no big deal. Right-click the word Favorites; from the shortcut menu, choose "Restore favorite links."

• **Rearrange** the icons by dragging them up or down in the list. Release the mouse when the thick black horizontal line lies in the desired new location.

Tip: You can also sort this list alphabetically. Right-click the word Favorites; from the shortcut menu, choose "Sort by name."

- **Install a new folder, disk, library, or saved search** by dragging its icon off of your desktop (or out of a window) into any spot in the list.

- **Adjust the width** of the pane by dragging the vertical divider bar right or left.

Tip: If you drag carefully, you can position the divider bar *just* to the right of the disk and folder icons, thereby hiding their names almost completely. Some people find it a tidier look; you can always identify the folder names by pointing to them without clicking.

Libraries

The next section of the Navigation pane lists your *libraries*. You can read about this new Windows 7 feature beginning on page 81.

POWER USERS' CLINIC

The Master Explorer-Window Keyboard-Shortcut List

If you arrive home one day to discover that your mouse has been stolen, or if you simply like using the keyboard, you'll enjoy the shortcuts that work in Windows Explorer:

F6 or Tab cycles the "focus" (highlighting) among the different parts of the window: Favorite Links, address bar, main window, and so on. (The only caveat: F6 skips over the Search box, for some reason.)

F4 highlights the address bar and pops open the list of previous addresses. (Press Alt+D to highlight the address bar without opening the pop-up menu.)

Alt+← opens the previously viewed window, as though you've clicked the Back button in a browser. Once you've used Alt+←, you can press Alt+→ key to move *forward* through your recently open windows.

Backspace does the same thing as Alt+←. It, too, walks you backward through the most recent windows you've had open. That's a change from Windows XP, when Backspace meant "up," as in, "Take me to the parent folder" (see Alt+↑, below).

Alt+double-clicking an icon opens the Properties window for that icon. (It shows the same sort of information you'd find in the Details pane.) Or, if the icon is already highlighted, press Alt+Enter.

Alt+↑ opens the parent window of whatever you're looking at now. For example, if you've drilled down into the USA→ Texas→Houston folder, you could hit Alt+↑ to pop "upward" to the Texas folder, again for the USA folder, and so on. If you hit Alt+↑ enough times, you wind up at your Desktop.

F11 enters or exits full-screen mode, in which the current window fills the entire screen. Even the taskbar is hidden. This effect is more useful in a Web browser than at the desktop, but you never know; sometimes you want to see everything in a folder.

Shift+Ctrl+N makes a new empty folder.

Shift+Ctrl+E adjusts the Navigation pane so that it reveals the folder path of whatever window is open right now, expanding the indented folder icons as necessary.

Press the Ctrl key while turning the mouse's scroll wheel to magnify or shrink the icons in your window. You can also press the letter keys to highlight a folder or file that begins with that letter, or the ↑ and ↓ keys to "walk" up and down a list of icons.

Homegroup

Next in the Nav pane is the Homegroup heading. Here's a list of all the Windows 7 computers in your house that you've joined into a harmonious unit, using the HomeGroup networking feature described in Chapter 26.

Computer

The next heading is Computer. When you expand this heading, you see a list of all of your drives (including the main C: drive), each of which is also expandable (Figure 2-13). In essence, this view can show you every folder on the machine at once. It lets you burrow very deeply into your hard drive's nest of folders without ever losing your bearings.

Figure 2-13:
When you click a disk or folder in the Navigation pane—including the Computer hierarchy—the main window displays its contents, including files and folders. Double-click to expand a disk or folder, opening a new, indented list of what's inside it; double-click again to collapse the folder list. (Clicking the flippy triangle accomplishes the same thing.)

At deeper levels of indentation, you may not be able to read an icon's full name. Point to it without clicking to see an identifying tooltip, as shown here.

Network

Finally, the Network heading shows your entire network. Not just Windows 7 PCs that have been connected as a homegroup, but the *entire* network—Macs, PCs running older Windows versions, Linux boxes, whatever.

Flippy triangles

As you can see, the Navigation list displays *only* disks and folders, never individual files. To see those, look at the main window, which displays the contents (folders *and* files) of whatever disk or folder you click.

To expand a folder or disk that appears in the Nav pane, double-click its name, or click the tiny ▸ next to its name. You've just turned the Nav list into an outline; the contents of the folder appear in an indented list, as shown in Figure 2-14. Double-click again, or click the flippy triangle again, to collapse the folder listing.

By selectively expanding folders like this, you can, in effect, peer inside two or more folders simultaneously, all within the single Navigation list. You can move files around by dragging them onto the tiny folder icons, too.

Libraries

All Versions

Libraries are new in Windows 7. They're like folders, except that they can display the contents of *other* folders from all over your PC—and even from other PCs on your network. In other words, a library doesn't really contain anything at all. It simply monitors *other* folders, and provides a single "place" to work with all their contents.

Windows 7 starts you out with four libraries: Documents, Music, Pictures, and Videos. Sure, XP and Vista came with *folders* bearing those names, but libraries are much more powerful. (You can make libraries of your own, too.)

The Pictures library, for example, seems to contain all your photos—but in real life, they may be scattered all over your hard drive, on external drives, or on other PCs in the house.

So what's the point? Well, consider the advantages over regular folders:

- **Everything's in one spot.** When it comes time to put together a year-end photo album, for example, you might be very grateful to find your pictures, your spouse's pictures from the upstairs PC, and the pictures from your kid's laptop all in one central place, ready for choosing. Figure 2-14 shows the idea.

- **Happy laptop reunions.** When you come home with your laptop and connect to the network, you're instantly reunited with all those music, pictures, and video files you store on other drives.

- **Easy backup or transfer.** You can back up or transfer all the files corresponding to a certain project or time period in one fell swoop, even though the originals are in a bunch of different places or reside on different collaborators' computers.

- **Manipulate en masse.** You can *work* with the contents of a library—slicing, dicing, searching, organizing, filtering—just as you would a folder's contents. But because you're actually working with folders from all over your computer and even your network, you can be far more efficient.

Working with Library Contents

To use a library, click its name in your Navigation pane. (Try Pictures, for example.)

A few clues tell you that you're not in a regular folder. First, there's the huge banner at the top of the window that says "Pictures library" or whatever (Figure 2-14). The subheading, "Includes: 2 locations," lets you know that you're actually looking at the consolidated contents of two folders.

The other giveaway is the "Arrange by:" pop-up menu. This awesome tool lets you sort the window contents according to useful criteria. For Pictures, you can sort by Folder, Month, Day, Rating, or Tag. For Music, it's Album, Artist, Song, Genre, and Rating. For Documents, it's Author, Date Modified, Tag, Type, or Name. You get the idea.

Actually sitting on
an external hard drive

Figure 2-14:
The Pictures library window seems to contain a bunch of photo folders, all in one place. As a bonus, you can access all this from within the Save and Open dialog boxes within your programs, too. But don't be fooled; in real life, these folders are scattered all over your system.

When you choose one of these Arrange commands, the icons in the library window clump together by type, like kids in a high-school cafeteria (Figure 2-15).

You can also *filter* a library window—that is, to hide all the files that don't meet certain criteria. You can show only the photos taken last year, only the songs recorded by The

---

Beatles, only documents written by your partner, and so on. Page 82 has more on filtering, but the point here is that you're now performing this action on files that have been rounded up from all over your system and your network—at once.

Tip: Remember, the icons in a library aren't really there; they're just a mirage. They're stunt doubles for files that actually sit in other folders on your hard drive.

Fortunately, when you're getting a bit confused as to what's really where, there's a way to jump to a file or folder's actual location. Right-click its icon in the library; from the shortcut menu, choose "Open file location" (or "Open folder location"). You jump right to the real thing, sitting in its actual Windows Explorer window.

Figure 2-15:
Top: The "Arrange by" pop-up menu does more than just sort things. It actually groups things. Here, when sorted by rating, Windows identifies each group of photos with its own headline, making the window look like an index. It's an inspired tool that makes it easier to hunt down specific icons among the haystack of thousands.

Bottom: When you're using "Arrange by" for your music, commands like Genre and Artist produce pseudo-folders—artificial holding tanks for all the music in that style or by that band.

Adding a Folder to an Existing Library

A library is nothing without a bunch of folders to feed into it. You can add a folder to a library (like Pictures or Music) in any of four ways, depending on where you're starting.

- **You can see the folder's icon.** If the folder is on the desktop or in a window, right-click it. From the shortcut menu, choose "Include in library"; the submenu lists all your existing libraries so you can choose the one you want. Figure 2-16 shows the idea.

Figure 2-16:
The path to adding a folder to a library may begin with the folder itself (left), the open window of the folder (bottom), or the library (right).

- **You can see the folder's icon (alternate).** Use the right mouse button to drag the folder onto a library's name in the Navigation pane. Release the mouse button when it's on the library name. From the shortcut menu, choose "Include in library."

- **You've opened the folder's window.** This one's even easier. On the toolbar of every folder window, there's a big fat "Include in library" menu staring you in the face. Use it to choose the library you want this folder to join.

- **You've opened the library window.** If you're already *in* the library, then where it says "Includes:" click where it says "3 locations" (or whatever the number is). You get the "Change how this library gathers its contents" dialog box, shown in Figure 2-16. Click Add, and then find and double-click the folder you want. You see it added to the "Library locations" list in the dialog box. Click OK.

The fine print

All the techniques above also work for folders on external drives, USB flash drives, and shared folders on your network. There is, however, some important fine print:

- You can't add a folder that's on a CD or a DVD.

- You *can* add a folder that's on a USB flash drive, as long as that flash drive's icon shows up in the Navigation pane when it's inserted, under the Computer/Hard Drives heading. (A few oddball models appear under Devices With Removable Storage; they're not allowed.) Furthermore, the folder won't be available in the library when the flash drive isn't inserted (duh).

- You can't add a networked folder to a library *unless* it's been *indexed for searching* on the PC that contains it; see page 134 for details on that process. (If it's a Windows 7 machine that's part of a homegroup [page 321], you're all set; it's been indexed.)

As an alternative, you can turn on the "available offline" feature for that networked folder, as described on page 636. The good news is that the folder can now be part of your library even when the other PC on the network is turned off. The bad news is that you've basically copied that folder to your own PC, which eats up a lot of disk space and sort of defeats the purpose of adding a networked folder to your library.

Removing a Folder from a Library

Getting rid of a folder is pretty straightforward, really. You can use any of these techniques:

- **If the library window is open:** Where it says "Includes:" click where it says "3 locations" (or whatever the number is). You get the "Change how this library gathers its contents" dialog box, shown in Figure 2-16. Click the folder you want to remove, click Remove, and click OK.

- **If the library's name is visible in the Navigation pane:** Expand the library to show the folder you want to remove. Right-click the folder's name. From the shortcut menu, choose "Remove location from library."

Remember: You're not deleting anything important. A library only *pretends* to contain other folders; the real ones are actually sitting in other places on your PC or network, even after the library is gone.

Creating a New Library

The starter libraries (Pictures, Music, Documents, and Videos) are awfully useful right out of the box. Truth is, they're as far as most people probably go with the libraries feature.

But you may have good reasons to create new ones. Maybe you want to create a library for each client—and fill it with the corresponding project folders, some of which have been archived away on external drives. Maybe you want to round up folders full of fonts, clip art, and text, in readiness for submitting a graphics project to a print shop.

In any case, here are the different ways to go about it:

- **From the Navigation pane.** Click the Libraries heading in the navigation pane, and then click "New library" in the toolbar. (Alternate method: Right-click the word "Library" in any window's Navigation pane. From the shortcut menu, choose New→Library.)

A new, empty library appears, both in the Libraries window and in the list of libraries in the Nav pane. It's up to you to add folders to it, as described earlier.

• **From a folder.** Right-click any folder. From the shortcut menu, choose "Include in library"→"Create new library." *Bing!* A new library appears in the Libraries list, named after the folder you clicked. As a handy bonus, this library already contains its first folder: the one you clicked, of course.

Tip: Once you've created a library, you can specify which canned library style it resembles most: General Items, Pictures, Music, Documents, or Videos. (Why does it matter? Because the library style determines which commands are available in the "Arrange by" pop-up menu. Pictures offer choices like Month and Day; Music offers choices like Rating and Genre.

Anyway, to make this choice, right-click the library's name in the Navigation pane of an Explorer window. From the shortcut menu, choose Properties. In the "Optimize this library for" list, click the type you want, and then click OK.

Tags, Metadata, and Properties
All Versions

See all that information in the Details pane—Date, Size, Title, and so on? It's known by geeks as *metadata* (Greek for "data about data"). (Drag the upper border of the Details pane upward to reveal more of this information.)

Different kinds of files provide different sorts of details. For a document, for example, you might see Authors, Comments, Title, Categories, Status, and so on. For an MP3 music file, you get Artists, Albums, Genre, Year, and so on. For a photo, you get Date Taken, Title, Author, and so on.

Oddly (and usefully) enough, you can actually edit some of this stuff (Figure 2-17).

POWER USERS' CLINIC

Hiding and Showing Libraries

Microsoft thinks libraries are very important. After all, libraries get one of the coveted spots in the Navigation pane at the left side of every single Explorer window.

You, however, may not consider all of them equally important. You might not use your PC for music at all. You might not have any videos.

Or maybe you love libraries, but you don't want all of them listed in the Nav pane, either for privacy reasons or clutter reasons.

In each of these cases, it's nice to know you can hide a library so that its name doesn't appear in the Nav pane. Just right-click the library's name; from the shortcut menu, choose "Don't show in navigation pane." Poof! It's gone (just the listing, not the library itself).

You can, fortunately, bring the library listing back. It's still sitting in your Personal folder→Libraries folder. To see it, click the word Libraries in any window's Navigation pane. Right-click the library's icon; from the shortcut menu, choose "Show in navigation pane." Foop! It's back in the list.

Some of the metadata is off limits. For example, you can't edit the Date Created or Date Modified info. (Sorry, defense attorneys of the world.) But you *can* edit the star ratings for music or pictures; in the row of five stars, click the rating star you want. Click the third star to give a song a 3, for example.

Figure 2-17:
Click the information you want to change; if a text-editing box appears, you've hit pay dirt. Type away, and then press Enter (or click the Save button at the lower-right corner of the dialog box). To input a list (of tags or authors, for example), type a semicolon (;) after each one.

Most usefully of all, you can edit the Tags box for almost *any* kind of icon. A tag is just a keyword. It can be anything you want: McDuffy Proposal, Old Junk, Back Me Up—anything. Later, you'll be able to round up everything on your computer with a certain tag, all in a single window, even though they physically reside in different folders.

You'll encounter tags in plenty of other places in Windows—and in this book, especially when it comes to searching for photos and music.

Note: Weirdly, you can't add tags or ratings to BMP, PNG, AVI, or MPG files.

Many of the boxes here offer autocompletion, meaning that Windows proposes finishing a name or text tidbit for you if it recognizes what you've started to type.

Tip: You can tag a bunch of icons at once. Just highlight them all (page 150) and then change the corresponding detail in the Details pane *once.* This is a great trick for applying a tag or star rating to a mass of files quickly.

Click Save when you're finished.

Properties

The Details pane shows some of the most important details about a file, but if you really want to see the entire metadata dossier for an icon, open its Properties dialog box using one of these tactics:

- Right-click it. From the shortcut menu, choose Properties.

- Alt+double-click it.

- If the icon is already highlighted, press Alt+Enter.

In each case, the Properties dialog box appears. It's a lot like the one in previous versions of Windows, in that it displays the file's name, location, size, and so on. But in Windows 7, it also bears a scrolling Details tab that's sometimes teeming with metadata details (Figure 2-18).

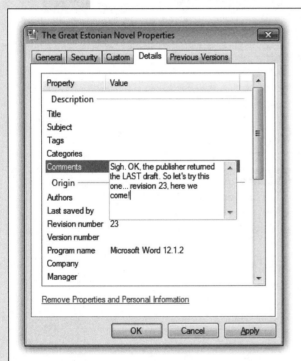

Figure 2-18:
If Windows knows anything about an icon, it's in here. Scroll, scroll, and scroll some more to find the tidbit you want to see—or to edit. As with the Details pane, many of these text morsels are editable.

Icon and List Views

All Versions

Windows's windows look just fine straight from the factory; the edges are straight, and the text is perfectly legible. Still, if you're going to stare at this screen for half of your waking hours, you may as well investigate some of the ways these windows can be enhanced.

For starters, you can view the files and folders in an Explorer window in either of two ways: as icons (of any size) or as a list (in several formats). Figure 2-19 shows some of your options.

Figure 2-19:
The Views pop-up menu is a little weird; it actually has two columns. At right, it displays the preset view options for the files and folders in a window. At left, a slider adjusts icon sizes to any degree of scaling—at least until it reaches the bottom part of its track.

In any case, here's a survey of the window views in Windows 7: Medium Icons, Content view, List view, and Details view. List and Details views are great for windows with lots of files. Extra Large Icons (not shown) is great if you're 30 feet away.

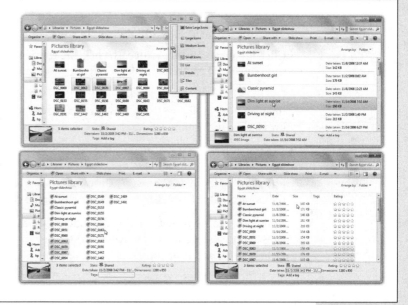

GEM IN THE ROUGH

How to Shed Your Metadata's Skin

At the bottom of the Details pane (of the Properties dialog box) is a peculiarly worded link: "Remove Properties and Personal Information."

This is a privacy feature. What it means is, "Clean away all the metadata I've added myself, like author names, tag keywords, and other insights into my own work routine."

Microsoft's thinking here is that you might not want other people who encounter this document (as an email attachment, for example) to have such a sweeping insight into the minutiae of your own work routine.

When you click this link, the Remove Properties dialog box appears, offering you a scrolling list of checkboxes: Title, Rating, Tags, Comments, and lots and lots of others.

You can proceed in either of two ways. If you turn on "Create a copy with all possible properties removed," then *all* the metadata that's possible to erase (everything but things like file type, name, and so on) will be stripped away. When you click OK, Windows instantly creates a duplicate of the file (with the word "Copy" tacked onto its name), ready for distribution to the masses in its clean form. The original is left untouched.

If you choose "Remove the following properties from this file" instead, you can specify exactly *which* file details you want erased from the original. (Turn on the appropriate checkboxes.)

Every window remembers its view settings independently. You might prefer to look over your Documents folder in List view (because it's crammed with files and folders), but you may prefer to view the Pictures library in Icon view, where the icons look like miniatures of the actual photos.

To switch a window from one view to another, you have three options, all of which involve the Views pop-up menu shown in Figure 2-19:

- **Click the Views button.** With each click, the window switches to the next view in this sequence: List, Details, Tiles, Content, Large Icons.

- **Use the Views pop-up menu.** If you click the ▾ triangle next to the word "Views," the menu opens, listing Extra Large Icons, Large Icons, Small Icons, List, and so on. Choose the option you want. (They're described below.)

- **Use the slider.** The Views menu, once opened, also contains a strange little slider down the left side. It's designed to let Windows's graphics software show off a little. The slider makes the icons shrink or grow freely, to sizes that fall *between* the canned Extra Large, Large, Medium, and Small choices.

   What's so strange is that partway down its track, the slider stops adjusting icon sizes and turns into a selector switch for the last four options in the menu: List, Details, Tiles, and Content.

Tip: You can enlarge or shrink all the icons in a window, quick as a wink, by turning your mouse's scroll wheel while you press the Ctrl key. This trick even works on desktop icons.

(If you didn't have that trick, the only way to adjust icon sizes on the desktop would be to right-click a blank spot and choose from the View command in the shortcut menu.)

So what *are* these various views? And when should you use which? Here you go:

- **Icon view.** In an icon view, every file, folder, and disk is represented by a small picture—an *icon*. This humble image, a visual representation of electronic bits, is the cornerstone of the entire Windows religion. (Maybe that's why it's called an icon.)

   Interestingly, in Windows 7, *folder* icons appear turned 90 degrees. Now, in real life, setting filing folders onto a desk that way would be idiotic; everything inside would tumble out. But in Windows-land, the icons within a folder remain exactly where they are. Better yet, at larger icon sizes, they peek out just enough so that you can see them. In the Music folder, for example, a singer's folder shows the first album cover within; a folder full of PowerPoint presentations shows the first slide or two; and so on.

Tip: If you have a multitouch screen, you can use the two-finger spreading gesture to enlarge icons, or the pinching gesture to shrink them, right on the glass.

- **List view.** This one packs, by far, the most files into the space of a window; each file has a tiny icon to its left, and the list of files wraps around into as many columns as necessary to maximize the window's available space.

- **Details view.** This is the same as List view, except that it presents only a single column of files. It's a table, really; additional columns reveal the size, icon type, modification date, rating, and other information.

- **Tiles view.** Your icons appear at standard size, with name and file details just to the *right*.

- **Content view.** This view, new in Windows 7, attempts to cram as many details about each file as will fit in your window (Figure 2-20). Yes, that's right: It's a table that shows not just a file's icon and name, but also its metadata (Properties) and, in the case of text and Word files, even the first couple of lines of text *inside* it. (If

---

Secrets of the Details View Columns

In windows that contain a lot of icons, Details view is a powerful weapon in the battle against chaos. Better yet, *you* get to decide how wide the columns should be, which of them should appear, and in what order. Here are the details on Details:

Add or remove columns.
Right-click any column heading (like Name or Size). When the shortcut menu opens, checkmarks appear next to the visible columns: Name, Date Modified, Size, and so on. Choose a column's name to make it appear or disappear.

But don't think that you're stuck with that handful of common columns. If you click More in the shortcut menu, you open the Choose Details dialog box, which lists *over 200 more*

column types, most of which are useful only in certain circumstances: Album Artist (for music files), Copyright, Date Taken, Exposure Time (for photos), Nickname (for people), Video Compression (for movies), and on and on. To make one of these columns appear, turn on its checkbox and then click OK; by the time you're done, your Explorer window can look like a veritable spreadsheet of information.

Rearrange the columns. You can rearrange your Details columns just by dragging their gray column headers horizontally. (You can even drag the Name column out of first position.) As you drag, a tiny bold divider line in the column-heading area snaps into place to show where it thinks you intend to drop the column you're dragging.

Change column widths. If some text in a column is too long to fit, Windows displays an ellipsis (...) after the first few letters of each word. In that case, here's a great trick: Carefully position your cursor at the right edge of the column's header (Name, Size, or whatever—even to the right of the ▼ button). When the cursor sprouts horizontal arrows from each side, double-click the divider line to make the column adjust *itself*, fitting automatically to accommodate the longest item in the column.

If you'd rather adjust the column width manually, then instead of double-clicking the dividing line between two column headings, just drag horizontally. Doing so makes the column to the *left* of your cursor wider or narrower.

---

you're not seeing all the file details you think you should, make the window bigger. Windows adds and subtracts columns of information as needed to fit.)

You'll get to know Content view very well indeed once you start using Windows 7's Search feature, which uses this view to display your results when you search in an Explorer window.

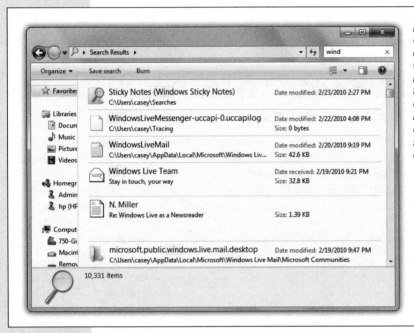

Figure 2-20:
Content view is especially useful when you're viewing search results, because the snippet of text revealed beneath each icon shows, with highlighting, the portion of text that matched your search query. Context is everything, dude.

Sorting, Grouping, and Filtering
All Versions

In Windows 7, sorting is only one way to impose order on your teeming icons. Grouping and filtering can be handy, too.

Note: In Windows Vista, there was actually a lot more of this stuff. There was a whole row of criteria buttons (Name, Size, Date…) across the top of every Explorer window—yes, another toolbar-like thing—that existed solely to help you sort, group, and filter. To make matters worse, Windows Vista offered still another organizational feature called stacking.

In the end, this was just too much; people's eyes glazed over. Today, the strip of sorting criteria lives on only in Details view, which is by far the best view for grouping and sorting. If you want to sort or group the contents of a window in any other view, you have to right-click, as described below.

Sorting Files

Sorting the files in a window alphabetically or chronologically is nice, but it's *so* 2005. In Windows 7, you can sort up, down, and sideways. The technique for doing so depends on which window view you're in.

Details view

In Details view, sorting is simple. See the column headings, like Name, Size, and Type? They aren't just signposts; they're also buttons. Click Name for alphabetical order, "Date modified" for chronological order, Size to view largest files at the top, and so on (Figure 2-21).

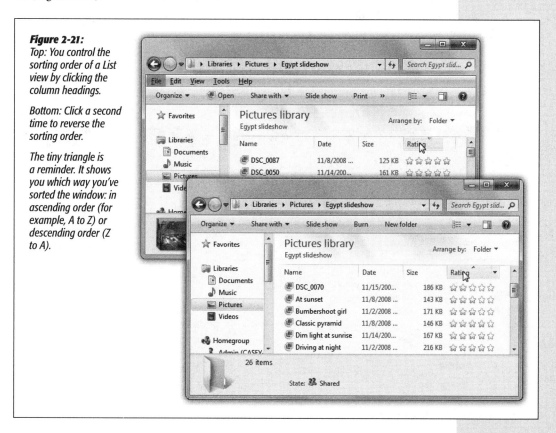

Figure 2-21:
Top: You control the sorting order of a List view by clicking the column headings.

Bottom: Click a second time to reverse the sorting order.

The tiny triangle is a reminder. It shows you which way you've sorted the window: in ascending order (for example, A to Z) or descending order (Z to A).

It's especially important to note the tiny ▲ or ▼ just *above* the heading you've most recently clicked. It shows you *which way* the list is being sorted. When the triangle points upward, oldest files, smallest files, or files whose names begin with numbers (or the letter A) appear at the top of the list, depending on which sorting criterion you've selected.

Tip: It may help you to remember that when the *smallest* portion of the triangle is at the top, the *smallest* files are listed first when viewed in size order.

To reverse the sorting order, just click the column heading a second time. The tiny triangle turns upside-down.

Note: Within each window, Windows groups *folders* separately from *files*. They get sorted, too, but within their own little folder ghetto.

All other views

You can sort your icons in the other window views, too, but it's a lot more work. For one thing, you have to know the secret: Right-click a blank spot in the window. From the shortcut menu, choose "Sort by" and choose the criterion you want (Name, Date, Type…) from the submenu.

There's no handy triangle to tell you *which way* you've just sorted things; is it oldest to newest or newest to oldest? To make *that* decision, you have to right-click the window a second time; this time, from the "Sort by" submenu, choose either Ascending or Descending.

Figure 2-22:
To group the icons in a window, right-click a blank spot. From the shortcut menu, choose "Group by," and then choose the criterion you want to use for grouping, like Name, Date, Size, or whatever.

Grouping

Grouping means "adding headings within the window and clustering the icons beneath the headings." The effect is shown in Figure 2-22, and so is the procedure. Try it out; grouping can be a great way to wrangle some order from a seething mass of icons.

Tip: Don't forget that you can flip the sorting order of your groups. Reopen that shortcut menu and the "Group by" submenu, and specify Ascending or Descending.

Filtering

Filtering, a feature available only in Details view, means hiding. When you turn on filtering, a bunch of the icons in a window *disappear*, which can make filtering a sore subject for novices.

Tip: In case you one day think you've lost a bunch of important files, look for the checkmark next to a column heading, as shown in Figure 2-23. That's your clue that filtering is turned on, and Windows is deliberately hiding something from you.

On the positive side, filtering means screening out stuff you don't care about. When you're looking for a document you know you worked on last week, you can tell Windows to show you *only* the documents edited last week.

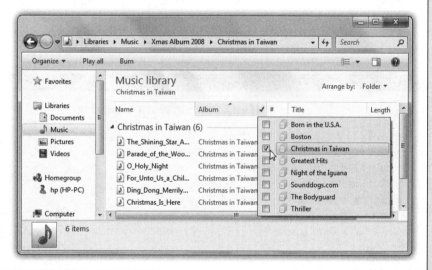

Figure 2-23:
You can turn on more than one checkbox. To see music by The Beatles or U2, turn on both checkboxes. In fact, you can turn on checkboxes from more than one heading—music by The Beatles or U2, rated four stars or higher.

You turn on filtering by opening the pop-up menu next to the column heading you want. For instance, if you want to see only your five-star photos in the Pictures folder, open the Rating pop-up menu.

Sometimes, you'll see a whole long list of checkboxes in one of these pop-up menus (Figure 2-23). For example, if you want to see only the songs in your Music folder by The Beatles, turn on the Beatles checkmark.

Note: Filtering, by the way, can be turned on *with* sorting or grouping.

Once you've filtered a window in Details view, you can switch to a different view; you'll still see (and not see) the same set of icons. The address bar reminds you that you've turned on filtering; it might say, for example, "Research notes→LongTimeAgo→DOC file," meaning "ancient Word files."

To stop filtering, open the heading pop-up menu again and turn off the Filter checkbox.

Note: The other window views offer a Search box in the upper right. Keep in mind that you can do quick-and-dirty filtering using that box, too, as described on page 125. It's not the same checkbox mechanism, but the results are pretty much the same.

Uni-Window vs. Multi-Window
All Versions

When you double-click a folder, Windows can react in one of two ways:

- **It can open a new window.** Now you've got two windows on the screen, one overlapping the other. Moving or copying an icon from one into the other is a piece of cake. Trouble is, if your double-clicking craze continues much longer, your screen will eventually be overrun with windows, which you must now painstakingly close again.

POWER USERS' CLINIC

The Little Filtering Calendar

Some of the column-heading pop-up menus in Details view—Date modified, Date created, Date taken, and so on—display a little calendar, right there in the menu. You're supposed to use it to specify a date or date range. You use it, for example, if you want to see only the photos taken last August, or the Word documents created last week. Here's how the little calendar works:

To change the month, click the ◄ or ► buttons to go one month at a time. Or click the month name to see a list of all 12 months; click the one you want.

To change the year, click the ◄ or ► buttons. Or, to jump farther back or forward, double-click the month's name. You're offered a list of all 10 years in this decade. Click a third time (on the decade heading) to see a list of *decades.* At this point, drill down to the year you want by clicking what you want. (The

calendar goes from 1601 to the year 9999, which should pretty much cover your digital photo collection.)

To see only the photos taken on a certain date, click the appropriate date on the month-view calendar.

To add photos taken on other dates, click additional squares. You can also drag horizontally, vertically, or diagonally to select blocks of consecutive dates.

If you "back out" until you're viewing the names of months, years, or decades, you can click or drag to choose, for example, only the photos taken in June or July 2010.

The checkboxes below the calendar offer one-click access to photos taken earlier this week, earlier this year, and before the beginning of this year ("a long time ago").

- **It can replace the original window with a new one.** This only-one-window-at-all-times behavior keeps your desktop from becoming crowded with windows. If you need to return to the previous window, the Back button takes you there. Of course, you'll have a harder time dragging icons from one window to another using this method.

Whatever you decide, you switch windows between these two behaviors like this: In an Explorer window, choose Organize→"Folder and search options." In the resulting dialog box, click "Open each folder in the same window" or "Open each folder in its own window," as you like. Then click OK.

Immortalizing Your Tweaks
All Versions

Once you've twiddled and tweaked an Explorer window into a perfectly efficient configuration of columns and views, you needn't go through the same exercises for each folder. Windows can immortalize your changes as the standard setting for *all* your windows.

Choose Organize→"Folder and search options"; click the View tab. Click "Apply to Folders," and confirm your decision by clicking Yes.

At this point, all your disk and folder windows open up with the same view, sorting method, and so on. You're still free to override those standard settings on a window-by-window basis, however. (And if you change your mind again and want to make all your maverick folder windows snap back to the standard settings, repeat the process, but click Reset Folders instead.)

The "Folder Options" Options
All Versions

In the battle between flexibility and simplicity, Microsoft comes down on the side of flexibility almost every time. Anywhere it can provide you with more options, it will.

Explorer windows are a case in point, as the following pages of sometimes preposterously tweaky options make clear. The good news: If Explorer windows already work fine for you the way they are, you can ignore all of this.

But if you'd like to visit the famed Folder Options dialog box, here are a few ways to get there:

- Choose Organize→"Folder and search options" from any Explorer window.

- Press the Alt key to make the old menu bar appear. Choose Tools→"Folder options."

- Open the Start menu. Start typing the word *folder* until you see Folder Options in the results list; click it.

- In the Control Panel, type *folder* into the Search box. Click Folder Options.

In each case, click the View tab to see the dialog box shown in Figure 2-24.

Here you see an array of options that affect *all* the folder windows on your PC. When assessing the impact of these controls, *earth-shattering* isn't the adjective that springs to mind. Still, you may find one or two of them useful.

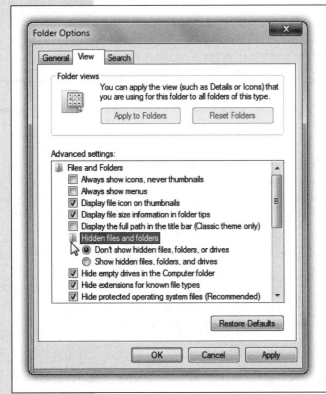

Figure 2-24:
Some of the options in this list are contained within tiny folder icons. A double-click collapses (hides) these folder options or shows them again. For example, you can hide the "Do not show hidden files and folders" option by collapsing the "Hidden files and folders" folder icon.

Here are the functions of the various checkboxes:

- **Always show icons, never thumbnails.** Windows takes great pride in displaying your document icons *as* documents. That is, each icon appears as a miniature of the document itself—a feature that's especially useful in folders full of photos.

  On a slowish PC, this feature can make your processor gasp for breath. If you notice that the icons are taking forever to appear, consider turning this checkbox on.

- **Always show menus.** This checkbox forces the traditional Windows menu bar (File, Edit, View, and so on) to appear in every Explorer window, without your having to tap the Alt key.

- **Display file icon on thumbnails.** Ordinarily, you can identify documents (think Word, Excel, PowerPoint) because their icons display the corresponding logo (a big W for Word, and so on). But in Windows's icon views (Medium and larger), you see the *actual document* on the icon—an image of the document's first page. So does that mean you can no longer tell at a glance what *kind* of document it is?

Don't be silly. This option superimposes, on each thumbnail icon, a tiny "badge," a sub-icon, that identifies what kind of file it is. (It works on only some kinds of documents, however.)

- **Display file size information in folder tips.** A *folder tip* is a rectangular balloon that appears when you point to a folder—a little yellow box that tells you what's in that folder and how big it is on the disk. (It appears only if you've turned on the "Show pop-up description" checkbox described below.) You turn off *this* checkbox if you want to see only the description, but not the size. Talk about tweaky!

Note: It's at this spot in the list where, in pre-Win7 versions, you used to find the "Display simple folder view" option. It added vertical dotted lines to designate each level of folder indenting in the Navigation pane, as in older versions of Windows. But simple folder view is no longer with us in Windows 7. Time marches on.

- **Display the full path in the title bar (Classic theme only).** Suppose you've rejected the millions of dollars Microsoft put into Windows's new look. You've opted instead for the clunky old Classic theme (page 176). In that case, when this option is on, Windows reveals the exact location of the current window in the title bar of the window—for example, *C:\Users\Chris\Documents*. See page 58 for more on folder paths. Seeing the path can be useful when you're not sure which disk a folder is on, for example.

- **Hidden files and folders.** Microsoft grew weary of answering tech-support calls from clueless or mischievous customers who had moved or deleted critical system files, rendering their PCs crippled or useless. The company concluded that the simplest preventive measure would be to make them invisible (the files, not the customers).

  This checkbox is responsible. Your personal and Windows folders, among other places, house several invisible folders and files that the average person isn't meant to fool around with. Big Brother is watching you, but he means well.

  By selecting "Show hidden files, folders, and drives," you, the confident power user in times of troubleshooting or customization, can make the hidden files and folders appear (they show up with dimmed icons, as though to reinforce their delicate nature). But you'll have the smoothest possible computing career if you leave these options untouched.

- **Hide empty drives in the Computer folder.** For years, the Computer window has displayed icons for your removable-disk drives (floppy, CD, DVD, memory-card slots, whatever) even if nothing was in them. In Windows 7, though, that's changed. Now you see icons only when you insert a *disk* into these drives. (It now works like the Mac, if that's any help.)

- **Hide extensions for known file types.** Windows normally hides the *filename extension* on standard files and documents (.doc, .jpg, and so on), in an effort to make Windows seem less technical and intimidating. Your files wind up named "*Groceries*" and "*Frank*" instead of "Groceries.doc" and "Frank.jpg."

There are some excellent reasons, though, why you should turn *off* this option. See page 242 for more on this topic.

- **Hide protected operating system files.** This option is similar to "Show hidden files and folders," above—except that it refers to even more important files, system files that may not be invisible, but are nonetheless so important that moving or deleting them might turn your PC into a $2,000 paperweight. Turning this off, in fact, produces a warning message that's meant to frighten away everybody but power geeks.

- **Launch folder windows in a separate process.** This geekily worded setting opens each folder into a different chunk of memory (RAM). In certain rare situations, this largely obsolete arrangement is more stable—but it slows down your machine slightly and unnecessarily uses memory.

- **Restore previous folder windows at logon.** Every time you log off the computer, Windows forgets which windows were open. That's a distinct bummer, especially if you tend to work out of your Documents window, which you must therefore manually reopen every time you fire up the old PC.

If you turn on this useful checkbox, then Windows will automatically greet you with whichever windows were open when you last logged off.

- **Show drive letters.** Turn off this checkbox to hide the drive letters that identify each of your disk drives in the Computer window (Start→Computer). In other words, "Local Disk (C:)" becomes "Local Disk"—an option that might make newcomers feel less intimidated.

- **Show encrypted or compressed NTFS files in color.** This option won't make much sense until you've read pages 163 and 675, which explain how Windows can encode and compact your files for better security and disk space use. It turns the names of affected icons green and blue, respectively, so you can spot them at a glance. On the other hand, encrypted or compressed files and folders operate quite normally, immediately converting back to human form when double-clicked; hence, knowing which ones have been affected isn't particularly valuable. Turn off this box to make them look just like any other files and folders.

- **Show pop-up description for folder and desktop icons.** If you point to an icon, a taskbar button, a found item in Search, or whatever (without clicking), you get a *tooltip*—a floating, colored label that identifies what you're pointing to. If you find tooltips distracting, turn off this checkbox.

- **Show preview handlers in preview pane.** This is the on/off switch for one of Windows's best features: seeing a preview of a selected document icon in the Preview pane. Turn it off only if your PC is grinding to a halt under the strain of all this graphics-intensive goodness.

- **Use check boxes to select items.** Now here's a weird one: This option makes a *checkbox* appear on every icon you point to with your mouse, for ease in selection. Page 151 explains all.

Tip: This option replaces the "Single-click to open an item" option of Windows XP.

- **Use Sharing Wizard (Recommended).** Sharing files with other computers is one of the great perks of having a network. As Chapter 26 makes clear, this feature makes it much easier to understand what you're doing. For example, it lets you specify that only certain people are allowed to access your files, and lets you decide how much access they have. (For example, can they change them or just see them?)

- **When typing into list view.** When you've got an Explorer window open, teeming with a list of files, what do you want to happen when you start typing?

In the olden days, that'd be an easy one: "Highlight an icon, of course!" That is, if you type *piz,* you highlight the file called *Pizza with Casey.jpg.* And indeed, that's what the factory setting means: "Select the typed item within the view."

But Windows 7 has a Search box in every Explorer window. If you turn on "Automatically type into the Search Box," then each letter you type arrives in that box, performing a real-time, letter-by-letter search of all the icons in the window. Your savings: one mouse click.

Taskbar 2.0
All Versions

For years, the *taskbar*—the strip of colorful icons at the bottom of your screen—has been one of the most prominent and important elements of the Windows interface (Figure 2-25). In Windows 7, you can call it Taskbar, Extreme Makeover Edition, because it does a lot of things it's never done before.

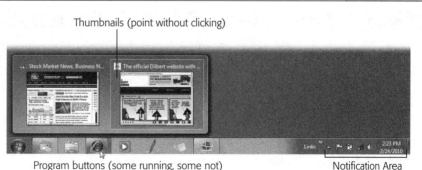

Figure 2-25:
On the left is the Start menu. In the middle are buttons for every program you're running–and every program you've pinned there for easy access later. .

Thumbnails (point without clicking)

Program buttons (some running, some not)

Notification Area

Here's an introduction to its functions, old and new:

- **The Start menu is at the left end.** As you'll soon see, the Start menu and taskbar are related in all kinds of ways.

- **The taskbar lists your open programs and windows.** The icons on the taskbar make it easy to switch from one open program to another—from your Web browser to your email programs, for example—or even to specific windows *within* those programs.

- **The taskbar lets you** open **your favorite programs.** If you just splurted your Sprite, you're forgiven; this is a new task for the taskbar, a Windows 7 special. The taskbar is now a *launcher,* just like the taskbar in Mac OS X or the QuickLaunch toolbar in old Windows versions.

- **The system tray (notification area) is at the right end.** These tiny icons show you the status of your network connection, battery life, and so on.

- **The Show Desktop button huddles at the** far right end. You can read more about this weird rectangular sliver on page 67.

You've already read about the Start menu; the following pages cover the taskbar's other functions.

Tip: You can operate the taskbar entirely from the keyboard. Press ⊞+T to highlight the first button on it, as indicated by a subtle glow. Then you can "walk" across its buttons by pressing the left/right arrow keys, or by pressing ⊞+T (add the Shift key to "walk" in the opposite direction). Once a button is highlighted, you can tap the space bar to "click" it, press Shift+F10 to "right-click" it, or press the Menu key on your keyboard to open the icon's jump list. Who needs a mouse anymore?

Taskbar as App Switcher

Every open window is represented by a button—in Aero, it's an actual miniature of the window itself—that sprouts from its program's taskbar icon. These buttons make it easy to switch between open programs and windows. Just click one to bring its associated window into the foreground, even if it has been minimized.

TROUBLESHOOTING MOMENT

No Thumbnails? No Previews? No Aero.

If your taskbar isn't offering up the goodies you're reading about here—pop-up thumbnails of your open windows, full-size window previews—then you must not have Aero working for you (page 23).

That could be because your computer is so feeble that it can't run Aero at all, as described on page 25. It could mean that your computer has Windows 7 Starter edition. Or it could mean that you've selected a cosmetic theme that comes with Aero turned off. (In that case, the problem is easy to fix. Right-click a blank spot on the desktop. From the shortcut menu, choose Personalize. In the resulting window, click one of the icons listed under Aero Themes. They offer the

Aero desktop features described in this book, whereas the Basic themes do not. (See Chapter 4 for more on themes.)

All right, but what if Aero is turned off and you can't, or don't want to, turn it on? The taskbar can still be useful to you!

In that case, clicking a taskbar thumbnail does not produce a miniature of its windows—instead, it produces a list of their names, which may not be as pretty but is often just as useful.

Also in that case, pointing to a thumbnail without clicking doesn't give a full-size window preview—but you're not out of luck. You can still enjoy full-size window previews—by Ctrl+clicking a taskbar icon. With each Ctrl+click, Windows shows you another open window in that program.

Handy Window Miniatures

On PCs with Aero (page 23), the taskbar does more than display each window's name. If you point to a program's button without clicking, it sprouts thumbnail images of *the windows themselves*. Figure 2-26 shows the effect. It's a lot more informative than just reading the windows' *names*, as in days of yore (your previous Windows versions, that is). The thumbnails are especially good at helping you spot a particular Web page, photo, or PDF document.

Tip: There's a tiny Close button (⊠) in each thumbnail, too, which makes it easy to close a window without having to bring it forward first. (Or click the thumbnail itself with your mouse's scroll wheel, or use your middle mouse button, if you have one.) Each thumbnail also has a hidden shortcut menu. Right-click to see your options!

Aero Peek

Those window miniatures are old news, at least if you've used Windows Vista. What's cool in Windows 7 is the *full-screen* previews of your windows.

To see them, point to one of the *thumbnails* without clicking. As you can see in Figure 2-26 (bottom), Windows now displays that window at full size, right on the screen, even if it was minimized, buried, or hidden. Keep moving your cursor across the thumbnails (if there are more than one); each time the pointer lands on a thumbnail, the full-size window preview changes to show what's in it.

When you find the window you want, click on the thumbnail you're already pointing to. The window pops open so you can work in it.

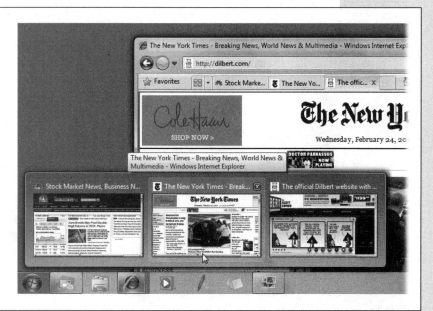

Figure 2-26:
Pointing to a taskbar button produces "live" thumbnail previews of the windows themselves, which can be a huge help. Click a thumbnail to open its window.

Then, as long as you're pointing around, try pointing to one of the thumbnails. You see a full-size preview of the corresponding window (in this case, a Web window). Click the thumbnail to make that window active.

Button Groups

In the old days, opening a lot of windows might produce a relatively useless display of truncated buttons. Not only were the buttons too narrow to read the names of the windows, but the buttons appeared in chronological order, not software-program order.

As you may have noticed, though, Windows 7 automatically consolidates open windows into a single program button. (There's even a subtle visual sign that a program

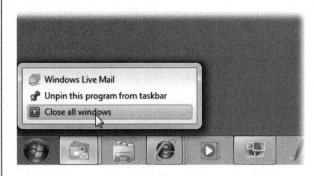

Figure 2-27:
An icon without a border is a program you haven't opened yet (the second and fourth ones here). A brightened background indicates the active (frontmost) program. Right-clicking one of these buttons lets you perform tasks on all the windows together, such as closing them all at once.

Figure 2-28:
Top: Cascading windows are neatly arranged so you can see the title bar for each window. Click any title bar to bring that window to the foreground as the active window.

Bottom: You may prefer to see your windows displayed stacked (left) or side-by-side (right).

has multiple windows open: Its taskbar icon appears to be "stacked," like the first and third icons in Figure 2-27.) All the Word documents are accessible from the Word icon, all the Excel documents sprout from the Excel icon, and so on.

Point to a taskbar button to see the thumbnails of the corresponding windows, complete with their names; click to jump directly to the one you want.

Despite all the newfangled techniques, some of the following time-honored basics still apply:

- If a program has only *one window* open, you can hide or show it by clicking the program's taskbar button—a great feature that a lot of PC fans miss. (To hide a *background* window, click its taskbar button *twice:* once to bring the window forward, then a pause, then again to hide it.)

- To minimize, maximize, restore, or close a window, even if you can't see it on the screen, point to its program's button on the taskbar. When the window thumbnails pop up, right-click the one you want, and choose from the shortcut menu.

NOSTALGIA CORNER

Bringing Back the Old Taskbar

The taskbar's tendency to consolidate the names of document windows into a single program button saves space, for sure.

Even so, it's not inconceivable that you might prefer the old system, in which there's one taskbar button for every single window. For example, the new consolidated-window scheme means you can't bring a certain application to the

While you're rooting around in here, consider also turning on "Use small icons." That step replaces the inch-tall, unlabeled, Mac-style taskbar icons with smaller, half-height ones. Click OK.

The only weirdness now: Icons representing programs that aren't open right now–icons you've pinned to the taskbar for quick access–appear only as icons, without labels, and

front just by clicking its taskbar button. (You must actually choose one particular window from among its thumbnails, which is a lot more effort.)

To make Windows display the taskbar the old way, right-click an empty area of the taskbar and choose Properties from the shortcut menu. From the "Taskbar buttons" pop-up menu, choose either "Never combine" or "Combine when taskbar is full" (meaning "only as necessary"). Click Apply; you now have the wider, text-labeled taskbar buttons from the pre-Win7 days, as shown here.

the effect is somewhat disturbing. You can get rid of them, if you want; just right-click each and choose "Unpin this program from taskbar."

Now you have a taskbar that looks almost exactly like the Windows XP taskbar—except that it still has a shiny, glass, modern look. If you want to complete your rewind fully, you can also choose the Classic theme (page 176), giving you a coarser, uglier, older look. It's as though the taskbar has just arrived in a time machine from 1995.

- Windows can make all open windows visible at once, either by *cascading* them, *stacking* them, or displaying them in side-by-side vertical slices. (All three options are shown in Figure 2-28.) To create this effect, right-click a blank spot on the taskbar and choose Cascade Windows from the shortcut menu.

Note: Actually, there's a *fourth* way to see all your windows at once: Flip 3D, described earlier in this chapter. The cascading/stacking business is an older method of plucking one window out of a haystack.

- To hide all open windows in one fell swoop, press ■+D. Or right-click a blank spot on the taskbar and choose "Show the desktop" from the shortcut menu. Or point to (or click) the Show Desktop rectangle at the far right end of the taskbar.

  To bring the windows back, repeat that step.

Tip: When the taskbar is crowded with buttons, it may not be easy to find a blank spot to click. Usually there's a little gap near the right end; you can make it easier to find some blank space by *enlarging* the taskbar, as described on page 114.

The Taskbar as App Launcher

Each time you open a program, its icon appears on the taskbar. That's the way it's always been. And when you exit that program, its icon disappears from the taskbar.

In Windows 7, however, there's a twist. Now you can *pin* a program's icon to the taskbar so that it's always there, even when it's not open. One quick click opens the app.

The idea, of course, is to put frequently used programs front and center, always on the screen, so you don't have to burrow into the Start menu to find them.

To pin a program to the taskbar in this way, use one of these two tricks:

- **Drag a program's icon** directly to any spot on the taskbar, as shown in Figure 2-29. You can drag them from any Explorer window, from the desktop, from the left side of the Start menu, or (most conveniently) from the Start menu's All Programs list.

- **Right-click a program's icon (or its shortcut icon),** wherever it happens to be. From the shortcut menu, choose "Pin to Taskbar." The icon appears instantly at the right end of the taskbar. This technique requires less mousing, of course, but it also deprives you of the chance to specify *where* the new icon goes.

Once an icon is on the taskbar, you can open it with a single click. By all means, stick your favorites there; over the years, you'll save yourself thousands of unnecessary Start-menu clicks.

Tip: If you Shift+click a taskbar icon, you open another window for that program—for example, a new Web-browser window, a new Microsoft Word document, and so on. (Clicking with your mouse's scroll wheel, or middle mouse button, does the same thing.) Add the Ctrl key to open the program as an administrator.

And if you Shift+right-click a taskbar icon, you see the same menu of window-management commands (Cascade, Restore, and so on) that you get when you right-click a blank spot on the taskbar.

If you change your mind about a program icon you've parked on the taskbar, it's easy to move an icon to a new place—just drag it with your mouse.

You can also remove one altogether. Right-click the program's icon—in the taskbar or anywhere on your PC—and, from the shortcut menu, choose "Unpin this program from taskbar."

Note: The taskbar is really intended to display the icons of programs. If you try to drag a file or folder, you'll succeed only in adding it to a program's jump list, as described next. If you want quick, one-click access to files, folders, and disks, you can have it—by using the Links toolbar (page 116).

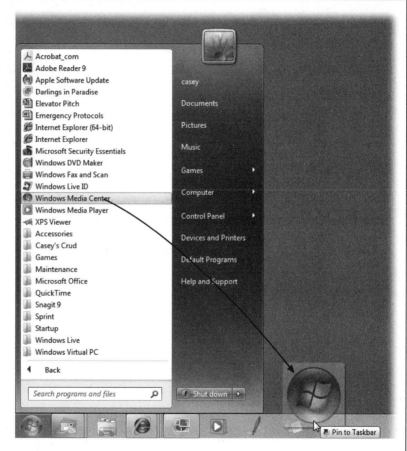

Figure 2-29:
To install a program on your taskbar, drag its icon to any spot; the other icons scoot aside to make room.

Jump Lists: Taskbar Edition

Jump lists, new in Windows 7, are submenus that list frequently or recently opened files in each of your programs. On the taskbar, each program's icon has its own jump list. (Jump lists can also sprout from your programs' icons in the Start menu, as described on page 52.)

To open a jump list, right-click an icon on your taskbar. The list pops right up, as shown in Figure 2-30.

All of this is designed to save you time, mousing, and folder-burrowing.

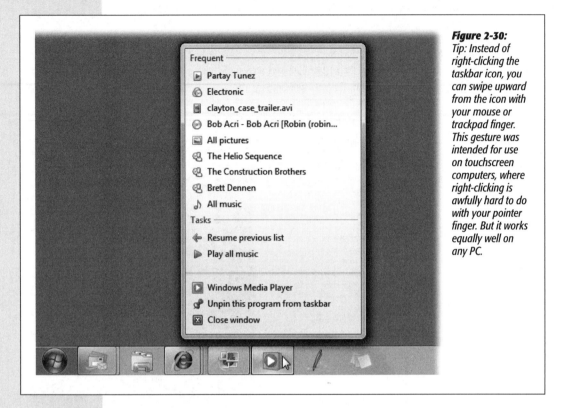

Figure 2-30:
Tip: Instead of right-clicking the taskbar icon, you can swipe upward from the icon with your mouse or trackpad finger. This gesture was intended for use on touchscreen computers, where right-clicking is awfully hard to do with your pointer finger. But it works equally well on any PC.

Ordinarily, Windows builds jump lists for you automatically, tracking the documents you open. Your Web browser's jump list tracks your recent and most-visited sites, for example. Your Excel icon's jump list shows the spreadsheets you've had open most recently.

But you can also install files *manually* into a program's jump list—in Windows-ese, you can *pin* a document to a program's jump list so that it's not susceptible to replacement by other items.

For example, you might pin the chapters of a book you're working on to your Word jump list. To the Windows Explorer jump list, you might pin the *folder and disk* locations you access often.

You can pin a file or folder to a jump list in any of three ways:

- **Drag an icon directly onto a blank spot on the taskbar.** You can drag a document (or its file shortcut) from the desktop, an Explorer window, or the Start menu.

(You can drag it onto its "parent" program's icon if you really want to, but the taskbar itself is a bigger target.)

As shown in Figure 2-31, a tooltip appears: "Pin to Adobe Photoshop" (or whatever the parent program is). Release the mouse. You've just pinned the document to its program's taskbar jump list.

Note: If the document's parent program doesn't already appear on the taskbar, it does now. In other words, if you drag a Beekeeper Pro document onto the taskbar, Windows is forced to install the Beekeeper Pro program icon onto the taskbar in the process. Otherwise, how would you open the jump list?

Figure 2-31:
Left: Drag a document icon to the taskbar and release.

Middle: That document's name now appears in its parent program's jump list.

Right: You can also pin something already in the jump list.

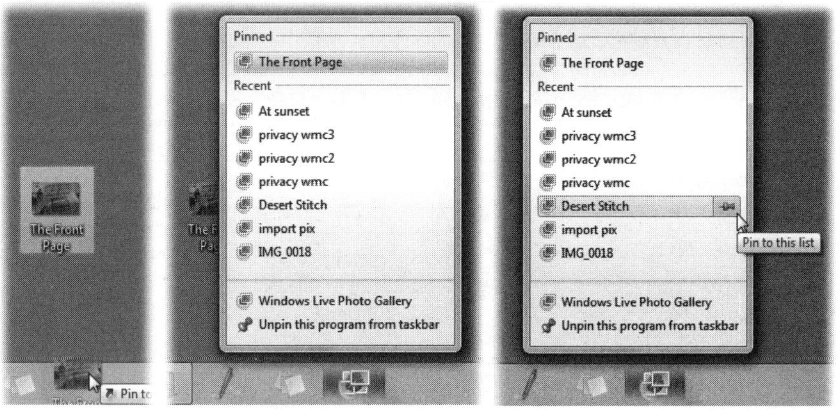

• **In an existing jump list, click the pushpin icon.** If the document already appears in a jump list, you can move it up into the Pinned list at the top of the jump list this way. Now it won't be dislodged over time by other files you open.

GEM IN THE ROUGH

Secret Keystrokes of the Taskbar Icons

There's secret keyboard shortcuts lurking in them taskbar icons.

It turns out that the first 10 icons, left to right, have built-in keystrokes that "click" them: the ⊞ key plus the numbers 1, 2, 3, and so on (up to 0, which means 10).

If you use this keystroke to "click" the icon of a program that's not running, it opens up as though you'd clicked it. If you "click" a program that has only one window open, that window pops to the front. If you "click" a program with more than one window open, the icon sprouts thumbnail previews of all of them, and the first window pops to the front.

Remember that you can drag icons around on the taskbar, in effect reassigning those 1-through-0 keystrokes.

Tip: If you drag a folder (or a shortcut of one) onto the taskbar, it gets pinned in the Windows Explorer icon's jump list.

- **If the file appears in** another **program's jump list, drag it onto the new program's taskbar icon.** For example, maybe you opened a document in WordPad (it's in WordPad's jump list), but you want to move it to Microsoft Word's jump list.

  To do that, drag the document's name out of WordPad's list and then drop it onto Word's taskbar icon. It now appears pinned in *both* programs' jump lists.

Removing things from your taskbar jump lists is just as easy. Open a program's jump list, point to anything in the Pinned list, and click the "Unpin from this list" pushpin.

Note: Once it's unpinned, the file's name may jump down into the Recent section of the jump list, which is usually fine. If that's not fine, you can erase it from there, too; right-click its name and, from the shortcut menu, choose "Remove from this list." (Of course, you're not actually deleting the file.)

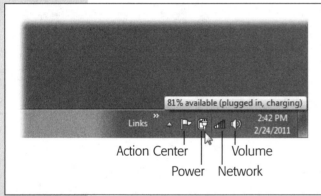

Figure 2-32:
You can point to a status icon's name without clicking (to see its name) or click one to see its pop-up menu of options.

Action Center
Power   Network
Volume

You can also erase your jump lists completely—for privacy, for example. For details, and for other caveats about jump lists, see page 54.

The Notification Area (System Tray)

The notification area gives you quick access to little status indicators and pop-up menus that control various functions of your PC (Figure 2-32).

This area has been a sore spot with PC fans for years. Many a software installer inserts its own little icon into this area: fax software, virus software, palmtop synchronization software, and so on. So before Windows 7 came along, the tray eventually filled with junky, confusing little icons that had no value to you—but made it harder to find the icons you *did* want to track.

In Windows 7, all that is history. Out of the box, only a handful of Windows icons appear here. Each one offers three displays: one when you *point without clicking,* one when you *click the icon,* and a third when you *right-click* the icon. Here's what you start with:

- **Action Center** (⚑). This humble, tiny icon is the front end for one of Win7's best new features: the Action Center. It's a single, consolidated command center for all the little nags that Windows used to bury you with.

  Nowadays, Windows may still whimper because you have no antivirus program, because your backup is out of date, because there are Windows updates to install, or whatever. But this icon will sprout a balloon just once, for a few seconds, and then leave you alone after that.

Note: When all is well, the Action Center icon looks like a tiny flag (⚑); when you've ignored some of its warnings, a circled X appears on the flag (⚑).

  If you ever actually care what Windows is griping about, you have several options. Point to the icon without clicking to see how many important messages are waiting. Click to see the most important messages (or click a link to take care of them). Right-click for links to the Action Center itself (Chapter 10), a troubleshooting wizard, or Windows Update (page 662).

- **Power** (🔋, **laptops only**). Point to the tiny battery icon without clicking to view the time-remaining (and percentage-remaining) readout for your laptop battery. Click for a choice of power plan (page 326)—and for a detailed battery juice–remaining readout, in minutes and in percentage of capacity. Right-click for access to the Power Options control panel and the Windows Mobility Center (see Chapter 19).

- **Network** (📶 or 🖥). Point to see the name of your current network and whether or not it's connected to the Internet. Click for a list of available networks; the wireless (WiFi) ones in the list come with icons for signal strength and "locked" (password-protected) status. You can switch networks by clicking one's name. Right-click for a shortcut menu that offers direct access to a troubleshooting screen and to the Network and Sharing Center.

- **Volume** (🔊). Point to see a tooltip that says, for example, "Speakers: 67%" (of full volume). Click for a volume slider that controls your PC's speakers. Right-click for a shortcut menu that offers direct access to various Control Panel screens, like Sounds, Recording Devices, and so on.

- **Clock.** Shows the current date and time. Point to see today's full date, with day of the week ("Thursday, January 17, 2013"). Click for a pop-up clock and mini-calendar, which you can use to check, for example, what day of the week March 9, 2016, falls on. (Right-clicking the Clock doesn't offer anything special—just the same shortcut menu that appears when you right-click a blank spot on the taskbar.)

Tip: You can drag system-tray icons around to rearrange them—not just these starter icons, but any that you install, as described below. A vertical insertion-point line appears to show you where the icon will go when you release the mouse.

Revealing the hidden status icons

So if these are the only authorized status icons, what happened to all the other junky ones deposited there by your software programs?

They're hidden until you summon them. Click the tiny ▲ at the left end of the system tray to see them, safely corralled in a pop-up palette (Figure 2-33).

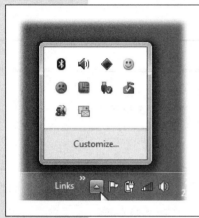

Figure 2-33:
Left: Nowadays, your taskbar isn't overrun by useless software-company icons. They're all hidden in this pop-up corral.

Right: You can drag them around within this bubble to rearrange them, or drag them into or out of the bubble to hide or un-hide specific icons.

Reinstating the hidden icons

OK, so now you know where the additional, non-Microsoft status icons are hidden. Thank you, Windows, for sparing us from Creeping Iconitus.

But what if you *want* one of those inferior icons to appear in the system tray? What if you *don't* want Windows to hide them away in the popup window (Figure 2-33)?

No big whoop. Just drag them *out* of the "hidden" corral and back onto the taskbar.

Or you can do it the long way, by opening the Notification Area control panel and bringing them back (see Figure 2-34).

Here, you see a list of all of those secondary, usually-hidden status icons. For each one, you can use the pop-up menu to choose from the following:

• **Show Icon And Notifications.** This icon will always appear in the system tray, unhidden at last.

• **Hide Icon And Notifications.** The icon is hidden. If the icon wants to get your attention by popping up a message, too bad; Windows stifles all notifications.

• **Only Show Notifications.** This icon is hidden, but if it needs your attention, Windows will still show you its notification pop-ups.

Hiding icons you rarely use is a noble ambition. Most of the time, you truly won't miss them, and their absence will make the icons you *do* use stand out all the more.

It's worth noting, by the way, that you have these options even for the basic Windows icons described above: Volume, Network, Power, and so on. If you don't want the date and time eating up taskbar space, then, by golly, you can hide it.

Tip: Actually, the Clock item doesn't appear in the dialog box shown in Figure 2-34. If you want to hide the date and time, click "Turn system icons on or off" at the bottom of that box. You arrive in another dialog box, this one dedicated exclusively to on/off switches for the basic Windows icons: Power, Action Center, Network, Volume—and, yes, Clock.

Figure 2-34:
To open this control panel, click the tiny ▲ at the left end of the system tray, and then click Customize. (Or open the Start menu; type as much of the word notification *as necessary until you see, and can click, Notification Area Icons.)*

Revealing all system-tray icons

One last thought: If your intention in visiting the Notification Area Icons box (Figure 2-34) is to turn on *all* system-tray icons—maybe to recreate the halcyon days of Windows XP—you can save yourself some time. Just turn on "Always show all icons and notifications on the taskbar." (It's at the bottom of the dialog box.)

Now all the icons appear in the system tray, the Behaviors pop-up menus are dimmed to show you've overridden them, and the little ▲ button at the left end of the system tray goes away. That's a lot faster than adjusting the Behaviors pop-up menu individually for each icon.

Tip: You have complete keyboard control over the system tray. Press ⊞+B to highlight the first icon—the little ▲ button. Then press the arrow keys to "walk" through the other icons. Press the space bar to "click" whatever icon is highlighted, opening its menu. (Press the Menu key or Shift+F10 to "right-click" the icon.)

Three Ways to Get the Taskbar Out of Your Hair

All Versions

The bottom of the screen isn't necessarily the ideal location for the taskbar. Virtually all screens are wider than they are tall, so the taskbar eats into your limited vertical screen space. You have three ways out: Hide the taskbar, shrink it, or rotate it 90 degrees.

Auto-Hiding the Taskbar

To turn on the taskbar's auto-hiding feature, start by right-clicking a blank spot on the taskbar, and then choose Properties from the shortcut menu. The dialog box that appears offers a checkbox called "Auto-hide the taskbar." This feature makes the taskbar disappear whenever you're not using it—a clever way to devote your entire screen to application windows and yet have the taskbar at your cursor tip when needed.

When this feature is turned on, the taskbar disappears whenever you click elsewhere, or whenever your cursor moves away from it. Only a thin line at the edge of the screen indicates that you have a taskbar at all. As soon as your pointer moves close to that line, the taskbar joyfully springs back into view.

Tip: On paper, an auto-hiding taskbar is ideal; it's there only when you summon it. In practice, however, you may find that the extra half-second the taskbar takes to appear and disappear makes this feature slightly less appealing. Fortunately, you can hide and show the taskbar at will by pressing the hide/show key—namely, the ⊞ key. Now you can make the taskbar pop in and out instantly, without requiring you to move the mouse.

Changing the Taskbar's Size

Even with the button-grouping feature, the taskbar can still accumulate a lot of buttons and icons. As a result, you may want to enlarge the taskbar to see what's what.

- **The draggy way.** First, ensure that the toolbar isn't *locked* (which means you can't move or resize it). Right-click a blank spot on the taskbar; from the shortcut menu, uncheck "Lock the taskbar," if necessary.

  Now position your pointer on the upper edge of the taskbar (or, if you've moved the taskbar, whichever edge is closest to the center of the screen). When the pointer turns into a double-headed arrow, drag to make the taskbar thicker or thinner.

Note: If you're resizing a taskbar that's on the top or bottom of the screen, it automatically changes its size in full taskbar-height increments. You can't fine-tune the height; you can only double or triple it, for example.

If it's on the left or right edge of your screen, however, you can resize the taskbar freely. If you're not careful, you can make it look really weird.

- **The dialog-box way.** In the Properties dialog box for the taskbar (right-click it; choose Properties from the shortcut menu), an option called "Use small icons" appears. As described in the box on page 105, it cuts those inch-tall taskbar icons down to half size, for a more pre-Win7 look.

Moving the Taskbar to the Sides of the Screen

Yet another approach to getting the taskbar out of your way is to rotate it so that it sits vertically against a side of your screen. You can rotate it in either of two ways:

- **The draggy way.** First, ensure that the toolbar isn't *locked*, as described above. (Right-click a blank spot; from the shortcut menu, uncheck "Lock the taskbar.")

  Now you can drag the taskbar to any edge of the screen, using any blank spot in the central section as a handle. (You can even drag it to the *top* of your screen, if you're a true rebel.) Release the mouse when the taskbar leaps to the edge you've indicated with the cursor.

Tip: No matter which edge of the screen holds your taskbar, your programs are generally smart enough to adjust their own windows as necessary. In other words, your Word document will shift sideways so that it doesn't overlap the taskbar you've dragged to the side of the screen.

- **The dialog-box way.** Right-click a blank spot on the taskbar; from the shortcut menu, choose Properties. Use the "Taskbar location on screen" pop-up menu to choose Left, Right, Top, or Bottom. (You can do this even if the taskbar is locked.)

You'll probably find that the right side of your screen works better than the left. Most programs put their document windows against the left edge of the screen, where the taskbar and its labels might get in the way.

Note: When you position your taskbar vertically, what was once the right side of the taskbar becomes the bottom. In other words, the Clock appears at the bottom of the vertical taskbar. So as you read references to the taskbar in this book, mentally substitute the phrase "bottom part of the taskbar" when you read references to the "right side of the taskbar."

Taskbar Toolbars

All Versions

You'd be forgiven if you've never even heard of taskbar *toolbars*; this is one obscure feature.

These toolbars are separate horizontal sections on the taskbar that offer special-function features. You can even build your own toolbars—for example, one stocked with documents related to a single project. (Somewhere in America, there's a self-help group for people who spend entirely too much time fiddling with this kind of thing.)

To make a toolbar appear or disappear, right-click a blank spot on the taskbar and choose from the Toolbars submenu that appears (Figure 2-35). The ones with check-marks are the ones you're seeing now; you can click to turn them on and off.

Tip: You can't adjust the toolbars' widths until you unlock the taskbar (right-click a blank spot and turn off "Lock the taskbar"). Now each toolbar is separated from the main taskbar by a dotted "grip strip." Drag this strip to make the toolbar wider or narrower.

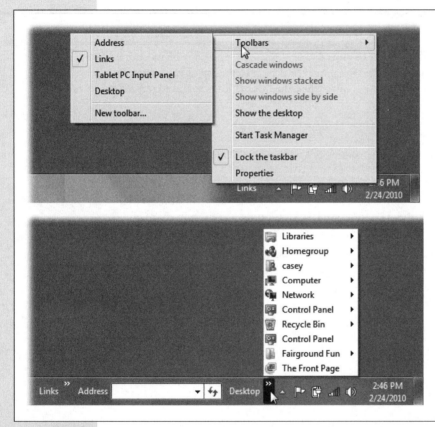

Figure 2-35:
Top: Make toolbars appear by right-clicking a blank area on the taskbar, if you can find one.

Bottom: Toolbars eat into your taskbar space, so use them sparingly. If you've added too many icons to the toolbar, a >> button appears at its right end. Click it to expose a list of the commands or icons that didn't fit.

Here's a rundown of the ready-made taskbar toolbars at your disposal.

Address Toolbar

This toolbar offers a duplicate copy of the address bar that appears in every Explorer window, complete with a Recent Addresses pop-up menu—except that it's always available, even if no Explorer window happens to be open.

Links Toolbar

From its name alone, you might assume that the purpose of this toolbar is to provide links to your favorite Web sites. And sure enough, that's one thing it's good for.

But in fact, you can drag *any icon at all* onto this toolbar—files, folders, disks, programs, or whatever—to turn them into one-click buttons.

In other words, the Links toolbar duplicates the "park favorite icons" function of the Start menu, taskbar, and Quick Launch toolbar. But in some ways, it's better. It can display *any* kind of icon (unlike the taskbar). It's always visible (unlike the Start menu). And it shows the icons' names.

> **Note:** The Links toolbar is a mirror of the Favorites toolbar in Internet Explorer (Tools→Toolbars→Favorites), just in case you were baffled. Edit one, you edit the other.

Here are a few possibilities of things to stash here, just to get your juices flowing:

- Install icons of the three or four programs you use the most (or a few documents you work on every day).

- Install the Recycle Bin's icon, so you don't have to mouse all the way over to… wherever you keep the real Recycle Bin.

- Install icons for shared folders on the network. This arrangement saves several steps when you want to connect to them.

- Install icons of Web sites you visit often so you can jump directly to them when you sit down in front of your PC each morning. (In Internet Explorer, you can drag the tiny icon at the left end of the address bar directly onto the Links toolbar to install a Web page there.)

You can drag these links around on the toolbar to put them into a different order, or remove a link by dragging it away—directly into the Recycle Bin, if you like. (They're only shortcuts; you're not actually deleting anything important.) To rename something here—a good idea, since horizontal space in this location is so precious—right-click it and choose Rename from the shortcut menu.

> **Tip:** Dragging a Web link from the Links toolbar to the desktop or an Explorer window creates an *Internet shortcut file.* When double-clicked, this special document connects to the Internet and opens the specified Web page.

Tablet PC Input Panel

This toolbar is useful only if you're working on a tablet PC, which has a touch screen and stylus. It provides quick access to Windows's handwriting-recognition software. Chapter 19 has the details.

Desktop Toolbar

The Desktop toolbar (Figure 2-35, bottom) offers quick access to whichever icons are sitting on your desktop—the Recycle Bin, for example, and whatever else you've put there. As a convenience, it also lists a few frequently used places that *aren't* on the desktop, including your Personal folder, your libraries, Homegroup, Network, Control Panel, and so on.

When it first appears, the Desktop toolbar takes the form of a >> button at the right end of the taskbar. You can widen the Desktop toolbar if you like, making its buttons appear horizontally on the taskbar. But if you leave it compressed, then many of its icons sprout pop-up *submenus* that give you direct access to their *contents*. That's a useful way to get at your stuff when your screen is filled with windows.

Redesigning Your Toolbars

To change the look of a toolbar, first unlock it. (Right-click it; from the shortcut menu, choose "Lock the taskbar," if necessary, so that the checkmark disappears. Later, repeat this procedure to lock the taskbar again.)

Next, right-click any blank spot on the toolbar. The resulting shortcut menu offers these choices, which appear *above* the usual taskbar shortcut menu choices:

NOSTALGIA CORNER

Bringing Back the Quick Launch Toolbar

The whole point of the old Quick Launch toolbar was to display the icons of programs you used a lot—exactly like the new Windows 7 taskbar itself. So Microsoft took the Quick Launch toolbar out behind the barn and shot it.

Besides, if "a toolbar filled with icons of my choosing, ready for one-click opening" is the idea behind the Quick Launch toolbar, why not use the Links toolbar or the "build your own" toolbar described on these pages?

Well, all right. If you really feel it's that important to have the Quick Launch toolbar—the actual, original one—you can bring it back.

Start by creating a folder that contains the icons for everything you want displayed on the toolbar.

Now right-click a blank spot on the taskbar. From the shortcut menu, choose Toolbars→New Toolbar. In the resulting dialog box, type this (AutoComplete is there to help you save typing)...

%appdata%\Microsoft\Internet Explorer\Quick Launch

...and then click Select Folder.

And presto: The Quick Launch toolbar now appears on your taskbar. It works exactly like the Links toolbar, in that you

can drag anything onto it for easy access: folder, file, disk, shortcut, program...anything with an icon.

It still doesn't look much like the old Quick Launch toolbar, though. But you can fix that.

First, unlock the taskbar. (Right-click it; from the shortcut menu, choose "Lock the taskbar," if necessary, so that the checkmark disappears.)

Now right-click the Quick Launch toolbar itself; turn off Show Title and Show Text. Drag the dotted "grip strip" handle at the toolbar's left edge all the way to the left so that it's right next to the Start menu, where the old Quick Launch toolbar used to be. Drag the right-side "grip strip" to adjust the width. Relock the taskbar, if you like.

From now on, you can install any file, folder, or disk onto this toolbar just by dragging it there. It shows up, tiny but legible, ready for opening with one click.

If you change your mind, you can get rid of the Quick Launch toolbar. Right-click the taskbar; from the shortcut menu, choose Toolbars→Quick Launch toolbar, so that the checkmark disappears.

- **View** lets you change the size of the icons on the toolbar.

- **Open Folder** works only with the Quick Launch and Links toolbars.

  It turns out that the icons on these toolbars reflect the contents of corresponding *folders* on your PC. To see one, right-click a blank spot on the toolbar itself; from the shortcut menu, choose Open Folder.

  Why is that useful? Because it means you can add, rename, or delete icons en masse, by working in the folder instead of on the toolbar itself. Of course, you can also delete or rename any icon on these toolbars by right-clicking it and choosing Delete or Rename from the shortcut menu. But a window isn't nearly as claustrophobic as the toolbar itself.

- **Show Text** identifies each toolbar icon with a text label.

- **Show Title** makes the toolbar's name (such as "Quick Launch" or "Desktop") appear on the toolbar.

- **Close Toolbar** makes the toolbar disappear.

Tip: How much horizontal taskbar space a toolbar consumes is up to you. Drag the border at the left edge of a toolbar to make it wider or narrower. That's a good point to remember if, in fact, you can't *find* a blank spot to right-click on. (Sub-Tip: In a pinch, you can right-click the clock.) Don't forget that you have to unlock the toolbar before you can change its size (right-click, and then choose "Lock the taskbar" so the checkmark disappears).

Figure 2-36:
To create a new toolbar, begin by making a folder. Stock it with the icons you want to access from the taskbar. Amaze your friends!

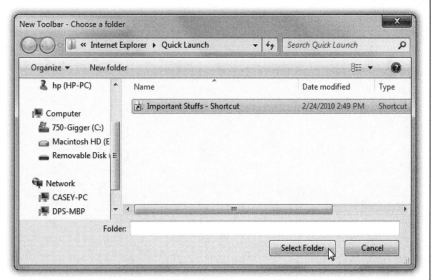

Build Your Own Toolbars

The Quick Launch and Links toolbars are such a delight that you may find that having only one isn't enough. You may wish to create several *different* Links toolbars, each stocked with the icons for a different project or person. One could contain icons for all the chapters of a book you're writing; another could list only your games.

Fortunately, it's easy to create as many different custom toolbars as you like, each of which behaves exactly like the Links toolbar.

Windows creates toolbars from *folders;* so before creating a toolbar of your own, you must create a folder and fill it with the stuff you want to toolbar-ize.

Next, right-click a blank spot on the taskbar. From the shortcut menu, choose Toolbars→New Toolbar to open the New Toolbar dialog box, as shown in Figure 2-36. Find and click the folder you want, and then click Select Folder.

Now there's a brand-new toolbar on your taskbar, whose buttons list the contents of the folder you selected. Feel free to tailor it as described—by changing its icon sizes, hiding or showing the icon labels, or installing new icons onto it by dragging them from other Explorer windows.

Searching & Organizing Your Files

Every disk, folder, file, application, printer, and networked computer is represented on your screen by an icon. To avoid spraying your screen with thousands of overlapping icons seething like snakes in a pit, Windows organizes icons into folders, puts those folders into *other* folders, and so on. This folder-in-a-folder-in-a-folder scheme works beautifully at reducing screen clutter, but it means that you've got some hunting to do whenever you want to open a particular icon.

Helping you find, navigate, and manage your files, folders, and disks with less stress and greater speed was one of the primary design goals of Windows 7—and of this chapter. The following pages cover Search, plus icon-management life skills like selecting them, renaming them, moving them, copying them, making shortcuts of them, assigning them to keystrokes, deleting them, and burning them to CD or DVD.

Tip: To create a new folder to hold your icons, right-click where you want the folder to appear (on the desktop or in any desktop window except Computer), and choose New→Folder from the shortcut menu. The new folder appears with its temporary "New Folder" name highlighted. Type a new name for the folder and then press Enter.

Meet Windows Search
All Versions

Every computer offers a way to find files. And every system offers several different ways to open them. But Search combines these two functions in a way that's so fast, so efficient, and so spectacular, it reduces much of what you've read in the previous chapters to irrelevance. It works like Google Desktop (or Spotlight on the Macintosh), in that it finds files *as you type* what you're looking for—not like Windows XP, which

---

doesn't start searching until you're finished typing and takes a very long time to find things at that.

It's important to note, though, that you can search for files on your PC using the superfast Search box in two different places:

- **The Start menu.** The Start Search box at the bottom of the Start menu searches *everywhere* on your computer.

- **Explorer windows.** The Search box at the top of every desktop window searches only *that window* (including folders within it). You can expand it, too, into something called the Search *pane*—a way to limit the scope of your search to certain file types or date ranges, for example.

Search boxes also appear in the Control Panel window, Internet Explorer, Windows Mail, Windows Media Player, and other spots where it's useful to perform small-time, limited searches. The following pages, however, cover the two main Search boxes, the ones that hunt down files and folders.

Search from the Start Menu
All Versions

Start by opening the Start menu, either by using the mouse or by pressing the ⊞ key.

The "Search programs and files" box appears at the bottom of the Start menu; you can immediately begin typing to identify what you want to find and open (Figure 3-1). For example, if you're trying to find a file called "Pokémon Fantasy League.doc," typing just *pok* or *leag* will probably work.

Capitalization doesn't count, and neither do accent marks; typing *cafe* finds files with the word "café" just fine. (You can change this, however; see page 136.)

As you type, the familiar Start menu items are replaced by search results (Figure 3-1). This is a live, interactive search; that is, Windows modifies the menu as you type—you do *not* have to press Enter after entering your search phrase.

The results menu lists every file, folder, program, email message, address book entry, calendar appointment, picture, movie, PDF document, music file, Web bookmark, and Microsoft Office document (Word, PowerPoint, and Excel) that contains what you typed, regardless of its name or folder location.

UP TO SPEED

Directories vs. Folders

Before Windows took over the universe, folders were called directories, and folders inside them were called subdirecto- ries. Keep that in mind the next time you're reading an old user guide, magazine article, or computer book.

Windows isn't just searching icon *names*. It's also searching their contents—the words inside your documents—as well as all your files' *metadata*. (That's descriptive text information about what's in a file, like its height, width, size, creator, copyright holder, title, editor, created date, and last modification date. Page 86 has the details.)

Note: Windows is constantly updating its invisible index (page 132) in real time. You can prove it to yourself like this: Open a text document (in WordPad, for example). Type an unusual word, like *wombat.* Save the document using a different name—say, "Fun Pets." Now *immediately* do a search. Hit the 🔲 key and type *wom,* for example. You'll see that Windows finds "Fun Pets" even though it's only moments old. That's a far cry from, for example, the old Windows Indexing Service, which updated its index only once a day, in the middle of the night!

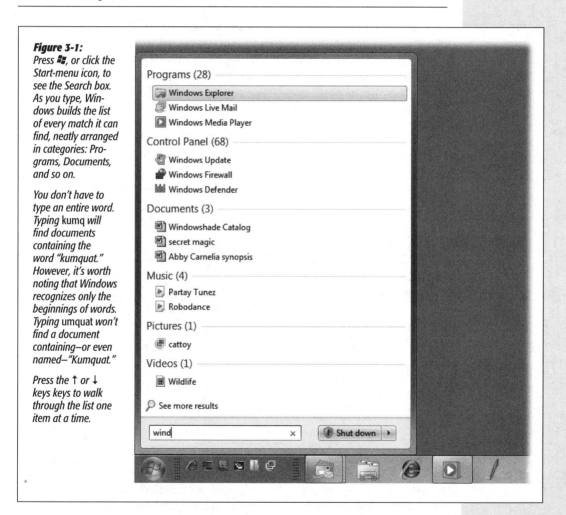

Figure 3-1:
Press 🔲, or click the Start-menu icon, to see the Search box. As you type, Windows builds the list of every match it can find, neatly arranged in categories: Programs, Documents, and so on.

You don't have to type an entire word. Typing kumq *will find documents containing the word "kumquat." However, it's worth noting that Windows recognizes only the* beginnings *of words. Typing* umquat *won't find a document containing—or even named—"Kumquat."*

Press the ↑ or ↓ keys keys to walk through the list one item at a time.

If you see the icon you were hoping to dig up, double-click it to open it. Or use the arrow keys to "walk down" the menu, and then press Enter to open it.

If you choose a program (programs are listed first in the results menu), well, that program pops onto the screen. Selecting an email message opens that message in your email program. And so on.

As you'll soon learn, Search threatens to make all that folders-in-folders business nearly pointless. Why burrow around in folders when you can open any file or program with a couple of keystrokes?

The "More Results" Window

Windows's menu shows you only about 15 results. Unless you own one of those extremely rare 60-inch Skyscraper Displays, there just isn't room to show you the whole list.

Instead, Windows uses some fancy behind-the-scenes analysis to calculate and display the 15 or so *most likely* matches for what you typed. They appear grouped into categories like Programs, Pictures, Control Panel, and Documents. The number in parentheses shows how *many* items are in each category.

Tip: If you click one of these category headings, you open a window containing just the search results in that category. Kind of handy, really.

Having such a short list of likely suspects means it's easy to arrow-key your way to the menu item you want to open. But at the bottom of the menu, a link called "See more results" is a reminder that there may be many other candidates. Click it to open the results *window*, shown in Figure 3-2.

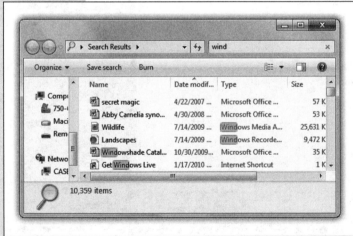

Figure 3-2:
You can open this window by clicking a link called "See more results" in the Start menu's results list. "More," in this case, means "everything Windows found except programs and Control Panel items."

Now you have access to the *complete* list of matches, listed in typical Explorer-window format, using the new Content view (so that you can read the first few lines of text in each file, for example). As a bonus, the text that matches your search query is highlighted in each file's name, also shown in Figure 3-2. You can sort this list, group it, or filter it exactly as described in Chapter 2.

The only difference is that the task toolbar (Organize, Views, and so on) offers a button that doesn't usually adorn standard folder windows, called "Save search." Details on this item later in this chapter.

This Search Results window offers a suite of additional tools for continuing your quest. For example, if you choose Organize→Layout→Preview pane, you open the right-hand Preview panel. It shows you the contents of each icon you click in the list (a picture, a playable movie or sound, the text in a Word file, and so on), which can be a great help in trying to figure out what these things are.

You can also click one of the "Search again in:" icons at the bottom of the results list. They represent specialized places where you can repeat the same search: just in your libraries, on the Internet, across your homegroup (page 775), or whatever. If you want to repeat the search in a *particular* folder or disk, click Custom to specify it.

Limit by Size, Date, Rating, Tag, Author...

Suppose you're looking for a file called *Big Deals.doc.* But when you type *big* into the Search box, you wind up wading through hundreds of files that *contain* the word "big."

It's at times like these that you'll be grateful for Windows's little-known *criterion* searches. These are syntax tricks that help you create narrower, more targeted searches. All you have to do is prefix your search query with the criterion you want, followed by a colon.

One example is worth a thousand words, so *several* examples should save an awful lot of paper:

- *name: big* finds only documents with "big" in their *names.* Windows ignores anything with that term *inside* the file.

- *tag: crisis* finds only icons with "crisis" as a tag—not as part of the title or contents.

- *created: 7/25/10* finds everything you wrote on July 25, 2010. You can also use *modified: today* or *modified: yesterday,* for that matter. Or don't be that specific. Just use *modified: July* or *modified: 2010.*

  You can use symbols like < and >, too. To find files created since yesterday, you could type *created: >yesterday.*

  Or use two dots to indicate a range. To find all the email you got in the first two weeks of March 2010, you could type *received: 3/1/2010..3/15/2010.* (That two-dot business also works to specify a range of file sizes, as in *size: 2 MB..5 MB.*)

Tip: That's right: Windows recognizes human terms like today, yesterday, this week, last week, last month, this month, and last year.

- *size: >2gb* finds all the big files on your PC.

- *rating: <**** finds documents to which you've given ratings of three stars or fewer.

- *camera model: Nikon D90* finds all the pictures you took with that camera.

- *kind: email* finds all the email messages.

That's just one example of the power of *kind*. Here are some other kinds you can look for: *calendar, appointment,* or *meeting* (appointments in Outlook, or iCal or vCalendar files); *communication* (email and attachments); *contact* or *person* (vCard and Windows Contact files, Outlook contacts); *doc* or *document* (text, Office, PDF, and Web files); *folder* (folders, .zip files, .cab files); *link* (shortcut files); *music* or *song* (audio files, Windows Media playlists); *pic* or *picture* (graphics files like JPEG, PNG, GIF, and BMP); *program* (programs); *tv* (shows recorded by Windows Media Center); and *video* (movie files).

- The *folder:* prefix limits the search to a certain folder or library. (The starter words *under:, in:,* and *path:* work the same way.) So *folder: music* confines the search to your Music library, and a search for *in: documents turtle* finds all files in your Documents library containing the word "turtle."

Tip: You can combine multiple criteria searches, too. For example, if you're pretty sure you had a document called "Naked Mole-Rats" that you worked on yesterday, you could cut directly to it by typing *mole modified: yesterday* or *modified: yesterday mole*. (The order doesn't matter.)

So where's the master list of these available criteria? It turns out that they correspond to the *column headings* at the top of an Explorer window that's in Details view: Name, Date modified, Type, Size, and so on.

You're not limited to just the terms you see now; you can use any term that *can* be an Explorer-window heading. To see them all, right-click any of the existing column headings in a window that's in Details view. From the shortcut menu, choose More. There they are: 115 different criteria, including Size, Rating, Album, Bit rate, Camera model, Date archived, Language, Nickname, and so on. Here's where you learn that,

---

GEM IN THE ROUGH

Wildcards

Windows recognizes two traditional wildcard characters—* and ?– in its searches.

A wildcard character means "whatever." So if you search for *tion, your search will find files named things like motion, nation, intimidation, intuition, and so on. A search like in*ble would match terms like intangible, incredible, and indistinguishable.

(Footnote: When placed at the beginning or in the middle of a search query, these wildcards don't work to find words inside your files—only filenames. And there's not much point in putting a wildcard character at the end of your search query, because Windows always acts as though there's a

wildcard at the end. That is, if you search for fil, you'll get results like filly, filibuster, filbert, and so on, even without * at the end. The * is more useful at the beginning or middle of search terms—when searching filenames.)

Here's a cool tip: When you open an Explorer window, typing * into the Search box produces a flat, simple list of every single file in it. That's a great time-saver when you want to scan for a certain file but don't feel like opening all the folders within folders within folders to find it.

Windows also recognizes the ? wildcard. The difference is that ? means "One character appears here," whereas the * can stand for any number of characters (or no characters).

for example, to find all your Ohio Address Book friends, you'd search for *home state or province: OH*.

Dude, if you can't find what you're looking for using all *those* controls, it probably doesn't exist.

Special Search Codes

Certain shortcuts in the Search boxes can give your queries more power. For example:

- **Document types.** You can type *document* to find all text, spreadsheet, and PowerPoint files. You can also type a filename extension—*.mp3* or *.doc* or *.jpg,* for example—to round up all files of a certain file type.

Tip: That sort of search will include both files whose names end with that filename extension as well as files whose text contains that extension. If you find that searching for (for example) .jpg produces too many results, you can try *ext: .jpg,* or *fileext: .jpg,* or *extension: .jpg,* or even *fileextension: .jpg.* They all work the same way: They limit the results to files whose names actually end with those filename extensions.

- **Tags, authors.** This is payoff time for applying *tags* or author names to your files (page 87). In a Search box, you can type, or start to type, *Gruber Project* (or any other tag you've assigned), and you get an instantaneous list of everything that's relevant to that tag. Or you can type *Mom* or *Casey* or any other author's name to see all the documents that person created.

- **Utility apps.** Windows comes with a bunch of geekhead programs that aren't listed in the Start menu and have no icons—advanced technical tools like RegEdit (the Registry Editor), (the command line), and so on. By far the quickest way to open them is to type their names into the Search box.

  In this case, however, you must type the *entire* name—*regedit,* not just *rege.* And you have to use the program's actual, on-disk name (regedit), not its human name (Registry Editor).

- **Quotes.** If you type in more than one word, Search works just the way Google does. That is, it finds things that contain both words *somewhere* inside.

  If you're searching for a phrase where the words really belong together, though, put quotes around them. For example, searching for *military intelligence* rounds up documents that contain those two words, but not necessarily side by side. Searching for *"military intelligence"* finds documents that contain that exact phrase. (Insert your own political joke here.)

- **Boolean searches.** Windows also permits combination-search terms like AND and OR, better known to geeks as Boolean searches.

  That is, you can round up a single list of files that match *two* terms by typing, say, *vacation AND kids.* (That's also how you'd find documents coauthored by two specific people—you and a pal, for example.)

Tip: You can use parentheses instead of AND, if you like. That is, typing *(vacation kids)* finds documents that contain both words, not necessarily together.

If you use OR, you can find icons that match *either* of two search criteria. Typing *jpeg OR mp3* will turn up photos and music files in a single list.

The word NOT works, too. If you did a search for *dolphins,* hoping to turn up sea-mammal documents, but instead find your results contaminated by football-team listings, then by all means repeat the search with *dolphins NOT Miami.* Windows will eliminate all documents containing "Miami."

Note: You must type Boolean terms like AND, OR, and NOT in all capitals.

You can even combine Boolean terms with the other special search terms described in this chapter. Find everything created in the past couple of months by searching for *created: September OR October,* for example. If you've been entering your name into the Properties dialog box of Microsoft Office documents, you can find all the ones created by Casey and Robin working together using *author: (Casey AND Robin).*

Results Menu Tips

It should be no surprise that a feature as important as Search comes loaded with options, tips, and tricks. Here it is—the official, unexpurgated Search Tip-O-Rama:

GEM IN THE ROUGH

Natural Language

OK, so very cool: You can search for *author: (Casey OR Robin NOT Smith) created: <yesterday.*

That's powerful, all right, but also totally intimidating. Ask yourself: Would your mother have any idea what that means?

The New Microsoft, the one that created Windows 7 and tried to make it user-friendly and elegant, is way ahead of you on this one. It has given you an alternative way to set up criteria searches: *natural-language searching.* That just means using plain English phrases instead of the usual codes.

To turn on this feature, open Folder Options. (Quickest route: Open the Start menu and type enough of the word *folder* until you see Folder Options in the results list. Click it.) Click the Search tab and turn on "Use natural language search." Click OK.

From now on, you can type in search phrases like these:

documents created last week

music by Beethoven

email from Xavier

email from Robin sent yesterday

pictures of Casey taken January 2009

classical music rated *****

It may take you some time to experiment to a point where you can trust these searches, but they're certainly easier than using a bunch of colons and parentheses. (Which you can still use, by the way, even when natural language search is turned on.)

- You can open anything in the results menu by highlighting it and then pressing Enter to open it.

It's incredibly convenient to open a *program* using this technique, because the whole thing happens very quickly and you never have to take your hands off the keyboard. That is, you might hit ⊞ to open the Start menu, type *calc* (to search for Calculator), and press Enter.

Why does pressing Enter open Calculator? Because it's the first item in the list of results, and its name is highlighted.

- If Windows doesn't find a *program* whose name matches what you've typed, it doesn't highlight anything in the list. In that case, pressing Enter has a different effect: It opens up the Search Results *window,* which has no length limit and offers a lot more features (page 125). (Pressing Enter, in this case, is the same as clicking the "See more results" list at the bottom.)

Alternatively, you can use the mouse or the arrow-key/Enter method described above to open one of the search results.

- You can learn more about a search result by pointing to it without clicking. The pop-up tooltip balloon shows you the details. For a file, you see size, date, and other info; for a program or control panel, you see a description.

- You can jump to the actual icon of a search result, sitting there in its actual window, instead of opening it. To do that, right-click its name, and, from the shortcut menu, choose "Open file location." The Esc key (top-left corner of your keyboard) is a quick "back out of this" keystroke. Tap it to close the results menu and restore the Start menu to its original form.

- To clear the Search box—either to try a different search or just to get the regularly scheduled Start menu back—click the little ✖ at the right end of the Search box.

GEM IN THE ROUGH

Beyond Your Own Stuff

Ordinarily, Windows searches only what's in *your* account—your Personal folder (page 33). From the Start menu, you can't search what's inside somebody else's stuff.

Yet you *can* search someone else's account—just not from the Start menu and not without permission.

Start by opening the Start menu→Computer→Users folder. Inside, you'll find folders for all other account holders. Open the one you want to search, and then search using the Search box at the top of the Explorer window.

You won't be given access, though, without first supplying an administrator's password. (You don't necessarily have to know it; you could just call an administrator over to type it in personally.) After all, the whole point of having different accounts is to ensure privacy for each person—and only the administrator, or *an* administrator, has full rein to stomp through anyone's stuff.

• When you need to look up a number in Address Book, don't bother opening Mail; it's faster to use Search. You can type somebody's name or even part of someone's phone number.

• Among a million other things, Windows tracks the *tags* (keywords) you've applied to your pictures. As a result, you can find, open, or insert any photo at any time, no matter what program you're using. This is a fantastic way to insert a photo into an outgoing email message, a presentation, or a Web page you're designing. (In a page-layout program, for example, use the Insert command, and then use the Search box that appears at the top of the Open dialog box.)

Explorer-Window Searches
All Versions

See the Search box at the top right of every Explorer window? This, too, is a piece of the Search empire. But there's a big difference: The Search box in the Start menu searches *your entire computer*. The Search box in an Explorer window searches *only that window* (and folders within it).

As you type, the window changes to show search results (in Content view) *as* you type into the Search box, much the way the Start menu changes. As described on the previous pages, a whole range of power tips is available to you, including file-type searches, AND searches, OR searches, and so on.

The beauty of an Explorer-window search is that it's not limited to 15 results, as the Start menu is. If there are a lot of results, you see all of them in one massively scrolling window.

Tip: What if you want to do an Explorer-window search, but no window is open? Press ⊞-F (for "Find," get it?) or F3. You get what amounts to an empty Explorer window, with the insertion point already in the Search box, ready for typing.

Unlike the Start menu search, though, the Explorer-window search offers a bonus search feature, which Microsoft calls Search Builder and normal people call *search filters.*

Search filters

As soon as you start typing into the Search box, a few words appear just beneath it—blue links that say things like "Authors," "Date modified," and "Size." These are *search filters* that help you weed down a big list of results.

When you click one, a pop-up menu appears to help you specify *what* author you want, or *which* dates modified, or *how big* the file is; Figure 3-3 should make this clear.

Which search filters appear depends on what kind of folder or library you're in. In the Documents library, your choices include Authors, Type, Date modified, Size, Name, Folder path, Tags, and Title; for the Pictures library, you get Date taken, Tags, Type,

Date modified, Name, Size, Folder Path, and Rating; for Music, you get Album, Artists, Genre, Length, Folder Path, Year, Rating, and Title; and so on.

Tip: If you make the Search box bigger—by dragging the divider bar (between the address bar and the Search box) to the left—then Windows has enough room to show you more search filters. Usually, there are eight in all.

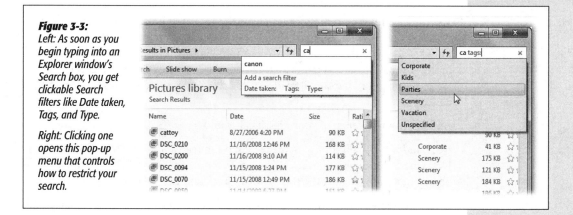

Figure 3-3:

Left: As soon as you begin typing into an Explorer window's Search box, you get clickable Search filters like Date taken, Tags, and Type.

Right: Clicking one opens this pop-up menu that controls how to restrict your search.

As soon as you set up a filter like this, two alarming things happen:

- **The Search box fills up with codes.** You'll see, for example, *datemodified:last week*, or *size:medium* in blue text. These are, in fact, exactly the same codes described on page 125. In other words, these clickable search filters are nothing more than user-friendlified, quicker ways of entering the same search codes. If you're more of a keyboard person than a mouse person, it's perfectly OK to type those codes into the Search box manually; the result is exactly the same.

  You can use as many of these filters as you want. The more you click them (or type the corresponding shorthand), the longer the codes are in the Search box. If you want to find medium files created by Casey last year with the tag *Murgatroid project,* go right ahead.

Tip: You can adjust the second part of each code just by clicking it. For example, if you chose size:small and you really wanted size:medium—or if the size:small query didn't produce any results—click the word small. The pop-up menu of sizes appears again so you can adjust your selection.

- **The results window changes.** Search filters work by *hiding* all the icons that don't match. So don't be alarmed if you click Size and then Small—and most of the files in your window suddenly disappear. Windows is doing what it thinks you wanted—showing you only the small files—in real time, as you adjust the filters.

  At any time, you can bring all the files back into view by clicking the little ⊠ at the right end of the Search box.

In any case, once the results appear in the main window, you can change the window view if that's helpful, or sort, filter, and group them, just as you would in any other Explorer window.

The Search Index

All Versions

You might think that typing something into the Search box triggers a search. But to be technically correct, Windows has already *done* its searching. In the first 15 to 30 minutes after you install Windows 7—or in the minutes after you attach a new hard drive—it invisibly collects information about everything on your hard drive. Like a kid cramming for an exam, it reads, takes notes on, and memorizes the contents of all your files.

And not just the *names* of your files. That would be *so* 2004!

No, Windows actually looks *inside* the files. It can read and search the contents of text files, email, Windows Contacts, Windows Calendar, RTF and PDF documents, and documents from Microsoft Office (Word, Excel, and PowerPoint).

In fact, Windows searches over 115 bits of text associated with your files—a staggering collection of tidbits, including the names of the layers in a Photoshop document, the tempo of an MP3 file, the shutter speed of a digital-camera photo, a movie's copyright holder, a document's page size, and on and on. (Technically, this sort of secondary information is called *metadata*. It's usually invisible, although a lot of it shows up in the Details pane described in Chapter 2.)

Windows stores all this information in an invisible, multimegabyte file called, creatively enough, the *index*. (If your primary hard drive is creaking full, you can specify that you want the index stored on some other drive; see page 137.)

Once it's indexed your hard drive in this way, Windows can produce search results in seconds. It doesn't have to search your entire hard drive—only that single card-catalog index file.

After the initial indexing process, Windows continues to monitor what's on your hard drive, indexing new and changed files in the background, in the microseconds between your keystrokes and clicks.

Where Windows Looks

Windows doesn't actually scrounge through *every* file on your computer. Searching inside Windows's own operating-system files and all your programs, for example, would be pointless to anyone but programmers. All that useless data would slow down searches and bulk up the invisible index file.

What Windows *does* index is everything in your Personal folder (page 33): email, pictures, music, videos, program names, entries in your Address Book and Calendar, Office documents, and so on. It also searches all your *libraries* (page 81), even if they contain folders from other computers on your network.

Similarly, it searches *offline files* that belong to you, even though they're stored somewhere else on the network (page 622). Finally, it indexes everything in the Start menu.

Note: Windows indexes all the drives connected to your PC, but not other hard drives on the network. You can, if you wish, add other folders to the list of indexed locations manually (page 133).

Windows does index the Personal folders of everyone else with an account on your machine (Chapter 23), but you're not allowed to search them from the Start menu. So if you were hoping to search your spouse's email for phrases like "meet you at midnight," forget it.

The Older, Slower Kind of Search

If you try to search anything Windows *hasn't* incorporated into its index—in a Windows system folder, for example, or a hard drive elsewhere on the network—a message appears. It lets you know that because you're working beyond the index's wisdom, the search is going to be slow, and the search will include filenames only—not file *contents* or metadata.

Furthermore, this kind of outside-the-index searching doesn't find things *as* you type. This time, you have to press Enter after typing the name (or partial name) of what you want to find.

Adding New Places to the Index

On the other hand, suppose there's some folder on another disk (or elsewhere on the network) that you really do want to be able to search the *good* way—contents and all, nice and fast. You can do that by adding it to your PC's search index.

And you can do *that* in a couple of ways:

- **Add it to a library.** Drag any folder into one of your libraries (page 81). After a couple of minutes of indexing, that folder is now ready for insta-searching, contents and all, just as though it were born on your own PC.

- **Add it to the Indexing Options dialog box.** Windows maintains a master list of everything in its search index. That's handy, because it means you can easily *add* folders to the index—folders from an external hard drive, for example—for speedy searches.

  You can *remove* folders from the index, too, maybe because you have privacy concerns (for example, you don't want your spouse searching your stuff while you're away from your desk). Or maybe you just want to create more focused searches, removing a lot of old, extraneous junk from Windows's database.

  Either way, the steps are simple. Open the Indexing Options control panel; the quickest way is to open the Start menu and start typing *indexing* until you see Indexing Options in the search results. Click it, and proceed as shown in Figure 3-4.

Tip: If you're trying to get some work done while Windows is in the middle of building the index, and the indexing is giving your PC all the speed of a slug in winter, you can click the Pause button. Windows will cool its jets for 15 minutes before it starts indexing again.

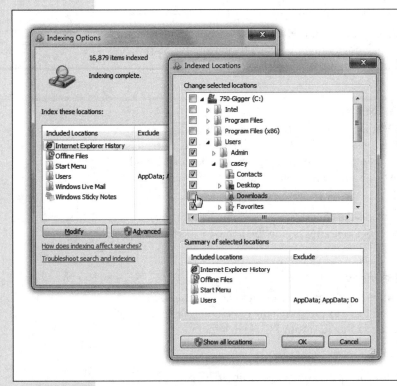

Figure 3-4:
You can add or remove disks, partitions, or folders in the list of searchable items. Start by opening Indexing Options (left), then click Modify. Now expand the flippy triangles, if necessary, to see the list of folders on your hard drive. Turn a folder's checkbox on (to have Windows index it) or off (to remove it from the index, and therefore from searches). In this example, you've just told Windows to stop indexing your Downloads folder. Click OK.

Customizing Search

You've just read about how Search works fresh out of the box. But you can tailor its behavior, both for security reasons and to customize it to the kinds of work you do.

Unfortunately for you, Microsoft has stashed the various controls that govern searching into three different places. Here they are, one area at a time:

Folder Options

The first source is in the Folder Options→Search dialog box. To open it, choose Organize→"Folder and search options" in any Explorer window. In the resulting dialog box, click the Search tab. You wind up at the dialog box shown in Figure 3-5.

- **What to search.** As the previous pages make clear, the Windows search mechanism relies on an *index*—an invisible database that tracks the location, contents, and metadata of every file. If you attach a new hard drive, or attempt to search another computer on the network that hasn't been indexed, Windows ordinarily just searches its files' *names*. After all, it has no index to search for that drive.

If Windows did attempt to index those other drives, you'd sometimes have to wait awhile, at least the first time, because index-building isn't instantaneous. That's why the factory setting here is: "In indexed locations, search file names and contents. In non-indexed locations, search file names only."

Figure 3-5:
Search actually works beautifully right out of the box. For the benefit of the world's tweakers, however, this dialog box awaits, filled with technical adjustments to the way Search works.

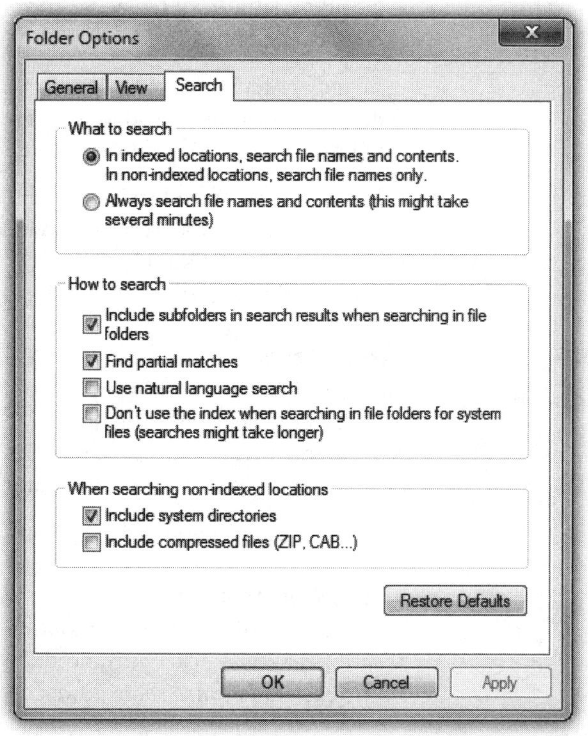

But if you really want Windows to search the text inside the other drives' files, even without an index—which can be painfully slow—turn on "Always search file names and contents" instead.

- **Include subfolders in search results when searching in file folders.** When you use the Search box at the top of an Explorer window, Windows ordinarily searches the currently open window *and* the folders inside it. Turn off this option if you want to search only what you see in the window before you.

- **Find partial matches.** Turn this off if you want Windows to find only whole-word matches, meaning that you'll no longer be able to type *waff* to find *Mom's Best Waffle Recipes of the Eighties.doc*.

- **Use natural language search.** See the box on page 128.

- **Don't use the Index when searching in file folders for system files.** If you turn this item on, Windows won't use its internal Dewey Decimal System for searching Windows itself. It will, instead, perform the names-only, slower type of search.

  So who on earth would want this turned on? You, if you're a programmer or system administrator and you're worried that the indexed version of the system files might be out of date. (That happens, since system files change often, and the index may take some time to catch up.)

- **Include system directories.** When you're searching a disk that hasn't been indexed, do you want Windows to look inside the folders that contain Windows itself (as opposed to just the documents people have created)? If yes, turn this on.

- **Include compressed files (.zip, .cab…).** When you're searching a disk that hasn't been indexed, do you want Windows to search for files inside compressed archives, like .zip and .cab files? If yes, turn on this checkbox. (Windows doesn't ordinarily search archives, even on an indexed hard drive.)

Indexing Options

The dialog box shown in Figure 3-6 is the master control over the search *index,* the massive, invisible, constantly updated database file that tracks your PC's files and what's in them. As described on page 133, you can use this dialog box to add or remove folders from what Windows is tracking.

But there are a few more handy options here, too:

Advanced Indexing Options

To find this third area of search options, start in the Indexing Options dialog box (Control Panel) and click Advanced. Authenticate if necessary (see page 726). Now you're ready to perform these powerful additional tweaks:

- **Index encrypted files.** Some Windows 7 versions (Professional, Enterprise, and Ultimate) can *encrypt* files and folders with a quick click, making them unreadable to anyone who receives one by email, say, and doesn't have the password. This checkbox lets Windows index these files (the ones that *you've* encrypted, of course; this isn't a back door to files you can't otherwise access).

- **Treat similar words with diacritics as different words.** The word "ole," as might appear cutely in a phrase like "the ole swimming pool," is quite a bit different from "olé," as in, "You missed the matador, you big fat bull!" The difference is a *diacritical mark* (øne öf mâny littlé lañguage märks).

  Ordinarily, Windows ignores diacritical marks; it treats "ole" and "olé" as the same word in searches. That's designed to make it easier for the average person who can't remember how to type a certain marking, or even which direction it goes. But if you turn on this box, Windows will observe these markings and treat marked and unmarked words differently.

- **Troubleshoot searching.** If the Search command ever seems to be acting wacky—for example, it's not finding a document you *know* is there—Microsoft is there to help you.

  Your first step should be to click "Troubleshoot search and indexing." (It appears both here, on the Advanced panel, and on the main Indexing Options panel.) The resulting step-by-step sequence may fix things.

  If it doesn't, click Advanced, and then click Rebuild. Now Windows *wipes out* the index it's been working with, completely deleting it—and then begins to rebuild it. You're shown a list of the disks and folders Windows has been instructed to index; the message at the top of the dialog box lets you know its progress. With luck, this process will wipe out any funkiness you've been experiencing.

- **Move the index.** Ordinarily, Windows stores its invisible index file on your main hard drive. But you might have good reason for wanting to move it. Maybe your main drive is getting full. Or maybe you've bought a second, faster hard drive; if you store your index there, searching will be even faster.

  In the Advanced Options dialog box, click "Select new." Navigate to the disk or folder where you want the index to go, and then click OK. (The actual transfer of the file takes place the next time you start up Windows.)

Figure 3-6:
Using the "How should this file be indexed" options at the bottom of the box, you can also make Windows stop searching these files' contents—the text within them—for better speed and a smaller index.

- **Teach Windows about new kinds of files.** Windows ordinarily searches for just about every kind of *useful* file: audio files, program files, text and graphics files, and so on. It doesn't bother peering inside things like Windows operating system files and applications, because what's inside them is programming code with little relevance to most people's work. Omitting these files from the index keeps the index smaller and the searches fast.

  But what if you routinely traffic in very rare Venezuelan Beekeeping Interchange Format (VBIF) documents—a file type your copy of Windows has never met before? You won't be able to search for their contents unless you specifically teach Windows about them.

  In the Advanced Options dialog box, click the File Types tab. Type the filename extension (such as VBIF) into the text box at the lower left. Click Add and then OK. From now on, Windows will index this new file type.

- **Turn off categories.** If you find that Windows uses up valuable search-results menu space listing, say, Web bookmarks—stuff you don't need to find very often—you can tell it not to bother. Now the results menu's precious 15 slots will be allotted to icon types you care more about.

  To remove file types from searches, click the Advanced button in the dialog box shown in Figure 3-4, authenticate if necessary, and then click the File Types tab in the resulting dialog box (Figure 3-6). Turn the checkboxes on or off to make Windows start or stop indexing them.

Saved Searches
All Versions

When you do a search that winds up in an Explorer window (for example, you hit "See more results" in the Start menu, or you started in an Explorer window to begin with), you may notice a little button in the toolbar called "Save search."

This button generates a *saved search*. Whenever you click it, you get an instantaneous update of the search you originally set up. (Behind the scenes, it's a special document with the filename extension *.search-ms*.)

To create a saved search, open an Explorer window and perform a search. By all means, use the *search filters* described on page 130 for more exactitude.

Now, as you survey the search results, click "Save search" in the task toolbar (Figure 3-7, top). You're asked to name and save your search. Windows proposes stashing it in your Saved Searches folder (which is in your Personal folder), but you can expand the Save As box and choose any location you like—including the desktop.

Either way, you also wind up with an icon for your saved search. Unless you changed the location manually, it shows up as an icon in the Favorites section of the Navigation pane in every Explorer window.

Here's a common example: Suppose that every week you want to round up all the documents authored by either you or your business partner that pertain to the Higgins proposal and burn them onto a CD. A search folder can do the rounding-up part with a single click.

So you open your Documents library (or even your Personal folder) and set up a search. In the search box, you type *tags: Higgins authors: casey OR authors: robin*. That text turns blue, meaning that Windows understands what you're looking for: anything with the Higgins tag that was written by Casey or Robin (or whatever your names are).

(Of course, you've been painstakingly tagging your documents with author names and tags, in readiness for this glorious moment.)

You click "Save search." You name the search something like "Our Higgins Files" and save it to your hard drive (Figure 3-7).

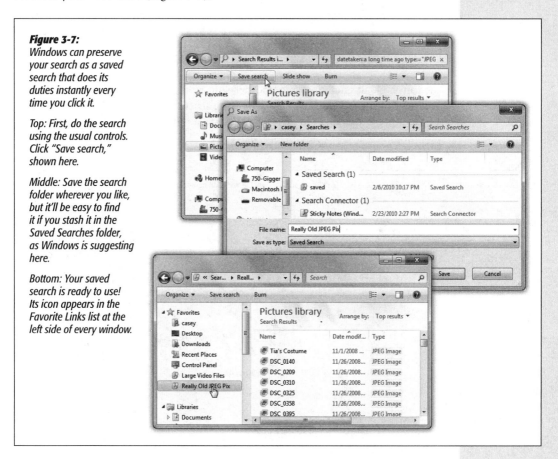

Figure 3-7:
Windows can preserve your search as a saved search that does its duties instantly every time you click it.

Top: First, do the search using the usual controls. Click "Save search," shown here.

Middle: Save the search folder wherever you like, but it'll be easy to find it if you stash it in the Saved Searches folder, as Windows is suggesting here.

Bottom: Your saved search is ready to use! Its icon appears in the Favorite Links list at the left side of every window.

From now on, whenever you click that Search icon in your Navigation pane, it opens to reveal all the files you've worked on that were tagged with "Higgins" and written by you or your partner. The great part is that these items' real locations may be all over the map, scattered in folders throughout your PC. But through the magic of the saved search, they appear as though they're all in one neat window.

Unfortunately, there's no easy way to edit a search folder. If you decide your original search criteria need a little fine-tuning, then the simplest procedure is to set up a new search—correctly this time—and save it with the same name as the first one; accept Windows's offer to replace the old one with the new.

Tip: Speaking of memorized searches: You might have noticed that the Search box in every Explorer window maintains a running list of all the searches you've performed so far. They appear in a drop-down menu when you click in the Search box.

If that list contains, ahem, some searches of a personal nature, or maybe just some annoying typos, you might wish you could delete individual items from this list. You can. Press ↑ or ↓ to highlight the one you want (or, rather, don't want), and then press Delete.

The Folders of Windows 7
All Versions

The top-level, all-encompassing, mother-ship window of your PC is the Computer window. From within this window, you have access to every disk, folder, and file on your computer. Its slogan might well be, "If it's not in here, it's not on your PC."

To see it, choose Start→Computer.

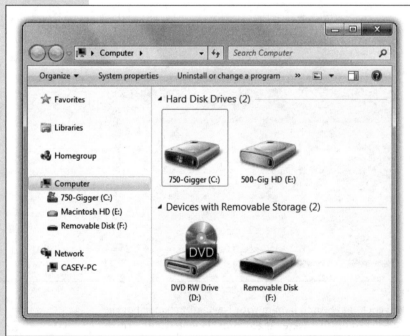

Figure 3-8:
The Computer window is the starting point for any and all folder-digging. It shows the "top-level" folders: the disk drives of your PC. If you double-click the icon of a removable-disk drive (such as your CD or DVD drive), you receive only a "Please insert a disk" message, unless there's actually a disk in the drive.

You wind up face to face with the icons of every storage gizmo connected to your PC: hard drives, CD and DVD drives, USB flash drives, digital cameras, and so on (Figure 3-8).

The Folders of Windows 7

Tip: Ordinarily, every drive has an icon in here, even if no disk or memory card is in it. That can be annoying if your laptop has, for example, four memory-card slots, each for a different kind of card, labeled D:, E:, F:, and G:, and your Computer window is getting a little hard to navigate.

Fortunately, a new option in Windows 7 hides your drive icons when they're empty, just as on the Mac. To turn it on or off, open Folder Options (type *folder* into the Start menu Search box to find it quickly). Click the View tab. Click "Hide empty drives in the Computer folder," and then click OK.

If you leave this option on, then your removable-disk/card drives appear only when something's in them—a CD, DVD, or memory card, for example.

Most people, most of the time, are most concerned with the Local Disk (C:), which represents the internal hard drive preinstalled in your computer. (You're welcome to rename this icon, by the way, just as you would any icon.)

Tip: The drive lettering, such as C: for your main hard drive, is an ancient convention that doesn't offer much relevance these days. (Back at the dawn of computing, the A: and B: drives were floppy drives, which is why you rarely see those letters anymore.)

Since Windows now displays icons and plain-English names for your drives, you might consider the drive-letter display to be a bit old-fashioned and cluttery. Fortunately, you can hide the drive letter (page 100).

What's in the Local Disk (C:) Window

If you double-click the Local Disk (C:) icon in Computer—that is, your primary hard drive—you'll find, at least, these standard folders:

PerfLogs
Windows Reliability and Performance Monitor is one of those hidden maintenance apps, as described on pages 706-707, that knowledgeable tech gurus can use to measure your PC's health and speed. This folder is where it dumps its *logs,* or reports.

Program Files
This folder contains all your applications—Word, Excel, Internet Explorer, your games, and so on.

Of course, a Windows program isn't a single, self-contained icon. Instead, it's usually a *folder,* housing both the program and its phalanx of support files and folders. The actual application icon itself generally can't even run if it's separated from its support group.

Program Files (x86)
If you've installed a 64-bit version of Windows 7 (page 263), this folder is where Windows puts all your older 32-bit programs.

Users

Windows's *accounts* feature is ideal for situations where different family members, students, or workers use the same machine at different times. Each account holder will turn on the machine to find her own separate, secure set of files, folders, desktop pictures, Web bookmarks, font collections, and preference settings. (Much more about this feature in Chapter 23.)

In any case, now you should see the importance of the Users folder. Inside is one folder —one *Personal folder*—for each person who has an account on this PC. In general, standard account holders (page 716) aren't allowed to open anybody else's folder.

Note: On page 81, you can read about libraries. Well, inside the Documents library, you'll see Public Documents; in the Music library, you'll see Public Music; and so on. These are nothing more than pointers to the master Public folder that you can also see here, in the Users folder. (Anything you put into a Public folder is available for inspection by anyone else with an account on your PC, or even other people on your network.)

Windows

Here's a folder that Microsoft hopes you'll just ignore. This most hallowed folder contains Windows itself, the thousands of little files that make Windows, well, Windows. Most of these folders and files have cryptic names that appeal to cryptic people.

In general, the healthiest PC is one whose Windows folder has been left alone.

Your Personal Folder

Everything that makes your Windows experience your own sits inside the Local Disk (C:)→Users→[your name] folder. This is your *Personal folder*, where Windows stores your preferences, documents, email, pictures, music, Web favorites, *cookies* (described below), and so on. You can get to it more directly by choosing your name from the top right of the Start menu.

Tip: Actually, it would make a lot of sense for you to install your Personal folder's icon in the Favorites list at the left side of every Explorer window. The easiest way to do that is to open your Personal folder (choose your name from the Start menu's right side) and then drag the tiny icon from the left end of the address bar directly into the Favorites list.

Inside your Personal folder, you'll find folders like these:

- **Contacts.** An address-book program called Windows Contacts came with Windows Vista, but Microsoft gave it the ol' pink slip for Windows 7. All that's left is this folder, where it used to stash the information about your social circle. The toolbar still has some buttons like New Contact and New Contact Group, but no other programs tap into whatever "cards" you make here. (Some other companies' address-book programs can use this folder, too.)

- **Desktop.** When you drag an icon out of a folder or disk window and onto your desktop, it may *appear* to show up on the desktop. But that's just an optical illusion—a visual convenience. In truth, nothing in Windows is ever really on the desktop; it's just in this Desktop *folder,* and mirrored on the desktop.

Remember that everyone who shares your machine will, upon logging in (page 737), see his own stuff sitting out on the desktop. Now you know how Windows does it; there's a separate Desktop folder in every person's Personal folder.

You can entertain yourself for hours trying to prove this. If you drag something out of your Desktop folder, it also disappears from the actual desktop. And vice versa.

Note: A link to this folder appears in the Navigation pane of every Explorer window.

- **Downloads.** When you download anything from the Web, Internet Explorer suggests storing it on your computer in this Downloads folder. The idea is to save you the frustration of downloading stuff and then not being able to find it later.

Tip: The Downloads folder appears in your Favorite Links list, too, so you can find your downloaded goodies with a single click.

- **Favorites.** This folder stores shortcuts of the files, folders, and other items you've designated as *favorites* (that is, Web bookmarks). This can be handy if you want to delete a bunch of your favorites all at once, rename them, or whatever.

- **Links.** This folder's icons correspond exactly to the easy-access links in the Favorite Links list at the left side of your Explorer windows (page 77). Knowing this little tidbit can be handy if you want to delete these links, rename them, or add to them. (Yes, you can perform these duties directly in the Favorite Links lists, but only one link at a time.)

FREQUENTLY ASKED QUESTION

Why "My" is Back

OK, I remember that Windows XP and earlier versions had "My" in front of all the folder names. You know: My Pictures, My Music, My Documents. I always thought it looked a little goofy, like, you know, it was My First Operating System.

Then the "My" disappeared in Windows Vista, which I thought was great.

But now "My" is back on those folder names in Windows 7! What gives?

In testing, Microsoft found that potential Windows 7 users were getting confused. They couldn't tell the difference between the Documents library and each individual's Documents folder. (Review Chapter 2 for the difference.)

Now, it's true that your My Documents folder is one of the folders that makes up the Documents library, but it's still really easy to get confused.

So Microsoft put "My" back on those folder names so you can tell them apart from the libraries that have similar names.

If the "My" on the names of your folders (in your Personal folder) bugs you, though, no biggie. You can rename these folders just as you would any other folder. Take off the "My," if you're so inclined. No harm done.

- **My Documents.** Microsoft suggests that you keep your actual work files in this folder. Sure enough, whenever you save a new document (when you're working in Word or Photoshop Elements, for example), the Save As box proposes storing the new file in this folder.

Tip: You can move the My Documents folder, if you like. For example, you can move it to a *removable* drive, like a pocket hard drive or USB flash drive, so that you can take it back and forth to work with you and always have your latest files at hand.

To do so, open your My Documents folder. Right-click a blank spot in the window; from the shortcut menu, choose Properties. Click the Location tab, click Move, navigate to the new location, and click Select Folder.

What's cool is that the Documents *link* in every Explorer window's Navigation pane still opens your My Documents folder. What's more, your programs still propose storing new documents there—even though it's not where Microsoft originally put it.

- **My Music, My Pictures, My Videos.** You guessed it: These are Microsoft's proposed homes for your multimedia files. These are where song files from ripped CDs, photos from digital cameras, and videos from camcorders go.

- **Saved Games.** When you save a computer game that's already in progress, it should propose storing it here, so you can find it again later. (Needless to say, it may take some time before all the world's games are updated to know about this folder.)

- **Searches.** This folder stores shortcuts that correspond to any search folders you create and lists the starter set that Microsoft provides. Its contents show up in the Favorites list of the Navigation pane.

Note: Your Personal folder also stores a few hidden items reserved for use by Windows itself. One of them is AppData, a very important folder that stores all kinds of support files for your programs (it was called Application Data in Windows XP). For example, it stores word-processor dictionaries, Web cookies, your Media Center recordings, Internet Explorer security certificates, changes you've made to your Start menu, and so on. In general, there's not much reason for you to poke around in them, but in this book, here and there, you'll find tips and tricks that refer you to AppData.

Life with Icons
All Versions

Windows Explorer, the program that runs automatically when you turn on your PC, has only one purpose in life: to help you manage your file, folder, and disk *icons.* You could spend your entire workday just mastering the techniques of naming, copying, moving, and deleting these icons—and plenty of people do.

Here's the crash course:

Renaming Your Icons

To rename a file, folder, printer, or disk icon, you need to open up its "renaming rectangle." You can do so with any of the following methods:

• Highlight the icon and then press the F2 key at the top of your keyboard.

• Click carefully, just once, on a previously highlighted icon's name.

• Right-click the icon and choose Rename from the shortcut menu.

Tip: You can even rename your hard drive so you don't go your entire career with a drive named "Local Disk." Just rename its icon (in the Computer window) as you would any other.

In any case, once the renaming rectangle has appeared, type the new name you want, and then press Enter. Use all the standard text-editing tricks: Press Backspace to fix a typo, press the ← and → keys to position the insertion point, and so on. When you're finished editing the name, press Enter to make it stick. (If another icon in the folder has the same name, Windows beeps and makes you choose another name.)

Tip: If you highlight a bunch of icons at once and then open the renaming rectangle for any *one* of them, you wind up renaming *all* of them. For example, if you've highlighted three folders called Cats, Dogs, and Fish, then renaming one of them *Animals* changes the original set of names to Animals (1), Animals (2), and Animals (3).

If that's not what you want, press Ctrl+Z (that's the keystroke for Undo) to restore all the original names.

A folder or filename can technically be up to 260 characters long. In practice, though, you won't be able to produce filenames that long; that's because that maximum must also include the *file extension* (the three-letter suffix that identifies the file type) and even the file's *folder path* (like C:\Users\Casey\My Pictures).

Note, too, that because they're reserved for behind-the-scenes use, Windows doesn't let you use any of these symbols in a Windows filename: \ / : * ? " < > |

You can give more than one file or folder the same name, as long as they're not in the same folder.

Note: Windows 7 comes factory-set not to show you filename extensions. That's why you sometimes might *think* you see two different files called, say, "Quarterly Sales, " both in the same folder.

The explanation is that one filename may end with .*doc* (a Word document), and the other may end with .*xls* (an Excel document). But because these suffixes are hidden (page 242), the files look like they have exactly the same name.

Icon Properties

Properties are a big deal in Windows. Properties are preference settings that you can change independently for every icon on your machine.

To view the properties for an icon, choose from these techniques, the first four of which open the Properties dialog box:

- Right-click the icon; choose Properties from the shortcut menu.

- Highlight the icon in an Explorer window; choose Organize→Properties.

- While pressing Alt, double-click the icon.

- Highlight the icon; press Alt+Enter.

- Open the Details pane in an Explorer window (page 75), and then click an icon in the window.

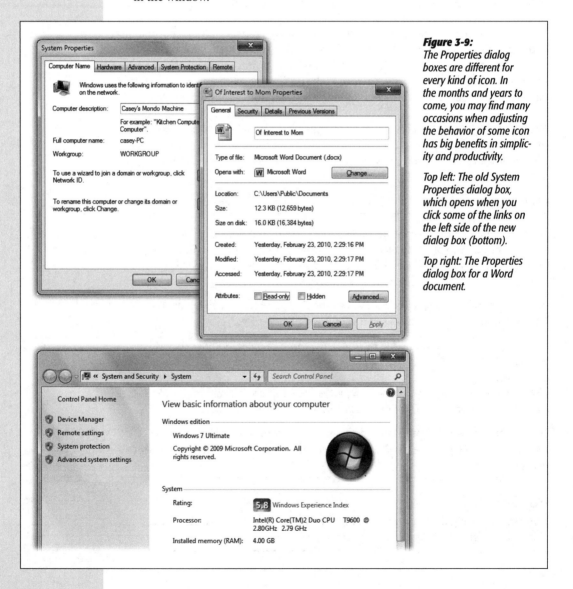

Figure 3-9:
The Properties dialog boxes are different for every kind of icon. In the months and years to come, you may find many occasions when adjusting the behavior of some icon has big benefits in simplicity and productivity.

Top left: The old System Properties dialog box, which opens when you click some of the links on the left side of the new dialog box (bottom).

Top right: The Properties dialog box for a Word document.

These settings aren't the same for every kind of icon, however. Here's what you can expect when opening the Properties dialog boxes of various icons (Figure 3-9):

Computer

There are about 500 different ways to open the Properties dialog box for your Computer icon. The quickest is to right-click Computer *in the Start menu.* Another is to open the System icon in the Control Panel (Chapter 8).

Either way, the System Properties window is packed with useful information about your machine: what kind of processor is inside, how much memory (RAM) your PC has, its overall "Experience Index" (horsepower score), and what version of Windows you've got.

The panel at the left side of the window (shown in Figure 3-9) includes some useful links—Device Manager, Remote settings, System protection, and Advanced system settings—all of which are described in the appropriate chapters of this book.

Note, however, that most of them work by opening the *old* System Properties Control Panel, also shown in Figure 3-9. Its tabs give a terse, but more complete, look at the tech specs and features of your PC. These, too, are described in the relevant parts of this book—all except "Computer Name." Here, you can type a plain-English name for your computer ("Casey's Laptop," for example). That's how it will appear to other people on the network, if you have one.

Disks

In a disk's Properties dialog box, you can see all kinds of information about the disk itself, like its name (which you can change), its capacity (which you can't change), and how much of it is full.

This dialog box's various tabs are also gateways to a host of maintenance and backup features, including Disk Cleanup, Error-checking, Defrag, Backup, and Quotas; all of these are described in Chapters 20 and 21.

Data files

The properties for a plain old document depend on what kind of document it is. You always see a General tab, but other tabs may also appear (especially for Microsoft Office files).

• **General.** This screen offers all the obvious information about the document—location, size, modification date, and so on. The *read-only* checkbox locks the document. In the read-only state, you can open the document and read it, but you can't make any changes to it.

Note: If you make a *folder* read-only, it affects only the files already inside. If you add additional files later, they remain editable.

Hidden turns the icon invisible. It's a great way to prevent something from being deleted, but because the icon becomes invisible, you may find it a bit difficult to open *yourself.*

The Advanced button offers a few additional options. *"File is ready for archiving"* means, "Back me up." This message is intended for the Backup and Restore program described in Chapter 22, and it indicates that this document has been changed since the last time it was backed up (or that it's never been backed up). *"Index this file for faster searching"* lets you indicate that this file should, or should not, be part of the quick-search index described earlier in this chapter.

"Compress contents to save disk space" is described later in this chapter. Finally, "Encrypt contents to secure data" is described on page 681. (These features aren't available in the cheaper versions of Windows 7.)

- **Custom.** As explained below, the Properties window of Office documents includes a Summary tab that lets you look up a document's word count, author, revision number, and many other statistics. But you should by no means feel limited to these 21 properties—nor to Office documents.

Using the Custom tab, you can create properties of your own—Working Title, Panic Level, Privacy Quotient, or whatever you like. Just specify a property type using the Type pop-up menu (Text, Date, Number, Yes/No); type the property name into the Name text box (or choose one of the canned options in its pop-up menu); and then click Add.

You can then fill in the Value text box for the individual file in question (so that its Panic Level is Red Alert, for example).

Note: This is an older form of tagging files—a lot like the tags feature described on page 86—*except* that you can't use Windows Search to find them. Especially technical people can, however, perform query-language searches for these values.

- The **Summary** tab reveals the sorts of details—tags, categories, authors, and so on—that *are* searchable by Windows's search command. You can edit these little tidbits right in the dialog box.

This box also tells you how many words, lines, and paragraphs are in a particular Word document. For a graphics document, the Summary tab indicates the graphic's dimensions, resolution, and color settings.

- The **Previous Versions** tab (Professional, Enterprise, and Ultimate editions of Windows only) lets you revert a document or a folder to an earlier version. It's part of the Shadow Copy automatic backup system described on page 700.

Folders

The Properties dialog box for a folder offers five (or six) tabs:

- **General.** Here you find the same sorts of checkboxes as you do for data files, described above.

- **Sharing** makes the folder susceptible to invasion by other people—either in person, when they log into this PC, or from across your office network (see Chapter 26).

- **Security** has to do with the technical NTFS permissions of a folder, technical on/off switches that govern who can do what to the contents (page 744). You see it only if your PC is running a high-end version of Windows 7, and only if the hard drive is formatted with NTFS.

- **Location.** This tab appears only for folders you've included in a library (page 81). It identifies where the folder *really* sits.

- **Previous Versions** lets you rewind a document to an earlier state; see page 700.

- **Customize.** The first pop-up menu here lets you apply a *folder template* to any folder: General Items, Documents, Pictures, Music, or Videos. A template is nothing more than a canned layout with a predesigned set of task toolbar buttons, icon sizes, column headings, and Search-box filters.

  You may already have noticed that your Pictures library displays a nice big thumbnail icon for each of your photos, and your Music library presents a tidy Details-view list of all your songs, with toolbar buttons like "Play all," "Share with," and "Burn." Here's your chance to apply those same expertly designed templates to folders of your own making.

  This dialog box also lets you change the *icon* for a folder, as described in the next section.

Program files

There's not much here that you can change yourself, but you certainly get a lot to look at. For starters, there are the General and Details tabs described above.

But there's also an important Compatibility tab, which may one day come to save your bacon. As described on page 259, it lets you trick a pre-Windows 7 program into running on Microsoft's latest.

Changing Your Icons' Icons

You can change the actual, inch-tall illustrations that Windows uses to represent the little icons replete in your electronic world. You can't, however, use a single method to do so; Microsoft has divided up the controls between two different locations.

Standard Windows icons

First, you can also change the icon for some of the important Windows desktop icons: the Recycle Bin, Documents, and so on. To do so, right-click a blank spot on the desktop. From the shortcut menu, choose Personalize. (This isn't available in the Starter edition of Windows 7.)

In the resulting window, click "Change desktop icons" in the task pane at the left side. You'll see a collection of those important Windows icons. Click one, and then click Change Icon to choose a replacement from a collection Microsoft provides. (You haven't *lived* until you've made your Recycle Bin look like a giant blue thumbtack!)

Folder or shortcut icons

Ordinarily, when your Explorer window is in Tiles, Content, or a fairly big Icon view, each folder's icon resembles what's in it. You actually see a tiny photo, music album, or Word document peeking out of the open-folder icon.

This means, however, that the icon may actually *change* over time, as you put different things into it. If you'd rather freeze a folder's icon so it doesn't keep changing, you can choose an image that will appear to peek out from inside that folder.

Note: The following steps also let you change what a certain shortcut icon looks like. Unfortunately, Windows offers no way to change an actual document's icon.

Actually, you have two ways to change a folder's icon. Both begin the same way: Right-click the folder or shortcut whose icon you want to change. From the shortcut menu, choose Properties, then click the Customize tab. Now you have a choice (Figure 3-10):

- **Change what image is peeking out of the file-folder icon.** Click Choose File. Windows now lets you hunt for icons on your hard drive. These can be picture files, icons downloaded from the Internet, icons embedded inside program files and .dll files, or icons you've made yourself using a freeware or shareware icon-making program. Find the graphic, click it, click Open, and then click OK.

  It may take a couple of minutes for Windows to update the folder image, but eventually, you see your hand-selected image "falling out" of the file-folder icon.

- **Completely replace the file-folder image.** Click Change Icon. Windows offers up a palette of canned graphics; click the one you want, and then click OK. Instantly, the original folder bears the new image.

Egypt slideshow

Egypt slideshow

Egypt slideshow

Figure 3-10:
Left: The original folder icon.

Middle: You've replaced the image that seems to be falling out of it.

Right: You've completely replaced the folder icon.

Selecting Icons
All Versions

Before you can delete, rename, move, copy, or otherwise tamper with any icon, you have to be able to *select* it somehow. By highlighting it, you're essentially telling Windows what you want to operate on.

Use the Mouse

To select one icon, just click it once. To select *multiple* icons at once—in preparation for moving, copying, renaming, or deleting them en masse, for example—use one of these techniques:

- **Select all.** Highlight all the icons in a window by choosing Organize→Select all. (Or press Ctrl+A, its keyboard equivalent.)

- **Highlight several consecutive icons.** Start with your cursor above and to one side of the icons, and then drag diagonally. As you drag, you create a temporary shaded blue rectangle. Any icon that falls within this rectangle darkens to indicate that it's been selected.

  Alternatively, click the first icon you want to highlight, and then Shift+click the last file. All the files in between are automatically selected, along with the two icons you clicked. (These techniques work in any folder view: Details, Icon, Content, or whatever.)

Tip: If you include a particular icon in your diagonally dragged group by mistake, Ctrl+click it to remove it from the selected cluster.

- **Highlight nonconsecutive icons.** Suppose you want to highlight only the first, third, and seventh icons in the list. Start by clicking icon No. 1; then Ctrl+click each of the others. (If you Ctrl+click a selected icon *again*, you *de*select it. A good time to use this trick is when you highlight an icon by accident.)

Tip: The Ctrl key trick is especially handy if you want to select *almost* all the icons in a window. Press Ctrl+A to select everything in the folder, then Ctrl+click any unwanted subfolders to deselect them.

Use the Keyboard

You can also highlight one icon, plucking it out of a sea of pretenders, by typing the first few letters of its name. Type *nak,* for example, to select an icon called "Naked Chef Broadcast Schedule."

Checkbox Selection

It's great that you can select icons by holding down a key and clicking—if you can remember *which* key must be pressed.

Turns out novices were befuddled by the requirement to Ctrl+click icons when they wanted to choose more than one. So Microsoft did something in Windows that nobody's ever done before—it created a checkbox mode. In this mode, any icon you point to temporarily sprouts a little checkbox that you can click to select (Figure 3-11).

To turn this feature on, open any Explorer window, and then choose Organize→Folder and search options. Click the View tab, scroll down in the list of settings, and then turn on "Use check boxes to select items." Click OK.

Now, anytime you point to an icon, an on/off checkbox appears. No secret keystrokes are necessary now for selecting icons; it's painfully obvious how you're supposed to choose only a few icons out of a gaggle.

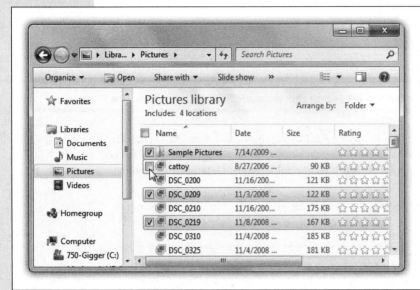

Figure 3-11:
Each time you point to an icon, a clickable checkbox appears. Once you turn it on, the checkbox remains visible, making it easy to select several icons at once. What's cool about the checkboxes feature is that it doesn't preclude your using the old click-to-select method; if you click an icon's name, you deselect all checkboxes except that one.

Eliminating Double-Clicks

In some ways, an Explorer window is just like Internet Explorer, the Web browser. It has a Back button, an address bar, and so on.

If you enjoy this PC-as-browser effect, you can actually take it one step further. You can set up your PC so that *one* click, not two, opens an icon. It's a strange effect that some people adore—and others turn off as fast as their little fingers will let them.

In any Explorer window, choose Organize→Folder and search options.

The Folder Options control panel opens. Turn on "Single-click to open an item (point to select)." Then indicate *when* you want your icon's names turned into underlined links by selecting "Underline icon titles consistent with my browser" (that is, *all* icons' names appear as links) or "Underline icon titles only when I point at them." Click OK. The deed is done.

Now, if a single click opens an icon, you're entitled to wonder how you're supposed to *select* an icon (which you'd normally do with a single click). Take your pick:

• Point to it for about a half-second without clicking. (To make multiple selections, press the Ctrl key as you point to additional icons. And to *drag* an icon, just ignore all this pointing stuff—simply drag as usual.)

• Turn on the checkbox mode described above.

Copying and Moving Folders and Files

All Versions

Windows offers two techniques for moving files and folders from one place to another: dragging them and using the Copy and Paste commands.

Whichever method you choose, you start by showing Windows which icons you want to copy or move—by highlighting them, as described on the previous pages. Then proceed as follows:

Copying by Dragging Icons

You can drag icons from one folder to another, from one drive to another, from a drive to a folder on another drive, and so on. (When you've selected several icons, drag any *one* of them, and the others will go along for the ride.)

Here's what happens when you drag icons in the usual way (using the left mouse button):

- Dragging to another folder on the same disk *moves* the folder or file.

- Dragging from one disk to another *copies* the folder or file.

- Holding down the Ctrl key while dragging to another folder on the same disk *copies* the icon. (If you do so within a single window, Windows creates a duplicate of the file called "[Filename] - Copy.")

- Pressing Shift while dragging from one disk to another *moves* the folder or file (without leaving a copy behind).

Tip: You can move or copy icons by dragging them either into an open window or directly onto a disk or folder *icon*.

The right-mouse-button trick

Think you'll remember all those possibilities every time you drag an icon? Probably not. Fortunately, you never have to. One of the most important tricks you can learn is to use the *right* mouse button as you drag. When you release the button, the menu shown in Figure 3-12 appears, letting you either copy or move the selected icons.

Tip: Press the Esc key to cancel a dragging operation at any time.

Dragging icons into the Navigation pane

You may find it easier to copy or move icons using the Navigation pane (page 77), since the two-pane display format makes it easier to see where your files are and where they're going.

Just expand the triangles of the Navigation pane until you can see the destination folder.

Tip: If you accidentally click a folder in the Navigation pane, its contents will pop up in the right pane, covering up the icon you wanted to copy. Click the Back button to get back to where you once belonged.

Figure 3-12:
Thanks to this shortcut menu, right-dragging icons is much easier and safer than left-dragging when you want to move or copy something. The handy numeric "badge" on the icon you're dragging reminds you how many things you're about to move or copy.

Then find the icon you want to move in the right pane, and drag it to the appropriate folder in the left pane (Figure 3-13), or vice versa. Windows copies the icon.

Figure 3-13:
A set of three documents is being dragged to the folder named A Deeply Nested Folder (in the My Documents folder). As the cursor passes each folder in the left pane, the folder's name darkens. Release the mouse when it's pointing to the correct folder or disk.

Tip: This situation is also a good time to use Windows 7's new Aero Snap feature. Drag the icon's home window against the right side of your screen; drag the destination window against the left side. Now they're perfectly set up for drag-copying between them.

Copying with Copy and Paste

Dragging icons to copy or move them feels good because it's so direct; you actually see your arrow cursor pushing the icons into the new location.

POWER USERS' CLINIC

Secrets of the "Send to" Command

If you find yourself copying or moving certain icons to certain folders or disks with regularity, it's time to exploit the "Send to" command that lurks in the shortcut menu for almost every icon. (If you press the Alt key to make the menu bar appear, the "Send to" command is also in the File menu of every Explorer window.)

This command offers a quick way to copy and move highlighted icons to popular destinations. For example, you can teleport a copy of a highlighted file directly to your CD burner by choosing Send to→DVD-RW Drive, or to the desktop background by choosing Send to→Desktop (create shortcut).

Then there's the Send to→Mail Recipient, which bundles the highlighted icon as an email attachment that's ready to send. You can also zip up a folder (see the end of this chapter) by choosing Send to→Compressed (zipped) Folder.

If you start getting into "Send to"—and you should—check this out. If you press Shift while you right-click, you get a much longer list of "Send to" options, including all the essential folders (Downloads, Desktop, Favorites, Links, Searches, and so on). Cool.

But if the folder you want isn't there, it's easy enough to make the "Send to" command accommodate your *own* favorite or frequently used folders. Lurking in your Personal folder

(page 33) is a folder called SendTo. Any shortcut icon you place here shows up instantly in the "Send to" menus within your desktop folders and shortcut menus.

Alas, this folder is among those Microsoft considers inappropriate for inspection by novices. As a result, the SendTo folder is *hidden*.

You can still get to it, though. In the address bar of any Explorer window, type shell:sendto, and then press Enter. (That's a quick way of getting to the C:\ Users\[your name]\AppData\ Roaming\Microsoft\Windows\ SendTo folder.)

Most people create shortcuts here for folders and disks (such as your favorite backup disk). When you highlight an icon and then choose "Send to"→Backup Disk, for example, Windows copies the icon to that disk. (Or, if you simultaneously press Shift, you *move* the icon to the other disk or folder.) You can even add shortcuts of *applications* (program files) to the SendTo folder. By adding WinZip to this "Send to" menu, for example, you can drop-kick a highlighted icon onto the WinZip icon (for decompressing) just by choosing Send to→WinZip. Or add a Web server to this menu, so you can upload a file with a quick right-click. You can even create shortcuts for your printer or fax modem so you can print or fax a document just by highlighting its icon and choosing File→"Send to"→ [printer or fax modem's name].

But you also pay a price for this satisfying illusion. That is, you may have to spend a moment or two fiddling with your windows, or clicking in the Explorer folder hierarchy, so you have a clear "line of drag" between the icon to be moved and the destination folder.

Fortunately, there's a better way. You can use the Cut, Copy, and Paste commands to move icons from one window into another. The routine goes like this:

1. **Highlight the icon or icons you want to move.**

   Use any of the tricks described on page 150.

2. **Right-click one of the icons. From the shortcut menu, choose Cut or Copy.**

   Alternatively, you can choose Organize→Cut or Organize→Copy, using the toolbar at the top of the window. (You may want to learn the keyboard shortcuts for these commands: Ctrl+C for Copy, Ctrl+X for Cut.)

   The Cut command makes the highlighted icons appear dimmed; you've stashed them on the invisible Windows Clipboard. (They don't actually disappear from their original nesting place until you paste them somewhere else—or hit the Esc key to cancel the operation.)

   The Copy command also places copies of the files on the Clipboard, but it doesn't disturb the originals.

3. **Right-click the window, folder icon, or disk icon where you want to put the icons. Choose Paste from the shortcut menu.**

   Once again, you may prefer to use the appropriate menu bar option, Organize→Paste (Ctrl+V).

   Either way, you've successfully transferred the icons. If you pasted into an open window, you see the icons appear there. If you pasted onto a closed folder or disk icon, you need to open the icon's window to see the results. And if you pasted right back into the same window, you get a duplicate of the file called "[Filename] - Copy."

The Recycle Bin
All Versions

The Recycle Bin is your desktop trash basket. This is where files and folders go when they've outlived their usefulness. Basically, the Recycle Bin is a waiting room for data oblivion, in that your files stay there until you *empty* it—or until you rescue the files by dragging them out again.

While you can certainly drag files or folders onto the Recycle Bin icon, it's usually faster to highlight them and then perform one of the following options:

- Press the Delete key.
- Choose File→Delete.
- Right-click a highlighted icon and choose Delete from the shortcut menu.

Windows asks if you're sure you want to send the item to the Recycle Bin. (You don't lose much by clicking Yes, since it's easy enough to change your mind, as noted below.) Now the Recycle Bin icon looks like it's brimming over with paper.

You can put unwanted files and folders into the Recycle Bin from any folder window or even from inside the Open File dialog box of many applications (see Chapter 6).

Note: All these methods put icons from your *hard drive* into the Recycle Bin. But deleting an icon from a removable drive (flash drives, for example), from other computers on the network, or from a .zip file, does *not* involve the Recycle Bin. Those files go straight to heaven, giving you no opportunity to retrieve them. (Deleting anything with the Command Prompt commands *del* or *erase* bypasses the Recycle Bin, too.)

Making the Recycle Bin Less Naggy

When you get right down to it, you really have to *work* to get rid of a file in Windows. First you have to put the thing in the Recycle Bin. Then you have to confirm that, yes, you're sure. Then you have to *empty* the Recycle Bin. Then you have to confirm that, yes, you're sure about *that.*

Fortunately, those are just the factory settings. There are all kinds of ways to eliminate some of these quadruplicate confirmations. For example:

Figure 3-14:
Use the Recycle Bin Properties dialog box to govern the way the Recycle Bin works, or even if it works at all. If you have multiple hard drives, the dialog box offers a tab for each of them so you can configure a separate and independent Recycle Bin on each drive.

- **Squelch the "Are you sure?" message.** Right-click the Recycle Bin. From the shortcut menu, choose Properties, and turn off "Display delete confirmation dialog." Now you'll never get that message when you put something into the Recycle Bin.

- **Bypass the Recycle Bin just this time.** Press the Shift key while you delete a file. Doing so—and then clicking Yes in the confirmation box (or hitting Enter)—deletes the file permanently, skipping its layover in the Recycle Bin. The Shift-key trick works for every method of deleting a file: pressing the Delete key, choosing Delete from the shortcut menu, and so on.

- **Bypass the Recycle Bin for good.** If you, a person of steely nerve and perfect judgment, never delete a file in error, then your files can *always* bypass the Recycle Bin. No confirmations, no second chances. You'll reclaim disk space instantly when you press the Delete key to vaporize a highlighted file or folder.

  To set this up, right-click the Recycle Bin. From the shortcut menu, choose Properties. Select "Don't move files to the Recycle Bin. Remove files immediately when deleted" (Figure 3-14).

  And voilà! Your safety net is gone (especially if you *also* turn off the "Display delete confirmation dialog" checkbox—then you're *really* living dangerously.)

Note: That really is living dangerously. The Shift-key trick might be a better safety/convenience compromise.

Restoring Deleted Files and Folders

If you change your mind about sending something to the software graveyard, simply open the Recycle Bin by double-clicking. A window like the one in Figure 3-15 opens.

To restore a selected file or a folder—or a bunch of them—click the "Restore this item" link on the task toolbar. Or right-click any one of the selected icons and choose Restore from the shortcut menu.

Restored means returned to the folder from whence it came—wherever it was on your hard drive when deleted. If you restore an icon whose original folder has been deleted in the meantime, Windows even recreates that folder to hold the restored file(s). (If nothing is selected, the toolbar button says "Restore all items," but be careful: If there are weeks' worth of icons in there, and Windows puts them all back where they came from, recreating original folders as it goes, you might wind up with a real mess.)

Tip: You don't have to put icons back into their original folders. By *dragging* them out of the Recycle Bin window, you can put them back into any folder you like.

Emptying the Recycle Bin

While there's an advantage to the Recycle Bin (you get to undo your mistakes), there's also a downside: The files in the Recycle Bin occupy as much disk space as they did when they were stored in folders. Deleting files doesn't gain you additional disk space until you *empty* the Recycle Bin.

That's why most people, sooner or later, follow up an icon's journey to the Recycle Bin with one of these cleanup operations:

- Right-click the Recycle Bin icon, or a blank spot in the Recycle Bin window, and choose Empty Recycle Bin from the shortcut menu.

- Click "Empty the Recycle Bin" on the toolbar in the Recycle Bin window.

- In the Recycle Bin window, highlight only the icons you want to eliminate, and then press the Delete key. (Use this method when you want to nuke only *some* of the Recycle Bin's contents.)

- Wait. When the Recycle Bin accumulates so much stuff that it occupies a significant percentage of your hard drive space, Windows empties it automatically, as described in the next section.

The first three of these procedures produce an "Are you sure?" message.

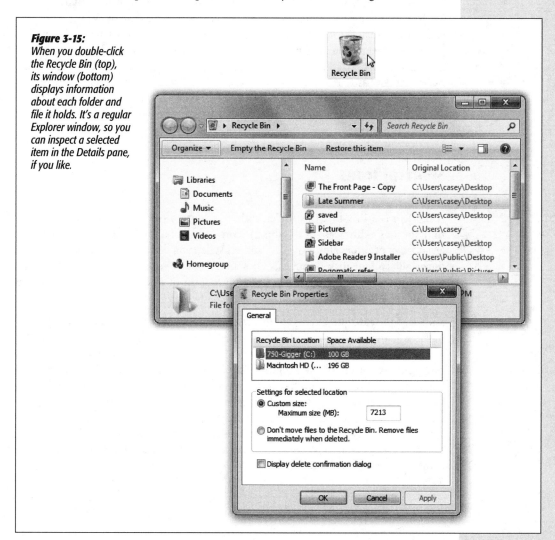

Figure 3-15:
When you double-click the Recycle Bin (top), its window (bottom) displays information about each folder and file it holds. It's a regular Explorer window, so you can inspect a selected item in the Details pane, if you like.

Auto-emptying the Recycle Bin

The Recycle Bin has two advantages over the physical trash can behind your house: First, it never smells. Second, when it's full, it can empty itself automatically.

To configure this self-emptying feature, you specify a certain fullness limit. When the Recycle Bin contents reach that level, Windows begins deleting files (permanently) as new files arrive in the Recycle Bin. Files that arrived in the Recycle Bin first are deleted first.

Unless you tell it otherwise, Windows reserves 10 percent of your drive to hold Recycle Bin contents.

To change that percentage, right-click the Recycle Bin. From the shortcut menu, choose Properties. Now you can edit the "Maximum size" number, in megabytes (Figure 3-15). Keeping the percentage low means you're less likely to run out of the disk space you need to install software and create documents. On the other hand, raising the percentage means you have more opportunity to restore files you decide to retrieve.

Note: Every disk has its own Recycle Bin, which holds files and folders you've deleted from that disk. As you can see in the Recycle Bin Properties dialog box, you can give each drive its own trash limit and change the deletion options shown in Figure 3-15 for each drive independently. Just click the drive's name before changing the settings.

Shortcut Icons
All Versions

A *shortcut* is a link to a file, folder, disk, or program (see Figure 3-16). You might think of it as a duplicate of the thing's icon—but not a duplicate of the thing itself. (A shortcut occupies almost no disk space.) When you double-click the shortcut icon, the original folder, disk, program, or document opens. You can also set up a keystroke for a shortcut icon so you can open any program or document just by pressing a certain key combination.

Shortcuts provide quick access to the items you use most often. And because you can make as many shortcuts of a file as you want, and put them anywhere on your PC, you can, in effect, keep an important program or document in more than one folder. Just create a shortcut to leave on the desktop in plain sight, or drag its icon onto the Start button or the Links toolbar. In fact, everything listed in the Start→All Programs menu *is* a shortcut. So is every link in the top part of your Navigation pane.

Tip: Don't confuse the term *shortcut,* which refers to one of these duplicate-icon pointers, with *shortcut menu,* the context-sensitive menu that appears when you right-click almost anything in Windows. The shortcut *menu* has nothing to do with the shortcut icons feature; maybe that's why it's sometimes called the *context* menu.

Among other things, shortcuts are great for getting to Web sites and folders elsewhere on your network, because you're spared having to type out their addresses or burrowing through network windows.

Creating and Deleting Shortcuts

To create a shortcut, use any of these tricks:

- Right-click an icon. From the shortcut menu, choose "Create shortcut."

- Right-drag an icon from its current location to the desktop. When you release the mouse button, choose "Create shortcuts here" from the menu that appears.

Tip: If you're not in the mood to use a shortcut menu, just left-drag an icon while pressing Alt. A shortcut appears instantly. (And if your Alt key is missing or broken—hey, it could happen—drag while pressing Ctrl+Shift instead.)

- Drag the tiny icon at the left end of the address bar onto the desktop or into a window.

Tip: This also works with Web sites. If your browser has pulled up a site you want to keep handy, drag that little address-bar icon onto your desktop. Double-clicking it later will open the same Web page.

You can delete a shortcut the same as any icon, as described in the Recycle Bin discussion earlier in this chapter. (Of course, deleting a shortcut *doesn't* delete the file it points to.)

Figure 3-16:
Left: You can distinguish a desktop shortcut from its original in two ways. First, the tiny arrow "badge" identifies it as a shortcut; second, its name contains the word "shortcut."

Right: The Properties dialog box for a shortcut indicates which actual file or folder this one "points" to. The Run drop-down menu (shown open) lets you control how the window opens when you double-click the shortcut icon.

Family Photos
Shortcut

Unveiling a Shortcut's True Identity

To locate the original icon from which a shortcut was made, right-click the shortcut icon and choose Properties from the shortcut menu. As shown in Figure 3-16, the resulting box shows you where to find the "real" icon. It also offers you a quick way to jump to it, in the form of the Open File Location button.

Shortcut Keyboard Triggers

Sure, shortcuts let you put favored icons everywhere you want to be. But they still require clicking to open, which means taking your hands off the keyboard—and that, in the grand scheme of things, means slowing down.

Lurking within the Shortcut Properties dialog box is another feature with intriguing ramifications: the Shortcut Key box. By clicking here and then pressing a key combination, you can assign a personalized keystroke for the shortcut. Thereafter, by pressing that keystroke, you can summon the corresponding file, program, folder, printer, networked computer, or disk window to your screen, no matter what you're doing on the PC. It's *really* useful.

Three rules apply when choosing keystrokes to open your favorite icons:

- The keystrokes work only on shortcuts stored *on your desktop or in the Start menu.* If you stash the icon in any other folder, the keystroke stops working.

- Your keystroke can't incorporate the space bar or the Enter, Backspace, Delete, Esc, Print Screen, or Tab keys.

- Your combination *must* include Ctrl+Alt and another key.

    Windows enforces this rule rigidly. For example, if you type a single letter key into the box (such as *E*), Windows automatically adds the Ctrl and Alt keys to your combination (Ctrl+Alt+E). This is the operating system's attempt to prevent you from inadvertently duplicating one of the built-in Windows keyboard shortcuts and thoroughly confusing both you and your computer.

Tip: If you've ever wondered what it's like to be a programmer, try this. In the Shortcut Properties dialog box (Figure 3-16), use the Run drop-down menu at the bottom of the dialog box to choose "Normal window," "Minimized," or "Maximized." By clicking OK, you've just told Windows what kind of window you want to appear when opening this particular shortcut. (See page 60 for a discussion of these window types.)

Controlling Windows in this way isn't exactly the same as programming Microsoft Excel, but you are, in your own small way, telling Windows what to do.

If you like the idea of keyboard shortcuts for your files and programs, but you're not so hot on Windows 7's restrictions, consider installing a free *macro program* that lets you make *any* keystroke open *anything anywhere.* The best-known one is AutoHot-Key, which is available from this book's "Missing CD" page at *missingmanuals.com*, but there are plenty of similar (and simpler) ones. (Check them out at, for example, *shareware.com.*)

Compressing Files and Folders

All Versions

Windows is especially effective at compressing files and folders to reduce the space they occupy on your hard drive—which is ironic, considering the fact that hard drives these days have enough capacity to stretch to Steve Ballmer's house and back three times.

Even so, compressing files and folders can occasionally be useful, especially when hard drive space is running short, or when you want to email files to someone without dooming them to an all-night modem-watching session. Maybe that's why Microsoft has endowed Windows with two different schemes for compressing files and folders: *NTFS compression* and *zipped folders*.

NTFS Compression

Windows 7, since you asked, requires a hard drive that's formatted using a software scheme called *NTFS* (short for NT file system; see page 676 for details). It's a much more modern formatting scheme than its predecessor, something called FAT32—and among its virtues is, you guessed it, NTFS *compression*.

This compression scheme is especially likable because it's completely invisible. Windows automatically compresses and decompresses your files, almost instantaneously. At some point, you may even forget you've turned it on. Consider:

- Whenever you open a compressed file, Windows quickly and invisibly expands it to its original form so you can edit it. When you close the file again, Windows instantly recompresses it.

- If you send compressed files (via disk or email, for example) to a PC whose hard drive doesn't use NTFS formatting, Windows once again decompresses them, quickly and invisibly.

- Any file you copy into a compressed folder or disk is compressed automatically. (If you only *move* it into such a folder from elsewhere on the disk, however, it stays compressed or uncompressed—whichever it was originally.)

There's only one downside to all this: You don't save a *lot* of disk space using NTFS compression (at least not when compared with Zip compression, described in the next section). Even so, if your hard drive is anywhere near full, it might be worth turning on NTFS compression. The space you save could be your own.

Compressing files, folders, or disks

To turn on NTFS compression, right-click the icon for the file, folder, or disk whose contents you want to shrink; from the shortcut menu, choose Properties. Proceed as shown in Figure 3-17.

Tip: To compress an entire hard drive, the steps in Figure 3-17 are even simpler. Just right-click the drive's icon (in your Computer window); choose Properties; and turn on "Compress this drive to save disk space." Click OK.

Many Windows veterans wind up turning on compression for the entire hard drive, even though it takes Windows several hours to do the job. (If you plan to go see a movie while Windows is working, though, wait until the appearance of the first message box letting you know about some "open file" that can't be compressed; then click Ignore All. A few files will remain uncompressed when you get back from the Cineplex, but at least you won't have had to stay home, manually clicking to dismiss every "open file" complaint box.)

Figure 3-17:
In the Properties dialog box for any file or folder, click Advanced. Turn on "Compress contents to save disk space," and then click OK. For a folder, Windows offers to compress all the files and folders inside this one, too.

When Windows is finished compressing files, their names appear in a different color, a reminder that Windows is doing its part to maximize your disk space.

Note: If the files don't change color, somebody—maybe you—must have turned off the "Show encrypted or compressed NTFS files in color" option (see page 100).

Zipped Folders

As noted above, NTFS compression is ideal for freeing up disk space while you're working at your PC. But as soon as you email your files to somebody else or burn them to a CD, the transferred copies bloat right back up to their original sizes.

Fortunately, there's another way to compress files: Zip them. If you've ever used Windows before, you've probably encountered Zip files. Each one is a tiny little suitcase, an *archive*, whose contents have been tightly compressed to keep files together, save space, and transfer them online faster (see Figure 3-18). Use this method when you want to email something to someone, or when you want to pack up a completed project and remove it from your hard drive to free up space.

Creating zipped folders

You can create a Zip archive in either of two ways:

- Right-click any blank spot on the desktop or an open window. From the shortcut menu, choose New→Compressed (zipped) Folder. Type a name for your newly created, empty archive, and then press Enter.

  Now, each time you drag a file or folder onto the archive's icon (or into its open window), Windows automatically stuffs a *copy* of it inside.

  Of course, you haven't exactly saved any disk space, since now you have two copies (one zipped, one untouched). If you'd rather *move* a file or folder into the archive—in the process deleting the full-size version and saving disk space—*right*-drag the file or folder icon onto the archive icon. Now from the shortcut menu, choose Move Here.

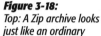
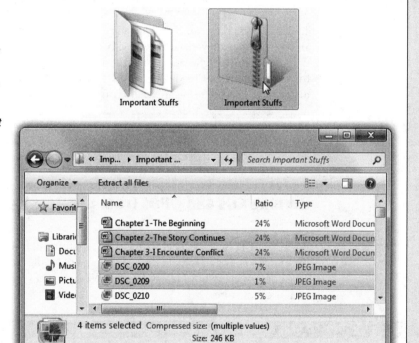

Figure 3-18:
Top: A Zip archive looks just like an ordinary folder—except for the tiny little zipper.

Bottom: Double-click one to open its window and see what's inside. Notice (in the Ratio column) that JPEG and GIF graphics usually don't become much smaller than they were before zipping, since they're already compressed formats. But word processing files, program files, and other file types reveal quite a bit of shrinkage.

- To turn an *existing* file or folder into a Zip archive, right-click its icon. (To zip up a handful of icons, select them first, and then right-click any one of them.) Now, from the shortcut menu, choose Send To→Compressed (zipped) Folder. You've just created a new archive folder *and* copied the files or folders into it.

Tip: At this point, you can right-click the zipped folder's icon and choose Send To→Mail Recipient. Windows automatically whips open your email program, creates an outgoing message ready for you to address, and attaches the zipped file to it. It's now set for transport.

Working with zipped folders

In many respects, a zipped folder behaves just like any ordinary folder. Double-click it to see what's inside.

If you double-click one of the *files* you find inside, however, Windows opens up a *read-only* copy of it—that is, a copy you can view, but not edit. To make changes to a read-only copy, you must use the File→Save As command and save it somewhere else on your hard drive first.

Note: Be sure to navigate to the desktop or Documents folder, for example, before you save your edited document. Otherwise, Windows will save it into an invisible temporary folder, where you may never see it again.

To decompress only some of the icons in a zipped folder, just drag them out of the archive window; they instantly spring back to their original sizes. Or, to decompress the entire archive, right-click its icon and choose Extract All from the shortcut menu (or, if its window is already open, click the "Extract all files" link on the toolbar). A dialog box asks you to specify where you want the resulting files to wind up.

Tip: Windows no longer lets you password-protect a zipped folder, as you could in Windows XP. But the Web is teeming with zip-file utilities, many of them free, that do let you assign a password. You might try, for example, SecureZIP Express. It's available from this book's "Missing CD" page at www.missingmanuals.com.

Burning CDs and DVDs from the Desktop
All Versions

Burning a CD or DVD is great for backing stuff up, transferring stuff to another computer, mailing to somebody, or archiving older files to free up hard drive space. These days, you can buy blank CDs and DVDs very inexpensively in bulk via the Web or a discount store.

FREQUENTLY ASKED QUESTION

Your Turn to Drive

Hey, my Dell has two CD/DVD burners. How do I specify which one is the default for burning blank discs?

All in good time, grasshoppa.

Choose Start→Computer. Right-click the icon of the burner you want; from the shortcut menu, choose Properties. Click the recording tab; use the drive menu to choose the one you want to do the heavy lifting. (Authenticate yourself if necessary, as described on page 726.)

In ancient times—you know, like 2002—every PC came with a CD-ROM drive. Nowadays, the drives on all new PCs can burn *both* CDs and DVDs.

Before you dig in, however, here's a brief chalk talk about CD data formats.

A Tale of Two Formats

Turns out Windows can burn blank CDs and DVDs using your choice of *two* formats:

• **Mastered (ISO).** This is what most of the world is used to. It's what everybody burned before Windows Vista and Windows 7 came along. The primary virtue of discs burned this way is compatibility; they play in just about any computer, including Macs, PCs, and CD or DVD players that play MP3 CDs and digital video.

To make one, insert the blank disc and then drag files and folders into its window. The PC duplicates the items, parking them in an invisible, temporary holding area until you're ready to burn. You burn all the files and folders at once.

Trouble is, you're therefore *doubling* the space requirement of the files you intended to burn. If you're burning a DVD to get older files off your hard drive because you're running low on space, you could wind up in a Catch-22. You can't free up drive space without burning a DVD—but you don't have enough drive space to burn a DVD!

Tip: To be fair, you *can* change the location of the temporary holding folder—if you have another hard drive. In your Computer window, right-click your burner's icon; from the shortcut menu, choose Properties. Click the Recording tab; from the drive menu, choose the hard drive you prefer, authenticating (page 726) when you're asked.

• **Live File System (UDF).** This newer, more modern format—Windows 7's factory setting—is light-years more convenient. It lets you use a blank CD or DVD exactly as though it's a USB flash drive. You can drag files and folders onto it, move icons around on it, rename them, and so on. There's no momentous Moment of Burn; files are copied to the CD in real time, whenever you put them there. You can leave a disc in your drive, dragging stuff onto it throughout the week as it's convenient—without ever having to click a Burn button.

What's more, you can then eject the CD, store it, or share it—and then, later, put it back into your PC and *burn more stuff onto it.* That's right—you can burn a single CD as many times as you like. And we're talking regular, cheapie CD-R discs, not CD-RW (rewritable).

What Windows creates, in other words, is a *multisession* disc.

Of course, the downside is that discs you burn this way play back only on relatively recent Macs and PCs. And you can record *more* stuff onto them only on a PC running Windows XP or later.

Tip: If it helps you to remember which format is which, here's a mnemonic for you: The last letter of the format name (ISO, UDF) lets you know whether this is the *Older* format or the *Future* one.

Burning, Step by Step

Now that, with luck, you understand the difference between the Mastered (ISO) and Live File System (UDF) formats, you're ready to proceed.

1. **Insert a blank disc into your PC.**

   The AutoPlay dialog box appears, asking whether you intend for this CD or DVD to hold computer files or music (Figure 3-19, top left). If you want to burn a music CD, skip ahead to Chapter 15.

Note: If you *always* want to create data CDs (or always burn music CDs), turn on "Always do this for blank CDs" to save yourself a step each time.

Windows duly records your preference in the AutoPlay applet of the Control Panel. If you ever change your mind, you can always open that applet and reverse yourself, as described in Chapter 8.

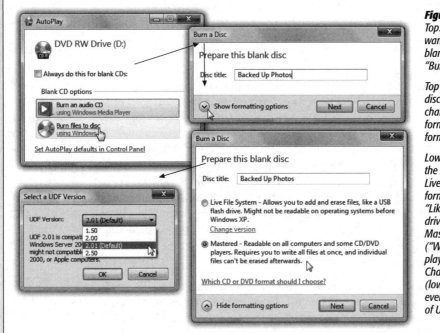

Figure 3-19:
Top: What do you want to do with the blank disc? Click "Burn files to disc."

Top right: Name your disc. If you want to change the burn format, click "Show formatting options."

Lower right: Choose the super-convenient Live File System format (here called "Like a USB flash drive") or the older Mastered format ("With a CD/DVD player"). If you click Change Version (lower left), you can even specify a version of UDF.

Otherwise, continue to step 2.

2. **Click the "Burn files to disc" link.**

   Windows asks you to name the CD or DVD.

3. **Type a name for the disc.**

But don't click Next yet. This crucial moment is your only chance to change the disc's format.

If you're OK with burning in the delicious, newfangled UDF format described above, leave "Like a USB flash drive" selected; skip to step 4.

If you want this disc to be usable by a CD or DVD player, or somebody using a version of Windows before Windows XP, though, you want to take this moment to click "With a CD/DVD player." Figure 3-19 shows the full life cycle of a disc you're burning.

Once that's done, you can go on to step 4.

4. **Click Next.**

Your PC takes a moment—a long one—to format the blank disc.

When it's finished, it presents a small window offering an "Open folder to view files" button. Click it.

5. **Begin putting files and folders into the disc's window.**

You can use any combination of these three methods:

First, you can scurry about your hard drive, locating the files and folders you want on the CD. Drag their icons into the open CD/DVD window, or onto the disc burner's icon in the Computer window.

Second, you can highlight the files and folders you want burned onto the CD. Choose Organize→Copy. Click in the CD or DVD's window, and then choose Organize→Paste to copy the material there.

Finally, you can explore your hard drive. Whenever you find a file or folder you'd like backed up, right-click it. From the shortcut menu, choose Send to→DVD/CD-RW Drive (or whatever your burner's name is).

To finish the job, see "The final steps," below, for the kind of disc you're burning.

Tip: The Details pane at the bottom of the CD/DVD window gives you a running tally of the disc space you've filled up so far. (It may say, for example, "223.2 MB of 702.8 used on disc.") At last you have an effortless way to exploit the blank disc's capacity with precision.

The final steps: Mastered (ISO) format

When you put files and folders into the disc's window, Windows actually *copies* them into a temporary, invisible holding-tank folder. (If you must know, this folder is in your Personal folder→Local Settings→AppData→Local→Microsoft→Windows→Burn→Temporary Burn Folder.)

In other words, you need plenty of disk space before you begin burning a CD—at least double the size of the CD files themselves.

Tip: Remember that a standard CD can hold only about 650 MB of files. To ensure that your files and folders will fit, periodically highlight all the icons in the Computer→CD window (choose Organize→Select All). Then inspect the Details pane to confirm that the size is within the legal limit.

What you see in the disc's window, meanwhile, is nothing but shortcuts (denoted by the downward arrows on their icons). The little down arrows mean, "This icon hasn't been burned to the disc yet. I'm just waiting my turn."

Tip: If you change your mind about including some of the files, highlight their icons in the disc window. On the task toolbar, click "Delete temporary files." You've just reclaimed the disc space those duplicates were using.

At last, when everything looks ready to go, click the "Burn to disc" link in the task toolbar. Or right-click the burner's icon, or any blank spot in its window, and, from the shortcut menu, choose "Burn to disc."

The CD Writing Wizard appears to guide you through the process of naming and burning the disc. The PC's laser proceeds to record the CD or DVD, which can take some time. Feel free to switch into another program and continue working.

When the burning is over, the disc pops out, and you have a freshly minted CD or DVD, whose files and folders you can open on any PC or even Macintosh.

POWER USERS' CLINIC

Closing the Session

Every time you eject a Live File System disc, Windows closes the session, which means sort of shrink-wrapping the disc so it can be used on other computers. (Even computers that can't understand Live File System, like Macs or pre-XP PCs, can play these discs. They just can't record more stuff onto them.)

But each time Windows does that, you lose another 20 megabytes of disc space and 2 minutes of your time.

If you, the power user, would like session-closing to be a decision left up to you, you can make Windows *stop* automatically closing sessions. Right-click the burner's icon in your Computer window; from the shortcut menu, choose Properties. In the dialog box, click the Recording tab and then the Global Settings button.

Here, you can turn off "Single session-only discs are ejected," which makes Windows stop auto-closing discs that can be burned only once (DVD-RW, DVD+RW, DVD-RAM, DVD+R DL, DVD-R DL, and BD-RE).

Or turn off "Multi session-capable discs are ejected," which refers to discs that you can record onto many times (CD-R, CD-RW, DVD+R, DVD-R, and BD-R discs).

From now on, Windows won't close your session—or use up 20 megabytes—unless *you* click the "Close session" link on the toolbar (or right-click your burner's icon in the Computer window and choose "Close session"). This way, you can maximize the space and speed of CDs and DVDs that you keep on your desk and *don't* distribute to other people.

Tip: If you try the CD or DVD in somebody else's machine and it doesn't work—and you realize that you forgot to close the session—all is not lost. You can always return the disc to your machine and close the session there.

And now, help yourself to some aspirin.

The final steps: Live File System (UDF) format

If you've been dragging files and folders into the window of a Live File System-formatted disc, there are no more steps. You can eject the disc and put it to use.

To eject the disc, right-click your burner's icon; from the shortcut menu, choose Eject. Windows takes a moment to "close the session" and then ejects the disc.

You can play this disc on Macs or PCs running Windows XP and later.

Better yet, you can put this disc back into any XP-or-later PC and pick up right where you left off, adding and erasing files as though it's a big flash drive.

Final Notes

Here are a few final notes on burning CDs and DVDs at the desktop:

- Not sure what kinds of disks your PC can burn? Choose Start→Computer. Study the name of the burner. There it is, plain as day: a list of the formats your machine can read and write (that is, burn). If you have a combo drive (can burn and play CDs, but can only play DVDs), for example, you'll see something like "DVD/CD-RW Drive." If your burner can *both* play and record *both* CDs and DVDs, it will say "DVD-RW Drive."

- To erase an RW type disc (rewritable, like CD-RW or DVD-RW), open your Computer window. Right-click the burner's icon; from the shortcut menu, choose Format. Change the file-system format if you like, and then turn on Quick Format. Finally, click Start to erase the disc.

Tip: Of course, you don't have to erase the disc completely. You can always select and delete individual icons from it using the Delete key.

- If you do a lot of disc burning, a full-fledged burning program like Nero adds myriad additional options. Only with a commercial CD-burning program can you burn MP3 music CDs, create *mixed-mode* CDs (containing both music and files), create Video CDs (low-quality video discs that play on DVD players), and so on.

Interior Decorating Windows

Without a doubt, Windows 7 looks a heck of a lot better than previous versions of Windows. The new system font alone, so much clearer and more graceful than the one that's labeled your icons for decades, contributes to the new look. (It must have been driving Microsoft nuts that little old Apple, with its 8 percent market share, was getting all the raves for the good looks and modern lines of its operating system.)

And then there's Aero, the visual design scheme described on page 23. Its transparent window edges may not add much to your productivity, but they do look cool.

Still, these changes aren't for everybody. Fortunately, Win7 is every bit as tweakable as previous versions of Windows. You can turn off Aero, or just selected parts of it. You can change the picture on your desktop, or tell Windows to change it *for* you periodically. You can bump up the text size for better reading by over-40 eyeballs.

As Microsoft might say, "Where do you want to redesign today?"

Note: Customizing the Start menu is described in Chapter 1; customizing the taskbar is covered in Chapter 2.

Aero or Not
Home Premium • Professional • Enterprise • Ultimate

If you ask Microsoft, the whole Aero thing is a key benefit of Windows 7.

"Aero" refers to a whole motley collection of eye-candy effects: transparent window edges, preview thumbnails of taskbar programs, full-size previews of windows when you press Alt+Tab, the Flip 3D display of all open windows, window buttons that glow when you point to them, shrinking/growing animations when you close or open windows, windows that snap against the edges of your screen, and so on.

All of it is neato—and all of it collectively saps your system of a little bit of memory and speed. It's not anything most people notice on modern PCs. But if your computer is older and slower, turning off Aero might make a noticeable speed difference.

Besides, some people just miss the less flashy, more utilitarian look of Windows XP.

Fortunately, Microsoft rarely takes a step forward without offering a step back to those who want it. Here's how to turn off Aero—one feature at a time.

Turning Off Only Transparent Window Edges

It's hard to think of how see-through window edges can boost your productivity. Truth is, depending on what's showing through them, they can look a little murky and ugly.

To turn them off, open the Start menu. In the Search box, start typing *transparency* until you see "Enable or disable transparent glass on windows." Click it.

In the resulting window, turn off "Enable transparency." Click "Save changes."

Turning Off Window Snapping and Shaking

In Windows 7, if you drag a window close to the top edge of your screen, the window expands to fill the *whole* screen. If you drag it close to a side of your screen, the window expands to fill *half* the screen. If all this auto-snapping makes you crazy, turn it off as described on page 65.

Turning Off the Inch-Tall Taskbar

The Windows 7 taskbar shows giant, inch-tall icons—with no text labels. And you no longer get one button for each open window; Windows consolidates open windows within each program to save taskbar space.

You can make the taskbar look like it did in Vista or even Windows XP, if you like. Details are on page 105.

Turn Off All Those Glitzy Animations

Then there are all those other things Windows does to show off: Windows seem to zoom open or closed; the Close, Minimize, and Maximize buttons glow when you point to them; menu commands and tooltips fade open and closed; and so on.

It turns out that there's a master list of these effects, filled with individual on/off switches for Win7's various animations, pop-up previews, simulated mouse and window shadows, and so on.

To see it, open the Start menu. Start typing *effects* until you see "Adjust the appearance and performance of windows." Click it.

Now you're in the Performance Options dialog box (see Figure 4-1). Now, these aren't exactly the kind of special effects they make at Industrial Light & Magic for use in *Star Wars* movies. In fact, they're so subtle, they're practically invisible. Some examples:

- **Enable Aero Peek.** Yes, you can turn off the Aero Peek feature, which lets you (a) point to a taskbar thumbnail to see its full-size window pop to the fore and (b) point to the Show Desktop button (right end of the taskbar) to make all windows transparent.

- **Smooth edges of screen fonts.** If you look very closely at the characters on your screen, they look a bit ragged on the curves. But when this option is turned on, Windows softens the curves, making the text look more professional (or slightly blurrier, depending on your point of view).

- **Show shadows under windows/mouse pointer.** Take a look: In Windows 7, open windows actually seem to cast faint, light gray drop shadows, as though floating an eighth of an inch above the surface behind them. It's a cool, but utterly superfluous, special effect.

- **Show window contents while dragging.** If this option is off, then when you drag a window, only a faint outline of its border is visible; you don't see all the items *in* the window coming along for the ride. As soon as you stop dragging, the contents reappear. If this option is on, however, then as you drag a window across your screen, you see all its contents, too—a feature that can slow the dragging process on really slow machines.

Figure 4-1:
Select "Adjust for best performance" to turn everything off, leaving you with, more or less, Windows XP. Alternatively, turn off only the animations you can live without.

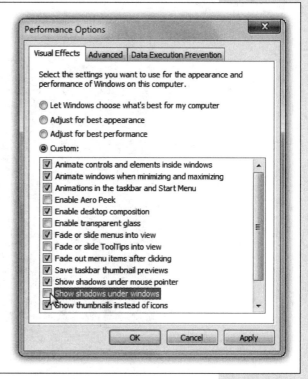

Turning Off the Aero Look (and Aero App Switchers)

Turning off the look of Aero—see-through window edges, taskbar thumbnail previews, and so on—is as easy as choosing a different *theme*. (A theme is a design scheme. Windows comes with a bunch of them.) For step-by-steps, read on.

A Gallery of Themes

Home Premium • Professional • Enterprise • Ultimate

As you can see in Figure 4-2, Windows includes a number of predesigned design themes that affect the look of your desktop and windows.

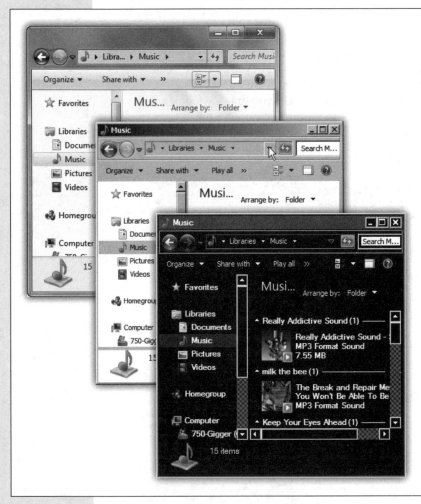

Figure 4-2:
Most people with fast enough computers use the Aero look of Windows (top). But your computer may look different, especially if you've turned on one of the other styles—like Windows Classic (middle) or a high-contrast theme (bottom)—or if you're running a netbook that has Windows Starter Edition installed.

Each design theme controls these elements of Windows:

- Your wallpaper (desktop picture).

- Your screen saver.

- The design of icons like Computer, Network, Control Panel, and Recycle Bin.

- The color scheme for your window edges, plus any tweaks you make in the Color and Appearance dialog box (font size, window border width, and so on).

- The size and shape of your arrow cursor.

- The sounds your PC uses as error and alert beeps.

It's fun to customize your PC (especially because it's your opportunity to replace, at last, that huge Dell or HP logo that came as your preinstalled wallpaper). This is also yet another way to shut off some of Aero's cosmetics.

To see your theme choices, right-click a blank spot on the desktop. From the shortcut menu, choose Personalize.

Note: There's no Personalize option in the Starter Edition of Windows 7. What few appearance options are available are described in the box on page 178.

The Personalization control panel opens, revealing a window full of factory-installed icons for different visual themes (Figure 4-3). Clicking one applies its look to your desktop world instantaneously, making it simple to try on different themes.

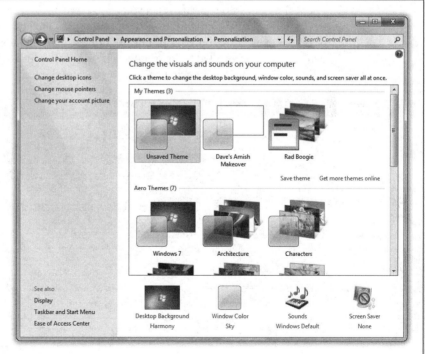

Figure 4-3:
A theme is more than a color scheme. It also incorporates a desktop background, a standard screen saver, and even a coordinated set of alert sounds. The four icons across the bottom show you the current desktop, color, sound, and screen saver settings for whatever theme you click.

Aero Themes

The Aero themes at the top come with all the Aero features turned on. There's also a "Get more themes online" link that takes you to a download-more-themes Web site.

Basic and High Contrast Themes

If you scroll down, you find the Basic and High Contrast themes. If you click one of these, you shut down much of what makes Aero, Aero.

Window edges are no longer transparent. The taskbar no longer offers thumbnail previews of open programs. The Show Desktop sliver (right end of the taskbar) no longer hides windows when you just point to it. Pressing ⊞+Tab no longer shows a 3-D stack of open programs for your switching pleasure, and pressing Alt+Tab shows a much more toned-down, XP-ish program switcher.

Notable here are Windows 7 Basic, which gives you the clean, modern look of Win7 windows and buttons, a rounded black glass look for the taskbar and Start menu, and so on; and Windows Classic, which returns your PC to the visual look of Windows Server 2003/Windows 2000.

Note: The High Contrast themes in the list are designed to help out people with limited vision, who require greater differences in color between window elements. High-contrast themes do not use any of the Aero features and more closely resemble the squared-off windows and dialog boxes of Windows 2000.

The real fun, however, awaits when you choose one of the canned themes and then *modify* it. Four of the modification tactics are represented by buttons at the bottom of the window (Desktop Background, Window Color, Sounds, and Screen Saver); two more are represented by links at the left side of the window (Desktop Icons and Mouse Pointers). The following pages cover each of these elements in turn.

FREQUENTLY ASKED QUESTION

Interior Decorating the Starter Edition

Man, when Microsoft strips down Windows, it doesn't kid around.

The Starter Edition of Windows 7, which comes on some netbooks and computers in poor countries, doesn't have the Personalize control panel. It doesn't even let you change your wallpaper, for heaven's sake.

In fact, personalizing the look of the Starter Edition pretty much boils down to what you can access from the Display control panel (Start→Control Panel→Appearance→Display).

For example, the "Change color scheme" link opens the Window Color and Appearance dialog box. You can choose from the Windows 7 Basic scheme, Windows Classic (for that Windows 2000 look), and four high-contrast schemes.

The "Change screen saver" link lets you choose one of the built-in screen savers.

In addition, you can change the screen resolution and make some low-level tweaks to your color calibration, ClearType font settings, and text DPI settings.

But that's about it.

Desktop Background (Wallpaper)

Home Premium • Professional • Enterprise • Ultimate

Windows 7 has a whole new host of desktop pictures, patterns, and colors for your viewing pleasure. You want widescreen images for your new flat-panel monitor? You got 'em. Want something gritty, artsy, in black and white? They're there, too. And you can still use any picture you'd like as your background as well.

To change yours, right-click the desktop; choose Personalize; and, at the bottom of the box, click Desktop Background.

Now you're looking at the box shown in Figure 4-4. It starts you off examining the Microsoft-supplied photos that come with Windows. Use the "Picture locations" pop-up menu to choose a category:

- **Windows Desktop Backgrounds** includes 37 absolutely gorgeous photos.

- **Pictures Library** displays all your *own* photos—at least those in your Pictures library. It's more fun to use one of your *own* pictures on the desktop. That might be an adorable baby photo of your niece, or it might be Britney Spears with half her clothes off; the choice is yours.

  Feel free to click Browse to forage through other photo folders on your PC, if you have them.

- **Top Rated Photos** displays the photos in your collection to which you've given the highest star ratings (page 544).

- **Solid Colors** is just a palette of simple, solid colors for your desktop background. It's not a bad idea, actually; it's a little easier to find your icons if they're not lost among the rocks and trees of a nature photo.

GEM IN THE ROUGH

Free Photos of Many Lands

You know how the standard set of Windows desktop backgrounds has a category called United States (or whatever your country is)? Yep, those are photos from your motherland. But unbeknownst to you, Windows comes with photos from other people's motherlands, too, and they all make great desktop pictures. Too bad Microsoft has hidden them—and then buried them.

But you, the enterprising Windows master, can unearth them. Open the Start menu. Start typing *location* until you see "Change location" in the results list; click it.

In the resulting dialog box, use the pop-up menu to select some other countries, clicking Apply after each selection. If you're using the U.S. version of Windows, for example, choose Australia, Great Britain, Canada, and South Africa. Finally, switch back to United States (or whatever your actual country is).

Now, when you right-click the desktop and choose Personalize, all of those countries' photo sets are available in the Desktop Background dialog box.

Click and enjoy your newfound desktop worldliness.

If you see something you like, you can click it to slap it across the entire background of your desktop.

Or—and this is a big *or*—you can use the new Windows 7 feature that *changes* your desktop picture periodically, so you don't get bored.

Figure 4-4:
Desktop backgrounds have come a long way since Windows 3.1. The desktop backgrounds include outdoors scenes, illustrations, and more. There are lots to choose from, so feel free to look around.

Auto–Picture Changing

The novelty of any desktop picture is likely to fade after several months of all-day viewing. Fortunately, in Windows 7, you can choose *multiple* desktop pictures from the gallery; see Figure 4-5.

Now, from the "Change picture every:" pop-up menu, specify when you want your background picture to change: every day, every hour, every 5 minutes, or whatever. (If you're *really* having trouble staying awake at your PC, you can choose every 10 seconds.)

Finally, turn on "Shuffle," if you like. If you leave it off, your desktop pictures change in the sequence shown in the gallery.

Now, at the intervals you specified, your desktop picture changes automatically, smoothly cross-fading between the pictures in your chosen source folder like a slide-show. You may never want to open another window, because you'd hate to block your view of the show.

Note: If you have a laptop, by all means turn on "When using battery power, pause the slide show to save power." Changing wallpapers is nice and all, but not if it means showing up for your talk with a dead laptop.

Making the Pictures Fit

No matter which source you use to choose a photo, you have one more issue to deal with. Unless you've gone to the trouble of editing your chosen photo so that it matches the precise dimensions of your screen (1280 × 800 or whatever), it probably isn't exactly the same size as your screen.

Figure 4-5:
To select an assortment of rotating wallpaper shots, turn on the checkboxes of the pictures you want. Or just use the usual icon-selection techniques; for example, Ctrl+click all the wallpapers you want to include, one at a time. Or click Select All, and then Ctrl+click the ones you don't want.

Fortunately, Windows offers a number of solutions to this problem. Using the "Picture position" pop-up menu, you can choose any of these options:

- **Fill.** Enlarges or reduces the image so that it fills every inch of the desktop without distortion. Parts may get chopped off, but this option never distorts the picture.

- **Fit.** Your entire photo appears, as large possible without distortion *or* cropping. If the photo doesn't precisely match the proportions of your screen, you get "letterbox bars" on the sides or at top and bottom.

• **Stretch.** Makes your picture fit the screen exactly, come hell or high water. Larger pictures may be squished vertically or horizontally as necessary, and small pictures are drastically blown up *and* squished, usually with grisly results.

• **Tile.** This option makes your picture repeat over and over until the multiple images fill the entire monitor.

• **Center.** Centers the photo neatly on the screen. If the picture is smaller than the screen, it leaves a swath of empty border all the way around. If it's larger, the outer edges get chopped off.

Other Ways to Choose Desktop Photos

Really, the Desktop Backgrounds screen described above is the wallpaper headquarters. But there are "Set as desktop background" commands hiding everywhere in Windows, making it simple to turn everyday images into wallpaper. You'll find that command, for example, when you do any of the following:

• Right-click a graphics icon in an Explorer window.

• Right-click a picture you've opened up in Windows Photo Viewer or Windows Live Photo Gallery.

• Right-click a photo you've found on a Web page.

• Open the first menu (to the left of the Home tab) in Paint, Windows's little painting program.

Window Color

All Versions

Choosing a theme or a desktop background is practically idiot-proof; even an adult could do it. The real geektastic fun, however, awaits when you click Window Color (at the bottom of the window shown in Figure 4-3) and then click "Advanced appearance settings."

Note: In Windows 7 Starter Edition, you get here by opening the Control Panel, then clicking Appearance→ Display→"Change color scheme"→Advanced.

Now you find yourself in a dialog box that lets you change every single aspect of the selected visual theme independently (Figure 4-6).

Note: The controls in this dialog box don't work if you're using one of the Aero themes as your starting point. Microsoft put a lot of work into the look of Windows 7, and it doesn't especially want people diluting it with their own random changes. "If you want the new look," the company is saying, "it's all or nothing."

In other words, you should start your customization odyssey by clicking a theme icon in the Basic and High Contrast category. Otherwise, the changes you make in the Window Color and Appearance box will have no effect.

Proceed with your interior-decoration crusade in either of two ways:

- Change the elements of the scheme one at a time. Start by choosing from the Item drop-down list (or by clicking a piece of the illustration at the top half of the dialog box, like a title bar or a button). Then use the Size, Color 1, and Color 2 drop-down lists to tailor the chosen element—such as Desktop or Scrollbar—to suit your artistic urges.

Figure 4-6:
Click a part of the View pane (Desktop, Scroll-bar, and so on). Then use the menus to choose colors and type sizes for the chosen interface element.

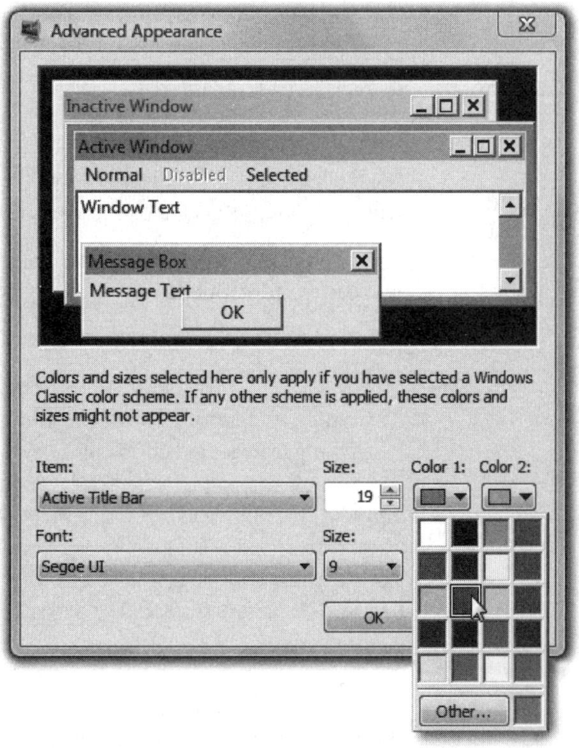

- Some of the screen elements named in the Item drop-down list have text associated with them: Icon, Inactive Title Bar, Menu, Message Box, ToolTip, and so on. When you choose one of these text items, the Font drop-down list at the bottom of the dialog box comes to life. Using this menu, you can change the typeface (font, color, and size) used for any of these screen elements. If you have trouble reading the type in dialog boxes (because you have a high-resolution, tiny-type screen), or you wish your icon names showed up a little more boldly, or you'd prefer a more graceful font in your menus, these controls offer the solution.

When you've exhausted your options—or just become exhausted—click OK to return to the Personalization dialog box.

Sounds
All Versions

Windows plays beeps and bloops to celebrate various occasions: closing a program, yanking out a USB drive, logging in or out, getting a new fax, and so on. You can turn these sounds on or off, or choose new sounds for these events.

Sounds, too, are part of a Windows 7 theme. To edit the suite of sounds that goes with your currently selected theme, click Sounds at the bottom of the Personalization dialog box (Figure 4-3).

Note: In Windows 7 Starter Edition, go to Control Panel, and then click Hardware and Sound→"Change system sounds." The Sound control panel opens, with the Sound tab ready to go.

See the list of Program Events? A speaker icon represents the occasions when a sound will play. Double-click a sound (or click the Test button) to see what it sounds like.

Or, if you click the name of some computer event (say, Low Battery Alert), you can make these adjustments:

- Remove a sound from the event by choosing (None) from the Sounds drop-down list.

- Change an assigned sound, or add a sound to an event that doesn't have one, by clicking Browse and choosing a new sound file from the list in the Open dialog box.

Tip: When you click the Browse button, Windows opens the Local Disk (C:)→Windows→Media folder, which contains the *.wav* files that provide sounds. If you drag *.wav* files into this Media folder, they become available for use as Windows sound effects. Many people download *.wav* files from the Internet and stash them in the Media folder to make their computing experience quirkier, more fun, and richer in *Austin Powers* sound snippets.

When you select a sound, its filename appears in the Sounds drop-down list. Click the Test button to the right of the box to hear the sound.

Tip: Each set of sounds is called a sound *scheme.* Sometimes the sound effects in a scheme are even sonically related. (Perhaps the collection is totally hip-hop, classical, or performed on a kazoo.) To switch schemes, use the Sound Scheme pop-up menu.

You can also define a new scheme of your own. Start by assigning individual sounds to events, and then click the Save As button to save your collection under a name that you create.

Screen Savers
All Versions

The term "screen saver" is sort of bogus; today's flat-panel screens *can't* develop "burn-in." (You're too young to remember, but screen savers were designed to bounce around a moving image to prevent burn-in on those old, bulky, CRT screens.)

No, screen savers are mostly about entertainment, pure and simple—and Windows's built-in screen saver is certainly entertaining.

The idea is simple: A few minutes after you leave your computer, whatever work you were doing is hidden behind the screen saver; passers-by can't see what's on the screen. To exit the screen saver, move the mouse, click a mouse button, or press a key.

Choosing a Screen Saver

To choose a screen saver, click Screen Saver at the bottom of the Personalize dialog box (Figure 4-3). The Screen Saver Settings dialog box appears.

Note: In Windows 7 Starter Edition, go to Control Panel, and then click Appearance→Display→"Change screen saver."

Now use the "Screen saver" drop-down list. A miniature preview appears in the preview monitor on the dialog box (see Figure 4-7).

To see a *full-screen* preview, click the Preview button. The screen saver display fills your screen and remains there until you move your mouse, click a mouse button, or press a key.

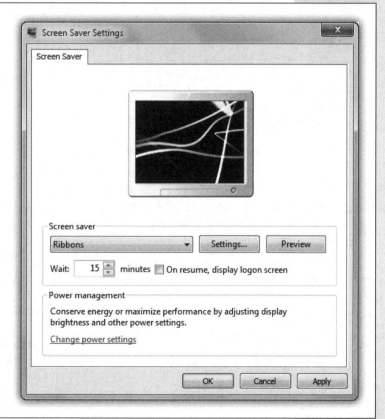

Figure 4-7:
"On resume, display logon screen" is a handy security measure. It means you'll have to input your password to get back into your PC once the screen saver has come on–a good barrier against nosy coworkers who saunter up to your PC while you're out getting coffee.

The Wait box determines how long the screen saver waits before kicking in, after the last time you move the mouse or type. Click the Settings button to play with the chosen screen saver module's look and behavior. For example, you may be able to change its colors, texture, or animation style.

POWER USERS' CLINIC

Desktop Icons: Sorting and Spacing

No matter how hard Microsoft tries to make people stop leaving icons out on the desktop—remember the Automatic Desktop Cleanup Wizard in Windows XP?—we keep doing it. People like leaving icons out on the desktop. Things are handy that way. Gives people a sense of control, of order.

"Well, fine," Microsoft seems to say. "But as long as you're going to leave your junk strewn everywhere, at least make it look neat." And sure enough, you can control the sorting, spacing, size, and even the visibility of the icons you put on the desktop.

Icon size. You can make all the desktop icons larger or smaller by turning your mouse's scroll wheel while pressing the Ctrl key. (Or use the View→Large, Medium, or Small commands.)

Visibility. You can also hide all those desktop icons—for example, when you're trying to show someone the beautiful baby photo that's your desktop wallpaper, but your Quarterly Expense Reports folder is covering her eye. To do that, right-click the desktop; from the shortcut menu, choose View→"Show desktop icons" so that the checkmark disappears—along with all your icons. Use the same command to make the icons reappear.

Align to grid. Right-click a blank spot on the desktop. In the shortcut menu, the View command offers submenus called "Auto arrange icons" and "Align icons to grid."

If both of these options are turned off, then you can drag icons anywhere. For example, some people like to keep current project icons at the top of the window and move older stuff to the bottom.

Ordinarily, though, Windows tries to impose a little discipline on you. It aligns your icons neatly to an invisible grid. If you choose this option, then all icons on the desktop jump to the closest positions on the invisible underlying grid.

Even so, this setting doesn't move icons into the most compact possible arrangement. If one or two icons have wandered off from the herd to a far corner of the window, then they're merely nudged to the grid points closest to their current locations. They aren't moved all the way back to the group of icons elsewhere in the window.

Consolidate. If you'd rather have icons sorted and bunched together on the underlying grid—no strays allowed—then choose View→"Auto arrange icons." This command places the icons as close as possible to one another on the desktop, rounding up any strays.

Sort. Right-click a blank spot on the desktop or in a window. The "Sort by" menu sorts the icons according to different criteria: name, date, and so on. Now if you add more icons to the window, they jump into correct alphabetical position; if you remove icons, the remaining ones slide over to fill in the gaps. This setup is perfect for neat freaks.

Adjust the grid spacing. Finally, you can control the spacing of the grid used for your desktop icons—in a place you'd never think of looking.

Open the Start menu. In the Search box, type enough of the word *metrics* until "Change window colors and metrics" appears in the results list; click it. (In Windows 7 Starter Edition, type enough of the word *color* until "Change the Color Scheme" appears in the results list; click it, and then click Advanced from the dialog box that appears.)

Now you see the dialog box shown in Figure 4-6. From the Items pop-up menu, choose Icon Spacing (Horizontal) or Icon Spacing (Vertical), and then adjust the Size number accordingly to nudge the grid spacing larger or smaller. Click Apply as you go to check your work; click OK when the desktop icons look perfect.

At the bottom of this tab, click "Change power settings" to open the Power Options window described on page 326.

***

Tip: If you keep graphics files in your Pictures folder, try selecting the Photos screen saver. Then click the Settings button and choose the pictures you want to see. When the screen saver kicks in, Windows puts on a spectacular slideshow of your photos, bringing each to the screen with a special effect (flying in from the side, fading in, and so on).

***

Desktop Icons
All Versions

Thanks to the "Change desktop icons" link at the left side of the Personalize screen, you can specify which standard icons sit on your desktop for easy access, and what they look like.

***

Note: In Windows 7 Starter Edition, open the Start menu, type *icons* into the Search box, and then click "Show or hide common icons on the desktop."

***

To choose your icons, just turn on the checkboxes for the ones you want (see Figure 4-8).

Figure 4-8:
Microsoft has been cleaning up the Windows desktop in recent years, and that includes sweeping away some useful icons, like Computer, Control Panel, Network, and your Personal folder. But you can put them back, just by turning on these checkboxes.

You can also substitute different *icons* for your icons. Click, for example, the Computer icon, and then click Change Icon. Up pops a collection of pre-drawn icons in a horizontally scrolling selection box. If you see a picture you like better, double-click it.

Click OK if you like the change, Cancel if not.

Mouse Makeover
All Versions

If your fondness for the standard Windows arrow cursor begins to wane, you can assert your individuality by choosing a different pointer shape. For starters, you might want to choose a *bigger* arrow cursor—a great solution on today's tinier-pixel, shrunken-cursor monitors.

Begin by clicking "Change mouse pointers" at the left side of the Personalize dialog box shown in Figure 4-3. In a flash, you arrive at the dialog box shown in Figure 4-9.

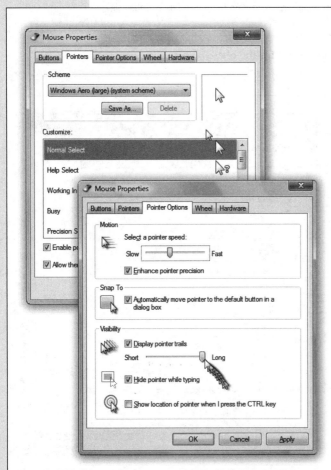

Figure 4-9:
Left: The Pointers dialog box, where you can choose a bigger cursor (or a differently shaped one).

Right: The Pointer Options tab. Ever lose your mouse pointer while working on a laptop with a dim screen? Maybe pointer trails could help. Or have you ever worked on a desktop computer with a mouse pointer that seems to take forever to move across the desktop? Try increasing the pointer speed.

Note: As usual, it's different In Windows 7 Starter Edition. Open the Control Panel, and then click Hardware and Sound→Mouse→Pointers.

At this point, you can proceed in any of three ways:

- **Scheme.** There's more to Windows cursors than just the arrow pointer. At various times, you may also see the spinning circular cursor (which means, "Wait; I'm thinking," or "Wait; I've crashed"), the I-beam cursor (which appears when you're editing text), the little pointing-finger hand that appears when you point to a Web link, and so on.

  All these cursors come prepackaged into design-coordinated sets called *schemes*. To look over the cursor shapes in a different scheme, use the Scheme drop-down list; the corresponding pointer collection appears in the Customize list box. The ones whose names include "large" or "extra large" offer jumbo, magnified cursors ideal for very large screens or failing eyesight. When you find one that seems like an improvement over the Windows Aero (system scheme) set, click OK.

- **Select individual pointers.** You don't have to change to a completely different scheme; you can also replace just one cursor. To do so, click the pointer you want to change, and then click the Browse button. You're shown the vast array of cursor-replacement icons (which are in the Local Disk (C:)→Windows→Cursors folder). Click one to see what it looks like; double-click to select it.

- **Create your own pointer scheme.** Once you've replaced a cursor shape, you've also changed the scheme to which it belongs. At this point, either click OK to activate your change and get back to work, or save the new, improved scheme under its own name, so you can switch back to the original when nostalgia calls. To do so, click the Save As button, name the scheme, and then click OK.

Tip: The "Enable pointer shadow" checkbox at the bottom of this tab is pretty neat. It casts a shadow on whatever's beneath the cursor, as though it's skimming just above the surface of your screen.

Pointer Options

Clicking the Pointer Options tab offers a few more random cursor-related functions (Figure 4-9, right).

- **Pointer speed.** It comes as a surprise to many people that the cursor doesn't move five inches when the mouse moves five inches on the desk. Instead, you can set things up so that moving the mouse one *millimeter* moves the pointer one full *inch*—or vice versa—using the "Pointer speed" slider.

  It may come as an even greater surprise that the cursor doesn't generally move *proportionally* to the mouse's movement, regardless of your "Pointer speed" setting. Instead, the cursor moves farther when you move the mouse faster. How *much* farther depends on how you set the "Select a pointer speed" slider.

The Fast setting is nice if you have an enormous monitor, since it prevents you from needing an equally large mouse pad to get from one corner to another. The Slow setting, on the other hand, can be frustrating, since it forces you to constantly pick up and put down the mouse as you scoot across the screen. (You can also turn off the disproportionate-movement feature completely by turning off "Enhance pointer precision.")

- **Snap To.** A hefty percentage of the times when you reach for the mouse, it's to click a button in a dialog box. If you, like millions of people before you, usually click the *default* (outlined) button—such as OK, Next, or Yes—then the Snap To feature can save you the effort of positioning the cursor before clicking.

  When you turn on Snap To, every time a dialog box appears, your mouse pointer jumps automatically to the default button so that all you need to do is click. (And to click a different button, like Cancel, you have to move the mouse only slightly to reach it.)

- **Display pointer trails.** The options available for enhancing pointer visibility (or invisibility) are mildly useful under certain circumstances, but mostly they're just for show.

  If you turn on "Display pointer trails," for example, you get ghost images that trail behind the cursor like a bunch of little ducklings following their mother. In general, this stuttering-cursor effect is irritating. On rare occasions, however, you may find that it helps locate the cursor—for example, if you're making a presentation on a low-contrast LCD projector.

- **Hide pointer while typing** is useful if you find that the cursor sometimes gets in the way of the words on your screen. As soon as you use the keyboard, the pointer disappears; just move the mouse to make the pointer reappear.

- **Show location of pointer when I press the CTRL key.** If you've managed to lose the cursor on an LCD projector or a laptop with an inferior screen, this feature helps you gain your bearings. After turning on this checkbox, Windows displays an animated concentric ring each time you press the Ctrl key to pinpoint the cursor's location.

Tip: You can also fatten up the insertion point—the cursor that appears when you're editing text. See page 288.

Preserving Your Tweaks for Posterity
Home Premium • Professional • Enterprise • Ultimate

The previous pages describe six ways to modify one of Windows 7's canned themes. You can change the desktop picture, the window color schemes, the sound scheme, the screen saver, the desktop icons, and the mouse-pointer shapes. The basic concept is simple: You choose one of Microsoft's canned themes as a starting point and then adjust these six aspects of it as suits your mood.

When that's all over, though, you return to the Personalization box, where all the modifications you've made are represented at the top of the screen—as an icon called Unsaved Theme (Figure 4-10).

Figure 4-10:
You may notice, after applying a theme, that its name seems to be "Unsaved Theme." This happens whenever you apply a theme and then change any single component of it, including the desktop background. Windows takes note and reports the theme you are using as modified.

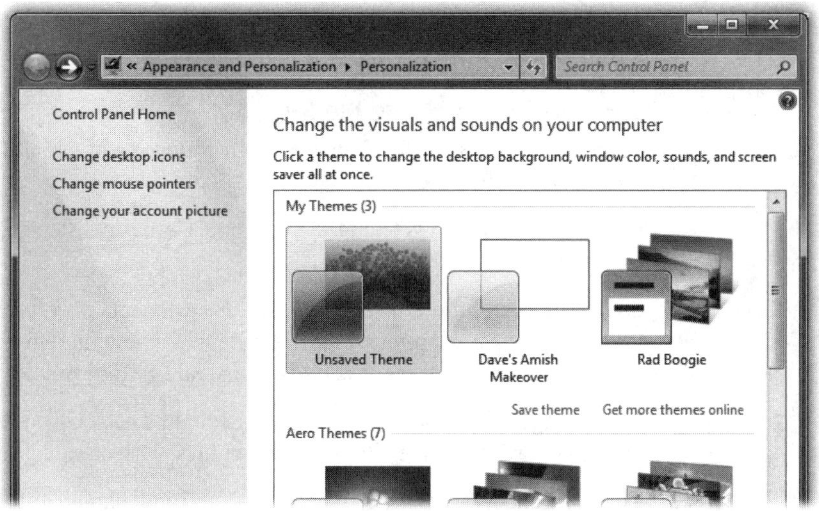

Well, you wouldn't want all that effort to go to waste, would you? So click "Save theme," type a name for your new, improved theme, and click Save.

From now on, the theme you've created (well, OK, *modified*) shows up in a new row of the Personalization dialog box called My Themes. From now on, you can recall the emotional tenor of your edited look with a single click on that icon.

If you make *further* changes to that theme (or any other theme), another Unsaved Theme icon appears, once again ready for you to save and name. You can keep going forever, adding to your gallery of experimentation.

You can also delete a less-inspired theme (right-click its icon; from the shortcut menu, choose Delete Theme). On the other hand, when you strike creative gold, you can package up your theme and share it with other computers—your own, or other people's online. To do that, right-click the theme's icon; from the shortcut menu, choose "Save theme for sharing." Windows asks you to name and save the new .themepak file, which you can distribute to the masses. (Just double-clicking a .themepak file installs it in the Personalize dialog box.)

Note: If your theme uses sounds and graphics that aren't on other people's PCs, they won't see those elements when they install your theme.

Monitor Settings
All Versions

You wouldn't get much work done without a screen on your computer. It follows, then, that you can get *more* work done if you tinker with your screen's settings to make it more appropriate to your tastes and workload. And boy, are there a lot of settings to tinker with.

Three Ways to Enlarge the Screen

There are two reasons why Windows 7 introduced a quick-and-easy way to magnify *everything* on the screen.

First, people tend to get older—even you. Come middle age, your eyes may have trouble reading smaller type.

Second, the resolution of computer screens gets higher every year. That is, more and more dots are packed into the same-sized screens, and therefore those dots are getting smaller, and therefore the *type and graphics* are getting smaller.

Microsoft finally decided enough was enough. That's why, in Windows 7, there's a one-click way to enlarge all type and graphics, with crisp, easier-to-see results.

There are also various older schemes for accomplishing similar tasks. Here's a run-down of all of them:

Change the resolution

Your screen can make its picture larger or smaller to accommodate different kinds of work. You perform this magnification or reduction by switching among different *resolutions* (measurements of the number of dots that compose the screen).

When you use a low-resolution setting, such as 800 × 600, the dots of your screen image get larger, enlarging (zooming in on) the picture—but showing a smaller slice of the page. Use this setting when playing a small movie on the Web, for example, so that it fills more of the screen.

At higher resolutions, such as 1280 × 1024, the screen dots get smaller, making your windows and icons smaller but showing more overall area. Use this kind of setting when working on two-page spreads in your page-layout program, for example.

Unfortunately, adjusting the resolution isn't a perfect solution if you're having trouble reading tiny type. On a flat-panel screen—that is, the *only* kind sold today—only one resolution setting looks really great: the maximum one. That's what geeks call the *native* resolution of that screen.

That's because on flat-panel screens, every pixel is a fixed size. At lower resolutions, the PC does what it can to blur together adjacent pixels, but the effect is fuzzy and unsatisfying. (On the old, bulky CRT monitors, the electron gun could actually make the pixels larger or smaller, so you didn't have this problem.)

If you still want to adjust your screen's resolution, here's how you do it. Right-click the desktop. From the shortcut menu, choose "Screen resolution." In the dialog box (Figure 4-11), use the Resolution pop-up menu.

Tip: Depending on your monitor, you may see a weird Orientation pop-up menu here. Believe it or not, this control lets you flip your screen image upside-down or left/right, forming a mirror image.

These options make hilarious practical jokes, of course, but they were actually designed to accommodate newfangled PC designs where, for example, the screen half of a laptop flips over, A-frame style, so people across the table from you can see it.

In any case, once you choose an orientation and click Apply or OK, a dialog box lets you either keep or discard the setting. Which is lucky, because if the image is upside-down on a regular PC, it's really hard to get any work done.

Figure 4-11:
Use the Resolution slider to change the magnification of the entire screen. On flat-panel screens, only the highest resolution is sharp, which is a good argument for leaving this setting alone.

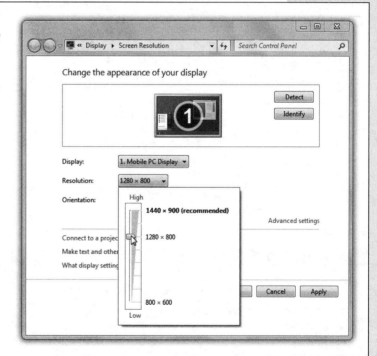

Enlarge just the type and graphics

This new Windows 7 feature is one of Microsoft's most inspired, most useful—and least publicized. It turns out that you can enlarge the type and graphics on the screen *without* changing the screen's resolution. So type gets bigger without getting blurrier, and everything else stays sharp, too.

To make this adjustment, right-click the desktop; from the shortcut menu, choose Resolution. In the resulting dialog box, click "Make text and other items larger or smaller."

Now you arrive at a new dialog box; proceed as directed in Figure 4-12.

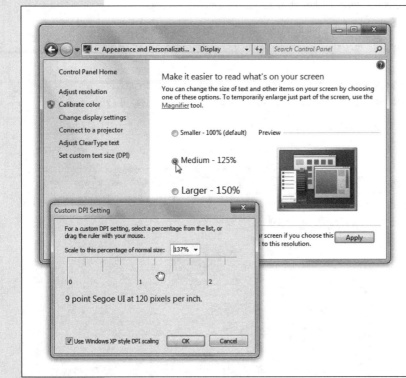

Figure 4-12:
Top: Click either Medium or Larger, and then click Apply. A message lets you know, "You must log off your computer." Click "Log off now." When the computer logs you in anew, you see larger type and graphics.

Bottom: If you prefer an in-between magnification, or a higher amount (up to 500%), drag right or left on the ruler until the sample text looks good to you; click OK. Older apps may not respond to the text-scaling feature, so you may get blurry text at large degrees of magnification. The "Use Windows XP style DP scaling" option is supposed to fix that, although it has side effects, too; it may produce weird-looking dialog boxes and chopped-off text in some programs.

TROUBLESHOOTING MOMENT

Blurry Bigger Text

This business about getting larger, easier-to-read type without changing your screen's resolution is a neat Windows 7 trick indeed. And it works beautifully on the pieces of your world controlled by Microsoft.

But older, pre-Windows 7 programs don't know anything about the new type-scaling features. If you've used one of the type-enlarging features described on these pages, the text might be blurry just in those apps.

If a particular program is giving you that sort of blurry text after you've scaled up your type, you can tell it not even to bother. Right-click the program's icon or its name in the Start menu. From the shortcut menu, choose Properties; click the Compatibility tab.

Turn on "Disable display scaling on high DPI settings."

Now the app won't magnify its text at all, but at least what's there will be crisp.

Tip: The box in Figure 4-12 offers only two fixed degrees of magnification: 125% and 150%. You can actually dial up any amount you like, though. Click "Set custom text size (DPI)" to produce the dialog box shown at bottom in Figure 4-12.

The Magnifier

If your "type is too small" problem is only occasional, you can call up Windows's Magnifier. It's like a software magnifying glass that fills the top portion of your screen; as you move your pointer around the real-size area beneath, the enlarged image scrolls around, too. Details are on page 195.

Colors

Today's monitors offer different *color depth* settings, each of which permits the screen to display a different number of colors simultaneously. You usually have a choice between settings like Medium (16-bit), which was called High Color in early versions of Windows; High (24-bit), once known as True Color; and Highest (32-bit).

POWER USERS' CLINIC

Some Clear Talk About ClearType

ClearType is Microsoft's word for a sneaky technology that makes type look sharper on your screen than it really is.

Imagine a lowercase s at a very small point size. It looks great on this page, because this book was printed at 1,200 dots per inch. But your monitor's resolution is far lower—maybe 96 dots per inch—so text doesn't look nearly as good. If you were to really get up close, you'd see that the curves on the letters are actually a little jagged.

Each dot on an LCD screen is actually composed of three subpixels (mini-dots): red, green, and blue. What ClearType does is simulate smaller pixels in the nooks and crannies of letters by turning on only some of those subpixels. In the curve of that tiny s, for example, maybe only the blue subpixel is turned on, which to your eye looks like a slightly darker area, a fraction of a pixel; as a result, the type looks finer than it really is.

In Windows 7, ClearType's behavior is adjustable. To see the options, open the Start menu. In the Search box, type enough of the word *cleartype* until "Adjust ClearType text" appears in the results list; click it.

On the first screen, you have an on/off checkbox for ClearType. It's there just for the sake of completeness, because text on an LCD screen really does look worse without it.

If you click Next, Windows walks you through a series of "Which type sample looks better to you?" screens, where all you have to do is click the "Quick Brown Fox Jumps Over the Lazy Dog" example that you find easiest to read. Behind the scenes, of course, you're adjusting ClearType's technical parameters without even having to know what they are. When it's all over, you'll have the best-looking small type possible.

Click the text sample that looks best to you (2 of 4)

The Quick Brown Fox Jumps Over the Lazy Dog. Lorem ipsum dolor sit amet, consectetuer adipiscing elit. Mauris ornare odio vel risus. Maecenas elit metus, pellentesque quis, pretium.

The Quick Brown Fox Jumps Over the Lazy Dog. Lorem ipsum dolor sit amet, consectetuer adipiscing elit. Mauris ornare odio vel risus. Maecenas elit metus, pellentesque quis, pretium.

The Quick Brown Fox Jumps Over the Lazy Dog. Lorem ipsum dolor sit amet, consectetuer adipiscing elit. Mauris ornare odio vel risus. Maecenas elit metus, pellentesque quis, pretium.

The Quick Brown Fox Jumps Over the Lazy Dog. Lorem ipsum dolor sit amet, consectetuer adipiscing elit. Mauris ornare odio vel risus. Maecenas elit metus, pellentesque quis, pretium.

The Quick Brown Fox Jumps Over the Lazy Dog. Lorem ipsum dolor sit amet, consectetuer adipiscing elit. Mauris ornare odio vel risus. Maecenas elit metus, pellentesque quis, pretium.

The Quick Brown Fox Jumps Over the Lazy Dog. Lorem ipsum dolor sit amet, consectetuer adipiscing elit. Mauris ornare odio vel risus. Maecenas elit metus, pellentesque quis, pretium.

In the early days of computing, higher color settings required a sacrifice in speed. Today, however, there's very little downside to leaving your screen at its highest setting. Photos, in particular, look best when you set your monitor to higher-quality settings.

To check your settings, right-click the desktop. From the shortcut menu, choose "Screen resolution." In the dialog box, click "Advanced settings" to open the Properties dialog box for your monitor. Click the Monitor tab, and use the Colors pop-up menu to choose your color depth.

Multiple Monitors

Home Premium • Professional • Enterprise • Ultimate

If your computer has a jack for an external monitor (most do these days—including the video-output jacks on laptops), then you can hook up a second monitor or a projector. You can either display the same picture on both screens (which is what you'd want if your laptop were projecting slides for an audience), or you can create a gigantic virtual desktop, moving icons or toolbars from one monitor to another. The latter setup also lets you keep an eye on Web activity on one monitor while you edit data on another. It's a *glorious* arrangement, even if it does make the occasional family member think you've gone off the deep end with your PC obsession.

What's especially great is that Windows 7 has a wicked-cool keystroke just for setups like this (two monitors, or laptop+projector): ⊞+P. When you press it, you see the display in Figure 4-13.

Tip: Actually, just plugging in a projector generally inspires Windows to present something like the options in Figure 4-13. This is an extremely thoughtful touch for laptop luggers, because it avoids the staggeringly confusing keyboard-based system you previously had to use. That's where you'd press, for example, F8 three times to cycle among the three modes: image on laptop only (projector dark), image on projector only (laptop screen dark), or image on both at once. Win7's method is much easier.

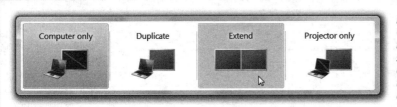

Figure 4-13:
Click how you want your two screens to work: one screen on and the other off, both screens showing the same thing, or some additional real estate.

You can also adjust the monitor settings independently for your two screens. To do that, right-click the desktop. From the shortcut menu, choose "Screen resolution."

In the resulting dialog box (Figure 4-14), you see icons for both screens (or even more, if you have them, you lucky thing). It's like a map. Click the screen whose settings (like resolution) you want to change. If Windows seems to be displaying these miniatures out of sequence—if your external monitor is really to the *left* of your main screen, and

Windows is showing it to the right—you can actually drag their thumbnails around until they match reality. (Click Identify if you get confused; that makes an enormous digit fill each real screen, which helps you match it to the digits on the miniatures.)

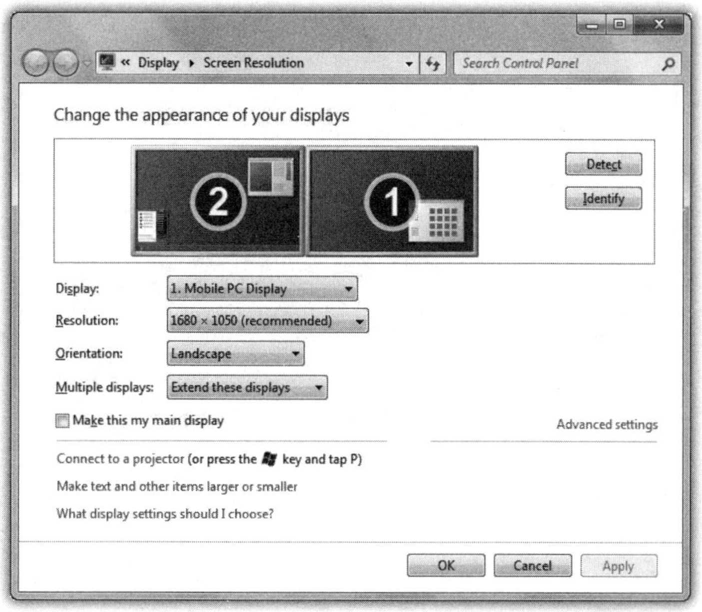

Figure 4-14:
When you have multiple monitors, the controls on the Settings tab change; you now see individual icons for each monitor. When you click a screen icon, the settings in the dialog box change to reflect its resolution, color quality, and so on.

To bring about that extended-desktop scenario, use the "Multiple displays" pop-up menu. It offers commands like "Duplicate these displays" and "Extend these displays."

Advanced Settings

If you click the Advanced button on the Settings tab, you're offered a collection of technical settings for your particular monitor model. Depending on your video driver, there may be tab controls here that adjust the *refresh rate* to eliminate flicker, install an updated adapter or monitor driver, and so on. In general, you rarely need to adjust these controls—except on the advice of a consultant or help-line technician.

Getting Help

Windows 7 may be better than any version of Windows before it, but improving something means changing it. And in Windows 7, a lot has changed; otherwise, you probably wouldn't be reading a book about it.

Fortunately, help is just around the corner—of the Start menu, that is. Windows's electronic Help system was completely new in Windows Vista and has been further enhanced in Win7; it's got little videos, links to Web articles, and even links that do certain jobs for you. It may take all weekend, but eventually you should find written information about this or that Windows feature or problem.

This chapter covers not only the Help system, but also some of the ways Windows can help you get help from a more experienced person via your network or the Internet.

Navigating the Help System
All Versions

To open the Help system, choose Start→Help and Support, or press ⊞+F1. The Help and Support window appears, as shown in Figure 5-1. From here, you can home in on the help screen you want using one of two methods: using the Search command, or clicking your way from the Help home page.

Search the Help Pages
By typing a phrase into the Search Help box at the top of the main page and then pressing Enter (or clicking the tiny magnifying glass button), you instruct Windows to rifle through its 10,000 help pages—and many more that reside online—to search for the phrase you typed.

Here are a few pointers:

- When you enter multiple words, Windows assumes you're looking for help screens that contain *all* those words. For example, if you search for *video settings*, then help screens that contain both the words "video" and "settings" (although not necessarily next to each other) appear.

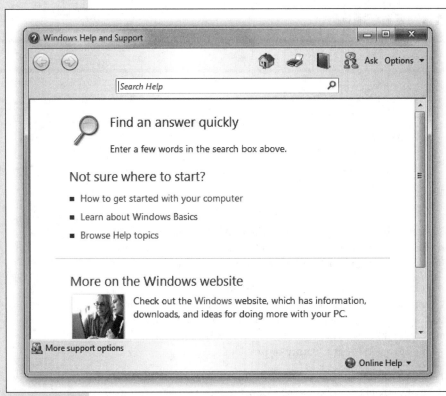

Figure 5-1:
The ⊙, ⊙, ⌂, and Search controls on the Help system's toolbar may look like the corresponding tools in a Web browser, but they refer only to your travels within the Help system. Other buttons at the top let you print a help article or change the type size.

Links in Help

Along with the nicely rewritten help information, you may find, here and there in the Help system, a few clickable links.

Sometimes you see a phrase that appears in green type; that's your cue that clicking it will produce a pop-up definition.

Sometimes you see blue links to other help screens.

And sometimes you see help links that *automate* the task you're trying to learn. These goodies, denoted by a blue compass icon, offer you two ways of proceeding: Either Windows can do the *whole* job for you, or it can show you step by step, using blinking, glowing outlines to show you exactly where to click.

There aren't nearly enough of these automated help topics—but when you stumble onto one, turn down the lights, invite the neighbors, and settle back for an unforgettable 5 minutes of entertainment.

- To search for an exact phrase, put quotes around it ("video settings").

- Once you've clicked your way to an article that looks promising, you can search within that page, too. Open the Options pop-up menu (upper-right corner of the Help window) and choose "Find (on this page)."

Tip: Unless you turn off "Improve my search results by using online Help" (under Options→Settings), Windows ordinarily searches both the Help system on your PC and additional articles online. But it doesn't search the entire Microsoft Knowledge Base, as Windows XP did. (That's an enormous technical Web site filled with troubleshooting and help articles.)

You can search it right from the Help screen, though. On the Help-screen toolbar, click Ask, and then click the link that says "Microsoft Customer Support. " Then take the phone off the hook for the rest of the afternoon.

Drilling Down

If you're not using the same terminology as Microsoft, you won't find your help topic by using the Search box. Sometimes, you may have better luck unearthing a certain help article by drilling down through the Table of Contents.

Figure 5-2:
As you arrive on each more finely grained subtable of subcontents, you'll see a "bread-crumb trail" of topics at the top of the window. These ▶ arrows illustrate the levels through which you've descended on your way to this help page; you can backtrack by clicking one of these links.

Start by clicking one of the three main browse options: "How to get started with your computer," "Learn about Windows Basics," or "Browse Help contents."

Each one lists subtopics. Keep clicking until you arrive at an actual help article (Figure 5-2).

Remote Assistance

All Versions

You may think you know what stress is: deadlines, breakups, downsizing. But nothing approaches the frustration of an expert trying to help a PC beginner over the phone—for both parties.

The expert is flying blind, using Windows terminology that the beginner doesn't know. Meanwhile, the beginner doesn't know what to look for and describe on the phone. Every little step takes 20 times longer than it would if the expert were simply seated in front of the machine. Both parties are likely to age 10 years in an hour.

Fortunately, that era is at an end. Windows's Remote Assistance feature lets somebody having computer trouble extend an invitation to an expert, via the Internet. The expert can actually see the screen of the flaky computer and can even take control of it by remotely operating the mouse and keyboard. The guru can make even the most technical tweaks—running utility software, installing new programs, adjusting hardware drivers, even editing the Registry (Appendix B)—by long-distance remote control. Remote Assistance really *is* the next best thing to being there.

Remote Assistance: Rest Assured

Of course, these days, most people react to the notion of Remote Assistance with stark terror. What's to stop some troubled teenager from tapping into your PC in the middle of the night, rummaging through your files, and reading your innermost thoughts?

Plenty. First of all, you, the help-seeker, must begin the process by sending a specific electronic invitation to the expert. The invitation has a time limit: If the helper doesn't respond within, say, an hour, then the electronic door to your PC slams shut again. Second, the remote-control person can only *see* what's on your screen. She can't actually manipulate your computer unless you grant another specific permission.

UP TO SPEED

Help for Dialog Boxes

In Windows XP, whenever you faced a dialog box containing a cluster of oddly worded options, the "What's This?" feature came to the rescue. It made pop-up captions appear for text boxes, checkboxes, option buttons, and other dialog box elements.

You summoned these pop-up identifiers by clicking the ? button in the upper-right corner of the dialog box and then clicking the element you wanted identified.

In Windows 7, there's still a ? button in some dialog boxes. But it doesn't offer anything like pop-up captions. Instead, it opens an article from the standard Windows Help center that explains the relevant dialog box as a whole.

Finally, you must be present *at your machine* to make this work. The instant you see something fishy going on, a quick tap on your Esc key disconnects the interloper.

Tip: If you still can't stand the idea that there's a tiny keyhole into your PC from the Internet, open the Start menu. Start typing *remote* until you see "Allow remote access to your computer" in the results list; click it. In the resulting dialog box, turn off "Allow Remote Assistance connections to this computer." Click OK. Now you've effectively removed the use of the Remote Assistance feature from Windows.

Starting Up Remote Assistance: If You're Both on Windows 7

There's a new feature in Windows 7 that greatly shortens the number of steps necessary to set up a Remote Assistance session. It's called, self-explanatorily enough, Easy Connect. But it works only if both of you are using Windows 7.

If the novice or the expert is using an older version of Windows, then skip to the next section.

Instructions for the novice

OK, let's say you're the one who needs help. And you're running Windows 7. And you know somebody else with Windows 7 who might be able to help you by remote control. Here's what you do:

1. **Open Windows Remote Assistance.**

    There are a bunch of ways to do that, but the quickest is to open the Start menu. Start typing *remote* in the Search box until you see "Windows Remote Assistance" in the results list; click it.

    You now arrive at a "Do you want to ask for or offer help?" screen.

POWER USERS' CLINIC

Invitation Expiration Dates

If you're the one who wants help, you'll be sending out an invitation to invade your machine. For security's sake, it has an expiration date. If your guru doesn't cash in on the opportunity within six hours, the ticket expires, and you'll have to reissue the invitation another time.

It's worth pointing out that you can adjust that expiration period. Open the Start menu. Start typing remote until you see "Allow remote access to your computer"; click it. In the System Properties dialog box, click Advanced (the button, not the tab). Here, you find two key security options:

Allow this computer to be controlled remotely. This is the master switch for permitting your guru to operate your PC from afar, not just see what's onscreen.

Invitations. Here's where you specify how quickly an invitation to a guru expires. It may give you an extra level of comfort knowing that after, say, three hours of waiting for your guru to come home and get your invitation, the window of opportunity will close. On the other hand, if you change it to, say, 99 days, and you're not especially worried that somebody might try to hack into your system (you do have to be present and approve the connection, of course), then you'll save yourself some time and effort the next time you need help.

Click OK twice to close the dialog boxes.

---

2. Click "Invite someone you trust to help you."

If you now see an error message ("This computer is not set up to send invitations"), click Repair. Usually, the problem is that the Windows Firewall (page 339) is blocking the outgoing signal—and usually, clicking Repair fixes it after a moment.

Note: You also may have trouble if your router doesn't offer a feature called Peer Name Resolution Protocol. How can you find out? Use the Internet Connectivity Evaluation Tool. It's available on Microsoft's Web site at *http://bit.ly/91EBbJ.*

At this point, what you see depends on whether you've used Easy Connect before. If so, you see a list of people who've helped you in the past; you can resend an invitation to your usual savior just by clicking that person's name.

If you're inviting someone new, on the other hand, you get the bottom box shown in Figure 5-3, offering three ways to send the invitation to your friendly neighborhood guru.

3. Click Use Easy Connect.

Now Windows shows you a 12-character password (Figure 5-3, middle).

4. Provide the password to your expert friend.

You can send it by email, read it to her over the phone, type it to her in a chat program, send a text message, whatever.

If your expert friend does indeed have a clue, then in a moment, you see a message from that person asking permission to see your screen ("Would you like to allow Casey to connect to your computer?"). Close whatever windows on the screen might be displaying incriminating information, and then—

5. Click Yes.

And voilà: Your guru friend can now see what you're doing—and what you're doing wrong.

Instructions for the expert

If you and your clueless friend are both using Windows 7 and you receive an invitation to help out—in the form of the 12-character Easy Connect password described above—here's what to do with it:

1. Open Windows Remote Assistance.

Once again, the quickest way is to start typing *remote* into the Start menu until you see "Windows Remote Assistance" in the results list; click it.

2. Click "Help someone who has invited you."

Now you're shown a list of people you've helped out before (if any). If you see your desperate friend's name, click it. Otherwise...

3. Click "Help someone new." In the next window, click Use Easy Connect.

Now Windows asks you for that 12-character password.

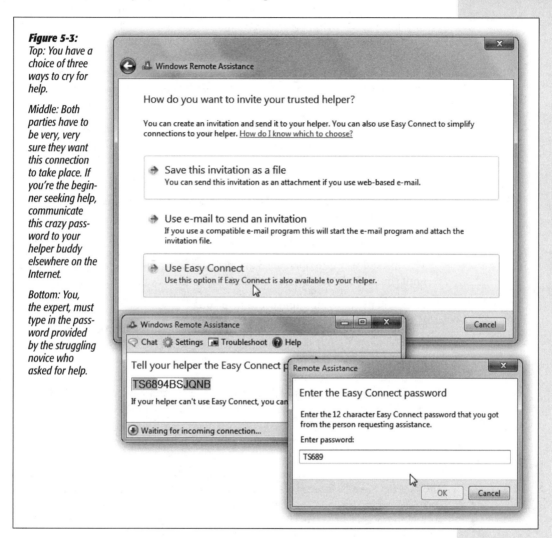

Figure 5-3:
Top: You have a choice of three ways to cry for help.

Middle: Both parties have to be very, very sure they want this connection to take place. If you're the beginner seeking help, communicate this crazy password to your helper buddy elsewhere on the Internet.

Bottom: You, the expert, must type in the password provided by the struggling novice who asked for help.

[Screenshot 1:]
Windows Remote Assistance

How do you want to invite your trusted helper?

You can create an invitation and send it to your helper. You can also use Easy Connect to simplify connections to your helper. How do I know which to choose?

→ Save this invitation as a file
You can send this invitation as an attachment if you use web-based e-mail.

→ Use e-mail to send an invitation
If you use a compatible e-mail program this will start the e-mail program and attach the invitation file.

→ Use Easy Connect
Use this option if Easy Connect is also available to your helper.

Cancel

[Screenshot 2:]
Windows Remote Assistance
Chat ⚙ Settings 🖥 Troubleshoot ❓ Help

Tell your helper the Easy Connect p

TS6894BSJQNB

If your helper can't use Easy Connect, you ca

Waiting for incoming connection...

[Screenshot 3:]
Remote Assistance

Enter the Easy Connect password

Enter the 12 character Easy Connect password that you got from the person requesting assistance.

Enter password:

TS689

OK   Cancel

4. Type in the 12-character password (Figure 5-3, bottom).

Capitals don't matter. Press Enter when you're finished.

If your inviter approves the connection, after a moment, the session begins, as described below.

Starting Up Remote Assistance: If You're Not Both on Windows 7

If the helper and the helpee aren't both using Windows 7, you can still use Remote Assistance; there are just more steps.

In fact, anybody with Windows XP, Vista, or Server 2003/2008 can help anyone else with one of those operating systems.

The steps, however, are different depending on whether you're the flailer or the helper. In the following steps, suppose you're running Windows 7. (It's a pretty good assumption; you're reading a book about Windows 7, aren't you?)

Tip: If you and your guru are both fans of Windows Live Messenger, Microsoft's chat program, you have at your disposal a more direct way of starting a Remote Assistance session. When you see that your guru is online in Messenger, choose Actions→Start Request Remote Assistance.

If the guru accepts, and you accept the acceptance, then a Remote Assistance session begins, without your having to go through all the email rigmarole described below.

Instructions for the novice

If you're the novice, and you have Windows 7, and you need help, here's how to request it from your more experienced friend:

1. **Open the Windows Remote Assistance program.**

   The quickest way is to open the Start menu. Start typing *remote* in the Search box until you see "Windows Remote Assistance" in the results list; click it.

2. **Click "Invite someone you trust to help you."**

   The phrase "you trust" is Microsoft's little way of reminding you that whomever you invite will be able to see anything you've got open on the screen. (Those who would rather keep that private know who they are.)

Note: If you now see an error message ("This computer is not set up to send invitations"), click Repair. As noted above, Windows will fix your Windows Firewall so that you can connect; then read on.

   In any case, now the "How do you want to invite your trusted helper?" screen appears.

Tip: If you click "Save this invitation as a file" at this point, then Windows invites you to save a *ticket file*—a standalone invitation file—to your hard drive. You have to do that if you have a Web-based email account like Gmail, Hotmail, or Yahoo Mail. (Make up a password first—see step 5, below, for an explanation—and then attach the file you've saved in this step when sending a message to your guru.)

Saving the file is also handy because you can save some steps by resending it to your guru the next time you're feeling lost.

---

3. **Click "Use email to send an invitation."**

   This assumes, of course, that you have a working email program on your PC. If not, set up your account as described in Chapter 12. Or get on the phone and ask your guru to drive over to your place to help you in person.

If you do have working email, your email program now opens, and Windows composes an invitation message *for* you. "Hi," it begins. "I need help with my computer. Would you please use Windows Remote Assistance to connect to my computer so you can help me?" (You're welcome to edit this message, of course—perhaps to something that does a little less damage to your ego.)

Now Windows displays a password like the one shown in Figure 5-3. It's designed to ensure that your guru, and only your guru, can access your machine.

4. **Type your guru's email address into the "To:" box, and then send the message.**

Windows sends an electronic invitation to your good Samaritan.

5. **Let your guru know the password.**

Of course, you need to find some way of *telling* that person the password—maybe calling on the phone, sending a text message, or sending a separate email. The password isn't automatically included in the invitation mail.

Now there's nothing to do but sit back, quietly freaking out, and wait for your guru to get the message and connect to your PC. (See the next section.)

If your buddy accepts the invitation to help you, then Windows asks if you're absolutely, positively sure you want someone else to see your screen. If you click Yes, the assistance session begins.

If you get a note that your expert friend wants to take control of your PC, and that's cool with you, click OK.

Now watch in amazement and awe as your cursor begins flying around the screen, text types itself, and windows open and close by themselves (Figure 5-4).

As noted earlier, if the expert's explorations of your system begin to unnerve you, feel free to slam the door by clicking the "Stop sharing" button on the screen—or just by pressing the Esc key. Your friend can still see your screen but can no longer control it. (To close the connection completely so that your screen isn't even visible anymore, click the Disconnect button.)

Instructions for the expert

When the novice sends you an email invitation, it arrives in your email program with an attachment—a tiny file called Invitation.msrcincident. This is your actual invitation, a Remote Assistance *ticket*.

When you open it, you're asked to supply the password that your helpless newbie created in step 5 above. Once that's done, the online help session can begin.

Tip: And by the way, if the novice, a trusting individual, sends you a Remote Assistance ticket that doesn't expire for a very long time (99 days, for example), keep it around on your desktop or in your Start menu. From now on, both of you can skip all of the invitation-and-response rigmarole. Now, whenever he needs your help, he can just call you up or email you. And all you have to do is double-click your ticket and wait for the OK from the other side.

Once You're Connected

Once you, the expert, and your little novice friend have completed all the inviting and permission-granting, you observe a strange sight: the other person's screen in a special Remote Assistance window (Figure 5-4). To communicate with your troubled comrade, chat on the phone, if you like, or click the Chat button to type back and forth.

Tip: If the victim's screen isn't exactly the same size as yours, click the "Actual size" button. With each click on that button, you cycle your display between two modes.

In the first one, the other person's screen is represented at full size, although you may have to scroll around to see all of it. With another click, Windows compresses (or enlarges) the other person's screen image to fit inside your Remote Assistance window, even though the result can be distorted and ugly.

The beginner's controls Your controls Beginner's desktop Your desktop

Figure 5-4:
This is what you see, wise master, as you watch the flailing beginner from across the Internet. You are now ready to tell him what he's doing wrong.

When you want to take control of the distant machine, click "Request control" on the toolbar at the top of your screen. Of course, all you've actually done is just ask *permission* to take control.

If it's granted, you can now use your mouse, keyboard, and troubleshooting skills to do whatever work you need to do. You can type messages back and forth (click Chat on the toolbar) or even send files back and forth (click Send Files on the toolbar).

You can do anything to the distant PC that the novice would be able to do—and you can't do anything the novice isn't allowed to do. (For example, if the novice doesn't have an administrative account, you won't be able to do administratory things like installing apps or creating accounts.)

When your job is done, click the window's Close button—or wait for your grateful patient to click Cancel on the toolbar.

Tip: Once you've taken control of the other person's screen, your first instinct might be to close the gargantuan Remote Assistance window that's filling most of the screen. Don't. If that window closes, the connection closes, too. What you really want is to *minimize* it, so it's out of your way but not closed.

If you're the person being helped, by the way, your toolbar has some useful options, too. "Stop sharing" is your emergency Off button if you think the remote guru is getting into places you consider private. You can also click Pause, which freezes the image the other person is seeing so that you can do something personal without fear of being watched.

Getting Help from Microsoft
All Versions

If you run into trouble with installation—or with any Windows feature—the world of Microsoft is filled with sources of technical help. For example, you can follow any of these avenues, all of which have direct links from the Ask page of the Help system (choose Start→Help and Support, and then click Ask on the toolbar):

- **Windows Answers.** This link takes you to a special Web site about Windows issues. You can post questions to the multitudes all over the Internet and return later to read the answers.

- **Microsoft Customer Support.** This Web site offers a summary of all the different ways you can get help from Microsoft: phone numbers, pricing plans, links to other help sources, and so on.

  You'll discover there that if you bought Windows separately (that is, it didn't come on your computer), then you can call Microsoft for free during business hours. The company is especially interested in helping you get Windows installed. In fact, you can call as often as you like on this subject.

  After that, you can call for everyday Windows questions for free—twice. You're asked to provide your 20-digit product ID number, which you can look up by right-clicking Computer in your Start menu and clicking the Properties tab. The not-toll-free number is listed in the packaging of your Windows installation DVD.

  (If Windows came preinstalled on your machine, on the other hand, you're supposed to call the computer company with your Windows questions.)

  Once you've used up your two free calls, you can still call Microsoft—for $35 per incident. (They say "per incident" to make it clear that if it takes several phone calls to solve a particular problem, it's still just one problem.) This service is available 24 hours a day; the U.S. number is (800) 936-5700.

Tip: If you're not in the United States, direct your help calls to the local Microsoft office in your country. You can find a list of these subsidiaries at *http://support.microsoft.com*.

- **Microsoft TechNet.** This link takes you to a special Web site for network administrators, programmers, and other IT (information technology) pros. At this site you'll find articles on deployment, corporate security, and so on.

- **Windows Web site.** This is the mother lode: the master Web site for help and instructions on running Windows. You can search it, use its links to other pages, read articles, study FAQs (frequently asked questions), or burrow into special-topic articles.

Of course, a lot of these online articles are built right into the regular Help system described at the beginning of this chapter. Unless you've opened the Help program, clicked Options→Settings, and turned off "Improve my search results by using online Help," you generally don't have to go online to search a second time.

Part Two:
Windows 7 Software

2

Programs, Documents, & Gadgets

W hen you get right down to it, an operating system is nothing more than a home base from which to launch applications (programs). And you, as a Windows person, are particularly fortunate, since more programs are available for Windows than for any other operating system on earth.

But when you launch a program, you're no longer necessarily in the world Microsoft designed for you. Programs from other software companies work a bit differently, and there's a lot to learn about how Windows handles programs that were born before it was.

This chapter covers everything you need to know about installing, removing, launching, and managing programs; using programs to generate documents; understanding how documents, programs, and Windows communicate with one another; and exploiting Windows 7's hybrid document/program entity, the gadget.

Opening Programs
All Versions

Windows lets you launch (open) programs in many different ways:

- Choose a program's name from the Start→All Programs menu.

- Click a program's icon on the taskbar.

- Double-click an application's program-file icon in the Computer→Local Disk (C:)→Program Files→application folder, or highlight the application's icon and then press Enter.

- Press a key combination you've assigned to be the program's shortcut (page 160).

- Press ⊞+R, type the program file's name in the Open text box, and then press Enter.

- Let Windows launch the program for you, either at startup (page 31) or at a time you've specified (see Task Scheduler, page 654).

- Open a document using any of the above techniques; its "parent" program opens automatically. For example, if you used Microsoft Word to write a file called Last Will and Testament.doc, then double-clicking the document's icon launches Word and automatically opens that file.

What happens next depends on the program you're using (and whether or not you opened a document). Most programs present you with a new, blank, untitled document. Some, such as FileMaker and Microsoft PowerPoint, welcome you instead with a question: Do you want to open an existing document or create a new one? And a few oddball programs don't open any window at all when launched. The appearance of tool palettes is the only evidence that you've even opened a program.

Exiting Programs
All Versions

When you exit, or quit, an application, the memory it was using is returned to the Windows pot for use by other programs.

If you use a particular program several times a day, like a word processor or calendar, you'll save time in the long run by keeping it open all day long. (You can always minimize its window when you're not using it.)

But if you're done using a program for the day, exit it, especially if it's a memory-hungry one like, say, Photoshop. Do so using one of these techniques:

- Choose File→Exit.

- Click the program window's Close box, or double-click its Control-menu spot (at the upper-left corner of the window).

- Right-click the program's taskbar button; from the shortcut menu, choose Close or Close Group.

- Point to the program's taskbar button; when the thumbnail preview pops up, point to the little ⊠ button in its upper-right corner. (If the program had only one window open, the program exits.)

- Press Alt+F4 to close the window you're in. (If it's a program that disappears entirely when its last document window closes, you're home.)

- Press Alt+F, then X.

After offering you a chance to save any changes you've made to your document, the program's windows, menus, and toolbars disappear, and you "fall down a layer" into the window that was behind it.

When Programs Die: The Task Manager

All Versions

Windows may be a revolution in stability (at least if you're used to, say, Windows Me), but that doesn't mean that *programs* never crash or freeze. They crash, all right—it's just that you rarely have to restart the computer as a result.

When something goes horribly wrong with a program, your primary interest is usually exiting it. But when a program locks up (the cursor moves, but menus and tool palettes don't respond) or when a dialog box tells you a program has "failed to respond," exiting may not be so easy. After all, how do you choose File→Exit if the File menu doesn't open?

As in past versions of Windows, the solution is to open up the Task Manager dialog box.

Tip: Actually, there may be a quicker solution. Try right-clicking the frozen program's taskbar button; from the shortcut menu, choose Close. This trick doesn't always work—but when it does, it's much faster than using the Task Manager.

UP TO SPEED

Sending an Error Report to Microsoft

Whenever Windows detects that a program has exited, shall we say, *eccentrically*—for example, it froze and you had to terminate it—your PC quietly sends a report back to Microsoft, the mother ship, via the Internet. It provides the company with the technical details about whatever was going on at the moment of the freeze, crash, or premature termination.

The information includes the name and version number of the program, the date and time, and other details. Microsoft swears that it doesn't collect any information about *you*.

Microsoft says it has two interests in getting this information. First, it collates the data into gigantic electronic databases, which it then analyzes using special software tools. The idea, of course, is to find trends that emerge from studying hundreds of thousands of such reports. "Oh, my goodness, it looks like people who own both Speak-it Pro 5 and Beekeeper Plus who right-click a document that's currently being printed experience a system lockup," an engineer might announce one day. By analyzing the system glitches of its customers en masse, the company hopes to pinpoint problems and devise software patches with much greater efficiency than before.

Second, Microsoft's computers may also react to the information on the spot and send you a dialog box that lets you know about an available fix.

Windows XP did this report-sending, too, but it asked you *each time* a program crashed. In Windows Vista, the report-sending feature was either turned *on* all the time or *off* all the time. In Windows 7, these automatic connections are once again up to you.

To adjust the settings, open the Start menu. In the search box, start typing *problems* until you see "Choose how to report problems"; click it. There, before you, are the controls for the auto-reporting. You can opt to have Windows check for solutions, check for solutions and report to Microsoft what happened, ask for permission before each sending, or never check for solutions.

This dialog box offers various other privacy controls. For example, you can "Select programs to exclude from reporting." (This one's for you, owners of Music Piracy Plus 4.0.)

For details on Windows's automatic error-reporting system, see page 705.

Here are three ways to do it:

- Invoke the new "three-fingered salute," Ctrl+Shift+Esc.

- Press the old "three-fingered salute," Ctrl+Alt+Delete. That keystroke opens the Windows Security screen (Figure 6-1). From *here* you can get to the Task Manager—by clicking Start Task Manager (Figure 6-1, top).

- Right-click the taskbar and, from the shortcut menu, choose Task Manager from the shortcut menu.

In any case, now you see a list of every open program. The Status column should make clear what you already know: that one of your programs—labeled "Not responding"—is ignoring you.

Tip: Now, "not responding" could just mean, "in the middle of crunching away." If the nonresponsive program is some huge mega-hog and you just chose some command that's going to take awhile, give it a chance to finish before you conclude that it's locked up.

Figure 6-1:
Top: Click the Task Manager button on the Windows Security dialog box to check on the status of a troublesome program.

Bottom: As if you didn't know, one of these programs is "not responding." Highlight its name and then click End Task to slap it out of its misery. Once the program disappears from the list, close the Task Manager and get on with your life. You can even restart the same program right away—no harm done.

As shown in Figure 6-1, shutting down the troublesome program is fairly easy; just click its name and then click the End Task button. (If yet another dialog box appears, telling you that "This program is not responding," click the End Now button.)

When you jettison a recalcitrant program this way, Windows generally shuts down the troublemaker gracefully, even offering you the chance to save unsaved changes to your documents.

If even this treatment fails to close the program, you might have to slam the door the hard way. Right-click the program's name on the Applications tab; from the shortcut menu, choose Go to Process. You switch to the Process tab, where the program's cryptic abbreviated name is already highlighted. Click the End Process button. (The Processes list includes dozens of programs, including many that Windows runs behind the scenes.)

Using this method, you lose any unsaved changes to your documents—but at least the frozen program is finally closed.

Tip: If you click a program's taskbar button but its window doesn't appear, the program may be frozen. In that case, try right-clicking the taskbar button; from the shortcut menu, choose Restore.

Saving Documents
All Versions

In a few programs, such as Calculator or Solitaire, you don't actually create any documents; when you close the window, no trace of your work remains.

Most programs, however, are designed to create *documents*—files you can reopen for further editing, send to other people, back up on another disk, and so on.

That's why these programs offer File→Save and File→Open commands, which let you preserve the work you've done, saving it onto the hard drive as a new file icon so that you can return to it later.

The Save Dialog Box
When you choose File→Save for the first time, you're asked where you want the new document stored on your hard drive (Figure 6-2). In Windows 7, this Save As dialog box is crystal-clear; in fact, it's a *full Explorer window*, complete with taskbar, Navigation pane, Search box, Views menu, and Organize menu. All the skills you've picked up working at the desktop come into play here; you can even delete a file or folder right from within the Save or Open box. (The Delete command is in the Organize menu.)

To give it a try, launch any Windows program that has a Save or Export command— WordPad , for example. (Not all programs from other software companies have updated their Save dialog boxes yet.) Type a couple of words and then choose File→Save. The Save As dialog box appears (Figure 6-2).

Saving into Your Documents Folder

The first time you use the File→Save command to save a file, Windows suggests putting your newly created document in your Documents library.

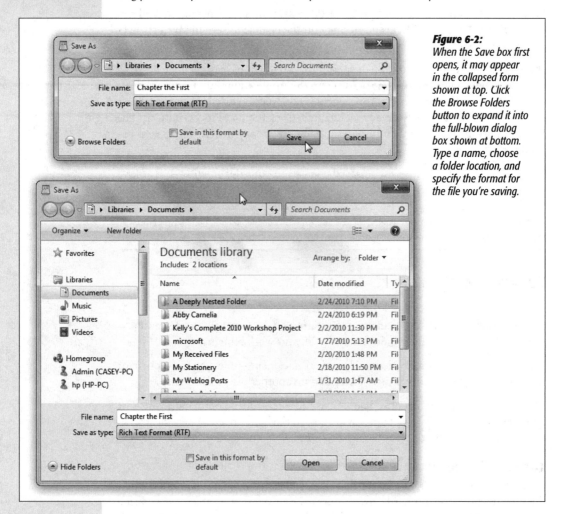

Figure 6-2:
When the Save box first opens, it may appear in the collapsed form shown at top. Click the Browse Folders button to expand it into the full-blown dialog box shown at bottom. Type a name, choose a folder location, and specify the format for the file you're saving.

For many people, this is an excellent suggestion. First, it means that your file won't accidentally fall into some deeply nested folder where you'll never see it again. Instead, it will be waiting in the Documents library, which is very difficult to lose.

Second, it's very easy to make a backup copy of your important documents if they're all in one folder. There's a third advantage, too: The Documents folder is also what Windows displays whenever you use a program's File→*Open* command. In other words, the Documents library saves you time both when *creating* a new file and when *retrieving* it.

Tip: If the Documents library becomes cluttered, feel free to make subfolders inside it to hold your various projects. You could even create a different default folder in Documents for each program. See page 81 for more on libraries.

Saving into Other Folders

Still, the now-familiar Navigation pane, address bar, and Search box also appear in the Save dialog box. (The Nav pane appears only in the Save box's expanded form; see Figure 6-2, bottom.) You always have direct access to other places where you might want to save a newly created file.

All the usual keyboard shortcuts apply: Alt+↑, for example, to open the folder that *contains* the current one. There's even a "New folder" button on the toolbar, so you can generate a new, empty folder in the current list of files and folders. Windows asks you to name it.

UP TO SPEED

Dialog Box Basics

To the delight of the powerful Computer Keyboard Lobby, you can manipulate almost every element of a Windows dialog box by pressing keys on the keyboard. If you're among those who feel that using the mouse to do something takes longer, you're in luck.

The rules for navigating a dialog box are simple: Press Tab to jump from one set of options to another, or Shift+Tab to move backward. If the dialog box has multiple *tabs,* like the one shown here, press Ctrl+Tab to "click" the next tab, or Ctrl+*Shift*+Tab to "click" the previous one.

Each time you press Tab, the PC's *focus* shifts to a different control or set of controls. Windows reveals which element has the focus by using text highlighting (if it's a text box or drop-down menu), or a dotted-line outline (if it's a button).

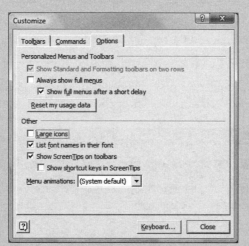

In the illustration shown here, the "Large icons" checkbox has the focus.

Once you've highlighted a button or checkbox, simply press the space bar to "click" it. If you've opened a drop-down list or a set of mutually exclusive *option buttons* (or *radio buttons*) then press the ↑ or ↓ keys. (Once you've highlighted a drop-down list's name, you can also press the F4 key to open it.)

Each dialog box also contains larger, rectangular buttons at the bottom (OK and Cancel, for example).

Efficiency fans should remember that tapping the Enter key is always the equivalent of clicking the *default* button—the one with the darkened or thickened outline (the Close button in the illustration here). And pressing Esc almost always means Cancel (or "Close this box").

In fact, if on some project you often find yourself having to navigate to some deeply buried folder, press ⊞+D to duck back to the desktop, open any Explorer window, and drag the folder to your Favorites list. From now on, you'll have quick access to it from the Save dialog box.

Tip: Many programs let you specify a different folder as the proposed location for saved (and reopened) files. In Microsoft Word, for example, you can change the default folders for the documents you create, where your clip art is stored, and so on.

Navigating the List by Keyboard

When the Save As dialog box first appears, the "File name" text box is automatically selected so you can type a name for the newly created document.

But a Windows dialog box is elaborately rigged for keyboard control. In addition to the standard Tab/space bar controls, a few special keys work only within the list of files and folders. Start by pressing Shift+Tab (to shift Windows's attention from the "File name" text box to the list of files and folders) and then do the following:

- Press various letter keys to highlight the corresponding file and folder icons. To highlight the Program Files folder, for example, you could type *PR*. (If you type too slowly, your keystrokes are interpreted as separate initiatives—highlighting first the People folder and then the Rodents folder, for example.)

- Press the Page Up or Page Down keys to scroll the list up or down. Press Home or End to highlight the top or bottom item in the list.

- Press the ↑ or ↓ keys to highlight successive icons in the list.

- When a folder (or file) is highlighted, you can open it by pressing the Enter key (or double-clicking its icon, or clicking the Open button).

GEM IN THE ROUGH

Why You See Document Names in the Save Dialog Box

In the Save dialog box, Windows displays a list of both folders *and documents* (documents that match the kind you're about to save, that is).

It's easy to understand why *folders* appear here: so you can double-click one if you want to save your document inside it. But why do *documents* appear here? After all, you can't very well save a document into another document.

Documents are listed here so you can perform one fairly obscure stunt: If you click a document's name, Windows copies its name into the "File name" text box at the bottom of the window. That's a useful shortcut if you want to *replace*

an existing document with the new one you're saving. By saving a new file with the same name as the existing one, you force Windows to overwrite it (after asking your permission, of course).

This trick also reduces the amount of typing needed to save a document to which you've assigned a different version number. For example, if you click the Thesis Draft 3.1 document in the list, Windows copies that name into the "File name" text box; doing so keeps it separate from earlier drafts. To save your new document as *Thesis Draft 3.2*, you need to change only one character (change the 1 to 2) before clicking the Save button.

The File Format Drop-Down Menu

The Save As dialog box in many programs offers a menu of file formats (usually referred to as file *types*) below or next to the "File name" text box. Use this drop-down menu when preparing a document for use by somebody whose computer doesn't have the same software.

For example, if you've typed something in Microsoft Word, you can use this menu to generate a Web page document or a Rich Text Format document that you can open with almost any standard word processor or page-layout program.

Closing Documents
All Versions

You close a document window just as you'd close any window, as described in Chapter 2: by clicking the close box (marked by an ⊠) in the upper-right corner of the window, by double-clicking the Control menu spot just to the left of the File menu, by clicking the ⊠ in its taskbar icon's preview thumbnail, or by pressing Alt+F4. If you've done any work to the document since the last time you saved it, Windows offers a "Save changes?" dialog box as a reminder.

Sometimes closing the window also exits the application, and sometimes the application remains running, even with no document windows open. And in a few *really* bizarre cases, it's possible to exit an application (like Windows Mail) while a document window (an email message) remains open on the screen, lingering and abandoned!

The Open Dialog Box
All Versions

To reopen a document you've already saved and named, you can pursue any of these avenues:

- Open your Documents library (or whichever folder contains the saved file). Double-click the file's icon.

- If you've opened the document recently, choose its name from the Start menu's jump list for that program, the taskbar's jump list, or the Start→Recent Items menu (if you've turned it on).

- If you're already in the program that created the document, choose File→Open. (Or check the bottom of the File menu, where many programs add a list of recently opened files.)

- Type the document's path and name into the Run dialog (⊞+R) or the address bar. (You can also browse for it.)

The Open dialog box looks almost identical to the Save As dialog box. Once again, you start out by perusing the contents of your Documents folder; once again, the dialog box otherwise behaves exactly like an Explorer window. For example, you can press Backspace to back *out* of a folder you've opened.

When you've finally located the file you want to open, double-click it or highlight it (from the keyboard, if you like), and then press Enter.

Most people don't encounter the Open dialog box nearly as often as the Save As dialog box. That's because Windows offers many more convenient ways to *open* a file (double-clicking its icon, choosing its name from the Start→Documents command, and so on), but only a single way to *save* a new file.

Moving Data Between Documents

All Versions

You can't paste a picture into your Web browser, and you can't paste MIDI music into your word processor. But you can put graphics into your word processor, paste movies into your database, insert text into Photoshop, and combine a surprising variety of seemingly dissimilar kinds of data. And you can transfer text from Web pages, email messages, and word processing documents to other email and word processing files; in fact, that's one of the most frequently performed tasks in all of computing.

Cut, Copy, and Paste

Most experienced PC users have learned to quickly trigger the Cut, Copy, and Paste commands from the keyboard—without even thinking.

Bear in mind that you can cut and copy highlighted material in any of three ways. First, you can use the Cut and Copy commands in the Edit menu; second, you can press Ctrl+X (for Cut) or Ctrl+C (for Copy); and third, you can right-click the highlighted material and, from the shortcut menu, choose Cut or Copy (Figure 6-3).

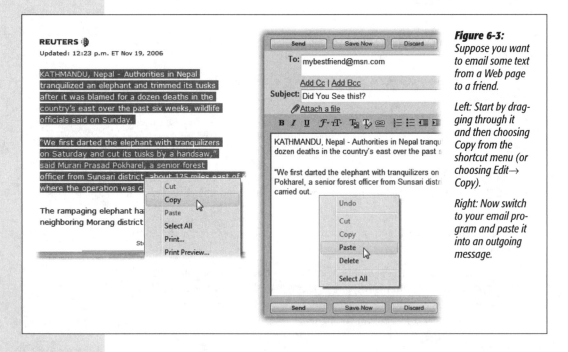

Figure 6-3:
Suppose you want to email some text from a Web page to a friend.

Left: Start by dragging through it and then choosing Copy from the shortcut menu (or choosing Edit→ Copy).

Right: Now switch to your email program and paste it into an outgoing message.

When you do so, Windows memorizes the highlighted material, stashing it on an invisible Clipboard. If you choose Copy, nothing visible happens; if you choose Cut, the highlighted material disappears from the original document.

Pasting copied or cut material, once again, is something you can do either from a menu (choose Edit→Paste), from the shortcut menu (right-click and choose Paste), or from the keyboard (press Ctrl+V).

The most recently cut or copied material remains on your Clipboard even after you paste, making it possible to paste the same blob repeatedly. Such a trick can be useful when, for example, you've designed a business card in your drawing program and want to duplicate it enough times to fill a letter-sized printout. On the other hand, whenever you next copy or cut something, whatever was previously on the Clipboard is lost forever.

Drag-and-Drop

As useful and popular as it is, the Copy/Paste routine doesn't win any awards for speed; after all, it requires four steps. In many cases, you can replace that routine with the far more direct (and enjoyable) drag-and-drop method. Figure 6-4 illustrates how it works.

Tip: To drag highlighted material offscreen, drag the cursor until it approaches the top or bottom edge of the window. The document scrolls automatically; as you approach the destination, jerk the mouse away from the edge of the window to stop the scrolling.

Figure 6-4:
You can drag highlighted text (left) to another place in the document—or a different window or program (right).

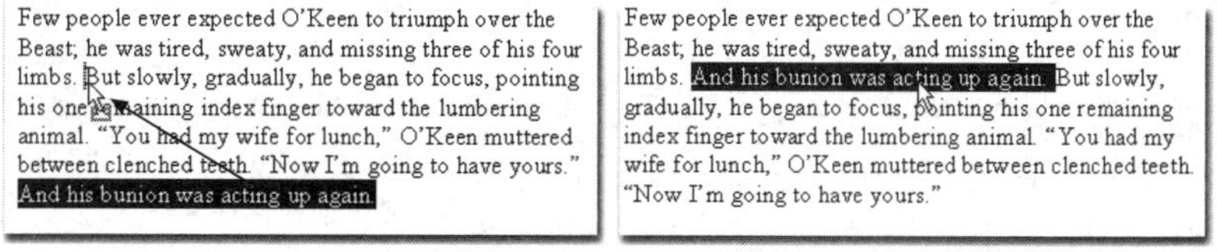

Several of the built-in Windows programs work with the drag-and-drop technique, including WordPad and Mail. Most popular commercial programs offer the drag-and-drop feature, too, including email programs and word processors, Microsoft Office programs, and so on.

Note: Scrap files—bits of text or graphics that you can drag to the desktop for reuse later—no longer exist in Windows.

As illustrated in Figure 6-4, drag-and-drop is ideal for transferring material between windows or between programs. It's especially useful when you've already copied something valuable to your Clipboard, since drag-and-drop doesn't involve (and doesn't erase) the Clipboard.

Its most popular use, however, is rearranging the text in a single document. In, say, Word or WordPad, you can rearrange entire sections, paragraphs, sentences, or even individual letters, just by dragging them—a terrific editing technique.

Tip: Using drag-and-drop to move highlighted text within a document also deletes the text from its original location. By pressing Ctrl as you drag, however, you make a *copy* of the highlighted text.

Export/Import

When it comes to transferring large chunks of information from one program to another—especially address books, spreadsheet cells, and database records—none of the data-transfer methods described so far in this chapter does the trick. For such purposes, use the Export and Import commands found in the File menu of almost every database, spreadsheet, email, and address-book program.

These Export/Import commands aren't part of Windows, so the manuals or help screens of the applications in question should be your source for instructions. For now, however, the power and convenience of this feature are worth noting. Because of these commands, your four years' worth of collected names and addresses in, say, an old address-book program can find its way into a newer program, such as Mozilla Thunderbird, in a matter of minutes.

FREQUENTLY ASKED QUESTION

When Formatting Is Lost

How come pasted text doesn't always look the same as what I copied?

When you copy text from Internet Explorer, for example, and then paste it into another program, such as Word, you may be alarmed to note that the formatting of that text (bold, italic, font size, font color, and so on) doesn't reappear intact. In fact, the pasted material may not even inherit the current font settings in the word processor. There could be several reasons for this problem.

First, not every program *offers* text formatting—Notepad among them. And the Copy command in some programs (such as Web browsers) doesn't pick up the formatting along with the text. So when you copy something from Internet Explorer and paste it into Word or WordPad, you may get plain, unformatted text. (There is some good news along these lines, however. Word maintains formatting pasted from the latest Internet Explorer.)

Finally, a note on *text wrapping.* Thanks to limitations built into the architecture of the Internet, email messages aren't like word processor documents. The text doesn't flow continuously from one line of a paragraph to the next, reflowing as you adjust the window size. Instead, email programs insert a press of the Enter key at the end of each line *within* a paragraph.

Most of the time, you don't even notice that your messages consist of dozens of one-line "paragraphs." When you see them in the email program, you can't tell the difference. But if you paste an email message into a word processor, the difference becomes painfully apparent—especially if you then attempt to adjust the margins.

To fix the text, delete the invisible carriage return at the end of each line. (Veteran PC users sometimes use the word processor's search-and-replace function for this purpose.) Or, if you just need a quick look, reduce the point size (or widen the margin) until the text no longer breaks oddly.

Speech Recognition

All Versions

For years, there's been quite a gulf between the promise of computer speech recognition (as seen on *Star Trek*) and the reality (as seen just about everywhere else). You say "oxymoron"; it types "ax a moron." (Which is often just what you feel like doing, frankly.)

Microsoft has had a speech-recognition department for years. But until recently, it never got the funding and corporate backing it needed to do a really bang-up job.

The speech recognition in Windows 7, however, is another story. It can't match the accuracy of its chief rival, Dragon NaturallySpeaking, but you might be amazed to discover how elegant its design is now, and how useful it can be to anyone who can't, or doesn't like to, type.

In short, Speech Recognition lets you not only *control* your PC by voice—open programs, click buttons, click Web links, and so on—but also *dictate text* a heck of a lot faster than you can type.

To make this all work, you need a PC with a microphone. The Windows Speech Recognition program can handle just about any kind of mike, even the one built into your laptop's case. But a regular old headset mike—"anything that costs over $20 or so," says Microsoft—will give you the best accuracy.

Take the Tutorial

The easiest way to fire up Speech Recognition for the first time is to open the Start menu and then type *spee*. Using the mouse takes *way* too much time (Start→All Programs→Accessories→Ease of Access→Windows Speech Recognition).

In any case, the first time you open Speech Recognition, you arrive at a very slick, very impressive full-screen tutorial/introduction, featuring a 20-something model in, judging by the gauzy whiteness, what appears to be heaven.

Click your way through the screens. Along the way, you're asked to do the following:

- Specify what kind of microphone you have. Headset, desktop, array, or built-in?

- Read a sample sentence, about how much Peter loves speech recognition, so your PC can gauge the microphone's volume.

- Give permission to Windows to study your documents and email collection. Needless to say, there's no human rooting through your stuff, and none of what Speech Recognition finds is reported back to Microsoft. But granting this permission is a great way to improve your ultimate accuracy, since the kinds of vocabulary and turns of phrase you actually use in your day-to-day work will be built right into Speech Recognition's understanding of your voice.

- Print the reference card. This card is critical when you're first learning how to operate Windows by voice. Truth is, however, you don't really need to print it. The same information appears in this chapter, and you can always call the reference card up on the screen by saying into your microphone, "What can I say?"

- Practice. The tutorial is excellent; it'll take you about half an hour to complete. It teaches you how to dictate and how to operate buttons, menus, windows, programs, and so on.

But there's another, better reason to try the tutorial: At the outset, Windows is just *simulating* its responses to what you say. But behind the scenes, it's actually studying your real utterances, learning about your voice, and shaping your voice profile. This, in other words, is the "voice training" session you ordinarily have to perform with commercial dictation programs.

Now you're ready to roll. Operating Windows by voice entails knowing three sets of commands:

- Controlling Speech Recognition itself.
- Controlling Windows and its programs.

Dictating.

The following sections cover these techniques one at a time.

Controlling Windows Speech Recognition

Slip on your headset, open Windows Speech Recognition, and have a gander at these all-important spoken commands:

- **"Start listening"/"Stop listening."** These commands tell your PC to start and stop listening to you. That's important, because you don't want it to interpret everything you say. It would not be so great if it tried to act when you said to your roommate, "Hey, Chris, close the window."

So say, "Start listening" to turn on your mike—you see the microphone button on the Speech palette (Figure 6-5) darken. Say "Stop listening" when you have to take a phone call.

Tip: Once you've opened the Speech Recognition program, you can hit a keystroke to turn listening on and off instead. That key combo is Ctrl+⊞. Get it? "Control Windows"?

- **"What can I say?"** This one's incredibly important. If you can't figure out how to make Windows do something, look it up by saying this. You get the Speech Recognition page of the Windows Help system, complete with a collapsible list of the things you can say.

- **"Show Speech Options."** This command opens the shortcut menu for the Speech palette, as shown in Figure 6-5. From this menu, you can leap into further training, open the "What can I say?" card, go to the Speech Recognition Web site, and so on.

- **"Hide Speech Recognition"/"Show Speech Recognition"** hides or shows the Speech palette itself when screen real estate is at a premium.

Controlling Windows and Its Programs

The beauty of controlling Windows by voice is that you don't have to remember what to say; you just say whatever you would click with the mouse.

For example, to open the little Calculator program using the mouse, you'd click the Start button (to open the Start menu), then All Programs, then Accessories, and finally Calculator. To do the same thing using speech recognition, you just *say* all that: "Start…All Programs…Accessories…Calculator." And presto—the Calculator appears.

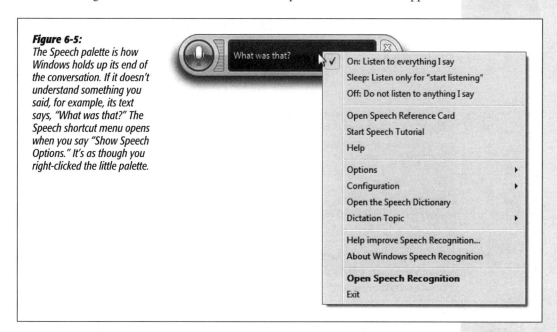

Figure 6-5:
The Speech palette is how Windows holds up its end of the conversation. If it doesn't understand something you said, for example, its text says, "What was that?" The Speech shortcut menu opens when you say "Show Speech Options." It's as though you right-clicked the little palette.

Actually, that's a bad example; you can open *any* program just by saying "Start Calculator" (or whatever its name is). But you get the idea.

Here's the cheat sheet for manipulating programs. In this list, any word in *italics* is meant as an example (and other examples that work just as well are in parentheses):

- Start *Calculator* (Word, Excel, Internet Explorer…). Opens the program you named, without your having to touch the mouse. Super convenient.

- Switch to *Word* (Excel, Internet Explorer…). Switches to the program you named.

- *File. Open.* You operate menus by saying whatever you would have clicked with the mouse. For example, say "Edit" to open the Edit menu, then "Select All" to choose that command, and so on.

- *Print* (Cancel, Desktop…). You can also click any button (or any tab name in a dialog box) by saying its name.

- *Contact us* (Archives, Home page…). You can also click any link on a Web page just by saying its name.

- Double-click *Recycle Bin*. You can tell Windows to "double-click" or "right-click" anything you see.

- Go to *Subject* (Address, Body…). In an email message, Web browser, or dialog box, "Go to" puts the insertion point into the text box you name. "Address," for example, means the address bar.

- *Close* that. Closes the frontmost window. Also "Minimize that," "Maximize that," "Restore that."

- Scroll *up* (down, left, right). Scrolls the window. You can say "up," "down," "left," or "right," and you can also append any number from one to 20 to indicate how many lines: "Scroll down 10."

- Press *F* (Shift-F, capital B, down arrow, X three times…). Makes Windows press the key you named.

Tip: You don't have to say "press" before certain critical keys: Delete, Home, End, Space, Tab, Enter, Backspace. Just say the key's name: "Tab."

Show numbers

It's great to know you can click any button or tab by saying its name. But what if you don't *know* its name? What if it's some cryptic little icon on a toolbar? You can't exactly say, "Click the little thing that looks like a guy putting his head between two rollers."

For this purpose, Microsoft has created a clever command called "Show numbers." When you say that, the program overlays *every clickable thing* with superimposed colorful numbers; see Figure 6-6.

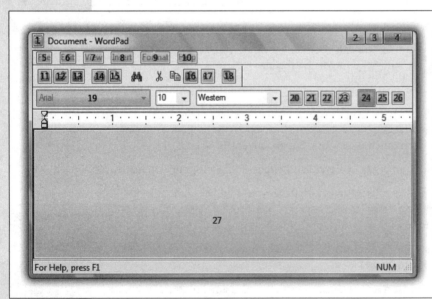

Figure 6-6:
When you say a number, that number turns green and changes into an OK logo—your clue that you must now say "OK" to confirm the selection. (You can run these utterances together without pausing—for example, "Three OK.") Not all programs respond to the "Show numbers" command, alas.

The numbers appear automatically if there's more than one button of the same name on the screen, too—several Settings buttons in a dialog box, for example. Say, "One OK."

Tip: This trick also works great on Web pages. Say "Show numbers" to see a number label superimposed on every clickable element of the page.

Controlling Dictation

The real Holy Grail for speech recognition, of course, is *dictation*—you speak, and Windows transcribes your words, typing them into any document. (This feature is especially important on Tablet PCs that don't have keyboards.)

Windows's dictation accuracy isn't as good as, say, Dragon NaturallySpeaking's. But it's a close second, it's free, and it's a lot of fun.

It's also very easy. You just talk—at regular speed, into any program where you can type. The only real difference is that you have to *say* the punctuation. You know: "Dear Mom (comma, new line), How are things going (question mark)? Can't believe I'll be home for Thanksgiving in only 24 more weeks (exclamation mark)!"

GEM IN THE ROUGH

Mousegrid

The voice commands described in this section are all well and good when it comes to clicking onscreen objects. But what about *dragging* them?

When you say "Mousegrid," Speech Recognition superimposes an enormous 3 x 3 grid on your screen, its squares numbered 1 through 9.

Say "Five" and a new, much smaller 3 x 3 grid, also numbered, appears in the space previously occupied by the five square. You can keep shrinking the grid in this way until you've pinpointed a precise spot on the screen.

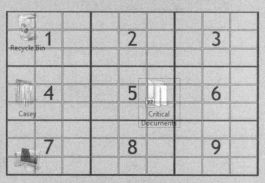

Dragging something—say, an icon across the desktop—is a two-step process.

First, use Mousegrid to home in on the exact spot on the screen where the icon lies; on your last homing-in, say, "Four mark." (In this example, the icon you want lies within the four square. "Mark" means "This is what I'm going to want to drag.")

When you say "mark," the Mousegrid springs back to the full-screen size; now you're supposed to home in on the *destination* point for your drag. Repeat the grid-shrinking exercise—but in the last step say, "Seven click."

Watch in amazement as Windows magically grabs the icon at the "mark" position and drags it to the "click" position.

You can use Mousegrid as a last resort for *any* kind of click or drag when the other techniques (like saying button or menu names, or saying, "Show numbers") don't quite cut it.

Correcting errors

Sooner or later—probably sooner—Speech Recognition is going to misunderstand you and type out the wrong thing. It's very important that you correct such glitches—for two reasons. First, you don't want your boss/family/colleagues to think you're incoherent. Second, each time you make a correction, Windows *learns*. It won't make that mistake again. Over time, over hundreds of corrections, Speech Recognition gets more and more accurate.

Suppose, then, that you said, "I enjoyed the ceremony," and Speech Recognition typed out, "I enjoyed this era money." Here's how you'd proceed:

1. Say, "Correct *this era money.*"

   Instantly, the Alternates panel pops up (Figure 6-7).

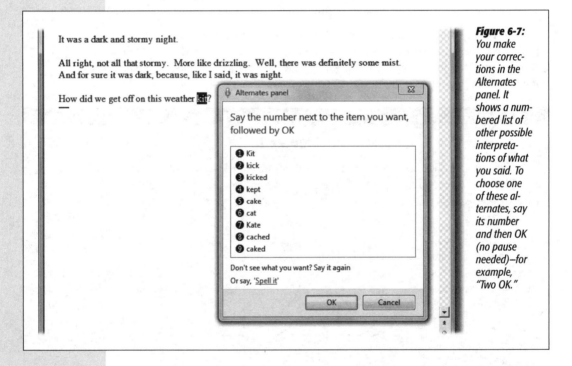

Figure 6-7:
You make your corrections in the Alternates panel. It shows a numbered list of other possible interpretations of what you said. To choose one of these alternates, say its number and then OK (no pause needed)—for example, "Two OK."

2. If the correct transcription is among the choices in the list, say its number and then "OK."

   As noted in Figure 6-7, you don't have to pause before "OK."

3. If the correct transcription *doesn't* appear in the list, then speak the correct text again.

   In this example, you'd say, "the ceremony." Almost always, the version you wanted now appears in the list. Say its number and then "OK."

4. **If the correct transcription** *still* **doesn't appear in the list, say "Spell it."**

You arrive at the Spelling panel; see Figure 6-8.

When you finally exit the Alternates panel, Speech Recognition replaces the corrected text *and* learns from its mistake.

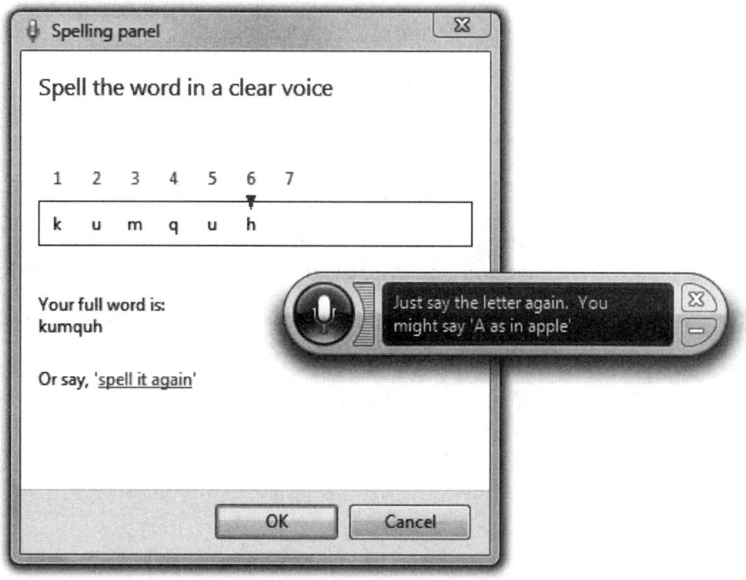

Figure 6-8:
Just spell out the word you really wanted: "F-I-S-H," for example. For greater clarity, you can also use the "pilot's alphabet": Alpha, Bravo, Charlie, Delta, and so on—or even "A as in alligator" (any word you like). If it mishears a letter you've spoken, say the number over it ("three") and then repronounce the letter. Say "OK" once you've gotten the word right.

More commands

Here are the other things you can say when you're dictating text. The first few are extremely important to learn.

- Select *next* (previous) *two* (10, 14, 20…) *words* (sentences, paragraphs). Highlights whatever you just specified—for example, "Select previous five sentences."

    At this point, you're ready to copy, change the font or style, say "Cap that" to capitalize the first words—or just redictate to replace what you wrote.

Tip: If the phrase you want to highlight is long, you can say, "Select *My country* through *land of liberty.*" Windows highlights all of the text *from* the first phrase *through and including* the second one.

- Correct *ax a moron.* Highlights the transcribed phrase and opens the Alternates panel, as described above. (You can say a whole phrase or just one word.)

- Undo. Undoes the last action.

- Scratch that. Deletes the last thing you dictated. ("Delete that" works, too.)

- Delete *your stupid parents.* Instantly deletes the text you identified.

Tip: If you use commands like *Delete, Select, Capitalize,* or *Add hyphens to* on a word that occurs *more than once* in the open window, Speech Recognition doesn't try to guess. It puts colorful numbered squares on every occurrence of that word. Say, "One OK" (or whatever the number is) to tell it *which* occurrence you meant.

- Go to *little.* Puts the insertion point right before the word "little."

- Go after *lamb.* Puts the insertion point right after the word "lamb."

- Go to the *start* (end) of the *sentence* (paragraph, document). Puts the insertion point where you said.

- Caps. Capitalizes the next word you dictate (no pause is necessary). Saying "All caps" puts the next word ENTIRELY in caps.

- Ready no space Boost. Types ReadyBoost—no space.

- He typed the word literal *comma.* The command "literal" tells Speech Recognition to type out the word that follows it ("comma"), rather than transcribing it as a symbol.

- Add hyphen to *3D.* Puts a hyphen in the word ("3-D").

- Start typing I, P, C, O, N, F, I, G; stop typing. When you say "Start typing" (and then pause), you enter Typing mode. Now you can spell out anything, letter by letter, in any program on earth. It's a handy way to dictate into programs that don't take dictation well, like PowerPoint and Excel.

Speech Recognition tips

There are zillions of secrets, tips, and tricks lurking in Speech Recognition—but here are a few of the most useful:

- You can teach Speech Recognition new words—unusual last names, oddball terminology—by adding them directly to its dictionary. Say "Show speech options" to open the shortcut menu, and then click (or say) "Open the Speech Dictionary."

GEM IN THE ROUGH

Text to Speech

The big-ticket item, for sure, is that speech-to-text feature. But Windows can also convert typed text *back* to speech, using a set of voices of its very own.

To hear them, open the Start menu. Start typing *text to* until you see "Change text to speech settings" in the results list; click it. Click Preview Voice to hear the astonishing realism of Microsoft Anna, the primary voice of Windows. You can even control her speaking rate using the "Voice speed" slider.

So when can you hear Microsoft Anna do her stuff? Primarily in Narrator (page 290). If you master the Narrator keyboard shortcuts, Anna can read back *whatever you want,* like stuff you've written or articles you find on the Web. Why not let her read the morning news to you while you're getting breakfast ready each day?

You're offered the chance to add words, change existing words, or stop certain words from being transcribed.

- When you want to spell out a word, say, "Spell it," and then launch right into the spelling: "F, R, E, A, K, A, Z, O, I, D." You don't have to pause between letters or commands.

- In the Spelling window, say the digit over the wrong letter, and then say "A," or "Alpha," or "A as in alligator" (or any word that starts with that letter).

- Beginning any utterance with "How do I" opens up Windows Help; the next part of your sentence goes into the Search box.

- "Computer" forces the interpretation of your next utterance as a command; "Insert" forces it to be transcribed.

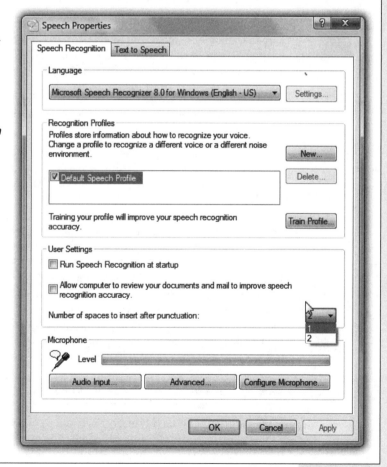

Figure 6-9:
In this dialog box, you can find the "Number of spaces to insert after punctuation" (meaning "periods") pop-up menu near the bottom. The other controls here let you create new voice files ("speech profiles")—one for your quiet home office, for example, and another for use in a busy, humming office.

- Out of the box, Speech Recognition puts two spaces after every period—a very 1980s thing to do. Nowadays, that kind of gap looks a little amateurish. Fortunately, you can tell Speech Recognition to use only one space.

Making this change requires you to visit the little-known Advanced Speech Options dialog box. Open the Start menu. Start typing *speech* until you see "Speech Recognition" in the results list; click it. In the task pane at left, click "Advanced speech options" (Figure 6-9).

Gadgets
All Versions

As you know, the essence of using Windows is running *programs,* which often produce *documents.* In Windows 7, however, there's a third category: a set of weird hybrid entities that Microsoft calls *gadgets.*

They debuted in Windows Vista, as part of a new entity called the Sidebar (which bore a startling resemblance to Mac OS X's Dashboard). They appeared, all at once, floating in front of your other windows, at the right side of the screen, when you first fired up Vista, or whenever you pressed ⊞+space bar.

In Windows 7, though, gadgets have been unleashed. Now they don't need no stinkin' Sidebar; they can stand tall on their own. You can park them anywhere on the screen, where they just float.

To make them appear, right-click the desktop; from the shortcut menu, choose Gadgets. You've just opened the Gadget Gallery, a semi-transparent catalog of all your gadgets, even the ones that aren't currently on the screen (Figure 6-10). Open one by double-clicking its icon.

Tip: You may have to scroll the Gadget Gallery to see all the gadgets, by clicking the Page arrows at the top left of the window. When you're finished opening new gadgets, close the Gadget Gallery by clicking its ⊠ button.

What are these weird hybrid entities, anyway? They're not really programs, because they don't create documents or have listings in the All Programs menu. They're certainly not documents, because you can't name or save them. What they *most* resemble, actually, are little Web pages. They're meant to display information, much of it from the Internet, and they're written using Web programming languages like DHTML, JavaScript, VBScript, and XML.

Note: They're generally distributed as .zip files that, when decompressed, have the filename extension *.gadget.*

Many gadgets require an Internet connection, preferably an always-on connection like a cable modem. If your PC loses its connection, the gadget displays the information from the last time it went online, and a little readout tells you exactly when that was.

Gadget Tip-o-Rama

The starter gadgets include a calculator, current weather reporter, stock ticker, clock, and so on. Mastering the basics won't take you long at all:

- To move a gadget, drag it around the screen. It doesn't have to stay where it first appeared.

Tip: If the gadget doesn't seem to want to move when you drag it, you're probably grabbing it by a clickable portion. Try to find a purely graphical spot—the spiral binding of the calendar, for example. Or use the grip strip (⋮⋮⋮) that appears off to the right when you point to it.

Figure 6-10:
The Gadgets gallery offers a selection of floating miniprograms that convey or convert all kinds of useful information. Click one, then click "Show details" to read about its function. Double-click one to make it appear on the right side of your screen, or just drag one out of the gallery to park it somewhere specific.

- To close a gadget, point to it. The square ⊠ button appears at the gadget's top-left corner; click it. (You can also right-click a gadget and choose Close Gadget from its shortcut menu.)

- To get rid of a gadget for good, right-click it; from the shortcut menu, choose Uninstall.

- Hide all gadgets by right-clicking a blank spot on the desktop. From the shortcut menu, choose View→"Show desktop gadgets" so that the checkmark disappears.

This technique just hides the gadgets. Any gadget you've moved onto your screen is still technically running, using memory. (To bring them back, use the same command again or just right-click the desktop and choose Gadgets.)

- Bring hidden gadgets to the front by pressing ⊞+G. (Do this when, for example, another window is covering them up.)

- Open more than one copy of the same gadget. Just double-click its icon more than once in the Gadget Gallery. You wind up with multiple copies of it on your screen: three clocks, two weather trackers, or whatever. That's a useful trick when, for example, you want to track the time or weather in more than one city, or when you maintain two different stock portfolios.

- Fiddle with a gadget's settings. If you point to a gadget without clicking, three or four tiny icons appear to its right. One is the ✕ (Close button), which you've already met. The ✎ button opens the gadget's Settings dialog box, where, for example, you can specify which stocks you want to track, or which town's weather you want to see. (As noted above, the ⋮⋮ icon is a "grip strip" that lets you drag the gadget to a new spot on the screen. Some icons, like Weather, have a ▣ icon, too, which means "make this gadget bigger.") See Figure 6-11.

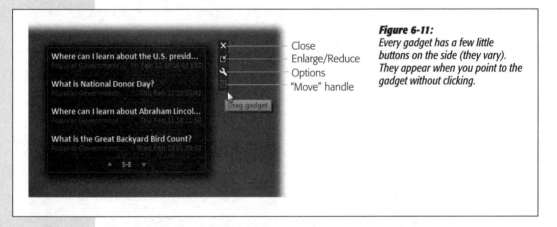

Figure 6-11:
Every gadget has a few little buttons on the side (they vary). They appear when you point to the gadget without clicking.

- "Tab" through the gadgets, highlighting one after another, by repeatedly pressing ⊞+G. When a certain gadget is highlighted, you can manipulate it. Close it, for example, by pressing Alt+F4.

- Search for a gadget in your Gallery window using the "Search gadgets" box in the top right. It's a real sanity saver for the hard-core gadget collector. But if you click the ▼ to its right, the pop-up menu lets you restrict your search to only "Recently installed gadgets."

Gadget Catalog

Here's a rundown of the standard gadgets that come preinstalled in Windows. True, they look awfully simple, but some of them harbor a few secrets.

Tip: If you right-click an individual gadget, the shortcut menu offers, among other commands, an Opacity control. That is, you can make any individual gadget more or less see-through—something that makes more sense for, say, the clock than the photo slideshow.

Calendar

Sure, you can always find out today's date by checking the right end of your taskbar. And this gadget isn't much of a calendar. It doesn't show your appointments, and it doesn't hook into Windows Calendar.

But it's much nicer looking than the taskbar one. And besides, you can use this calendar to look ahead or back. Here's the scheme of things you can click:

- Double-click today's orange "page" to open the month-view calendar.

- Navigate to a different month by clicking the ◄ or ► buttons. Change the year by clicking the current year digits at the top of the month view.

- Double-click a date square to see its "page," identifying its day and date. (Not that you learn much by doing this—clicking Wednesday, June 22, makes the big date squares read "Wednesday, June 22." Ooooh!)

- Click the red peeking corner to return to the month-view calendar.

- Click 🔳 icon to see both the month-view calendar and the big today's-date display simultaneously.

FREQUENTLY ASKED QUESTION

The Disappearing Notes, Stocks, or Weather

Hey! I filled my Notes gadget with grocery lists and Web addresses, and now they're gone!

Hey! I set up my home city in the Weather gadget, and now it's showing Redmond, Washington!

Hey! I painstakingly typed in all my stocks, and now it's forgotten them all!

Welcome to gadget hell, buddy.

Remember, gadgets are not actually programs. They don't, therefore, have their own preference files stashed away on the hard drive.

And so—here's the bad news—anytime you close a gadget, you *lose all the data you had typed into it.* When you reopen Weather, it always shows Redmond, Washington (Microsoft's hometown); when you reopen Stocks, it always shows the NASDAQ and S&P indexes; when you reopen Notes, the sticky notes are always empty; and so on.

And so, a word to the wise: Don't click that ⊠ button unless you really mean it!

Clock

Sure, this clock shows the current time, but your taskbar does that. The neat part is that you can open up several of these clocks—double-click Clock in the Gadget Gallery repeatedly—and set each one up to show the time in a different city. The result looks like the row of clocks in a hotel lobby, making you look Swiss and precise.

- Point to the analog clock without clicking to see a digital rendition of the current time ("5:34 p.m.").

- Click the ✎ button for a choice of eight good-looking analog clock faces. The Options dialog box also lets you choose each clock's time zone, add a sweep-second hand, and name this clock—"New York" or "London," for example. This name appears on the clock's face.

CPU Meter

A power user's dream—now you can watch your PC wheeze and gasp under its load in real time, with statistical accuracy.

CPU Meter has two gauges. The left-side one shows how hard you're driving your CPU (central processing unit—that is, your Intel or AMD chip), expressed as a percentage of its capacity. The smaller dial shows how much of your computer's RAM (memory) you're using at the moment. Watch the needles rise and fall as you open and close your programs! (Watch them go nuts when you open Microsoft Office!)

Currency

This one's for you, world travelers (or global investors). This little gadget can convert dollars to euros, or pounds to francs, or whatever to whatever.

From the upper pop-up menu, choose the currency type you want to convert *from:* U.S. Dollar, Norwegian Krone, or whatever. Into the text box, type how *many* of those you want to convert.

Use the lower pop-up menu to specify which units you want to convert *to.*

You don't have to click anything or press any key; the conversion is performed for you instantly and automatically as you type. (Never let it be said that technology isn't marching forward.)

Some of Currency's features are available only when you click this gadget's ▣ button on the right side. For example:

- See more details about your currency's current situation by clicking the little ~ button to the left of each pop-up menu. (This button is visible only in the gadget's enlarged state.) Your Web browser opens and takes you to the MSN Money Web site, already opened to a details page about that currency and its history.

- Convert more currencies at once by clicking the **+** button (lower-right of the gadget). That is, you can see $20 represented as dinars, baht, and shekels simultaneously.

- Find out where the data comes from by clicking the words Data Providers.

Note: This gadget actually does its homework. It goes online to download up-to-the-minute currency rates to ensure that the conversion is accurate.

Feed Headlines

An *RSS feed* is a newfangled Internet feature, in which the headlines from various Web sites are sent to you automatically (see page 414 for details). Internet Explorer can accept RSS feeds, of course—but you don't have to fire it up every time you want to know the news of the world. Just take a look at this little gadget.

Actually, don't look yet; out of the box, this gadget doesn't show much at all. But if you click its "View headlines" link, you get to see 100 recent headlines, mostly from Microsoft and U.S. government news sources.

- Substitute your own feeds. This gadget is much more attractive when you fill it with your own favorite feeds—*The New York Times*, sports-score sites, favorite online columnists, and so on. Fortunately, the gadget inherits its list of feeds from those you've subscribed to in Internet Explorer, as described on page 417.

  Once you've subscribed to a feed there, click this gadget's ✎ button. Use the "Display this feed" list to choose the feed you want displayed.

Tip: You can choose only *one* item from the "Display this feed" pop-up menu. Fortunately, that doesn't mean only one feed. If you take the effort to create a *folder* for your favorite feeds when storing them in Internet Explorer, you can choose that *folder's* name in this gadget, thereby getting a rotating list of *multiple* favorite feeds.

- Scroll the list by clicking the ▲ or ▼ buttons.
- See more of each headline by clicking the ▣ button on the right side.

Picture Puzzle

For generations, Microsoft Windows fans had their Solitaire game—and only occasionally looked over the backyard fence to see the Tile Game that their Macintosh friends were playing. The idea, of course, is to click the tiles of the puzzle, using logic to rearrange them back into the original sequence, so that they eventually slide together into the put-together photograph.

- Change the photo by clicking the ✎ button.
- Pause the timer (upper-left corner) by clicking the tiny clock.
- See the finished photo, so you know what the goal is, by holding the cursor down on the little ? button.
- Give up by clicking the double-arrow button in the upper-right corner of the puzzle window. (The same button rescrambles the puzzle.)

Slide Show

So you've got a digital camera and a hard drive crammed with JPEGs. What are you gonna do with 'em all?

Slide Show offers an ingenious way to savor your handiwork all day long. It's just what it says: a small slideshow that presents one photo at a time for a few seconds each. Think of it as an electronic version of the little spouse 'n' kids photo that cubicle dwellers prop up on their desks—except that the picture changes every 15 seconds.

The buttons in the tiny translucent control bar at the bottom of the picture correspond to Previous Photo, Pause/Resume, Next Photo, and View (which opens up the picture—much larger now—in Windows Photo Gallery).

- Substitute your own photos. When you first install Windows, this gadget presents Microsoft's favorite nature photos. But where's the fun in that? Once you're sick of them, click the ✎ button. In the dialog box, use the Folder controls to choose a folder full of your own pictures.

- Set up the show timing. Fifteen seconds is an awfully long time to stare at one photo, of course. Then again, if the pix change too often, they'll be distracting, and you won't get any work done. Nonetheless, the Options dialog box lets you keep each slide on the screen for as little as 5 seconds or as long as 5 minutes.

  The Options box also lets you create a crossfade effect as one slide morphs into the next. And the Shuffle checkbox, of course, makes Slide Show present your pix in a random order, rather than their alphabetical order in the folder.

Tip: If you click this gadget's ▣ icon on the right side, you get to see your photos at a larger, more pleasant size.

Weather

This gadget shows a handy current-conditions display for your city (or any other city) and, at your option, even offers a three-day forecast.

Before you get started, the most important step is to click the ✎ button. In the Options dialog box, you see where you can specify your city and state or Zip code. Type it in and press Enter; the gadget goes online to retrieve the latest *Weather.com* info. You can also specify whether you prefer degrees Celsius or degrees Fahrenheit. Click OK.

Now the front of the gadget displays the name of your town, general conditions, and current temperature.

- See more details by clicking the ▣ button. Now you see today's predicted high and low, the sky situation (like "Clear"), the current temperature, and the three-day forecast.

- See the complete weather report by clicking the underlined location (such as "Central Park, NY") to open your Web browser and call up the full-blown *Weather.com* page for that location.

More Gadgets

The gadgets that come with Windows are meant to be only examples—a starter collection. The real beauty of gadgets is that people can write new ones for the whole world to enjoy: gadgets that show your local movie listings, regional gas prices, your email Inbox, upcoming Outlook appointments, and so on (Figure 6-12).

Figure 6-12:
Not all good things come from Microsoft. Here's a handful of neat gadgets written by other people.

To see the current list of goodies that have been vetted by Microsoft, click "Get more gadgets online" in the Gadget Gallery described above. That takes you to the Microsoft Gadgets Gallery downloads page. (Alternatively, go straight to *http://gallery.microsoft.com.*)

You should have no problem finding gadgets that tell you local traffic conditions, let you know if your flight will be on time, help you track FedEx packages, provide a word (or joke, or comic strip) of the day, and so on.

Installing a gadget

Downloading and installing a gadget isn't hard, but there are a number of warnings and permission boxes along the way. Fortunately, once it's over, the new gadget should be proudly floating on your screen.

Uninstalling a gadget

If you decide you don't want a gadget, you can just close it (right-click it; from the shortcut menu, choose "Close gadget"). That leaves it on your PC, but dormant.

If, on the other hand, you really doubt you'll ever need it again, open your Gadget Gallery. Right-click the offending gadget; from the shortcut menu, choose Uninstall. Now it's really, truly gone.

Filename Extensions and File Associations
All Versions

Every operating system needs a mechanism to associate documents with the applications that created them. When you double-click a Microsoft Word document icon, for example, Word launches and opens the document.

In Windows, every document comes complete with a normally invisible *filename extension* (or just *file extension*)—a period followed by a suffix that's usually three letters long.

Here are some common examples:

When you double-click this icon...	...this program opens it.
Fishing trip.docx	Microsoft Word
Quarterly results.xlsx	Microsoft Excel
Home page.htm	Internet Explorer
Agenda.wpd	Corel WordPerfect
A home movie.avi	Windows Media Player
Sudoku.gadget	Sidebar gadget
Animation.dir	Macromedia Director

Tip: For an exhaustive list of every file extension on the planet, visit *www.whatis.com*; click the link for "Every file extension in the world."

Behind the scenes, Windows maintains a massive table that lists every extension and the program that "owns" it. More on this in a moment.

Displaying Filename Extensions

It's possible to live a long and happy life without knowing much about these extensions. Because file extensions don't feel very user-friendly, Microsoft designed Windows to *hide* the suffixes on most icons (Figure 6-13). If you're new to Windows, you may never have even seen them.

Some people appreciate the way Windows hides the extensions, because the screen becomes less cluttered and less technical-looking. Others make a good argument for the Windows 3.1 days, when every icon appeared with its suffix.

Figure 6-13:
As a rule, Windows shows filename extensions only on files whose extensions it doesn't recognize. The JPEG graphics at left, for example, don't show their suffixes.

Right: You can ask Windows to display all extensions, all the time.

For example, in a single Explorer window, suppose one day you discover that three icons all seem to have exactly the same name: PieThrower. Only by making filename extensions appear would you discover the answer to the mystery: that one of them is called PieThrower.ini, another is an Internet-based software updater called PieThrower.upd, and the third is the actual PieThrower program, PieThrower.exe.

If you'd rather have Windows reveal the file suffixes on *all* icons, open an Explorer window. Choose Organize→"Folder and search options." In the Folder Options dialog box, click the View tab. Turn off "Hide extensions for known file types," and then click OK.

Now the filename extensions for all icons appear (Figure 6-13).

Hooking Up an Unknown File Type

Every now and then, you might try to open a mystery icon—one whose extension is missing, or whose extension Windows doesn't recognize. Maybe you've been sent some weirdo document created by a beekeeper or a banjo transcriber using a program you don't have, or maybe you're opening a document belonging to an old DOS program that doesn't know about the Windows file-association feature. What will happen when you double-click that file?

Windows *asks* you.

In the dialog box shown in Figure 6-14, Windows offers you two buttons:

• **Use the Web service to find the appropriate program.** In other words, Windows will take your PC onto the Internet and look up the mystery file extension on the Microsoft Web site.

• **Select the program from a list of installed programs.** Windows displays a dialog box that looks like the one at bottom in Figure 6-14. Click the name of the program you want, and then turn on "Always use the selected program to open this kind of file," if you like.

Hooking Up a File Extension to a Different Program

Windows comes with several programs that can open text files with the extension *.txt*—Notepad and WordPad, for example. *There are also at least two* Windows apps (Paint and Photo Gallery) that can open picture files with the extension *.jpg*. So how does it decide *which* program to open when you double-click a .txt or .jpg file?

Easy—it refers to its internal database of preferred *default programs* for various file types. But at any time, you can reassign a particular file type (file extension) to a different application. If you've just bought Photoshop, for example, you might want it to open up your JPEG files, rather than Photo Gallery.

This sort of surgery has always confused beginners. Yet it was important for Microsoft to provide an easy way of reprogramming documents' mother programs; almost everyone ran into programs like RealPlayer that, once installed, "stole" every file association they could. The masses needed a simple way to switch documents back to their preferred programs.

So in Vista (and Windows 7), Microsoft ripped up its File Types dialog boxes and started from scratch. Whether or not the *three* new file-association mechanisms are actually superior to the *one* old one from XP—well, you be the judge.

Tip: The File Types tab of the Folder Options dialog box, once the headquarters of document-to-program relationships, no longer exists in Windows 7.

Method 1: Start with the document

Often, you'll discover a misaligned file-type association the hard way. You double-click a document and the wrong program opens it.

For that reason, Microsoft has added a new way of reprogramming a document—one that starts right in Explorer, with the document itself.

Right-click the icon of the file that needs a new parent program. From the shortcut menu, choose Open With.

If you're just trying to open this document into the new program *this once,* you may be able to choose the new program's name from the Open With submenu (Figure 6-15, top). Windows doesn't always offer this submenu, however.

If you choose Choose Default Program from the submenu, or if there's no submenu at all, then the new Open With dialog box appears, as shown in Figure 6-15 (bottom). It's supposed to list every program on your machine that's capable of opening the document.

And now, a critical decision: Are you trying to make *this document only* open in a different program? Or *all documents of this type?*

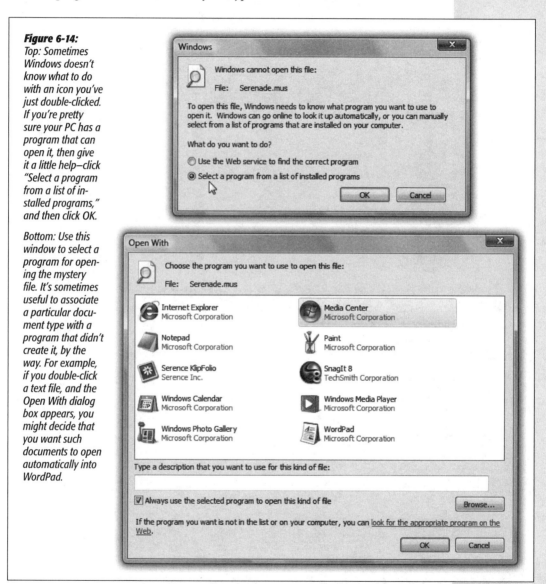

Figure 6-14:

Top: Sometimes Windows doesn't know what to do with an icon you've just double-clicked. If you're pretty sure your PC has a program that can open it, then give it a little help—click "Select a program from a list of in-stalled programs," and then click OK.

Bottom: Use this window to select a program for open-ing the mystery file. It's sometimes useful to associate a particular docu-ment type with a program that didn't create it, by the way. For example, if you double-click a text file, and the Open With dialog box appears, you might decide that you want such documents to open automatically into WordPad.

If it's just this one, click OK and stop reading. If it's *all* files of this type (all JPEGs, all MP3s, all .doc files…), then also turn on "Always use the selected program to open this kind of file," and click OK.

You should now be able to double-click the original document—and smile as it opens in the program you requested.

Note: *If the program isn't listed, click the Browse button and go find it yourself. And if you don't seem to have* any *program on your PC that will open the document, click "look for the appropriate program on the Web." You go online to a File Associations Web page, which lists programs that Microsoft knows can open the file.*

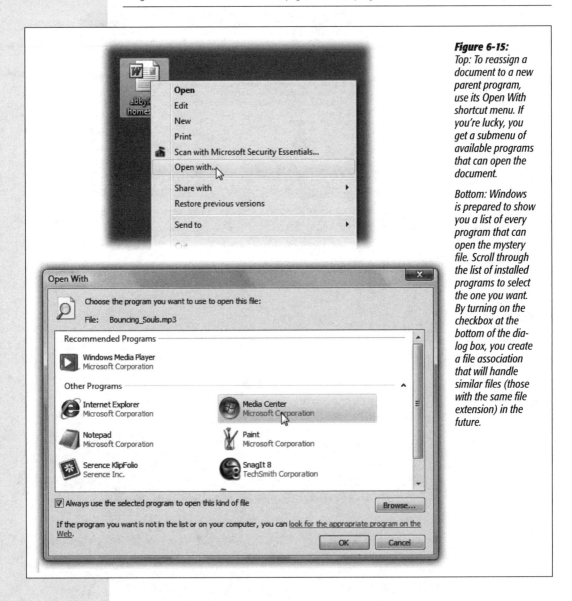

Figure 6-15:
Top: To reassign a document to a new parent program, use its Open With shortcut menu. If you're lucky, you get a submenu of available programs that can open the document.

Bottom: Windows is prepared to show you a list of every program that can open the mystery file. Scroll through the list of installed programs to select the one you want. By turning on the checkbox at the bottom of the dialog box, you create a file association that will handle similar files (those with the same file extension) in the future.

Method 2: Start with the program

If you'd prefer to edit the master database of file associations directly, a special control panel awaits. You can approach the problem from either direction:

- Choose a program and then choose which file types you want it to take over; or

- Choose a filename extension (like .aif or .ico) and then choose a new default program for it.

Here's how to perform the first technique:

1. **Open the Start menu. Start typing default until you see "Set your default programs" in the results list; click it.**

   The Default Programs control panel opens.

2. **Click "Set your default programs."**

   A curious dialog box appears, as shown in Figure 6-16 at top. It's a list of every program on your machine that's capable of opening multiple file types.

3. **Click the name of a program.**

   For example, suppose a program named FakePlayer 3.0 has performed the dreaded Windows Power Grab, claiming a particular file type for itself without asking you. In fact, suppose it has elected itself King of *All* Audio Files. But you want Windows Media Player to play everything *except* FakePlayer (.fkpl) files.

   In this step, then, you'd click Windows Media Player.

   If you want Media Player to become the default player for *every* kind of music and video file, you'd click "Set this program as default." But if you want it to open only *some* kinds of files, proceed like this:

4. **Click "Choose defaults for this program."**

   Now yet another dialog box opens (Figure 6-16, bottom). It lists every file type the selected program knows about.

5. **Turn on the checkboxes of the file types for which you want this program to be the default opener.**

   Of course, this step requires a certain amount of knowledge that comes from experience—how the heck would the average person know what, say, a .wvx file is?—but it's here for the power user's benefit.

6. **Click Save, and then OK.**

Method 3: Start with the file type

Finally, you can approach the file-association problem a third way: by working through a massive alphabetical list of filename extensions (.aca, .acf, .acs, .aif, and so on) and hooking each one up to a program of your choice.

1. Open the Start menu. Start typing *defaults* until you see Default Programs in the
results list; click it.

The Default Programs control panel opens.

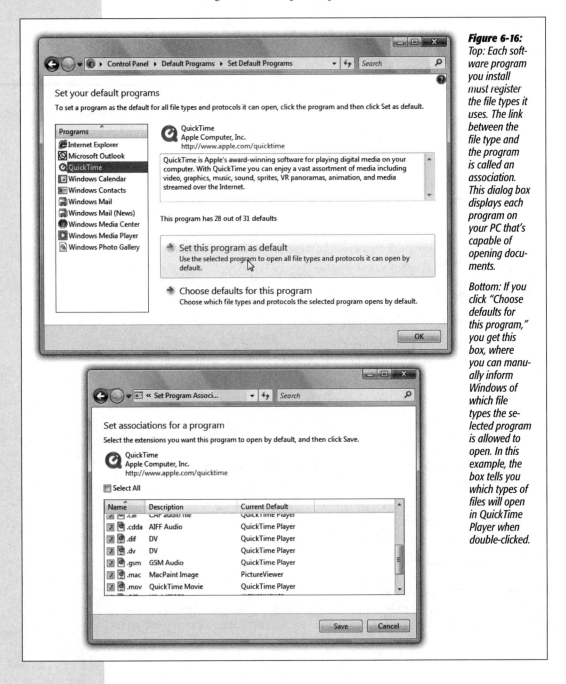

Figure 6-16:
*Top: Each software program
you install
must register
the file types it
uses. The link
between the
file type and
the program
is called an
association.
This dialog box
displays each
program on
your PC that's
capable of
opening documents.*

*Bottom: If you
click "Choose
defaults for
this program,"
you get this
box, where
you can manually inform
Windows of
which file
types the selected program
is allowed to
open. In this
example, the
box tells you
which types of
files will open
in QuickTime
Player when
double-clicked.*

Program Access and Defaults

OK, I've just barely understood your description of the control panel where I can hook up documents to programs or programs to documents. So what, exactly, is this other link in that panel, called "Set program access and computer defaults?"

Well, it's kind of a long story.

In its 2002 agreement with the U.S. Department of Justice, Microsoft agreed to give other companies a fighting chance at competing with programs like Internet Explorer, Outlook Express, and Windows Media Player.

If you open the Default Programs applet and click "Set program access and computer defaults," you get the dialog box shown here. After you authenticate yourself (page 726), you're offered three or four options:

Microsoft Windows means, "Use all of Microsoft's utility programs, just as Windows has been doing from Day One." You're saying you prefer Microsoft's Web browser (Internet Explorer), email program (Windows Mail), music/video player (Windows Media Player), and instant messaging program (Windows Messenger).

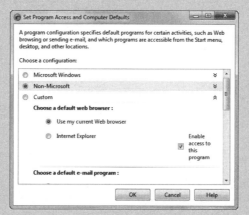

Selecting this option doesn't *prevent* you from using other browsers, email programs, and so on—you can still find them listed in the Start→All Programs menu. But this option does put the Internet Explorer and Windows Mail icons, for example, into prime positions at the top of your Start menu for quick and easy access.

Non-Microsoft means, "Use *anything* but Microsoft's programs! Instead, use Netscape Navigator, Eudora, RealPlayer, Sun's Java, or whatever—just nothing from Microsoft."

You should install your preferred alternate programs *before* selecting this option. Otherwise, the only programs this feature "sees" are Microsoft programs, which would make selecting this option a tad pointless.

As with the "Microsoft" option, choosing this option places your preferred programs' icons at the top of your Start menu. Unlike the "Microsoft" option, however, this option *removes access* to the corresponding Microsoft programs. If you choose a non-Microsoft program as your email program, for example, Windows Mail disappears completely from the All Programs menu and its folder (in C:→Program Files).

Of course, Microsoft's programs aren't really gone—they're just hidden. They pop right back when you choose the "Microsoft Windows" option, or when you choose Custom and then click the associated "Enable access to this program" checkbox. Just remember to click OK to apply your changes.

Computer Manufacturer means, "Use whatever programs are recommended by Dell" (or whoever made the PC and signed deals with AOL, Real, and so on). This option doesn't appear on all PCs.

Custom lets you choose each kind of program independently, whether it comes from Microsoft or not. For example, you can choose Firefox, Internet Explorer, or any other Web browser as your default browser. (They'll all be listed here when you click the double-arrow button to expand the dialog box.)

During your selection process, note the "Enable access to this program" checkbox. It really means, "List this baby at the top of the Start menu, and also put its icon on the Quick Launch toolbar, the Desktop, and wherever else important programs are listed."

2. Click "Associate a file type or protocol with a program."

   After a moment, a massive filename extensions list opens, as shown in Figure 6-17.

3. **Select the filename extension you want, and then click "Change program."**

   Now the Open With dialog box appears (the same one shown in Figure 6-15).

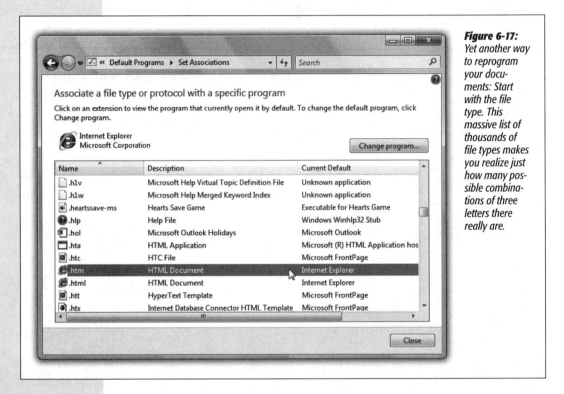

Figure 6-17:
Yet another way to reprogram your documents: Start with the file type. This massive list of thousands of file types makes you realize just how many possible combinations of three letters there really are.

4. **Click the name of the new default program.**

   Once again, if you don't see it listed here, you can click Browse to find it yourself.

5. **Click OK and then Close.**

Installing Software
All Versions

As you probably know, Microsoft doesn't actually sell PCs (yet). Therefore, you bought your machine from a different company, which probably installed Windows on it before you took delivery.

Many PC companies sweeten the pot by preinstalling other programs, such as Quicken, Microsoft Works, Microsoft Office, more games, educational software, and so on. The great thing about preloaded programs is that they don't need installing. Just double-click their desktop icons, or choose their names from the Start→All Programs menu, and you're off and working.

Sooner or later, though, you'll probably want to exploit the massive library of Windows software and add to your collection. Today, almost all new software comes to your PC from one of two sources: a disc (CD or DVD) or the Internet.

An installer program generally transfers the software files to the correct places on your hard drive. The installer also adds the new program's name to the Start→All Programs menu, tells Windows about the kinds of files (file extensions) it can open, and makes certain changes to your *Registry* (Appendix B).

The Preinstallation Checklist

You can often get away with blindly installing some new program without heeding the checklist below. But for the healthiest PC and the least time on hold with tech support, answer these questions before you install anything:

- **Are you an administrator?** Windows derives part of its security and stability by handling new software installations with suspicion. For example, you can't install most programs unless you have an *administrator account* (see page 716).

POWER USERS' CLINIC

Who Gets the Software?

As you're probably becoming increasingly aware, Microsoft designed Windows to be a *multiuser* operating system, in which each person who logs in enjoys an independent environment—from the desktop pattern to the email in Windows Mail. The question thus arises: When someone installs a new program, does every account holder have equal access to it?

In general, the answer is yes. If an administrator (page 716) installs a new program, it usually shows up on the Start→All Programs menu of *every* account holder.

Occasionally, a program's installer may offer you a choice: Install the new software so that it's available *either* to everybody *or* only to you, the currently logged-in account holder.

Also occasionally, certain programs might just install software into your own account, so nobody else who logs in even knows the program exists.

In that case, you can proceed in either of two ways. First,

you can simply log into each account, one after another, reinstalling the program.

Second, you may be able to get away with moving the program's shortcut from your Personal folder to the corresponding location in the All Users folder. Windows actually maintains two different types of Programs folders: one that's shared by everybody, and another for each individual account holder.

Here's where that information pays off. Open your Start→All Programs menu; right-click the name of the program you want everyone to be able to access, and then choose Copy from the shortcut menu. Now right-click the Start→All Programs menu (not the Start menu itself, as in previous Windows versions); from the shortcut menu, choose Open All Users. In the window that appears, right-click the Programs folder, and then choose Paste from the shortcut menu. The program now appears on the Start menu of everybody who uses the machine.

- **Does it run in Windows 7?** If the software or its Web site specifically says it's compatible with 7, great. Install away. Otherwise, consult the Microsoft Web site, which includes a list—not a complete one, but a long one—of Win7-compatible programs.

Tip: See "Running Pre-Win7 Programs" later in this chapter for compatibility tips.

- **Is the coast clear?** Exit all your open programs. You should also turn off your virus-scanning software, which may take the arrival of your new software the wrong way.

- **Am I prepared to backtrack?** If you're at all concerned about the health and safety of the software you're about to install, remember that the System Restore feature (page 695) takes an automatic snapshot of your system just before any software installation. If the new program turns out to be a bit hostile, you can rewind your system to its former, happier working condition.

Installing Software from a Disc

Most commercial software these days comes on a CD or DVD. On each one is a program called Setup.exe, which, on most installation discs, runs automatically when you insert the disc into the machine. You're witnessing the *AutoPlay* feature at work.

If AutoPlay is working (page 315), a few seconds after you insert the disc, the "wait" cursor appears. A few seconds later, the welcome screen for your new software appears, and you may be asked to answer a few onscreen questions (for example, to specify the folder into which you want the new program installed). Along the way, the program may ask you to type in a serial number, which is usually on a sticker on the disc envelope or the registration card.

When the installation is over—and sometimes after restarting the PC—the words All Programs appear with orange highlighting in the Start menu. If you click, the new program's name also appears highlighted in orange, and your Start→All Programs menu is now ready for action.

Installing Downloaded Software

When you download a new program from the Internet (see Figure 6-18), you have a couple of decisions to make:

FREQUENTLY ASKED QUESTION

Microsoft InstallShield?

I'm a bit confused. I bought a program from Infinity Workware. But when I run its installer, the Welcome screen says InstallShield. Who actually made my software?

Most of the time, the installer program isn't part of the software you bought or downloaded, and doesn't even

come from the same company. Most software companies pay a license to installer-software companies. That's why, when you're trying to install a new program called, say, JailhouseDoctor, the first screen you see says InstallShield. (InstallShield is the most popular installation software.)

- **Are you darned sure?** Internet downloads are the most common sources of PC virus infections. If you're downloading from a brand-name site like Shareware.com or Versiontracker.com (or a software company's site, like Microsoft.com), you're generally safe. But if the site is unfamiliar, be very, very afraid.

- **Run or Save?** As shown in Figure 6-18, when you download a program from the Web, you're asked if you want to Run its installer or Save it. Most of the time, Run is fine; that means your PC will download the installer program to your hard drive, open the installer, install the software you wanted, and then completely disappear. There's no cleanup to worry about.

  If you click Save instead, your browser will download the installer program to your hard drive—and that's it. Your job is to find that installer program, double-click it, install the program—and then delete the installer program later, if you have no further use for it.

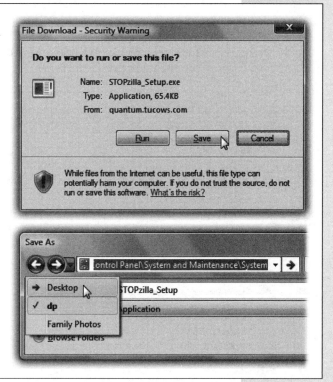

Figure 6-18:
You can find thousands of Windows programs (demos, free programs, and shareware) at Web sites like www.download.com, www.tucows.com, or www.versiontracker.com.

Top: When you click a link to download something, this box appears. Click the Run button to download and install the program, or Save to retain the installer program on your hard drive for later.

Bottom: Internet Explorer proposes storing a download in your Downloads folder; some people prefer clicking the Desktop button in the left-side pane instead so the download will be easier to find. After the download is complete, quit your browser. Unzip the file, if necessary, and then run the downloaded installer.

Installing Windows Components

The Windows installer may have dumped over a gigabyte of software onto your hard drive, but it was only warming up. Plenty of second-tier programs and features came on the Windows DVD—stuff that Microsoft didn't want to burden you with right off the bat, but copied to your hard drive just in case.

Want to see the master list of software components you have and haven't yet installed? The quickest method is to open the Start menu. Start typing *features* until you see "Turn Windows features on or off" in the results list; click it.

You've just opened the Windows Features Wizard—basically a list of all the optional Windows software chunks. Checkmarks appear next to some of them; these are the ones you already have. The checkboxes that aren't turned on are the options you still haven't installed. As you peruse the list, keep in mind the following:

- To learn what something is, point to it without clicking. A description appears in a tooltip balloon.

- Turn on the checkboxes for software bits you want to install. Turn off the checkboxes of elements you already have but that you'd like Windows to hide.

Note: Turning off an optional feature *doesn't* remove it from your hard drive, as it did in Windows XP. Turning off a feature simply hides it and doesn't return any disk space to you. You can make a feature magically reappear just by turning the checkbox back on (without having to hunt down your Windows installation disc).

- Some of these checkboxes' titles are just catch-alls for bigger groups of independent software chunks (see Figure 6-19).

Figure 6-19:
Most of the optional installations involve networking and administrative tools designed for corporate computer technicians. Still, you might want to turn off Games if you don't have that kind of time to kill, or Tablet PC Optional Components if your computer doesn't have a touch screen.

(On the other hand, turning off Tablet PC Optional Components also turns off the Snipping Tool described on page 279.)

Uninstalling Software

All Versions

When you've had enough of a certain program and want to reclaim the disk space it occupies, don't just delete its folder. The typical application installer tosses its software components like birdseed all over your hard drive; therefore, only some of the program is actually in the program's folder.

Instead, ditch software you no longer need using the Programs and Features program. (Open the Start menu. Start typing *programs* until you see "Programs and Features" in the results list; click it.)

Now your master list of installed programs (and driver updates) appears, as shown in Figure 6-20. Click the one you no longer want, and then click Uninstall on the toolbar.

Tip: If your computer is a member of a workgroup and you're using Fast User Switching (see page 736), then don't delete a program until you've verified that it isn't running in somebody else's account behind the scenes.

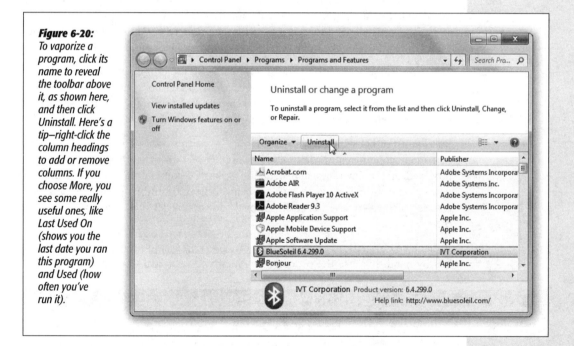

Figure 6-20:
To vaporize a program, click its name to reveal the toolbar above it, as shown here, and then click Uninstall. Here's a tip—right-click the column headings to add or remove columns. If you choose More, you see some really useful ones, like Last Used On (shows you the last date you ran this program) and Used (how often you've run it).

Even after you uninstall a program, the folder that contained it may still exist, especially if it contains configuration files, add-ons, or documents you created while the program was still alive. If you're sure you won't need those documents, it's safe to remove the folder (discussed later in this section), along with the files inside it.

Note: In Windows XP, the list in this dialog box was cluttered up with dozens upon dozens of "Windows Hotfixes"—the little security patches Microsoft sends out weekly or monthly via the Internet just to make your life interesting.

In Windows 7, though, they get a list of their own. Click "View installed updates" (one of the links in the task pane at the left side). That's useful to remember if you suspect one day that a certain patch has broken something on your PC.

When Uninstalling Goes Wrong

That's the *theory* of uninstalling Windows programs, of course. In practice, you'll probably find that the Programs and Features program should more accurately be called the "Add or I'll-Make-My-Best-Effort-to-Remove-Programs-But-No-Guarantees" program. A disappointing percentage of the time, one error message or another pops up, declaring that the uninstallation can't proceed because Windows can't find this or that component.

Most of the time, it's not the fault of Windows. Programs and Features is simply a list of links, like the All Programs section of your Start Menu. When you highlight an entry and click Uninstall, Windows just fires up the program's own uninstaller program. When the uninstaller doesn't work, thanks to some bug or glitch, the fun begins.

The truth is, the world won't end if you just leave the crippled program on board your PC. You can join millions of other PC fans who slog along, hard drives corroded with bits of software they can't seem to remove. Apart from the waste of space and the uneasy feeling that your PC is getting clogged arteries, there's no harm done.

But if you'd rather wipe the slate clean, start by visiting the Web site of the company that made your program. Dig into its support section to see if the company has provided a fix or any removal instructions. (Some companies discover bugs in their uninstaller utilities just like they might in any other part of their programs, and then release patches—or even special removal tools—that let their customers remove their software.)

If that step doesn't lead anywhere, you can get serious by eliminating the stubborn bits by hand. Because the process is manual and technical—and because, heaven

---

willing, you won't need it often—it's been offloaded to a free bonus article called "Removing Stubborn Programs." You can find it on this book's "Missing CD" page at *www.missingmanuals.com*.

Program Compatibility Modes

All Versions

"You can't make an omelet without breaking a few eggs." If that's not Microsoft's motto, it should be. Each successive version of Windows may be better than the previous one, but each inevitably winds up "breaking" hundreds of programs, utilities, and drivers that used to run fine.

Microsoft is well aware of this problem and has pulled every trick in the book to address it. Here, for example, is the chain of second chances you'll experience:

Warning When You Upgrade to Windows 7

In theory, you'll know about incompatible programs well in advance. You'll have run the Windows 7 Upgrade Advisor app (page 819) before you even installed Windows 7, for example, and learned which programs will give you trouble. Even if you skip that step, the Windows installer is supposed to quarantine all incompatible programs (369).

FREQUENTLY ASKED QUESTION

Really Ancient Apps

Will Windows 7 run my really old, really important app?

You'll never really know until you try. And this chapter outlines all the tools available to help you make the old app run. But here are some specifics on what you can expect.

16-bit programs are so old, they were written when Windows 3.1 roamed the earth and the first George Bush was president. (Programs written for Windows 95 and later are known as *32-bit* programs; Windows 7 can even run *64-bit* programs.) But amazingly enough, the 32-bit versions of Windows 7 (though not the 64-bit versions) can run most of these programs. They do so in a kind of software simulator—a DOS-and-Windows 3.1 PC impersonation called a *virtual machine*.

As a result, these programs don't run very fast, don't understand the long filenames of modern-day Windows, and may crash whenever they try to "speak" directly to certain components of your hardware. (The simulator stands in their way, in the name of keeping Windows stable.) Furthermore,

if just one of your 16-bit programs crashes, *all* of them crash, because they all live in the same memory bubble.

Even so, it's impressive that they run at all, 10 years later.

DOS programs are 16-bit programs, too, and therefore they run just fine in 32-bit versions of Windows, even though DOS no longer lurks beneath the operating system.

To open the black, empty DOS window that's familiar to PC veterans, press ⊞+R, type *command.com*, and press Enter. (See page 272.)

For the best possible compatibility with DOS programs—and to run DOS programs in a 64-bit copy of Windows—try out DOSBox (*www.dosbox.com/*), which emulates a classic 16-bit computer, complete with DOS compatibility. It's great for those old DOS games that haven't run correctly on Windows since the days of Windows 95.

Programs written for Windows 95, 2000, and XP usually run OK in the Compatibility mode described on these pages.

Warning Right When You Install an Older App

If you try to install an old, incompatible program later, the Program Compatibility Assistant may appear to bring you the bad news.

This app works by consulting a database of programs that Microsoft has determined to have problems with Windows 7. It might tell you a newer version is available for downloading.

Or it might announce that the installation didn't go smoothly. In that case, you can click "Reinstall using recommended settings," which makes Windows run the installer again using different compatibility settings. (For example, it might use one of the compatibility modes described below.)

Compatibility Mode

In principle, programs that were written for recent versions of Windows should run fine in Windows 7. Unfortunately, some of them contain software code that deliberately sniffs around to find out what Windows version you have. These programs (or even their installer programs) may say, "Windows *what?*"—and refuse to open.

Fortunately, Windows 7's Compatibility mode has some sneaky tricks that can fool them into running. You can use it to make "let me run!" changes to a stubborn app either the non-techie way (you just answer questions in a screen-by-screen interview format, and let Windows make the changes behind the scenes) or the expert way (changing compatibility settings manually).

Compatibility mode: the wizardy way

To let Windows fix your compatibility headache, open the Start menu. Start typing *compatibility* until you see "Run programs made for previous versions of Windows" in the results list. Press Enter.

Tip: Here's another way to get to the wizard: Right-click a program's icon, or its shortcut's icon, or even its name in the Start menu; from the shortcut menu, choose "Troubleshoot compatibility."

The Program Compatibility program opens. It's a wizard—a series of dialog boxes that interview you. On the way, you're asked to click the name of the program you're having trouble with. On the following screen, you have a choice of automatic or manual modes:

- Try recommended settings means, "Let Windows try to figure out how to make my stubborn program run. I don't really care what it has to tinker with under the hood."

- Troubleshoot program means, "Let me adjust the compatibility settings myself."

  You'll be asked to choose from options like, "The program worked in earlier versions of Windows," "The program opens but doesn't display correctly," and so on. Work through the question screens the best you can. When it's all over, you get a "Start the program" button that lets you see if the program finally runs without problems.

Whether things are fixed or not, after you've checked out the app, return to the troubleshooting wizard and click Next. You'll be able to (a) save the fixed settings for the future, (b) start a new round of troubleshooting, or (c) send a report to Microsoft that you never did solve the problem.

Compatibility mode: the manual way

If you know what you're doing, you can save some time and cut to the chase by invoking Compatibility mode yourself. To do that, right-click a program's icon (or its shortcut's icon). From the shortcut menu, choose Properties; click the Compatibility tab.

Now the dialog box shown in Figure 6-21 appears. The options here are precisely the same choices Windows makes for you automatically when you use the wizard described above—it's just that now you can adjust them yourself. Here's what you get:

Figure 6-21:
By turning on "Run this program in compatibility mode for" and choosing the name of a previous version of Windows from the list, you can fool that program into thinking it's running on Windows 95, Windows Me, Windows NT, or whatever.

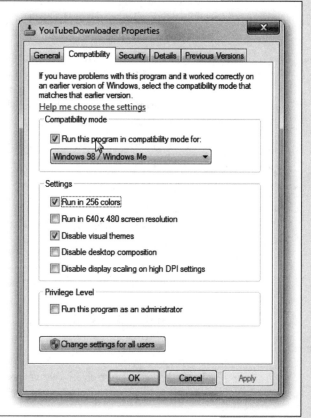

- **Compatibility mode.** This is the part that tricks the program into believing you're still running Windows 95, Windows XP, or whatever.

- **Run in 256 colors.** Makes the program switch your screen to certain limited-colors settings required by older games.

- **Run in 640 × 480 pixel resolution.** Runs the app in a small window—the size monitors used to be in the olden days. You might try this option if the app doesn't look right when it runs.

- **Disable visual themes.** Turns off the new Windows look, which often solves problems when the program's menus or buttons look odd.

- **Disable desktop composition** refers to the fancy eye candy in Windows 7, like transparent window edges and animations. Once again, turn this off if you're seeing weird cosmetic glitches.

- **Disable display scaling on high DPI settings.** If you've bumped up the type size for your screen as described on page 193, but your fonts are looking really weird in an older app, turn on this checkbox.

- **Run this program as an administrator** lets you run the program as though you have an administrator account (page 716; it's not available if you are *actually* logged in as an administrator).

  This mode is designed to accommodate poorly written programs that, in the XP days, had to be run in administrative mode, back when everyone ran their PCs that way and didn't realize how many virus doors that left open. The downside of turning on this option is that you'll have to authenticate yourself (page 726) every time you run the program.

- **Change settings for all users.** If more than one person has an account on this PC, this applies the changes you've just made to everyone's accounts.

Finally, two footnotes:

- You're much better off securing an updated version of the program, if it's available. Check the program's Web site to see if a Win7-compatible update is available.

- Don't try this "fake out the app" trick with utilities like virus checkers, backup programs, CD-burning software, and hard drive utilities. Installing older versions of these with Windows 7 is asking for disaster.

Windows XP Mode

Professional • Enterprise • Ultimate

Microsoft would love it if the whole world embraced each new version of Windows, but let's not kid ourselves. Two years after the introduction of Windows Vista, the most popular, most-used Windows version on earth was still—Windows XP.

It should come as no surprise, then, that there are more programs for Windows XP than any other version of Windows—including Win7.

Unfortunately, a huge number of those XP programs won't be updated for Windows 7 compatibility. Maybe the company that wrote the app is out of business. Maybe your company commissioned a specialty app, and the people who wrote it are long gone. Maybe the company that made your fancy graphics or sound card has no intention of rewriting a more modern driver, because it would much rather have people buy an all-new card.

But if you have a high-end version of Windows 7, you won't care. You can download a free copy of Windows XP and run it on top of Windows 7, with 100 percent XP compatibility. It's a wild arrangement (see Figure 6-22).

Note: No matter how cool this arrangement is, however, it's a lot more trouble (and uses up a lot more memory and disk space) than the easier tweaks described on the previous pages. Running an old app right in Windows 7 means better speed, convenience, and security. (For example, Microsoft emphasizes that you'll want to install another antivirus program within your Windows XP world to protect it.)

In short, Windows XP Mode is a last-ditch solution. If you can make your older app work with one of the simpler steps described above, you probably should.

Figure 6-22:
Windows XP Mode, anybody? Yes, it's a full-blown XP computer running in a window on your Windows 7 machine, thanks to the magic of emulation.

You're running XP in a window...in Windows 7.

To set this up, you need a few special ingredients:

- **The right hardware.** You need a PC whose processor can do hardware-assisted virtualization (the geek name for this "pretending to be a different operating system" feature). Some processors do, some don't.

  It's easy enough to find out if your processor is one of the blessed, however; just download (what else?) the Hardware-Assisted Virtualization Detection Tool. It's on Microsoft's Web site here— *http://bit.ly/9QfSY*—and it will give you a simple yes or no.

- **The right software.** You also have to download two big, free software chunks from Microsoft. One is called Windows Virtual PC, which is the software that simulates a PC-within-your-PC. The other is called Windows XP Mode, which includes a full working copy of Windows XP. You can download both of these programs here: *http://bit.ly/lvAjC.*

Follow the Web site's instructions for installing these two software chunks.

When it's all over, you can fire up Windows XP whenever you want. Choose Start→All Programs→Windows Virtual PC→Windows XP Mode (or just type *xp mode* into the Search box).

The first time you start up XP Mode, you're asked to assign a password to the starter (administrator) account. (Unless you turn off the "Remember" checkbox, you won't have to enter the password again.) You're also asked to turn on Automatic Updates (a good idea), and to wait a good while, while XP Mode is fired up for the first time.

- Then that's it! You have a full-blown Windows XP computer running in a window on your Windows 7 PC's screen. Here's everything you have to know: Make the window fill your screen by clicking its Maximize button, by dragging the title bar against the top of your screen, or by choosing Action→View Full Screen. (Click Restore on the toolbar to go back to floating-window mode.)

- You can copy and paste between Windows XP and Windows 7 programs.

- To install software on a CD or DVD, you can't just insert the disc and expect the installer to open automatically, as it does in Windows 7; after all, your computer doesn't know which operating system the installer should open into. So to run it in Windows XP, you have to open the Setup program manually. Choose Start→ Computer, double-click the CD or DVD's name, and then double-click the Setup program.

- When you want to open a program you've installed in Windows XP, choose its name from the Windows 7 Start→All Programs→Windows XP Mode Applications menu. That is, you can open them directly, without having to start up XP Mode first.

XP Mode programs take longer to open, but they run at full speed. What's especially wild is that when you open them from the Start menu that way, you don't even see the rest of the Windows XP world; these programs just act like regular Windows 7 programs, with very few reminders that they're actually running a simulated operating system.

- In the Computer window of your Windows XP world, the XP computer's "hard drive" shows up as its C: drive as usual. The real hard drive, the one running Windows 7, shows up as a D: drive.

- External USB storage drives like hard drives, memory cards, and flash drives show up in both worlds (XP and Windows 7).

- Other USB gadgets, like music players, are a little more complicated. You have to tell your computer when Windows XP is allowed to use them.

To make one available to your XP world, connect it, turn it on, and then choose USB→Attach iPod (or whatever the thing's name is). Then, when you're finished using it in the XP world, choose USB→Release iPod so you can use it in Windows 7 again.

- Exit XP Mode by clicking the Close button on the toolbar or title bar.

UP TO SPEED

A Little Bit About 64 Bits

Every version of Windows 7 except Starter is available in both 32-bit and 64-bit versions. (Both come in the same package.)

Right. 64-what?

If you want your eyes to glaze over, you can read the details on 64-bit computing in Wikipedia. But the normal-person's version goes like this:

For decades, the roadways for memory and information passed through PCs were 32 "lanes" wide–they could manage 32 chunks of data at once. It seemed like plenty at the time. But as programs and even documents grew enormous, and computers came with the capacity to have more and more memory installed, engineers began to dream of 64-lane circuitry.

To reach 64-bit nirvana, however, you need a 64-bit computer running the 64-bit version of Windows.

Sometimes, you don't have a choice. For example, if your PC comes with at least 4 gigabytes of memory, it has 64-bit Windows, like it or not. And if you buy a netbook, it probably comes with the 32-bit version.

Otherwise, though, you probably have a choice. Which version should you go for?

In the short term, the most visible effect of having a 64-bit computer is that you can install a lot more memory. A top-of-the-line 32-bit PC, for example, is limited to 4 GB of RAM–and only about 3 GB is actually available to your programs. That once seemed like a lot, but it's suffocatingly small if you're a modern video editor, game designer, or number-crunchy engineer.

On a 64-bit PC with 64-bit Windows, though, you can install just a tad bit more memory: 192 GB. (In the Home Premium version of Windows 7, the cap is 16 GB).

Eventually, there may be other benefits to a 64-bit PC. Programs can be rewritten to run faster. Security can be better, too. For now, though, there are some downsides to going 64-bit.

For example, much of the world's software has yet to be rewritten as 64-bit apps. The older, 32-bit programs mostly run fine on a 64-bit machine. But some won't run at all, and 32-bit drivers for your older hardware (sound card, graphics card, printer, and so on) may give you particular headaches.

(That's why, for example, 64-bit Windows 7 actually runs the 32-bit version of Internet Explorer–because the world's Internet Explorer plug-ins are mostly 32-bit, and they wouldn't work with the 64-bit version of Internet Explorer.)

You can't run 16-bit programs at all in 64-bit Windows, either (at least not without an add-on program like DOSBox).

If you have taken the 64-bit plunge, you generally don't have to know whether your apps are running in 32- or 64-bit mode; every kind of program runs in the right mode automatically. If you ever want to see how many of your apps are actually 32-bitters, though, press Ctrl+Shift+Esc to open the Task Manager; then click the Processes tab. The 32-bit programs you have open are indicated by "*32" after their names.

Note: Your XP machine goes into the old Hibernate mode, meaning that all your open windows and programs will be right where they were the next time you start up your Windows XP "computer." If you'd rather have the Close box mean Shut Down or Turn Off, change the settings in Settings→Tools.

The Freebie Apps

E ven after a fresh installation of Windows 7, a glance at your Start→All Programs menu reveals a rich array of preinstalled programs—as an infomercial might put it, they're your *free bonus gifts*. This chapter offers a tour of these programs. (A few of them merit chapters of their own in this book.)

For your reference pleasure, they're described here semi-alphabetically—that is, just as they appear in the All Programs menu (Figure 7-1).

For example, Accessories doesn't appear here first, because it appears way down the list in your All Programs menu.

Windows Live Essentials
All Versions

Before the software tour begins, however, a word about Windows Live Essentials.

If you can believe it, this version of Windows doesn't come with an email program! It doesn't come with a chat program, calendar, address book, video-editing app, or even basic photo-management software, either.

It's not because Microsoft doesn't have the talent; Windows Vista, after all, came with all this stuff.

No, it's because of the lawyers. Microsoft grew sick and tired of defending itself in antitrust lawsuits ("If you include all the software anybody would ever need, you're stifling your competition!"). So in Windows 7, Microsoft left out all those controversial programs.

Well, they've been left out, but that doesn't mean they're actually gone. These programs are one click away, a one-shot free download from the Web, in a package called Windows Live Essentials (formerly known as Microsoft Lawsuit Bait).

Figure 7-1:
In Windows 7, many of the listings in the All Programs menu are nothing more than links to other programs and places on your PC. Many of the big-ticket items that appear in the All Programs menu have their own chapters or sections in this book.

Most of them, anyway. The Windows Live Essentials suite includes these apps:

- **Mail.** Yes, it's the classic free Microsoft email program. Once, long ago, it went by the name Outlook Express.

- **Photo Gallery.** This is Microsoft's "digital shoebox" program for managing, organizing, and touching up all your photos.

- **Messenger.** It's the chat program that uses Microsoft's chat network, rival to AIM and Yahoo IM.

- **Movie Maker, DVD Maker.** Simple video-editing/DVD-burning programs.

- **Family Safety.** A naughty-Web-page blocker for your kids.

- **Toolbar.** A toolbar for your Web browser that taps into Microsoft's mail, chat, and other services.

- **Writer.** A tool for composing blog posts.

If you're observant, you might have noticed what this list does *not* include: Windows Calendar and Windows Contacts. They came with Vista, but they're no longer available for Windows 7, even as a download.

Microsoft says, "Hey, there's a calendar and a contacts list built right into Mail! Just use that!" Well, great, except that those are super-basic programs that can't sync with your cellphone, can't hook into online sites like Google Calendar, and require opening up your email program just to check your calendar.

Ah, well. Steve Ballmer giveth, and Steve Ballmer taketh away.

The following pages assume that you have, in fact, downloaded the Windows Live Essentials, which you do like this:

Open the Start menu. Start typing *essentials* until you see "Go online to get Windows Live Essentials" in the results list; click it. Your Web browser opens to the download page. Click Download and follow the instructions.

Default Programs
All Versions

This item is a link to the Default Programs control panel. It's described in Chapter 6.

Desktop Gadget Gallery
All Versions

Choose this item to make your *gadgets* (small, floating, single-purpose apps) appear on the screen. (It's the same thing as right-clicking the desktop and choosing Gadgets.) Chapter 6 covers gadgets in detail.

Internet Explorer
All Versions

Yes, it's *that* Internet Explorer—Microsoft's world-famous Web browser. Full details are in Chapter 11.

Note: If you've installed the 64-bit version of Internet Explorer, you see listed in your All Programs menu both "Internet Explorer" and "Internet Explorer (64-bit)." In general, the plain Internet Explorer version will give you fewer headaches, because it works with all the existing browser plug-ins, and the 64-bit version doesn't.

Windows Anytime Upgrade

Starter • Home Basic • Home Premium • Professional

As you're probably aware, Windows 7 comes in a number of different editions: Home Premium, Business, Ultimate, and so on. (Details are in the Introduction.)

But what if you buy, say, the Home Premium version, but you later decide that you really want the file-encryption and laptop-projector features of Professional? Or maybe you bought Professional, but you crave the BitLocker drive encryption features of Ultimate?

Not to worry; Microsoft has made sure you'll be taken care of. Believe it or not, *you already have the Ultimate version on your hard drive.* Microsoft has simply hidden the additional features from you, disk space be damned.

Using Anytime Upgrade, you can *upgrade* your version of Windows 7 to a higher version; all you need is a valid credit-card number and a few bucks in your account.

Tip: The scheme of upgrades is complicated, actually. You can use Anytime Upgrade only in certain countries. You can't switch from the 32-bit version to the 64-bit or vice versa. If you upgraded from Windows Vista, then whatever you started with affects what you can migrate to. And so on.

If you value your sanity, download the Windows 7 Upgrade Advisor before you begin; it will analyze your current installation, your free hard drive space, and what programs may run into trouble with the upgrade, and provide you with a concise report. This free little program is available at *http://windows.microsoft.com/ upgradeadvisor*.

When you open Windows Anytime Upgrade, a dialog box appears that offers two choices:

- **Go online to choose the edition of Windows 7 that's best for you.** Click this to go online to see which versions you can buy, and the prices. Once you plug in your credit-card information, the Web site shows you a long serial number; you'll need it only if you decide to reinstall Windows 7 later. Otherwise, the upgrade is fairly automatic—and quick, about 10 minutes. (It's nothing like the complete Windows reinstallation that was required by Windows Vista's Anytime Upgrade.)

  The upgrade process doesn't disturb any of your programs, settings, or documents. Everything remains exactly where it was.

- **Enter an upgrade key.** You can also buy Windows 7 upgrade kits in stores, containing that long Microsoft serial number. In that case, click this option and type the thing in.

During the upgrade, the PC will restart once, and then you're good to go, with your new, fancier edition of Windows 7.

Windows DVD Maker

Home Premium • Professional • Enterprise • Ultimate

DVD Maker can turn your camcorder (or digital-camera) masterpieces into standard DVDs that play on the TVs of your adoring public. For details on DVD Maker, download the free PDF appendix, "Movie Maker & DVD Maker," from this book's "Missing CD" at www.missingmanuals.com.

Windows Fax and Scan

All Versions

See Chapter 17 for full details on sending and receiving faxes from your PC—and on scanning documents using a scanner.

Windows Media Center

Home Premium • Professional • Enterprise • Ultimate

The software that once required a special-edition PC is now available to anyone with the right version of Windows. See Chapter 16 for more.

Windows Media Player

All Versions

This massive music and video player is described in Chapter 15.

Note: What happened to Windows Meeting Space, which would ordinarily appear here in the alphabetical list? It's gone. Microsoft has eliminated it. The requirements were too steep, the setup was too confusing, and pretty much nobody used it. Then again, Microsoft SharedView offers pretty much the same features in a free, simpler form: *http://connect.microsoft.com/site94*.

Windows Live Movie Maker

Home Premium • Professional • Enterprise • Ultimate

It's Microsoft's basic video-editing program—the iMovie of the PC world. It's part of Windows Live Essentials, and it's described in the free PDF appendix to this book, "Windows Live Movie Maker & DVD Maker." You can download it from this book's "Missing CD" page at *www.missingmanuals.com*.

Windows Update

All Versions

This program is Microsoft's system for patching your copy of Windows via the Internet. Full coverage appears in Chapter 20.

XPS Viewer

All Versions

This little app is dedicated to letting you read XPS files that people send you. (Hint: Nobody will.) For details on XPS, see the box below.

Accessories

All Versions

The programs in this suite have two things in common: First, they're all smallish, single-purpose programs (or just links to them) that you'll probably use only occasionally. Second, you get to them from the Start→All Programs→Accessories menu.

Bluetooth File Transfer

This program lets you send and receive files over Bluetooth, a wireless networking technology that lets computers and devices exchange information quickly. It's not as fast as WiFi, but Bluetooth—if your computer has this feature—is good for quick and dirty ad-hoc exchanges of files.

FREQUENTLY ASKED QUESTION

Microsoft XPS = Adobe PDF

What, exactly, is Microsoft XPS? I see an icon for it in my Print dialog box.

Well, you know how Microsoft always comes up with its own version of anything popular? PalmPilot, iPod, Web browser, whatever?

Its latest target is the PDF document, the brainchild of Adobe.

A PDF document, of course, is a file that opens up on any kind of computer–Mac, Windows, Unix, anything–looking exactly the way it did when it was created, complete with fonts, graphics, and other layout niceties. The recipient can't generally make changes to it, but can search it, copy text from it, print it, and so on. It's made life a lot easier for millions of people because it's easy, free, and automatic.

And now Microsoft wants a piece o' dat. Its new Microsoft XPS document format is pretty much the same idea as PDF, only it's Microsoft's instead of Adobe's.

To turn any Windows document into an XPS document, just choose File→Print. In the Print dialog box, choose Microsoft XPS Document Writer as the "printer," and then click Print. You're asked to name it and save it.

The result, when double-clicked, opens up in Internet Explorer. (Yes, Internet Explorer is the new Acrobat Reader.) You might not even notice the two tiny toolbars that appear above and below the main browser window, but they offer the usual PDF-type options: Save a copy, find a phrase, jump to a page, zoom in or out, switch to double-page view, and so on.

Microsoft plans to release XPS readers for other versions of Windows–and, eventually, other kinds of computers. Even so, Microsoft has a long battle ahead if it hopes to make the XPS format as commonplace as PDF.

But then again, long battles have never fazed it before.

Calculator

At first glance, this calculator looks like nothing more than a thinner version of every pocket calculator you've ever seen (Figure 7-2). You can operate it either by clicking the buttons with your mouse or by pressing the corresponding keys on your keyboard.

Tip: Choosing View→Digit Grouping instructs Calculator to display numbers with commas (123,456,789), making large numbers (123456789) a lot easier to read.

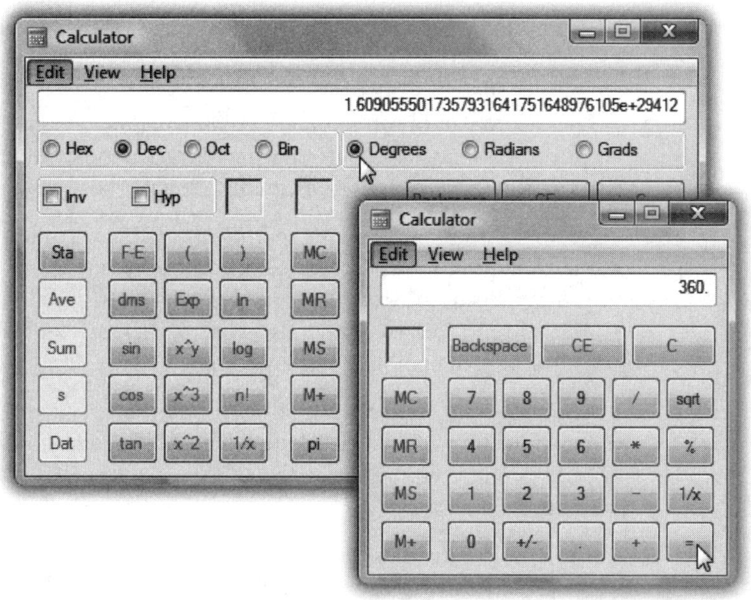

Figure 7-2:
After ducking into a phone booth, the humble Calculator (lower right) emerges as Scientific Calculator (upper left), which contains a hexadecimal/decimal/octal/binary converter for programmers, mathematical functions for scientists, and enough other buttons to impress almost anyone.

Most of the buttons look just like the ones on the plastic calculator that's probably in your desk drawer at this very moment, but several require special explanation:

- **/.** The slash means "divided by" in computerese.

- ***.** The asterisk is the multiplication symbol.

- **sqrt.** Click this button to find the square root of the currently displayed number.

- **%.** Type in one number, click the * button, type a second number, and then click this button to calculate what percentage the first number is of the second.

- **1/x.** Here's a ratio button. It makes the currently displayed number appear as the denominator of a fraction. That is, it turns 4 into ¼, which it expresses as 0.25.

Tip: This calculator may appear to have almost every feature you could desire, but it lacks a paper-tape feature—and we all know how easy it is to get lost in the middle of long calculations.

The solution is simple: Type your calculation, such as *34+(56/3)+5676+(34*2)=*, in a word processor. Highlight the calculation you've typed, choose Edit→Copy, switch to Calculator, and then choose Edit→Paste. The previously typed numbers fly into the calculator in sequence, finally producing the grand total on its screen. (You can then use the Edit→Copy command to copy the result back out of the calculator, ready for pasting into another program.)

But by choosing View→Scientific, you turn this humble five-function calculator into a full-fledged scientific number-cruncher, as shown in Figure 7-2.

Command Prompt

The Command Prompt opens a *command line interface:* a black, empty screen with the time-honored *C:>* prompt where you can type out instructions to the computer. This is a world without icons, menus, or dialog boxes; even the mouse is almost useless.

Surely you can appreciate the irony. The whole breakthrough of Windows was that it *eliminated* the DOS command-line interface that was still the ruling party on the computers of the day. Most nongeeks sighed with relief, delighted that they'd never have to memorize commands again. Yet here's Windows 7, Microsoft's supposedly ultramodern operating system, complete with a command line! What's going on?

Actually, the command line never went away. At universities and corporations worldwide, professional computer nerds kept right on pounding away at the little *C:>* prompts, appreciating the efficiency and power such direct computer control afforded them.

You never *have* to use the command line. In fact, Microsoft has swept it far under the rug, obviously expecting that most people will use the beautiful icons and menus of the regular desktop.

Tip: You can also open the Command Prompt directly from the Start menu. Just type *command* into the Search box, and then press Enter.

FREQUENTLY ASKED QUESTION

Clipboard Viewer

Hey, what happened to the Clipboard Viewer? It used to be in the System Tools group of my Start→Programs→Accessories menu, and now it's gone.

Yes, Clipboard Viewer was a cool little program for seeing the material you'd most recently copied.

It's gone. You can't even use the Run command to issue the *Clipbrd.exe* command anymore.

Fortunately, the shareware world is ready to step into the breach. Take a look, for example, at AccelClip (available, among other places, from this book's "Missing CD" page at *www.missingmanuals.com*).

If you have a little time and curiosity, however, the Command Prompt opens up a world of possibilities. It lets you access corners of Windows that you can't get to from the regular desktop. (Commands for exploring network diagnostics are especially plentiful—*ping, netstat,* and so on.) It lets you perform certain tasks with much greater speed and efficiency than you'd get by clicking buttons and dragging icons. And it gives you a fascinating glimpse into the minds and moods of people who live and breathe computers.

Here are a few examples:

Command	Purpose	Example
control	Opens a Control Panel applet	*control date/time*
ping	Checks to see if a server is responding	*ping nytimes.com*
ipconfig	Reveals your PC's IP address and other network info	*ipconfig*
mkdir	Make directory (that is, create a folder)	*mkdir \Reports*
copy	Copy files from one folder to another	*copy c:\Reports*.* \Backup*

You can also type the true, secret name of any program to open it, quickly and efficiently, without having to mouse around through the Start menu. For example, you can type *winword* to open Word, or *charmap* to open Character Map.

To learn a few of the hundreds of commands at your disposal, consult the Internet, which is filled with excellent lists and explanations. To find them, visit a search page like *www.google.com* and search for *Windows command line reference.* You'll find numerous ready-to-study Web sites that tell you what to type at the Command Prompt. (Here's an example from Microsoft: *http://bit.ly/bx0xo4.*)

Tip: You can open a Command Prompt for any folder just by Shift+right-clicking a folder. From the shortcut menu, choose Open Command Window Here.

Connect to a Network Projector

Professional • Enterprise • Ultimate

Talk about a program you won't use every day!

This little wizard is designed to detect, and connect your PC to, a *network projector*—a video projector that can project the image from any computer on the network. You, the pitchmaster, can stand in the conference room on the eighth floor (where the projector is), showing your awestruck coworkers a PowerPoint presentation that's actually sitting on your PC in Accounting down on the fourth.

Note: This feature isn't available in the Home Basic or Home Premium versions of Windows 7.

If such a projector is already set up and turned on, you should be able to find it and connect to it by clicking "Search for a projector." You're asked for a password, if necessary, and whether you want to *mirror* (display the same thing as) or *extend* (act as additional area of) the screen on your fourth-floor PC.

If the projector is not on the same *subnet* (chunk of the network), however, the wizard won't see it. In that case, you need to click "Enter the projector address" instead. Tap in the projector's network address (supplied by your friendly network administrator, of course).

Note: Don't use videos in your network-projected pitches. They'll show up choppy when transmitted over the network.

Connect to a Projector

Choosing this program's name is the same as pressing ⊞+P. It brings up the handy choice of multi-monitor displays shown on page 196.

Getting Started

Opens the Getting Started guide that appears at the top of the Start menu after you installed Windows 7, complete with links to personalizing Windows, transferring files from an old PC, backing up files, adjusting screen type size, and so on.

Math Input Panel

Home Premium • Professional • Enterprise • Ultimate

This new, unsung little freebie is intended for an elite group indeed: mathematicians with touchscreen computers. You're supposed to write out math equations in the writing area using your finger or a touchscreen stylus and marvel as Windows 7 translates your handwriting into a typed-out mathematical expression. (You *can* use this program with a mouse; it just might feel a little odd.)

Most of the time, you'll want to use MIP when you're writing in a word processor—preparing a math test for students, writing a white paper, whatever.

Note: This program can insert its finished math expressions only into programs that recognize something called MathML (Mathematical Markup Language). Microsoft Word, Excel, and PowerPoint do, and so does the free OpenOffice.org. (Yes, the software itself has the same name as its Web site.)

In the unlikely event that you have a tablet PC and you're working in the Windows Journal program, you can also use MIP to analyze your previously *handwritten* math expressions and make them properly typeset. (Use the selection tool to highlight your handwriting, then drag the expression *into* the MIP window.)

To use MIP on any other computer, write out the mathematical expression, as neatly as you can, in the writing area. In the Preview area (see Figure 7-3), you see Windows's stab at recognizing your handwriting.

If it's all correct, tap Insert to drop the equation into your word processor.

If something needs correcting, you can show MIP what it got wrong in one of several ways:

- Right-click the mistake. Or, if the mistaken transcription is more than one symbol, circle the error while pressing the right mouse button.

- Tap the mistake while pressing your stylus's button. (Or, again, circle the mistake while pressing the pen's button.)

  Click the Select and Cancel button. Now tap the erroneous symbol, or circle the larger part that's wrong.

Tip: It's better to correct errors after you've written out the whole thing.

Immediately, a pop-up menu of alternative transcriptions appears. Proceed as shown in Figure 7-3.

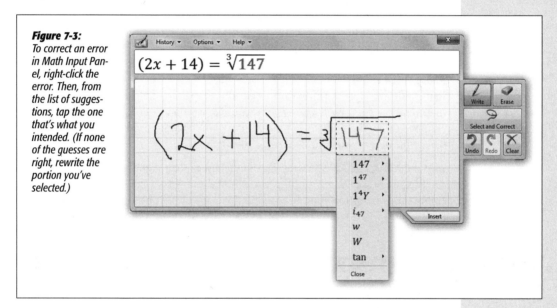

Figure 7-3:
To correct an error in Math Input Panel, right-click the error. Then, from the list of suggestions, tap the one that's what you intended. (If none of the guesses are right, rewrite the portion you've selected.)

If the expression is now complete, tap Insert. If you have more to write, just keep on going. (If you got into symbol-correction mode by tapping Select and Cancel, then you have to tap Write before you continue.)

Tip: You can tap any entry in the History menu to re-input an expression you've entered before. When you're working on, for example, a proof, or a drill with many similar problems, that can save you a lot of time.

Notepad

Notepad is a bargain-basement *text editor,* which means it lets you open, create, and edit files that contain plain, unformatted text, like the ReadMe.txt files that often accompany new programs. You can also use Notepad to write short notes or to edit text that you intend to paste into your email program after editing it.

Notepad basics

Notepad opens automatically when you double-click text files (those with the file extension *.txt*). You can also open Notepad by choosing Start→All Programs→ Accessories→Notepad—or, more efficiently, by typing *notep* into the Start menu's Search box.

You'll quickly discover that Notepad is the world's most frill-free application. Its list of limitations is almost longer than its list of features.

For example, the Notepad window has no toolbar and can work with only one file at a time.

Above all, Notepad is a *text* processor, not a *word* processor. That means you can't use any formatting at all—no bold, italic, centered text, and so on. That's not necessarily bad news, however. The beauty of text files is that any word processor on any kind of computer—Windows, Mac, Unix, whatever—can open plain text files like the ones Notepad creates.

About Word Wrap

In the old days, Notepad didn't automatically wrap lines of text to make everything fit in its window. As a result, chunks of text often went on forever in a single line or got chopped off by the right side of the window, which could produce disastrous results when you were trying to follow, say, a soufflé recipe.

In Windows 7, lines of text wrap automatically, exactly as they do in a word processor. But you're still seeing nothing more than the effects of the Format→Word Wrap command—an option you can turn off, if you like, by choosing the command again. (You can tell when Word Wrap is on by the presence of a checkmark next to the command in the Format menu.)

GEM IN THE ROUGH

Notepad Log Files

As stripped-down as it is, Notepad has one surprising feature not available in any other text processor or word processor: automated log files. Every time you open a certain file, Notepad can automatically insert the current date and time at the bottom of the file, creating a tidy record of when you last worked on it—a nifty way to keep any type of a log, like a record of expenditures or a secret diary.

To set this up, create a new Notepad document (choose File→New). Then type the phrase *.LOG* at the top of the new document. (Capitalize "LOG," and put nothing, not even a space, before the period.)

Now save the document (File→Save) wherever you like, and give it a name. (Notepad adds the extension *.txt* automatically.)

When you next open the file, Notepad types out the date and time automatically and puts your cursor on the next line. Now you're ready to type the day's entry.

To make your log file easier to read, press the Enter key to insert a blank line after each entry before saving the file.

Paint

You can use Paint to "paint" simple artwork or to edit graphics files from other sources. You might say Paint is something like Adobe Photoshop (well, in the same way you might say the local Cub Scout newsletter is something like *The New York Times*). Common tasks for this program include making quick sketches, fixing dust specks on scanned photos, and entertaining kids for hours on end.

When you first open Paint, you get a small, empty painting window. It's been visually overhauled in Windows 7—there's a tool "ribbon" now—but the essentials haven't changed. Go like this:

1. **From the Paint menu (to the left of the Home tab), choose Properties to specify the dimensions of the graphic you want to create. Click OK.**

    Later in your life, you can revisit that command to adjust your graphic's dimensions.

2. **Click a tool on the Home tab, like the Pencil.**

    If you need help identifying one of these tools, point to it without clicking. A tooltip identifies the icon by name, and a help message appears at the bottom of the window.

3. **Click a "paint" color from the palette.**

    You may also want to change the "brush" by clicking the Brushes palette, like the spray-paint splatter shown in Figure 7-4.

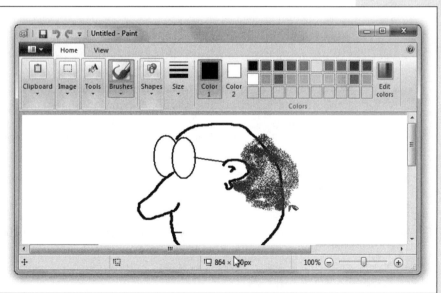

Figure 7-4:
The Paint tools include shapes, pens for special uses (straight lines and curves), and coloring tools (including an airbrush). The Select tools don't draw anything. Instead, they select portions of the image for cutting, copying, or dragging to a new location.

4. **If you've selected one of the enclosed-shape tools, use the Fill pop-up menu to specify a texture (Watercolor, Crayon, or whatever); click Color 2, and then a color swatch, to specify the color for the inside of that shape.**

Some tools produce enclosed shapes, like squares and circles. You can specify one color for the border, and a second color for the fill color inside.

5. **Finally, drag your cursor in the image area (see Figure 7-4).**

   As you work, don't forget that you can click the Undo button (the counterclockwise arrow at the very top edge of the window), "taking back" the last painting maneuvers you made.

   For fine detail work, click the View tab, and then click Zoom In. You've just enlarged it so every dot is easily visible.

Paint can open and create several different file formats, including BMP, JPEG, and GIF—every file format you need to save graphics for use on a Web site.

Tip: Paint also offers a nifty way to create wallpaper (see page 179). After you create or edit a graphic, open the Paint menu. Choose "Set as desktop background"; from the submenu, choose Fill, Tile, or Center to transfer your masterpiece to your desktop.

Remote Desktop Connection

Remote Desktop Connection lets you sit at your home PC and operate your office PC by remote control. Details are in Chapter 27.

Run

When you want to open something with just a few keystrokes, the little Run command-line window is there for you. See page 55 for details.

Snipping Tool

Snipping Tool takes pictures of your PC's screen, for use when you're writing up instructions, illustrating a computer book, or collecting proof of some secret screen you found buried in a game. You can take pictures of the entire screen or capture only the contents of a rectangular selection. When you're finished, Snipping Tool displays your snapshot in a new window, which you can print, close without saving, edit, or save (as a JPEG, GIF, PNG, or embedded HTML file), ready for emailing or inserting into a manuscript or page-layout program.

Note: Snipping Tool isn't available in the Starter Edition of Windows 7.

Now, as experienced PC enthusiasts already know, Windows has *always* had shortcuts for capturing screenshots: Press the Print Screen (or PrtScn) key to print a picture of the whole screen; add the Alt key to copy it to your Clipboard.

So why use Snipping Tool instead? Because it's infinitely more powerful and flexible. Here's how it works:

1. **Open Snipping Tool.**

   The screen goes foggy and light, and the Snipping Tool palette appears on your screen.

2. **From the New shortcut menu, specify what area of the screen you want to capture.**

These are your choices:

Free-form Snip, which means you can drag your cursor in any crazy, jagged, freehand, nonrectangular shape. Snipping Tool conveniently outlines it with a red border.

Tip: You can change the border color in the Options dialog box. It appears when you click Options on the main Snipping palette, or when you choose Tools→Options in the editing window.

Rectangular Snip lets you drag diagonally across the frozen screen image, thus capturing a square or rectangular area. Unfortunately, you can't adjust the rectangle if your aim was a little off; the instant you release the mouse button, the program captures the image in the rectangle.

A **Window Snip** neatly captures an entire window, automatically cropping out the entire background. And *which* window does it capture? That's up to you. As you point to each window, a red border appears around it to illustrate what Snipping Tool *thinks* you intend to capture. When the correct one is highlighted, click the mouse to capture.

Tip: A "window," in this context, doesn't have to be a window. It can also be the taskbar, a Sidebar gadget, the Start menu logo, a dialog box, and so on.

And a **Full-screen Snip,** of course, captures the entire screen.

3. **Specify what you want to capture, if necessary.**

That is, drag across the screen for a Free-form or Rectangular snip, or click the window (object) you want for a Window Snip. (Skip this step if you chose Full-

---

POWER USERS' CLINIC

May I Please See a Menu?

Snipping Tool, as you've already seen, is a heck of a lot better than the old PrtScn keystroke. But at first glance, you might assume that it still can't take a picture of a menu or a shortcut menu. After all, the instant you try to drag to highlight the menu, the menu closes!

Actually, you can capture menus—if you know the secret.

Open Snipping Tool, and then *minimize* it, which hides its window but keeps it running.

Now open the menu you want to capture, using the mouse or keyboard. Once the menu is open, press Ctrl+PrtScn.

That's all it takes; Snipping Tool is smart enough to know that you intend to capture just the menu.

That's workable, but still a bit complicated. That's why, if you're *actually* going to write a computer book or manual, you probably want a proper screen-capture program like Snagit (*www.techsmith.com*). It offers far more flexibility than any of Windows's own screenshot features. For example, you have a greater choice of file formats and capture options, you can dress up the results with arrows or captions, and (with its companion program, Camtasia) you can even capture *movies* of screen activity.

---

screen Snip. In that case, Snipping Tool pretty much knows what to do.) Now the editing window appears (Figure 7-5).

What you do with your finished graphic is up to you. For example:

- **Paste it.** The edited image may be in the window in front of you, but the original, unedited image is *also* on your invisible Windows Clipboard. Close the editing window without saving changes, pop into your graphics, word processing, or email program, and paste (Ctrl+V) what you've copied. Often, that's exactly what you want to do.

Tip: On the other hand, the Snipping Tool's tendency to copy everything to the Clipboard can be *bad* if there was already something *on* the Clipboard you wanted to keep. (The Clipboard can hold only one thing at a time.) If that syndrome is driving you nuts, you can turn off the copy-to-Clipboard feature in Options.

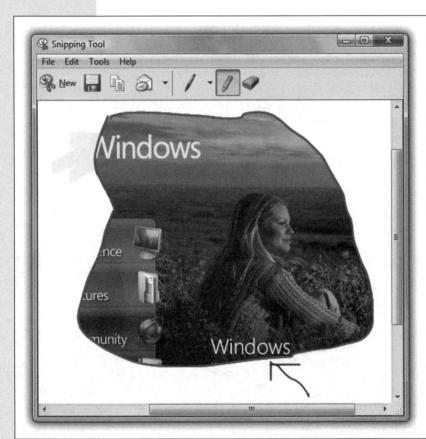

Figure 7-5:
After you capture a snip, the editing window appears, with your screen grab right in the middle of it. The Pen, Highlighter, and Eraser tools are there to help you annotate, draw attention to, or erase parts of your illustration. (The Eraser works only on pen and highlighter strokes—not the snip itself.)

- **Send it.** The little envelope button on the editing-window toolbar automatically prepares an outgoing email message with your graphic already pasted in (or, if your email program is set to send plain, unformatted text messages only, as an attachment).

- **Save it.** If your intention is to save the capture as a file, click the Save (floppy-disk) icon, or choose File→Save, or press Ctrl+S. When the Save As dialog box appears, type a name for your graphic, choose a file format for it (from the "Save as type" pop-up menu), specify a folder location, and then click Save.

Tip: If you capture the screen of a Web page and save it in HTML format, Snipping Tool helpfully prints the original URL (Web address) at the bottom of the image, so you'll know where it came from. You can turn off this "subtitling" feature in the Options dialog box of Snipping Tool.

Sound Recorder

Windows comes with a generous assortment of sound files you can use as error beeps, as described in Chapter 4. But no error beep is as delightful as one you've made yourself—of your 2-year-old saying, "Nope!" for example, or your own voice saying, "Dang it!"

Using Sound Recorder (Figure 7-6) requires a sound card, speakers, and a microphone. If your PC is appropriately equipped, you can use this little program to record various snippets of your life, which can serve a number of purposes, including becoming error beeps.

Recording a new sound

Here's how to do it:

1. **Choose Start→All Programs→Accessories→Sound Recorder.**

   Or start typing *recorder* into the Start menu Search box until Sound Recorder pops up in the list. The window shown in Figure 7-6 appears.

2. **Click Start Recording. Make the sound, and then click Stop Recording as soon as possible thereafter.**

   If you see the green animated bar dance in the Sound Recorder window, great; that's your VU (sound level) meter. It tells you that the PC is hearing you. If you don't see this graphic, however, then the sound isn't getting through. Most likely, the problem is that your PC control panel isn't set to record the appropriate sound source. Visit the Control Panel and open the Sound panel to investigate.

   As soon as you click Stop Recording, the Save As box appears.

Figure 7-6:
Sound Recorder has been lobotomized since the Windows XP version, but it does the job.

---

3. Type a name for your sound file in the "File name" text box, choose a folder for it, and then click the Save button.

You've just created a .wma file, a standard kind of Windows sound file.

What to do with sounds

When you double-click a .wma file, the file opens in Windows Media Player and plays back immediately. (Press Esc to halt playback.) Sound files are ideal for emailing to other people, posting on Web sites, transferring over the network, and so on. Many a Bart Simpson sound bite proliferates via the Internet in exactly this way.

Sticky Notes

Sticky Notes creates virtual Post-it notes that you can stick anywhere on your screen—a triumphant software answer to the thousands of people who stick notes on the edges of their actual monitors.

You can type quick notes and to-do items, paste in Web addresses or phone numbers you need to remember, or store any other little scraps and snippets of text you come across (Figure 7-7).

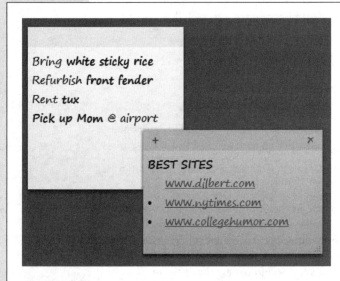

Figure 7-7:
You can apply some limited formatting to your sticky notes, but only by using keyboard shortcuts. Sticky Notes doesn't come with Windows 7 Starter Edition, by the way.

Creating notes

To create a new note, click the **+** button in the upper-left corner of the starter note, or press Ctrl+N. Then fill the note by typing or pasting.

Note the resize handle on the lower-right corner of each note. Drag it to make notes larger or smaller onscreen.

Formatting notes

You can format the text of a note—a *little* bit. There are no menus, of course, so you have to use keyboard shortcuts:

- **Bold, Italic, Underline.** Press Ctrl+B, Ctrl+I, or Ctrl+U.

- **Strikethrough style.** Press Ctrl+T.

- **Create a bulleted list.** Press Ctrl+Shift+L.

Tip: Press Ctrl+Shift+L a second time to produce a numbered list.

- **Change the type size.** Press Ctrl+Shift+> (larger font) or Ctrl+Shift+< (smaller).

You can also change the "paper" color for a note to any of five other pastel colors. To do that, right-click the note and then choose from the shortcut menu.

Deleting notes

To get rid of a note, click the little ✕ in the upper-right corner. (You may have to point to it to see it.) When the program asks if you're sure, click Yes.

On the other hand, you can *exit* Sticky Notes without worrying that you'll lose what you've already typed. Right-click the Sticky Notes icon on the taskbar, for example, and choose "Close window" from the shortcut menu. The program disappears, but all your notes will be there the next time you open it.

Sync Center

This program is the terminal for Windows's offline files feature. (This feature is great for laptop owners who want to take work home from the office network, or network domain members who want to keep working on documents even if the server that houses them goes down.) See page 635 for Sync Center details.

Windows Explorer

Windows Explorer just means "desktop windows." Choosing this command opens one up for you—namely, your Libraries window.

Windows Mobility Center

Home Premium • Professional • Enterprise • Ultimate

The Mobility Center gives you a single, centralized dashboard for managing laptop features. Here, in one window, you can turn wireless networking on and off, change display settings to suit the environment, change the display orientation, and even sync your palmtop or phone with your PC. Page 621 has the full rundown.

WordPad

WordPad is a basic word processor (see Figure 7-8), and it received a major face-lift in Windows 7. Among other blessings, WordPad now has a toolbar ribbon for quick access to formatting commands, and it can now open and create Microsoft Word files. Yes, you can get away with not buying Microsoft Office, and none of your email business partners will ever know the difference.

Figure 7-8:
WordPad's new formatting ribbon makes it an even closer relative to Microsoft Word .

And it's not just Word files. WordPad also can open and create plain text files, Rich Text Format (RTF) documents, and OpenOffice.org files.

Using WordPad

When WordPad first opens, you see an empty sheet of electronic typing paper. Just above the ruler, you find a ribbon full of drop-down menus and buttons that affect

Text-Selection Fundamentals

Before doing almost anything to text in a word processor, like making it bold, changing its typeface, or moving it to a new spot in your document, you have to *highlight* the text you want to affect. For millions of people, this entails dragging the cursor extremely carefully, perfectly horizontally, across the desired text. And if they want to capture an entire paragraph or section, they click at the beginning, drag diagonally, and release the mouse button when they reach the end of the passage.

That's all an enormous waste of time. Selecting text is the cornerstone of every editing operation in a word processor, so there are faster and more precise ways of going about it.

For example, double-clicking a word highlights it, instantly and neatly. In fact, by keeping the mouse button pressed on the second click, you can now drag horizontally to highlight text in crisp one-word chunks—a great way to highlight text faster and more precisely. These tricks work anywhere you can type.

In most programs, including Microsoft's, additional shortcuts await. For example, *triple*-clicking anywhere within a paragraph highlights the entire paragraph. (Once again, if you *keep* the button pressed at the end of this maneuver, you can then drag to highlight your document in one-paragraph increments.)

In many programs, including Word and WordPad, you can highlight exactly one sentence by clicking within it while pressing Ctrl.

Finally, here's a universal trick that lets you highlight a large blob of text, even one that's too big to fit on the current screen. Start by clicking to position the insertion point cursor at the very beginning of the text you want to capture. Now scroll, if necessary, so the ending point of the passage is visible. Shift+click there. Windows instantly highlights everything between your click and your Shift+click.

the formatting of your text, as shown in Figure 7-9. As in any word processor, you can apply these formats (like bold, italic, or color) to two kinds of text:

- Text you've highlighted by dragging the mouse across it.

- Text you're *about* to type. In other words, if you click the *I* button, the next characters you type will be italicized. Click the *I* button a second time to turn off the italics.

The Font formatting buttons let you change the look of selected text: font, size, color, subscript, and so on. The Paragraph formatting buttons affect entire paragraphs, as shown in Figure 7-9.

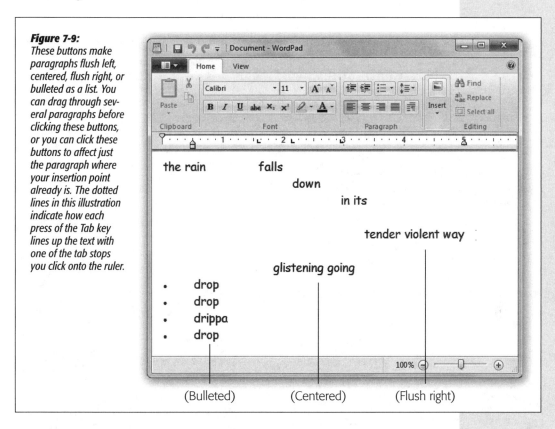

Figure 7-9:
These buttons make paragraphs flush left, centered, flush right, or bulleted as a list. You can drag through several paragraphs before clicking these buttons, or you can click these buttons to affect just the paragraph where your insertion point already is. The dotted lines in this illustration indicate how each press of the Tab key lines up the text with one of the tab stops you click onto the ruler.

(Bulleted) (Centered) (Flush right)

WordPad doesn't offer big-gun features like spell checking, style sheets, or tables. But it does offer a surprisingly long list of core word-processing features. For example:

- **Find, Replace.** Using the Find button (right end of the Home toolbar), you can locate a particular word or phrase instantly, even in a long document. The Replace command takes it a step further, replacing that found phrase with another one (a great way to change the name of your main character throughout your entire novel, for example).

- **Indents and Tab stops.** As shown in Figure 7-9, you click on the ruler to place tab stops there. Each time you press the Tab key, your insertion point cursor jumps in line with the next tab stop.

- **Bulleted lists.** You're reading a bulleted list right now. To apply bullets to a bunch of paragraphs, click the Bullets button (▤). If you click the ▾ next to it, you can create a numbered or lettered list instead.

- **Insert object.** This button lets you create or slap in a picture, graph, chart, sound, movie, spreadsheet, or other kind of data. (The "Paint drawing" button opens up a temporary Paint window so that you can whip up a quick sketch that then gets dropped into your WordPad document.)

UP TO SPEED

Mouse Keys, Sticky Keys, Toggle Keys, Filter Keys

The Ease of Access center offers a single page of options designed to make the keyboard easier to use if you have limited dexterity. There are four primary features here:

Mouse Keys lets you use the number keypad to control the arrow cursor. (It's useful if you can't use the mouse, or if you can but you want more precision in a graphics program.) Pressing the 2, 4, 6, and 8 keys on this pad moves the mouse around your screen—down, left, up, and right.

If you click "Set up mouse keys," you see where you can control how *fast* the cursor moves. You can also turn on "Hold down Ctrl to speed up and Shift to slow down" to do just what it says: Make the cursor jump in larger increments when you press Ctrl or smaller increments when you press Shift. As a convenience, you can also indicate that when the NumLock key is tapped, you want the numbers to type *numbers* instead of moving the cursor.

Sticky Keys is for people who have difficulty pressing two or more keys (such as Ctrl, Alt, and Shift combinations) at once.

Once this feature has been turned on, you can press keys of a specified combination one at a time instead of simultaneously. To do so, press the first key (Ctrl, Alt, or Shift) *twice,* which makes it "stick." Then press the second key (usually a letter key). Windows responds exactly as though you had pressed the two keys simultaneously.

Here again, a setup page awaits—click "Set up Sticky Keys." Here, you can indicate that you want to be able to turn on Sticky Keys by pressing the Shift key five times in a row. Another option makes Windows beep when a key is double-pressed and "stuck"—a confirmation that you're about to trigger a keyboard shortcut.

Toggle Keys makes the computer beep whenever you press the Caps Lock, Num Lock, or Scroll Lock keys. You don't have to be disabled to find this option attractive, since the confirmation beep prevents you from looking up after five minutes of typing to find a page of text tHAT lOOKS lIKE tHIS.

Finally, there's **Filter Keys**. In Windows, holding down a key for longer than a fraction of a second produces repeated keystrokes (such as TTTTTTT). When you turn on Filter Keys, though, Windows treats a repeated key as a *single* keystroke, which can be useful if you have trouble pressing keys lightly and briefly.

The "Set up Filter Keys" link offers an option that lets you use the right-side Shift key as the on/off switch for the filtering mode (by pressing Shift for 8 seconds): "Turn on Filter Keys when right SHIFT [key] is pressed for 8 seconds." It's also the home to the new Bounce Keys option, which helps filter out unwanted keystrokes, and an option that puts a stopwatch-like icon in the Notification Area when you're in Filter Keys mode.

Tip: If you click "Date and time," you get a dialog box full of date and time formats (12/18/2010; 12-Dec-2010; Saturday, December 18, 2010, and so on). Double-click one to insert that date into your document at the insertion point.

- **Drag-and-drop editing.** Instead of using the three-step Copy and Paste routine for moving words and phrases around in your document, you can simply drag highlighted text from place to place on the screen. See page 223 for details.

Ease of Access

If you have trouble using your keyboard or making out small text on the screen, the programs in the Start→All Programs→Accessories→Ease of Access folder may be just what you need. (In previous versions of Windows, this accessibility center was called Universal Access, which pretty much explains why its keyboard shortcut is 🪟+U.)

Windows gets disability-friendlier with every new version. It includes a long list of features that let the PC magnify, speak, or otherwise boost the elements of the screen.

The Ease of Access item in the Start menu is actually yet another *folder.* It contains these items:

Ease of Access Center

This new control panel gathers together all of Windows 7's accessibility features under one roof.

At the top of the window are the triggers for four of the big-ticket accessibility items: Magnifier, On-Screen Keyboard, Narrator, and High Contrast. You can click one of these buttons with your mouse, or, if you can't use the mouse, just wait; a blue rectangle highlights one after another, pausing a few seconds at each stop. Tap the space bar to open a highlighted option. (The four features are described below.)

At the bottom of the window, you find a tidy list of controls that tweak the PC's audio, visual, mouse, and keyboard settings in special ways to help out people with limited hearing, vision, or mobility. When you click one of these links (such as "Use the computer without a display"), a special, very peculiar window opens, half Explorer window and half dialog box, that's filled with checkboxes. Here's the rundown.

Tip: These features aren't useful only to people with disabilities. If you have a flat-panel screen, for example, you may have noticed that everything on the screen is smaller than it might be on a traditional CRT screen. The result is that the cursor is sometimes hard to find, and the text is sometimes hard to read—but these features let you make it more visible.

- **Use the computer without a display.** If you have trouble seeing the screen, turn on Narrator (described on page 290) here. You can also turn on Audio Description, in which a disembodied voice *describes* the action in movies. (Of course, this assumes that the movie comes with a description *track,* and few do.) This screen also lets you make Windows alert boxes go away by themselves after a while—a solution to a blind person's typical dilemma (the PC doesn't seem to react to anything, because, unbeknownst to you, there's a dialog box on the screen holding up the works).

• **Make the computer easier to see.** Here's the on/off switch for High Contrast mode (Figure 7-10)—or, rather, the on/off switch for the *keystroke* that turns on High Contrast mode (Alt+Left Shift+PrtScn).

This screen also offers yet another way to turn on Narrator and Magnifier (described on page 289), plus a link to the control panel where you can make text

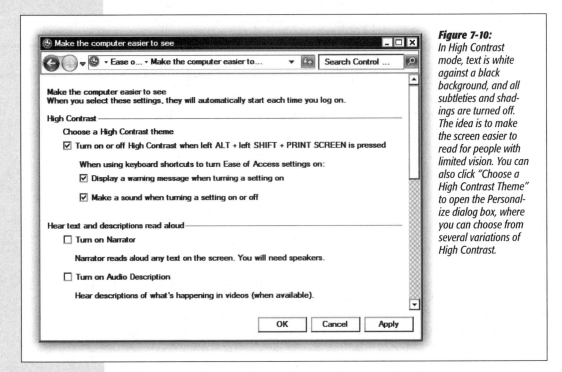

Figure 7-10:
In High Contrast mode, text is white against a black background, and all subtleties and shadings are turned off. The idea is to make the screen easier to read for people with limited vision. You can also click "Choose a High Contrast Theme" to open the Personalize dialog box, where you can choose from several variations of High Contrast.

and icons bigger.

Most interesting of all, you can use the options at the bottom of the box to make the "focus" rectangle, or even the blinking word processor insertion point, thicker and easier to see.

• **Use the computer without a mouse or keyboard.** This window offers an on/off switch for the onscreen keyboard (described below), and a link to turn on Speech Recognition (page 225).

• **Make the mouse easier to use.** Very cool: a palette of nine cursor (and insertion-point) styles, in various color schemes and enlarged sizes. One click is all it takes.

Also here: an on/off switch for Mouse Keys (described below) and "Activate a window by hovering over it with the mouse" (switch windows by *pointing*, not *clicking*).

- **Make the keyboard easier to use.** These features—Mouse Keys, Sticky Keys, and so on—have been with Windows for several generations, but they finally have a home that makes sense. See the box on page 286 for full details.

- **Use text or visual alternatives for sounds.** If you're deaf, a computer that beeps to get your attention isn't especially helpful. But this feature, formerly called Sound Sentry, instructs Windows to make your screen flash or blink when a sound occurs. You choose which part of the screen you want to use as a warning: the title bar ("caption bar") of the window, the window itself, or the entire desktop.

Note: "Turn on text captions for spoken dialog" refers to subtitles on DVDs and videos. It works only if (a) subtitles have been prepared for the movie you're watching, and (b) the video-playback software is Win7-capable.

- **Make it easier to focus on tasks.** Man, who doesn't occasionally wish it were easier to focus on tasks?

  Of course, Microsoft has a slightly more literal meaning in mind here. In truth, this page is nothing more than yet *another* set of on/off switches for features that appear on other Ease of Access pages: Narrator, Sticky Keys, Toggle Keys, and so on.

Magnifier

Magnifier is like a software magnifying glass that fills the top portion of your screen. (The actual-size version appears in the bottom half.) The magnified area scrolls as you move your cursor, tab through a dialog box, or type, enlarging whatever part of the screen contains the action. Using the Magnifier Settings dialog box shown in Figure 7-11, you can specify how much magnification you want (1 to 16 times), which area of the screen gets magnified, and so on.

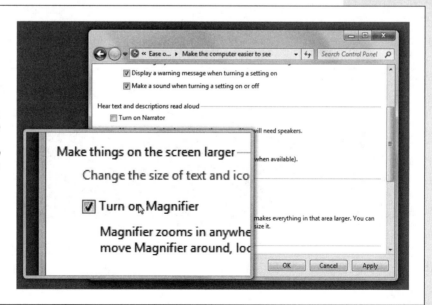

Figure 7-11:
Magnifier enlarges whatever part of the screen your cursor is touching. You can adjust the size of the magnification pane by dragging its edge. You can also tear the pane away from the edge of the screen so it becomes a floating window; just drag anywhere inside it.

Tip: Whenever Magnifier is turned on, you can zoom in or out by pressing Ctrl+plus sign or Ctrl+minus sign, respectively.

Narrator

As the little welcome screen tells you, Narrator is a program that can read aloud whatever text appears on the screen—dialog boxes, error messages, menus, text you've typed, and so on. Narrator doesn't work in all programs, and it sounds a little bit like a Norwegian who's had a few beers. Still, if you have trouble reading text on the screen, or if you just like to hear your email read back to you, it's better than nothing.

In the Windows XP days, Narrator could read only what you see listed in the Narrator dialog box:

- **User's Keystrokes.** That is, Narrator pronounces each letter as you type it—a handy safeguard if you can't see what you're doing.

- **System Messages.** Windows error messages and other alert boxes.

- **Scroll Notification.** You're be told when the screen has scrolled, to better keep your bearings.

In Windows 7, however, Narrator is quite a bit more flexible. If you click the Quick Help button, you can scroll down to see an elaborate chart of keystrokes that tell Narrator what to read. Here are a few of the most useful commands:

Read the frontmost window	Ctrl+Shift+space bar
Stop reading	Ctrl
Read the selected word	Insert+F4
Read the selected line	Insert+F5
Read the selected paragraph	Insert+F6
Read the whole document	Insert+F8
Read you the details about the highlighted icon	Ctrl+Shift+Enter

Figure 7-12:
Use the Keyboard menu to choose a different key layout, and the Settings menu to change the typeface that appears on the keys.

Tip: You can fiddle with Anna, if you like. She's the voice of Windows, and she's adjustable.

If you click Voice Settings, you open a dialog box where you can use pop-up menus to make Anna speak faster or slower, louder or softer, and higher or lower.

On-Screen Keyboard
If you're having trouble typing, keep the On-Screen Keyboard program in mind. It lets you type just by clicking the mouse (Figure 7-12)—an option you may find useful in a pinch.

Windows Speech Recognition
Windows 7 offers a surprisingly useful (and accurate) speech-recognition feature. You can read all about it in Chapter 6.

System Tools
This folder (Start→All Programs→Accessories→System Tools) is designed to be a toolbox for basic Windows administration, maintenance, and troubleshooting programs. Many of these programs are described elsewhere in this book:

Computer	Chapter 1
Control Panel	Chapter 8
Disk Cleanup	Chapter 20
Disk Defragmenter	Chapter 20
Resource Monitor	Chapter 20
System Restore	Chapter 22
Task Scheduler	Chapter 20
Windows Easy Transfer	Appendix A

Three items in this submenu, however, have nothing to do with PC health and fitness, and were stashed here perhaps because Microsoft couldn't find a more logical place to stash them: Character Map, Internet Explorer (No Add-ons), and Private Character Editor.

Character Map
Your computer is capable of creating hundreds of different typographical symbols—the currency symbols for the yen and British pound, diacritical markings for French and Spanish, various scientific symbols, trademark and copyright signs, and so on. Obviously, these symbols don't appear on your keyboard; to provide enough keys, your keyboard would have to be the width of Wyoming. You *can* type the symbols, but they're hidden behind the keys you do see.

The treasure map that reveals their locations is the Character Map. When first opening this program, use the Font pop-up menu to specify the font you want to use (because every font contains a different set of symbols). Now you see every single symbol in the font. As you click on each symbol, a magnified version of it appears to help you distinguish them. See Figure 7-13 for details on transferring a particular symbol to your document.

Tip: Some email programs can't handle the fancy kinds of symbols revealed by the Character Map. That explains why your copyright symbols, for example, can turn into a gibberish character on the receiving end.

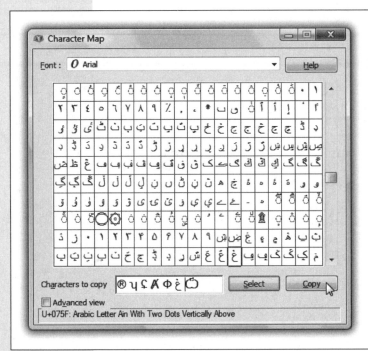

Figure 7-13:
Double-click a character to transfer it to the "Characters to copy" box, as shown here. (Double-click several in a row if you want to capture a sequence of symbols.) You may have to scroll down quite a bit in some of today's modern Unicode fonts, which contain hundreds of characters. Click Copy, and then Close. When you've returned to your document, use the Paste command to insert the symbols.

Internet Explorer (No Add-ons)

Internet Explorer is far more secure than it was in the XP days. Its behavior can still get flaky, however, especially when you go gunking it up with add-ons and plug-ins. There may come a day when your main copy is behaving oddly, but you don't have the time to troubleshoot. In that case, choose this command. It opens a fresh, virginal copy of Internet Explorer, with all of your add-on junk stripped away—a copy that, in theory, should perform as smoothly as the day it was born.

Private Character Editor

If the Character Map doesn't have enough strange characters for you, this cranky little oddball app lets you create new font symbols all by yourself.

Note: As the name implies, these characters are private, which means they won't appear on anyone else's computer.

When you open Private Character Editor (and authenticate yourself, if necessary), you're shown the strange little character grid shown in Figure 7-14. Click an empty square to proceed as shown in the figure.

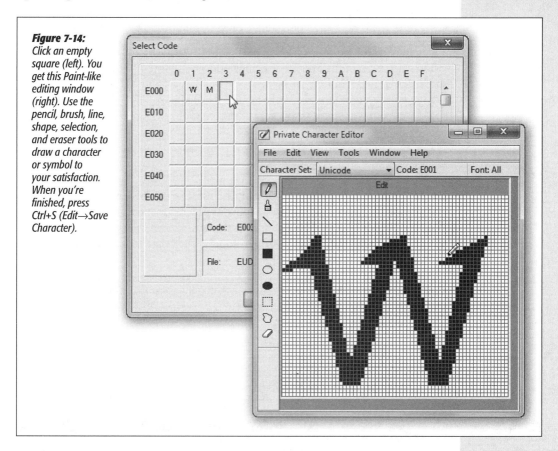

Figure 7-14:
Click an empty square (left). You get this Paint-like editing window (right). Use the pencil, brush, line, shape, selection, and eraser tools to draw a character or symbol to your satisfaction. When you're finished, press Ctrl+S (Edit→Save Character).

Once you've designed a symbol or two, you can insert them into your everyday documents using the Character Map program described above. Just remember that you won't see your hand-drawn masterpiece in Character Map until you choose, from the Font pop-up menu, All Fonts (Private Characters).

Tablet PC

Home Premium • Professional • Enterprise • Ultimate

These links take you to three programs that are especially (or exclusively) useful to people who use PCs with touch screens—tablet PCs, as they're known. All three—Personalize Handwriting Recognition, Tablet PC Input Panel, and Windows Journal—are described in Chapter 19.

Windows PowerShell

Windows 7 introduces PowerShell 2.0, a command console and scripting language. If you're a programmer, PowerShell lets you write your own simple programs, called *cmdlets* ("commandlets") that can perform all kinds of automated drudgery for you: Copy or move folders, manipulate files, open or quit programs, and so on.

You harness all this power by typing up *scripts* in PowerShell's command-line interface (which means no mouse, no menus, no windows—all text, like in the DOS days). In short, PowerShell is not for the layperson. If you're an *ambitious* layperson, however, a Google search for *PowerShell tutorial* unveils all kinds of Web sites that teach you, step-by-step, how to harness this very advanced tool.

Games
All Versions

Even if you have a corporate version of Windows, like the Professional or Enterprise version, you still get a bunch of games for your procrastination pleasure. Happily, the Windows 7 complement of games includes the return of Internet games, meaning that you can play them against other people online. (They were removed from Windows Vista as a security precaution.)

Note: Well, OK–Microsoft isn't quite as generous as all that. The Starter Edition of Windows 7 is missing several of the games described here—including the two Titans titles and all the Internet games.

Here's the suite of Windows 7 games, all of which are listed in the Start→All Programs→Games submenu.

Tip: Complete instructions lurk within the Help menu of each game.

In Every Game, a Gem

Many of the games in Windows 7 bear the same names as the ones in Windows XP and Vista–but they're actually all new. All nine have a consistent look, consistent menus, and consistent options.

Each has two menus, Game and Help. The Game menu always offers a way to start a new game, plus these intriguing options:

Statistics reveals your personal game-playing history: how many times you've won, and so on.

Options lets you turn animations and pop-up tip boxes off if you find them annoying or insulting. Here, too, you find checkboxes for "Always save game on exit" and "Always continue saved game," which can help lend a through line to your otherwise fractured, chaotic life.

And **Change Appearance** lets you redecorate your game world. For example, if, in Chess Titans, you choose Game→Change Appearance, you can choose all kinds of wacky materials for the look of your pieces (Wood, Porcelain, or Frosted Glass) and for your game board (Porcelain, Marble, or Wood).

Use *those* options if you don't have *enough* variety in your life.

Chess Titans

It's not just chess—it's computer-generated chess on a gorgeously rendered board with a set of realistic 3-D pieces. You can rotate the board in space, as described in Figure 7-15.

Figure 7-15:
How did this chess board get rotated like this? On Aero-capable PCs, you can right-click a corner of the board and rotate it in 3-D space to study your situation from a different angle. (It snaps back to its original angle when you let go—unless, of course, you choose Game→Options and turn off "Rotate board back after free view.") Cool!

When you launch Chess, you're asked what difficulty level you want. Then you're offered a fresh, new game that's set up in Human vs. Computer mode—meaning that you (the human, with the light-colored pieces) get to play against the computer (your PC, on the dark side). Drag the chess piece of your choice into position on the board, and the game is afoot.

If you'd rather trade piece colors with the PC, no biggie. Choose Game→Options and select "Play against computer as black."

Tip: Click a piece without dragging to see where it's allowed to move, courtesy of light-up chessboard squares.

If you and a buddy are looking for something to do, you can play against each other. Choose Game→"New game against human," and enjoy the way Windows rotates the chessboard after each person's turn.

FreeCell

You might think of this card game as solitaire on steroids. When you choose Game→New Game, the computer deals eight piles of cards before you. The goal is to sort them into four piles of cards—one suit each and sequentially from ace to king—in the spaces (the "home stacks") at the upper-right corner of the screen. (To move a card, click it once and then click where you want it moved to. You're allowed to move only the bottom card from one of your eight stacks, or the cards in the free cells, described next.)

You can use the upper-left placeholders, the "free cells," as temporary resting places for your cards. From there, cards can go either onto one of the upper-right piles or onto the bottom of one of the eight piles in the second row. However, when moving cards to the eight piles, you must place them alternating red/black, and in descending sequence.

Games Explorer

This is just a standard Explorer window containing all nine of Windows's games.

Hearts

The object of this card game is to get rid of all the hearts you're holding by passing them off to other players. At the end of each round, all players count up their points: one point for each heart, and 13 points for the dreaded queen of spades. The winner is the person with the fewest points when the game ends (which is when somebody reaches 100).

What makes it tricky is that even while you're trying to ditch your hearts, somebody else may be secretly trying to collect them. If you can collect *all* the hearts *and* the queen of spades, you win big-time; everybody else gets 26 big fat points, and you get off scot-free.

You can play Classic Hearts only against Windows, which manages the hands and strategies of three other fictional players to play against you (named North, West, and East).

Internet Backgammon, Internet Checkers, Internet Spades

Yes, kids, they're back—three classic games, now playable against perfect strangers on the Internet.

When you fire up one of the Internet games, a message appears to tell you that you'll be matched up at random with somebody else online, and that Microsoft won't spy on you.

Once the game begins, it's assumed that you and your anonymous partner both know the rules. You can "chat" with your opponent, but only by using a pop-up menu of 24 canned phrases (like "Hello," "Nice try," and "Good game").

Overall, it's good and creepy to see those pieces moving by themselves on your screen, driven by some unknowable opponent, maybe thousands of miles away, with only one thing in common for sure: You're both bored enough to want to kill a little time with these games.

Tip: If your unsportsmanlike opponent bails on you midgame, Microsoft's computers are kind enough to take over for her, so you don't feel like you've wasted a game.

Mahjong Titans

Here's yet another kind of solitaire. In Mahjong, you use tiles instead of cards. When the game begins, click the starting tile pile you want to work with. The idea is to click pairs of matching tiles to make them disappear—but only free tiles (not pinned under any others) can disappear.

Most of the time, the tiles have to match *exactly*, both in pattern and in number. Flower tiles let you off easy, though—any flower is considered a match of any other. Season tiles, same deal; any matches any.

Tip: If you get stuck, press the letter H key for a hint. Well, not so much a hint as a blatant giveaway; the next pair of available matching tiles blinks at you.

Minesweeper

Under some of the grid cells are mines; under others, hints about nearby mines. Your goal: Find the mines without blowing yourself up.

When clicking random squares, you run the risk of getting blown up instantly. If that happens, you lose; them's the breaks. But if you get lucky, you uncover little numbers around the square you clicked. Each number reveals how many mines are hidden in the squares surrounding it. Using careful mathematical logic and the process of elimination, you can eventually figure out which squares have mines under them. (To

---

GEM IN THE ROUGH

Why Mimesweeper Didn't Make the Cut

Windows Vista was the first version of Windows to be written in the age of blogs (Web diaries)—and Microsoft actually permitted its programmers to participate by keeping Windows fans updated on its progress.

Most of the blogs were pretty mundane, filled with programmery stuff. But Microsoft researcher David Vronay had PC nuts splurting their coffee in laughter with this posting:

"One of the most common requests I get from people is a list of features that didn't make it [into Windows Vista]. I thought it would be interesting for readers to hear about some of these things.

"As you may know, we have taken flack in the past for Minesweeper and the use of mines. Although we don't have land mines in the USA, in many countries they are experienced in daily life, and not something to make light of in a video game.

"So for Vista, we wanted to replace mines with something that people also wanted to avoid finding. Thus we came up with the concept of Mimesweeper.

"In Mimesweeper, you uncover street intersections on a black-and-white striped grid in which several mimes are hidden. Just like wandering around Paris, the goal is to figure out where all of the mimes are without actually encountering one.

"Unfortunately, beta feedback revealed a tremendous amount of controversy over the use of mimes. Although we do not have many mimes in the USA, apparently there are many countries where running into a mime is common occurrence and not something to make light of in a video game.

"In the end, we pulled the concept and replaced it with a garden of flowers."

---

help keep track, you can right-click the squares to plant little flags that mean, "Don't step here.") You win if you mark all the mine squares with flags.

Purble Place

Meet Microsoft's nod to the next generation of Windows fans: Purble Place, which is geared toward the elementary-school (or even preschool) set (Figure 7-16).

Figure 7-16:
All three of the games here smack of the games you find on educational CDs like Reader Rabbit.

Which game you play depends on which of the three Fisher-Price-style buildings you click first:

- **Purble Pairs.** It's Ye Olde Memory Matching Game. Click any two tiles to reveal what's on their faces. If they match, they disappear. If not, they spin facedown again; as the game goes on, you have to remember where you saw that darned hat, or cake, or whatever. You're racing against the clock.

- **Comfy Cakes.** The TV shows you what kind of cake the chef needs. As the naked cake moves down the assembly lines, you have to click the right pan shape, batter color, frosting flavor, and decoration by clicking the appropriate buttons below the belt. The idea is to make the cake match the one shown on the TV. As you get better, the conveyor belt speeds up (can you say *I Love Lucy*?).

- **Purble Shop.** Your mission is to build a Purble character whose features match the mystery dude (marked by the question mark). Each time you assemble some features from the shelves (eyes, nose, mouth) and click the checkmark button, the game tells you how many of these features you got right—but not which ones. Through trial and error, you're supposed to deduce what the mystery dude actually looks like.

Solitaire

Here it is: the program that started it all, the application that introduced millions of people to the joys of a graphic interface like Windows. (Ask the advanced-beginner Windows fan to identify a good program-file code to type into the Start→Run dialog box, and he might not know *winword* or *msconfig*—but he'll probably know *sol.)*

In Solitaire, the object is to build four piles of cards, one for each suit, in ascending order (starting with aces). To help achieve this, you maintain seven smaller stacks of cards in the second row. You can put cards onto these piles as long as you alternate red and black, and as long as the cards go in descending order (a four of hearts can be placed on a five of spades, for example). Click a facedown card on one of these piles to turn it over. If it helps you to continue the red/black/red/black sequence you've started, you can drag around stacks of faceup cards on these piles. And when you can't find any more moves to make, click the deck in the upper-left corner to reveal more cards.

Spider Solitaire

If your spirit needs a good game of solitaire, but you just don't have the time or patience for Solitaire or FreeCell, this kinder, gentler, *easier* game may be just the ticket. Thanks to the built-in cheat mechanism, which suggests the next move with

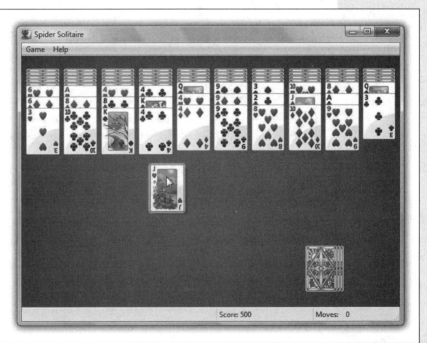

Figure 7-17:
In the easiest level, there's no need to worry about color or suit, because the game gives you only spades. If you run out of imagination, just press the M or H key to make the program propose a move. And if even the game can't find a legal move, simply click the deck in the lower-right corner to distribute another round of cards, which opens up a new round of possibilities.

no penalty, you can blow through this game with all the satisfaction and none of the frustration of traditional solitaire games.

You play with 104 cards. You get 10 stacks across the top of the screen, and the rest in a pile in the lower-right corner of the screen (Figure 7-17). All you have to do is create stacks of cards in descending order, from king down to ace, by dragging cards around. As soon as you create such a stack, the cards fly off the playing board. The goal is to remove *all* the cards from the playing board.

Sticking with the game to the very end delivers an animated fireworks display—and a tiny, budding sense of achievement.

Maintenance

This folder contains four PC maintenance tools that may one day save your bacon:

- **Backup and Restore** is described in Chapter 22.
- **Create a System Repair Disc** is covered on page 689.
- **Help and Support** is the main online help system for Windows (Chapter 5).
- **Windows Remote Assistance** is the online connection mechanism that lets a guru see your screen, and even operate your mouse, from afar (page 202).

Startup

The Startup folder contains documents, disks, folders, and programs you want to run *automatically* when you log in. Maybe you begin your day with an email or calendar check, for example; if so, drop their icons into this folder. Page 31 has the details.

Windows Live

Here, in the Windows Live folder, is the suite of Windows Live Essentials described at the beginning of this chapter. These programs are described in the appropriate chapters of this book:

- **Windows Live Call** is nothing more than a link to Windows Messenger, Microsoft's chat program. It's just a reminder that you can use Windows Messenger to make free voice calls over the Internet—from PC to PC rather than phone to phone. (You can call from your PC to someone's phone, too, but that part's not free.) It's described in Chapter 13.
- **Windows Live Family Safety** is an Internet porn blocker, and it's covered in Chapter 10.
- **Windows Live Mail**, your basic email program, is described in Chapter 12.
- **Windows Live Messenger** is Microsoft's chat program; it's described at the end of this chapter.

- **Windows Live Movie Maker** is for editing your camcorder videos and other videos. You can read all about it in "Movie Maker," a free bonus PDF appendix to this chapter that's available from this book's "Missing CD" page at *www.missingmanuals.com*.

- **Windows Live Photo Gallery** is the subject of Chapter 14.

- **Windows Live Writer** is described next.

Windows Live Writer

Windows Live Writer makes its debut in Windows 7. If WordPad is a basic word processor, and Notepad is a basic text processor, then Writer is a basic *blog* processor. It's a simple program for composing blogs (Web logs—frequently updated Web pages full of text and photos) and, more important, posting them online. If you don't already have a blog, Writer makes it easy to create one that's hosted by Microsoft for free.

When you first open Writer, you're asked to set up your new blog. After the welcome screen, you have to specify *where* on the Web you want your blog to live:

- **If you don't already have a blog account,** click "I don't have a blog; create one on Windows Live for me." You're asked for your Windows Live name and password. Then, after a moment, Writer will create a brand-new blog Web site for you on Microsoft's free Windows Live blogging service.

- **If you already have a blog account,** either on one of Microsoft's sites (Windows Live Spaces or SharePoint) or one of its rivals (Blogger, WordPress, TypePad, or some other site), click the appropriate button. When you click Next, you're asked for the blog's Web address and your account name and password.

Note: There's no reason you can't maintain multiple blog accounts. Just choose Tools→Accounts at any time, and click Add to add on a new account.

Then, after a moment, you name your new blog ("Cat Diaries" or whatever)—and then you're ready to begin writing!

The process goes like this:

- **Make up a title for your post.** Each new post (mini-article) on your blog needs a title. Type it into the "Enter a post title" headline box.

- **Write.** Go ahead and type or paste into the big empty, white box. You can use the formatting tools on the toolbar (see Figure 7-18) to dress up the formatting. (Don't miss the first pop-up menu at the left, which offers different canned styles for headings.)

- **Add pictures, links, tables, or videos.** You can add a link to another Web page by clicking the "Insert hyperlink" button, drop in a photo by clicking the "Insert picture" button, or even insert a table ("Insert table"). In fact, you can even insert a video or a map, using the Insert pop-up menu at the right end of the toolbar.

Tip: When you click a photo you've inserted, the options pane at the right side of the window changes. It now offers all kinds of options: You can make your text wrap around the photo, you can add a drop shadow border, and so on. On the Advanced tab, you can even change the size of the photo, crop it, rotate it, or adjust its contrast. The Effects tab even lets you apply cheesy special effects, like Black and White, Sharpen, Emboss, and so on.

When it's all over, and everything looks good, and you've checked your spelling (choose Tools→Check Spelling), and you've clicked Preview to see what the thing will look like on the Web, you can publish your little writeup for your fans worldwide to enjoy. Just click Publish on the toolbar (or choose File→Publish to Blog).

After a moment, your Web browser opens, with your fresh, hot, piping blog post in all its glory. Now all you have to do is send the address of your blog to your friends and loved ones so your fan base can start to grow.

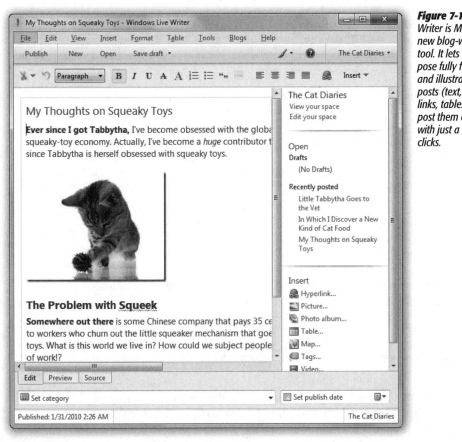

Figure 7-18:
Writer is Microsoft's new blog-writing tool. It lets you compose fully formatted and illustrated blog posts (text, graphics, links, tables) and post them online with just a couple of clicks.

Note: The free Windows Live blog-hosting service is very nice. It lets people leave comments about your writings, subscribe to RSS feeds of them (automated summaries), sign up to have your posts sent to their cellphones, and more. Of course, rival services like Blogger (Google's similar free service) do the same thing. It's a glorious world for the cheapskate blogger.

Windows Live Messenger

Somewhere between email and the telephone lies a unique communication tool called *instant messaging*. Messenger, of course, is Microsoft's very own instant messenger program.

Messenger does four things very well:

- **Instant messaging.** If you don't know what instant messaging is, there's a teenager near you who does.

  It's like live email. You type messages in a chat window, and your friends type replies back to you in real time. Instant messaging combines the privacy of email and the immediacy of the phone.

- **Free long distance.** If your PC has a microphone, and your buddy's does, too, the two of you can also chat *out loud*, using the Internet as a free long-distance phone.

- **Free videoconferencing.** If you and your buddies all have broadband Internet connections and cameras, you can have *video* chats, no matter where you happen to be in the world. This arrangement is a jaw-dropping visual stunt that can bring distant collaborators face to face without plane tickets—and it costs about $99,900 less than professional videoconferencing gear.

- **File transfers.** Got an album of high-quality photos or a giant presentation file that's too big to send by email? Forget about using some online file-transfer service

---

GEM IN THE ROUGH

Status Messages

On the buddy-list (startup) screen, using the pop-up menu just to the right of your name at the top, you can display your current mental status to other people's buddy lists. You can announce that you're Available, Away, Busy, or—sneakiest of all—"Appear offline." (But of course you're not; you can still monitor who's coming and going, without being bothered.)

If you have music playing in Windows Media Player, you can tell the world what you're listening to at the moment by choosing "Show what I'm listening to" from the pop-up menu below your name.

Best of all, if you click that status line beneath your name, you open a text box where you can type any status message at all ("Having soup," "Makin' copies"—or whatever). That's what other people will see beneath your name in their buddy lists.

---

or networked server; you can drag that monster file directly to your buddy's PC, through Messenger, for a direct machine-to-machine transfer.

Tip: The following pages assume that you've made the Messenger menu bar appear (which it doesn't normally). To do that, click the 📑 button near the top of the buddy list; from the shortcut menu, choose "Show the menu bar."

Building the Buddy List

The first thing you need is a chatting companion, what's called a *buddy* in instant-messaging circles. It can be anyone with a Microsoft account (Hotmail, Xbox, Windows Live, Messenger), or anyone with a Yahoo Messenger account. (The three big chat networks are Microsoft's, Yahoo's, and AOL's; only AOL chatters can't communicate with Windows Live Messenger.)

All your buddies are listed in the startup window, as shown 7-19.

Figure 7-19:
On this buddy list, your favorite chat partners appear at the top. (And how do you designate someone a Favorite? Right-click his name and choose "Add to favorites," of course.)

Getting hold of these people's chat addresses is up to you. Several tools are at your disposal: the Search box at the top of the Messenger window, for example, and especially the "Add contacts from other services" command. (To see it, click the Add button next to the Search box at the top.) This command lets you invite contacts from Facebook, Windows Live, LinkedIn, AOL, hi5, or your Google address book to become part of your Messenger or Windows Live network.

Text Chats

As with any conversation, somebody has to talk first. In chat circles, that's called *inviting* someone to a chat.

Figure 7-20:
When someone wants to chat, this message pops up on your taskbar (top). Click it to begin the conversation (bottom).

They invite you

When someone tries to "page" you for a chat, a notification bubble pops up on your system tray, and a little chime plays (Figure 7-20).

Tip: If you're getting hassled by someone, right-click his name and choose "Block contact" from the shortcut menu.

You invite them

To invite somebody in your buddy list to a chat, point to a name in the Messenger buddy list without clicking. From the shortcut menu, choose "Send an instant message."

You can invite more than one person to the chat. Once you're chatting away, click Invite on the toolbar; you're shown your list of buddies, so you can invite an additional chatter. Everyone sees all the messages anyone sends.

Text chatting

A typed chat works like this: Each time you or your chat partner types something and then presses Enter, the text appears on both of your screens (Figure 7-20).

Messenger displays each typed comment next to an icon—a profile picture. You can change yours at any time by clicking the little ▾ next to it.

Tip: You can also make it not so huge. Click that little ▾ and, from the shortcut menu, choose Size→Small. You can make the other guy's picture smaller this way, too—or even make it disappear completely ("Hide display pictures").

In-Chat Fun

Typing isn't the only thing you can do during a chat. You can also perform any of these stunts:

- **Insert a smiley.** When you choose a face (like Undecided, Angry, or Frown) from this quick-access menu of smiley options (at the left end of the button bar), Messenger inserts it as a graphic into your response.

  On the other hand, if you know the correct symbols to produce smileys—that ":)" means a smiling face, for example—you can save time by typing them instead of using the pop-up menu. Messenger converts them into smiley icons on the fly, as soon as you send your reply.

- **Format your text.** You can click the A|B button beneath the text box to open the Change Font dialog box. Here, you can choose a font, style, size, and color for the text you're typing. (If you use some weird font that your chat partners don't have installed, they won't see the same typeface.)

- **Send a file.** Choosing File→"Send a file or photo" lets you send a file to *all* the participants in your chat.

Easier yet, you can drag a file's icon from your Windows desktop right into the box where you normally type. (This trick works well with pictures, because your conversation partner sees the graphic right in his chat window.)

This is a fantastic way to transfer a file that would be too big to send by email. A chat window never gets "full," and no attachment is too large to send. And it even works to send files between PCs and Macs.

This method halves the time of transfer, too, since your recipients get the file *as* you upload it. They don't have to wait 20 minutes for you to send the file and then another 20 minutes to download it, as they would with email or FTP.

- **Send email.** If someone messages you, "Hey, will you email me directions?" you can do so on the spot. Point to the person's name in your buddy list; from the shortcut menu, choose "Send e-mail." Your email program opens up automatically so you can send the note along; if your buddy's email address is part of his profile, the message is even preaddressed.

- **Send a text message to a cellphone.** This is *really* cool: You can send text messages directly to your friends' cellphones. Just point to the person's name in your buddy list and, from the shortcut menu, choose "Send mobile text (SMS)."

Note: If you've never entered this person's cellphone number, the command says, "Enter a mobile number" instead. Do it.

In the box that pops up, type a short message (a couple of sentences, tops), and then press Enter. Instantly, that message shows up on the person's cellphone!

Amazingly, you can even carry on an interactive conversation this way. If the person writes you back from the phone, the message appears right in the Messenger window, as though you were actually chatting.

- **Change the background.** You can change the white background to a faded, pale photo, if that's the kind of thing that floats your boat. Just click the Background button at the bottom of the chat window (the sixth icon). You're offered an array of ready-to-use window backgrounds; you can see one of them in Figure 7-20.

To get rid of the background and revert to soothing white, choose the slashed-circle background (lower right of the pop-up menu).

Audio Chats

Messenger becomes much more exciting when you exploit its AV Club capabilities. You can conduct audio chats, speaking into your microphone and listening to the responses from your speaker.

To begin an audio chat, you have two choices:

- In the buddy list, choose Actions→Call→"Call a contact's computer." (To see the Actions menu, tap Alt, or click the tiny Menu icon 🖹 in the upper-right.)

- If you're already in a text chat, click Call→"Call computer" on the toolbar.

Once your invitation is accepted, you can begin speaking to each other. World-over long distance, computer to computer, absolutely free. There may be a delay, like you're calling overseas on a bad connection, but hey—it's free.

Tip: You can also place a call to an actual phone number, thanks to a feature called Windows Live Call. To do that, choose Actions→Call→"Call a contact's phone" (or →"Call phone," to enter a number not already in your address book). Click the contact name (or enter the phone number, complete with 1 plus the area code) and then click Call.

(Another way: Point to a contact's name; from the shortcut menu, choose "Call mobile.")

You'll discover that this kind of calling is not free. However, it's very cheap—2 cents a minute from the U.S. to Europe, for example. You'll be guided through the setup procedure, which involves depositing some money up front, via a Web site.

Video Chats

If you and your partner both have broadband Internet connections and Web cameras, an even more impressive feat awaits: You can conduct a free video chat. This isn't the jerky, out-of-audio-sync, Triscuit-sized video of days gone by. If you've got the PC muscle and bandwidth, your partners are as crisp, clear, bright, and smooth as television.

Tip: You and your buddy don't both need the gear. If only you have a camera, for example, your less-equipped buddy can see you but has to speak (audio only) or type in response.

To begin a video chat, you have the usual two choices:

- In the buddy list, choose Actions→Call→"Start a Video Call." (To see the Actions menu, tap Alt, or click the 🖹 icon in the upper-right.)

Tip: If you want to see the other guy but you're not presentable enough to show yourself, you can use "View a contact's webcam" instead, for a one-way effect.

- If you're already in a text chat, click Video on the toolbar.

A window opens, showing both you and your pal (Figure 7-21).

And now, some video-chat notes:

- If your conversation partners seem unwilling to make eye contact, it's not because they're shifty. They're just looking at *you,* on the screen, rather than at the camera—and chances are you aren't looking into your camera, either.

- A headset gives much better sound quality (both ends) than mike and speaker.

- This cutting-edge technology can occasionally present cutting-edge glitches. The video quality deteriorates, the transmission aborts suddenly, the audio has an annoying echo, and so on. When problems strike, choose Tools→"Audio and video setup" to see if Messenger can fix it.

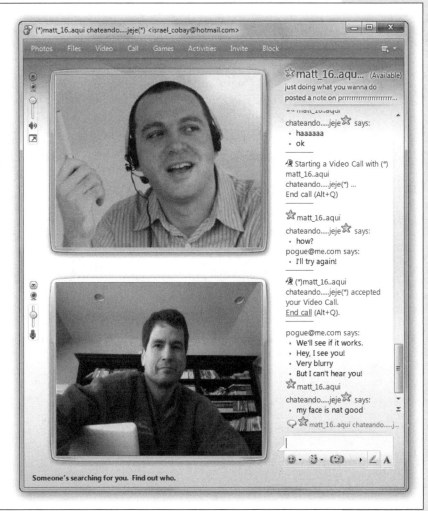

Figure 7-21:
You'll probably discover that you need some kind of light in front of you to avoid being too shadowy. Don't forget that you can keep type-chatting in the right-side area—great when what you need to say is, "I can see you, but I can't hear you!"

- You can save your typed transcripts of instant message conversations. Choose Tools→Options→Messages, and then turn on "Automatically keep a history of my conversations." Use the Change button to specify which folder you want to contain the transcripts.

Cosmetic Tweaks

If you've done nothing but chat in Messenger, you haven't even scratched the surface. You can customize and tailor this thing to within an inch of its life.

To see your options, click the little Options button (the middle of the three next to the Search box on the buddy list). In the Options dialog box, you have an enormous number of settings to fiddle with. Some of the highlights:

- **Personal.** Controls how you want other people to see you: your name, your picture, your profile, your status message, your Webcam.

- **Layout.** Governs what sections of your buddy list appear. For example, you can hide the groups, the favorites, the what's-new list, and so on. You also get to choose how big people's icons appear: Large, Medium, Small, or Invisible.

- **Sign in.** Do you want Messenger to open and sign in automatically when you turn on the PC? Do you want to be able to sign in from more than one place (for example, your PC and your phone)?

- **Messages.** Do you want to get nudges, winks, photos, and voice clips as people send them to you? Do you want to hide smileys (because they are, after all, insufferable)? Do you want Messenger to keep a transcript of your chats?

- **Alerts.** Do you want Messenger to beep and pop up a message when contacts come online? When you get email? When your message is received?

- **Sounds.** What sounds do you want to hear when someone signs in? When someone invites you to chat? When someone "nudges" you?

- **File Transfer.** Where do you want transferred files to go? Do you want them scanned for viruses?

- **Privacy.** Here are the lists of people you want to block.

- **Security.** Various checkboxes for features intended to stop you from stumbling onto viruses or spyware.

- **Connection.** Troubleshooting tools to use if you're not getting good audio or video quality.

The Control Panel

L ike the control panel in the cockpit of an airplane, the Control Panel is an extremely important feature of Windows 7. It's teeming with miniature applications (or *applets*) that govern every conceivable setting for every conceivable component of your computer. Some are so important that you may use them (or their corresponding notification-area icons) every day. Others are so obscure that you'll wonder what on earth inspired Microsoft to create them. This chapter covers them all.

Note: Here and there, within the Control Panel, you'll spot a little Windows security-shield icon. It tells you that you're about to make an important, major change to the operating system, something that will affect everyone who uses this PC—fiddling with its network settings, for example, or changing its clock. To prove your worthiness (and to prove that you're not an evil virus attempting to make a nasty change), you'll be asked to *authenticate* yourself; see the box on page 726 for details.

Many Roads to Control Panel
All Versions

There are two ways to change a setting on your PC. There's the traditional way, which begins with opening the Control Panel and drilling down from there. And there's the Windows 7 way, which involves jumping directly to the setting you want, using the Start menu's Search box. Herewith: the steps for both methods.

The Control Panel Itself
To have a look at your Control Panel applet collection, choose Start→Control Panel to open the Control Panel window.

You see that for the fourth-straight Windows edition, Microsoft has rejiggered the layout in an attempt to make the thing easier to navigate. (Figure 8-1).

The "View by" pop-up menu (upper right) shows that there are three ways to view the complete collection of control panels: by category or as a list of small or large icons.

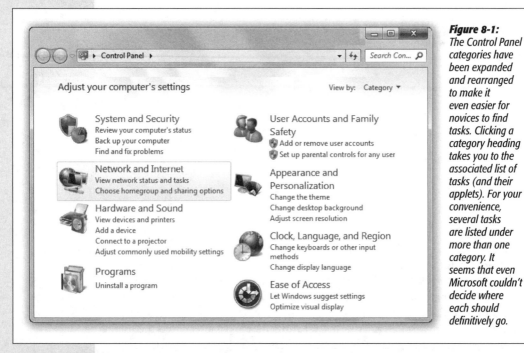

Figure 8-1:
The Control Panel categories have been expanded and rearranged to make it even easier for novices to find tasks. Clicking a category heading takes you to the associated list of tasks (and their applets). For your convenience, several tasks are listed under more than one category. It seems that even Microsoft couldn't decide where each should definitively go.

Control Panel Terminology Hell

The Control Panel continues to be an object of bafflement for Microsoft, not to mention its customers; from version to version of Windows, this window undergoes more reorganizations than a bankrupt airline.

Windows 7 presents the most oddball arrangement yet. There are far more icons in the Control Panel than ever before—about 50 of them, in fact. But they're not all the same kind of thing.

Some are the traditional *applets,* meaning mini-applications (little programs). Others are nothing more than tabbed dialog boxes. Some open up wizards (interview dialog boxes that walk you through a procedure) or even ordinary Explorer windows. And even among the applets, the look and substance of the Control Panel panels vary widely.

So what are people supposed to call these things? The world needs a general term for the motley assortment of icons in the Control Panel window.

To help you and your well-intentioned author from going quietly insane, this chapter refers to all the Control Panel icons as either icons (which they definitely are), control panels, or applets (which most of them are—and besides, that's the traditional term for them).

Category view

Here's a rundown of the new, improved Control Panel home categories:

- **System and Security.** In this category are system and administrative tasks like backing up and restoring, setting your power options, and security options (firewall, encryption, and so on).

- **Network and Internet.** This category contains settings related to networking, Internet options, offline files (page 635), and Sync Center (to manage synchronizing data between computers and network folders).

- **Hardware and Sound.** Here you find everything for managing gadgets connected to your computer: printer settings, projector settings, laptop adjustments, and so on.

- **Programs.** You'll probably use this one a lot. Here's how you uninstall programs, choose which program is your preferred one (for Web browsing or opening graphics, for example), turn Windows features on and off, and manage your desktop gadgets.

- **User Accounts and Family Safety.** This category contains the settings you need to manage the accounts on the computer (Chapter 23), including the limited accounts that parents can create for their children.

- **Appearance and Personalization.** Here's a big category indeed. It covers all things cosmetic, from how the desktop looks (plus taskbar, Sidebar, and personalization settings) to folder options, fonts, and ease-of-access settings.

- **Clock, Language, and Region.** These time, language, and clock settings all have one thing in common: They differ according to where in the world you are.

- **Ease of Access.** This revamped category replaces the Accessibility Options dialog box from Windows XP. It's one-stop shopping for every feature Microsoft has dreamed up to assist the disabled. It's also the rabbit hole into Speech Recognition Options.

Classic view

The category concept sounds OK in principle, but it'll drive veterans nuts. You don't want to guess what category Fax wound up in—you just want to open the old Print and Fax control panel, right now.

Fortunately, Classic view is still available. That's where the Control Panel displays all 50 icons in alphabetical order (Figure 8-2).

Use the "View by" pop-up menu in the upper-right, and choose either "Small icons" or "Large icons." Then double-click the icon of the applet you'd like to use.

Control Panel via Search

Ever try to configure a setting in the Control Panel but forget which applet it's in? Happens all the time. It's perfectly possible to waste some time, clicking likely categories, opening and closing a few applet icons, backing out, and trying again.

Use the Search box in the Start menu instead. It's uncannily good at taking you to the control panel you really want.

Quick: Where do you go to set up your monitor's color settings? Would it be under the System and Security category? Hardware and Sound? Appearance and Personalization?

Figure 8-2:
Classic view might be overwhelming for novices, because the task icons give little indication about what settings they actually contain. Here's a hint: Remember that you can just move your mouse over a task and pause there. A tooltip pops up, giving you an idea of what's inside.

Don't worry about it. Press the ⊞ key to open the Start menu; type *color*; when you see Color Management highlighted in the results list, press Enter to open it. (On other quests, you might type *fonts, sound, battery, accounts, date, CDs, speech,* or whatever.)

Yes, you've had to type, just like in the ancient DOS days—but you saved a lot of time, steps, and fumbling. It just works really well. (There's a similar Search box right in the Control Panel window itself.)

Tip: There are other shortcuts to the Control Panel, too, that don't require typing.

First, you can turn on the feature that lets you choose a certain control panel's name *directly* from the Start menu, as described on page 44.

Or, if you don't mind a cluttered desktop, make a shortcut for the applets you access most. To do that, open the Control Panel. Right-click the icon you want; from the shortcut menu, choose "Create shortcut." It automatically places it on the desktop for you. Or, what the heck—drag an applet right out of the Control Panel *into* the Start menu to install it there!

The Control Panel, Applet by Applet

All Versions

Icon view is the perfect structure for a chapter that describes each Control Panel applet, since it's organized in alphabetical order. The rest of this chapter assumes you're looking at the Control Panel in one of the two Icon views.

Action Center

Here's the new Windows 7 Action Center: a single, consolidated window listing every security- and maintenance-related concern that Windows has at the moment. Be grateful: These all used to be separate balloons harassing you from the right end of the taskbar. For details, see Chapter 20.

Administrative Tools

This icon is actually a folder containing a suite of very technical administrative utilities. These tools, intended for serious technowizards only, are explained in Chapter 20.

AutoPlay

What do you want to happen when you insert a CD? Do you want to see a window of what's on it? Do you want the music on it to start playing? Do you want to auto-run whatever software installer is on it? Do you want whatever photos it contains to get copied to your Pictures library?

The answer, of course, is, "Depends on what kind of CD it is," and also, "That should be up to me."

That's the purpose of the AutoPlay feature of Windows 7. It differentiates between different kinds of audio CDs and DVDs, video CDs and DVDs, programs (like software and games), pictures, video and audio files, blank CDs and DVDs, and even proprietary kinds of discs, like Blu-ray, HD, and Super Video. It even lets you manage how externally attached devices (like a camera or USB drive) are handled.

Each time you insert such a disc or drive, you get the dialog box shown at top in Figure 8-3, asking how you want to handle it—this time, and every time you insert

---

FREQUENTLY ASKED QUESTION

What happened to AutoRun?

What the heck? I've inserted a flash drive that I know contains a software installer, but it doesn't run automatically like it did in Windows Vista. What's going on?

Microsoft made a big change in Windows 7: It turned off the ability for software installers to autorun from USB gadgets like flash drives.

Why? Because the bad guys were using the AutoRun feature as an evil backdoor for installing viruses and other nasties on your PC. You'd insert a flash drive, and bing!—something would auto-install without your awareness.

Nowadays, if you really want to run an installer from a flash drive, choose Start→Computer, open the drive's icon, and run the installer manually by double-clicking it.

---

a similar gadget thereafter. For each kind of disc, the pop-up menu offers you obvious choices by disc type (like "Play audio CD" for music CDs), as well as standard options like "Open folder to view files using Windows Explorer," "Take no action," or "Ask me every time."

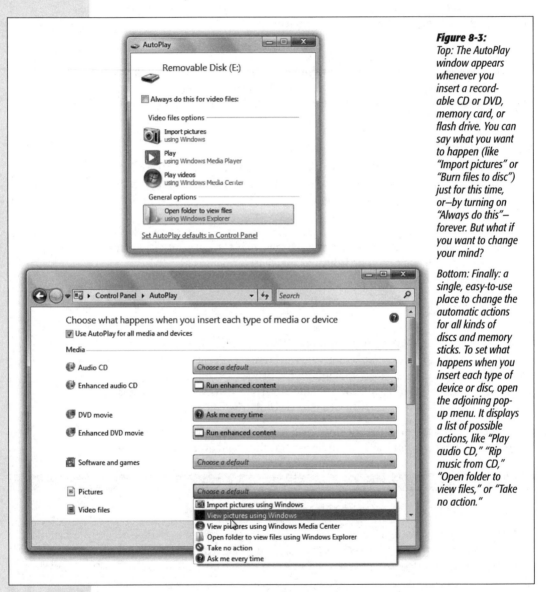

Figure 8-3:
Top: The AutoPlay window appears whenever you insert a recordable CD or DVD, memory card, or flash drive. You can say what you want to happen (like "Import pictures" or "Burn files to disc") just for this time, or—by turning on "Always do this"—forever. But what if you want to change your mind?

Bottom: Finally: a single, easy-to-use place to change the automatic actions for all kinds of discs and memory sticks. To set what happens when you insert each type of device or disc, open the adjoining pop-up menu. It displays a list of possible actions, like "Play audio CD," "Rip music from CD," "Open folder to view files," or "Take no action."

Behind the scenes, your choices are recorded in the AutoPlay control panel, where you can change your mind or just look over the choices you've made so far (Figure 8-3, bottom).

Tip: If you've never liked AutoPlay and you don't want Windows to do *anything* when you insert a disc, just turn off "Use AutoPlay for all media and devices" at the top of the window.

Backup and Restore Center

Backup and Restore Center controls how you back up your computer (and restore it). Check out Chapter 22 for more detailed information.

BitLocker Drive Encryption

BitLocker encrypts the data on your drives to keep them from being accessed by the bad guys who might steal your laptop. For details, see Chapter 21.

Color Management

Microsoft created this applet in conjunction with Canon in an effort to make colors more consistent from screen to printer. Details are in Chapter 17.

Credential Manager

Credential Manager, formerly called "Stored User Names and Passwords," lets you teach Windows to memorize your corporate account names and passwords. It's not the same thing as the Web-browser feature that memorizes your passwords for every-day Web sites (like banking sites). Instead, Credential Manager stores passwords for shared network drives and corporate-intranet Web sites, the ones where you have to enter a name and password before you even see the home page.

Date and Time

Your PC's concept of what time it is can be very important. Every file you create or save is stamped with this time, and every email you send or receive is marked with it. When you drag a document into a folder that contains a different draft of the same thing, Windows warns that you're about to replace an older version with a newer one (or vice versa)—but only if your clock is set correctly.

This program offers three tabs:

• **Date and Time.** Here's where you can change the time, date, and time zone for the computer (Figure 8-4)—if, that is, you'd rather not have the computer set its own clock (read on).

Tip: In the "Time zone" section of the Date and Time tab, you can find exactly when Windows thinks daylight saving time is going to start (or end, depending on what time of year it is). In addition, there's an option to remind you a week before the time change occurs, so you don't wind up unexpectedly sleep-deprived on the day of your big TV appearance.

• **Additional Clocks.** If you work overseas, or if you have friends, relatives, or clients in different time zones, you'll like this one; it's the only thing that stands between you and waking them up at three in the morning because you forgot what time it is where they live.

This feature shows you, at a glance, what time it is in other parts of the world. You can give them any display name you want, like "Paris" or "Mother-in-Law time." Note that the additional clocks' times are based on the PC's own local time. So if the computer's main clock is wrong, the other clocks will be wrong, too.

Figure 8-5 shows how to check one of your additional clocks.

Tip: If you *click* the time on the taskbar instead of just pointing to it (Figure 8-5), you get three large, beautiful *analog* clocks in a pop-up window.

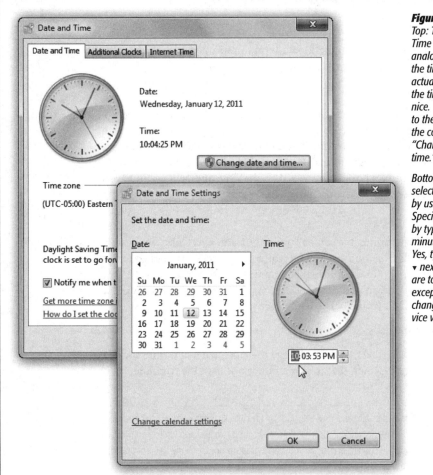

Figure 8-4:
Top: The Date and Time tab has a lovely analog clock displaying the time. You can't actually use it to set the time, but it looks nice. To make a change to the date or time of the computer, click "Change date and time."

Bottom: At that point, select the correct date by using the calendar. Specify the correct time by typing in the hour, minute, and seconds. Yes, type it; the ▲ and ▼ next to the time field are too inefficient, except when you're changing AM to PM or vice versa.

- **Internet Time.** This option has nothing to do with Swatch Internet Time, a 1998 concept of time that was designed to eliminate the complications of time zones. (Then again, it introduced complications of its own, like dividing up the 24-hour day into 1,000 parts called "beats," each one being 1 minute and 26.4 seconds long.)

Instead, this tab teaches your PC to set its own clock by consulting one of the highly accurate scientific clocks on the Internet. To turn the feature on or off, or to specify which atomic Internet clock you want to use as the master clock, click Change Settings. (No need to worry about daylight saving time, either; the time servers take that into account).

Note: Your PC resets its clock once a week–*if* it's connected to the Internet at the time. If not, it gives up until the following week. If you have a dial-up modem, in other words, you might consider connecting to the Internet every now and then and using the "Update now" button to compensate for all the times your PC unsuccessfully tried to set its own clock.

Figure 8-5:
To see the time for the additional clocks, point without clicking over the time in the notification area. You get a pop-up displaying the time on the additional clock (or clocks) that you configured.

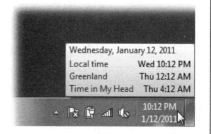

Default Programs

In an age when Microsoft is often accused of leveraging Windows to take over other realms of software, like Web browsing and graphics, the company created this command center. It's where you choose your preferred Web browser, music-playing program, email program, and so on—which may or may not be the ones provided by Microsoft.

You're offered four links:

- **Set your default programs.** Here's where you teach Windows that you want your own programs to replace the Microsoft versions. For instance, you can say that, when you double-click a music file, you want to open iTunes and not Windows Media Player. For details, see page 319.

- **Associate a file type or protocol.** This window lets you specify exactly what kind of file you want to have opened by what program. (That's essentially what happens in the background when you set a default program.) File associations are covered in more depth on page 242.

- **Change AutoPlay Settings.** This option opens the AutoPlay applet described on page 315.

- **Set program access and computer defaults.** Here, you can not only manage what programs are used by default, like browsing with Internet Explorer or getting email with Windows Mail, but also disable certain programs so that they can't be used at all. It's organized in rather combative schemes: You can choose to prefer Micro-soft products (disabling access to the non-Microsoft interlopers), Non-Microsoft products (pro-third party, anti-Microsoft), or create a Custom scheme, in which you can specifically choose a mix of both. See page 249 for more information.

Desktop Gadgets

This icon is nothing more than a shortcut to the Gadgets window described on page 235.

Device Manager

The Device Manager console shows you where all your hardware money was spent. Here, you or your tech-support person can troubleshoot a flaky device, disable and enable devices, and manage device drivers. If you're comfortable handling these more advanced tasks, then Chapter 18 is for you.

Devices and Printers

Double-click to open the new Devices and Printers window, where everything you've attached to your PC—Webcam, printer, scanner, mouse, whatever—appears with its own picture and details screen. Chapter 17 has the details.

Display

This one opens the "Make it easier to read what's on your screen" window described on page 192. The task pane on the left side offers links to other screen-related controls, like "Adjust resolution," "Change display settings" (meaning resolution), and so on.

Ease of Access Center

The Ease of Access Center is a completely revamped version of the Accessibility Options of Windows XP. It's designed to make computing easier for people with disabilities, although some of the options here can benefit anyone. See page 287 for details.

Folder Options

This program offers three tabs—General, View, and Search—all of which are described in Chapter 3.

Fonts

This icon is a shortcut to a folder; it's not an applet. It opens into a window that reveals all the typefaces installed on your machine, as described in Chapter 17.

Getting Started

What's this thing doing here? It's not a control panel at all. Instead, it's the welcome screen that greets you every single time you log in (until you turn off the "Run at startup" checkbox). This window conveniently displays how to get started with Win-dows, transfer stuff from your old PC, and so on. For a more detailed look at this window and its offerings, see Chapter 1.

HomeGroup

The HomeGroup icon opens the "Change homegroup settings" screen, where you can change the password or perform other administrative tasks related to your homegroup (home file-sharing network). Homegroups are described in Chapter 26.

Indexing Options

The Start menu's Search box is so magnificently fast because it doesn't actually root through all your files. Instead, it roots only through an *index* of your files, an invisible, compact database file that Windows maintains in the background.

This dialog box lets you manage indexing functions and change what gets indexed, and it lets you know how many items have been indexed. To learn more about the particulars of indexing and how to use it, see Chapter 3.

Internet Options

A better name for this program would have been "Web Browser Options," since all its settings apply to Web browsing—and, specifically, to Internet Explorer. As a matter of fact, this is the same dialog box that opens from the Tools→Internet Options menu command within Internet Explorer. Its tabs break down like this:

- **General, Security, Privacy, and Content.** These tabs control your home page, cache files, search-field defaults, and history list. They also let you define certain Web pages as off-limits for your kids, and manage RSS feeds, as well as block pop-up windows. Details on these options are in Chapter 10.

- **Connections.** Controls when your PC modem dials.

- **Programs.** Use this tab to manage browser add-ons, decide whether or not Internet Explorer should warn you whenever it is not the default browser (for your protection, of course), or choose the default programs that open, should you click a link to email someone, open a media file, or view the HTML source of a Web page (View→Source).

- **Advanced.** On this tab, you find dozens of checkboxes, most of which are useful only in rare circumstances and affect your Web experience only in minor ways. For example, "Enable personalized favorites menu" shortens your list of bookmarks over time, as Internet Explorer hides the names of Web sites you haven't visited in a while. (A click on the arrow at the bottom of the Favorites menu makes them reappear.)

  Similarly, turning off the "Show Go button in Address bar" checkbox hides the Go button at the right of the address bar. After you've typed a Web address (URL), you must press Enter to open the corresponding Web page instead of clicking a Go button on the screen. And so on.

iSCSI Initiator

This applet is not for the faint of heart. In fact, it requires tech support or your network administrator to set up properly and is completely useless for computers not on a network. Just opening it could wind up opening holes in your Windows Firewall. You've been warned.

Keyboard

You're probably too young to remember the antique known as a *typewriter*. On some electric versions of this machine, you could hold down the letter X key to type a series of XXXXXXXs—ideal for crossing something out in a contract, for example.

On a PC, *every* key behaves this way. Hold down any key long enough, and it starts spitting out repetitions, making it easy to type, "No WAAAAAY!" or "You go, grrrrrl!" for example. (The same rule applies when you hold down the arrow keys to scroll through a text document, hold down the = key to build a separator line between paragraphs, hold down Backspace to eliminate a word, and so on.) The Speed tab of this dialog box (Figure 8-6) governs the settings.

- **Repeat delay.** This slider determines how long you must hold down the key before it starts repeating (to prevent triggering repetitions accidentally).

- **Repeat rate.** The second slider governs how fast each key spits out letters once the spitting has begun.

  After making these adjustments, click the "Click here and hold down a key" test box to try out the new settings.

POWER USERS' CLINIC

iSCSI Initiator

You've already been warned that iSCSI Initiator is for system administrators, and you still want to know about it?

OK, fine.

iSCSI Initiator is a way of connecting your computer to hard drives on almost any kind of network—even across the Internet.

In the old days, accessing such externally stored data was painfully slow. If you needed a file on that distant hard drive, you didn't dare work on it "live" from across the network; it would be just too slow. So you'd download the files to your computer first, work on it, and then upload it when you were done.

And that's why Microsoft created iSCSI. It's not as fast as using your computer's internal hard drive, but it's a big improvement. Ever walked on one of those moving sidewalks between airport terminals, zooming past the people who

are walking on the ground? That's the kind of speed boost iSCSI gives you.

To make this work, your computer *initiates* the process of finding and connecting to the *target* iSCSI storage device across the network. (That's why this applet is called iSCSI Initiator, get it?)

Your computer must have an iSCSI service running on it, and the ports that iSCSI uses must be open on your computer's firewall. (The applet offers to do this part for you.) Once the service is started and the ports are open (or you've canceled through the prompts), you can get to the iSCSI Initiator dialog box and configure its settings. It's at that point that you really need a highly paid network professional to configure the settings, because it's filled with such fun settings as CHAP or IPsec authentication, the IP address of the RADIUS server, the IP address of the target device, and more.

- **Cursor blink rate.** The "Cursor blink rate" slider actually has nothing to do with the *cursor,* the little arrow that you move around with the mouse. Instead, it governs the blinking rate of the *insertion point,* the blinking marker that indicates where typing will begin when you're word processing, for example. A blink rate that's too slow makes it more difficult to find your insertion point in a window filled with data. A blink rate that's too rapid can be distracting.

Figure 8-6:
How fast do you want your keys to repeat?
This dialog box also offers a Hardware tab,
but you won't go there very often. You'll use
it exclusively when you're trying to trouble-
shoot your keyboard or its driver.

Location and Other Sensors

These days, small computers like netbooks come equipped with sensors, like tilt sensors and GPS location sensors. Well, OK, they don't really come with sensors, but Microsoft wishes they would.

Just in case these ever do become standard PC components, Microsoft has built this panel, which lets you turn these sensors on and off individually. The real point here is the location sensor, which bothers people with a strong sense of privacy.

Mouse

All the icons, buttons, and menus in Windows make the mouse a very important tool. And the Mouse dialog box is its configuration headquarters (Figure 8-7).

Buttons tab

This tab offers three useful controls: "Button configuration," "Double-click speed," and "ClickLock."

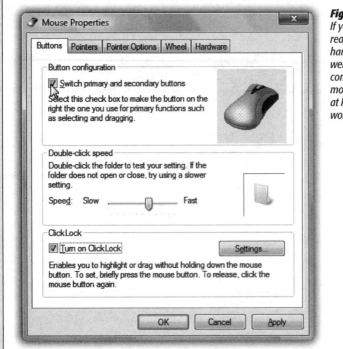

Figure 8-7:
If you're a southpaw, you've probably realized that the advantages of being left-handed when you play tennis or baseball were lost on the folks who designed the computer mouse. It's no surprise, then, that most mice are shaped poorly for lefties—but at least you can correct the way the buttons work.

- **Button configuration.** This checkbox is for people who are left-handed and keep their mouse on the left side of the keyboard. Turning on this checkbox lets you switch the functions of the right and left mouse buttons so that your index finger naturally rests on the primary button (the one that selects and drags).

- **Double-click speed.** Double-clicking isn't a very natural maneuver. If you double-click too slowly, the icon you're trying to open remains stubbornly closed. Or worse, if you accidentally double-click an icon's name instead of its picture, Windows sees your double-click as two single clicks, which tells it that you're trying to rename the icon.

  The difference in time between a double-click and two single clicks is usually well under a second. That's an extremely narrow window, so let Windows know what you consider to be a double-click by adjusting this slider. The left end of the slider bar represents 0.9 seconds, and the right end represents 0.1 seconds. If you need more time between clicks, move the slider to the left; by contrast, if your reflexes are highly tuned (or you drink a lot of coffee), try sliding the slider to the right.

Each time you adjust the slider, remember to test your adjustment by double-clicking the little folder to the right of the Speed slider. If the folder opens, you've successfully double-clicked. If not, adjust the slider again.

- **ClickLock.** ClickLock is for people blessed with large monitors or laptop trackpads who, when dragging icons onscreen, get tired of keeping the mouse button pressed continually. Instead, you can make Windows "hold down" the button automatically, avoiding years of unpleasant finger cramps and messy litigation.

  When ClickLock is turned on, you can drag objects on the screen like this: First, point to the item you want to drag, such as an icon. Press the left mouse or trackpad button for the ClickLock interval. (You can specify this interval by clicking the Settings button in this dialog box.)

  When you release the mouse button, it acts as though it's still pressed. Now you can drag the icon across the screen by moving the mouse (or stroking the trackpad) without holding any button down.

  To release the button, hold it down again for your specified time interval.

Pointers tab
See page 188 for details on changing the shape of your cursor.

Pointers Options tab
See page 189 for a rundown of these cursor-related functions.

Wheel tab
The scroll wheel on the top of your mouse may be the greatest mouse enhancement since they got rid of the dust-collecting ball on the bottom. It lets you zoom through Web pages, email lists, and documents with a twitch of your index finger.

Use these controls to specify just how *much* each wheel notch scrolls. (You may not see this tab at all if your mouse doesn't have a wheel.)

Hardware tab
The Mouse program provides this tab exclusively for its Properties buttons, which takes you to the Device Manager's device properties dialog box. Useful if you have to troubleshoot a bad driver.

Network and Sharing Center
This network command center offers, among other things, a handy map that shows exactly how your PC is connected to the Internet. It also contains a tidy list of all networking-related features (file sharing, printer sharing, and so on), complete with on/off switches. See Chapter 26 for details.

Notification Area Icons
Double-click to open up a screen where you can hide or show specific icons in your system tray (at the right end of your taskbar), as described in Chapter 2.

Parental Controls

This applet lets you, the wise parent, control what your inexperienced or out-of-control loved one (usually a child, but sometimes a spouse) can and cannot do on (or with) the computer. For more information, see Chapter 10.

Pen and Input Devices

This applet opens up a dialog box where you can configure how your stylus (pen) interacts with the desktop and windows. (You need this control panel primarily if you have a tablet PC or a graphics tablet.) For details, see Chapter 19.

Performance Information and Tools

Windows 7 needs a fast computer. Just how fast is yours? This control panel breaks it down for you, even going so far as giving your PC a grade for speed.

In addition, this window has convenient links to tabs of several other applets (like Power Options, Indexing Service, and System Performance), as well as access to the old Disk Cleanup utility. For power users, there's even a kickin' Advanced Tools window stocked with speed-related goodies, logs, and reports. For details, see Chapters 20 and 21.

Personalization

Have you ever admired the family photo or space shuttle picture plastered across a coworker's PC desktop? Wished the cursor were bigger? Been annoyed that you have to log in again every time your screen saver kicks in?

All these are aspects of the Personalization applet. It's such a big topic, it gets its own chapter: Chapter 4.

Phone and Modem

You'll probably need to access these settings only once: the first time you set up your PC or laptop to dial out. Details in Chapter 9.

Power Options

The Power Options program manages the power consumption of your computer. That's a big deal when you're running off a laptop's battery, of course, but it's also important if you'd like to save money (and the environment) by cutting down on the juice consumed by your *desktop* PC.

The options you see depend on your PC's particular features. Figure 8-8 displays the Power Options for a typical computer.

In Windows 7, Microsoft has tried to simplify the business of managing the electricity/speed tradeoff in two ways. First, it has abandoned the old name *power scheme* and adopted a new one: *power plan*. You can feel the clouds breaking up already.

(A power plan dictates things like how soon the computer goes to sleep, how bright the screen is, what speed the processor cranks at, and so on.)

The Story of God Mode

It started on a blog called *jkontherun.com:* the crazy rumor that Microsoft had created a secret Control Panel view called God Mode, and that only power users could access it.

Crazy thing is, it's true. "God Mode" is a simple folder that brings all aspects of Windows 7 control—Control Panel functions, interface customization, accessibility options—to a single location.

To create this all-powerful Control Panel folder, start by creating an empty folder anywhere. Give it this name:

GodMode.{ED7BA470-8E54-465E-825C-99712043E01C}

One typo, and you're toast. But if you type it correctly, the folder transforms into a strange little icon called GodMode. Open it, and you get the super-cool Control Panel view shown here, with major headings and minor ones in a tidy alphabetical list—and even a "Search GodMode" box at the top. Fantastic! Convenient! Slick! Secret!

Or not.

As it turned out, the bloggers had gotten just about everything about God Mode wrong. It isn't unique to Windows 7, it isn't unique to the Control Panel, and it isn't actually called God Mode.

Turns out it was in Vista, too. And "God Mode" is a name the bloggers came up with; in fact, you can type any folder name you want before the first period. Call it Master Control Panel, or All Tasks, or whatever.

And it turns out, finally, that this Control Panel thing isn't secret; it's a documented shortcut for programmers. Actually, "God Mode" is only one of a dozen summary folders you can create. You can also create folders that offer lists of what's in the Action Center, desktop gadgets, the Devices and Printers window, and so on.

Here are a few of the folders you can create. In each case, you can type anything you want before the period, as long as the hexadecimal code that follows is correct.

AutoPlay. {9C60DE1E-E5FC-40f4-A487-460851A8D915}

DateandTime. {E2E7934B-DCE5-43C4-9576-7FE4F75E7480}

FolderOptions. {6DFD7C5C-2451-11d3-A299-00C04F8E-F6AF}

Fonts. {93412589-74D4-4E4E-AD0E-E0CB621440FD}

Homegroup. {67CA7650-96E6-4FDD-BB43-A8E774F73A57}

InternetOptions. {A3DD4F92-658A-410F-84FD-6FBBBEF2FFFE}

NetworkandSharingCenter. {8E908FC9-BECC-40f6-915B-F4CA0E70D03D}

PowerOptions. {025A5937-A6BE-4686-A844-36FE4BEC8B6D}

Sound. {F2DDFC82-8F12-4CDD-B7DC-D4FE1425AA4D}

SpeechRecognition. {58E3C745-D971-4081-9034-86E34B30836A}

Troubleshooting.{C58C4893-3BE0-4B45-ABB5-A63E4B8C8651}

Mobility Center. {5ea4f148-308c-46d7-98a9-49041b1dd468}

There are many more, as a quick Google search will tell you. Not all of them work in Windows 7 (sometimes, the folder you're renaming with the magic name simply doesn't change its icon and adopt its new personality). And of course, there's not a whole lot of point in going to this trouble; if you really want direct access to a certain Control Panel applet, you can simply drag it to your desktop right from the Control Panel window!

But even if it's not that secret, not that special, and not that new, it's still cool.

Second, it presents you right up front with three premade power plans:

- **Balanced,** which is meant to strike a balance between energy savings and performance. When you're working hard, you get all the speed your PC can deliver; when you're thinking or resting, the processor slows down to save juice.

- **Power saver** slows down your computer, but saves power—a handy one for laptop luggers who aren't doing anything more strenuous than word processing.

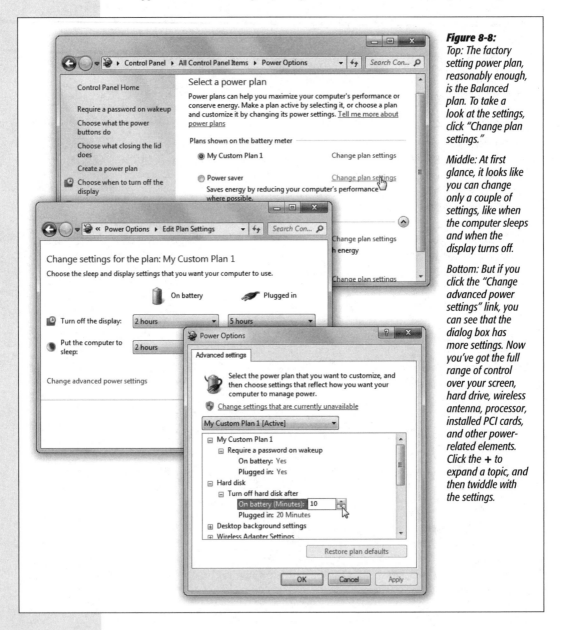

Figure 8-8:
Top: The factory setting power plan, reasonably enough, is the Balanced plan. To take a look at the settings, click "Change plan settings."

Middle: At first glance, it looks like you can change only a couple of settings, like when the computer sleeps and when the display turns off.

Bottom: But if you click the "Change advanced power settings" link, you can see that the dialog box has more settings. Now you've got the full range of control over your screen, hard drive, wireless antenna, processor, installed PCI cards, and other power-related elements. Click the + to expand a topic, and then twiddle with the settings.

- **High performance** (click "Show additional plans" to see it) sucks power like a black hole but grants you the computer's highest speed possible.

Tip: You don't have to open the Control Panel to change among these canned plans. On a laptop, for example, you can just click the battery icon on your notification area and choose from the pop-up menu.

Creating your own plan

But adding to Microsoft's three starter plans can be useful, not only because you gain more control, but also because you get to see exactly what a plan is made of. In Windows 7, you create a new plan by modifying one of Microsoft's three starter plans.

Start by clicking "Create a power plan" (left side of the window). On the next screen, click the plan you want to modify, type a name for your plan (say, PowerPoint Mode), and then click Next.

The "Change settings" dialog box now appears. Yeah, yeah, you can use the pop-up menus to specify how soon your PC sleeps and turns off its monitor; if you're using a laptop, you can even specify *different* timings depending on whether you're running on battery power or plugged into the wall. Boring!

The real fun begins when you click "Change advanced power settings" (Figure 8-8, bottom). Lots of these subsettings are technical and tweaky, but a few are amazingly useful (click the **+** button next to each one to see your options):

- **Require a password on wakeup.** Nice security feature if you're worried about other people in your home or office seeing what you were working on before your machine went to sleep to save power.

- **Hard disk.** Making it stop spinning after a few minutes of inactivity saves a lot of juice. The downside: The PC takes longer to report in for work when you return to it and wake it up.

- **Wireless Adapter Settings.** If you're not using your computer, you can tell it to throttle back on its WiFi wireless networking signals to save juice.

- **Sleep.** How soon should the machine enter low-power sleep state after you've left it idle? And should it sleep or hibernate (page 39)?

- **Power buttons and lid.** What should happen when you close the lid of your laptop or press its Power or Sleep button (if it has one)?

- **PCI Express.** If you've got any adapter cards installed, and they're modern and Windows 7-aware, then they, too, can save you power by sleeping when not in use.

- **Processor power management.** When you're running on battery, just how much are you willing to let your processor slow down to save juice?

- **Display.** These controls govern how fast your monitor turns off to save power.

- **Multimedia settings.** These controls have little to do with electricity, and everything to do with not ruining your big PowerPoint pitch. They let you specify that the computer should not sleep if you're in the middle of playing a song, movie, or PowerPoint deck.

- **Battery.** "Critical battery action" dictates what the laptop should do when the battery's all out: hibernate, sleep, or shut down. The other settings here let you govern when Windows's two low-battery warnings appear (that is, at what percentage-remaining levels).

Some of these options also appear in the task pane at the left side of the Power Options control panel, for your convenience. They affect whatever plan is currently selected.

In any case, click OK to close the "Advanced settings" box. Click "Save changes" to immortalize your newly created power plan. From now on, you can choose its name from the Battery icon on the system tray (if you have a laptop), or switch to it right in the control panel (if you have a desktop).

Tip: To delete a plan you've created, open the Power Options control panel; click "Change plan settings," and then click "Delete this plan."

Programs and Features

Programs and Features is about managing the software you have installed, managing updates, and buying software online. It replaces the old Add/Remove Programs program. ("Add" was dropped from the name because it was unnecessary; all programs these days come with their own installer. When was the last time you installed a program through Add/Remove Programs?)

This window is useful for fixing (which might simply mean reinstalling), changing, or uninstalling existing programs, and it's the only place you can go to turn on (or off) Windows features like Fax and Scan, Games, Meeting Space, and more.

Recovery

The new Recovery icon is nothing more than a quick-access button for triggering a System Restore, as described on page 695. It saves you a few steps when you want to rewind your PC back to an earlier, better-behaved state.

Region and Language

Windows can accommodate any conceivable arrangement of date, currency, and number formats; comes with fonts for dozens of Asian languages; lets you remap your keyboard to type non-English symbols of every ilk; and so on.

The revamped Regional and Language Options allow you to install multiple input language kits on your computer and switch between them when the mood strikes. The key term here is *default input language*; the language for the operating system doesn't change. If you installed Windows 7 in English, you still see the menus and dialog boxes in English.

But when you switch the input language, your keyboard can type the characters necessary for the selected language.

Formats tab

If you think that 7/4 means July 4 and that 1.000 is the number of heads you have, skip this section.

But in some countries, 7/4 means April 7, and 1.000 means one thousand. If your PC isn't showing numbers, times, currency symbols, or dates in a familiar way, choose your country from the "Current format" pop-up menu. (Or, if you're a little weird, use the "Customize this format" button to rearrange the sequence of date elements; see Figure 8-9.)

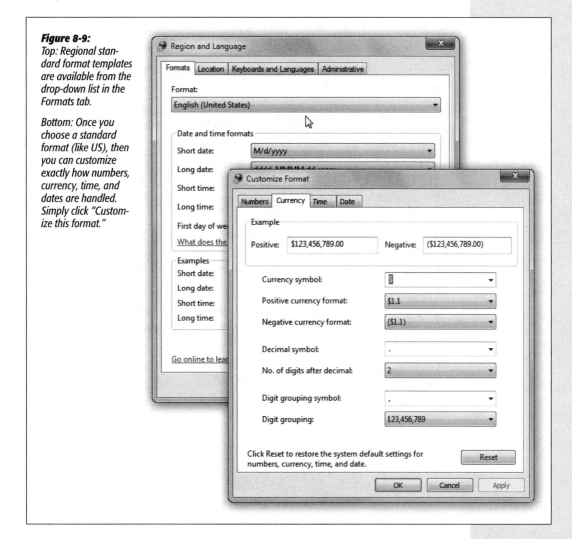

Figure 8-9:
Top: Regional standard format templates are available from the drop-down list in the Formats tab.

Bottom: Once you choose a standard format (like US), then you can customize exactly how numbers, currency, time, and dates are handled. Simply click "Customize this format."

Tip: The Customize Regional Options box (Figure 8-9) is where you can specify whether you prefer a 12-hour clock ("3:05 PM") or a military or European-style, 24-hour clock ("1505").

Location tab

This tab identifies your computer's location. The point is so when you go online to check local news and weather, you get the *right* news and weather—a handy feature if you're traveling with a laptop.

Keyboards and Languages tab

The symbols you use when you're typing in Swedish aren't the same as when you're typing in English. Microsoft solved this problem by creating different *keyboard layouts,* one for each language (or more, like Qwerty or Dvorak for English). Each keyboard layout rearranges the letters that appear when you press the keys. For example, in the Swedish layout, pressing the semicolon key produces an ö.

There are two buttons on the Keyboards and Languages tab: "Change keyboards" and "Install/uninstall languages."

The "Install/uninstall languages" button lets you install additional language packs to your computer (you can download them from Microsoft's Web site). The "Change keyboards" button takes you to another dialog box with three tabs:

- **General tab.** In order to even use Windows 7, you must have an input language. The default is US English. If yours is different, then choose it from the drop-down list. This is the language Windows will use to communicate with you, and the standard language for your keyboard.

  To change your keyboard language and/or the keyboard layout, click Add, and then scroll to the language of your choice. (Expand the **+** buttons to see the available keyboard layouts. For English, the traditional Qwerty layout is the factory setting, but you can choose from several Dvorak offerings.) See Figure 8-10.

  Once you've selected your keyboard layouts, you need to access them. There are two ways to manage and switch between keyboard layouts: through the Language bar, and by creating keyboard combinations.

- **Language bar.** The Language bar is a floating toolbar that lets you switch input languages on the fly; it appears automatically as soon as you add more than one language or keyboard layout (or when you use handwriting or speech recognition). The options on this tab can make the Language bar transparent, display text labels, and even add additional Language bar icons in the taskbar. See page 332 for more on the Language bar.

- **Advanced Key Settings.** On this tab, you can set up a keyboard combination to use to switch between layouts. The factory setting is the left Alt key+Shift, which scrolls through your layouts sequentially with each press, but you can also assign a combination to each specific layout.

Administrative

The "Change system locale" button on this tab lets you specify which language handles error messages and the occasional dialog box. (Just changing your input language may not do the trick.)

The "Copy to reserved account" button lets the newly configured language settings apply to new user accounts, so anyone who gets a new account on this computer will have your language, format, and keyboard settings conveniently available to them.

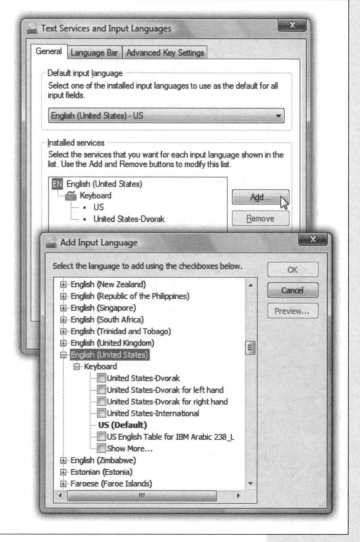

Figure 8-10:
Top: Although all languages that you choose are technically input languages, there can be only one base, default input language. From there you can add new languages (and see what you already have) by clicking Add.

Bottom: Talk about a polyglot! Windows knows more languages than you've even heard of. To see what keyboard input options are available for a language, click the + button next to it.

RemoteApp and Desktop Connections

With Windows 7, Microsoft continues its service to the world's corporate IT nerds. As in the past, these corporate system administrators can "publish" certain programs, or even entire computers, at the company headquarters—and you, using your laptop or home computer, can use them as though you were there.

But in Windows 7, these "published" resources behave even more like programs right on your PC. They're listed right in your Start menu, for heaven's sake (in a folder in All Programs called, of course, "RemoteApp and Desktop Connections"), and you can search for them as you'd search for any apps.

The whole cycle begins when your company's network nerd provides you with the URL (Internet address) of the published program. Once you've got that, open the RemoteApp and Desktop Connections control panel, and then click "Set up a new connection with RemoteApp and Desktop Connections."

A wizard now appears; its screens guide you through pasting in that URL and typing in your corporate network name and password.

When it's all over, you see a confirmation screen; your new "connection" is listed in the control panel; and the folder full of "published" remote programs appears in your Start menu, ready to use.

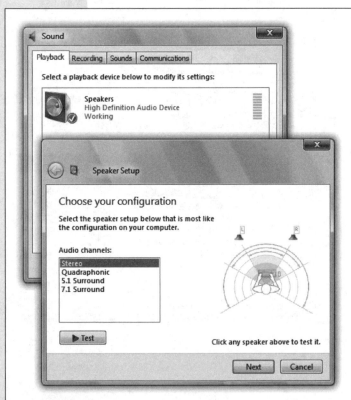

Figure 8-11:
Top: The Playback and Recording tabs display the devices your computer has for playing or recording sounds. If you select the device, you can see its properties or configure it.

Bottom: Here are some of the configurations you can set from the Playback tab, from simple stereo to 7.1 surround sound. Your setup may vary.

Sound

Since Windows XP, the Sound dialog box has been simplified. It now contains only four tabs that control every aspect of your microphone and speakers: Playback, Recording, Sounds, and Communications. See Figure 8-11.

Playback and Recording tabs

These tabs simply contain the icons for each attached sound device. To change a device's settings, select it, and then click Configure.

If you're configuring an output ("playback") device like a speaker or headset, then you get a quick wizard that lets you set the speaker configuration (stereo or quadraphonic, for example). If you're configuring a microphone ("recording"), then you're taken to the Speech Recognition page, where you can set up your microphone.

Sounds tab

Windows comes with a tidy suite of little sound effects—beeps, musical ripples, and chords—that play when you turn on the PC, trigger an error message, empty the Recycle Bin, and so on. This tab lets you specify which sound effect plays for which situation; see page 184 for details.

Communications tab

This tab, new in Windows 7, is designed for people who make phone calls using the PC, using a program like Skype, Google Talk, or Windows Live Messenger. Here, you can tell your PC to mute or soften other sounds—meaning music you've got playing—whenever you're on a PC call.

Nice touch.

Speech Recognition

This little program sets up all the speech-related features of Windows. See Chapter 6 for complete details.

Sync Center

The Sync Center used to be where you managed connected devices (like smartphones or palmtops) and synchronized them with your calendar and address book. In Windows 7, it's strictly for syncing your files with folders elsewhere on your corporate network, so you'll always be up to date. For details, see page 635.

System

This advanced control panel window is the same one that appears when you right-click your Computer icon and choose Properties from the shortcut menu (or press ⊞+Break key). It contains the various settings that identify every shred of circuitry and equipment inside, or attached to, your PC.

When you open the System icon in Control Panel, you're taken to the System window (Figure 8-12). Here you can find out:

- What edition of Windows is installed on your computer. As you know, Windows 7 comes in several editions. Not all editions are made equal; if you're flailing to find some feature that you could have sworn is supposed to be in Windows 7, it's good to check here. You might find out that the feature you want is available only on higher-priced versions.

- Your PC's performance rating. See page 25.

- The model name and speed of your PC's processor (such as Intel Core 2 Duo, 2.8 GHz).

- How much memory your PC has. That's a very helpful number to know, particularly if you need to improve your computer's speed.

- Your computer's name, domain, or workgroup, which can be modified with the "Change settings" button. Remember, your computer name and description are primarily useful on a network, since that's how other people will identify your computer. Unless you tell it otherwise, Windows names your computer after your login name, something like Casey Robbins-PC.

- Whether or not your operating system is activated. For more on Activation, check Appendix A.

- What the Product ID key is for your system. Every legal copy of Windows has a Product ID key—a long serial number that's required to activate Microsoft software. For more information about Product ID keys, see Appendix A.

Tip: In the Windows Activation section, you can do something unprecedented (and this is a really good thing): You can change your product key without having to reinstall your operating system. Now you can change your product ID simply by clicking "Change product key" in the System window. That's progress.

At the left side of the window, you find a few links:

- **Device Manager.** This very powerful console lists every component of your PC: CD-ROM, Modem, Mouse, and so on. Double-clicking a component's name (or clicking the **+** symbol) discloses the brand and model of that component. For more on the Device Manager, see Chapter 18.

- **Remote settings.** To read about Remote Assistance—the feature that lets a technical help person connect to your PC (via the Internet) to help you troubleshoot—turn to page 202.

- **System Protection.** This link takes you to the System Protection tab in the System dialog box. Here, you can keep track of the automatic system restores (snapshot backups of a system), or even create a new restore point. And if your computer has begun to act like it's possessed, you can go here to restore it to a previous restore point's state. Check out Chapter 22 for more details.

- **Advanced system settings.** Clicking this link opens the Advanced tab of the System Properties dialog box. This tab is nothing more than a nesting place for four buttons that open other dialog boxes—some of which aren't "advanced" in the least.

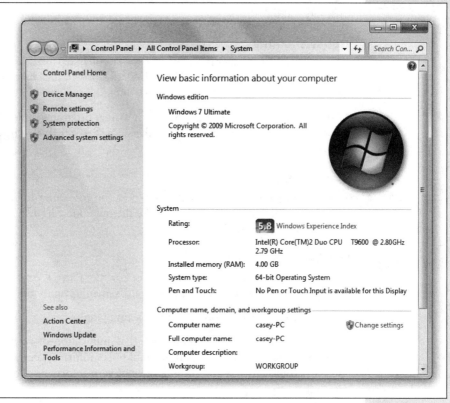

Figure 8-12:
The System window is a one-stop shop for all things computer-related. From your hardware (and what Windows thinks of it) to your product ID key, System's got you covered.

The first Settings button opens the **Performance Options** dialog box, described on page 174. The second Settings button opens the **User Profiles** box, which is covered in Chapter 23. The third Settings button opens a **Startup and Recovery** window. It contains advanced options related to *dual-booting* (Appendix A) and what happens when the system crashes.

Finally, the **Environment Variables** button opens a dialog box that will get only technically minded people excited. It identifies, for example, the path to your Windows folder and the number of processors your PC has. If you're not in the computer-administration business, avoid making changes here.

Taskbar and Start Menu

This program controls every conceivable behavior of the taskbar and Start menu. You can read all about these options—the same ones that appear when you right-click the taskbar or the Start button and choose Properties from the shortcut menu—in Chapters 1 and 2.

Troubleshooting

Here's a list of Windows 7's troubleshooters—step-by-step interview screens that walk you through fixing various problems. [Insert your own joke here about Windows's need for an entire program dedicated to troubleshooting.]

Anyway, you can find links here for running older programs under Windows 7, getting online, figuring out why your speakers aren't working, sleuthing out why your PC is getting so slow, and so on.

User Accounts

This control panel is the master switch and control center for the user-accounts feature described in Chapter 23. If you're the only one who uses your PC, you can (and should) ignore it.

Windows CardSpace

Ever have to fill out a form on the Internet—name, address, email address—only to go to a different site that requests exactly the same information?

Of course you have. Everyone has, and it's annoying as heck.

CardSpace is Microsoft's attempt to solve that duplication-of-effort problem. You're supposed to create a profile containing this kind of information, like a digital ID card. You show your card at a site, and the site gets your information off the card, saving you all that retyping.

Before you get too excited, though, there is a catch. CardSpace works only with Web sites that are, ahem, CardSpace-compatible—and there aren't many of them.

To get started, click "Add a card." Specify whether you want to create a Personal card or a Managed one.

Personal cards store your name, email, address, phone, birthday, and so on. You can even add a photo. Managed cards are cards given to you by a business or institution, like a bank or credit card company. They contain some information about you, but mostly they point at the company that is managing the card. When you use a Managed card in a transaction with a Web site, the site retrieves private information (such as a credit card number) from the company that issued the CardSpace card. It confirms that you are who you say you are, have the right to use the card, and the right to use the private information the managing company has for you.

Tip: Clearly, CardSpace cards can be a serious security worry. Fortunately, Windows lets you back up, restore, and lock your card.

Locking a card means assigning it a password so nobody can open or send it without authentication. Open a card and click "Lock card" on the right side.

Backing up the card means saving an encrypted copy of it in a file somewhere of your choosing. To back up a card, click "Back up cards" on the main screen, and follow the instructions. (If the worst should come to pass, you can use the "Restore cards" link to find and bring them back from the dead.)

Windows Defender

Windows Defender is Microsoft's free anti-spyware product, built into Windows 7. For an extensive look at what it can do for you, see Chapter 10.

Windows Firewall

In this age of digital technology, when most people's computers are connected at all times to the Internet (and therefore always vulnerable to the Internet), it's a good and reasonable idea to have a firewall protecting your computer from possible attacks and exploitation. To learn more about Windows Firewall, see Chapter 10.

Windows Mobility Center

The Windows Mobility Center icon appears only if you have a laptop. It (the Mobility Center, not the laptop) is described on page 111.

Windows Update

Because Windows is a constant work in progress, Microsoft frequently releases updates, fixes, patches, and drivers, in hopes of constantly (or at least one Tuesday a month) improving your computer's speed and security. Windows Update is the tool used to acquire, install, and track those useful fixes. For a more in-depth look at Windows Update, see Chapter 20.

Part Three: Windows 7 Online

3

Hooking Up to the Internet

P lenty of people buy a PC to crunch numbers, scan photos, or cultivate their
kids' hand-eye coordination. But for millions of people, Reason One for using a PC is to get on the Internet. Few computer features have the potential to
change your life as profoundly as the Web and email.

There are all kinds of ways to get your PC onto the Internet these days:

- **WiFi.** Wireless hot spots, known as WiFi, are glorious conveniences, especially
  if you have a laptop. Without stirring from your hotel bed, you're online at high
  speed. Sometimes for free.

- **Cable modems, DSL.** Over half of the U.S. Internet population connects over
  higher-speed wires, using broadband connections that are always on: cable modems, DSL, or corporate networks. (These, of course, are often what's at the other
  end of an Internet hot spot.)

- **Cellular modems.** A few well-heeled individuals enjoy the go-anywhere bliss of
  USB cellular modems, which get them online just about anywhere they can make
  a phone call. These modems are offered by Verizon, Sprint, AT&T, and so on, and
  usually cost $60 a month.

- **Tethering.** Tethering is letting your cellphone act as a glorified Internet antenna
  for your PC, whether connected by a cable or a Bluetooth wireless link. In general,
  the phone company charges you a hefty fee for this convenience.

- **Dial-up modems.** It's true: Plenty of people still connect to the Internet using a
  modem that dials out over ordinary phone lines. They get cheap service but slow
  connections, and their numbers are shrinking.

This chapter explains how to set up each one of these. (For the basics of setting up your own network, see Chapter 24.)

Tip: If you upgraded to Windows 7 from an earlier version of Windows, then you can already get online, as the installer is thoughtful enough to preserve your old Internet settings. (So is Windows Easy Transfer, described in Appendix A.) That's the best news you'll hear all day.

Your New Network Neighborhood

The old Network Neighborhood is long gone. Now you set up and control your network and Internet connections using two essential tools: the Network icon and the Network and Sharing Center.

Network Icon

The Network icon on your taskbar (📶 or 🖥) is a handy status meter, no matter how you're getting online. See Figure 9-1.

Tip: If you point without clicking, you see your current network's name and (if it's wireless) the signal strength. And if you right-click the icon, you get links to a troubleshooting app and the Network and Sharing Center.

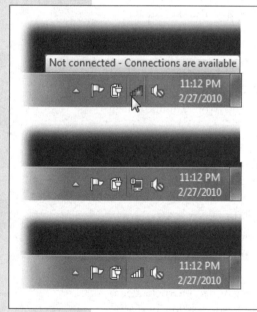

Figure 9-1:
Top: Hey, look! My 📶 icon is glowing orange—there's WiFi here!

Middle: Hey, look! I'm plugged into an Ethernet cable, and I'm on the network!

Bottom: Hey, look! I've chosen a WiFi network, and now I'm online, and the bars show my signal strength!

(If the taskbar icon bears a red X, it means your PC isn't connected to any network at all.)

Network and Sharing Center

Over and over again in this chapter, you're directed to open the all-powerful Network and Sharing Center. That's the master control center for creating, managing, and connecting to networks of all kinds (Figure 9-2). Knowing how to get there might be useful.

There are all kinds of ways, but the quickest is to click the ▪ or ▪ icon on your taskbar system tray. When the list of networks appears, click the "Open Network and Sharing Center" link at the bottom.

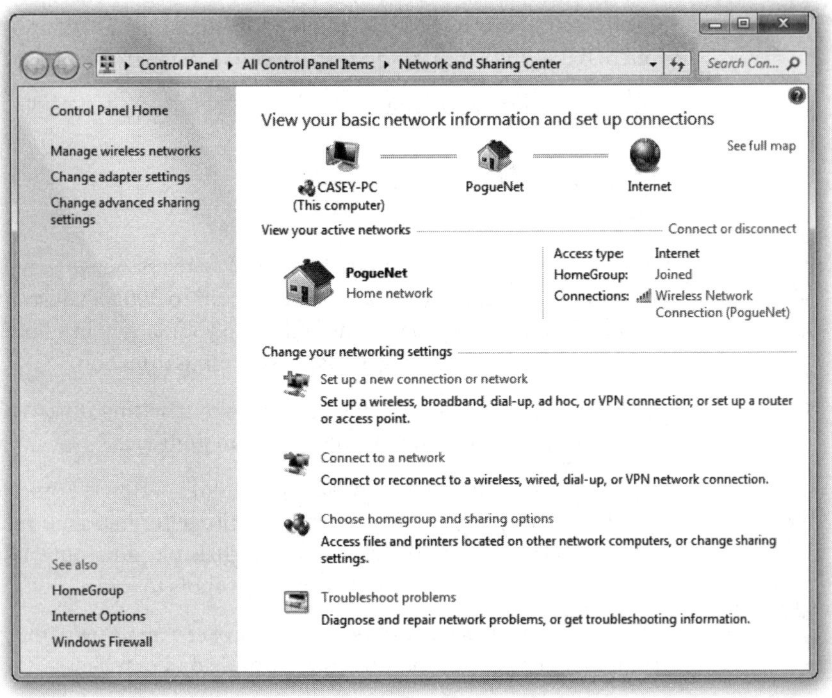

Figure 9-2:
Once it's open, the Network and Sharing Center offers links that let you connect to a network, create a new network, troubleshoot your connection, fiddle with your network or network adapter card settings, and so on. It also shows you a handy map of how, exactly, your computer is connected to the Internet.

Wired Connections
All Versions

The beauty of Ethernet connections is that they're superfast and supersecure. No bad guys sitting across the coffee shop, armed with shareware "sniffing" software, can intercept your email and chat messages, as they theoretically can when you're on wireless.

And 99 percent of the time, connecting to an Ethernet network is as simple as connecting the cable to the computer. That's it. You're online, fast and securely, and you never have to worry about connecting or disconnecting.

Automatic Configuration

Most broadband wired connections require no setup whatsoever. Take a new PC out of the box, plug in the Ethernet cable to your cable modem, and you can begin surfing the Web instantly.

That's because most cable modems, DSL boxes, and wireless base stations use DHCP. It stands for dynamic host configuration protocol, but what it means is: "We'll fill in your Network Control Panel automatically." (Including techie specs like IP address and DNS Server addresses.)

Manual Configuration

If, for some reason, you're not able to surf the Web or check email the first time you try, it's remotely possible that your broadband modem or your office network doesn't offer DHCP. In that case, you may have to fiddle with the network settings manually.

See "Connection Management" on page 354 for details.

WiFi Hot Spots

All Versions

If your PC has WiFi—the 802.11 (WiFi) wireless networking technology—it can communicate with a wireless base station up to 300 feet away, much like a cordless phone. Doing so lets you surf the Web from your laptop in a hotel room, for example, or share files with someone across the building from you.

Chapter 24 has much more information about setting up a WiFi network. The real fun begins, however, when it comes time to join one.

Sometimes you just want to join a friend's WiFi network. Sometimes you've got time to kill in an airport, and it's worth a $7 splurge for half an hour. And sometimes, at some street corners in big cities, WiFi signals bleeding out of apartment buildings might give you a choice of several free hot spots to join.

If you're in a new place, and Windows discovers, on its own, that you're in a WiFi hot spot, then the ▦ icon (on the system tray) glows orange.

Here's how to proceed:

1. **Click the Network icon (▦).**

POWER USERS' CLINIC

PPPoE and DSL

If you have DSL service, you may be directed to create a PPPoE service.

It stands for PPP over Ethernet, meaning that although your DSL "modem" is connected to your Ethernet port, you still have to make and break your Internet connections manually, as though you had a dial-up modem.

To set this up, open the Network and Sharing Center (page 755). Click "Set up a new connection or network." In the next box, click "Connect to the Internet."

In the next box—which is known as the "Connect to the Internet" wizard—click "Broadband (PPPoE)." Fill in the PPPoE box as directed by your ISP (usually just your account name and password). From here on in, you start and end your Internet connections exactly as though you had a dial-up modem—for example, by clicking the ▦ icon on your taskbar tray, and then clicking the network name.

The delightful display shown in Figure 9-3 appears. This is the Connect To menu, a convenient pop-up list of all the networks that Windows sees, both wired and wireless.

Note: The tiny caution icon (⚠) identifies networks that are not password-protected.

Point to a network's name to see a pop-up box that identifies its name, signal strength, network type, and so on.

2. **Click the name of the network (hot spot) you want to join.**

   The Connect button appears. You can click it now—but if you first turn on "Connect automatically," you'll spare yourself all this clicking the next time your PC is in range. It'll just hop on that network by itself.

3. **Click Connect.**

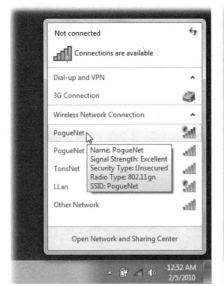

Figure 9-3:
Left: Your PC has a multitude of ways to get online! You even get to see the signal strength of a hot spot right in the menu. Point to a network's name to find out the details.

Right: Click a network's name to see the "Connect" button—and the "Connect automatically" checkbox that will save you all this effort next time. A ⚠ icon indicates an open network, not password-protected.

Some hot spots (most these days, actually) are protected by a password. It serves two purposes: First, it keeps everyday schlumps from hopping onto that network, and it also encrypts the connection so that hackers armed with sniffing software can't intercept the data you're sending and receiving.

4. **In the "Type the network security key" box, if it appears, type in the network's password. Click OK.**

   If someone's peeking over your shoulder, you can also turn on "Hide characters." That way, you fill the box with only dots as you type.

Tip: Some modern WiFi routers offer a feature called WPS (Wi-Fi Protected Setup). If you press it at this point, it will transmit the password automatically to your PC, saving you the trouble of filling in the password yourself. (This technology is great because it transmits a huge, complicated password that nobody would ever be able to guess. But it's not so great because if any other WiFi gadget—one that doesn't have the WPS feature—tries to get online, you'll have to type in that endless password manually.)

5. **Click Public, Work, or Home.**

   This gets a little technical, so hold on to your hat.

   The first time you connect to a new network—the first time you use a wireless hot spot, the first time you connect to a dial-up ISP, the first time you plug into an office network—you see the dialog box shown in Figure 9-4.

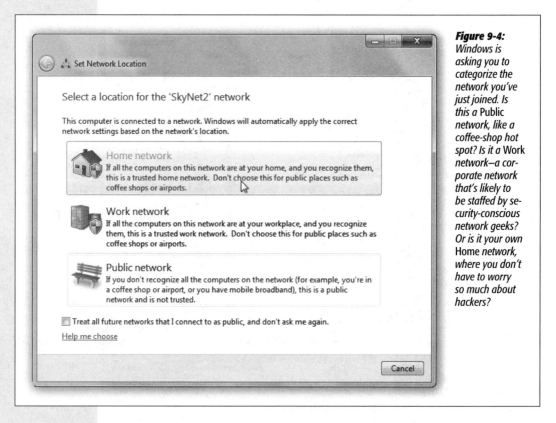

Figure 9-4:
Windows is asking you to categorize the network you've just joined. Is this a Public *network, like a coffee-shop hot spot? Is it a* Work *network—a corporate network that's likely to be staffed by security-conscious network geeks? Or is it your own* Home *network, where you don't have to worry so much about hackers?*

The choice you make here has absolutely nothing to do with the physical *location*, no matter what the dialog box says. Instead, it tells Windows how much *security* to apply to the network you've just joined.

If you choose Public, for example, Windows makes your computer invisible to other computers nearby. (Technically, it turns off the feature called *network discovery*.)

That's not ideal for file sharing, printer sharing, and so on—but it means hackers have a harder time "sniffing" the airwaves to detect your presence.

If you say a network is Public, you may be visited quite a bit by the "Unblock?" messages from the Windows firewall. That's just Windows being insecure, asking for permission every time any program (like a chat program) tries to get through the firewall.

Note: The only difference between Home and Work is that you can use the new HomeGroups feature (Chapter 8) on a Home network.

When You Can't Get On

That should be all that's necessary to get you onto a WiFi hot spot. You should now be able to surf the Web or check your email.

Before you get too excited, though, some lowering of expectations is in order. There are a bunch of reasons why your ⚹ icon might indicate that you're in a hot spot, but you can't actually get online:

- **It's locked.** If there's no little ⚹ icon next to the hot spot's signal strength in the pop-up list of networks, then the hot spot has been password-protected. That's partly to prevent hackers from "sniffing" the transmissions and intercepting messages, and partly to keep random passersby like you off the network.

- **The signal's not strong enough.** Sometimes the WiFi signal is strong enough to make the hot spot's name show up in your Connect To menu, but not strong enough for an actual connection.

- **You're not on the list.** Sometimes, for security, hot spots are rigged to permit only specific computers to join, and yours isn't one of them.

- **You haven't logged in yet.** Commercial hot spots (the ones you have to pay for) don't connect you to the Internet until you've supplied your payment details on a special Web page that appears automatically when you open your browser, as described below.

TROUBLESHOOTIING MOMENT

Wrong Network Type—Oops

Oh dear. When I connected to my home WiFi network, I clicked Public by accident. Now I can't see any of my shared files, music, printers, and so on. What to do?

You should change the location to the Home or Work settings, which are less paranoid. In these settings, network discovery is turned on, so you and your PCs can see each other on the network and share files, music, printers, and so on.

To change a connection from one "location" (that is, security scenario) to another, connect to the network in question. Now open the Network and Sharing Center (page 755). There, you see the name of the miscategorized network—and you see "Public network" (or "Home network" or "Work network") under its name. Click that phrase to reopen the box shown in Figure 9-4, where you can choose another location type.

- **The router's on, but the Internet's not connected.** Sometimes wireless routers are broadcasting, but their Internet connection is down. It'd be like a cordless phone that has a good connection back to the base station in the kitchen—but the phone cord isn't plugged into the base station.

Tip: If you point to the ▦ icon window clicking, you'll know. It will say either "Internet access" (good) or "No Internet access" (bad).

Commercial Hot Spots

Choosing the name of the hot spot you want to join is generally all you have to do—if it's a home WiFi network.

Unfortunately, joining a commercial hot spot—one that requires a credit card number (in a hotel room or an airport, for example)—requires more than just connecting to it. You also have to sign into it before you can send so much as a single email message.

To do that, open your browser. You see the "Enter payment information" screen either immediately or as soon as you try to open a Web page of your choice. (Even at free hot spots, you might have to click OK on a welcome page to initiate the connection.)

Supply your credit card information or (if you have a membership to this WiFi chain, like Boingo or T-Mobile) your name and password. Click Submit or Proceed, try not to contemplate how this $8 per hour is pure profit for somebody, and enjoy your surfing.

POWER USERS' CLINIC

Secret Hot Spots

It's entirely possible for you to be standing right in the middle of a juicy, strong WiFi hot spot —and not even know it. Its name doesn't show up in the Connect To list.

It turns out that the owner can choose whether or not the hot spot should broadcast its name. Sometimes, he might want to keep the hot spot secret–to restrict its use to employees at a coffee shop, for example, so that the common customer riffraff can't slow it down. In these cases, you'd have to know (a) that the hot spot exists, and (b) what its name is.

If you do know the name of one of these secret hot spots, open the Connect To list from your system tray. You see the invisible hot spot identified here, sure enough, but only as "Other Network." Click it, and then click Connect. Now you have to type in the network's exact name (and password, of course, if there is one) before you can proceed.

This method is great for quick encounters with hidden hot spots. If you want the option to have your laptop hop onto the secret hot spot automatically whenever it's nearby, the process is slightly more complex.

Click your Network icon (▦); click "Open Network and Sharing Center." Click "Set up a new connection or network"; in the next box, click "Manually connect to a wireless network." Now you're asked to type the hot spot's name and password–and you have the option to turn on "Start this connection automatically." Also turn on "Connect even if the network is not broadcasting," despite the warning (which is saying that a dedicated hacker nearby could learn the hot spot's name by using special "sniffing" software). Click Next, Next, and Close.

Memorized Hot Spots

If you turned on "Connect automatically," then whenever your laptop enters this hot spot, it will connect to the network automatically. You don't have to do any clicking at all.

Behind the scenes, Windows is capable of piling up quite a list of these hot spots, representing a bread-crumb trail of the hot spots you've used at every hotel, airport, coffee shop, and buddy's house.

If you ever want to clean out this list, or just look at it, open the Network and Sharing Center (page 755). In the panel at left, click "Manage wireless networks."

You now see the list of hot spots you've told Windows to memorize. See Figure 9-5 for details.

Figure 9-5:
If you click a memorized network's name, the toolbar offers you options like "Remove," "Adapter properties," and "Move down." That last option is important. It lets you answer the question, "What if I'm in the presence of more than one memorized hot spot? Which should I connect to first?" Answer: Whichever hot spot appears at the top of this list.

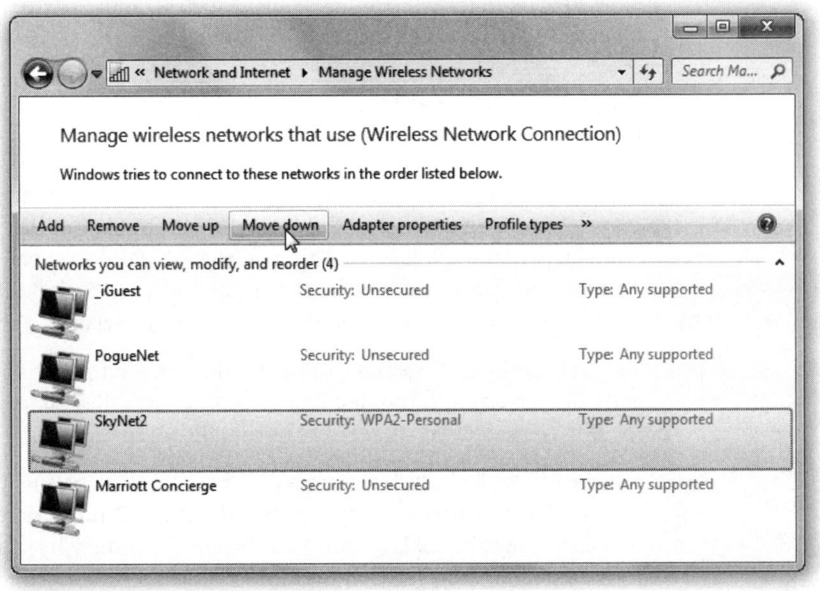

Cellular Modems

All Versions

WiFi hot spots are fast and usually cheap—but they're hot spots. Beyond 150 feet away, you're offline.

No wonder laptop luggers across America are getting into cellular Internet services. All the big cellphone companies offer ExpressCards or USB sticks that let your laptop get online at high speed anywhere in major cities. Plenty of laptops and netbooks even have this circuitry built right inside, so you have nothing to insert or eject.

Imagine: No hunting for coffee shops. With cellular Internet service, you can check your email while zooming down the road in a taxi. (Outside the metropolitan areas, you can still get online wirelessly, though much more slowly.)

Verizon, Sprint, T-Mobile, and AT&T all offer cellular Internet networks with speeds approaching a cable modem. So why isn't the world beating a path to this delicious technology's door? Because it's expensive—usually $60 a month on top of your phone bill.

To get online, insert the card or USB stick, if you have one; it may take about 15 seconds for the thing to latch on to the cellular signal.

Note: This assumes, of course, that you've installed the modem's software. Sometimes it comes on a CD. Sometimes it's right on the modem itself, which doubles as a flash drive.

Now, to make the connection, click the ⊿ icon on your system tray; from the Connect To pop-up list, just click the modem's name and then click Connect.

Dial-Up Connections
All Versions

High-speed Internet is where it's at, baby! But there are plenty of reasons why you may be among the 10 percent of the Internet population that connects via dial-up modem, slow though it is. Dial-up is a heck of a lot less expensive than broadband. And its availability is incredible—you can find a phone jack in almost any room in the civilized world, in places where the closest Ethernet or WiFi network is miles away.

To get online by dial-up, you need a PC with a modem—not a sure thing anymore—and a dial-up *account*. You sign up with a company called an Internet service provider (or *ISP*, as insiders and magazines inevitably call them).

National ISPs like EarthLink and AT&T have local telephone numbers in every U.S. state and many other countries. If you don't travel much, you may not need such broad coverage. Instead, you may be able to save money by signing up for a local or regional ISP. In fact, you can find ISPs that are absolutely free (if you're willing to look at ads), or that cost as little as $4 per month (if you promise not to call for tech support). Google can be your friend here.

Even if you have a cable modem or DSL, you can generally add dial-up access to the same account for another few bucks a month. You'll be happy to have that feature if you travel a lot (unless your cable modem comes with a *really* long cord).

In any case, dialing the Internet is a local call for most people.

Microsoft no longer tries to steer you to its own MSN service, as it once did. Instead, Windows expects that you've contacted an ISP on your own. It assumes that you're equipped with either (a) a setup CD from that company or (b) a user name, password, and dial-up phone number from that ISP, which is pretty much all you really need to get online.

Your only remaining task is to plug that information into Windows. (And, of course, to plug your computer into the phone jack on the wall.)

Here's how you do it.

1. **Open the Network and Sharing Center.**

   See the beginning of this chapter for instructions.

2. **In the main window, click "Set up a new connection or network."**

   The "Choose a connection option" dialog box opens.

3. **Double-click "Set up a dial-up connection."**

   Now the creatively named "Create a Dial-up Connection" box appears.

4. **Fill in the phone number, user name, and password your ISP provided.**

   You can call your ISP for this information, or consult the literature it mailed you when you signed up.

   If you were given a setup CD instead, click "I don't have an ISP," and then click "Use the CD I received from an ISP." Insert the disc when you're asked.

   Otherwise, complete the final step.

5. **Click Connect.**

   Assuming a phone line is plugged in, your PC dials and makes its connection with the mother ship.

6. **Make a decision: Is this network Public or Private?**

   When the "Choose a location" dialog box appears (Figure 9-4), click Home, Work, or Public after you've read what the heck that means (see page 348). (Hint: "Public" is the most secure option for dial-up.)

UP TO SPEED

IP Addresses and You

Every computer connected to the Internet, even temporarily, has its own exclusive *IP address* (IP stands for Internet Protocol). When you set up your own Internet account, as described on these pages, you're asked to type in this string of numbers. As you'll see, an IP address always consists of four numbers separated by periods.

Some PCs with high-speed Internet connections (cable modem, DSL) have a permanent, unchanging address called a *static* or *fixed* IP address. Other computers get as-

signed a new address each time they connect (a *dynamic* IP address). That's always the case, for example, when you connect via a dial-up modem. (If you can't figure out whether your machine has a static or fixed address, ask your Internet service provider.)

If nothing else, dynamic addresses are more convenient in some ways, since you don't have to type numbers into the Internet Protocol (TCP/IP) Properties dialog box shown in Figure 9-6.

From now on, whenever you want to go online, you can choose your dial-up connection's name from the Connect To list shown in Figure 9-3.

Tip: Or you can make your PC dial automatically whenever one of your programs needs an Internet connection. To set that up, and to read about the other tweaks you can make to your dial-up connection, download the free PDF appendix to this chapter called "Details on Dial-Up." You'll find it on this book's "Missing CD" page at www.missingmanuals.com.

Connection Management
All Versions

No matter what crazy combination of Internet connections you've accumulated on your computer, Windows represents each one as a *connection icon.* You can view them, rename them, change their settings, or just admire them by opening the window shown at top in Figure 9-6.

To get there, open the Network Connections window. Here's the quickest way to go about it: Open the Start menu. Type *view network* until you see "View network connections" in the results; click it or press Enter.

These icons are handy because their Properties dialog boxes are crammed with useful information. A dial-up connection icon stores your name, password, phone number, and so on; a broadband or wireless icon stores various technical Internet connection details.

In these and other situations, you need a way to make manual changes to your connections. Here, for example, is how you might change the Internet settings for a cable modem, DSL, or wireless connection:

1. **Double-click a connection icon.**

   You get the dialog box shown in Figure 9-6, lower left.

FREQUENTLY ASKED QUESTION

Laptop's Lament: Away from the Cable Modem

When I'm home, I connect my laptop to my cable modem. But when I'm on the road, of course, I have to use my dial-up ISP. Is there any way to automate the switching between these two connection methods?

If there weren't, do you think your question would have even appeared in this chapter?

The feature you're looking for is in the Internet Options control panel. (Quickest way to open it: Open the Start menu;

start typing *Internet options* until you see Internet Options in the results list; press Enter to open it.

Click the Connections tab, and then turn on "Dial whenever a network connection is not present."

From now on, your laptop will use its dial-up modem only when it realizes that it isn't connected to your cable modem.

---

2. **Click Properties.**

   Authenticate yourself, if necessary (page 726).

3. **Double-click the listing that says Internet Protocol Version 4.**

   An even more intimidating dialog box now appears (Figure 9-6, lower right).

4. **Edit the connection details.**

   Most of the time, your cable or phone company has instructed you to turn on "Obtain an IP address automatically" and "Obtain DNS server address automati-

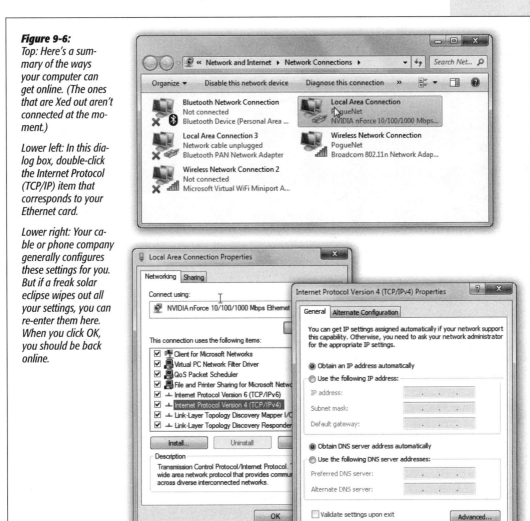

Figure 9-6:
Top: Here's a summary of the ways your computer can get online. (The ones that are Xed out aren't connected at the moment.)

Lower left: In this dialog box, double-click the Internet Protocol (TCP/IP) item that corresponds to your Ethernet card.

Lower right: Your cable or phone company generally configures these settings for you. But if a freak solar eclipse wipes out all your settings, you can re-enter them here. When you click OK, you should be back online.

cally." You don't know how lucky you are—you've been saved from typing in all the other numbers in this dialog box. Otherwise, turn on "Use the following IP address" and type in the appropriate numbers. Do the same with "Use the following DNS server addresses."

5. **Click OK.**

As a courtesy, Windows doesn't make you restart the computer in order for your new network settings to take effect.

Internet Security

If it weren't for that darned Internet, personal computing would be a lot of fun. After all, it's the Internet that lets all those socially stunted hackers enter our machines, unleashing their viruses, setting up remote hacking tools, feeding us spyware, trying to trick us out of our credit-card numbers, and otherwise making our lives an endless troubleshooting session. It sure would be nice if they'd cultivate some other hobbies.

In the meantime, these lowlifes are doing astronomical damage to businesses and individuals around the world—along the lines of $100 billion a year (the cost to fight viruses, spyware, and spam).

A big part of the problem was the design of Windows itself. In the quaint old-fashioned days of 2000, when Windows XP was designed, these sorts of Internet attacks were far less common. Microsoft left open a number of back doors that were intended for convenience (for example, to let system administrators communicate with your PC from across the network) but wound up being exploited by hackers.

Microsoft wrote Windows Vista, and later Windows 7, for a lot of reasons: to give Windows a cosmetic makeover, to give it up-to-date music and video features, to overhaul its networking plumbing—and, of course, to make money. But Job Number One was making Windows more secure. Evil strangers will still make every attempt to make your life miserable, but one thing is for sure: They'll have a much, much harder time of it.

Note: This chapter focuses on Windows's self-protection features—all of them. It's only called "Internet Security" because, in fact, virtually all the infectious unpleasantness that can befall a PC these days comes from the Internet. A PC that never goes online probably won't get infected.

So why is Internet Explorer (IE) the most popular hacking target? First, it's by far the most popular browser on the planet. Second, Internet Explorer includes hooks directly into Windows itself, so a hacker can wreak havoc on Windows by using Internet Explorer as a back door.

Lots of Win7's security improvements are invisible to you. They're deep in the plumbing, with no buttons or controls to show you. If you're scoring at home, they include the following features:

- **Application isolation.** A program can't take over important tasks performed by Windows itself.

- **Service hardening.** Windows *services* are programs that run in the background: the print spooler that comes with Windows, virus checkers from other companies, and so on. Service hardening prevents rogue services (or services that have been surreptitiously modified by nasties from the Internet) from making changes to parts of the system they're not supposed to touch; for example, they can't change important system files or the Registry (Appendix B).

- **Protected Mode.** Protected Mode shields the operating system from actions taken by Internet Explorer or its add-ons. So even if a nasty piece of software breaks through all of Internet Explorer's security features, it can't do harm to your PC, because Protected Mode locks IE inside a safe box. What happens in Internet Explorer stays in Internet Explorer.

- **Address Space Layout Randomization.** When a program is running, it keeps a lot of information in system memory. Because many viruses and worms depend on their author's knowledge of *how* vulnerable programs keep that information organized, ASLR scrambles that information—though not so much that the programs can't run—to make it harder for them to break into your system.

- **Network Access Protection.** On a corporate domain network, this feature prevents you from connecting to an insufficiently protected PC on the network—one lacking virus protection, for example.

- **PatchGuard.** This prevents non-Microsoft software from touching the beating heart of Windows.

- **Code Integrity.** Software is checked before it runs to make sure it hasn't been modified somehow.

The rest of this chapter describes features that *aren't* invisible and automatic—the ones you can control.

Note: And does it work? Do all these tools and patches actually reduce the number of virus and spyware outbreaks?

Apparently yes. The years of annual front-page headlines about national virus outbreaks—called things like Melissa (1999), Blaster (2003), and Sasser (2004)—seem to be over. There will always be clever new attacks—but they'll be much less frequent and much harder to write.

Note, however, that built-in security tools can't do the whole job of keeping your PC safe; you play a role, too. So keep in mind these basic tips before you or your family go online:

- **Don't trust a pretty face.** It doesn't take much expertise to build a snazzy-looking Web site. Just because a Web site looks trustworthy doesn't mean you can trust it. If you're visiting a little-known Web site, be careful what you do there.

- **Don't download from sites you don't know.** The Web is full of free software offers. But that free software may, in fact, be spyware or other *malware*. (Malware is a general term for viruses, spyware, and other Bad Software.) So be very careful when downloading anything online.

- **Don't click pop-up ads.** Pop-up ads are more than mere annoyances; some of them, when clicked, download spyware to your PC. As you'll see later in this chapter, Internet Explorer includes a pop-up blocker, but it doesn't block all pop-ups. So to be safe, don't click.

With all that said, you're ready to find out how to keep yourself safe when you go online.

Microsoft Security Essentials

All Versions

It's historic. It's amazing. It's free. After all these decades, Microsoft has finally decided to offer free antivirus software. At long last, you have no excuse not to protect your PC.

If you don't already have an antivirus program, go this minute to *www.microsoft. com/security_essentials* and download and install this software. At last: The X on the system-tray nag flag (⚑), complaining that your PC is unprotected, will go away.

Like any good antivirus program, this one (Figure 10-1) has two functions:

- It watches over your PC constantly, as a barrier against new infections of viruses and spyware. Each day, the program auto-downloads new *definitions files*—behind-the-scenes updates to its virus database, which keep it up to date with the latest new viruses that Microsoft has spotted in the wild.

Note: If you haven't been online in awhile, a system-tray balloon lets you know. Click the balloon to go online to download the latest definitions.

- Second, it has a scanning function that's designed to clean out infections you already have (a feature that, thank heaven, you'll rarely need).

Ordinarily, the program scans your PC automatically every Sunday at 2 a.m. (If the computer isn't turned on at that point, then it will scan the next time it's on but you're not using it.) But you can also scan a particular file or folder that seems to be acting flaky.

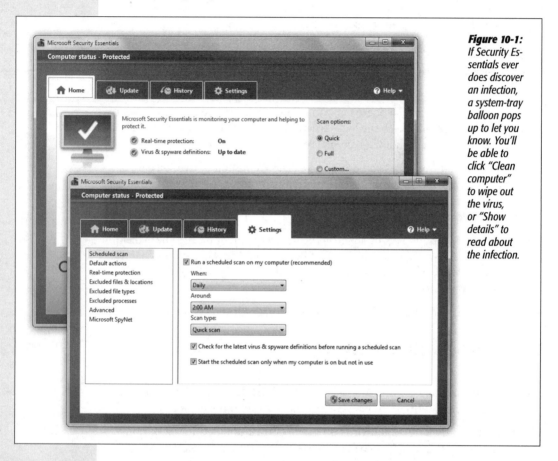

Figure 10-1:
If Security Essentials ever does discover an infection, a system-tray balloon pops up to let you know. You'll be able to click "Clean computer" to wipe out the virus, or "Show details" to read about the infection.

That's all there is to it—it's mostly automatic and in the background. But if you like to poke around, open Microsoft Security Essentials from your Start menu. You find four tabs:

- **Home.** A summary of your protection status, definitions status, and so on. There's also a Scan Now button for times of panic.

- **Update.** Shows you what definitions database you've got and offers a big fat Update button to download the latest one right now.

- **History.** A list of viruses and spyware programs Essentials has found. You can see All, Quarantined (infected files the program has just disabled instead of deleting), and Allowed ("infected" files you've told Windows you want to keep alive anyway).

- **Settings.** Here's where you can specify when your PC scans the computer, in case Sunday at 2 a.m. isn't ideal. Here, too, is where you can exclude certain files, folders, and disks from being scanned (handy if, for example, if you're writing PC viruses and don't want them removed). You can also turn off the real-time protection feature if you think it's slowing down your PC.

Now, Microsoft Security Essentials is certainly not the only antivirus program on the planet; it's not even the best one.

Several rival antivirus programs are free for personal use, like Avast (*www.avast.com*). These do have their downsides—some nag you to buy the Pro versions, for example, and there's nobody to call for tech support.

Meanwhile, almost every new PC comes with a trial version of a commercial antivirus program like Norton or McAfee; you have to pay an annual fee to keep it up to date.

In any case, the bottom line is this: If your PC doesn't have antivirus software working for you right now, then getting some should be at the top of your To Do list. *Important:* Get antivirus software written especially for Windows 7. Antivirus software from the Windows XP days won't work.

Action Center
All Versions

One of the biggest annoyances in Windows Vista was the nagginess. The thing was constantly bugging you, popping up balloons, popping up "Attention!" boxes, demanding your name and password at every turn. It's great that Microsoft tightened up security, but come on; it was like living with a needy 5-year-old.

Windows 7 harangues you much less. In fact, 10 categories of not-that-urgent, security-related nags don't interrupt your work at all; instead, they quietly collect themselves into a new, central message station called the Action Center. You can poke in there from time to time to have a look.

The only indication you have that Windows is still on the job, in fact, is Action Center's front man: the tiny ⚑ icon on your taskbar tray. When there's an X on it like this ⚑, Windows has something to say to you (Figure 10-2, top). If Windows considers the problem to be urgent, then a message balloon sprouts from the flag, too.

Tip: If you point to the flag icon without clicking, a status balloon appears to let you know how many messages Windows has saved up for you.

If you click the ⚑, you get a pop-up summary of the problem (and others that Windows has noticed). Sometimes, there's a link you can click to solve the problem right in the summary bubble. Other times, you may want to just click Open Action Center in the shortcut menu; the Action Center appears, as shown in Figure 10-2, bottom. (If you ever see a message balloon appearing from the ⚑ icon, you can also open the Action Center by clicking the balloon itself.)

Here's where Windows collects all messages related to antivirus software, antispyware software, Windows Update settings, Internet security settings, your firewall software, and your backup settings.

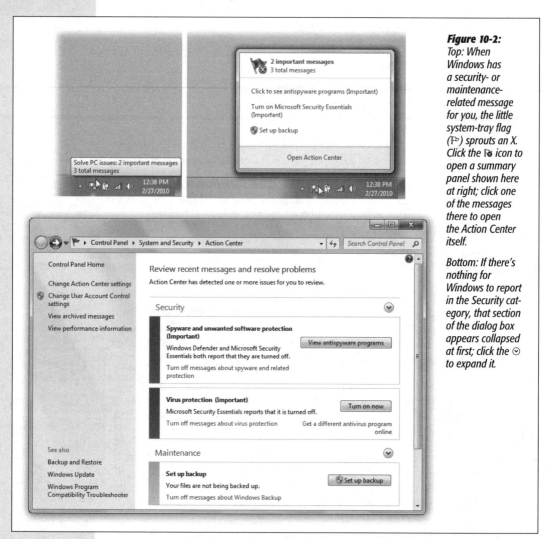

Figure 10-2:
Top: When Windows has a security- or maintenance-related message for you, the little system-tray flag (⚑) sprouts an X. Click the ⚑ icon to open a summary panel shown here at right; click one of the messages there to open the Action Center itself.

Bottom: If there's nothing for Windows to report in the Security category, that section of the dialog box appears collapsed at first; click the ⊙ to expand it.

If the Security heading is collapsed and you see no messages, then Windows thinks that all is well. Expand the ⊙ button next to the Security heading, if …you like, to see the full panoply of security settings. Here, you see the state of firewall security, automatic updating, malware protection, and other security settings. "On" or "OK" means you're protected.

Tip: Each message comes with a "Turn off" link. Click it if you no longer want to be bothered by messages on this subject. Or click "Change Action Center settings"; you're shown a complete list of the kinds of situations Action Center monitors—and you can turn off a bunch of them at once.

A color-coded bar indicates the urgency of the messages here: red for dire (for example, you don't have an antivirus program), yellow for not-so-urgent messages (for example, you don't have Windows Update set to auto-download patches). Each message comes with a button that proposes an action Windows thinks you should take: turning on your antivirus program, setting up an automatic backup system, and so on.

Conveniently enough, both Microsoft and non-Microsoft security programs can patch into Action Center; if you use Norton Antivirus, for example, you see its messages here, too.

Windows Firewall
All Versions

If you have a broadband, always-on connection, you're connected to the Internet 24 hours a day. It's theoretically possible for some cretin to use automated hacking software to flood you with files or take control of your machine. Fortunately, the Windows *Firewall* feature puts up a barrier to such mischief.

The firewall acts as a gatekeeper between you and the Internet. It examines all Internet traffic and lets through only communications that it knows are safe; all other traffic is turned away at the door.

How It Works
Every kind of electronic message sent to or from your PC—instant messaging, music sharing, file sharing, and so on—conducts its business on a specific communications channel, or *port.* Ports are numbered tunnels for certain kinds of Internet traffic.

POWER USERS' CLINIC

Inbound vs. Outbound

These days, the Windows Firewall can protect both inbound and outbound traffic. (The Windows XP firewall handled only inbound traffic.) But the factory setting is not to block outgoing signals.

Now, inbound signals are a much bigger threat than outgoing ones. Still, some spyware, Trojans, and malicious software "phone home"—that is, once secretly installed, it sends out an invisible note telling the world that it's ready to be used to attack your PC. Some may try to attack other computers near it. And some turn your PC into a zombie: basically a spam relay station. Your PC could be pumping out millions of junk-mail messages a day, and you wouldn't even know it.

Windows Vista didn't have an outbound-blocking firewall at all. So why did Microsoft add outbound-blocking to Windows 7, and then ship it turned off?

The theory is that if your PC is locked down tight enough with antivirus software, antispyware software, and an inbound firewall, you won't get any infection that could send outbound signals in the first place. Meanwhile, you're saved the incessant pinging of the "Are you sure?" messages you'd get every time a normal program tried to connect to the Internet.

The problem with Windows before Vista came along was that Microsoft left all your ports *open* for your convenience—and, as it turns out, for the bad guys'. Starting with Vista, all the ports arrive on your PC *closed*.

The firewall blocks or permits signals based on a predefined set of rules. They dictate, for example, which programs are permitted to use your network connection, or which ports can be used for communications.

You don't need to do anything to turn on the Windows Firewall. When you turn on Windows, it's already at work. But the Windows Firewall *can* be turned off.

To do that, or to fiddle with any of its settings, there are plenty of ways to find it:

- Open the Start menu. Start typing *firewall* until you see "Windows Firewall" in the results list; click it.

- Choose Start→Control Panel. In Icon view, double-click Windows Firewall. Or, in Category view, click "System and Security" and then Windows Firewall.

As you can see in Figure 10-3, the Firewall screen is pretty simple.

Tip: It's perfectly OK to use the Windows Firewall and another company's firewall software—a first for Windows. Each can be assigned to handle different technical firewall functions—if you're a supergeek.

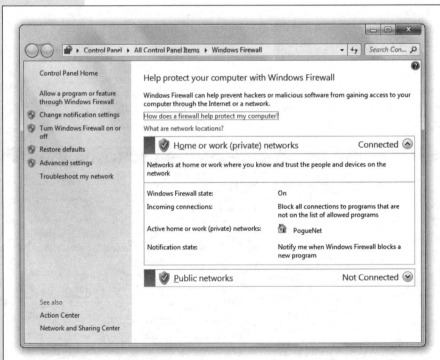

Figure 10-3:
The firewall is basically a dashboard that tells you if your firewall is turned on, the name of your network, and what the settings are for each kind of network location—Domain (Work), Private, or Public. See page 715 for details on these network types.

Firewall Settings

To see the ways you can adjust the Windows Firewall, click "Turn Windows Firewall on or off" in the left-side task panel. (Authenticate yourself if necessary.)

The resulting screen lets you tweak the settings for each location (Public, Private, Domain) independently. You have these options:

- Block all incoming connections, including those in the list of allowed programs. When you're feeling especially creeped out by the threat of hackerishness—like when you're at the coffee shop of your local computer-science grad school—turn on this box. Now your computer is pretty much completely shut off from the Internet except for Web browsing, email, and instant messaging.

- Notify me when Windows Firewall blocks a new program. Windows will pop up a message that lets you know when a new program has attempted to get online, on the off chance that it's some evil app. Most of the time, of course, it's some perfectly innocent program that you happen to be using for the first time; just click Allow in the box and go on with your life.

Note: If you really are on a domain (Chapter 25), then you may not be allowed to make any changes to the firewall settings, because that's something the network nerds like to be in charge of.

- Turn off Windows Firewall. Yes, you can turn the firewall off entirely. There's very little reason to do that, though, even if you decide to install another company's firewall; its installer turns off the Windows Firewall if necessary.

  You also might be tempted to turn off the firewall because you have a *router* that distributes your Internet signal through the house—and most routers have *hardware* firewalls built right in, protecting your entire network.

  Still, there's no harm in having *both* a hardware and software firewall in place. In fact, having the Windows Firewall turned on protects you from viruses you catch from other people on your own network (even though you're both "behind" the router's firewall). And if you have a laptop, this way you won't have to remember to turn the firewall on when you leave your home network.

Punching Through the Firewall

The firewall isn't always your friend. It can occasionally block a perfectly harmless program from communicating with the outside world—a chat program or game that you can play across the Internet, for example.

Fortunately, whenever that happens, Windows lets you know with a message like the one shown in Figure 10-4. Most of the time, you know exactly what program it's talking about, because it's a program you just opened *yourself*—a program you installed that might legitimately need Internet access. In other words, it's not some rogue spyware on your machine trying to talk to the mother ship. Click "Allow access" and get on with your life.

Alternatively, you can set up permissions for your apps in advance. At the left side of the firewall screen shown in Figure 10-3, click "Allow a program or feature through Windows Firewall." Proceed as shown in Figure 10-5.

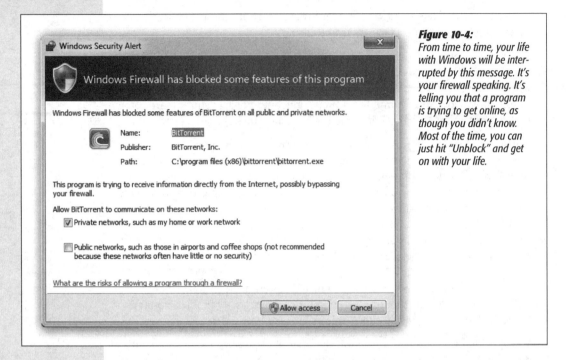

Figure 10-4:
From time to time, your life with Windows will be interrupted by this message. It's your firewall speaking. It's telling you that a program is trying to get online, as though you didn't know. Most of the time, you can just hit "Unblock" and get on with your life.

Advanced Firewall

The Windows Firewall screen gives you a good deal of control over how the Windows Firewall works. But it doesn't offer nearly the amount of tweakiness that high-end geeks demand, like control over individual ports, IP addresses, programs, and so on. It also offers no way to create a log (a text-file record) of all attempts to contact your PC from the network or the Internet, which can be handy when you suspect that some nasty hacker has been visiting you in the middle of the night.

There is, however, an even more powerful firewall control panel. In an effort to avoid terrifying novices, Microsoft has hidden it, but it's easy enough to open. It's called the Windows Firewall with Advanced Security.

Get there by typing *firewall* into the Start menu Search box; when you see "Windows Firewall with Advanced Security" in the list, hit Enter. Or, if you've already opened Windows Firewall, click "Advanced settings" in the left-side taskbar. Either way, authenticate if necessary.

Figure 10-5 shows you the very basics. But if you're really that much of an Advanced Security sort of person, you can find Microsoft's how-to guide for this console at *http://bit.ly/hxR0i.*

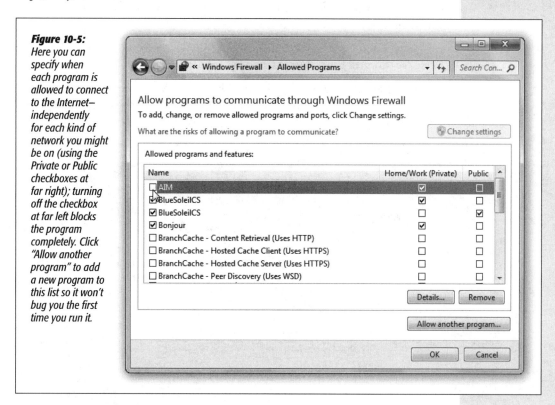

Figure 10-5:
Here you can specify when each program is allowed to connect to the Internet— independently for each kind of network you might be on (using the Private or Public checkboxes at far right); turning off the checkbox at far left blocks the program completely. Click "Allow another program" to add a new program to this list so it won't bug you the first time you run it.

Windows Defender
All Versions

Spyware is software you don't know you have. You usually get it in one of two ways. First, a Web site may try to trick you into downloading it. You see what looks like an innocent button in what's actually a phony Windows dialog box, or maybe you get an empty dialog box—and clicking the Close button actually triggers the installation.

Second, you may get spyware by downloading a program you *do* want—"cracked" software (commercial programs whose copy protection has been removed) is a classic example—without realizing that a secret program is piggybacking on the download.

Once installed, the spyware may make changes to important system files, install ads on your desktop (even when you're not online) or send information about your surfing habits to a Web site that blitzes your PC with pop-up ads related in some way to your online behavior.

Spyware can do much damage beyond simply tracking what you do on the Internet. It can, for example, hijack your home page or search page so that every time you open your browser, you wind up at a Web page that incapacitates your PC with a blizzard of pop-ups. *Keylogger* spyware can record all your keystrokes, passwords and all, and send them to a snooper.

Fortunately, Windows 7 comes with a free anti-spyware program. It's called Windows Defender (Control Panel→System and Security→Windows Defender).

You don't need to do anything to turn Windows Defender on. It runs every time you start Windows. It protects you against spyware in two ways: by protecting you continuously, in real time, and by removing spyware after you're infected.

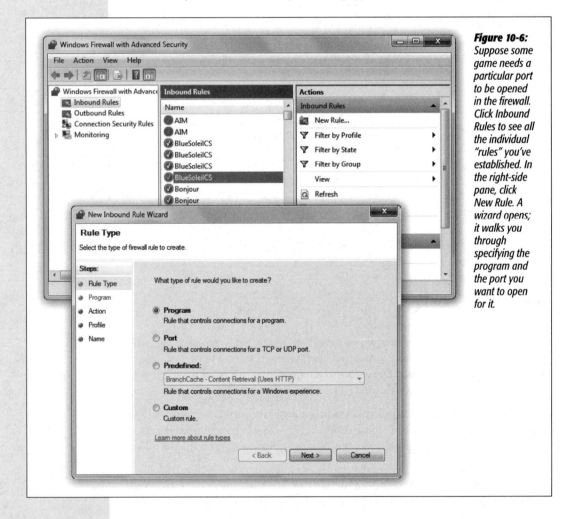

Figure 10-6:
Suppose some game needs a particular port to be opened in the firewall. Click Inbound Rules to see all the individual "rules" you've established. In the right-side pane, click New Rule. A wizard opens; it walks you through specifying the program and the port you want to open for it.

Note: Defender used to be called Microsoft Windows AntiSpyware. Microsoft changed the name because Defender not only scans your PC looking for spyware, just like several free programs, but also monitors important corners of the operating system that are common spyware targets. The watched areas include startup programs, system preference settings, Internet Explorer settings and downloads, and so on.

Real-Time Protection

Defender is a kind of silent sentinel that sits in the background, watching your system and even the files you download from the Web or get via email.

- If it recognizes a piece of spyware on your PC, Defender zaps it automatically. (How does it recognize spyware? Because every week, Windows downloads the latest spyware definitions database that tells Defender how to recognize the latest threats.)

- If it sees something that acts like spyware, an alert message pops up and asks if you want to allow the questionable software to keep working, or instead remove it.

  If the alert level is **Severe, High,** or **Medium,** let Windows Defender remove the spyware immediately. If the alert level is **Low,** read the message for details. If you don't like what you read, or if you don't recognize the publisher of the software, tell Windows Defender to block or remove the software. **Not yet classified** generally denotes a harmless program. If you recognize the software's name, let it run normally. If not, search the program's name with Google to help you decide whether to let it run or not.

  In each case, you can click in the Action column to choose Quarantine (move the software to a special "sandboxed" folder where it can't run, whereupon you can delete it or restore it); Remove; or Allow (adds the program to the "allowed" list for Defender, so that Defender will quit bugging you about it).

Scanning

Defender also scans your hard drive for infections every night at 2 a.m. and removes what it finds.

UP TO SPEED

Is It Spyware or Adware?

Spyware has a less-malignant cousin called *adware*, and the line between the two types is exceedingly thin.

Adware is free software that displays ads (the free version of Eudora, for example). In order to target those ads to your interest, it may transmit reports on your surfing habits to its authors. (Windows Defender doesn't protect against adware.)

So what's the difference between adware and spyware? If it

performs malicious actions, like incapacitating your PC with pop-ups, it's spyware for sure.

Proponents of adware say, "Hey—we've gotta put bread on our tables, too! Those ads are how you pay for your free software. Our software doesn't identify you personally when it reports on your surfing habits, so it's not really spyware."

But other people insist that any software that reports on your activities is spyware, no matter what.

If you're feeling a little antsy, you can also trigger a scan manually. To do that, open Defender. (Quickest way: Open the Start menu. Start typing *defender* until you see "Windows Defender" in the results list; press Enter to open it. If a message tells you that Defender is turned off, click the link to turn it on.) See Figure 10-7.

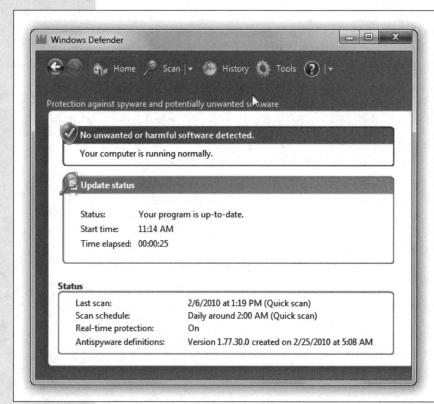

Figure 10-7:
This screen tells when you last scanned for spyware, whether Defender found any spyware, and your daily scanning schedule. Pay particular attention to the "Definition version." This tells you how up-to-date your spyware definitions are. If they're more than a week old, use Windows Update (page 662) to get the latest definitions.

Across the top of the screen, you see four links: Home, Scan, History, and Tools. You know all about Home already; it's where you are when you first run the program, as shown in Figure 10-7. Here's what you need to know about the rest:

Scan

This link scans your PC for spyware. Click it to start a scan, or click the ▾ button to change the *kind* of scan. Your choices:

- Quick Scan is what Windows Defender does every night. It scans those parts of your PC most likely to be infected by spyware, plus any programs you're currently running. (Why would you run a Quick Scan if it just ran last night? Maybe because you've just installed a piece of software, or you've visited a dubious Web site.)

- The Full Scan is more thoroughgoing; it looks at every single file on all your hard disks, as well as any programs currently running. If you suspect you've been infected by spyware, run the Full Scan to whack it. It takes considerably longer than a Quick Scan.

- The Custom option lets you specify which folders you want to scan, just in case you think spyware might be lurking in a nonobvious spot.

History

This tab offers a log of all the actions Windows Defender has taken. Most of what you see in its history are decisions to permit software to continue to function, because the programs don't appear to be malicious.

For each program it's taken action on, it lists the name, the alert level, the action it took, the date, and whether the action was successful. Click a listing to find out more details about it, like its location, file name, and description of why Defender considered the program suspicious.

Techies will be glad to see more rarefied information here, such as the Registry key each program uses.

Tools

Here's where Microsoft has assembled Windows Defender's advanced tools:

- **Options.** Schedule how and when Windows Defender should run, and what actions it should take when it comes across suspicious software, among other options.

  The factory setting is to scan your system every night at 2 a.m. Of course, there's a good chance your PC won't be turned on at that hour—so use these options to specify a time when your PC *is* turned on.

  You can also select a Quick Scan or Full Scan. It's set to Quick Scan, but if you set it to run at a time when you're not using the PC, it can't hurt to set it to do a Full Scan. This section also lets you specify what Defender should do when it comes across High, Medium, and Low alert items. "Default action," which tells Defender to use its own judgment, is the best setting.

Tip: Here's also where you can exclude a certain program, or program type, from being scanned. That's a handy trick when Defender keeps insisting that some perfectly innocuous program is spyware.

- **Microsoft SpyNet.** One of Defender's most potent tricks is learning about emerging spyware types from the Microsoft SpyNet network, which harnesses the collective wisdom of Windows fans all over the Internet.

  Suppose, for example, that Windows Defender can't determine whether or not some new program is spyware. It can send out an online feeler to see how people in the network have handled the same program—for example, if other Windows fans removed it (having determined that it's spyware)—and then use what it finds out to handle your own copy of that program.

  Microsoft says all this information is anonymous. If you're OK with that, you can opt into the SpyNet community here.

- **Quarantined items.** When Defender finds spyware, it puts the offending software into a quarantine area where it can't do any more harm. This tab lets you see the quarantined software, delete it, or restore it (take it out of quarantine). In general, restoring spyware is a foolhardy move.

- **Allowed items.** If Defender announces that it's found a potential piece of malware, but you allow it to run anyway, it's considered an Allowed Item. From now on, Defender ignores it, meaning that you trust that program completely. Allowed programs' names appear on this list.

  If you highlight a program's name and then click Remove From List, it's *gone* from the Allowed list, and therefore Defender monitors it once again.

- **Windows Defender website.** This link takes you to the Windows Defender site, which contains a few moderately useful help resources about spyware.

POWER USERS' CLINIC

Data Execution Prevention

Data Execution Prevention (DEP), one of Windows 7's advanced security features, isn't well-known, but it protects you against a variety of threats. It monitors important Windows services (background programs) and programs to make sure that no virus has hijacked them to your PC from within its own system memory. If DEP finds out an attack is under way, it automatically closes the offending service or program.

DEP comes set to protect only Windows itself—not other programs. You can, though, ask DEP to monitor *every* program on your system, or just programs that you specify. The upside is better protection; the downside is that DEP could conflict with those programs, causing them to run erratically or not at all. In such cases, though, you can always turn off DEP protection for the affected programs.

(Note: If DEP suddenly starts interfering with important Windows files and features, a recently installed program could be at fault. Try uninstalling it, or inquire if the publisher has a DEP-friendly version; that may solve the problem.)

To turn on DEP for some or all programs: Open the Start menu. Start typing *advanced system* until you see "View advanced system settings" in the results list; click it. In the Performance section, click Settings, and then click the Data Execution Prevention tab, shown here. Select "Turn on DEP for all programs and services except those I select," and then click OK.

Should you find that DEP interferes with a program, click Add, and then follow the directions for selecting it.

Incidentally, at the bottom of the Data Execution Prevention screen, you can see whether or not your PC offers DEP *circuitry,* which reduces its speed impact. If not, Windows runs a software-based version of DEP.

- **Microsoft Malware Protection Center.** It's a Web site maintained by Microsoft's virus/spyware experts, full of articles and details.

SmartScreen Filter
All Versions

The criminal mind knows no bounds. How else do you explain the clever nefariousness of *phishing* attacks?

In a phishing attack, you're sent what appears to be legitimate email from a bank, eBay, PayPal, or some other financial Web site. The message tells you the site needs to confirm account information, or warns that your account has been hacked, and needs you to help keep it safe.

If you, responsible citizen that you are, click the provided link to clear up the supposed problem, you wind up on what looks like the bank/eBay/PayPal Web site. But it's a fake, carefully designed to look like the real thing; it's run by a scammer. If you type in your password and login information, as requested, then the next thing you know, you're getting credit-card bills for $10,000 charges at high-rolling Las Vegas hotels.

The fake sites look so much like the real ones that it can be extremely difficult to tell them apart. (That's *can* be; on some of the phishing sites, spelling mistakes a fourth-grader wouldn't make are a clear giveaway.) To make the site seem more realistic, the scam artist often includes legitimate links alongside phony ones. But if you click the login link, you're in trouble.

Internet Explorer 8's SmartScreen filter protects you from these scams. You don't need to do anything to turn it on; it's always running. It's always comparing the sites you visit with a master list of sites run by the bad guys.

FREQUENTLY ASKED QUESTION

Sherlock Explorer

How does Internet Explorer know what's a phishing site and what's not?

IE uses three bits of information to figure out whether a site is legitimate or a phishing site.

Its first line of defense is a Microsoft-compiled, frequently updated database of known phishing sites that, believe it or not, sits right on your own hard drive. Whenever you head to a Web site, Internet Explorer consults that database. If the Web site appears in the list, you get the warning. (The database is compiled from several phish-tracking companies,

including Cyota, Internet Identity, and MarkMonitor, as well as from direct user feedback.)

Second, Internet Explorer uses *heuristics,* a sort of low-level artificial intelligence. It compares characteristics of the site you're visiting against common phishing-site characteristics. The heuristics tool helps IE recognize phishing sites that haven't yet made it into the database of known sites.

Finally, Internet Explorer quietly sends addresses of some of the sites you visit to Microsoft, which checks it against a frequently updated list of reported phishing sites (not the database on your PC).

Note: In Internet Explorer 7, this feature was called the phishing filter, and it protected you only from phishing sites. Nowadays, it watches for both phishing sites and sites that are known to contain malware (viruses and spyware); it alerts you about both of them. (The addition of the spyware sites explains the name change.)

One day, when you least expect it, you'll be on your way to visit some Web site—and Internet Explorer will stop you in your tracks with a pop-up warning that you're about to open to a "reported phishing website" or "reported malware site" (Figure 10-8). The address bar turns red to emphasize the danger.

Note: You may sometimes see a weaker version of this message—a screen that says, "Are you trying to visit this site?" (Um, yes? Duh.) This message means the site isn't actually on the list of known phishing/malware sites, but it sure smells like one to Microsoft.

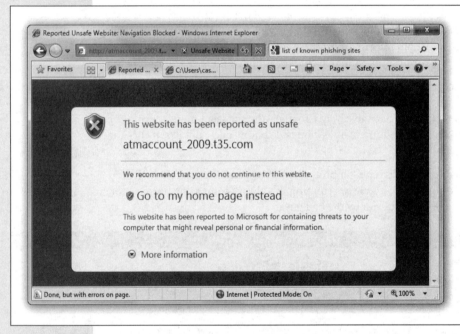

Figure 10-8:
Danger! You're sitting on a known phishing site. (This site was a particularly malicious one; if you clicked a link on it, the site would attempt to silently install a virus on your PC without your knowledge.)

In that situation, close the page, or click "Go to my home page instead," or go to another site. (If you're just researching phishing sites, and you know full well what trouble you're getting yourself into, and you really want to proceed, click "More information" and then "Disregard and continue"; you'll go through to the phony site.)

If Internet Explorer isn't quite sure about a certain site's phishiness, but it has a funny feeling in its bones, a yellow button appears next to the address bar that says, "Suspicious Website." Unless you absolutely know the site is legitimate, it's a good idea to head somewhere else.

Phine-Tuning the Philter

There's not much to controlling the phishing-filter feature; you can turn it on and off and check a certain Web site to see if it's legitimate. In Internet Explorer, choose Safety→SmartScreen Filter to view the following options:

- **Check this Website.** This command sends the address of the Web site you're visiting to Microsoft's computers, where it's checked against the massive real-time database of phishing and malware sites.

Note: The first time you try this command, you get a pop-up message that explains, for the sake of your privacy paranoia, that you're about to transmit anonymous information to Microsoft. Click OK to proceed; if you want the warning to never appear again, check the box next to "Don't show this again."

After a moment, a message appears to let you know whether the site is legitimate, suspicious, or a phishing site. If it's legitimate, a box pops up telling you so; if it's suspicious or a phishing site, the warning appears in the address bar.

- **Turn Off/On SmartScreen Filter.** This option brings up the on/off dialog box for the filter feature. (The first time you run Internet Explorer, you're encouraged to turn the filter on. This is your opportunity to change your mind.)

Note: Why would you ever want to turn this feature off? Because maybe you're a privacy nut. SmartScreen works by sending the Web address of each page you visit back to Microsoft, where it's compared against the list of evil sites. Actually, Internet Explorer also sends your computer's IP address, browser type, and filter version number. It's all transmitted in encrypted form, and none of it, according to Microsoft, is stored anywhere. And no information associated with the site is sent, like search terms you've used, information you've entered into forms, or cookies.

Still. If that transmitting business creeps you out, you can turn the whole thing off.

- **Report Unsafe Website.** If you stumble onto a Web site you think is a phishing site, click here. A new browser window opens; turn on "I think this is a phishing Website." Specify what you think is wrong with the site ("I think this is a phishing site" or "I think this website contains malicious software"), fill in the rest of the form, and then click Submit.

Also use this option in the opposite situation: when you're visiting what you *know* is a legitimate site, but Internet Explorer identifies it as a phishing site. Just above the Submit button are two choices: one for reporting that you don't think the Web site is a phishing site, and the other to report that you *know* it's not a phishing hole because you *own* it.

Privacy and Cookies
All Versions

Cookies are something like Web-page preference files. Certain Web sites—particularly commercial ones like Amazon.com—deposit them on your hard drive like little bookmarks so that they'll remember you the next time you visit. On Amazon, in fact, a greeting says "Hello, Casey" (or whatever your name is), thanks to the cookie it uses to recognize you.

Most cookies are perfectly innocuous—and, in fact, are extremely helpful. They can let your PC log into a site automatically, or let you customize what the site looks like and how you use it.

But fear is on the march, and the media fan the flames with tales of sinister cookies that track your movement on the Web. Some Web sites rely on cookies to record which pages you visit on a site, how long you spend on a site, what kind of information you like to find out, and so on.

If you're worried about invasions of privacy—and you're willing to trade away some of the conveniences of cookies—Internet Explorer is ready to protect you.

The Terminology of Cookies

Before you begin your cookie-fortification strategy, you'll have to bone up on a little terminology. Here are a few explanations to get you started:

- A **first-party cookie** is created by the site you're currently visiting. These kinds of cookies generally aren't privacy invaders; they're the Amazon type described above, designed to log you in or remember how you've customized, for example, the Google home page.

- **Third-party cookies** are deposited on your hard drive by a site other than the one you're currently visiting—often by an advertiser. Needless to say, this kind of cookie is more objectionable. It can track your browsing habits and create profiles about your interests and behaviors.

- A **compact privacy statement** is a Web site's publicly posted privacy policy that describes how its cookies are used. Here you'll find out why cookies are used, for

---

POWER USERS' CLINIC

Examine Individual Cookies

Want to see the actual cookies themselves as they sit on your hard drive—the individual cookie files?

They're sitting on your hard drive in your Personal folder→AppData→Roaming→Microsoft→Windows→ Cookies folder. (You won't be able to see it until you visit Folder Options—page 97. Click "Show hidden files, folders, and drives," and turn off "Hide protected operating system files." Remember to switch these back to the factory settings when you're finished with this little experiment.)

Each cookie is named something like *casey@abcnews.*

com[1].txt. The name of the Web site or ad network usually appears after the @, but not always—sometimes you just see a number.

To inspect a cookie, open the file as you would any other text file (in Notepad or WordPad, for example). Usually, there's nothing but a list of numbers and letters inside, but you might occasionally find useful information like your user name and password for the Web site.

If you don't want the cookie on your hard disk, simply delete it as you would any other text file.

---

example, and how long they stay on your PC. (Some cookies are automatically deleted when you leave a Web site, and others stay valid until a specified date.)

• **Explicit consent** means you've granted permission for a Web site to gather information about your online activity; that is, you've "opted in."

• **Implicit consent** means you haven't OK'd that info gathering, but the site assumes that it's OK with you because you're there on the site. If a Web site uses the implicit-consent policy, it's saying, "Hey, you're fair game, because you haven't opted out."

Cookie Options

In Internet Explorer, choose Tools→Internet Options→Privacy to get to the Privacy tab shown in Figure 10-9.

Tip: You can also accept or reject cookies on a site-by-site basis. To do that, click the Sites button on the Privacy tab (Figure 10-9). The Per Site Privacy Actions dialog box appears. Type the name of the site in question, and then click either Block or Allow.

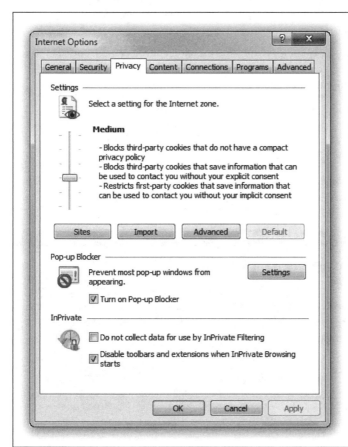

Figure 10-9:
This screen helps you keep your private information private—it lets you control how your PC works with cookies, which are bits of data put on your hard disk by Web sites. Medium High is a good setting that balances your privacy with Web sites' needs to use cookies for purposes like automated logins.

The slider on the left side lets you pick your compromise on the convenience/privacy scale, ranging from Accept All Cookies to Block All Cookies. Here are a few examples (and good luck with the terminology):

- **Block All Cookies.** No cookies, no exceptions. Web sites can't read existing cookies, either.

- **High.** No cookies from any Web site that doesn't have a compact privacy policy. No cookies from sites that use personally identifiable information without your explicit consent.

- **Medium High.** Blocks third-party cookies from sites that don't have a compact privacy policy or use personally identifiable information without your explicit consent. Blocks first-party cookies that use personally identifiable information without your implicit consent.

- **Medium (Default).** Blocks third-party cookies from sites that don't have a compact privacy policy or that use personally identifiable information without your implicit consent. Accepts first-party cookies from sites that use personally identifiable information without your implicit consent, but deletes them when you close Internet Explorer.

- **Low.** Blocks third-party cookies from sites that don't have a compact privacy policy. Accepts third-party cookies that use personally identifiable information without your implicit consent, but deletes them when you close Internet Explorer.

- **Accept All Cookies.** All cookies OK. Web sites can read existing cookies.

Choose the setting you want, and then click OK, and you're ready to start browsing.

Note: Some sites don't function well (or at all) if you choose to reject all cookies. So if you choose High Privacy, and you run into trouble browsing your favorite sites, return here and change the setting to Medium High. (The factory setting is Medium.)

Backing Up Your Cookies

This is probably deeper cookie information than you really wanted to know, but here it is: You may want to consider *backing up* your cookies. You could do that, for example, and transfer your cookies to another PC, for your auto-login convenience. Or you could back up the cookies just in case yours get somehow deleted.

To export or back up your cookies, open Internet Explorer. Press the Alt key to make the menus appear. Then choose

File→Import and Export. The Import/Export Wizard appears. Choose Export Cookies and follow the directions. A single text file containing all your cookies is created in your Documents folder (or a folder you specify).

To import cookies to another computer (or the same one after a disaster), launch the Import/Export Wizard, choose Import Cookies, and then browse to the folder where you stashed the backup file.

If you're ever curious whether a Web site you've visited in your current browser session has placed any cookies on your hard disk, press the Alt key to make Internet Explorer's menu bar appear. Choose View→Webpage Privacy Policy. You'll see a list of the sites you've visited, and whether any have placed cookies on your PC.

History: Erasing Your Tracks
All Versions

You'd be shocked to see the kinds of information Internet Explorer stores about you. Behind the scenes, it logs every Web site you ever visit. It stashes your cookies, of course, plus passwords and information you type into Web forms (your name and address, for example). Your hard drive also keeps cache files—graphics and text files that make up the Web pages themselves, stored on your hard drive to speed up their reappearance if you visit those sites again.

Now, some people find it unnerving that Internet Explorer maintains a complete list of every Web site they've seen recently, right there in plain view of any family member or coworker who wanders by.

Fortunately, you can delete any or all of these tracks easily enough.

- To delete just one particularly incriminating History listing, right-click it in the History list (page 412). From the shortcut menu, choose Delete. You've just re-written History.

POWER USERS' CLINIC

Add-On Manager

Internet Explorer is more than just a browser. In fact, it's practically a kind of mini-operating system that lets lots of little add-on programs run inside of it. The most common category of these plug-ins is called ActiveX controls. They grant all kinds of superpowers to Internet Explorer; for example, the Flash add-on makes possible animations and movies on YouTube and many other sites.

But ActiveX controls and other add-ons can cause problems. Install too many, and your browser can get sluggish. Sometimes add-ons conflict with one another, resulting in an Internet Explorer crash. And some—this is the really nasty part—may actually be malicious code, designed to gum up your browser or your PC.

You'll know when some page needs an ActiveX control to proceed. You'll see a yellow warning bar just under the address bar, letting you know you have to click to proceed. (If you're pretty sure this is a reliable Web site that really

needs to install this add-on feature, click the information bar; from the shortcut menu, choose Allow Blocked Content.) Gone are the days when evildoers could invade your PC by downloading these things without your knowledge.

To help you get a handle on your plug-in situation, choose Tools→Manage Add-ons. You get a list of all your add-ons and ActiveX controls. They're listed in several different categories, like those that are currently loaded into Internet Explorer and ActiveX controls you've downloaded.

Highlight one to read details about it, and to summon the Disable, Enable, and (in some categories) Remove buttons.

(Hint: Before clicking any of these buttons, do a Google search on the name or the file name. You'll find out soon enough if the plug-in is trustworthy. Be especially wary of add-ons in the Browser Helper Objects [BHOs] category. These can be useful, but also very dangerous.)

- You can also delete any other organizer icon in the History list: one of the little Web-site folders, or even one of the calendar folders like "Three Weeks Ago."

- To erase the entire History menu, choose Safety→Delete Browsing History, and then click "Delete history."

- The same dialog box (Figure 10-10) offers individual buttons for deleting the other kinds of tracks—the passwords, cache files, and so on. Or, if you really want a clean slate, you can click Delete All to purge all of it at once.

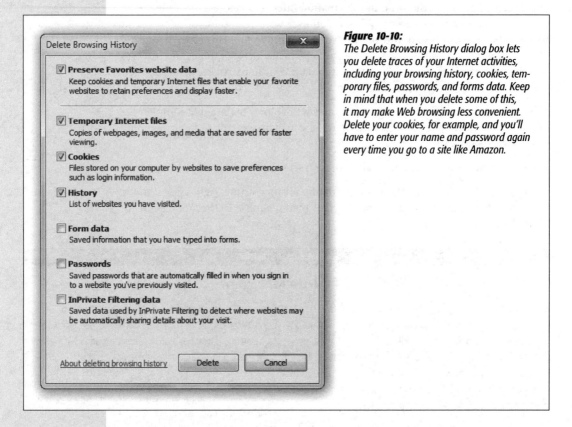

Figure 10-10:
The Delete Browsing History dialog box lets you delete traces of your Internet activities, including your browsing history, cookies, temporary files, passwords, and forms data. Keep in mind that when you delete some of this, it may make Web browsing less convenient. Delete your cookies, for example, and you'll have to enter your name and password again every time you go to a site like Amazon.

This is good information to know; after all, you might be nominated to the Supreme Court some day.

The Pop-Up Blocker
All Versions

The ad banners at the top of every Web page are annoying enough—but nowadays, they're just the beginning. The world's smarmiest advertisers have begun inundating us with *pop-up* and *pop-under* ads: nasty little windows that appear in front of the browser window or, worse, behind it, waiting to jump out the moment you close your

browser. They're often deceptive, masquerading as error messages or dialog boxes…
and they'll do absolutely anything to get you to click inside them (Figure 10-11).

Pop-ups are more than just annoying; they're also potentially dangerous. They're a favorite trick that hackers use to deposit spyware on your PC. Clicking a pop-up can begin the silent downloading process. That's true even if the pop-up seems to serve a legitimate purpose—asking you to participate in a survey, for example.

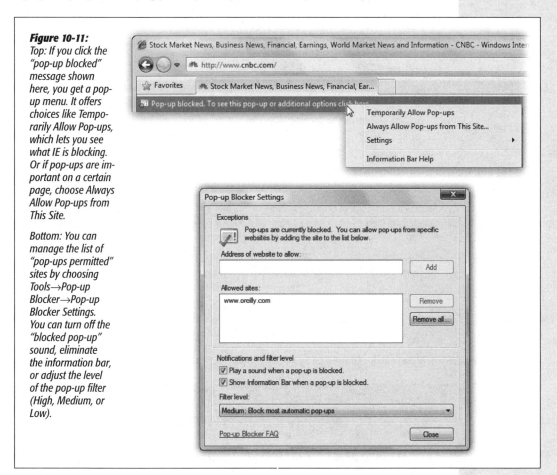

Figure 10-11:
Top: If you click the "pop-up blocked" message shown here, you get a pop-up menu. It offers choices like Temporarily Allow Pop-ups, which lets you see what IE is blocking. Or if pop-ups are important on a certain page, choose Always Allow Pop-ups from This Site.

Bottom: You can manage the list of "pop-ups permitted" sites by choosing Tools→Pop-up Blocker→Pop-up Blocker Settings. You can turn off the "blocked pop-up" sound, eliminate the information bar, or adjust the level of the pop-up filter (High, Medium, or Low).

Internet Explorer, fortunately, has a pop-up *blocker*. It comes automatically turned on; you don't have to do anything. You'll be browsing along, and then one day you'll see the "Pop-up blocked" message in the yellow information bar (Figure 10-11, top).

Tip: At the outset, IE does more than just show the info bar message. It also opens a little dialog box—yes, a pop-up—to brag that it's blocked a pop-up. For best results, click "Don't show this message again," and then click OK. (The "pop-up blocked" message still shows on the information bar, so you'll always know when a pop-up is sent into the ether.)

Note that IE blocks only pop-ups that are spawned *automatically,* not those that appear when you click something (like a seating diagram on a concert-tickets site). And it doesn't block pop-ups from your local network, or from Web sites you've designated as Trusted (choose Tools→Internet Options→Security, click "Trusted sites," and then click Sites).

Tip: As you can read in Figure 10-11, there *is* a High setting that blocks *all* pop-ups, even the ones that appear when you click a link. Even then, you still have a way to see the occasional important pop-up: Hold down the Ctrl key as your Web page is loading.

Overriding the Pop-up Block

Sometimes, though, you *want* to see the pop-up. Some sites, for example, use pop-up windows as a way to deliver information—a seating chart when you're buying plane or concert tickets, for example.

Tip: When a useful pop-up makes it through the pop-up blocker, it usually appears in its own small, separate window. But you can exploit Internet Explorer's tabbed-browsing feature (page 405) by making the pop-up open in a new tab.

Choose Tools→Internet Options, click the General tab, and then, under the Tabs section, click Settings. In the Tabbed Browsing Settings dialog box, click "Always open pop-ups in a new tab," and then click OK.

In those situations, click the information bar. A dialog box appears that lets you manage pop-ups from this particular Web site (Figure 10-11, top).

Your options:

- **Temporarily Allow Pop-ups** lets this Web site's pop-ups through just for this browsing session. Next time, pop-ups will be blocked again.

- **Always Allow Pop-ups from This Site** does what it says.

FREQUENTLY ASKED QUESTION

The Wisdom of Internet Explorer

How does the pop-up blocker know a good pop-up from a bad one, anyway?

Internet Explorer generally tries to distinguish between pop-ups it considers necessary for a site to run and those it considers annoying or dangerous.

Although it doesn't always succeed, there is some logic behind its thinking.

At the factory setting, some pop-ups get through. For example, it allows pop-ups that contain "active content"–for

example, important features, brought to you by ActiveX controls and browser add-ons, that are integral to the proper functioning of a Web site: seating charts, flight-details screens, and so on.

The blocker doesn't block pop-ups from sites in your Local Intranet or Trusted Sites zones, either (page 387).

Finally, if you already have a spyware infection, pop-ups may appear constantly; the pop-up blocker isn't designed to block spyware pop-ups.

- **Settings** lets you configure the pop-up blocker. From the menu that appears, select Turn Off Pop-up Blocker to turn the blocker off. Turn off Show Information Bar for Pop-ups if you don't even want the yellow information bar to appear when a pop-up is blocked. Select More Settings, and a screen appears that lets you always allow or block pop-ups from specific sites.

  This dialog box also lets you control how you're notified in the event of a pop-up: with a sound, with a note in the information bar, or neither. You can also use the Filter Level pop-up menu to tone down Internet Explorer's aggressiveness in blocking pop-ups. The High level, for example, blocks *all* pop-ups, even the ones Internet Explorer determines to be necessary for the site to run properly.

Tip: If you've installed some other company's pop-up blocker, you can turn off IE's version by choosing Tools→Pop-up Blocker→Turn Off Pop-up Blocker.

InPrivate Browsing

If, ahem, not everything you do on the Web is something you want your spouse/parents/boss/teacher to know about, then Microsoft has heard you.

Of course, you can erase individual History entries, as described earlier. But those aren't the only tracks you leave as you browse the Web. Your hard drive collects cookies and temporary files; Internet Explorer collects passwords and other stuff you type into boxes; the address bar memorizes addresses you type, so you'll have AutoFill working for you later; and so on.

But in Internet Explorer 8, a feature called InPrivate browsing lets you surf wherever you like within a single browser window. Then, when you close that window, all that stuff is wiped out. No History items, no cookies, no saved password list, no AutoFill entries, and so on. In other words, what happens in InPrivate browsing stays in InPrivate browsing.

- To start InPrivate browsing, choose Safety→InPrivate Browsing, or press Shift+Ctrl+P. A new window opens (Figure 10-12). Nothing you do in this window—or in the tabs within it—will leave tracks.

- To stop InPrivate browsing, just close the window. Open a new Internet Explorer window to continue browsing "publicly."

Note: Casual snoopers will never know you've been looking over the racy photos on the Midwestern Shirtless Accountants Web site. But you're not completely untraceable. Nobody using your PC can see where you've been, but your network administrator, or a nearby hacker, could watch you from across the network.

InPrivate Filtering

Just in case your head hasn't exploded yet, here's yet another new Internet Explorer privacy feature. The short version: This feature can stop Web sites from tracking you.

The long version:

Suppose you visit a site called ChihuahuaGifts.com. On that site, you see a lot of great info about gifts for Chihuahuas, sure—but there's also an ad there. You might not realize it, but this ad isn't actually sitting on the ChihuahuaGifts.com computers. It's

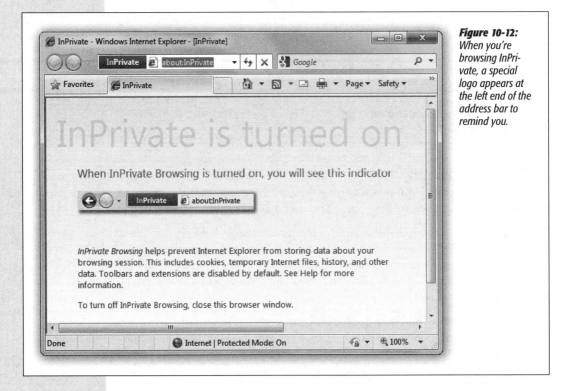

Figure 10-12:
When you're browsing InPrivate, a special logo appears at the left end of the address bar to remind you.

"patched through" from some other company—let's say DoggieAdServers.net—and automatically inserted onto the ChihuahuaGifts.com home page.

This kind of thing goes on all the time: You're seeing some map, or ad, or Web analysis tool on Site A, but it actually originates from Site B.

Trouble is, when you visit ChihuahuaGifts.com, some information about you (your computer's IP address, for example) is sent back to DoggieAdServers.net, to help it study how effective its ads are.

The problem is, DoggieAdServers.net might have ads on lots of sites. If you wind up visiting more of them, DoggieAdServers.net might be able to put together a picture of where you go on the Web. (Well, not you—they don't know who you are—but they can follow your computer's IP address.)

Note: Sometimes, you can't even see the object that originates from Site B. It might be a Web beacon—a 1-pixel graphic that exists on Site A exclusively to gather information about visitors' browsing habits and send it to Site B.

InPrivate Filtering is the answer. It lets you block the ads (or other triggers) that might transmit your information to a third-party Web site.

You have to remember to turn it on every time you start browsing. Choose Safety→In-Private Filtering, or press Shift+Ctrl+F.

The dialog box shown in Figure 10-13 (top) appears. These are your options:

- **Block for me.** Internet Explorer won't send information about you to any of those shadow sites.

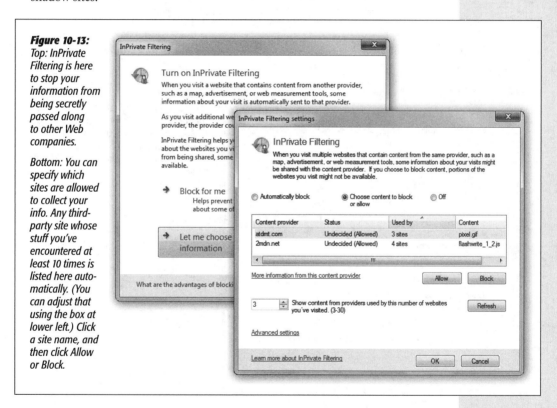

Figure 10-13:
Top: InPrivate Filtering is here to stop your information from being secretly passed along to other Web companies.

Bottom: You can specify which sites are allowed to collect your info. Any third-party site whose stuff you've encountered at least 10 times is listed here auto-matically. (You can adjust that using the box at lower left.) Click a site name, and then click Allow or Block.

- **Let me choose which providers receive my information.** Now you get the box shown in Figure 10-13 (bottom). Here, you can see the list of shadow sites that are receiving information about your Web travels—and block them individually.

Internet Security Zones

All Versions

In the real world, you usually have a pretty good sense of where the bad parts of town are, and how to avoid them after dark. On the Web, it's not so easy. The most elegant-looking Web page may be a setup, a trick by sleazy hackers to install viruses on your PC.

Security zones is an older Internet Explorer feature designed to limit the number of paths the bad guys have into your PC. It's fairly confusing, which is why almost nobody uses it.

Under this scheme, if you have tons of time, you can place individual Web sites into different classifications (zones) according to how much you trust them. Internet Explorer refuses to download potential bad stuff (like those ActiveX plug-ins) from sites in the seedier zones. Your PC, sanitized for your protection.

For example, internal company Web sites, right there on the corporate network, are pretty unlikely to be booby-trapped with spyware and viruses (unless you have a really

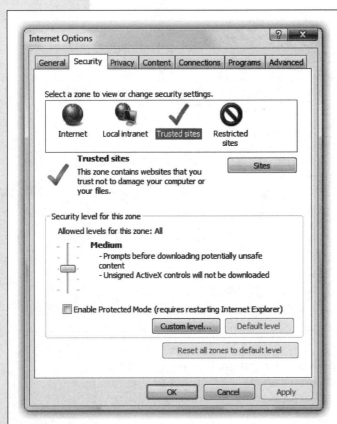

Figure 10-14:
The Internet Options Security tab lets you control Internet Explorer's security settings for browsing the Web. You can customize the settings for each zone by moving the slider up for more security, or down for less security.

twisted network administrator). Such internal sites are automatically part of the low-security Local Intranet zone. If you maintain a Web site at home, it's in that zone, too.

The rest of the Internet starts out in the very big Internet zone (medium security). As you browse, though, you can manually place them into zones called Trusted Sites (medium security) or Restricted Sites (high security).

To see your options, choose Tools→Internet Options→Security from within Internet Explorer (Figure 10-14).

Security Levels

And what, exactly, is meant by "Medium security" or "High security"? These settings control what can and can't be done when you're visiting such a site. For example, they govern whether or not you're allowed to download files, and whether or not Internet Explorer runs embedded Web-page programs like Java applets or ActiveX controls. (Java applets are little programs that offer interactivity on Web sites, like games and interactive weather maps.)

Here's the cheat sheet:

- **High** security blocks all kinds of features that could conceivably be avenues for bad guys to infect your browser: ActiveX controls, Java and Java applets, and downloads.

- **Medium** security means that whenever a Web site triggers an ActiveX control to run, you're asked for permission. Unsigned ActiveX controls—those whose origins aren't clear to Internet Explorer—don't get run at all. Downloads and Java applets are OK.

- **Medium-Low.** Same as Medium, but some ActiveX programs run without first checking with you.

- **Low.** Runs all ActiveX controls and other little Web programs. Rarely asks you for permission for things.

Classifying Sites by Hand

To place a certain Web site into the Trusted or Restricted zone, choose Tools→Internet Options→Security. Click either Trusted Sites or Restricted Sites, and then click the Sites button.

In the resulting dialog box, the current Web site's address appears automatically. Click Add, and then Close.

Hot Spot Security

All Versions

One of the greatest computing conveniences of the new millennium is the almighty public wireless hot spot, where and your WiFi-enabled laptop can connect to the Internet at high speed, often for free. There are thousands of them at cafés, hotels, airports, and other public locations (see *www.jiwire.com* for a national directory).

But unless you're careful, you'll get more than a skinny latte from your local café if you connect to their hot spot—you may get eavesdropped on as well. It's possible for someone sitting nearby, using free shareware programs, to "sniff" the transmissions from your laptop. He can intercept email messages you send, names and passwords, and even the images from the Web pages you're visiting.

Now, you don't have to sell your laptop and move to the Amish country over this. There are a few simple steps that will go a long way toward keeping yourself safe:

- **Tell Windows it's a public network.** When you first connect to a wireless network, Windows asks whether it's a public or private one. Choosing Public gives you extra protection. Technically speaking, Windows turns off *network discovery*, the feature that makes your PC announce its presence to others on the network. (Unfortunately, lurking hackers using special scanning software can still find you if they're determined.)

- **Turn off file sharing.** You certainly don't want any of your over-caffeinated neighbors to get access to your files. Open the Start menu. Start typing *sharing* until you see "Manage advanced sharing settings" in the results list; click it. In the resulting window, turn of all the Sharing options.

- **Watch for the padlock.** You generally don't have to worry about online stores and banks. Whenever you see the little padlock icon in your Web browser (or whenever the URL in the address bar begins with https instead of http), you're visiting a secure Web site. Your transmissions are encrypted in both directions and can't be snooped.

- **Look over your shoulder.** Hacking isn't always high-tech stuff; it can be as simple as "shoulder surfing," in which someone looks over your shoulder to see the password you're typing. Make sure no one can look at what you're typing.

- **Don't leave your laptop alone.** Coffee has a way of moving through your system fast, but if you have to leave for the rest room, don't leave your laptop unattended. Pack it up into its case and take it with you, or bring along a lock that you can use to lock it to a table.

- **Use a virtual private network (VPN).** If somebody intercepts your "Hi, Mom" email, it may not be the end of the world. If you're doing serious corporate work, though, and you want maximum safety, you can pay for wireless virtual private network (VPN) software that encrypts all the data that you're sending and receiving. Nobody will be able to grab it out of the air using snooping software at a hot spot.

  For example, HotSpotVPN (*www.hotspotvpn.com*) costs $3.88 per day or $8.88 per month. You get a password, user name, and the Internet address of a VPN server.

  Open the Network and Sharing Center (quickest link to it: Click the Network icon on your system tray). Click "Set up a new connection or network." Select "Connect to workplace" and follow the prompts for creating a new VPN connection with the information provided to you by HotSpotVPN.

Protect Your Home Wireless Network

All Versions

Public wireless hot spots aren't the only ones that present a theoretical security risk; your wireless network at home harbors hacker potential, too. It's theoretically possible (barely) for so-called war drivers (people who drive around with laptops, looking for unprotected home WiFi networks) to piggyback onto home networks to download child pornography or send out spam.

This one's easy to nip in the bud:

- **Turn on wireless encryption.** When you first set up your WiFi router (your base station or access point), you're offered the chance to create a password for your network. Take the chance. (Modern wireless routers offer two different types of password-protected encryption, called WEP and WPA. If it's available, choose the more modern, more secure one, which is WPA.)

  You then have to enter the password when you first connect to that hot spot from each wireless PC on your network.

Note: You won't have to type this password every time you want to get onto your own network! Windows offers to memorize it for you.

- **Ban unwanted PCs.** Many routers include a feature that lets you limit network access to specific computers. Any PC that's not on the list won't be allowed in. The feature is called MAC address filtering, although it has nothing to do with Macintosh computers. (A Media Access Control address is a serial number that uniquely identifies a piece of networking hardware.)

  Not all routers can do this, and how you do it varies from router to router, so check the documentation. In a typical Linksys router, for example, you log into the router's administrator's screen using your Web browser, and then select Wireless→Wireless Network Access. On the screen full of empty boxes, type the MAC address of the PC that you want to be allowed to get onto the network.

Tip: To find out the MAC address of a PC, press ⊞+R to open the Run dialog box, type *ipconfig /all*, and press Enter. In the resulting info screen, look for the Physical Address entry. That's the MAC address.

  Type all the MAC addresses into the boxes on the Linksys router, click Save Settings, and you're all done.

- **Place your router properly.** Placing your WiFi router centrally in the house minimizes the "leaking" of the signal into the surrounding neighborhood.

Parental Controls

All Versions

Many parents reasonably worry about the volatile mixture of kids+computers. They worry about kids spending too much time in front of the PC, rotting their brains instead of going outside to play stickball in the street like we did when we were their age, getting fresh air and sunshine. They worry that kids are rotting their brains by playing disgusting, violent video games. They worry that kids are using programs they really shouldn't be using, corrupting themselves with apps like Skype or Quicken. (That's a joke.)

Above all, parents worry that their kids might encounter upsetting material on the Internet: violence, pornography, hate speech, illegal drug sites, and so on.

A special Windows feature gives you a fighting chance at keeping this stuff off your PC: Parental Controls. They're easy to use and fairly complete.

Note: Weirdly, Microsoft took out the feature of Parental Controls that blocks dirty Web sites, even though it was in Windows Vista. Fortunately, you can restore it easily enough. That software is now called Family Safety, and it's an easy download as part of the free Windows Live Essentials suite.

To get it, open the Start menu. Start typing *essentials* until you see "Go online to get Windows Live Essentials" in the results list; press Enter. Your Web browser opens to the download page. Click Download and follow the instructions.

Time Limits, Game Limits, Software Restrictions

Before you can set up parental controls, some housekeeping is required. You, the parent, are presumably in charge of the computer, and therefore you should have an Administrator account (page 716). (And it should be password-protected; if it's not, then the kid whose innocence you're trying to preserve can just log in as you and turn Parental Controls off.)

Your children, on the other hand, should have Standard accounts. You can create one account that all your kids share, or you can set up a different account for each kid; that way, you can set up different safety restrictions for each person.

Now sign in using your administrative account. You turn on Parental Controls like this:

- Open the Start menu. Start typing *parental* until you see "Parental Controls" in the results list; press Enter to open it.

- Choose Start→Control Panel. In the "User Accounts and Family Safety" category, click "Set up parental controls for any user." Authenticate yourself if necessary (page 726).

The dialog box shown in Figure 10-15 appears, listing all the user *accounts* on the PC (Chapter 23).

Note: If you've downloaded the Windows Live Essentials suite (page 265), you're prompted, at this point, to enter your Windows Live email address and password. That's because Windows thinks now is a good time to turn on Family Safety, a feature that's part of those Essentials. Details begin on page 393; for now, just close the window and continue with the instructions here.

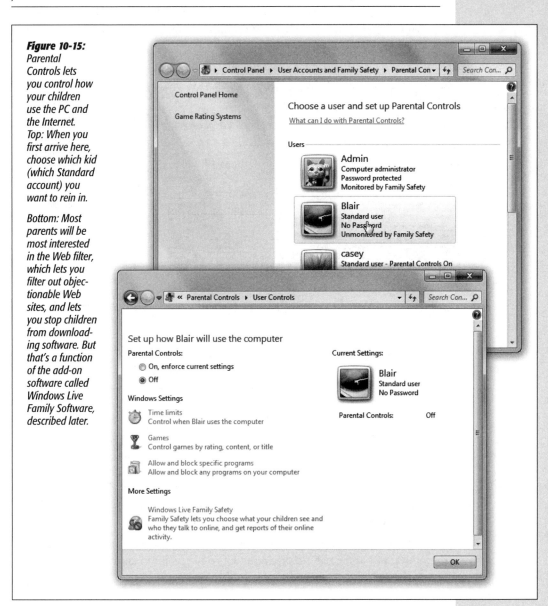

Figure 10-15:
Parental Controls lets you control how your children use the PC and the Internet.

Top: When you first arrive here, choose which kid (which Standard account) you want to rein in.

Bottom: Most parents will be most interested in the Web filter, which lets you filter out objectionable Web sites, and lets you stop children from downloading software. But that's a function of the add-on software called Windows Live Family Software, described later.

One of the key advantages of the accounts system is that you can set up separate "worlds" for each person in your family—and now comes the payoff. Click your kid's account to open up its parental controls screen.

Under the Parental Controls setting, click "On, enforce current settings"—the master switch (Figure 10-15, bottom). You can now set up these limits for your offspring's PC use:

- **Time Limits** lets you set the times and days of the week that your little tyke can use the Internet. You might, for example, decide to keep your kids off the PC on school nights. When you click "Time limits," a calendar opens where you can block times by selecting them (Figure 10-16).

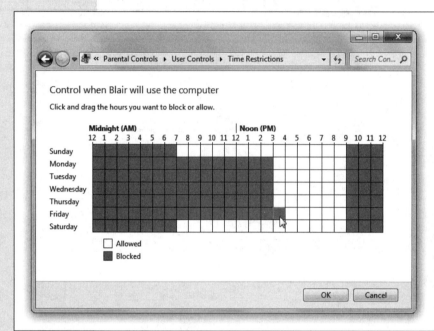

Figure 10-16:
If you set up time limits for your little rug rats, they won't be able to log in outside of the permitted hours. And if they're signed in when the time block ends, they get dumped off, and a taskbar message lets them know they're out of time. (Their programs and windows remain open in the background, in suspended animation until the next approved time slot.)

- **Games** prevents your youngsters from playing games altogether, or lets you specify which kinds of games they can play.

  For example, if you click "Set game ratings," you see that you can permit only games in a certain age bracket: Early Childhood, say, or Adults Only. If you scroll down, you see that you can even customize any level, by blocking specific upsetting depictions within the games—everything from "Animated Blood" to "Use of Drugs" and everything in between.

  (Caution: Not all game programs on your PC identify themselves as games. Some appear just as regular old programs. Of course, you can always block them using the "specific programs" options described next.)

Note: To make this feature work, Windows consults a tiny GDF (game definition file) that software companies can put into their game. Game companies usually use ratings bestowed by a ratings board like the Entertainment Software Ratings Board (ESRB).

If a publisher uses information from a different ratings board, or doesn't have a rating file (GDF) at all, Windows consults Microsoft's own 2,000-game database. And if even *that* source draws a blank, Windows considers the game unrated. You may have noticed that the Games screen in Parental Controls offers a "Block games with no rating" option, which is designed just for such situations.

- **Allow and block specific programs** lets you declare individual programs on your PC to be off-limits. On the configuration screen, turn on "Casey [or whoever] can only use the programs I allow." Windows presents you with a staggering list of every single program on your PC; turn on the checkboxes of the programs you consider appropriate for your kid. Click OK.

    If your lovable young ruffian does attempt to run an off-limits program, a box appears that says, "Parental Controls has blocked this program." If he clicks "Ask an administrator for permission," the UAC box appears (page 726) so he can call you or some other older, wiser account holder over to the PC. You can type in a name and administrator password to "unlock" the program—just for this time.

The final step is explaining the new limits to the young account holder. (Windows has no new features to help you with that one.)

Family Safety

Windows no longer comes with built-in software that protects your kids from objectionable Web sites. Instead, Microsoft invites you to supply your own. Microsoft makes a free Web filter called Family Safety (it's part of the free Windows Live Essentials, as described on page 265), or you can buy a similar program from another company.

Once it's installed, the Web filter's name appears in the "Select a provider" pop-up menu on the Parental Controls screen.

Note: The rest of this section describes using Family Safety, since it's free and easy to use.

Here's how to use Family Safety. Before you begin, make sure the name of your filtering software appears in the "Select a provider" pop-up menu (Family Safety, in this case).

1. **Open Parental Controls. Click the account holder's name to set up the filtering.**

    Quick way to get to Parental Controls: Open the Start menu. Start typing *parental* until you see "Parental Controls" in the results list; press Enter to open it.

    The first time you click someone's name after installing Family Safety, you're asked to sign in with your Windows Live ID and password (page 468). Proceed carefully.

You're designating yourself as the only parent who can change settings and get the activity reports.

Now you're shown a list of Standard account holders on your PC—presumably, your kids.

Tip: For this feature, each kid should really have a separate Windows account. That way, you'll be able to see what each child is doing online. And by the way: Turn off the Guest account (page 725), so your wily kid can't get around the controls just by using that.

2. **Turn on the checkboxes of the account holders you want to protect and track online. Click Next.**

Now you may see a screen that says, "Match each Windows account with a Family Safety member" (Figure 10-17).

Figure 10-17:
Forgive Microsoft for its red tape. Turns out Family Safety has accounts for each of your family members—but that's not the same as the accounts on your PC. Here's where you're supposed to match up the former with the latter. (If the pop-up menu doesn't already show the person's name, use the Add command at the bottom.)

3. **From the pop-up menu next to each account holder, choose the matching account holder's name. Click Save.**

Now you've successfully turned on Family Safety.

Note: The restrictions won't kick in until the next time each person logs in.

So far, you've managed to turn on basic Web filtering for each Standard account holder you specified in step 2. If those young whippersnappers try to call up a porn Web site (or stumble onto one), they'll see only a "This page is blocked" message. They can ask you for permission to unblock it, though; see Figure 10-18.

Figure 10-18:
Busted! Your naughty child has tried to look at dirty pictures. If he feels that Windows's site blocker is being too zealous, he can email you for permission to proceed. (The email you get will contain a link to the Family Safety Web site, where you can unblock the site from now on.) Or, if you're nearby, he can click "Ask in person"; that will let you enter your administrator's name and password to OK an override of the block, now and henceforth.

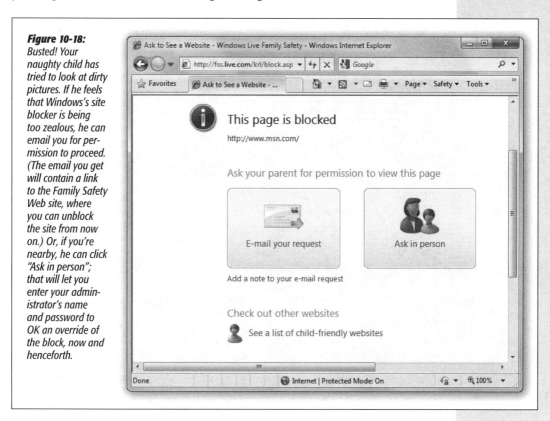

Customizing Family Safety

Out of the box, Family Safety does a reasonable job of keeping your kids from seeing raunchy Web sites. (It does nothing about sites that pertain to violence, hate, religion, and so on, however.)

On the Family Safety Web site (*familysafety.live.com*), you can have all kinds of fine-tuning fun. Specifically, you can do the following:

- **Adjust the filtering intensity.** To do that, click "Edit settings" under your kid's name (Figure 10-19). On the next screen, click "Web filtering."

  Now you see the on/off switch for Web filtering, as well as a choice of filtering styles. Strict blocks all Web sites except a list of 8,000 sites especially for children, as inspected by Microsoft's experts (and any sites you've added to that list. Basic blocks pornographic sites (and "anonymizer" sites that let you surf the Web without leaving tracks).

If you click Custom, you get a new panel (Figure 10-19, bottom) that lists other categories of stuff you might not want your kid involved with: social-networking sites like MySpace and Facebook; Webmail sites like Gmail and Hotmail; and sites Microsoft hasn't evaluated.

Alternatively, you can type in the addresses of *individual* Web sites that you want to declare off-limits (or on-limits), as shown at bottom in Figure 10-19.

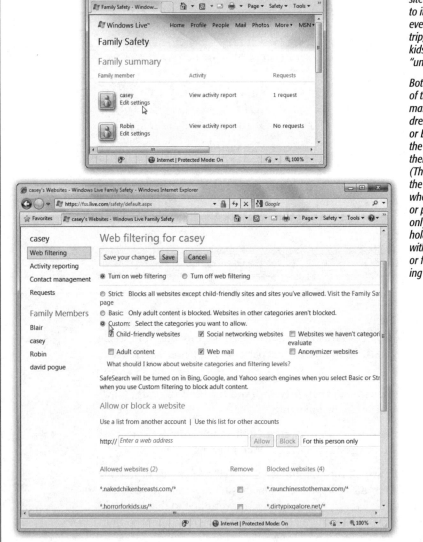

Figure 10-19:
Top: The advantage of the Family Safety Web site is that you can get to it wherever you are, even at work or on a trip, to monitor your kids' activity and see "unblock" requests.

Bottom: At the bottom of this screen, you can manually add Web addresses to the Allowed or Blocked lists. Type in the Web address, and then click Allow or Block. (The pop-up menu on the right lets you specify whether you're blocking or permitting this site only for this account holder, for all your kids with Standard accounts, or for everyone including yourself.)

Finally, don't miss the "Allow [kid's name] to download files online" checkbox. If you really want a safe PC, turn this one off. Your kid won't be able to download anything from the Web at all: no songs, games, videos—and no viruses, spyware, or worms.

Click Save to preserve your changes.

- **Activity reporting.** The Parental Report brings Big Brother home to you. It shows every Web site your kid has visited (or tried to visit), every program or game your kid has run, the files they've downloaded, and so on—on all your PCs. You also see how often your kid logged onto the PC, and the amount of time spent during each session.

- **Contact management.** Family Safety can even limit who your kid emails and chats with—if the kid doesn't use any email or chat services other than Microsoft's (Messenger, Hotmail, and Spaces). Which means it's pretty useless unless you've locked your kid into those services. (Your kid also needs a Windows Live ID, as described on page 468.)

  If you're interested, click "Contact management," click "Sign in," and then enter your kid's Windows Live name and password.

  Turn on the services you want to let your kid use: Messenger, Hotmail, Spaces.

  At the outset, your kid is allowed to communicate only with you. If you want to expand her social circle a bit, type in that person's name and email address, and then click Add.

Note: Ordinarily, you are the only one who can add people to the list of Approved Communications Partners. When your child wants to contact someone else, they'll see a link that lets them email you for permission, exactly as with the blocked Web sites. Once again, you'll get a message that offers a link to the Requests tab, described below, so you can approve or decline the permission request.

If you want your kid to be able to add people without your involvement, on the other hand, then turn on the grammatically excruciating checkbox called "Allow child to manage their own contact list."

  When it's all over, click Save.

- **Requests.** Here's where you can see the blocked Web sites your child wants you to override. ("But, Dad! I need to see *Playboy.com* for my social-studies report on Social Norms in the 20th Century!")

  Check out the requested site by clicking the link in the "Web address" column. If it seems harmless enough, use the pop-up menu in the Response column to choose "Approve for this account only" (just this kid) or "Approve for all accounts" (all kids). If not, then click Deny.

  There's a separate tab here for Contact requests—people your kid wants to email or chat with who aren't on the approved list. You can approve or deny these people, too.

Internet Explorer 8

Internet Explorer is the most famous Web browser on earth, thanks in part to several years of Justice Department scrutiny and newspaper headlines. It also has more syllables than any other Web browser, which is probably why most people just call it IE.

The revamped version 8 offers plenty of new features. A bunch of them are dedicated, as always, to privacy and security—features like SmartScreen filter (blocks phishing and virus/spyware sites), InPrivate Browsing (blocks certain ads and other Web graphics that can track your Web movements), and InPrivate Filtering (lets you surf without leaving any tracks like cookies or History-list items). There are so many security features in IE, in fact, that they'd weigh this chapter down with all their negative energy. They've been offloaded to Chapter 10.

There are lots of great new productivity features, too, though: a better Search box; accelerators for instant mapping, translation, or searching; a command that lets you reopen a tab you've closed by accident; and so on.

All these goodies and more are described in this chapter.

Note: Internet Explorer 8 is better than previous Internet Explorer versions—it's more secure, it has more modern features, and it's much more compatible with today's Web standards.

Nonetheless, you should be aware that there are other free browsers out there, like Firefox (*www.getfirefox. com*), Safari (*apple.com/safari*), and Chrome (*google.com/chrome*), which are all much faster than IE. The Web intelligentsia greatly prefer these non-Microsoft alternatives.

IE8: The Grand Tour
All Versions

You can open Internet Explorer in a number of ways:

- Choose its name from the Start→All Programs menu.

- Open the Start menu; start typing *Internet* until "Internet Explorer" is highlighted in the results list; press Enter.

- Click its icon on the taskbar.

- Type a Web address—a *URL* (Uniform Resource Locator)—into a window's address bar. A Web page URL usually begins with the prefix *http://*, but you can leave that part off when typing into the address bar.

- Click a blue, underlined link on a Windows Help screen, in an email message, and so on.

As you can see in Figure 11-1, the Internet Explorer window is filled with tools designed to facilitate a smooth trip around the World Wide Web.

Figure 11-1:
The Internet Explorer window offers tools and features that let you navigate the Web almost effortlessly; these various toolbars and status indicators are described in this chapter. Chief among them: the address bar, which displays the address (URL) of the Web page you're currently seeing, and the standard buttons, which let you control the Web-page loading process.

The first time you open Internet Explorer, you're asked to make a couple of quick decisions:

- **Turn on Suggested Sites.** You can read about the new Suggested Sites feature later in this chapter; for now, it's enough to know that this feature suggests Web sites you might like based on Web sites you've already visited. This sort of artificial-intelligence suggestions feature seems to work on Amazon and iTunes, but if you think Microsoft is tracking you in far too many ways already, you can turn Suggested Sites off here. Either way, click Next.

- **Choose your settings.** There are lots of choices to make in Internet Explorer. Whose search (Google's or Microsoft Bing's) do you want to power the Search box? Do you want to turn on the new SmartScreen filter? Is it OK for IE to download updates to itself automatically? Here's where you can accept Microsoft's factory settings for all of this, or click "Choose custom settings" to change them one by one. (Of course, you can change any of these settings at any time later.)

Click Finish to exit the interview—and start using the darned program.

The Raw Basics

A link (or hyperlink) is a bit of text, or a little graphic, that's been programmed to serve as a button. When you click a link, you're transported from one Web page to another. One may be the home page of General Motors; another might have baby pictures posted by a parent in Omaha. About a billion pages await your visit.

Tip: Text links aren't always blue and underlined. In fact, modern Web designers sometimes make it very difficult to tell which text is clickable and which is just text. When in doubt, move your cursor over some text. If the arrow changes to a pointing-finger cursor, you've found yourself a link.

Actually, you can choose to hide *all* underlines, a trick that makes Web pages look cleaner and more attractive. Underlines appear only when you point to a link (and wait a moment). If that arrangement appeals to you, open Internet Explorer. Choose Tools→Internet Options, click the Advanced tab, scroll down to "Underline links," select the Hover option, and then click OK.

Menus and Gizmos

Internet Explorer doesn't have a traditional menu bar (although you can make the old one come back if you press Alt or F10). Instead, it offers five tiny menu *icons* at the upper-right corner. Each little ▾ is, in fact, a menu.

Here's a look at the other basic controls—the doodads that surround your browser window.

The Address Bar

When you type a new Web page address (URL) into this strip and press Enter, the corresponding Web site appears. (If only an error message results, then you may have mistyped the address, or the Web page may have been moved or dismantled—a relatively frequent occurrence.)

Because typing out Internet addresses is so central to the Internet experience and such a typo-prone hassle, the address bar is rich with features that minimize keystrokes. For example:

- You don't have to click in the address bar before typing; just press Alt+D.

- You don't have to type out the whole Internet address. You can omit the *http://www* and *.com* portions if you press Ctrl+Enter after typing the name; Internet Explorer fills in those standard address bits for you.

  To visit Amazon.com, for example, you can press Alt+D to highlight the address bar, type *amazon,* and then press Ctrl+Enter.

- Even without the Ctrl+Enter trick, you can still omit the *http://* from any Web address. (Most of the time, you can omit the *www.,* too.) To jump to today's Dilbert cartoon, type *dilbert.com* and then press Enter.

- When you begin to type into the address bar, the AutoComplete feature compares what you're typing against a list of Web sites you've recently visited. IE displays a drop-down list of Web addresses that seem to match what you're typing. To save typing, just click the correct complete address with your mouse, or use the ↓ key to reach the desired listing and then press Enter. The complete address you selected then pops into the address bar.

  (To make AutoComplete *forget* the Web sites you've visited recently—so that nobody will see what you've been up to—delete your History list, as described on page 379.)

- Press F4 (or click the ▾ inside the right end of the address bar) to view a list of URLs you've visited recently—your History list, in other words—as well as sites you've

---

GEM IN THE ROUGH

Let AutoFill Do the Typing

Internet Explorer can remember the user names and passwords you type into those "Please sign in" Web sites.

You can't miss this feature; each time you type a password into a Web page, this dialog box appears.

It's a great time- and brain-saver, even though it doesn't work on all Web sites. (Of course, use it with caution if you share an account on your PC with other people.)

When you want IE to "forget" your passwords–for security reasons, for example–choose Tools→Internet Options. In the AutoComplete section,click Settings, and then click "Delete AutoComplete history."

You get the box shown on page 380, where you can delete all kinds of stuff Internet Explorer memorizes: cookies, forms (your name, address, and so on), your History list, user names and passwords, and so on. Turn on the checkboxes you want (or, rather, don't want), and then click Delete.

---

bookmarked (which Microsoft calls Favorites). Once again, you can click the one you want—or press the ↓ or ↑ keys to highlight one, and the Enter key to select it.

Tip: When you first press F4 (or click the ▼ button), you see only the most recent five items in your History or Favorites list. Click the down-arrow button to see a more complete list.

Topside Doodads

Around the address bar, you'll find several important buttons. Some of them lack text labels, but all offer tooltip labels:

- **Back button, Forward button.** Click the Back button to revisit the page you were just on. (*Keyboard shortcut:* Backspace and Shift+Backspace, or Alt+← and Alt+→.)

Tip: Pressing Shift as you turn your mouse's scroll wheel up or down also navigates forward and back. Cool.

Once you've clicked Back, you can then click the Forward button (or press Alt+→) to return to the page you were on *before* you clicked the Back button. Click the white ▼ button for a list of all the Web pages you've visited during this online session (that is, within this browser window, as opposed to your long-term History list).

- **Refresh button.** Click this double-arrow button (↔) just to the right of the address bar if a page doesn't look or work quite right, or if you want to see the updated version of a Web page that changes constantly (such as a stock ticker). This button forces Internet Explorer to redownload the Web page and reinterpret its text and graphics.

- **Stop (✕) button.** Click this button, at the far right end of the address bar, to interrupt the downloading of a Web page you've just requested (by mistake, for example). (*Keyboard shortcut:* Esc.)

- **Search bar.** There's no tidy card catalog of every Web page. Because Web pages appear and disappear hourly by the hundreds of thousands, such an exercise would be futile.

The best you can do is to use a search engine, a Web site that searches *other* Web sites. You might have heard of the little engine called Google, for example, or Microsoft's rival service called Bing.

But why waste your time plugging in *www.google.com?* Here's one of Internet Explorer's most profoundly useful features—a Search box that accesses Google automatically—or any other search page you like. Type something you're looking for into this box—*electric drapes*, say—and then press Enter. You go straight to the Google results page.

In IE8, it's much easier to switch from Google to Bing, or Bing to Google: As you type in your search term, tiny icons for both appear just below the box. Click the icon for the search engine you want to use for this search.

Or make Internet Explorer use a different engine for all searches by choosing its name from the ▾ button next to the magnifying glass icon; Google and Bing appear here already.

If you prefer some oddball off-brand search service, you can add its icon and name to the Search box so it appears right alongside Bing and Google. See Figure 11-2 for the steps.

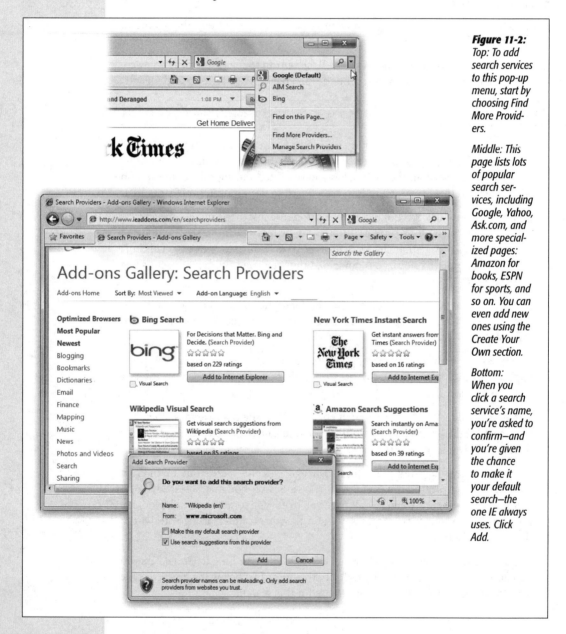

Figure 11-2:
Top: To add search services to this pop-up menu, start by choosing Find More Providers.

Middle: This page lists lots of popular search services, including Google, Yahoo, Ask.com, and more specialized pages: Amazon for books, ESPN for sports, and so on. You can even add new ones using the Create Your Own section.

Bottom: When you click a search service's name, you're asked to confirm—and you're given the chance to make it your default search—the one IE always uses. Click Add.

Tip: Truth is, it's often faster to type your search phrase into the *address bar itself,* if for no other reason than you have a keyboard shortcut to get your cursor in there (Alt+D). When you press Enter, IE does a Web search for that term, using the same search service you've set up for the Search box.

Window Controls

These last items wrap up your grand tour of Internet Explorer's window gizmos:

- **Scroll bars.** Use the scroll bar, or the scroll wheel on your mouse, to move up and down the page—or to save mousing, press the space bar each time you want to see more. Press Shift+space bar to scroll *up.* (The space bar has its traditional, space-making function only when the insertion point is blinking in a text box or the address bar.)

  You can also press your ↑ and ↓ keys to scroll. Page Up and Page Down scroll in full-screen increments, while Home and End whisk you to the top or bottom of the current Web page.

- **⌂ button.** Click to bring up the Web page you've designated as your home page— your starter page.

  And which page is that? Whichever one you designate. Open a good startup page (Google, NYTimes.com, Dilbert.com, whatever), and then choose Add or Change Home Page from this icon's pop-up menu.

- **Status bar.** The status bar at the bottom of the window tells you what Internet Explorer is doing (such as "Opening page…" or "Done"). When you point to a link without clicking, the status bar also tells you which URL will open if you click it.

  And when you're opening a new page, a graph appears here, showing that your PC is still downloading (receiving) the information and graphics on the Web page. In other words, you're not seeing everything yet.

  If you consult all this information only rarely, you can hide this bar to conserve screen space. To do so, choose View→Toolbars→Status Bar from the classic menu bar (press Alt).

Tabbed Browsing
All Versions

Beloved by hard-core surfers the world over, *tabbed browsing* is a way to keep a bunch of Web pages open simultaneously—in a single, neat window, without cluttering up your taskbar with a million buttons.

Figure 11-3 illustrates.

Tip: Here's a New!! feature in IE8: When you open new tabs by clicking links on a Web page, the tabs are color-coded to match the color of the originating page, so you can tell where they came from. The newly sprouted tab appears right next to its source tab, too, instead of appearing at the end of the row of tabs.

Shortcut-O-Rama

Turning on tabbed browsing unlocks a whole raft of Internet Explorer shortcuts and tricks, which are just the sort of thing power surfers gulp down like Gatorade:

- **To open a new, empty tab** in front of all others, press Ctrl+T (for tab), or click the New Tab stub identified in Figure 11-3, or double-click anywhere in the empty area of the tab row. From the empty tab that appears, you can navigate to any site you want.

- **To open a link into a new tab,** Ctrl+click it. Or click it with your mouse wheel.

  Or, if you're especially slow, right-click it and, from the shortcut menu, choose Open in New Tab.

Note: Ctrl+clicking a link opens that page in a tab *behind* the one you're reading. That's a fantastic trick when you're reading a Web page and see a reference you want to set aside for reading next, but you don't want to interrupt whatever you're reading now.

But if you want the new tab to appear in *front,* add the Shift key.

- **To close a tab,** click the ⊠ on it, press Ctrl+W, or click the tab with your mouse wheel or middle mouse button, if you have one. (If you press Alt+F4, you close all tabs. If you press Ctrl+Alt+F4, you close all tabs *except* the one that's in front.)

Tip: New in IE8: If you close a tab, or a group of tabs, by accident, you can now call them back from the dead. Click the New Tab button (see Figure 11-3). The resulting New Tab page displays the addresses of tabs you've recently closed; click the one you want.

If you've exited Internet Explorer in the meantime, you lose your chance to recover those closed tabs. But speaking of which: If that happens, you can always choose Tools→Reopen Last Browsing Session, another new command that brings back all the pages you had open when you quit the program.

- **Switch from one tab to the next** by pressing Ctrl+Tab. Add the Shift key to move backward through them.

- **Jump to a specific tab** by pressing its number along with the Ctrl key. For example, Ctrl+3 brings the third tab forward.

- **Save a tab configuration.** If there's a certain set of Web sites you like to visit daily, open them all into tabs. Click the Favorites button, and then, from the Add to Favorites pop-up menu, choose Add Current Tabs to Favorites. Type a name for the group, and then click Add.

  Later, you can recreate your current setup—with all of them in a tabbed window— by selecting the resulting listing in the Favorites menu and then clicking the blue ➔ button beside its name. The beauty of this arrangement is that you can start reading the first Web page while all the others load into their own tabs in the background.

One more note to tab fans: When you close Internet Explorer, a dialog box appears asking if you really want to close *all* the tabs. If you click Show Options at this point, you're offered an opportunity to "Open these the next time I use Internet Explorer." Turn that on and click Close Tabs; the next time you go a-browsing, you'll pick up right from the tabs where you left off.

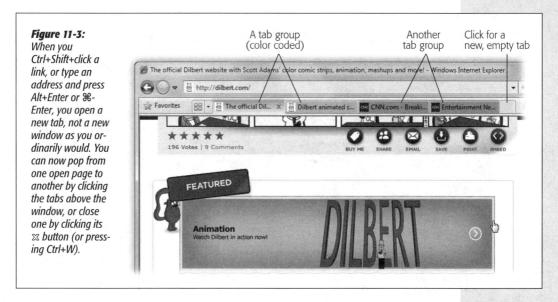

Figure 11-3:
When you Ctrl+Shift+click a link, or type an address and press Alt+Enter or ⌘-Enter, you open a new tab, not a new window as you ordinarily would. You can now pop from one open page to another by clicking the tabs above the window, or close one by clicking its ⊠ *button (or pressing Ctrl+W).*

A tab group (color coded)   Another tab group   Click for a new, empty tab

Quick Tabs (Thumbnails)

Once you've got a bunch of tabs open, you may face a horizontal screen-space crunch. How much, exactly, of the text "Welcome to Bass World—The Internet's Global Resource for Bass Fisherfolk" can you see on a half-inch tab?

Not much. But how, then, are you supposed to tell your tabs apart?

By using another feature called Quick Tabs. Figure 11-4 shows all.

Tip: You can *close* a tab directly from the Quick Tabs screen, too—just click the ⊠ button in the upper-right corner of the thumbnail.

Tab Settings

People get *really* obsessive over tabs for some reason. They want tabs to behave *just* the way they expect, or it's back to Firefox they go.

No worries—IE lets you customize tabs' behavior to within an inch of their lives. Start by choosing Tools→Internet Options→General; in the Tabs section of the dialog box, click Settings. Here's the most useful of what you'll find:

• **Enable Tabbed Browsing.** This is the on/off switch for the whole tab feature.

- **Warn me when closing multiple tabs.** If tabs are open when you close Internet Explorer, a confirmation box appears: "Do you want to close all tabs?" It's semi-annoying but semi-useful, because you may not realize that you're about to close all your tabs.

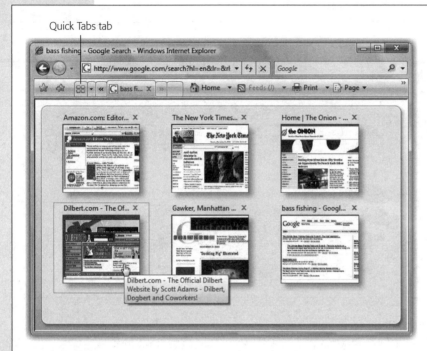

Quick Tabs tab

Figure 11-4:
Quick Tabs shows you thumbnails of all the Web pages you've opened into tabs, making it simple to tell them apart. One click on a thumbnail returns it to full size, with that tab in front of the others. All you have to learn is the Quick Tabs keystroke, which is Ctrl+Q—or the location of the Quick Tabs button, shown here. (Repeat the trigger to exit the Quick Tabs view without changing anything.)

- **Always switch to new tabs when they are created.** Makes every new tab appear in front of the others, even if you Ctrl+click a link rather than Ctrl+Shift+click it. (Even if you leave this option off, though, Ctrl+Shift+clicking a link still opens the tab in front.)

- **Show previews for individual tabs in the taskbar.** Ordinarily, pointing to the Internet Explorer icon on the taskbar produces the handy pop-up thumbnails for each tab you have open. Turn this option off if you want only a thumbnail for each window.

- **Enable Quick Tabs.** This is the on/off switch for the feature shown in Figure 11-4.

- **Enable Tab Groups.** When you're on one tab, and you open a new tab from it (for example, by right-clicking a link and choosing Open Link in New tab), IE color-codes the two tabs, so you can tell that they sprouted from the same source. It also puts them together on the row of tabs. This feature, new in Internet Explorer 8, is called tab grouping, and you can turn it off here.

- **Open only the first home page when Internet Explorer starts.** Got a tab group set as your home page (page 406)? Turn on this box if you want only the first tab to open when IE starts, rather than the whole tab group.

- **When a new tab is opened, open:.** When you click the New Tab tab (Figure 11-3), a special, mostly blank New Tab page opens, graced by links like "Reopen closed tabs" and "Browse with InPrivate." This pop-up menu lets you choose to have your home page appear instead, or even a completely blank page.

- **When a pop-up is encountered.** When a "good" pop-up window opens, should it open in a new window or a new tab? Or should Internet Explorer try to figure out which would be most helpful? (If the Web programmer has specified a specific size for the pop-up, it appears in a window; otherwise, in a new tab.)

- **Open links from other programs in:.** If you click a link in an email message, should the resulting Web page open in a new window or a new tab? Or should it replace whatever's currently in the frontmost window or tab? Only you can decide.

Actually, there's one more useful tabbed-browsing setting that's *not* here—for some reason, Microsoft stuck it on the Tools→Internet Options→Advanced tab. It's "Use most recent order when switching tabs with Ctrl+Tab."

Ordinarily, pressing Ctrl+Tab moves you through your tabs from left to right; adding Shift moves you backward.

But if you turn this option on, then Ctrl+Tab jumps through the tabs you've visited in *reverse chronological order.* It's just the way Alt+Tab works when you're switching between Windows programs. This arrangement makes it very easy to compare two Web pages, because pressing Ctrl+Tab bounces you back and forth between them.

Note: This option also affects what happens when you hit Ctrl+W repeatedly to *close* tabs. They close in reverse chronological order.

Favorites (Bookmarks)
All Versions

When you find a Web page you might like to visit again, press Ctrl+D. That's the keyboard shortcut for the Add to Favorites command. (The long way is to click the ★ Favorites button to make the Favorites pane appear, and then click the Add to Favorites button, identified in Figure 11-5—but who's got the time?) Type a shorter or more memorable name, if you like, and click Add.

Tip: Actually, there's a new Windows 7 trick that may save you even more time. You can drag a Web site's icon (the tiny one just to the left of its address in the address bar) directly onto Internet Explorer's taskbar icon. (This works with any browser, actually—Firefox or whatever.) When you release the mouse, that site's name appears at the top of the icon's jump list, in the pinned area. Next time you want to visit that site, just click the Internet Explorer icon (even if it's not running) and click the site's name in the jump list.

The page's name appears instantly in the Favorites Center, which is the panel indicated by the yellow star (Figure 11-5). The next time you want to visit that page, open this menu—or press Alt+C—and click the Web site's name in the list. (Your Favorites also appear in a tidy list that appears when you click the ▾ at the right end of the address bar.)

Tip: You can send your list of Favorites to or from other browsers or other PCs, which can save you a lot of time.

To do that, open the Add to Favorites menu (Figure 11-5); choose Import and Export. The Import/Export wizard appears to guide you through the process. Consider saving them onto, for example, a flash drive, for ease in transporting to another location or computer.

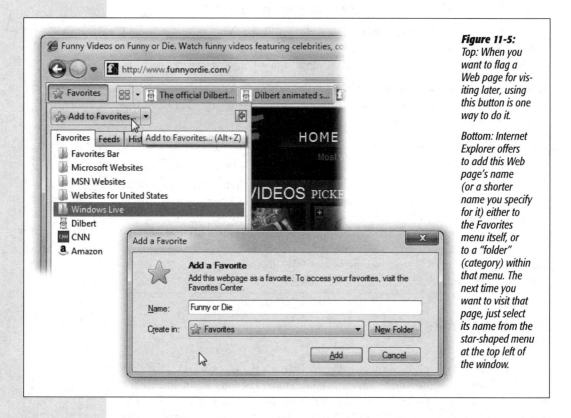

Figure 11-5:
Top: When you want to flag a Web page for visiting later, using this button is one way to do it.

Bottom: Internet Explorer offers to add this Web page's name (or a shorter name you specify for it) either to the Favorites menu itself, or to a "folder" (category) within that menu. The next time you want to visit that page, just select its name from the star-shaped menu at the top left of the window.

You can rearrange the commands in your Favorites menu easily enough. Open the Favorites Center (Figure 11-6), and then drag the bookmarks up and down in the list.

Or, for more elaborate organizing tasks—creating and deleting folders, renaming sites, and so on—click the Add to Favorites button (Figure 11-5) and, from the shortcut menu, choose Organize Favorites. You get a little dialog box that makes all those tasks easy.

The Favorites Toolbar

The Favorites pane is one way to maintain a list of Web sites you visit frequently. But opening a Web page in that pane requires *two mouse clicks*—an exorbitant expenditure of energy. The Favorites toolbar, on the other hand, lets you summon a few, very select, *very* favorite Web pages with only *one* click.

You make the toolbar appear by choosing Tools→Toolbars→Favorites Bar. Figure 11-7 illustrates how to add buttons to, and remove them from, this toolbar. Once they're there, you can rearrange these buttons simply by dragging them horizontally. (Whatever you stash here also turns up on the Links toolbar at the desktop, weirdly enough.)

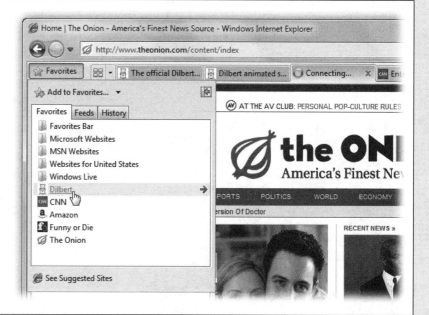

Figure 11-6:
When the Favorites menu opens, you can drag names up or down to rearrange the list, as shown. Or right-click one to access the commands that rename, delete, or file a favorite into a folder. (Unfortunately, the Favorites menu covers up part of the Web page you're reading. It hides itself soon enough, but you might also want to freeze the Favorites Center open so that it doesn't cover the page. To do that, click the Pin the Favorites Center button shown here.)

Figure 11-7:
Drag the tiny page icon to the Links bar. Right-click a link to choose Rename (to pick a shorter name that fits better).

Tip: As shown in Figure 11-7, you can drag a link from a Web page onto your Favorites toolbar. But you can also drag it directly to the desktop, where it turns into a special Internet shortcut icon. To launch your browser and visit the associated Web page, just double-click this icon whenever you like.

Better yet, stash a few of these icons in your Start menu for even easier access. (Moreover, if you open your Computer→(C:) drive→Users→[Your Name]→Favorites folder, you see these shortcut icons for *all* your favorite links. Feel free to drag them to the desktop, Links toolbar, or wherever you like.)

History List

All Versions

This *history* is a list of the Web sites you've visited. It's the heart of three IE features: AutoComplete, described at the beginning of this chapter; the drop-down list at the right side of the address bar; and the History list itself.

That's the pane that appears when you click the Favorites (★) button and then click History—or just press Ctrl+H. Figure 11-8 presents the world's shortest History class.

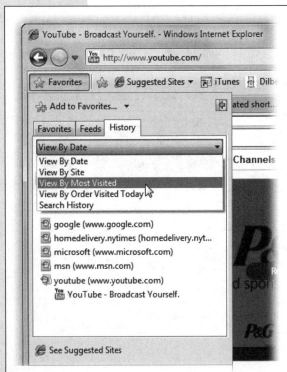

Figure 11-8:
The pop-up menu here lets you sort the list by Web site, date, frequency of visits—or you can see only the sites you've visited today, in order. The same little pop-up menu offers a command called Search History, so that you can search for text in the History list—not the actual text on those pages, but text within the page addresses and descriptions.

The History pane lists the Web sites you've visited in the past week or so, neatly organized into subfolders like "Today" and "Last Week." These are great features if you can't recall the URL for a Web site you remember having visited recently.

Click one of the time-period icons to see the Web sites you visited during that era. Click the name of a Web site to view a list of each visited page *within* that site—and click an actual URL to reopen that Web page in the main window.

You can configure the number of days for which you want your Web visits tracked. To do so, choose Tools→Internet Options→General; where it says "Browsing history," click Settings. At the bottom of the dialog box, you see the "Days to keep pages in history" control.

For details on *erasing* your History list for security purposes, see page 379.

Tip: The more days IE tracks, the easier it is for you to refer to those addresses quickly. On the other hand, the more days it tracks, the longer the list becomes, which may make it harder to use the list efficiently.

Oh, and if you set "Days to keep pages in history" to 0, Internet Explorer won't track your movements at all. (You know who you are.)

WORKAROUND WORKSHOP

Compatibility View

For years, Internet Explorer didn't respect the programming conventions of the Web. Web-page designers would carefully follow the rules to create, say, a picture with a 3-point blue box around it—but in Internet Explorer, it would look wrong. Microsoft just said: "We're the 800-pound gorilla. We do things our own way."

So Web designers had to use all sorts of programming hacks and kludges, writing the HTML code for their sites so that they'd look right in Internet Explorer. (Many went to the effort of designing a different site just for the "all other browsers" category. Which version you'd see when you visited that page depended on what browser you had.)

But with millions of people choosing other free Web browsers, Microsoft realized that it couldn't remain cocky forever. So in Internet Explorer 8, it cleaned up its act; this version, for the first time, strictly sticks to modern Web standards.

The irony, of course, is that now all those millions of pages written for the old IE now look funny in the new IE!

Now Microsoft gets to know what it feels like to be one of the other browsers, the ones that have always worked properly.

In any case, if you find a Web page that looks odd, or the text spills out of its box, or the buttons don't line up, or whatever, you can use Compatibility View. You can turn it on in either of two ways:

- Click the Compatibility View button (🖹). It appears on the address bar automatically whenever you're on a page that hasn't been updated for IE8.

- Choose Tools→Compatibility View.

In this mode, IE8 impersonates IE6, believe it or not, displaying the page the way the creator intended. IE will remember to use this view for this Web site until (a) you turn Compatibility View off, or (b) the site is rewritten for IE8.

RSS: The Missing Manual

All Versions

In the beginning, the Internet was an informational Garden of Eden. There were no banner ads, pop-ups, flashy animations, or spam messages. People thought the Internet was just the greatest.

Those days, unfortunately, are long gone. Web browsing now entails a constant battle against intrusive advertising and annoying animations. And with the proliferation of Web sites and blogs, just reading your favorite sites can become a full-time job.

Enter RSS, a technology that lets you subscribe to *feeds*—summary blurbs provided by thousands of sources around the world, from Reuters to Microsoft to your nerdy next-door neighbor. News and blog sites usually publish RSS feeds, but RSS can also bring you podcasts (recorded audio broadcasts), photos, and even videos.

You used to need a special RSS *reader* program to tune into them—but no longer. Internet Explorer can "subscribe" to updates from such feeds so you can read any new articles or postings at your leisure.

The result? You spare yourself the tedium of checking for updates manually, plus you get to read short summaries of new articles without ads and blinking animations. And if you want to read a full article, you can click its link in the RSS feed to jump straight to the main Web site.

Note: RSS stands for either Rich Site Summary or Really Simple Syndication. Each abbreviation explains one aspect of RSS—either its summarizing talent or its simplicity. (Web feeds and XML feeds are the same thing.)

Viewing an RSS Feed

So how do you sign up for these free, automatic RSS "broadcasts"? Watch your tab bar as you're surfing the Web. When the Feeds button (🔊) turns orange, IE is telling you, "This site has an RSS feed available."

(Sometimes, in fact, the site has *multiple* feeds available—for example, in different formats—in which case you can choose among them using the ▾ menu next to the 🔊 icon.)

Tip: To find more RSS feeds, visit a site like *www.syndic8.com*.

By the way, Internet Explorer isn't the only RSS reader. If you catch the RSS bug, you might want to try out a more powerful RSS reader. Visit *www.downloads.com,* for example, and search for *RSS readers,* or try a Web-based one like *www.reader.google.com*.

To see what the fuss is all about, click that button. Internet Explorer switches into RSS-viewing mode, as shown in Figure 11-9.

At this point, you have three choices:

• **Subscribe.** Click "Subscribe to this feed." Name and save the feed into a folder, if you like. From now on, you'll be able to see whether the RSS feed has had any new articles posted—without actually having to visit the site. Figure 11-9 has the details.

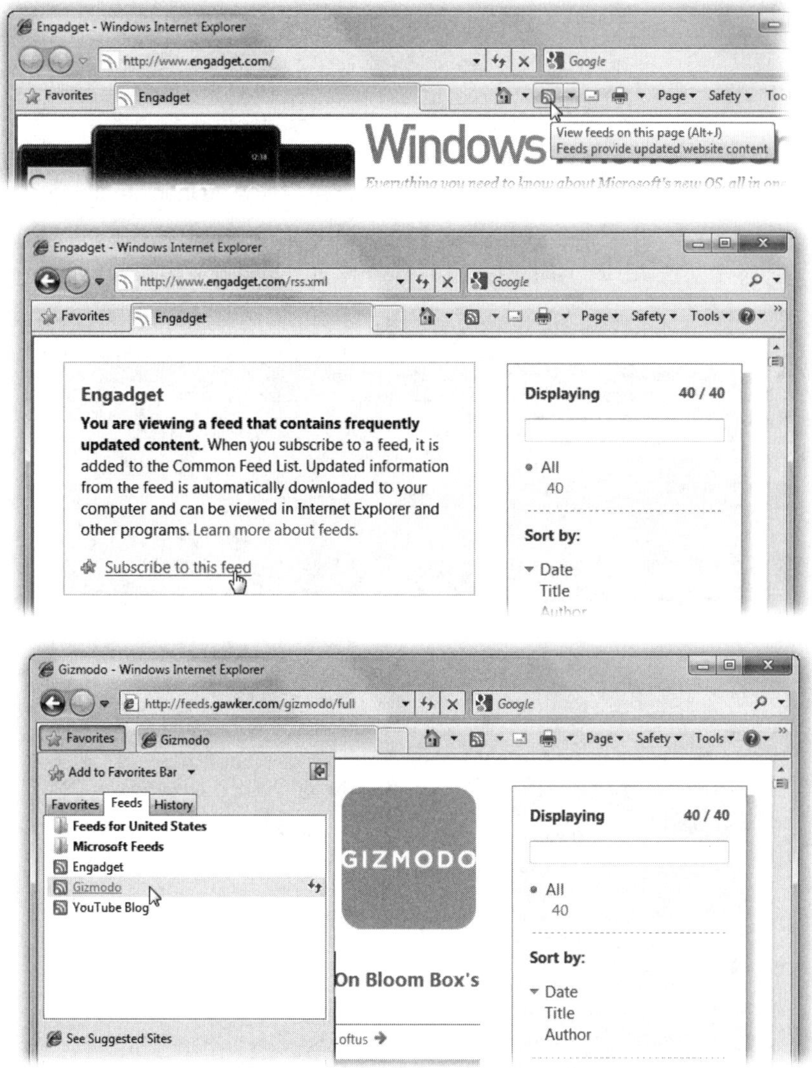

Figure 11-9:
Top: When the Feeds button changes color, you've got yourself a live one: a Web site that publishes a feed. Click the Feeds button.

Middle: Now you get a sneak peek at what the feed looks like. If you like, subscribe, as shown here.

Bottom: To read your feed, click the Favorites button (★) and, at the top of the pane, click Feeds. Click the one you want to read.

Note: Once you've subscribed to a feed, Internet Explorer checks the originating Web site once a day for updates.

You can make it check a bit more obsessively, if you like (as often as every 15 minutes), or cool its jets (once a week). To adjust the schedule, choose Tools→Internet Options→Content; click Settings at the bottom of the dialog box. Use the "Every:" pop-up menu to specify the frequency.

While you're here, turn on "Play a sound" if you want a little sonic heads-up, too, when IE finds that a Web page you've just opened has an available RSS feed.

- **Massage the feed.** Once you're looking at the feed, you can sort the headline items by date, title, and author, or use the Search box to find text among all the articles.

- **Close the RSS feed altogether.** To do so, just click the Feeds button again. You're left back where you started, at whatever Web page you were visiting.

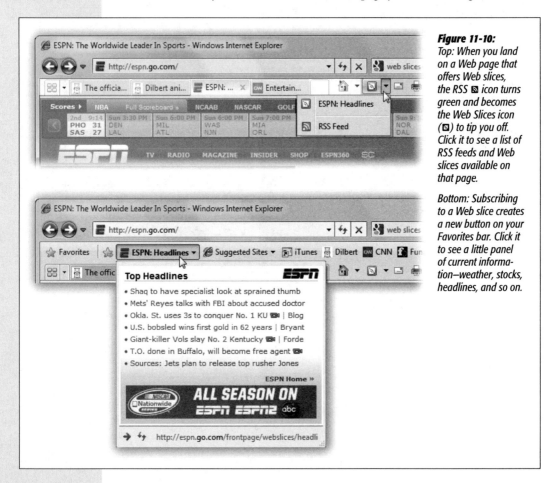

Figure 11-10:
Top: When you land on a Web page that offers Web slices, the RSS ☒ icon turns green and becomes the Web Slices icon (☒) to tip you off. Click it to see a list of RSS feeds and Web slices available on that page.

Bottom: Subscribing to a Web slice creates a new button on your Favorites bar. Click it to see a little panel of current information—weather, stocks, headlines, and so on.

Tip: Once you've subscribed to some feeds, you don't actually have to fire up Internet Explorer just to see what's new in your world. Remember the Gadgets described in Chapter 6?

One of them, you may recall, is called Feed Headlines. Yes, right there on your desktop, you see headlines from your subscribed Web sites, updating themselves as the news breaks. Click a headline to open a minipreview window; double-click to open Internet Explorer and view the actual Web page.

Web Slices

A Web slice, a new feature in Internet Explorer 8, has a lot in common with an RSS feed: It's information from other Web sites, automatically updated and placed in front of you for easy reviewing.

But a Web slice is a pop-up panel that sprouts from a button on your Favorites toolbar. That is, you don't lose your place on the Web; you stay on whatever page you were on and just pop up a Web slice panel for a quick look at the weather, the latest headlines, current stock prices, your Hotmail inbox, or whatever (Figure 11-10).

You'll know when a Web site offers a Web slice because the Slices icon (◨) appears and lights up green. Click it, or press Alt+J, to see a list of the RSS feeds and Web slices that are available on that page. Click the one you want to subscribe to.

From now on, you can click that button on the toolbar to see the latest information. If the slice's name appears in bold, that means it's been updated since the last time you looked.

Not every Web page offers a Web slice—in fact, hardly any do. A Web page's programmer would have to create a Web slice. And since they're a brand-new concept, and Internet Explorer 8 is the only Web browser that can exploit them, Web slices are very slow to catch on.

Tip: To remove a Web slice, right-click its button on the Favorites toolbar; from the shortcut menu, choose Delete.

Tips for Better Surfing
All Versions

Internet Explorer is filled with shortcuts and tricks for better speed and more pleasant surfing. For example:

Full-Screen Browsing

The Web is supposed to be a *visual* experience; losing a bunch of your monitor's real estate to toolbars and other window dressing isn't necessarily a good thing.

But if you press F11 (or choose View→Full Screen from the Classic menus), all is forgiven. The browser window explodes to the very borders of your monitor, hiding the Explorer bar, toolbars, and all. The Web page you're viewing fills your screen, edge to edge—a glorious, liberating experience.

You can return to the usual crowded, toolbar-mad arrangement by pressing F11 again—but you'll be tempted never to do so.

Picking a Home Page

The first Web site you encounter when IE connects to the Internet is a Microsoft Web site—or one of Dell's, or EarthLink's; the point is, *you* didn't choose it. This site is your factory-set *home page.*

Unless you actually work for Microsoft, Dell, or EarthLink, you'll probably find Web browsing more fun if you specify your *own* favorite Web page as your startup page.

The easiest way to go about it is to follow the instructions shown in Figure 11-11.

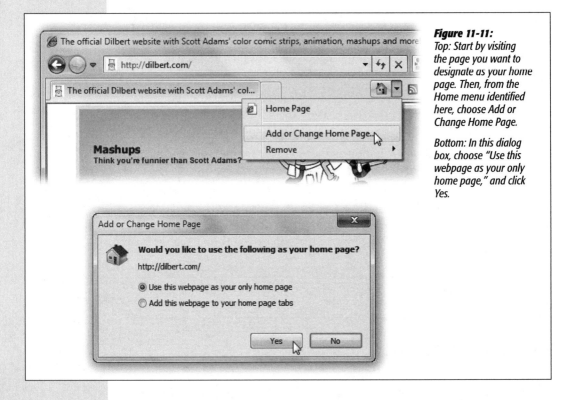

Figure 11-11:
Top: Start by visiting the page you want to designate as your home page. Then, from the Home menu identified here, choose Add or Change Home Page.

Bottom: In this dialog box, choose "Use this webpage as your only home page," and click Yes.

Google makes a nice home page; so does a news site. But here are a couple of possibilities that might not have occurred to you:

• **A blank page.** If you can't decide on a home page, or if your mood changes from day to day, set up a blank—empty—home page. This setup makes IE load very quickly when you first launch it. Once this window opens, *then* you can tell the browser where you want to go today.

To set this up, open the Home menu (Figure 11-11) and choose Remove→Remove All; in the confirmation box, click Yes.

- **Multiple home page tabs.** This is a cool one. You can designate a bunch of tabs to open all at once each time you fire up Internet Explorer. It's a great way to avoid wasting time by calling up one site after another, because they'll all be loading in the background as you read the first one.

Note: Choose "Tab settings" on page 407; a few settings there pertain exclusively to home page tab groups.

The quickest way to set up a Home tab set: Open all the Web sites into their own tabs, just the way you'll want IE to do automatically in the future. Then, from the Home menu, choose Add or Change Home Page. Next, in the dialog box (Figure 11-11, bottom), select "Use the current tab set as your home page," and click Yes.

Thereafter, you can always add additional tabs to this starter set by choosing "Add this webpage to your home page tabs," the bottom option shown in Figure 11-11.

Note: Although it's a little more effort, you can also edit your home page (or home page tab sets) manually in a dialog box, rather than opening them up first.

Choose Tools→Internet Options→General. In the "Home page" text box, type each address, complete with *http://* and so on. If you want to create a home page tab set, type each address on its own line. (Leave the box empty for a blank home page.) Click OK, OK?

Bigger Text, Smaller Text

When your eyes are tired, you might like to make the text bigger. When you visit a site designed for Macintosh computers (whose text tends to look too large on PC screens), you might want a smaller size. You can adjust the point size of a Web page's text using the Page→Text Size command.

Zooming In and Out

So much for magnifying the *text;* what about the whole Web page?

There are plenty of ways to zoom in or out of the whole affair:

- If you have a scroll-wheel mouse, press the Ctrl key as you turn the mouse's wheel. (This works in Microsoft Office programs, too.)

- Press Ctrl+plus or Ctrl+minus on your keyboard.

- Use the pop-up menu in the lower-right corner of the window (where it probably says "100%" at the moment). Just clicking the digits repeatedly cycles the page among 100, 125, and 150 percent of actual size. Alternatively, you can use its ▾ menu to choose a degree of zoom from 50 to 400 percent—or choose Custom to type anything in between.

Online Photos

Internet Explorer is loaded with features for handling graphics online. Right-clicking an image on a Web page, for example, produces a shortcut menu that offers commands like Save Picture As, E-mail Picture, Print Picture, and Set as Background (that is, wallpaper).

Tip: To turn off IE's picture-shrinking feature, choose Tools→Internet Options. Click the Advanced tab, scroll down to the Multimedia heading, and then turn off "Enable automatic image resizing." Click OK.

By the way, when you see a picture you'd like to keep, right-click it and choose Save Picture As from the shortcut menu. After you name the picture and then click the Save button, the result is a new graphics file on your hard drive containing the picture you saved. (You can also choose Set as Background, which makes the picture part of your desktop image itself.)

Saving Pages

You can make Internet Explorer *store* a certain Web page on your hard drive so that you can peruse it later—on your laptop during your commute, for example.

The short way is to choose Page→Save As. For greatest simplicity, choose "Web Archive, single file (*.mht)" from the "Save as type" drop-down list. (The other options here save the Web page as multiple files on your hard drive—a handy feature if you intend to edit them, but less convenient if you just want to read them later.) Name the file and click the Save button. You've just preserved the Web page as a file on your hard drive, which you can open later by double-clicking it.

Sending Pages

Internet Explorer provides two different ways of telling a friend about the page you're looking at. You might find that useful when you come across a particularly interesting news story, op-ed piece, or burrito recipe.

Hiding in the Page menu are commands that let you e-mail the page to someone, email only the link to it, or send it to your Windows Live blog or Hotmail account (E-mail with Windows Live).

Tip: If the email options are dimmed and unavailable, it means that Internet Explorer thinks you haven't officially chosen your email program yet. Use the "Set program access and computer defaults" to specify your email program as described on page 249.

Accelerators

Accelerators, new in Internet Explorer 8, are time-saving commands that process selected Web text in useful ways. Highlight an address: An accelerator can show you where it is on a map. Highlight a sentence or paragraph in another language: An accelerator can translate it into your language. Highlight a term you want to look up online: An accelerator feeds it directly to Google or Bing. And so on.

Better yet, accelerators are a kind of plug-in; you can add new ones as other people write them.

Note: The first time you open Internet Explorer, you're asked if you want a starter set of accelerators installed. If you decline them at that time, you can always install them (or a different set) later, as described below.

How to use an accelerator

When you see some text that you want to map, define, translate, or otherwise process with one of your accelerators, highlight it. When you point to the highlighted text, the little Accelerator icon (⊡) appears at the corner of the selection. Click it to see the menu of accelerators (Figure 11-12).

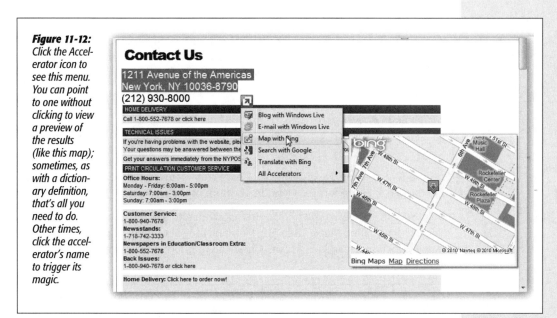

Figure 11-12:
Click the Accelerator icon to see this menu. You can point to one without clicking to view a preview of the results (like this map); sometimes, as with a dictionary definition, that's all you need to do. Other times, click the accelerator's name to trigger its magic.

As you can see in the figure, some accelerators reveal their goodies when you just point to their names. That's handy, since you don't lose your place on the Web. Other times, you have to click the accelerator's name, which takes you to a different Web page containing the desired info.

Here's what the starter accelerators do:

- **Blog with Windows Live.** This option appears if you've installed the Windows Live Essentials described at the beginning of Chapter 7. When you click this accelerator's name, you flip to your Windows Live blog site, where the highlighted text is auto-pasted into a new post, quotation style, so you can comment on it.

- **Email with Windows Live.** Again, this option appears if you've installed the Essentials. The accelerator sends the highlighted text into a new, outgoing email message. Great for little "I told you so" notes! ("According to this article, I was right about the Steelers' starting lineup in 1973!")

- **Search with Bing/Search with Google.** Copies the selected text into the Bing or Google Search box—and actually performs the search for you.

- **Map with Bing.** If you've highlighted a street address, this opens up the Bing maps site and shows you the address on a map.

- **Translate with Bing.** Sends the highlighted text to the Bing translation Web site. Use the pop-up menus there to specify what languages you want the text translated from and to. (Keep in mind that it's a computer, not a person; there may be some goofy words and phrases in the automated translation.)

Turning off accelerators

If you find your shortcut menu of accelerators cluttered by commands you never use, you can turn them off. Highlight some text, click the Accelerator button (◨), and then choose All Accelerators→Manage Accelerators. Click the one you're tired of, and then click either Disable or Remove.

Adding more accelerators

The starter accelerators are only the beginning; you can install a world of additional ones.

Choose Tools→"Manage Add-ons," click Accelerators (in the "Add-on Types" column), and then click Find More Accelerators (bottom of the screen).

On the site that appears, you find additional accelerators that send the selected text to Google Maps, Yahoo Maps, LinkedIn, Hotmail, Bing Shopping, Digg, eBay, Facebook search, a dictionary, and on and on. Click Add to Internet Explorer for each one you want to try out.

Tip: A lot of these features duplicate one another. There's Yahoo Maps, Bing Maps, Google Maps, and so on. That's why, when you add a new accelerator in an existing category, the confirmation box offers a "Make this my default provider for the Accelerator Category" option. Turn it on to make that your main Maps option, for example.

If you have several accelerators in a single category, you can always get to the nondefault ones by choosing All Accelerators from the Accelerator (◨) shortcut menu.

Later, you can always change the default option for each category in the Manage Accelerators box described previously.

Happy accelerating!

Printing Pages

The decade of chopped-off printouts is over. In IE8, when you press Ctrl+P or choose Print (the little printer icon), *all* the page's text is auto-shrunk to fit within the page.

Tip: You can print only *part* of a page, too. Drag through the portion you want, press Ctrl+P, click Selection, and then click Print.

Better yet, if you choose Print Preview from the little printer icon, you get a handsome preview of the end result. The icons in the Print Preview window include buttons like these:

- Portrait, Landscape (Alt+O, Alt+L) controls the page orientation: upright or sideways.

- Turn headers and footers on or off (Alt+E) hides or shows the header (the text at the top of the printout, which usually identifies the name of the Web site you're printing and the number of pages) and the footer (the URL of the Web page and the date).

- View Full Width (Alt+W) blows up the preview to fill your screen, even if it means you have to scroll down to see the whole page. (This option has no effect on the printout itself.)

- View Full Page (Alt+1) restores the original view, where the entire print preview is shrunk down to fit your screen.

- The 1 Page View pop-up menu governs how many pages fit in the preview window at a time.

- The Change Print Size pop-up menu affects the size of the image on the printed pages. Shrink to Fit adjusts the printout so that it won't be chopped off, but you can manually magnify or reduce the printed image by choosing the other percentage options in this menu.

Tip: Lots of Web sites have their own "Print this Page" buttons. When they're available, use them instead of Internet Explorer's own Print command. The Web site's Print feature not only makes sure the printout won't be chopped off, but it also eliminates ads, includes the entire article (even if it's split across multiple Web pages), and so on.

UP TO SPEED

Faster Browsing Without Graphics

Sure, sure, graphics are part of what makes the Web so compelling. But they're also responsible for making Web pages take so long to arrive on the screen. Without them, Web pages appear almost instantaneously. You still get fully laid-out Web pages; you still see all the text and headlines. But wherever a picture would normally be, you see an empty rectangle containing a generic "graphic goes here" logo, usually with a caption explaining what that graphic would have been.

To turn off graphics, choose Tools→Internet Options, which opens the Internet Options dialog box. Click the Advanced

tab, scroll halfway down into the list of checkboxes, and turn off "Show pictures" (in the Multimedia category of checkboxes).

Now try visiting a few Web pages. You should feel a substantial speed boost, especially if you're connected by dial-up modem.

And if you wind up on a Web page that's nothing without its pictures, you can still summon them individually. Just right-click a picture's box and choose Show Picture from the shortcut menu.

Turn Off Animations

If blinking ads make it tough to concentrate as you read a Web-based article, choose Tools→Internet Options→Advanced tab, and then scroll down to the Multimedia heading. Turn off "Play animations in web pages" to stifle most animated ads. Alas, it doesn't stop *all* animations; the jerks of the ad-design world have grown too clever for this option.

Take a moment, too, to look over the other annoying Web page elements that you can turn off, including sounds.

Internet Options

Internet Explorer's Options dialog box offers roughly 68,000 tabs, buttons, and nested dialog boxes. Most of the useful options have been described, in this chapter, with their appropriate topics (like Tabbed Browsing). Still, by spending a few minutes adjusting Internet Explorer's settings, you can make it more fun (or less annoying) to use.

To open this cornucopia of options, choose Tools→Internet Options (Figure 11-13).

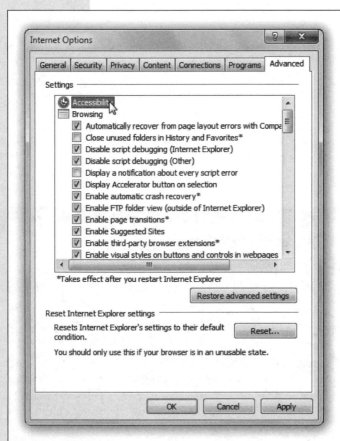

Figure 11-13:
Choosing Tools→Internet Options opens this dialog box, the identical twin of the Internet Options program in the Control Panel. Two of its tabs are shown here. Double-click one of the headings (like "Accessibility") to collapse all of its check-boxes. Your sanity is the winner here.

The Keyboard Shortcut Master List
All Versions

Before you set off into the Internet Explorer sunset, it's worth admitting that surfing the Web is one of the things most people do *most* with their PCs. And as long as you're going to spend so much time in this single program, it's worth mastering its keyboard shortcuts. Once you've learned a few, you save yourself time and fumbling.

Here it is, then: the complete master list of every Internet Explorer keyboard shortcut known to Microsoft. Clip and save.

Viewing

Full Screen mode (on/off)	F11
Cycle through links on a page	Tab
Search the text on a page	Ctrl+F
Open the current page in a new window	Ctrl+N
Print this page	Ctrl+P
Select all items on the page	Ctrl+A
Zoom in/out by 10 percent	Ctrl+plus, Ctrl+minus
Zoom to 100%	Ctrl+0
Override pop-up blocker	Ctrl+Alt
Shut up this page's background sounds	Esc

Bars and menus

Highlight the address bar	Alt+D
Open URL in the address bar in a new tab	Alt+Enter
View previously typed addresses	F4
Highlight the information bar	Alt+N
Open Home menu	Alt+M
Open Feeds menu	Alt+J
Open Print menu	Alt+R
Open Page menu	Alt+P
Open Tools menu	Alt+O
Open Help menu	Alt+L
Open Favorites menu	Alt+C, Ctrl+I
Open Favorites in pinned mode (won't auto-close)	Ctrl+Shift+I
Organize Favorites dialog box	Ctrl+B
Open Feeds list	Ctrl+J
Open Feeds in pinned mode	Ctrl+Shift+J
Open History	Ctrl+H
Open History in pinned mode	Ctrl+Shift+H Add *http://www.*
Add *http://www.* and *.com* to the text in address bar	Ctrl+Enter
Add *http://www.* and *.net* or *.org* to the text in address bar	Ctrl+Shift+Enter

---

Tip: To set up this last trick, open Tools→Internet Options→General tab→Langauges. In the Suffix box, enter whatever suffix you want IE to insert when you press Ctrl+Shift+Enter: *.org, .net, .edu, .jp,* or whatever you like.

Navigation

Scroll down a screenful	Space bar (or Page Down)
Scroll up a screenful	Shift+space bar (or Page Up)
Go to home page	Alt+Home
Go back a page	Alt+←
Go forward a page	Alt+→
Refresh page	F5
Super refresh (ignore any cached elements)	Ctrl+F5
Stop downloading this page	Esc
Open link in a new window	Shift+click
Add current page to Favorites	Ctrl+D
"Right-click" any highlighted item	Shift+F10

Search bar

Highlight the Search bar	Ctrl+E
Open list of search services	Ctrl+↓
Open search results in new tab	Alt+Enter

Tabbed browsing

Open link in new background tab	Ctrl-click*
Open link in new foreground tab	Ctrl+Shift+click (left or middle button)
Close tab (closes window if only one tab is open)	Ctrl+W, Ctrl+F4*
Quick Tab view	Ctrl+Q
Open new empty tab	Ctrl+T
View list of open tabs	Ctrl+Shift+Q
Switch to next tab	Ctrl+Tab
Switch to previous tab	Ctrl+Shift+Tab
Switch to tab #1, #2, etc.	Ctrl+1, Ctrl+2, etc.
Switch to last tab	Ctrl+9

* or scroll wheel–click, or middle button–click

Windows Live Mail

E mail is a fast, cheap, convenient communication medium; these days, it's almost embarrassing to admit you don't have an email address. To spare you that humiliation, Microsoft offer you Windows Live Mail. It's a renamed, revamped version of the program that, through the years, has been called Windows Mail and Windows Live Desktop Mail. It lets you receive and send email and read

---

GEM IN THE ROUGH

The "Windows Live" in Windows Live Mail

If you downloaded Windows Live Essentials, then you probably have a free Windows Live account (a Windows Live ID, in other words). But in Mail's case, "Windows Live" isn't just a name; the program really does hook into Microsoft's vast Windows Live suite of services.

For example, if you're signed into Windows Live when you're using Mail, you can pull off some nifty stunts:

You can send huge photo files as attachments—files that would ordinarily be too big for email. But although your friends will receive only thumbnail-sized images, the email they get contains "Play slideshow" and "Download picture" links that take them to the full-size versions on the Windows

Live Web site. (The thumbnail link remains live for 30 days.)

When you click Contacts (lower-left corner of Mail), you see your email address book—but if any of your Windows Messenger chat partners are online, special icons let you know. Sometimes a quick live chat is better than an email exchange. (If you're not signed into Windows Live, you just see the address book that's stored on your PC.)

You can place voice calls or send text messages to cellphones, right from within Mail.

Mail can show you your Windows Live online calendars.

So how do you sign into Windows Live? By clicking "Sign in" (upper-right corner of the screen), of course!

---

newsgroups (Internet bulletin boards), and it's also the only calendar program you get in Windows 7.

If you do have an email address, or several, Mail can help you manage your email accounts, messages, and contacts better than ever.

Now, Mail doesn't exactly come *with* Windows 7; the lawyers saw to that. But it is part of the free, easy-to-download Windows Live Essentials suite (page 265), so you have very little excuse for not having an email program.

Note: In trying to make Mail look less threatening, Microsoft has chosen to hide the usual menu bar (File, Edit, View, and so on). The menus reappear temporarily when you tap the Alt key. But you'll use them so often, it's probably better to make the menus appear all the time. To do that, press Alt+M twice. (Or choose "Show menu bar" from the Menus button, which is right next to the Help icon on the toolbar.)

This chapter assumes that you have, in fact, made the menus visible—for good.

Setting Up Windows Mail
All Versions

To start up Mail for the first time, you can use either of the two standard Windows methods:

- **The long, mousy way.** Choose Start→All Programs→Microsoft Live Essentials→ Windows Live Mail.

Figure 12-1:
To set up an email account in Windows Mail, start by filling in the Display Name. This is the name people will see when you send them email, in the "From:" field. It does not have to be the same as your email address; it can be your full name, a nickname, or anything you like. When you're done, click Next to continue.

- **The quick, keyboard way.** Open the Start menu (press the ⊞ key), type *mail*, and press Enter when you see Windows Live Mail highlighted.

Either way, you'll find that setting up your account is a lot easier than it once was. If you had Outlook Express or Windows Mail on your PC, Windows Live Mail imports *everything* automatically: mail, address book, calendar, account settings. You're ready to start doing email.

If not, it's fairly easy to enter your email settings information for the first time. Microsoft has rounded up the acronym-laden server settings for all the common email services—Hotmail, Gmail, Yahoo, Comcast, and so on—and built them right in.

All you have to do is type your email name and password into the box (Figure 12-1). If Mail recognizes the suffix (for example, *@gmail.com),* then it does the heavy lifting for you.

Now, if you use a service provider that Mail *doesn't* recognize when you type in your name and password—you weirdo!—then you have to set up your mail account the long way. Mail prompts you along, and you confront a dialog box where you're supposed to type in various settings to specify your email account. Some of the information may require a call to your Internet service provider (ISP).

Note: If you used the Easy Transfer Wizard (page 830) to bring over your files and settings from an older PC, then Windows Mail is probably already set up quite nicely. If that's the case, skip to the next section.

UP TO SPEED

POP, IMAP, and Web-based Mail

When it comes to email, there are three flavors of accounts: POP (also known as POP3), IMAP (also known as IMAP4), and Web-based. Each has its own distinct feeling, with different strengths and weaknesses.

POP accounts are the most common. A POP server transfers your incoming mail to your hard drive before you read it, and then deletes the original copies on the Internet. From now on, those messages live on your computer, and it's up to you to save them, back them up, or delete them. (You can configure Mail not to delete the messages from the server, but most ISPs don't give you much disk space. If your mailbox gets too full, the server may begin rejecting your incoming messages.)

IMAP servers are newer than, and have more features than, POP servers, but as a result, they're not quite as common. IMAP servers are Internet computers that store all your mail for you, rather than making you download it each time you

connect. The benefit? You can access the same mail regardless of which computer you use. IMAP servers remember which messages you've read and sent, too.

One downside to this approach, of course, is that you can't work with your email except when you're online, because all your mail is on an Internet server, not on your hard drive. And if you don't conscientiously delete mail manually after you've read it, your online mailbox eventually overflows. Sooner or later, the system starts bouncing fresh messages back to their senders, annoying your friends and depriving you of the chance to read what they have to say.

Free Web-based servers like Hotmail also store your mail on the Internet. You can use a Web browser on any computer to read and send messages; then again, most POP accounts these days offer that feature, too. Web email is slower and more cumbersome to use than "regular" email accounts.

Click Next to step through the wizard's interview process, during which you'll provide the following information:

- **Incoming mail server details.** Enter the information your ISP provided about its mail servers: the type of server (POP3, IMAP, or HTTP), the name of the incoming mail server, and the name of the outgoing mail server. Most of the time, the incoming server's name is connected to the name of your ISP. It might be *pop. gmail.com, for example, or mail.comcast.net.*

  The outgoing mail server (the *SMTP server*) usually looks something like *smtp. gmail.com or smtp.comcast.net.*

- **Security settings.** All that stuff about "This server requires a secure connection" and "requires authentication"? You'll never guess it. Contact your ISP (or its Web pages, which almost always include these details).

When you click Next, if all is well, you get a congratulations message, and then you return to the main Mail screen, where your latest messages come flooding in automatically (Figure 12-2).

Figure 12-2:
Windows Live Mail has pretty much the same design as every other email program: mail folders on the left, toolbar up top, list of messages on the upper right, the currently highlighted message contents below. (You can also opt for a center message list, and a right-side pane showing the message itself; choose View→Layout.)

To sort the message list, click a column heading: From, Subject, and so on. Yoou can rearrange or adjust the widths of the columns, too.

After a moment, you see that Mail has created a folder representing your email account in the list at the left side, complete with subfolders like Inbox, Drafts, and Sent Items.

To add another email account, click "Add e-mail account" at the bottom of the folder list at the left side of the window. The wizard you worked through previously reappears. You've just met a great feature of Mail: It can manage a bunch of different email accounts all in one place.

Tip: If you want to import a stash of mail from an older email program, like Outlook Express, choose File→Import→Messages.

Sending Email

Whenever you want to receive and send new mail, you use the Sync command (which, in most email programs, would be called Send & Receive).

Note: In all the instructions having to do with email, this chapter assumes that you've clicked Mail in the list of modules at the lower-left corner of the Mail window. Not Calendar, not Contacts; Mail. (Pressing Shift+Ctrl+J also selects the Mail module.)

You can trigger the Sync command in three ways:

- Click the Sync button on the toolbar (Figure 12-3).
- Press Ctrl+M.
- Or press F5.

Tip: You can set up Mail to check your email accounts automatically according to a schedule. Choose Tools→Options. On the General tab, you see the "Check for new messages every __ minutes" checkbox, which you can change to your liking.

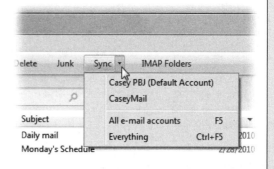

Figure 12-3:
The Sync button is on the toolbar. The arrow beside it lets you choose which mail you'd like to get, if you don't want to check all your accounts.

Now Mail retrieves new messages and sends any outgoing messages.

In the second column on your screen, the names of new messages show up in bold type; in the "Quick views" list at the left side of the window, parentheses show how many unread messages are waiting in each folder.

Tip: Mail can, at your command, group your inbox into conversations or threads, meaning that related back-and-forths on a certain subject, with a certain person, appear as a single item marked by a flippy triangle (▸). Click that triangle to expand the listing, showing all the individual messages within that flurry of communication.

To make this happen, choose View→"View by conversation," so that a checkmark appears.

Mail Folders in Windows Mail

At the left side of the screen, Mail organizes your email into *folders*. To see what's in a folder, click it once:

- **Inbox** holds mail you've received.

- **Outbox** holds mail you've written but haven't sent yet.

- **Sent Items** holds copies of messages you've sent.

- **Deleted Items** holds mail you've deleted. (There's a separate Deleted folder for each account.) It works a lot like the Recycle Bin, in that messages placed there don't actually disappear. Instead, they remain in the Deleted Items folder, awaiting rescue if you opt to retrieve them. To empty this folder, right-click it and then choose "Empty 'Deleted Items' Folder" from the shortcut menu.

Tip: To make the folder empty itself every time you exit Mail, choose Tools→Options, click the Advanced tab, and then click the Maintenance button. From the Maintenance dialog box, turn on "Empty messages from the 'Deleted Items' folder on exit."

- **Drafts** holds messages you've started but haven't finished—and don't want to send just yet.

- **Junk E-Mail** holds messages deemed as junk (spam) by Mail's Junk E-Mail Protection. (More about that later.)

GEM IN THE ROUGH

Checking a Specific Email Account

You don't have to check *all* your email accounts whenever you want to get mail. To check just one particular account, click the ▾ beside the Sync button and choose that account's name from the pop-up menu.

But what if you never want all accounts checked? What if you want to leave out one particular account from the automated periodic checking, so that you get its mail only when you ask for it?

Excluding an account (or several accounts) from the "Send and receive all" routine is easy enough. Open the Accounts window (Tools→Accounts), select the account to turn off, and then click Properties. Turn off "Include this account when receiving mail or synchronizing," click OK, and, finally, close the Accounts window.

Now you'll see that account's mail only when you manually request it from the Sync pop-up menu.

You can also add to this list, creating folders for your own organizational pleasure—Family Mail, Work Mail, or whatever. See page 442.

Composing and Sending Messages

To send a message, click New on the toolbar (or press Ctrl+N). The New Message form opens (Figure 12-4).

Tip: You can also start writing a message by clicking Contacts (lower left). In the Contacts window (page 437), click the person's name, and then click E-Mail on the toolbar. A blank, outgoing piece of mail appears, already addressed to the person whose name you clicked.

Come to think of it, it's faster to hit Ctrl+N.

The Mighty Morphing Interface

You don't have to be content with the factory-installed design of the Mail screen; you can control which panes are visible, how big they are, and which columns show up in List views.

To change the size of a pane, drag its border to make it larger or smaller, as shown here.

There's also a vast array of layout options hiding in the View→Layout command. For example, you can control where the Preview pane appears: under the message list, as usual, or to its right—a great arrangement if you have a very wide screen.

You can show one-line or two-line previews. You can make "Storage folders" appear in the folder list (that is, folders that hold messages on your PC, as opposed to the Web-based folders from a Gmail, Yahoo, or Hotmail account).

Mail lets you decide what columns are displayed in the List pane. For example, if you don't particularly care about seeing the Flag column, you can hide it, leaving more space for the Subject and Received columns. To switch columns on or off, choose from the list in the View→Columns dialog box.

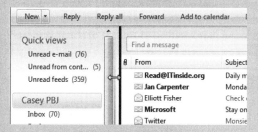

You can also *rearrange* the columns, which can be handy if you'd rather see the Subject column first instead of the sender, for example. Just drag the column's name *header* horizontally; release when the vertical dotted line is where you want the column to wind up. To make a column wider or narrower, drag the short black divider line between column names horizontally, much the way you'd resize a folder window List view column.

Finally, about that toolbar—the one with plain-English words like New, Reply, Forward, and so on—you can customize it. You can get rid of the commands you never use (or the commands you've learned the keyboard shortcuts for), and add ones that you do use but that don't appear at first (like Print).

To do it, use the Menu menu (to the left of the Help icon on the toolbar); choose "Customize toolbar." In the resulting dialog box, you can use the ◄ and ► buttons to move the missing but available buttons (left list) onto the toolbar (right list). You can even specify their relative left-to-right positions on the toolbar by clicking, nonobviously enough, the ▼ and ▲ buttons.

To specify which format Windows Mail *proposes* for all new messages (plain text or HTML), choose Tools→Options→Send tab. Next, in the section labeled Mail Sending Format, choose either the HTML or Plain Text button, and then click OK.

No matter which setting you specify there, however, you can always switch a *particular* message you're writing to the opposite format. Just choose Format→Rich Text (HTML), or Format→Plain Text.

Whenever you're creating a formatted HTML message, the HTML toolbar's various buttons control the formatting, font, size, color, paragraph indentation, line spacing, and other word processor–like formatting controls (Figure 12-5).

Just remember: Less is more. If you go hog wild formatting your email, the message may be difficult to read, especially if you also apply stationery (a background).

Figure 12-5:
When you're composing an email using the HTML format, the New Message window gives you options for choosing fonts, formatting options like bold, italic, and underline, and colors (from a handy color palette).

5. **Enter the message in the message box (the bottom half of the message window).**

   You can use all standard editing techniques, including Cut, Copy, and Paste, to rearrange the text as you write it.

Tip: If Microsoft Word is installed on your PC, you can also spell check your outgoing mail. Just choose Tools→Spelling (or press F7) in the New Message window.

---

6. **Add a signature, if you wish.**

   Signatures are bits of text that get stamped at the bottom of outgoing email messages. They typically contain a name, a mailing address, or a *Star Trek* quote.

To create a signature, choose Tools→Options→Signatures tab; click the New button. The easiest way to compose your signature is to type it into the Edit Signatures text box at the bottom of the window. (If you poke around long enough in this box, you'll realize that you can actually create multiple signatures—and even assign each one to a different outgoing email account.)

Once you've created a signature (or several), you can tack it onto your outgoing mail for all messages (by turning on "Add signatures to all outgoing messages" at the top of this box) or on a message-by-message basis (press Shift+Ctrl+S, or choose Insert→Signature).

7. **Click the Send button.**

Alternatively, press Alt+S, or Ctrl+Enter. Your PC connects to the Internet and sends the message.

Tip: If you seem to be able to receive mail but can't send it, your Internet service provider might require Mail to log into its server before sending email. To try that approach, first click Tools→Accounts. From there, click your account's name, and then open the Properties→Servers tab. Turn on "My server requires authentication." Click OK and then Close.

If you're working offline, you might prefer Mail to place each message you write in the Outbox folder, saving them up until you click the Sync button on the toolbar; see "Send Tab," on page 451.

The Contacts List

Accumulating names in a Contacts list eliminates the need to enter complete email addresses whenever you want to send a message. Click the Contacts button (lower left of the window), or press Ctrl+Shift+B; then, to begin adding names and email addresses, click New Contact.

Tip: Windows Mail offers a convenient timesaving feature: the Tools→"Add contact"→Sender (or "Add contact"→"Everyone on the To line") command. Whenever you choose it, Mail automatically stores the email address of the person whose message is open on the screen. (Alternatively, you can right-click an email address in a list of messages and choose "Add sender to contacts" from the shortcut menu.)

Attaching Files to Messages

Sending little text messages is fine, but it's not much help when you want to send somebody a photograph, a sound recording, a Word or Excel document, and so on. Fortunately, attaching such files to email messages is one of the world's most popular email features.

To attach a file to a message, use either of two methods:

- **The long way.** Click the Attach button on the New Message toolbar. Alternatively, you could select Insert→"File as attachment." When the Open dialog box appears, locate the file and select it. (In the resulting navigation window, you can Ctrl+click multiple files to attach them all at once.)

Now the name of the attached file appears in the message, in the Attach text box. When you send the message, the file tags along.

- **The short way.** If you can see the icon of the file you want to attach—in its folder window behind the Mail window, on the Desktop, or wherever—then attach it by *dragging* its icon directly into the message window. That's a handy technique when you're attaching many different files.

Tip: To remove a file from an outgoing message before you've sent it, just click it and then press the Delete key.

Reading Email
All Versions

Just seeing a list of the *names* of new messages in Mail is like getting wrapped presents—the best part's yet to come. There are two ways to read a message: using the Preview pane, and opening the message into its own window.

To preview a message, click its name in the List pane; the body of the message appears in the Preview pane below or to the right. Don't forget that you can adjust the relative sizes of the List and Preview panes by dragging the border between them up or down.

To open a message into a window of its own, double-click its name in the List pane. An open message has its own toolbar, along with Previous and Next buttons.

Once you've read a message, you can view the next one in the list either by pressing Ctrl+→ (next message), by pressing Ctrl+U (next *unread* message), or by clicking its name in the List pane. (If you're using Preview mode and haven't opened a message into its own window, you can also press the ↑ or ↓ key to move from one message to the next.)

Tip: To mark a message you've read as an *unread* message, so that its name remains bolded, right-click its name in the List pane and then choose "Mark as unread" from the shortcut menu.

Here's another timesaver: To hide all the messages you've already read, just choose View→"Show or hide"→"Hide read messages." Now only unread messages are visible in the selected folder. To bring the hidden messages back, choose View→"Show or hide"→"Show all messages."

When Pictures are Part of the Message

Sending pictures in email is a globally popular activity—but Mail doesn't want you to see them.

Mail comes set up to block images, because these images sometimes serve as "bugs" that silently report back to the sender whether you received and opened the message. At that point, the spammers know that they've found a live, working email address—

and, better yet, a sucker who opens email from strangers. And presto, you're on their "safe senders" list, and the spam flood *really* begins.

You'll know if pictures were meant to appear in the body of a message; see the strip that appears at the top in Figure 12-6.

Figure 12-6:
To view blocked images in a message, press F9, choose View→"Blocked images," or click "Show images" in the yellow strip above the message. Or, to make Mail quit blocking pictures altogether, choose Tools→Options→ Security; next, turn off "Block images and other external content in HTML messages."

Selecting Messages

In order to process a group of messages simultaneously—to delete, move, or forward them, for example—you must first master the art of multiple message selection.

To select two or more messages that appear consecutively in your message list, click the first message, and then Shift+click the last. Known as a *contiguous selection*, this trick selects every message between the two that you clicked.

To select two or more messages that *aren't* adjacent in the list (that is, skipping a few messages between selected ones), Ctrl+click the messages you want. Only the messages you click get selected—no filling in of messages in between this time.

After using either technique, you can also *deselect* messages you've managed to highlight—just Ctrl+click them again.

How to Process a Message

Once you've read a message and savored the feeling of awe brought on by the miracle of instantaneous electronic communication, you can handle the message in any of several ways.

Deleting messages

Sometimes it's junk mail, sometimes you're just done with it; either way, it's a snap to delete a message. Click the Delete button on the toolbar, press the Delete key, hit Ctrl+D, or choose Edit→Delete. (You can also delete a batch of selected messages simultaneously.)

The messages don't actually disappear. Instead, they move to the Deleted Items folder for that email account. If you like, click this folder to view a list of the messages you've deleted. You can even rescue some simply by dragging them into another folder (even right back into the Inbox).

Mail doesn't truly vaporize messages in the Deleted Items folder until you "empty the trash." You can empty it in any of several ways:

- Right-click the Deleted Items folder. Choose "Empty 'Deleted Items' Folder" from the shortcut menu.

- Click the X button to the right of the Deleted Items folder's name.

- Click a message, or a folder, within the Deleted Items folder list and then click the Delete button on the toolbar (or press the Delete key). You're asked to confirm its permanent deletion.

- Set up Mail to delete messages automatically when you quit the program. To do so, choose Tools→Options→Advanced. Click the Maintenance button, and then turn on "Empty messages from the 'Deleted Items' folder on exit." Click OK.

Replying to Messages

To reply to a message, click the Reply button in the toolbar, or press Ctrl+R. Mail creates a new, outgoing email message, preaddressed to the sender's return address. (If the message was sent to you *and* a few other people, and you'd like to reply to all of them at once, click "Reply all" in the toolbar.)

To save additional time, Mail pastes the entire original message at the bottom of your reply (either indented, if it's HTML mail, or marked with the > brackets that serve as Internet quoting marks); that's to help your correspondent figure out what you're talking about.

Note: To turn off this feature, choose Tools→Options, click the Send tab, and then turn off "Include message in reply."

Mail even tacks "*Re:*" (meaning "regarding") onto the front of the subject line.

Your insertion point appears at the top of the message box. Now, just begin typing your reply. You can also add recipients, remove recipients, edit the subject line or the message, and so on.

Tip: Use the Enter key to create blank lines within the bracketed original message in order to place your own text within it. Using this method, you can splice your own comments into the paragraphs of the original message, replying point by point. The brackets preceding each line of the original message help your correspondent keep straight what's yours and what's hers. Also, if you're using HTML formatting for the message, you can format what you've written in bold, italic, underline, or even in another color for easier reading.

Forwarding Messages

Instead of replying to the person who sent you a message, you may sometimes want to *forward* the message—pass it on—to a third person.

To do so, click Forward in the toolbar, choose Message→Forward, or press Ctrl+F. A new message opens, looking a lot like the one that appears when you reply. Once again, before forwarding the message, you have the option of editing the subject or the message. (For example, you may wish to precede the original message with a comment of your own, along the lines of, "Frank: I thought you'd be interested in this joke about Congress.")

All that remains is for you to specify who receives the forwarded message. Just address it as you would any outgoing piece of mail.

Printing Messages

Sometimes there's no substitute for a printout of an email message—an area where Mail shines. Choose File→Print, or press Ctrl+P. The standard Windows Print dialog box pops up so you can specify how many copies you want, what range of pages, and so on. Make your selections, and then click Print.

UP TO SPEED

About Mailing Lists

During your email experiments, you're likely to come across something called a mailing list—a discussion group conducted via email. By searching Yahoo.com or other Web directories, you can find mailing lists covering just about every conceivable topic.

You can send a message to all members of such a group by sending a message to a single address—the list's address. The list is actually maintained on a special mail server. Everything sent to the list gets sent to the server, which forwards the message to all the individual list members.

That's why you have to be careful if you're actually trying to reply to *one person* in the discussion group; if you reply to the list and not to a specific person, you'll send your reply to every address on the list—sometimes with disastrous consequences.

Filing Messages

Mail lets you create new folders in the Folders list; by dragging messages from your Inbox onto one of these folder icons, you can file away your messages into appropriate cubbies. You might create one folder for important messages, another for order confirmations from shopping on the Web, still another for friends and family, and so on. In fact, you can even create folders *inside* these folders, a feature beloved by the hopelessly organized.

To create a new folder, see Figure 12-7.

Tip: To rename an existing folder, right-click it and choose Rename from the shortcut menu.

Figure 12-7:
To create a new folder, click File→Folder→ "Create new folder," or press Shift+Ctrl+D, or click the ▼ next to the New toolbar button and choose Folder from the pop-up menu. No matter which way you choose, this window appears. Name the folder and then, by clicking, indicate which folder you want this one to appear in. Usually, you want to click Storage Folders (that is, not inside any other folder).

To move a message into a folder, proceed like this:

• **Drag it out of the List pane and onto the folder icon.** You can use any part of a message's "row" in the list as a handle. You can also drag messages en masse into a folder after selecting them.

• **Right-click a message (or one of several you've highlighted).** From the shortcut menu, choose "Move to folder." In a dialog box, the folder list appears; select the one you want, and then press Enter or click OK.

Tip: When you click a ▸ triangle in the Folder list, you see all folders contained within that folder, exactly like in Windows Explorer. You can drag folders inside other folders, nesting them to create a nice hierarchical folder structure. (To drag a nested folder back into the list of "main" folders, just drag it to the Storage Folders icon.)

You can also drag messages between folders; just drag one from the message list onto the desired folder at the left side of the screen.

This can be a useful trick when you apply it to a message in your Outbox. If you decide to postpone sending it, drag it into any other folder. Windows Mail won't send it until you drag it *back* into the Outbox.

Flagging Messages

Sometimes, you'll receive an email message that prompts you to some sort of action, but you may not have the time or the fortitude to face the task at the moment. ("Hi there…it's me, your accountant. Would you mind rounding up your expenses for 1996 through 2004 and sending me a list by email?")

That's why Mail lets you *flag* a message, positioning a small, red flag in the corresponding column next to a message's name. These little flags are visual indicators that mean whatever you want them to mean. You can bring all flagged messages to the top of the list by choosing View→"Sort by"→Flag, or by clicking the tiny flag icon in the list of message columns.

To flag a message in this way, see Figure 12-8.

Figure 12-8:
To flag a message, click in the Flag column. (That's the short way. The advantage of the long way–choosing Action→"Flag message"–is that you can flag a whole batch of selected messages that way.)

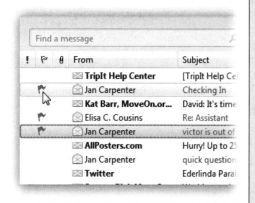

Opening Attachments

Just as you can attach files to a message, people can send files to you. You know when a message has an attachment because a paper-clip icon appears next to its name in the Inbox.

To free an attached file from its message, releasing it to the wilds of your hard drive, use one of the following methods:

• **Right-click the attachment's name (in the message)**, select "Save as" from the shortcut menu, and then specify a folder for the saved file (Figure 12-9).

- Double-click the attachment's name. After you click Open to confirm the risk (it's *always* risky to open an email attachment), it opens right up in Word, Excel, or whatever.

- If you've double-clicked the message so it appears in its own window, then drag the attachment icon out of the message window and onto any visible portion of your desktop.

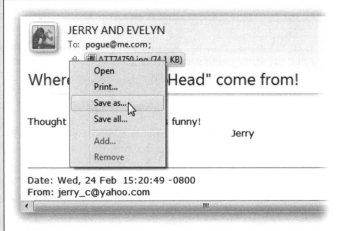

Figure 12-9:
One way to rescue an attachment from an email message is to right-click its name and choose "Save as." You can also drag an attachment's icon onto your desktop. Either way, you take the file out of the Mail world and into your standard Windows world, where you can file it, trash it, open it, or manipulate it as you would any file.

Message Rules

Once you know how to create folders, the next step in managing your email is to set up *message rules*. These are filters that can file, answer, or delete an incoming message *automatically* based on its subject, address, or size.

Message rules require you to think like the distant relative of a programmer, but the mental effort can reward you many times over. In fact, message rules can turn Mail into a surprisingly smart and efficient secretary.

Setting up message rules

Now that you're thoroughly intrigued about the magic of message rules, here's how to set one up:

1. **Choose Tools→"Message rules"→Mail.**

   If you've never created a message rule, you see what's shown in Figure 12-10. If you *have* created message rules before, you see the Message Rules window first. Click New to open the New Mail Rule window shown in Figure 12-10.

2. **Use the top options to specify how Mail should select messages to process.**

   For example, if you'd like Mail to watch out for messages from a particular person, you would choose, "Where the From line contains people."

To flag messages containing *"loan," "$$$$," "XXX," "!!!!,"* and so on (favorites of spammers), choose, "Where the Subject line contains specific words."

If you turn on more than one checkbox, you can set up another condition for your message rule. For example, you can set up the first criterion to find messages *from* your uncle, and a second that watches for subject lines that contain "joke." If you click the Options button, you get to specify whether the message has to contain *all* the words you've specified, or *any* of them.

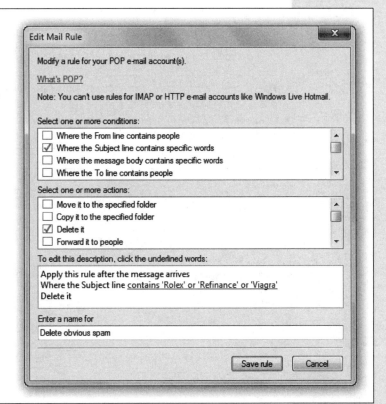

Figure 12-10:
Building a message rule entails specifying which messages you want Mail to look for—and what to do with them. By adding the underlined words, as shown here, you specify what criteria you're looking for. Here, any email with the words "Rolex," "Refinance," or "Viagra" in the Subject line is automatically deleted.

3. **Using the second set of checkboxes, specify what you want to happen to messages that match the criteria.**

   If, in step 2, you told your rule to watch for messages from your uncle containing the word "joke" somewhere in the message body, here's where you can tell Mail to delete or move the message into, say, a Spam folder.

   With a little imagination, you'll see how these checkboxes can perform absolutely amazing functions with your incoming email. Windows Mail can delete, move, or print messages; forward or redirect them to somebody; automatically reply to certain messages; and even avoid downloading files bigger than a certain number of kilobytes (ideal for laptop lovers on slow hotel room connections).

4. **Specify *which* words or people you want the message rule to watch out for.**

In the bottom of the dialog box, you can click any of the underlined phrases to specify which people, which specific words, which file sizes you want Mail to watch out for—a person's name, or "*Viagra*," in the previous examples.

If you click "contains people," for example, a dialog box appears that lets you open your Contacts list to select certain individuals whose messages you want handled by this rule. If you click "contains specific words," you can type in the words you want a certain rule to watch out for. And so on.

5. **In the very bottom text box, name your mail rule. Click OK.**

Now the Message Rules dialog box appears (Figure 12-11).

Tip: Windows Mail applies rules as they appear—from top to bottom—in the Message Rules window. If a rule doesn't seem to be working properly, it may be that an earlier rule is intercepting and processing the message before the "broken" rule even sees it. To fix this, try moving the rule up or down in the list by selecting it and then clicking the Move Up or Move Down buttons.

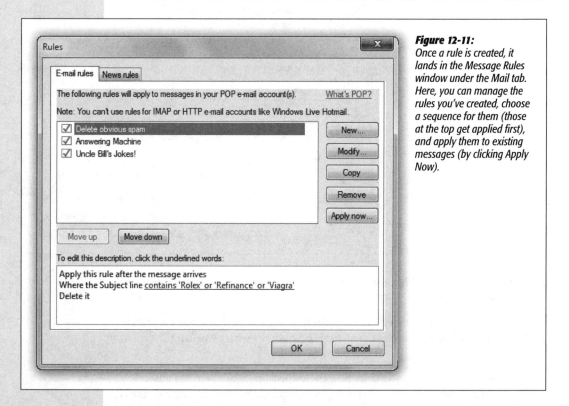

Figure 12-11:
Once a rule is created, it lands in the Message Rules window under the Mail tab. Here, you can manage the rules you've created, choose a sequence for them (those at the top get applied first), and apply them to existing messages (by clicking Apply Now).

Two sneaky message-rules tricks
You can use message rules for many different purposes. But here are two of the best:

- **File mail from specific people.** For instance, if you have a few friends who constantly forward their idea of funny messages, create a rule that sends any email from them to a specific folder automatically. At the end of the day, look through the folder just to make sure you haven't missed anything, and if you have time, read the "most excellent funny emails in the whole wide world."

- **The email answering machine.** If you're going on vacation, turn on "For all messages" in step 2, and then "Reply with message" in step 3. In other words, you can turn Windows Mail into an email answering machine that automatically sends a canned "I'm away until the 15th" message to everyone who writes you.

Tip: Unsubscribe from, or turn off, any email mailing lists before you turn on "For all messages." Otherwise, you'll incur the wrath of the other list members by littering their email discussion groups with copies of your autoreply message.

Junk Email
All Versions

Mail's Junk filter automatically channels what it believes to be spam into the "Junk E-mail" folder in the folder list.

FREQUENTLY ASKED QUESTION

Canning Spam

Help! I'm awash in junk email! How do I get out of this mess?

Spam is a much-hated form of advertising that involves sending unsolicited emails to thousands of people. While there's no instant cure for spam, you can take certain steps to protect yourself from it.

1. Above all, never post your main e-mail address online, ever. Use a different, dedicated email account for online shopping, Web site and software registration, and newsgroup posting.

   Spammers have automated software robots that scour every Web page, automatically recording email addresses they find. These are the primary sources of spam, so at least you're now restricting the junk mail to one secondary mail account.

2. Even then, when filling out forms or registering products online, look for checkboxes requesting permission for the company to send you email

or share your email address with its "partners." Just say no.

3. When posting messages in a newsgroup, insert the letters NOSPAM, SPAMISBAD, or something similar somewhere into your email address. Anyone replying to you via email must manually remove it from your email address, which, though a hassle, keeps your email address away from the spammer's robots. (They're getting smarter every day, though; a trickier insert may be required, along the lines of REMOVETOEMAIL or SPAMMERSARESCUM.)

4. Create *message rules* to filter out messages containing typical advertising words such as *casino, Rolex, herbal,* and so forth. (Instructions are on page 444.)

5. Buy an antispam program like SpamAssassin.

Tip: You may not have a "Junk E-mail" folder for Web-based email accounts like Gmail and Yahoo. Those online mail services usually have their own spam filters.

The Junk filter's factory setting is Low, meaning that only the most obvious spam gets sent to the "Junk E-mail" folder. You'll probably still get a ton of spam, but at least almost no legitimate mail will get mistakenly classified as spam.

You can configure the level of security you want in the Junk E-Mail Options window, shown in Figure 12-12.

Figure 12-12:
To visit this dialog box, choose Tools→Safety Options. Choose No Automatic Filtering, Low, High, or Safe List Only. You can also opt to permanently delete suspected spam instead of moving it to the Junk E-Mail folder. No matter what setting you choose, though, always go through the Junk E-Mail folder every few days to make sure you haven't missed any important messages that were flagged as spam incorrectly.

Junk E-Mail Safety Options

Junk E-Mail Safety Options offers six tabs. The Options tab is shown in Figure 12-12. These are the other tabs:

- **Safe Senders.** Messages from any contacts, email addresses, or domain names that you add to this list are never treated as junk email. (A domain name is what comes after the @ sign in an email address, as in bob@*herbalviagra.com*.) Click Add to begin.

Tip: The two checkboxes below the list are also useful in preventing "false positives." The first, "Also trust e-mail from my Contacts," means that anyone in your own address book is not a spammer. The second, "Automatically add people I e-mail to the Safe Senders list," means that if you send mail *to* somebody, it's someone you don't consider a spammer.

- **Blocked Senders.** This one's the flip side of Safe Senders: It's a list of contacts, email addresses, and domain names that you always want flagged as spam.

- **International.** You can also block email in foreign languages or messages that originate overseas. (A huge percentage of spam originates overseas, since U.S. antispam laws have no jurisdiction there.) See Figure 12-13.

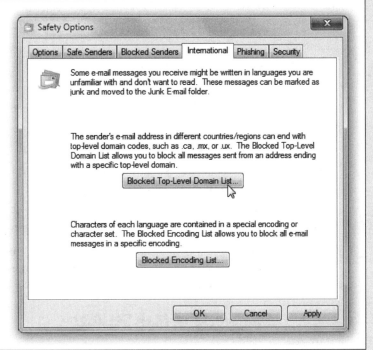

Figure 12-13:
If you find you're getting email from specific countries or domains, you can select the top-level domains (.ca for Canadian mail, .uk for British mail, and so on) for those countries. All email from those domains now gets treated as junk email.

- **Phishing.** For a complete description of phishing scams, see page 373. In brief, phishing email is designed to look like it came from your bank, eBay, or PayPal—but it's a trick to get you to surrender your account information so the bad guys can steal your identity.

  Mail keeps phishing email out of your inbox unless you turn off this feature on this tab.

- **Security.** This tab contains options for sending secure mail, using digital IDs, and encryption. If you're using Mail in a business that requires secure email, the system administrator will provide instructions. Otherwise, you'll find that most of these settings have no effect.

  The exceptions are the antivirus and antispam features, like "Do not allow attachments to be saved or opened that could potentially be a virus" and "Block images," described earlier in this chapter. For best results, leave these settings as they are.

Tip: One of these options is very useful in the modern age: "Warn me when other applications try to send mail as me." That's a thinly veiled reference to viruses that, behind the scenes, send out hundreds of infected emails to everybody in your Contacts list, with you identified as the sender. This option ensures that if some software—not you—tries to send messages, you'll know about it.

When the Junk Filter Goes Wrong

Windows Live Mail doesn't always get it right. It labels some good messages as junk, and some spam messages as OK.

Over time, though, it's supposed to get better—*if* you patiently help it along. Every time you see a good piece of email in the "Junk E-mail" folder, click it, and then click "Not junk" on the toolbar.

Better yet, use the Actions→"Junk e-mail" submenu to choose one of these two options:

• **Add sender to safe senders list.** No future mail from this person will be misfiled.

• **Add sender's domain to safe senders list.** No future mail from this person's entire company or ISP will be marked as spam.

On the other hand, you can reverse all this logic if you find a piece of spam in your inbox. That is, click it and then click the Junk button on the toolbar.

You can also use the Actions→"Junk e-mail"→"Add sender to blocked senders list" (or "Add sender's domain"); unfortunately, spammers rarely use the same address or domain twice, so it's probably faster just to hit the Delete key.

The World of Mail Settings

All Versions

Mail has enough features and configuration options to fill a very thick book. You can see them for yourself by choosing Tools→Options. Here's a brief overview of some of the most useful options (Figure 12-14).

General Tab

Most of the controls here govern what Mail does when you first open the program. Take note of the options to connect automatically; you can opt to have Mail check for messages every few minutes and then use the drop-down list to say how, and whether, to connect at that time if you're not already online.

Read Tab

Use these options to establish how the program handles messages in the Inbox. One of these options marks a message as having been read—changing its typeface from bold to nonbold—if you leave it highlighted in the list for 1 second or more, even without opening it. That's one option you may want to consider turning off. (This tab is also where you choose the font you want to use for the messages you're reading, which is an important consideration.)

Receipts Tab

You can add a *return receipt* to messages you send. When the recipient reads your message, a notification message (receipt) is emailed back to you under two conditions: *if* the recipient agrees to send a return receipt to you, and *if* the recipient's email program offers a similar feature. (Mail, Outlook, and Eudora all do.)

Send Tab

The options here govern outgoing messages. One option to consider turning *off* here is the factory-set option "Send messages immediately." That's because as soon as you click the Send button, Mail sends messages immediately, even if you haven't had time to fully consider the consequences of the rant inside it—aimed at an ex, a boss, or a coworker—which could land you in hot water.

Tip: It's also a good choice if you're on a dial-up connection. All this dialing—and *waiting* for the dialing—drives some people crazy, especially in households with only one phone line.

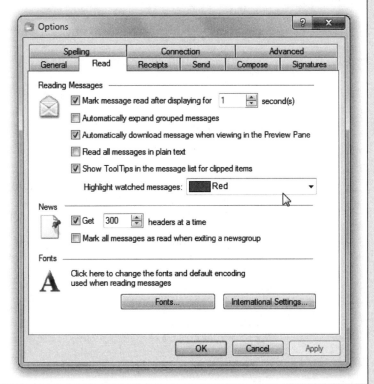

Figure 12-14:
The Options dialog box has 10 tabs, each loaded with options. Most tabs have buttons that open additional dialog boxes. Coming in 2012: Windows Mail Options: The Missing Manual.

If you turn this option off, then clicking the Send button simply places a newly written message into the Outbox. As you reply to messages and compose new ones, the Outbox collects them. They're not sent until you click the Sync button, or press Ctrl+M. Only at that point does Mail send your email.

Tip: To see the messages waiting in your outbox, click the Outbox icon at the left side of the screen. At this point, you can click a message's name (in the upper-right pane of the screen) to view the message itself in the *lower*-right pane, exactly as with messages in your inbox.

Don't bother to try *editing* an outgoing message in this way, however; Mail won't let you do so. Only by double-clicking a message's name (in the upper-right pane), thus opening it into a separate window, can you make changes to a piece of outgoing mail.

The Send tab also includes features for configuring replies. For example, you can disable the function that includes the original message in the reply.

Finally, the "Automatically put people I reply to in my address book after the third reply" option can be a real timesaver. It means that if somebody seems to have become a regular in your life, his email address is automatically saved in your Contacts list. The next time you want to write him a note, you won't need to look up the address—just type the first few letters of it in the "To:" box.

Tip: The option here called "Upload larger images to the Web when sending a photo e-mail" works if you have signed into Windows Live, as described at the beginning of this chapter. It means you don't have to worry about photo file sizes; your big mama files will be "hosted" on the Windows Live site (for 30 days). Your recipient gets a smaller version of the photos, which she can click to see or download the bigger ones.

Compose Tab

Here's where you specify the font you want to use when writing messages and news-group messages.

This is also the control center for *stationery* (custom-designed templates, complete with fonts, colors, backgrounds, borders, and other formatting elements that you can use for all outgoing email).

To choose a stationery style for all outgoing messages, turn on the Mail checkbox, and then click the Select button. You're offered a folder full of Microsoft stationery templates; click one to see its preview. You can also click the Create New button, which launches a wizard that walks you through the process of creating your own background design.

Tip: You don't have to use one particular stationery style for all outgoing messages. When composing a message, use the Stationery pop-up menu to view the list of stationery templates. In other words, you can choose one on a message-by-message basis.

Signatures Tab

Use this tab to design a *signature* for your messages (page 436). By clicking the New button and entering more signature material in the text box, you can create several *different* signatures: one for business messages, one for your buddies, and so on.

To insert a signature into an outgoing message, choose Insert→Signature, and then choose from the list that appears.

Spelling Tab

The Spelling tab offers configuration options for the Mail spell-checking feature. You can even force the spell checker to correct errors in the *original* message when you send a reply, although your correspondent may not appreciate it.

Tip: Mail's spelling checker is so smart, it's supposed to be able to recognize the language of the message and to use the appropriate spelling dictionary automatically.

Connection Tab

Here, you can tell Mail to hang up automatically after sending and receiving messages (and reconnect the next time you want to perform the same tasks). As noted in the dialog box, though, Mail otherwise uses the same Internet settings described in Chapter 9.

Advanced Tab

This tab is your housekeeping and settings center for Mail. You can configure what you want Mail to do with your contacts' vCards (virtual business cards), whether you want to compose your replies at the bottom of emails instead of at the top, and whether you want to mark message threads in newsgroups as "watched."

Don't miss the Maintenance button. It lets you clear out old deleted messages, clean up downloads, purge newsgroup messages, and so on.

Calendar

All Versions

Windows 7 doesn't come with a calendar program, not even the basic one that came with Windows Vista. But there is a simple calendar built into Windows Live Mail. Sometimes, its integration with Mail makes sense (like when potential appointments come to you via email), and sometimes not so much (like when you have to fire up Mail just to see what you're doing on Thursday night).

It's pretty basic—there's no to-do list, no alarms, no subscribing to Web calendars. On the other hand, all those features are available if you have a free Windows Live account—and the online Windows Live calendar *brings* those features to the simple one in Mail. Details to follow.

To open the calendar, click the Calendar button in the lower-left corner of the screen, or choose Go→Calendar, or press Shift+Ctrl+X.

Note: If you've upgraded to Windows 7 from Windows Vista, all your old Windows Calendar appointments are automatically imported into Mail's calendar. (It's a one-time import, though; if you add more appointments to the old Windows Calendar app, they don't make it into Mail's calendar.)

In many ways, this calendar is not so different from those "Hunks of the Midwestern Police Stations" paper calendars people leave hanging on the walls for months past their natural life spans. But this calendar offers several advantages over paper calendars. For example:

- It can automate the process of entering repeating events, such as weekly staff meetings or gym workout dates.

- The calendar can give you a gentle nudge (with a dialog box and a sound, if you like) when an important appointment is approaching.

- Your Mail calendar is synced with your Windows Live online calendar. Make a change on the Web calendar, you'll find it changed on your PC, and vice versa.

Tip: Truth be told, the online calendar has even more features than this one. For example, the Windows Live one has a to-do list, which the Mail calendar lacks.

- You can "subscribe" to calendars on the Internet, like the ones published by your family members/classmates/baseball team members/downtrodden employees. For example, you can subscribe to your spouse's Google calendar, thereby finding out if you've been committed to after-dinner drinks on the night the big game's on TV.

Working with Views

When you open Calendar, you see something like Figure 12-15. By clicking the buttons on the toolbar (or pressing Ctrl+Alt+1, 2, or 3), you can switch among any of these views:

- **Day** shows the appointments for a single day in the main calendar area, broken down by time slot.

Tip: Calendar provides a quick way to get to the current day's date: click "Go to today," a link just below the mini-month calendar at left.

- **Week** fills the main display area with seven columns, reflecting the current week.

- **Month** shows the entire current month. Double-click a date square or date number to create a new appointment.

Tip: Your mouse's scroll wheel can be a great advantage in this calendar. For example, when entering a date, turning the wheel lets you jump forward or backward in time. It also lets you change the time zone as you're setting it.

Making an Appointment

The basic calendar is easy to figure out. After all, with the exception of one unfortunate Gregorian incident, we've been using calendars successfully for centuries.

Even so, there are two ways to record a new appointment: a simple way and a more flexible, elaborate way.

The easy way

You can quickly record an appointment using any of several techniques:

- In any view, double-click a time slot on the calendar.

- In any view, right-click a date or a time slot, and then choose either "New event" or "New all day event" from the shortcut menu.

- Click New on the toolbar.

- Press Ctrl+Shift+E (for *event*).

Figure 12-15:
Top: Week view. The miniature navigation calendar provides an overview of adjacent months. You can jump to a different week or day by clicking the triangle buttons and then clicking within the numbers. If the event is recurring, it bears an icon that looks like two curly arrows chasing each other.

Bottom: Month view. Pretty lame—you don't see what time any appointment is for—but it's something. You can make more room by hiding the Navigation and/or Details panes.

Tip: In Day or Week view, drag vertically through the time slots for the appointment you're trying to create (10 a.m. down to 12:30 p.m., for example) before taking one of the steps above. That way, you've already specified the start and end times, saving yourself a lot of tedious typing.

In each case, the New Event dialog box appears, where you type the details for your new appointment. (In Month view, you can drag the entire appointment to a new date.)

The long way

The Details pane shown in Figure 12-16 contains all the information about a certain appointment. Here, you can create far more specific appointments, decked out with far more bells and whistles.

Figure 12-16:
You can open this info pane by double-clicking any appointment on your calendar. It's also the window that appears when you create an appointment.

For each appointment, you can tab your way to the following information areas:

- **Subject.** That's name of your appointment. For example, you might type, *Fly to Phoenix.*

- **Location.** This field makes a lot of sense; if you think about it, almost everyone needs to record *where* a meeting is to take place. You might type a reminder for yourself like *My place,* a specific address like *212 East 23rd,* or some other helpful information like a contact phone number or flight number.

- **Start, End.** Most appointments have the same Start and End dates, thank heaven (although we've all been in meetings that don't seem that way). But you can click the little calendar buttons to change the dates.

Tip: If you specify a different ending date, you get a *banner* across the relevant dates in the Month view.

Then set the start and end time for this appointment, either by using the pop-up menu or by editing the text (like "9:30 a.m.") with your mouse and keyboard.

- **All day.** An "all-day" event, of course, is something with no specific time of day associated with it: a holiday, a birthday, a book deadline. When you turn on this box, the name of the appointment jumps to the top of the daily- or weekly-view screen, in the area reserved for this kind of thing.

- **My Calendar.** A *calendar,* in Microsoft's confusing terminology, is a subset—a category—into which you can place various appointments. You can create one for yourself, another for whole-family events, another for book-club appointments, and so on. Later, you'll be able to hide and show these categories at will, adding or removing them from the calendar with a single click. For details, read on.

Tip: Use this same pop-up menu to *change* an appointment's category. If you filed something in Company Memos that should have been in Sweet Nothings for Honey-Poo, open the event's dialog box and reassign it. Quick.

- **No recurrence.** The pop-up menu here contains common options for repeating events: "Daily," "Weekly," and so on. It starts out saying "No recurrence."

The somewhat goofy part is that if you choose any of those convenient commands in the pop-up menu, the calendar assumes that you want to repeat this event every day/week/month/year *forever.* You don't get any way to specify an end date. You'll be stuck seeing this event repeating on your calendar until the end of time. That may be a good choice for recording your anniversary, especially if your spouse might be consulting the same calendar. But it's not a feature for people who are afraid of long-term commitments.

If you want the freedom to *stop* your weekly gym workouts or monthly car payments, choose Custom from the pop-up menu instead.

The dialog box that appears offers far more control over how this event repeats itself. You can make the repeating stop after a certain number of times, which is a useful option for car and mortgage payments. And if you choose "After," you can specify the date (or the number of times) after which the repetitions come to an end; use this option to indicate the last day of school, for example.

Tip: This dialog box also lets you specify days of the week. For example, you can schedule your morning runs for Monday, Thursday, and Saturday mornings.

- **Busy.** This pop-up menu lets you block off time during which you're unavailable (or tentatively available). The point here is for coworkers who might be looking over your calendar online to know when you're *not* available for meetings.

- **Reminder.** This pop-up menu tells the calendar that you want to be notified when a certain appointment is about to begin. Unfortunately, this feature isn't built into the Mail calendar—it's actually a function of the Windows Live Web service.

  If you're cool with that, then the news is good: Windows Live can remind you of an event by email, as a notice in the Windows Live Messenger chat program, or even with a text message to your cellphone.

Note: To set these reminders up, choose Tools→"Deliver my reminders to." Your Web browser opens up to the Windows Live page where you change your mail, chat, and cellphone options for getting reminders.

  Use the pop-up menu to specify how much advance notice you want. If it's a TV show you like to watch, you might set up a reminder only five minutes before airtime. If it's a birthday, you might set up a two-day warning to give yourself enough time to buy a present, and so on.

- **Notes.** Here's your chance to customize your calendar event. In the big, empty part of the window, you can type, paste, or drag any text you like in the notes area— driving directions, contact phone numbers, a call history, or whatever.

When you're finished entering all the details, click "Save & close" (or press Ctrl+S). Your newly scheduled event now shows up on the calendar, complete with the color coding that corresponds to the calendar category you've assigned.

What to Do with an Appointment

Once you've entrusted your agenda to Calendar, you can start putting it to work. Here are a few of the possibilities:

Editing events

To edit a calendar event's name or details, double-click it. You don't have to bother with this if all you want to do is *reschedule* an event, however, as described next.

Rescheduling events

If an event in your life gets rescheduled, you can move an appointment just by dragging the rectangle that represents it. In Day or Week view, drag the event vertically in its column to change its time on the same day; in Week or Month view, you can drag it to another date.

Note: You can't reschedule the *first* occurrence of a recurring event by dragging it—you have to edit the date in the Details pane. You can drag subsequent occurrences, though.

If something is postponed for, say, a month or two, it's more of a hassle; you can't drag an appointment beyond its month window. You have no choice but to open the Details pane and edit the starting and ending dates or times—or just cut and paste the event to a different date.

Lengthening or shortening events

If a scheduled meeting becomes shorter or your lunch hour becomes a lunch hour-and-a-half (in your dreams), changing the length of a selected calendar event is as easy as dragging the top or bottom border of its block in Day or Week view (see Figure 12-17).

Tip: In Week view, if you've grabbed the top or bottom edge of an appointment's block so that the cursor changes, you can drag *horizontally* to make an appointment cross the midnight line and extend into a second day.

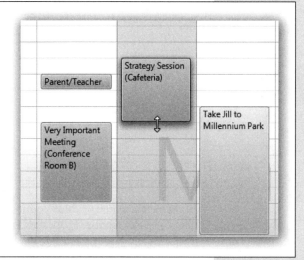

Figure 12-17:
You can resize any calendar event just by dragging its border. As your cursor touches the bottom edge of a calendar event, it turns into a double-headed arrow. You can now drag the event's edge to make it take up more or less time on your calendar.

Printing events

To commit your calendar to paper, choose File→Print, or press Ctrl+P. The resulting Print dialog box lets you specify a range of dates and which view you want (Week, Month, or whatever).

Deleting events

To delete an appointment, just click its box and then press the Delete key. If you delete a recurring event (like a weekly meeting), the calendar asks whether you want to delete only that particular instance of the event or the entire series.

The "Calendar" Category Concept

Everyone in your house (or office) can have a different set of appointments on the same calendar, color-coded so you all can tell your schedules apart. The red appointments might be yours; the blue ones, your spouse's; the green ones might be your kid's. You can overlay all of them simultaneously to look for conflicts (or mutually available meeting times), if you like.

Each such set of appointments is called, confusingly enough, a *calendar* (Figure 12-18).

To create a calendar, click "Add calendar" (in the left-side panel), or press Shift+Ctrl+D. Type a name that defines the category in your mind, and choose the color you want for its appointments.

Tip: Whenever you're about to create an appointment, click a calendar name *first.* That way, the appointment will already belong to the correct calendar.

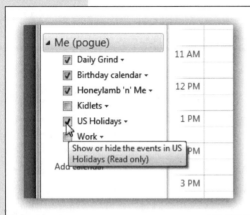

Figure 12-18:
You might create calendars (color-coded categories) called Home, Work, and TV Reminders. A small business could have categories called Deductible Travel, R&D, and R&R. Hide or show a category using the checkboxes here.

To change the name or color-coding of an existing category, click its name; from the shortcut menu, choose Properties to reopen the dialog box.

You assign an appointment to one of these categories using the pop-up menu on its Details pane. After that, you can hide or show an entire category of appointments at once just by turning on or off the appropriate checkbox in the list of calendars.

Syncing Calendars with Windows Live

If you've signed into your Windows Live account (use the Sign In button in the upper-right corner of Mail, for example), a great feature awaits: Your Mail calendar and your Windows Live calendar on the Web are automatically brought up to date with each other. In other words, you can check your schedule from any PC in the world over the Internet.

You don't have to do anything to make this happen; it's automatic.

Publishing Calendars

One of Windows Live Calendar's best features is its ability to post your calendar on the Web so that other people—or you, using a different computer—can subscribe to it, which adds *your* appointments to *their* calendars. For example, you might use this feature to post the meeting schedule for a club you manage, or to share the agenda for a series of upcoming financial meetings that all your coworkers will need to consult.

Note: This isn't the same thing as the Windows Live syncing described above. Publishing a calendar lets you control which appointments people see, which people see them, and what permission they have to make changes to it.

And you're not the only one who can publish a calendar. The Web is full of such schedules published by *other* people, ready for adding to your *own* calendar: team schedules, company meetings, national holidays, and so on.

Unfortunately, the calendar in *Mail* can't do any of this publishing; only the Web-based copy of it at the Windows Live Web site can. Fortunately, your Mail calendar is a mirror of what's online, so the difference may not be so huge. For details, see page 453.

RSS Feeds

RSS feeds are like free headline services, reporting what's new on different Web sites (news, sports, tech, whatever). There's a great description of them on page 239.

Microsoft must think a lot of RSS feeds, because Windows 7 is *crawling* with different ways to read them. There's a gadget that can show them; Internet Explorer can show them; and Windows Live Mail can show them.

Tip: In fact, if you subscribe to feeds in Internet Explorer, they show up in Mail, and vice versa.

Start by clicking the ▧ Feeds button (lower left of the Mail window), or pressing Shift+Ctrl+K. The main window is empty, but the Navigation pane displays a bunch of harmless starter feeds from Microsoft and the government. Keep expanding the flippy triangles until you see the list of individual headlines in the center column, where email messages would normally appear. Click one to read, in the Preview pane, the summary that it represents.

You can work with feeds exactly the way you work with email: forward them, file them in folders, print them, and so on.

If you're an RSS fan, then you're an executive-summary kind of person—and so here's the executive summary:

- **To add a new feed**, click "Add feed"; in the resulting box, paste or type in the URL (the Web address) of that feed. Click OK.

- **To change the frequency of a feed (and how many headlines to keep)**, click "Manage feeds" on the toolbar. In the Manage Your Feeds dialog box, expand the flippy triangles until you can see the feed in question. Click its name, and then click Edit Feed.

- **To remove a feed,** click its name and then click Delete on the toolbar (and confirm the deletion).

Newsgroups
All Versions

Newsgroups have nothing to do with news; in fact, they're Internet bulletin boards. There are hundreds of thousands of them, on every conceivable topic: pop culture, computers, politics, and every other special (and *very* special) interest; in fact, there are thousands just about Windows. You can use Mail to read and reply to these messages almost exactly as though they were email messages.

Subscribing to a Microsoft Newsgroup

Subscribing to your first newsgroup can be quite an experience, simply because there are just so many newsgroups to choose from.

To get started with newsgroups, click the Newsgroups button (lower left of the Mail window), or press Shift+Ctrl+L. At the outset, the top of the window says, "Would you like to view a list of available newsgroups now?"

Yes, you would. Click View Newsgroups. Mail downloads a list of the available newsgroups, which may take awhile.

Scroll through the list, or use the Search box, to pluck out something that looks good. If you're interested in learning more about the Mail program, for example, you could click *Microsoft.public.windows.live.mail.desktop.*

Tip: You can select more than one newsgroup by Ctrl+clicking their names.

Then click Subscribe. The newsgroup(s) you subscribed to are now available in Mail, under Microsoft Communities. Each discussion sits in its own folder, with its own flippy triangle.

Other Newsgroups

Hard though it may be to believe, there are other subjects worth newsgrouping about than just Microsoft's. Fortunately, Mail lets you see them, too.

UP TO SPEED

Newsgroups Explained

Newsgroups (often called *Usenet*) started out as a way for people to conduct discussions via a bulletin board–like system, in which a message is posted for all to see and reply to. These public discussions are divided into categories called newsgroups, which cover the gamut from photographic techniques to naval aviation.

These days, Usenet has a certain seedy reputation as a place to exchange pornography, pirated software, and MP3 files with doubtful copyright pedigrees. Even so, there are tens of thousands of interesting, informative discussions going on, and newsgroups are great places to get help with troubleshooting, to exchange recipes, or just to see what's on the minds of your fellow Usenet fans.

To have at it, click "Add newsgroup account" in the left-side panel. A wizard walks you through adding your name (as you'll be represented in these discussions); your email address (*do not use your main one* unless you want an ocean of spam!); and your news server address.

Right: Your *what?*

A news server is a central computer that lists and manages the thousands of newsgroups. Your Internet service provider has one—call to find out what its address is—or you can type in a free one like *www.eternal-september.org*. (You have to go to that Web site and sign up for a free account first.)

When you finally click Finish, Mail asks if you'd like to view a list of the available newsgroups, and if so, whether or not they work with Microsoft's Communities features (which include message ratings and rankings). May as well let Mail try. Then click OK.

When you're finished with the wizard, Mail downloads a list of newsgroups available on your server. Wait patiently; the list can be quite long—tens of thousands of entries. Fortunately, it's a one-time deal.

Now you're ready to find yourself some good online discussions; see Figure 12-19.

Figure 12-19:
In the box at the top, type the term you're hoping to find in a newsgroup's title (such as kittensandcats—*in cyberspace, nobody can hear you use the space bar). If you turn up a good-sounding topic in the gigantic list beneath, click its name and click Subscribe to subscribe to it. Now, each time you connect, Mail will download the latest messages on that topic.*

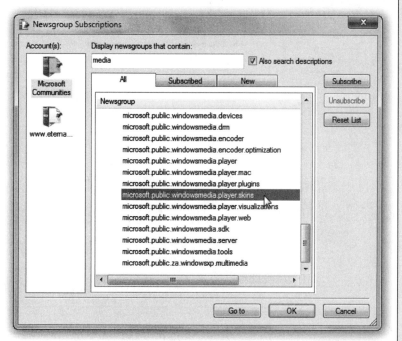

Reading Messages

Once you've subscribed to a newsgroup, Mail downloads all the message summaries in the discussions to which you've subscribed. (There may be just a few messages, or several hundred; they may go back only a few days or a couple of weeks, depending on the amount of "traffic" in each discussion and the storage space on the news server.)

To read the messages in a newsgroup, either click an entry in the list of messages to display it in the Preview window (Figure 12-20), or double-click an entry to open the list of messages in a new window.

Tip: You can set up message rules for newsgroups to screen out messages from certain people, messages with certain phrases in their Subject lines, and so on. It works exactly like the message rules for email, as described earlier in this chapter. Just go to Tools→Message Rules→News.

Figure 12-20:
If you've been using Mail for email, the newsgroup interface should look familiar. The Folders pane lists news servers to which you've subscribed, the top-right pane lists the names of messages in a selected newsgroup, and the bottom-right pane displays the actual text of the message you've highlighted in the message list.

Replying, Composing, and Forwarding Messages

Working with newsgroup messages is very similar to working with email messages, except that you must be conscious of whether you're replying to the individual sender of a message or to the entire group. Otherwise, you can reply to messages, forward them, or compose them exactly as described earlier in this chapter. You can include file attachments, too, by using the Attach toolbar button, for example.

Tip: Aside from posting ads and HTML-formatted messages, the best way to irritate everyone on a newsgroup is to ask a question that has already been answered recently on the newsgroup. Before asking a question, spend 5 minutes reading the recent newsgroup messages to see whether someone has already answered your question. Also consider visiting the Groups tab at *www.google.com,* a Web site that lets you search all newsgroups for particular topics.

Windows Live Services

This much we know about Windows Live: It's free. It's on the Web. And not one average person out of a thousand can tell you exactly what it is. (Maybe that's because Microsoft keeps *changing* what it is, year by year. And slapping the "Live" name on other features, like XBox Live and Office Live, that have nothing to do with Windows Live.)

For the moment, Windows Live is a suite of Internet features that connect to your PC's copy of Windows in various useful ways. For example:

- **Windows Live Calendar.** A Web-based calendar and to-do list that syncs with the calendar in Mail on your PC.

- **Windows Live Events.** An online invitation service; adds events to your Windows Live Calendar automatically.

- **Windows Live Groups.** Discussion pages. Great for organizing team, club, or family events.

- **Windows Live Hotmail.** A free email account.

- **Windows Live People.** An online master address book, incorporating both your Mail and Messenger chat addresses. Can even import Facebook contacts.

- **Windows Live Photos.** A Web site of your very own to show off your pictures. Syncs with Windows Live Photo Gallery on your PC (Chapter 14).

- **Windows Live SkyDrive.** A free, 25-gigabyte virtual hard drive on the Internet, accessible from any computer.

- **Windows Live Spaces.** Blogging and "make your own Web page" site. You can use Windows Live Writer (Chapter 7) to post to it.

Note: Many of these services have special cellphone versions, too.

Two things make the Windows Live concept very confusing. First, the whole thing is in a constant state of flux; Microsoft routinely adds new services and kills off old ones. What you read in this chapter may be different by the end of the year, or even by the end of this paragraph.

Second, Microsoft also applies the term "Windows Live" to all kinds of things, some of which aren't on the Web at all. For example, "Windows Live" also refers to a bunch of free *programs* that you're supposed to download and install (Windows Live Writer, Windows Live Photo Gallery, Windows Live Mail, Windows Live Family Safety, and so on; see Chapters 7, 10, 12, and 14).

Nonetheless, there are some gems among the masses of online software; here's a guide to some of the best.

Note: Before you can use any of this stuff, you have to sign up for a free Windows Live ID (account). If you already have a Hotmail, Xbox, or Messenger ID, then you're in good shape—that is your Windows Live ID. Otherwise, go to *http://home.live.com* and register.

You can either supply your existing email address when asked, or you can sign up for one that ends with @live.com, meaning that you gain a free Hotmail email account in the process.

Home

This screen, at *home.live.com,* is a sort of dashboard for the whole Live archipelago. It shows your most recent incoming email messages, updates from your contacts, the current weather, news headlines, and a lot of ads for Windows Live features. It also has links to all the other Live services, including the calendar.

Profile

The Profile page (on the Home screen, click Profile) is Microsoft's small attempt to be Facebook. Here, you list information about yourself that you want other people to see: profession, favorite music, interests, and so on. Other people can leave public messages here, too, just the way people can write messages on your Facebook "wall."

Tip: If you click "Add" under "Web activities," you can direct Live to fill your Profile page with your Twitter, Facebook, MySpace, or Flickr updates. That way, you don't have to update your status, or post your daily thoughts, in more than one place.

Spaces

Spaces is a build-your-own blog-page feature. You can use it as a blog, a photo gallery, a news page, whatever you want (Figure 13-1).

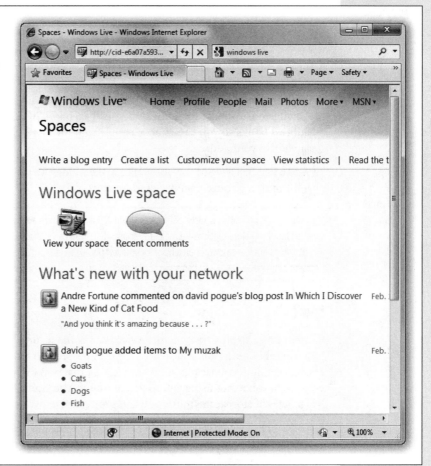

Figure 13-1:
As you create your blog, each new entry pushes the older ones down the page.

Of course, it's not *quite* the same as having a real Web page; Microsoft puts ads on it, for example. And some of it feels a little crude and unfinished.

Still, it's free and easy. Click "Create your space" to get started. At the top of the page, there are icons representing your Web-building tools:

- **Web address.** You don't really want your Web page to reside at *http://cid-4bf-489cb9cf10cee.home.spaces.live.com*, do you? Fortunately, if you click this button, you get to choose a much simpler Web address, in the form of *http://yourname.spaces.live.com*.

- **Share photos.** You're walked through the process of adding photos from your hard drive and building an album (and controlling who sees it—everyone, or just a few people from your address book).

- **Add blog entry.** Sometimes, a thousand pictures are worth a word or two. Click here to write up your thoughts.

Tip: It's a lot easier to do this using the free Windows Live Writer program, described on page 301. If you do your writing on the Web page instead, you're expected to know HTML formatting codes like </b> for bold, instead of just clicking the Bold button.

- **Invite your friends.** Your blog isn't very useful if nobody knows it exists. Click "Invite your friends" to connect to your Facebook, AOL, LinkedIn, or MySpace address books so you can choose people to notify. Or just email people who are already in your address book.

- **Add a list.** Just a weird way for you to make a blog entry consisting of nothing but a list of things: music, books, random stuff.

Tip: You can also email blog posts to the Live Web site; it will post them automatically for you. To set this up, choose Options→More Options→Email Publishing. Here, you can specify which email addresses Live will accept entries from; a password; an album for emailed photos to go into; and if you want emailed entries to be posted immediately (rather than saved as Drafts for you to review when you get home).

Mail

Hotmail, Microsoft's free email service, has come a long way since its days as a junkyard of blinking ads and spam overruns. It's great to have as a second (or third) email account—as a backup, for example, one that's on the Web so you can get to it even when you're not using your own computer. Microsoft doesn't even limit you to 5 gigabytes of storage anymore; you can pretty much save as much email as you get.

It works pretty much like any other email program, including Windows Live Mail (Chapter 12); it's just not quite as fast, slick, or pretty. For example, clicking a message opens it to fill the screen, so you no longer see the list of messages.

Hotmail can consolidate multiple *other* email accounts—Gmail, Yahoo, AOL, and so on—which can be mighty handy. At the same time, you can check your Hotmail account using regular desktop email programs like Windows Live Mail and Microsoft Outlook.

The one downside, of course, is the huge advertisement on the right side of the screen. Then again, that's what's paying for your free account.

Photos

Photos (Figure 13-2) is an online photo gallery—Microsoft's version of Flickr. Getting your pictures online is as easy as 1-2:

1. Click "Create album."

   You're asked to type a name for it and then to specify who can see this album: everyone on the Internet, only people in your address book ("My network"), or only you. Make your choice from the pop-up menu and then click Next.

2. Add photos.

   On the next screen, you get five Choose File buttons. Each one lets you browse your hard drive for a photo to upload. Once you've manually selected them, click Upload. It's a slow, manual, tedious way to get photos online. So if you value your sanity, use the Windows Live Photo Gallery program to upload your photos instead (Chapter 14).

   Or, if you don't use Photo Gallery, take advantage of the yellow message bar right before you that says, "Install the upload tool now!" Figure 13-2 shows you why.

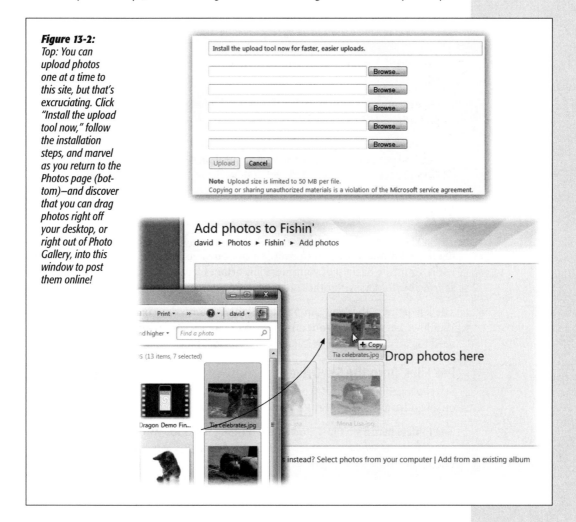

Figure 13-2:
Top: You can upload photos one at a time to this site, but that's excruciating. Click "Install the upload tool now," follow the installation steps, and marvel as you return to the Photos page (bottom)—and discover that you can drag photos right off your desktop, or right out of Photo Gallery, into this window to post them online!

Tip: You can also email photos; they'll get posted automatically, if you like. To set this up, choose Options→ More Options→Email Publishing.

Once you've got some albums on your Photos page, people can view and interact with them like this:

- **Open an album, then a photo.** When you're viewing a photo, you see its size, camera details, and other information on the right side.

- **Tag people in a photo.** Once you've opened a picture, the "Tag someone" link at the top lets you type in the names of anyone you recognize in the picture (or "That's me!" if it's you). That way, visitors know who's in the picture.

Tip: If you don't trust the vast unwashed masses to tag your photos responsibly, you can block tagging. Click the Options button (upper right) and then choose "People tagging." You can specify that only you can tag photos on your site—and also, intriguingly, you can stop other people from tagging you in their photos (which would make those photos show up on your profile page).

- **Download.** Yep, your loved ones can download your pictures to have and to hold when they're offline.

- **Comment.** Your admirers can type into the Comments box to remark on your pictures.

- **View a slideshow.** Click an album to open it, and then click the "Slide show" button. You get a full-screen, black-background presentation of the photos, complete with playback controls and thumbnails at the right side so you can jump around.

SkyDrive

The SkyDrive is an Internet-based hard drive that makes a perfect intermediate parking place for files you want to shuttle from one computer to another. You can also use it for offsite backup of your most important files, or as a handy intermediary for sharing big folders with other people far away.

The key point is that you can pull the SkyDrive onto *any* computer's screen—Mac, Windows, whatever—at your office, at your home, at your friend's house, so you don't need to carry around a physical disk to transport files.

Put Files Onto the SkyDrive

Start by logging into *http://skydrive.live.com,* or choose More→SkyDrive when you're on any other part of the Live Web site (Figure 13-3).

The folders here aren't just convenient holding tanks for your files; they're also how you determine *who can see what's in them.* Microsoft starts you off with folders like Public (everyone in the world can see the contents); Documents; Favorites (only you can see them); and "Shared favorites" (only people in your address book can see them).

Tip: You can change these "who can see them" settings easily enough. Open the folder, and then click More→"Edit permissions." (You can't change the settings for Public or Documents, however.)

You can create your own folders, too: Click "Create folder." (You can even create folders within folders.) You're asked to name the new folder, but also to specify who has access to it. Your choices:

- **Everyone (public).** The whole Internet can see the files you post here.

- **My network.** Only people in your Live address book can see the files.

- **Just me.** For personal use only.

- **Select people.** You're offered a chance to specify individual names (from your address book) or email addresses. This is a great way to share files only with specific coworkers—especially files that are too big to send by email.

Tip: If you do a lot of this, you might want to visit your Profile page to create some categories of people (that is, predefined groups), like Office, Family, Kids, or Bert & Steve. That way, if you tend to share stuff with the same cluster of people, you'll save a lot of time.

Figure 13-3:
SkyDrive in all its glory. Microsoft starts you off with several folders; you'll notice right away, for example, that any photo albums you've created appear as folders here. Yes, the SkyDrive is where your uploaded photos sit, behind the scenes.

When you click Next, you're shown the "Add files" screen, where five Choose File buttons await—or a "Drop files here" notation, if you've added the Upload tool (Figure 13-2). (You can also get here by clicking "Add files" on the main SkyDrive page.)

Each time you click a Choose File button, you can browse your hard drive to find a file to transfer to that SkyDrive folder. (Max file size: 50 megabytes.) Click Upload once you've loaded them up.

Tip: Frankly, this is a slow, limited, horrible way to interact with your SkyDrive. What you really want is to have your SkyDrive show up on your Windows desktop, just like a real hard drive, so you can simply drag files in and out of its folders.

Fortunately, that's exactly what the free SDExplorer program does. If you intend to use the SkyDrive, you really, really need this app. You can download it from this book's "Missing CD" page at *www.missingmanuals.com*.

(There, you'll also find a free Microsoft app called Windows Live Upload Tool. It lets you drag and drop files, too, but only from within Internet Explorer.)

Windows Live Sync—and Mesh

If you think the SkyDrive is cool, wait till you see Live Sync.

SkyDrive is great for transferring stuff between computers, but what if you didn't have to do that manually? What if your computers kept your important folders synced between your work and home machines (or upstairs and downstairs machines) *automatically*? Even if one of them's a Mac?

That's the magic of Windows Live Sync.

Suppose, for example, that you have a PC at work and a Mac at home. Go to *https://sync.live.com/clientdownload. aspx* on each machine. Download and install the little Live Sync app. It puts a tiny Sync icon on your menu bar (Mac) or system tray (PC).

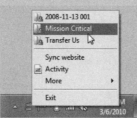

To set things up, sit at the PC and go to *http://live.sync. com*. Sign in. Click "Create a personal folder." Navigate to the PC folder that you want to sync; select it by opening it, right there on the Sync Web page, and then clicking "Sync folder here." (You can also create a new folder at this point.)

You're shown a list of the computers on which you've installed the Sync program (and that are turned on and online).

Click the one you want this folder to sync with, and then, on the "Select a folder" screen, specify which folder on the *Mac* you want synced with the PC folder you chose. Finally, choose either Automatic or On-demand synchronization, and click Finish.

And that is all. When you add, change, or delete anything in a synced folder on one machine, it's automatically updated on the other, over the Internet. It's totally great for keeping the latest versions of everything accessible at all times.

The fine print: You can synchronize up to 20 folders, each containing up to 20,000 files, max. Files can't be larger than 4 gigabytes. Files can be synced with Windows XP, Windows Vista, Windows 7, and Macs.

Windows Llive *Mesh* is the same idea but even more powerful and complicated. It creates a Web-based "desktop" with 5 gigabytes of storage—and your Macs, PCs, smartphones, and even authorized friends can sync up to it. Details are at *www.mesh.com*.

Happy syncing!

Retrieving the Files

Once you've got some files and folders on your SkyDrive, the fun begins.

You can retrieve the files yourself, from any Internet-connected computer. Just log into Windows Live, click SkyDrive, open the folder, click the file, and then click Download.

The 50-Megabyte Email Attachment

People use the SkyDrive for all kinds of things: as backup, as a bucket to carry files between computers far away, and so on. But here's one of the coolest features of all: You use your SkyDrive to "send" huge files to anyone.

Ordinarily, you can't attach anything bigger than 5 or 10 megabytes to an email message. But SkyDrive files can be much bigger—50 megs each. They're not really attached to the email at all; you're simply sending your colleague a *link* to download something from a SkyDrive folder.

To use this feature, open the SkyDrive folder that contains what you want to give your pals—it has to be a folder you've actually made public, or at least available to your lucky recipient—and then proceed as shown in Figure 13-4.

Figure 13-4:
Top: Click "Send a link" once you've opened the folder you want to share.

Bottom: Then click the To button to choose recipients, or categories of them, from your address book. Add a message, if you like. Be sure to turn on "Don't require recipients to sign in with Windows Live ID," unless you want to fill their lives with red tape. Click Send.

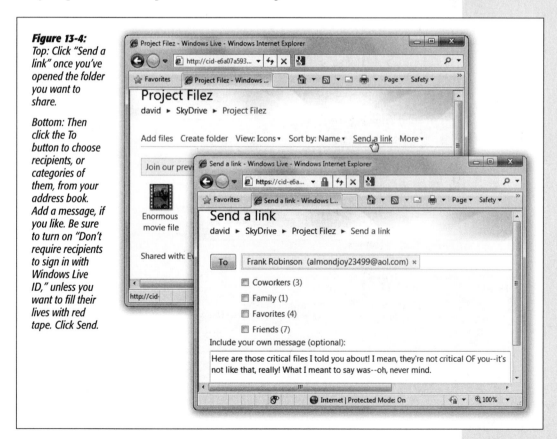

Once your colleagues receive your email, they have but to click the link in the message to visit your folder and download the huge file immediately.

Calendar

Odd as it may seem, the online Windows Live Calendar is actually a *superset* of the calendar built into the Mail program described in Chapter 12. That is, it has *more features,* including a to-do list, an Agenda (list) view, and the ability to publish and subscribe to calendar categories.

Fortunately, since it syncs with the calendar on your own PC, it doesn't much matter.

To learn the basics of the Windows Live Calendar, including how to operate the views and how to add appointments to it, see Chapter 12. (You'll notice only a few differences: For example, to see the *entire* list of options for a new appointment you're creating, like auto-repeating and alarms, click "Add more details.")

Here, though, is a tour of two of the most powerful additional features: publishing and subscribing to Internet calendars.

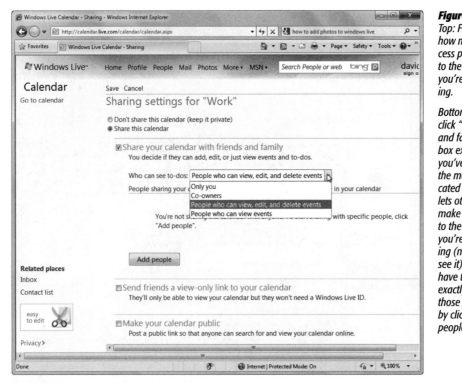

Figure 13-5:
Top: First, decide how much access people have to the calendar you're publishing.

Bottom: If you click "Friends and family," the box expands— you've selected the most complicated option. It lets other people make changes to the calendar you're publishing (not just see it), but you have to specify exactly who gets those privileges by clicking "Add people."

Publishing a Calendar

Once you've painstakingly entered a bunch of appointments onto your calendar, it can make life a lot easier if you can share it with other people over the Internet. Enter a sports team or company agenda, travel arrangements for your whole family, birthdays for your entire family tree, whatever—and let the interested parties import them onto their *own* calendars.

Begin by choosing Share→Company Schedule (or whatever the name of the calendar category is). On the next screen, click "Share this calendar" (Figure 13-5).

Now you have to decide *how* you want this calendar shared:

- **With friends and family.** Since this is a small, trusted group (right?), they'll be allowed to see *and edit* your calendar. Click "Add people." In the resulting dialog box, you can choose names from your address book or even type in email addresses of people who aren't in it.

Note: These people must be Windows Live members, and they'll have to sign in to see your calendar.

At the bottom of the dialog box is a powerful but confusing pop-up menu. It lets you specify *how much* control these people have over your published calendar. "Co-owner" means they have as much power as you do—they can *add* appointments, and they can also change the permissions settings that you're making right now. (They can't delete a calendar category or change *your* permissions.)

The remaining options represent decreasing amounts of freedom.

"View, edit, and delete items" gives people the ability to edit the appointments already on the calendar; "View details" means they can only *see* what's on the calendar. The two remaining "View" options let people see fewer and fewer details about each appointment.

Tip: You'll be able to change these settings for each person individually after you click Add and return to the sharing screen.

Finally, click Add to return to the main Sharing screen. When you click Save, and then OK, your PC fires off emails to the people in question, notifying them that your calendar is now available and providing a link for them to see it.

- **Send friends a view-only link to your calendar.** This time, the recipients don't have to be Windows Live members. On the other hand, they won't be able to make any changes—they can only *see* your calendar.

Note: When you click this "Send friend" option, or the next one ("Make your calendar public"), you have to click "Get your calendar links" (and confirm that you want to publish the calendar) before you can make any further decisions.

Whether they get to see only when you're busy, or the full details of every appointment, depends on which of the two link types you click. For each one, you can send your friends (a) a link to a Web-based version of the calendar (HTML), (b) a link that lets another calendar program on Mac or Windows import these appointments (ICS), or (c) a link that puts your appointments into an RSS feed, for viewing in a program like Internet Explorer or Mail (RSS).

Incidentally, this option doesn't actually *send* your friends anything. When you click one of these links, you just get a dialog box displaying an endless Web address. It's up to you to copy it and paste it into an email that you send around.

- **Make your calendar public.** Here's how you make your calendar visible to everyone on the Web, no muss, no fuss. Use the Permission pop-up menu to specify how much detail people see, and then click the appropriate link.

This option, too, just displays a long URL that you're supposed to copy and distribute or post online.

Subscribing

You're not the only one who can publish your calendar. The Web is full of such schedules published by *other* people, ready for adding to your *own* calendar: team schedules, company meetings, national holidays, sports teams, movies, and so on.

Tip: Lots of these public calendars await at *www.icalshare.com* and *www.calendardata.com*.

All you have to do is figure out the Web addresses of these feeds. They usually end with *.ics*.

To add one to your own Live Calendar, click "Subscribe." Now you have two options:

- **Subscribe to a public calendar.** Paste the address into the Calendar URL box. Type the name you want for this calendar, and a color for its appointments; it will show up as its own, noneditable category on your calendar. Click "Subscribe to calendar."

- **Import from an ICS file.** Sometimes people send you a calendar feed's address as a *file*—by email, for example. If you have one of these ICS files, click this option, and then click Choose File to browse your hard drive and open the thing. Specify if you want these appointments added to an existing category or if you want to create a new one (and what name and color you want, in that case). Finally, click "Import calendar."

When it's all over, you see a new "calendar" category in your left-side list, representing the published appointments. Whenever the publisher of the calendar makes changes to it, you'll see the appointments magically change on your own calendar.

Part Four: Pictures, Music, & TV

4

Windows Live Photo Gallery

Y our digital camera is brimming with photos. You've snapped the perfect gradu-
ation portrait, captured that jaw-dropping sunset over the Pacific, or compiled
an unforgettable photo essay of your 2-year-old attempting to eat a bowl of
spaghetti. It's time to use your PC to gather, organize, and tweak all these photos so
you can share them with the rest of the world.

Until recently, all Windows offered for digital photos was Paint. That's right, Paint—a
feeble holdover from 1985 that sat in your Programs→Accessories folder and opened
one picture at a time. Barely.

Microsoft has addressed photo organizing/editing with a vengeance. Pathetic little
Paint is still there, for the benefit of change-phobic Windows veterans. But now there's
also Windows Live Photo Gallery, a beautiful, full-blown digital camera companion
that has nothing to be ashamed of. The current version has been smartly enhanced—
among other things, it can now display video clips from your camera as well as stills.

It's not built into Windows 7 the day you get it. You have to download it as part of
the Windows Live Essentials software suite described on page 265. But once you have
it, you'll realize that it's an important part of Windows. And beyond—it syncs with
your free Windows Live account, so you can post your photos to free online slideshow
galleries with a single click.

Tip: Then again, you may prefer Google's Picasa—a free photo-editing program that you could argue is faster,
easier, and more powerful. It, too, connects to a beautiful online photo gallery. Just sayin'.

Photo Gallery: The Application

All Versions

Photo Gallery approaches digital photo management as a four-step process: importing the photos to your Pictures folder; organizing, tagging, and rating them; editing them; and sharing them (via prints, onscreen slideshows, design DVD slideshows, email, your screen saver, and so on).

To open Windows Live Photo Gallery, choose its name from the Start→Programs menu, or double-click a photo in your Pictures folder.

The first time you open it, you're subjected to a battery of interview questions:

- **Sign in with your Windows Live name and password.** (Why? So Photo Gallery will be able to post your photos online when you're ready for that.)

- **Do you want Photo Gallery to open when you double-click common photo types (like JPEG, PNG, and TIFF)?** Probably. Otherwise, they'll continue to open in Windows Photo Viewer, which does nothing but *show* photos—it doesn't let you organize or edit them.

- **Some photos can't be displayed.** If you have any video clips that are in a format Photo Gallery doesn't understand—specifically, Apple's QuickTime format—this dialog box appears to let you know. Click Download to go get the necessary adapter software that lets Photo Gallery recognize those file types.

Figure 14-1:
Here's what Photo Gallery looks like once you've added a few photos. The viewing area is where thumbnails of your photos appear. The buttons at top represent all the stuff you can do with them. To adjust their size, drag the lower-right slider. All the thumbnails expand or contract simultaneously. Cool!

Once you do that, you finally arrive at the program's main window, the basic elements of which are shown in Figure 14-1.

Getting Pictures into Photo Gallery
All Versions

The very first time you open it, Photo Gallery displays all the digital photos it can find in your Pictures and Videos folders (Start→Pictures and Start→Videos).

This is important: You're looking at the *actual files* on your hard drive. If you delete a picture or a movie from Photo Gallery, you've just deleted it from your PC. (Well, OK, you've actually moved it to your Recycle Bin. But still, that's a step closer to oblivion.)

If you store your photos in other folders, you can make Photo Gallery aware of those, too. You can go about this task in either of two ways:

- **The menu way.** Choose File→"Include a folder in the gallery"; navigate to and select the additional folder, and then click OK.

- **The draggy way.** Find the folder on your desktop or in any Explorer folder. Drag the folder directly onto the heading "All photos and videos" in the left-side list, or directly into Photo Gallery's window (see Figure 14-2). Windows not only makes the contents appear in Photo Gallery, but also copies them to your Pictures folder for safekeeping.

Note: If you don't have a photo-management program like Photo Gallery or Picasa, Windows 7 can still import pictures. When you connect a camera, the AutoPlay box pops up; click "Import pictures and videos using Windows." You're offered the chance to tag the incoming photos and to erase the memory card after the import. When it's all over, the pictures are in a new folder in your Pictures library. Double-click one to view it in the bare-bones Windows Photo Viewer program.

Figure 14-2:
You can add a "watched folder" to Photo Gallery by dragging it off the desktop (or any folder window) right onto a Pictures heading or into the main window, as shown here. The cursor changes to let you know that Photo Gallery understands your intention.

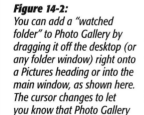

Photos from a Digital Camera

In Windows Live Photo Gallery, Microsoft has done a lot of work to make the camera-importing process smoother and smarter. Here's how it goes:

1. **Connect your camera to the PC. Turn the camera on.**

   Now, if this is the first time you've ever connected a camera, you may be shown the standard AutoPlay dialog box—otherwise known as the "What am I supposed to do with this thing?" box.

   You don't want it. Turn on "Always do this for pictures," and then scroll down and click "No action."

2. **Open Windows Live Photo Gallery.**

   For example, open the Start menu. Type *gallery* until you see the program's name; click it.

3. **In Photo Gallery, choose File→"Import from a camera or scanner."**

   A dialog box appears, displaying the camera's memory card as though it's a disk. Make sure the disk is highlighted (Figure 14-3, top).

4. **Click Import.**

   Now the Import Photos and Videos dialog box appears (Figure 14-3, middle). Here, the steps branch. If you'd like to review the photos and import only certain batches (by date), go on to step 5a. If you'd rather just import them all now, without all the examining and grouping, skip to step 5b.

5a. **Click "Review, organize and group items to import," and then click Next.**

   Now you see the impressive new dialog box shown in Figure 14-3 (bottom).

   In the old days, Photo Gallery just imported everything on your camera in one gigantic clump—even if it included photos from several different events, shot weeks apart. Now it automatically analyzes the time stamps in the incoming photos and puts them into individually named groups according to when you took them.

   Your job here, then, is to click "Enter a name" and type a name for each event whose photos you're about to import. It could be *Disney Trip, Casey's Birthday,* or *Baby Meets Lasagna,* for example—anything that helps you organize and find your pictures later.

5a. **Click "Import all new items now." Enter a description, like "Fall Fun."**

   Photo Gallery also invites you to type in *tags* to each of the incoming photos, separated by semicolons. More on tags later in this chapter; for now, it's enough to know that you can use them to specify who was on the trip, the circumstances of the shoot, and so on.

   Click Import when you're ready. Photo Gallery brings the photos onto your PC.

Tip: So what constitutes an "event?" Out of the box, Photo Gallery starts a new group after every 30 minutes of no picture-taking. But you can drag the "Adjust groups" slider to make that interval greater–a couple of hours, a whole day, even a whole month–which results in fewer separate groups. You can even drag the slider all the way to the right for "All items in one group," if you like.

Click "View 20 items" (or whatever the number is) to see thumbnail previews of the photos in each batch, so you know what you're talking about.

Figure 14-3:
The importing process is impressively smart in Windows 7 (and it takes considerably more steps).

Top: You're asked to click the memory card that contains your photos. Usually, it's like, "Duh–the one in my camera? Hello?"

Middle: Do you want to examine the various clumps of photos before importing them? Or do you want to just slurp them all in at once, and organize them later?

Bottom: In this box, you can break up the camera's contents into batches by date. You can also apply tags (keywords) to each batch, as described above. Above all, you can also turn each group's checkbox on or off, thereby importing only certain ones.

6. **Click Import.**

Windows sets about sucking in the photos from the camera and placing them into your Pictures folder.

Not all loose and squirming—that'd be a mess. Instead, it neatly creates a Photo Gallery folder bearing the name or description you provided in step 5. (If you were to choose Start→Pictures, you'd discover that there's a new folder *there*, too, bearing the same name. Photo Gallery is just a mirror of what's in your Pictures folder.) See Figure 14-4.

Tip: You can fiddle with Windows's folder- and photo-naming conventions by choosing File→Options→Import in Photo Gallery. For example, you can opt to have the subfolder named after the date the pictures were *taken* instead of the date they were *imported.*

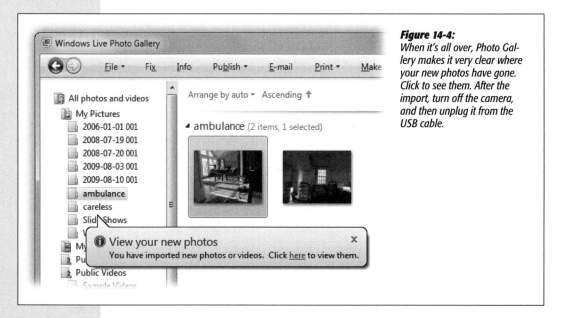

Figure 14-4:
When it's all over, Photo Gallery makes it very clear where your new photos have gone. Click to see them. After the import, turn off the camera, and then unplug it from the USB cable.

Photos from a USB Card Reader

A USB *memory card reader* offers another convenient way to transfer photos into Photo Gallery. Most of these card readers, which look like tiny disk drives, are under $15; some can read more than one kind of memory card.

If you have a reader, then instead of connecting the camera to the PC, you can slip the camera's memory card directly into the reader. Windows, or Photo Gallery, recognizes the reader as though it's a camera and offers to import the photos, just as described on the previous pages.

This method eliminates the considerable battery drain involved in pumping the photos straight off the camera. Furthermore, it's less hassle to pull a memory card out of your camera and slip it into your card reader (which you can leave always plugged in) than it is to constantly plug and unplug camera cables.

The File Format Factor

Photo Gallery is a bit finicky about digital pictures' file formats. It's not a universal graphics manager by any means; in fact, it really prefers JPEG and TIFF files. Here are the details.

Common graphics formats

Photo Gallery recognizes the most common photo file formats—but not all of them. Here's the rundown:

- **JPEG.** Just about every digital camera on earth saves photos as JPEG files—and Photo Gallery handles this format beautifully. JPEG is the world's most popular file format for photos, because even though a JPEG photo is compressed to occupy a *lot* less disk space than it would otherwise, the visual quality is still very high. JPEG is also the most common format for photos on the Web.

Note: While most digital photos you work with are probably JPEG files, they're not always *called* JPEG files. You may also see JPEG referred to as JPG or *JFIF* (JPEG File Interchange Format). Bottom line: The terms JPEG, JFIF, JPEG JFIF, and JPEG 2000 all mean the same thing.

GEM IN THE ROUGH

Auto Card Erase

Ordinarily, each time your camera's card is full, you'll want to dump all the selected pictures onto your PC. And ordinarily, each time you've finished dumping them, you'll want to erase the memory card so that it's empty and ready to reuse.

Windows does that for you automatically. There's zero risk that you'll lose pictures if lightning strikes in mid-import; Photo Gallery doesn't delete

your pictures until *after* it has successfully copied them all to the Pictures folder.

Still, if you want Windows to stop erasing the card after importing the pix, you can change the setting.

In Photo Gallery, choose File→Options. Click the Import tab. There you see the "Delete files from this device after importing" checkbox.

- **TIFF.** Some cameras offer you the chance to leave your photos *uncompressed* on the camera, in what's called TIFF format. These files are huge. Fortunately, they retain 100 percent of the picture's original quality.

    Along with JPEG, TIFF is Photo Gallery's other favorite photo format.

- **GIF** is the most common format used for non-photographic images on Web pages (borders, backgrounds, and logos). Unfortunately, Photo Gallery doesn't much care for GIF files. In fact, it can't display them at all.

- **PNG** files are also used in Web design, though not nearly as often as JPEG and GIF. They often display more complex graphic elements. Photo Gallery works with PNG files just fine.

- **BMP** was once a popular graphics file format in Windows. Its files are big and bloated by today's standards, though; even so, they work in Photo Gallery.

- **WPD** is a new Microsoft graphics protocol intended for cellphones and palmtops. (Actually, only the technology is called WPD; the images are still labeled .jpg.) Photo Gallery handles them fine.

- **Photoshop** refers to Adobe Photoshop, the world's most popular image-editing and photo-retouching program. Photo Gallery can't recognize, open, or fix Photoshop files.

Movies

In addition to still photos, most consumer digital cameras these days can also capture cute little digital movies. Some are jittery, silent affairs the size of a Wheat Thin; others are full-blown, 30-frames-per-second, fill-your-screen movies (which eat up a memory card plenty fast). Either way, Photo Gallery can import and organize them, *if* you've installed Windows Live Movie Maker (page 269) and *if* the movies are in a format that Movie Maker can understand, like .mov, .wmv, .asf, .mpeg, or .avi format.

UP TO SPEED

Scanning Photos

Microsoft has outsourced the task of scanning to two different programs. When you want to scan documents, you're supposed to use Windows Fax and Scan. When you want to scan photos, though, stay right where you are—in Photo Gallery.

When a scanner is turned on and connected to the PC, choose File→"Import from a camera or scanner," clicking the scanner's name in the next dialog box and then clicking Import. The New Scan dialog box appears. From the Profile list, choose Photo. You can also specify a color format, file format, resolution, and so on.

Click Preview to see what lies ahead. If it all looks good, click Scan.

As usual, Photo Gallery offers to tag the picture; click Import. After a moment, the freshly scanned photo pops up in the Photo Gallery viewer, ready for you to fix and organize it.

Behind the scenes, Photo Gallery dumps the scanned file into the Pictures folder. (You can override this setting by choosing File→Options→Import tab within Photo Gallery. Click "Settings for," choose Cameras, click Browse, and then find the folder you prefer.)

You don't have to do anything special to import movies; they get slurped in automatically. To play one of these movies once they're in Photo Gallery, see Figure 14-5.

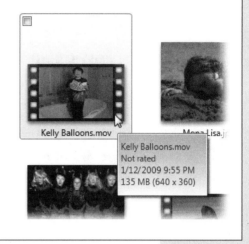

Figure 14-5:
The first frame of each video clip shows up as though it's a photo in your library. Your only clues that it's a movie and not a photo are the film sprocket holes along the sides and the tooltip that identifies the movie's running time. If you double-click one, it opens up and begins to play immediately.

Kelly Balloons.mov

Kelly Balloons.mov
Not rated
1/12/2009 9:55 PM
135 MB (640 x 360)

RAW format

Most digital cameras work like this: When you squeeze the shutter button, the camera studies the data picked up by its sensors. The circuitry then makes decisions about sharpening level, contrast, saturation, white balance, and so on—and then saves the processed image as a compressed JPEG file on your memory card.

For millions of people, the result is just fine, even terrific. But all that in-camera processing drives professionals nuts. They'd much rather preserve every last shred of original picture information, no matter how huge the resulting file—and then process the file *by hand* once it's been safely transferred to the PC, using a program like Photoshop.

That's the idea behind the RAW file format, an option in many pricier digital cameras. (RAW stands for nothing in particular.) A RAW image isn't processed at all; it's a complete record of all the data passed along by the camera's sensors. As a result, each RAW photo takes up much more space on your memory card.

But once RAW files open up on the PC, image-manipulation nerds can perform astounding acts of editing to them. They can actually change the lighting of the scene—retroactively! And they don't lose a speck of image quality along the way.

Most people use a program like Photoshop or Photoshop Elements to do this kind of editing. But humble little Photo Gallery can at least open and organize them—usually. Its success at this depends on *which* kind of RAW files you've added to your Pictures folder. Each camera company (Canon, Nikon, and so on) has created a different flavor of RAW files—their filename suffixes are things like .cr2, .crw, .dng, .nef, .orf, .rw2, .pef, .arw, .sr2, and .srf—and it's up to Microsoft to keep Photo Gallery updated. If there are RAW files in your Pictures folder but they're not showing up in Photo Gallery, well, now you know the reason.

Note: You can open a RAW file for editing in Photo Gallery, but you're never making changes to the original file. Photo Gallery automatically creates a *copy* of the photo–in JPEG format–and lets you edit *that.*

The Post-Dump Slideshow
All Versions

If you're like most people, the first thing you want to do after dumping the photos from your camera into your PC is to see them at full size, filling your screen. That's the beauty of Photo Gallery's slideshow feature.

To begin the slideshow, specify which pictures you want to see. For example:

- To see the pictures you most recently imported, click the folder Photo Gallery just created.

- Click a folder, tag, rating row, or another heading in the Navigation pane at the left side of the screen.

- If "All photos and videos" (your whole library) is selected, then click one of the photo-batch headings in the main window—for example, "C:\Users\Public\Pictures\Ski Trip."

Now click the Slideshow button at the bottom of the window (🖥), or just hit Alt+S. Photo Gallery fades out of view, and a big, brilliant, full-screen slideshow of the new photos—and even self-playing videos—begins (Figure 14-6).

What's really useful is the slideshow control bar shown in Figure 14-6. You make it appear by wiggling your mouse as the show begins.

Click Exit, or press any key, to end the slideshow.

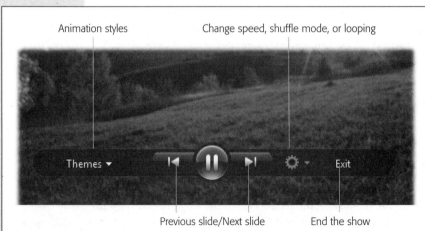

Animation styles

Change speed, shuffle mode, or looping

Themes ▼   Exit

Previous slide/Next slide   End the show

Figure 14-6:
As the slideshow progresses, you can pause the show, go backward, rotate a photo, or change the transition effects, all courtesy of this control bar.

Note: Photo Gallery can't play music with your slides. (Bummer.) Microsoft cheerfully suggests that if you want music, you can first pop into another program (like Windows Media Player) to start playback, then return to Photo Gallery to start the slides.

Or, if you're really serious and you're willing to put in some effort, choose Make→"Make a movie." Photo Gallery hands off the project to Movie Maker, where you can add music there (and even upload the result to YouTube).

Slideshow Themes

If you wiggle the mouse during a slideshow to make the control bar appear, you see an odd little button called Themes at the left side.

A Theme is a canned special-effect set for a slideshow. On a powerful PC, you can call up slideshows with multiple photos parading into and out of view, with special backdrops filling in the gaps.

If your PC doesn't have the horsepower for such elaborate effects, your Themes menu is much shorter. You can give the show an olde-tyme, mottled brown or monochrome look by choosing "Sepia" or "Black and white" from the Themes menu.

Choosing "Pan and Zoom" makes the pictures smoothly crossfade, panning and zooming as they go, as in a Ken Burns documentary on PBS. Your other choices include "Fade," meaning a crossfade, and "Classic," meaning Windows XP style: no transition effect at all.

The Digital Shoebox

All Versions

If you've imported your photos into Photo Gallery using any of the methods described above, you should now see a neatly arranged grid of thumbnails in Photo Gallery's main photo-viewing area. This is, presumably, your entire photo collection, including every last picture you've ever imported—the digital equivalent of that old shoebox you've had stuffed in the closet for the past 10 years.

Your journey out of chaos has begun. From here, you can sort your photos, give them titles, group them into smaller subcollections (called *albums*), and tag them with keywords so you can find them quickly.

The Bigger Picture

If you point to a photo thumbnail without clicking, Photo Gallery is kind enough to display, at your cursor tip, a larger version of it. Think of it as a digital version of the magnifying loupe that art experts use to inspect gemstones and paintings.

Tip: If this feature gets on your nerves, choose File→Options, and then turn off "Show photo and video previews in tooltips."

You can also make *all* the thumbnails in Photo Gallery grow or shrink using the Size slider—the horizontal slider at the lower-right corner of the window. Drag the slider all the way left, and you get micro-thumbnails so small that you can fit 200 or more of them in the window. If you drag it all the way to the right, you end up with such large thumbnails that only a few fit the screen at a time.

For the biggest view of all, though, double-click a thumbnail. It opens all the way, filling the window. At this point, you can edit the picture, too, as described below.

The Navigation Tree

Even before you start naming your photos, assigning them keywords, or organizing them into albums, Photo Gallery imposes an order of its own on your digital shoebox.

The key to understanding it is the *Navigation tree* at the left side of the Photo Gallery window. This list grows as you import more pictures and organize them—but right off the bat, you find icons like these:

- **All photos and videos.** The first icon in the Navigation tree is a very reassuring little icon, because no matter how confused you may get in working with subsets of photos later in your Photo Gallery life, clicking this icon returns you to your entire picture collection. It makes *all* your photos and videos appear in the viewing area.

  Click the My Pictures or My Videos subhead to filter out the thumbnails so that *only* photos or *only* videos are visible.

- **Date Taken.** Photo Gallery's navigation tree also offers miniature calendar icons named for the years (2010, 2009, and so on). You can click, say, the 2007 icon to see just the ones you took during that year.

  By clicking the flippy triangle next to a year's name, furthermore, you expand the list to reveal the individual *months* in that year; click a month's flippy triangle to see the individual *dates* within that month. Photo Gallery shows *only* the months and dates in which you actually took pictures; that's why 2008, for example, may show only April, July, and October (Figure 14-7).

- **People Tags, Descriptive Tags.** As you work with your photos, you'll soon discover the convenience of adding *tags* (keywords) to them, like Family, Trips, or Baby Pix. Then, with one click on one of the tag labels in this list, you can see *only* the photos in your collection that match that keyword.

Tip: You can Ctrl+click several items in the Tags list at once. For example, if you want to see both Family photos *and* Vacation photos, click Family, and then Ctrl+click Vacation.

This trick also works to select multiple months, years, folders, or any mix thereof.

Working with Your Photos

All right: Enough touring Photo Gallery's main window. Now it's time to start *using* it.

Browsing, selecting, and opening photos is straightforward. Here's everything you need to know:

- Use the vertical scroll bar, or your mouse's scroll wheel, to navigate through your thumbnails.

- To create the most expansive photo-viewing area possible, you can temporarily hide the details pane at the right side of the window. To do so, click the tiny ✕ button at its top. (The red ☒ button *above* the Help button closes Photo Gallery.) Bring the Info pane back by clicking Info in the toolbar.

Figure 14-7:
The year and month icons are very helpful when you're creating a slideshow or trying to pinpoint one certain photo. After all, you usually can re-member what year you took a vacation or when some-one's birthday was. These icons help you narrow down your search so you don't have to scroll through your entire library.

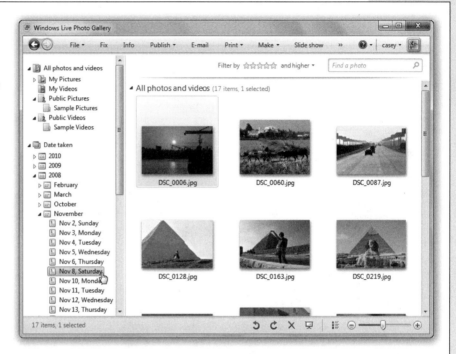

Category Groupings

Each time you import a new set of photos into Photo Gallery—whether from your hard drive, a camera, or a memory card—it appears with its own heading in Photo Gallery. Each batch is like one film roll you've had developed. Photo Gallery starts out sorting your photo library chronologically, meaning that the most recently imported photos appear at the top of the window.

Tip: If you'd prefer that the most recent items appear at the *bottom* of the Photo Gallery window instead of the top, click the Ascending/Descending button on the toolbar.

You can exploit these mini-categories within Photo Gallery in several ways:

- For speed in scrolling through a big photo collection, you can *collapse* these groupings so only their names are visible. To do that, just click the tiny ▶ button at the left end of each horizontal line.

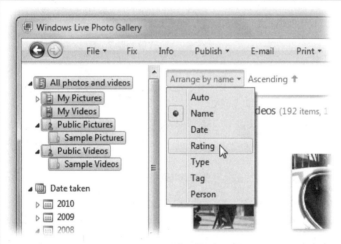

Figure 14-8:
This pop-up menu is the master sorting control for the display of photos. You can use it to sort your collection by name, date, tag or person (alphabetically), rating, or type (meaning all videos and all photos clumped together).

FREQUENTLY ASKED QUESTION

Your Own Personal Sorting Order

I want to put my photos in my own order. I'm making a slideshow, and I want to dictate the sequence. How do I do that?

You can't.

At least not without a lot of effort—namely, by manually renaming the photos so that their names are 000 Beach, 001 Sunset, and so on.

To rename a photo, click it once. See the Info pane at the right side of the window? (If not, click Info in the toolbar.) Click the photo's name to open its photo-editing box.

If you want to *drag* photos into a new order—say, for the purposes of a slideshow movie—you have to do it in Movie Maker.

- The "categories" don't have to be chronological. You can also ask Photo Gallery to cluster your photos into other logical groups: by rating (all the five-starrers together), by date taken, and so on; see Figure 14-8.

Selecting Photos

To highlight a single picture in preparation for printing, opening, duplicating, or deleting, click its thumbnail once with the mouse.

That much may seem obvious. But first-time PC users may not know how to manipulate *more* than one icon at a time—an essential survival skill.

To highlight multiple photos, use one of these techniques:

- **To select all the photos.** Select all the pictures in the set you're viewing by pressing Ctrl+A (the equivalent of the Edit→Select All command).

- **To select several photos by dragging.** You can drag diagonally to highlight a group of nearby photos, as shown in Figure 14-9. You don't even have to enclose the thumbnails completely; your cursor can touch any part of any icon to highlight it. In fact, if you keep dragging past the edge of the window, the window scrolls automatically.

Figure 14-9:
You can highlight several photos simultaneously by dragging a box around them. To do so, start from somewhere outside the target photos and drag diagonally across them, creating a whitish enclosure rectangle as you go. Any photos touched by this rectangle are selected when you release the mouse.

- **To select consecutive photos.** Click the first thumbnail you want to highlight, and then Shift+click the last one. All the files in between are automatically selected, along with the two photos you clicked (Figure 14-10, top). This trick mirrors the way Shift+clicking works in a word processor, the Finder, and many other kinds of programs.

- **To select nonconsecutive photos.** If you want to highlight only, for example, the first, third, and seventh photos in a window, start by clicking the photo icon of the first one. Then Ctrl+click each of the others. Each thumbnail sprouts colored shading to indicate that you've selected it (Figure 14-10, bottom).

Figure 14-10:

Top: To select a block of photos (as indicated by the faint colored border on each one), click the first one, and then Shift+click the last one. Photo Gallery selects all the files in between your clicks.

Bottom: To select nonadjacent photos, Ctrl+click each of them. (To remove one of the photos from your selection, Ctrl+click it again.)

If you're highlighting a long string of photos and then click one by mistake, you don't have to start over. Instead, just Ctrl+click it again, and the highlighting disappears. (If you do want to start over from the beginning, however, just deselect all selected photos by clicking any empty part of the window.)

The Ctrl-key trick is especially handy if you want to select *almost* all the photos in a window. Press Ctrl+A to select everything in the folder, then Ctrl+click any unwanted photos to deselect them. You'll save a lot of time and clicking.

Tip: You can also combine the Ctrl+clicking business with the Shift+clicking trick. For instance, you could click the first photo, then Shift+click the 10th, to highlight the first 10. Next, you could Ctrl+click photos 2, 5, and 9 to *remove* them from the selection.

Once you've highlighted multiple photos, you can manipulate them all at once. For example, you can drag them en masse out of the window and onto your desktop—a quick way to export them.

In addition, when multiple photos are selected, the commands in the shortcut menu (which you can access by right-clicking any *one* of the icons)—like Rotate, Copy, Delete, Rename, or Properties—apply to all the photos simultaneously.

Deleting Photos

As every photographer knows—make that every *good* photographer—not every photo is a keeper. You can relegate items to the Recycle Bin by selecting one or more thumbnails and then performing one of the following:

- Right-click a photo, and then choose Delete from the shortcut menu.

- Click the red, slashy ✕ button at the bottom of the window.

- Press the Delete key on your keyboard.

Note: That's the forward-delete key, not the regular delete (Backspace) key. In Photo Gallery, the Backspace key means "go back to the previous view," just as in a Web browser.

If you suddenly decide you don't really want to get rid of any of these trashed photos, it's easy to resurrect them. Switch to the desktop, open the Recycle Bin, and then drag the thumbnails out of the window and back into your Pictures folder.

(Of course, if you haven't deleted the imported pictures from your camera, you can still recover the original files and reimport them even after you empty the Recycle Bin.)

Duplicating a Photo

It's often useful to have two copies of a picture. For example, a photo whose dimensions are appropriate for a slideshow or a desktop picture (that is, a 4:3 proportion) isn't proportioned correctly for ordering prints (4 × 6, 8 × 10, or whatever). To use the same photo for both purposes, you really need to crop two copies independently.

To make a copy of a photo, you can copy and paste it right back where it is. Or double-click its thumbnail to open it, and then choose File→"Make a copy." You're asked to name the duplicate and choose a folder location for it. Do so, and then click Save.

The Info Panel

Behind the scenes, Photo Gallery stores a wealth of information about each individual photo in your collection. To take a peek, highlight a thumbnail; if you don't already see the Info pane at the right side of the window (Figure 14-11), then click the Info button on the toolbar.

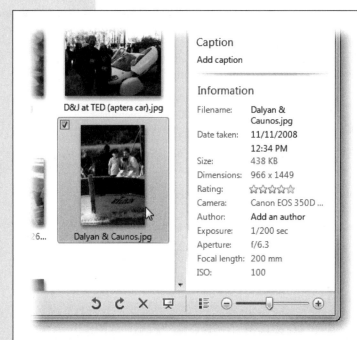

Figure 14-11:
The Info pane reveals a picture's name, rating, creation time and date, dimensions (in pixels), file size, camera settings, and any comments you've typed into the Captions area. It isn't just a place to look at the details of your pictures, though. You can also edit a lot of it. You can even change the date a photo was taken—a good tip to remember if you're a defense attorney.

How does Photo Gallery know so much about how your photos were taken? Most digital cameras embed a wealth of image, camera, lens, and exposure information in the photo files they create, using a standard data format called *XMP* or *EXIF* (Exchangeable Image Format). With that in mind, Photo Gallery automatically scans photos for XMP or EXIF data as it imports them (see Figure 14-12).

Note: Some cameras do a better job than others at embedding EXIF data in photo files. Photo Gallery can extract this information only if it's been properly stored by the camera when the digital photo was created. Of course, most of this information is missing if your photos didn't come from a digital camera (if they were scanned in, for example).

Titles

You can rename a photo easily enough. Just click its existing name in the Info panel, and then retype it.

Tip: Most people find this feature especially valuable when it comes to individual photographs. When you import them from your digital camera, the pictures bear useless gibberish names like CRS000321.JPG, CRS000322.JPG, and so on. If you highlight a *bunch* of photos and then change the title, you're renaming *all* of them at once. Photo Gallery even numbers them (Snowstorm 1.jpg, Snowstorm 2.jpg, and so on).

Figure 14-12:
The Properties dialog box reports details about your photos by reading the XMP or EXIF tags that your camera secretly embeds in your files. This is even more information than you see in the Info pane (Figure 14-11).

To open this box, right-click any photo in Photo Gallery. From the shortcut menu, choose Properties.

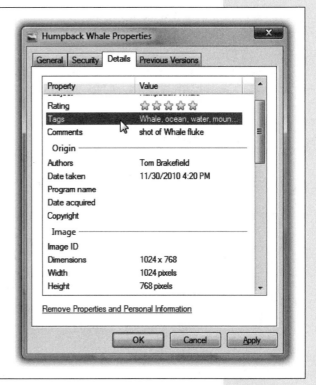

While you can make a photo's title as long as you want, it's smart to keep it short (about 10 characters or so). This way, you can see all or most of the title in the Title field (or under the thumbnails).

Tip: Once you've gone to the trouble of naming your photos, remember that you can make these names appear right beneath the thumbnails for convenient reference. Use the "Arrange by"→Name command (upper left) to make it so.

Dates

Weirdly enough, you can even edit the dates the pictures were taken—a handy fix if, for example, the camera's clock wasn't set right. Just click the date or time, and then either retype the date digits or click the ▾ button to open a clickable calendar.

Captions

Sometimes you need more than a one- or two-word title to describe a picture. If you want to add a lengthier description, you can type it in the Captions area of the Info pane (click where it says "Add caption").

Even if you don't write full-blown captions for your pictures, you can use the Captions box to store little details such as the names, places, dates, and events associated with your photos.

The best thing about adding comments is that they're searchable. After you've entered all this free-form data, you can use it to quickly locate a photo using Photo Gallery's search command.

Tags and Ratings
All Versions

Tags are descriptive keywords—like *Family*, *Vacation*, or *Kids*—that you can use to label and categorize your photos and videos. Ratings are, of course, star ratings from 0 to 5, meaning that you can categorize your pictures by how great they are.

The beauty of tags and ratings is that they're searchable. Want to comb through all the photos in your library to find every closeup taken of your children during summer vacation? Instead of browsing through dozens of folders, just click the tags *Kids*, *Vacation*, *Closeup*, and *Summer* in the Navigation tree. You'll have the results in seconds.

Or want to gather only the cream of the crop into a slideshow or DVD? Let Photo Gallery produce a display of only your five-star photos.

Editing Tags

You can create as many tag labels as you want to create a meaningful, customized list. To build your list, you can operate in either of two ways:

• **In the Navigation tree.** To add a tag, click "Add a new tag" in the Navigation tree, either under the "People tags" heading or the "Descriptive tags" heading. Type the tag label and click OK.

Note: People tags are new in Photo Gallery, and they simply identify who's in the picture. Microsoft starts you out with some generic people-tag groups (Coworkers, Family, and others), and also creates one called Favorites, starring the same people identified as your Favorites in Windows Live Messenger and your other Windows address books.

- **In the Info pane.** Click Info in the toolbar. In the Info pane, click either "Add people tags" or "Add descriptive tags."

To edit or delete a tag, right-click it, and then, from the shortcut menu, choose Delete or Rename.

Note: Be careful about renaming tags after you've started using them; the results can be messy. If you've already applied the keyword *Fishing* to a batch of photos but later decide to replace it with *Romantic* in your keyword list, then all the fishing photos automatically inherit the keyword Romantic. Depending on you and your interests, this may not be what you intended.

It may take some time to develop a really good master set of keywords. The idea is to assign labels that are general enough to apply across your entire photo collection, but specific enough to be meaningful when conducting searches.

Applying Tags and Ratings

Photo Gallery offers two methods of applying tags and ratings to your pictures:

- **Method 1: Drag the picture.** One way to apply tags to photos is, paradoxically, to apply the *photos* to the *tags*.

  That is, drag relevant photos directly onto the tags in the Navigation tree, as shown in Figure 14-13.

  To give a photo a new star rating, drag its thumbnail onto the appropriate row in the Navigation tree.

Tip: You can apply as many tags to an individual photo as you like. A picture of your cousin Rachel at a hot dog–eating contest in London might bear all of these keywords: Rachel, Relatives, Travel, Food, Humor, and Medical Crises. Later, you'll be able to find that photo no matter which of these categories you're hunting for.

Figure 14-13:
You can drag thumbnails onto tags one at a time, or you can select the whole batch first, using any of the selection techniques described on page 495.

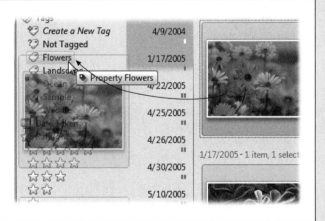

This method is best when you want to apply a whole bunch of pictures to one or two keywords. It's pretty tedious, however, when you want to apply a lot of different keywords to a single photo. That's why Microsoft has given you a second method, described next.

• **Method 2: Info Pane.** Highlight a thumbnail. On the Info panel, you find a simple list of all the tags you've applied to this photo. Add a tag by clicking Add Tag and then typing a tag name (or as much as necessary for Photo Gallery to AutoComplete it). To change the photo's rating, click the number of stars you want in the lower half of the Info panel.

The beauty of this system is that you can *keep the little Info pane open* on the screen as you move through your photo collection. Each time you click a photo—or, in fact, select a group of them—the tags list updates itself to reflect the tags of whatever is now selected.

(To *remove* tag assignments from a certain picture, right-click the name of the tag. From the shortcut menu, choose Remove Tag.)

Tip: You can drag thumbnails onto other Navigation-tree elements, too—not just tags and ratings. For example, you can drag them onto a different month or year to *change* their internal records of when they were taken. You can also drag them onto folders in the Folder list to sort them into different locations. (Yes, you can actually move them around the hard drive this way.)

GEM IN THE ROUGH

Face Recognition?

If you're fooling around in Photo Gallery, and you double-click a photo with people in it, you might be astounded to see, on the full-size view, small white rectangles around their faces. (Try pointing to the third word of the phrase "Person found – Identify" if you don't see the white rectangles.)

Why, it looks just like the face-recognition feature of a modern digital camera! If you click Identify, you get a pop-up palette of people's names, so you can tag the right face with the right name.

Could it be? Does Photo Gallery recognize faces, like iPhoto and Picasa do? If you flag someone as your mom, will

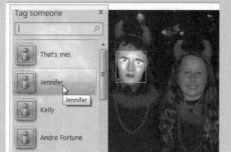

Photo Gallery autotag all the other photos of your mom, since you've told it what she looks like?

Well, no.

Photo Gallery recognizes that something is a face, but it makes no attempt to figure out whose face it is, even if you've manually flagged that person's face in dozens of photos.

So why even bother? No reason, except that when you post these photos online, your friends will be able to search for photos containing the people whose faces you've identified.

Using Tags and Ratings

The big payoff for your diligence arrives when you need to get your hands on a specific set of photos, because Photo Gallery lets you *isolate* them with one quick click.

To round up all the photos with, say, the Kids tag, just click Kids in the Navigation tree at the left side of the window. Photo Gallery immediately rounds up all photos labeled with that tag, displays them in the photo-viewing area, and hides all others. Or, to find all your five-star photos, click the row of five stars ("Filter by") at the top of the screen. (Use the pop-up menu beside it to choose "and higher," "and lower," or "only." That is, "three stars and higher," "three stars and lower," or "only three stars.")

Note: Windows can't embed metadata (and therefore tags or star ratings) to BMP, PNG, GIF, or MPEG files. Actually, you can apply such identifying information to those file types *in Photo Gallery,* but it won't show up in Explorer windows or anywhere else in Windows (like the Photo Viewer program).

You also won't be able to apply Windows-wide metadata to files that are locked, in use by another program, or corrupted.

More tips:

- To find photos that match multiple keywords, Ctrl+click additional tag labels. For example, if you click Travel, and then Ctrl+click Holidays, Photo Gallery reveals all the pictures that have *either* of those keywords. (There's no way to perform an "and" keyword roundup—that is, to find pictures that have *both* Travel *and* Holidays tags.)

- You can also Ctrl+click *unrelated branches* of the Navigation tree. For example, you can click the Casey tag, and then Ctrl+click the five-star rating row, to find only the very best pictures of Casey. You could then even Ctrl+click "2009" in the Navigation tree to further restrict the photos you're seeing.

  But why stop there? Ctrl+click Videos at the top of the Navigation tree, and now you're seeing only the five-star *videos* of Casey in 2009.

- You can drag tags up or down in the Navigation tree (to rearrange them). And if you drag a tag *on top of* another one, it becomes a *subtag* (nested tag). That is, you could have a tag called Trips, and then subtags called Vermont, Florida, and Ohio. As the tag list grows, remember that you can collapse any branch of the tree by clicking its flippy triangle.

Searching for Photos by Text

The tag mechanism described above is an adequate way to add textual descriptions to your pictures, but there are other ways. The name you give a picture might be significant, and so might the picture's caption or its folder location (that is, its folder *path).*

The Search box at the top of Photo Gallery searches *all* these text tidbits. It works essentially like the Start menu's Search box:

- Just start typing. As you type, you filter the thumbnails down to just the pictures that match what you've typed so far. You don't have to finish a word, press Enter, or use wildcard characters (*). See Figure 14-4.

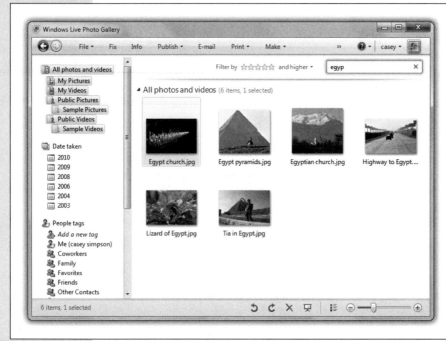

Figure 14-14:
As you type into the Search box, Photo Gallery hides all pictures except the ones that have your typed phrase somewhere in their names, captions, file-names, or folder paths. (To cancel your search and reveal all the pictures again, click the tiny X at the right end of the Search box.)

- You can type two words (or parts of words) to find pictures that match both. To find all photos of Zelda in Brazil, typing *zel br* will probably do the trick.

- Only beginnings of words count. Typing *llweg* won't find pictures of Renee Zellweger, but *zell* will.

Editing Your Shots
All Versions

Straight from the camera, digital snapshots often need a little bit of help. A photo may be too dark or too light. The colors may be too bluish or too yellowish. The focus may be a little blurry, the camera may have been tilted slightly, or the composition may be somewhat off.

Fortunately, Photo Gallery lets you fine-tune digital images in ways that, in the world of traditional photography, would have required a fully equipped darkroom, several bottles of smelly chemicals, and an X-Acto knife.

In Photo Gallery, you can't paint in additional elements, mask out unwanted backgrounds, or apply 50 different special-effects filters, as you can with editing programs like Photoshop and Photoshop Elements. Nonetheless, Photo Gallery handles basic photo fix-up tasks, many of which work with a single click.

All Photo Gallery editing is performed in a special editing mode, in which the photo appears at nearly full-screen size, and tool icons appear at the top (Figure 14-15). You enter Edit mode by clicking a photo's thumbnail and then clicking the Fix button on the toolbar. (If you've double-clicked the photo to open it into the larger viewing window, you can click Fix there, too.)

Figure 14-15:
Photo Gallery's editing tools appear in a special toolbar. There's no Save command. Any changes you make to a photo are automatically saved. But don't worry; Photo Gallery always keeps the untouched, unedited original behind the scenes.

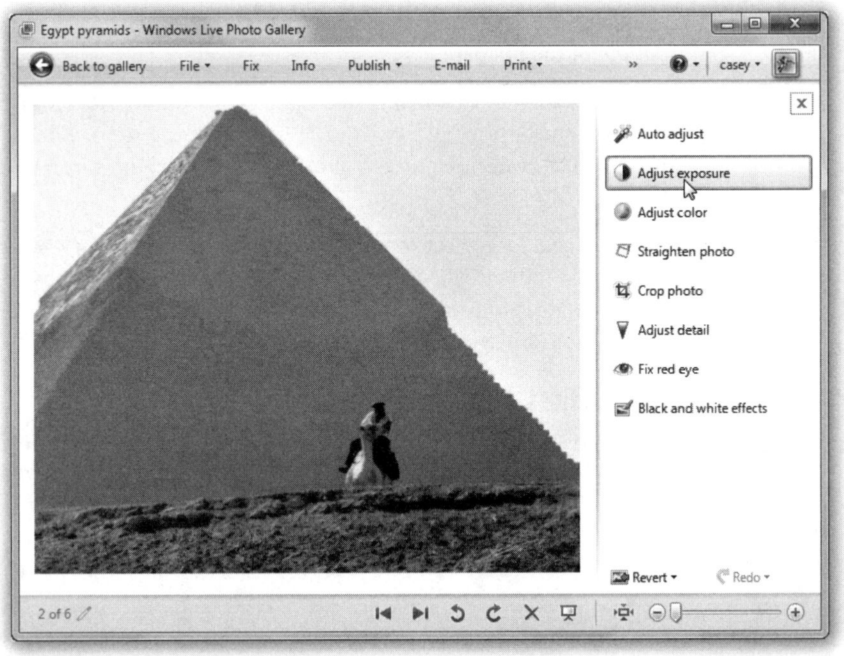

You exit Edit mode by clicking "Back To Gallery" (top left of the window) or tapping the Esc key.

Ways to Zoom

Before you get deeply immersed in the editing process, it's well worth knowing how to zoom and scroll around, since chances are you'll be doing quite a bit of it.

- **Maximize.** One way to zoom is to change the size of the window itself. Maximize Photo Gallery to enlarge the image.

- **The Size pop-up menu.** Use the Size slider (lower-right) to zoom in or out.

- **The mouse wheel.** If your mouse has a scroll wheel on the top, you can zoom in or out by turning that wheel, which is surely the most efficient way of all.

Note: The icon beside the size slider means, "Fit the photo in the window once again, no matter how much zooming I did." Pressing Ctrl+0 does the same thing.

When you're zoomed in, the cursor changes to a friendly little white glove—your clue that you can now scroll the photo in any direction just by dragging. That's more direct than fussing with two independent scroll bars.

Ten Levels of Undo

As long as you remain in Edit mode, you can back out of your latest 10 changes. To change your mind about the *last* change you made, just click the Undo button at the *bottom* of the Fix pane.

To retrace even more of your steps, click the ▾ button next to the Undo button. The resulting pop-up menu lists your latest 10 editing steps. Choose how far you want to "rewind," or click Undo All to back out of everything you've done since opening the photo.

But once you leave Edit mode—by returning to the gallery—you lose the ability to undo your individual edits. At this point, the only way to restore your photo to its original state is to use the Revert command, which removes all the edits you've made to the photo since importing it (page 512).

Auto Adjust

The "Auto adjust" button at the top of the Fix panel provides a simple way to improve the appearance of less-than-perfect digital photos. One click makes colors brighter,

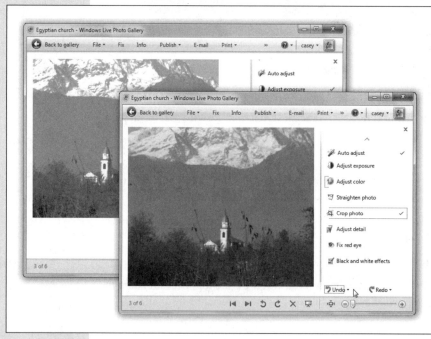

Figure 14-16:
The "Auto adjust" command works particularly well on photos that are slightly dark and that lack good contrast, like the original photo on the top. Using Photo Gallery's Brightness and Contrast sliders alone might have helped a little, but the "Auto adjust" button produces a faster and overall better result, as shown at the bottom.

skin tones warmer, and details sharper, as shown in Figure 14-16. (This button is a lot like the Auto Levels command in Photoshop.)

It works by analyzing the relative brightness of all the pixels in your photo and attempting to balance the image by dialing the brightness or contrast up or down and intensifying dull or grayish-looking color. Usually, this approach at least makes pictures look somewhat richer and more vivid.

You may find that Auto Adjust has no real effect on some photos and only minimally improves others. Remember, too, that you can't enhance just one part of a photo. If you want to selectively adjust specific portions of a picture, you need a true photo-editing program like Photoshop Elements.

Cropping

You'd be surprised at how many photographs can benefit from selective cropping. You can eliminate parts of a photo you just don't want, improve a photo's composition (filling the frame with your subject often has greater impact), or fit a photo to specific proportions (an important step if you're going to turn your photos into standard-size prints).

Here are the steps for cropping a photo:

1. **Open the photo for editing.**

   For example, double-click it, and then click Fix on the toolbar.

Figure 14-17:
When you crop a picture, you draw a rectangle in any direction using the crosshairs pointer to define the part of the photo you want to keep. (To deselect this area—when you want to start over, for example—click anywhere in the dimmed area.) Once you've drawn the rectangle and clicked Crop, the excess falls to the digital cutting room floor, thus enlarging your subject.

2. **In the Fix pane, click "Crop photo."**

The Crop controls appear.

3. **Make a selection from the Proportion pop-up menu, if you like (Figure 14-17).**

The **Proportion** pop-up menu controls the behavior of the cropping tool. When the menu is set to Original, you can draw a cropping rectangle of any size and proportion, in essence going freehand.

When you choose one of the other options in the pop-up menu, however, Photo Gallery constrains the rectangle you draw to preset proportions. It prevents you from coloring outside the lines, so to speak.

Most digital cameras produce photos whose proportions are 4:3 (width to height). This size is ideal for onscreen slideshows and DVDs, because most PC screens and TVs use 4:3 dimensions, too—but it doesn't divide evenly into standard print photograph sizes.

That's why the Proportion pop-up menu offers canned choices like 4 × 6, 5 × 7, and so on. Limiting your cropping to one of these preset sizes guarantees that your cropped photos will fit perfectly into Kodak (or Shutterfly) prints. (If you don't constrain your cropping this way, Kodak—not you—will decide how to crop them to fit.)

As soon as you make a selection from this pop-up menu, Photo Gallery draws a preliminary cropping rectangle—of the proper dimensions—on the screen, turning everything outside it slightly dim.

In general, this rectangle always appears in landscape (horizontal) orientation. To make it vertical, click "Rotate frame" just below the Proportion pop-up menu.

Often, you'll want to give the cropping job the benefit of your years of training and artistic sensibility by *redrawing* the cropping area. Here's how:

4. **Drag the tiny white control handles to reshape the cropping rectangle.**

Drag inside the rectangle to move it relative to the photo itself.

5. **When the cropping rectangle is just the way you want, click Apply.**

Photo Gallery throws away all the pixels outside the rectangle. Of course, the Undo and Revert commands are always there if you change your mind.

Note: Remember that cropping always shrinks your photos. Remove too many pixels, and your photo may end up too small (that is, with a resolution too low to print or display properly).

Red Eye

You snap a near-perfect family portrait: The focus is sharp, the composition is balanced, everyone's smiling. And then you notice it: Uncle Mitch, standing dead center in the picture, looks like a vampire. His eyes are glowing red, as though illuminated by the evil within.

Red eye is light reflected back from your subject's eyes. The bright light of your flash passes through the pupil of each eye, illuminating and bouncing off of the blood-red retinal tissue at the back of the eye. Red-eye problems worsen when you shoot pictures in a dim room, because your subject's pupils are dilated wider, allowing even more light from the flash to shine on the retina.

The best course of action is to avoid red eye to begin with—by using an external (not built-in) flash, for example. But if it's too late for that, and people's eyes are already glowing demonically, there's always Photo Gallery's Red Eye tool. It lets you alleviate red-eye problems by digitally removing the offending red pixels. Figure 14-18 shows how.

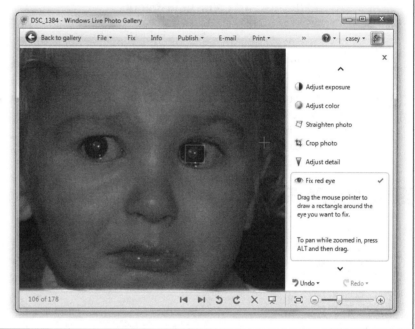

Figure 14-18:
Top: To fix red eye, zoom in and scroll so that you have a closeup view of the eye with the red-eye problem. Click "Fix red eye," and then drag a box around each affected eye.

Photo Gallery neutralizes the red pixels, painting them solid black. Of course, this means that everybody winds up looking like they have black eyes instead of red ones—but at least they look a little less like the walking undead.

Truth be told, the Red Eye tool doesn't know an eyeball from a pinkie toe. It just turns any red pixels black, regardless of what body part they're associated with. Friends and family members look more attractive—and less like *Star Trek* characters—after you touch up their phosphorescent red eyes with Photo Gallery.

Rotate

If your digital camera has a built-in orientation sensor, Photo Gallery attempts to figure out which orientation the photos are supposed to be (horizontal or vertical) at the time you import them.

If it missed a few, however, you can use either of these methods to turn them right-side up:

- Click one of the blue Rotate buttons at the bottom of the main Photo Gallery window.

- Right-click a thumbnail; from the shortcut menu, choose one of the Rotate commands.

Tip: After importing a batch of photos, you can save a lot of time and mousing if you first select *all* the thumbnails that need rotating (by Ctrl+clicking each, for example). Then use one of the rotation commands above to fix all the selected photos in one fell swoop.

Exposure and Color Adjustments

Plenty of photos need no help at all. They look fantastic right out of the camera. And plenty of others are ready for prime time after only a single click on the "Auto adjust" button, as described earlier.

If you click "Adjust exposure" "Adjust color" on the Fix pane, though, you can make *gradations* of the changes that the "Auto adjust" button makes. For example, if a photo looks too dark and murky, you can bring details out of the shadows without blowing out the highlights. If the snow in a skiing shot looks too bluish, you can de-blue it. If the colors don't pop quite enough in the prize-winning-soccer-goal shot, you can boost their saturation levels.

POWER USERS' CLINIC

The Histogram

The histogram, the little graph in the Exposure panel, is a self-updating visual representation of the dark and light tones that make up your photograph, and it's a tool that's beloved by photographers.

If the mountains of your graph seem to cover all the territory from left to right, you already have a roughly even distribution of dark and light tones in your picture, so you're probably in good shape. But if the mountains seem clumped up at either the left side or the right side of the graph, your photo is probably either muddy/too dark or overexposed/too bright. (Your eye could probably have told you that, too.) Anyway, you might want to make an adjustment.

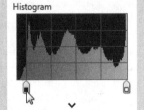

To fix this situation, drag the right or left pointer on the slider inward, toward the base of the "mountain." If you move the right indicator inward, the whites become brighter, but the dark areas stay pretty much the same; if you drag the left indicator inward, the dark tones change, but the highlights remain steady.

In general, avoid moving these endpoint handles inward beyond the outer edges of the mountains. Doing so adds contrast, but it also throws away whatever data is outside the handles, which generally makes for a lower-quality printout.

In short, there are fixes the Adjust panels can make that no one-click magic button can touch.

Exposure

When you move the Brightness slider, you're making the *entire* image lighter or darker. In other words, if the picture's contrast is already exactly as you want it, but the whole picture could use darkening or lightening, Brightness should be your tool of choice.

The Contrast slider, on the other hand, affects the difference between the darkest and lightest tones in your picture. If you increase the contrast, you create darker blacks and brighter whites. If you decrease the contrast (too much), you create flat or muddy tones.

The new Shadows slider attempts to recover lost detail in the darkest parts of the photo, and the Highlights slider attempts to recover detail from white, blown-out parts. Both of them work surprisingly well—in moderation. (Too much makes the photo look weird.)

Color balance

One of the most common failings of digital cameras (and scanners) is that they don't capture color very accurately. Digital photos sometimes have a slightly bluish or greenish tinge. Or maybe you just want to take color adjustment into your own hands, not only to get the colors right, but to also create a specific mood for an image—icy blue for a freezing day, for example.

Figure 14-19:
You can drag the handle of a slider, of course, but that doesn't give you much accuracy. Sometimes you may prefer to click directly on the slider, which makes the handle jump to the spot. The checkmark means, "You've fooled with this parameter."

The Adjust Color panel offers three sliders that wield power over this sort of thing (Figure 14-19):

- **Color Temperature.** This slider adjusts the photo along the blue-orange spectrum. Move the slider to the left to make the image "cooler," or slightly bluish—a good way to improve overly yellowish scenes shot in incandescent lighting. Move the slider to the right to warm up the tones, or make them more orange—a particularly handy technique for breathing life back into subjects that have been bleached white with a flash.

- **Tint.** Nudge the slider to the right to add a greenish tint, left to add red.

  Adjusting this slider is particularly helpful for correcting skin tones and compensating for difficult lighting situations, like pictures you took under fluorescent lighting.

- **Saturation.** When you increase the saturation of a photo's colors, you make them more vivid; you make them "pop" more. You can also improve photos that have harsh, garish colors by dialing *down* the saturation, so that the colors end up looking a little less intense than they appeared in the original snapshot. That's a useful trick in photos whose *composition* is so strong that the colors are almost distracting.

Tint: Drag the Saturation slider all the way to the left for an instant black-and-white rendition of your shot.

Reverting to the Original

Photo Gallery includes built-in protection against overzealous editing—a feature that can save you much grief. If you end up cropping a photo too much, or cranking up the brightness of a picture until it seems washed out, or accidentally turning someone's lips black with the Red-Eye tool, then you can undo all your edits at once with the Revert command. Revert strips away *every change you've ever made* since the picture arrived from the camera. It leaves you with your original, unedited photo—even if it's been months or years since you made the changes.

FREQUENTLY ASKED QUESTION

Originals-Folder Auto-Cleanup

Let me get this straight: Every time I edit a photo, even slightly, I wind up with a duplicate copy of it in some hidden folder on my hard drive? Seems like that's a recipe for wasting a lot of disk space.

True enough: The auto-backup feature means you wind up with *two* copies of every photo you ever edit, the edited one visible in Photo Gallery, and the original stashed on your hard drive. If left unchecked, all those originals could wind up eating up a distressingly large chunk of your hard drive.

For that reason, Photo Gallery can auto-delete the secret originals after a certain amount of time has passed. If it's been a year since you touched a photo, after all, you're probably happy with the changes you made to it, and you may not need the space-eating safety net any more.

To turn on this feature, choose File→Options within Photo Gallery. In the Options dialog box, under the Original Images heading, you can specify how long Windows should keep those unedited originals on hand.

The secret of the Revert command: Whenever you use any editing tools, Photo Gallery—without prompting and without informing you—instantly makes a duplicate of your original file. With an original version safely tucked away, Photo Gallery lets you go wild on the copy. Consequently, you can remain secure in the knowledge that in a pinch, Photo Gallery can always restore an image to the state it was in when you first imported it.

Note: Windows keeps your unedited original photos in your Personal→AppData→Local→Microsoft→Windows→Original Images folder. (It's OK to open this folder to inspect its contents and even open photos inside, but don't delete, move, or rename any of them; you'll wind up completely confusing Photo Gallery.)

To restore a selected photo to its original, choose File→"Revert to original," or press Ctrl+R, or click the Revert button at the bottom of the Fix panel. Photo Gallery asks you to confirm the change; if you click OK, it swaps in the original version of the photo. You're back where you started.

Tip: Clearly, Photo Gallery has all the basics covered. But if you want more editing control—for example, if you want to edit only *part* of an image, or you want to add text or something—you'll have to rely on another program.

Fortunately, Photo Gallery plays well with others. Once you've opened a photo, you can use the Extras→"Open with" submenu to send it off to any other graphics program—say, Photoshop Elements—for additional tweaking.

But even if you make changes in that other program, you're still protected by the warmth and security of the Revert command.

Finding Your Audience

All Versions

The last stop on your digital photos' cycle of greatness is, of course, a showing for other people. Photo Gallery offers several ways to make that happen.

Tip: A subset of these options, including Slide Show, Print, E-mail, and Burn, are available right in the toolbar of your Pictures window. That is, you don't have to open Photo Gallery first (although in most cases, all you're doing is handing off the task *to* Photo Gallery).

Make Prints

If you highlight some photo thumbnails and then click Print (in the Photo Gallery toolbar), the pop-up menu offers you two choices:

- **Print.** Here, you can specify what printer, paper, and quality options you want in order to print your own pictures at home—on an inkjet printer, for example.

- **Order Prints.** Even if you don't have a high-quality color printer, traditional prints of your digital photos are only a few clicks away—if you're willing to spend a little money, that is. Figure 14-20 has the details.

The best part is that you get to print only the prints you actually want, rather than developing a roll of 36 prints only to find that just two of them are any good.

> **Tip:** If you plan to order prints, first crop your photos to the proper proportions (4 × 6, for example), using the Crop tool described earlier in this chapter. Most digital cameras produce photos whose shape doesn't quite match standard photo-paper dimensions. If you send photos to Shutterfly uncropped, you're leaving it up to Shutterfly to decide which parts of your pictures to lop off to make them fit. (More than one PC fan has opened the envelope to find loved ones missing the tops of their skulls.) You can always restore the photos to their original uncropped versions using the Revert command.

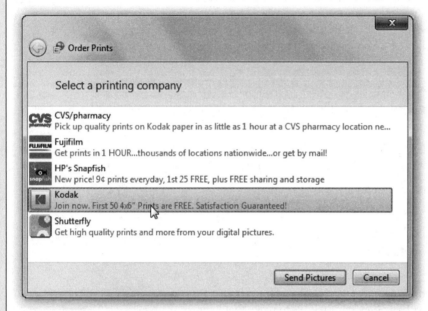

Figure 14-20:
Thanks to deals that Microsoft has cut with online photo print shops, you can order prints directly from within Photo Gallery. After you select the size and quantity of the pictures you want, one click is all it takes to transmit your photos and bill your credit card. The rates range from 19 cents for a single 4 × 6 print to about $4 for 8 × 10s. You get photos printed on high-quality glossy paper in the mail.

Slideshows

See "The Post-Dump Slideshow" on page 490.

Email

The most important thing to know about emailing photos is this: *Full-size photos are usually too big to email.* They're big files, and the original camera shots won't even fit on a modern PC monitor—they're much bigger, in terms of pixels—without shrinking.

In Photo Gallery, the problem has been neatly solved in an automated, amazingly slick way—*if* Windows Live Mail (Chapter 12) is your email program:

1. **Select the thumbnails of the photo(s) you want to email.**

   You can use any of the picture-selecting techniques described on page 495.

2. **Click Email on the toolbar.**

   Photo Gallery hands off the photos to your email program. It prepares an outgoing message with the photos already attached.

3. **Choose a size for your photo(s).**

   The size options are at the right side of the photo-formatting strip (Figure 14-21). Medium, for example, pares your photos down to about 1 megabyte each, so beware if you try to send more than five of them in one email message; you may overflow your friends' email boxes.

Figure 14-21:
Photo Gallery hands off the photos to Windows Live Mail, if you have it; here, you see an impressive new strip of photo-attachment controls. Add borders, control the size—even rotate them or correct the color! (If you click Layout, you can specify how the photos appear—with what layout? With text or without? What size?)

4. **Format the photos.**

   The other buttons in the formatting strip let you add frames around each photos—sweet—and even correct the colors (Autocorrect) or convert the shots to black-and-white.

5. **Address the message, add a note if you like, and click Send.**

   At this point, Mail processes your photos—converting them to JPEG format and, if you requested it, resizing them. Your photos are on their merry way.

Now then. What if you *don't* have Windows Live Mail as your email program? In that case, see Figure 14-22.

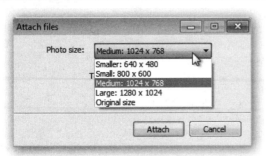

Figure 14-22:
If you don't have Windows Live Mail, then when you click Email on Photo Gallery's toolbar, you're offered an opportunity to shrink down your multimegabyte photo files before attaching them.

Burn to a Disc

If you highlight some photo thumbnails, the Make menu offers two ways to burn them onto a blank CD or DVD:

- **Burn a data CD.** This is a great way to back up or archive your pictures and movies. Insert a blank CD or DVD when you're asked.

- **Burn a DVD.** The "Burn a data CD" option makes a *data* disc. It doesn't play on your TV—only in a computer.

  This command, however, hands off the photos to Windows Live DVD Maker for burning to a DVD, so you can share your masterpieces on your friends' TV sets. For details on DVD Maker, download the free PDF appendix, "Movie Maker & DVD Maker," from this book's "Missing CD" at *www.missingmanuals.com.*

Make a Slideshow Movie

If you highlight some photo thumbnails and then choose Make→"Make a movie," Photo Gallery automatically hands them off to Windows Movie Maker and lays them out in the timeline as a slideshow, all ready to go.

All you have left to do is rearrange them, add music and credits, and save as a digital movie file for publishing online or distributing to your hip friends. (Once again, check out the free PDF appendix "Movie Maker & DVD Maker" from this book's "Missing CD" at *www.missingmanuals.com.*)

Build a Photo Screen Saver

This feature's really nice. You can turn any arbitrary batch of photos into your PC's very own screen saver. After half an hour (or whatever) of inactivity, the screen darkens, thunder rolls, and *your* friends and family begin to appear, gracefully panning and zooming and crossfading, as your coworkers spill their coffee in admiration and amazement.

The hard part is specifying *which* pictures you want to be part of the show; you can't just highlight a bunch of them and say, "Use these." Instead, you have to isolate your screen saver–bound shots, either by giving them a certain tag, applying a certain rating, or confining them to a certain folder.

Begin by choosing File→"Screen saver settings" to open the Screen Saver Settings control panel. Make sure the "Screen saver" pop-up menu says "Windows Live Photo Gallery." Then click Settings.

Now you can choose how you want your photos selected for their big moment in the spotlight. You can specify only the photos with certain tags, only photos *without* certain tags, photos with certain star ratings, or photos from a particular folder. You can also choose a theme (animation style), a speed, and whether or not you want the photos presented in a random order.

When you've finished setting up the slideshow—that is, screen saver—click Save. When you return to the Screen Saver Settings dialog box, you can either click Preview to manually trigger the screen saver for your inspection, or click OK and wait 20 minutes for the screen saver to kick in by itself.

GEM IN THE ROUGH

The Automatic Panorama

If you're one of those clever shutterbugs who tries to capture really wide-angle scenes by taking multiple side-by-side photos, Photo Gallery is here to help you. Its new automatic panorama-stitching feature can combine those side-by-side shots into one superwide megavista.

To make this work, select all the side-by-side shots in Photo Gallery. Choose Make→"Create a panoramic photo."

After the program crunches away for a while, it proposes a name for the resulting shot ("Flower stitch," for example);

fix the name, if you like, and then click Stitch.

Now the panorama opens up at full size. Usually, you see that the edges don't quite align, or the exposure was slightly different from shot to shot.

Click Fix on the toolbar, and use the cropping tool to shave away the jagged edges. (There's not much you can do about the mismatched lighting—except to remember that the next time you take panorama shots, it's best to turn off your camera's automatic mode. Choose one exposure and stick with it for all the side-by-side shots.)

Make a Blog Post

If you've got yourself a Windows Live blog (page 469), you can fire photos to it directly from Photo Gallery. Choose Make→"Make a blog post," and then specify whether you

Figure 14-23:
Top: Here, you can specify a name for your new album (or add the photos to an existing album); choose who can see the pictures (everyone, just you, or only people in your online address book); and specify how big you want the pictures to be. When you click Publish, Photo Gallery shoots them up to your Windows Live account (Chapter 13).

Bottom: When it's all over, your photos are online in a handsome gallery for all your fans to see. They can click a thumbnail to see the photo at full size.

want the photos to appear pasted into your post or separately as an album.

Now Windows Live Writer appears (page 301), with your photos already in place. (If you chose "as album," you see only a link to them, just as your audience will see.) Type up a few words about your masterpieces, and then click Publish.

Publish a Web Photo Gallery

Ahh, now we're talking. Here's the quickest, easiest, freest way ever to let your admirers far and wide enjoy your pictures: Post them in a Web gallery.

Just highlight the pictures you want, and then choose Publish→"Online album." Proceed as shown in Figure 14-23.

Tip: Microsoft generously permits you to upload photos directly to Flickr.com, or videos directly to YouTube.com—it's not all about Microsoft.

Just select the photos or videos, and then choose Publish→More Services→"Publish on Flickr" or "Publish on YouTube."

The first time you try this, you'll be asked for your Flickr or YouTube account information. After that, though, it's one-stop publishing.

Windows Media Player

I n the beginning, Windows Media Player was the headquarters for music and video on your PC. It was the Grand Central Terminal for things like music CDs (you could play 'em, copy songs off 'em, and burn 'em); MP3 files and other digital songs (you could sort 'em, buy 'em online, and file 'em into playlists); pocket music players of the non-iPod variety (fill 'em up, manage their playlists); Internet radio stations; DVD movies (watch 'em); and so on.

Media Player still does all that, and more. But it's no longer clear that this is the program you'll use for these activities. Gradually, the Media Player audience is splintering. Nowadays, a certain percentage of people are using alternative programs like these:

- **iTunes.** If you have an iPod or an iPhone, you use Apple's iTunes software to do your music and video organizing.

- **Zune software.** If you have a Zune music player, you have to use yet *another* juke-box program—the software that came with it—for loading up and organizing your player.

- **Media Center.** Many of Media Player's functions are now duplicated in Windows Media *Center,* the vast playback engine described in Chapter 16.

Still, most of the Windows world continues to use Windows Media Player as their music-file database. Version 12 has some excellent new features, including a cleaner design, free streaming through your house—or even over the Internet—to other computers, and playback of more kinds of audio and video files (the new types include H.264, AAC, Xvid, and DivX). It's worth getting to know.

Note: In its insatiable quest to dominate the world of digital music and video, Microsoft keeps updating Windows Media Player, usually redesigning it beyond recognition with each update. For example, this chapter describes Media Player version 12, included with Windows 7 out of the gate. But sure as shootin', version 13 will be coming your way within a year or so. (Windows's automatic-update feature will let you know when version 13 is fully baked and ready to download.)

The Lay of the Land
All Versions

The first time you open Windows Media Player, you confront the usual Microsoft interrogation about your privacy tolerance. If it's pretty much OK with you for Microsoft to do what it wants with (anonymous) details of your Media Center habits, click Recommended and get on with your life.

If you click Custom instead, you can opt out of that kind of invisible data transfer, decline the auto-connection to Microsoft's online music store, and avoid making Media Player the automatic playback program for all kinds of different file types.

In any case, eventually, you wind up at the main Media Player screen (Figure 15-1). It looks quite a bit different from its predecessors. In fact, if you've perused the previous chapter, you'll realize that Media Player and Photo Gallery share a very similar design.

Figure 15-1:
When you click a label at left, the main portion of the window changes to show you your music collection, using the actual album-cover artwork as icons. It's very visual, but not especially stingy with screen space. Fortunately, you also have a more compact List view available—choose Details from the View Options pop-up menu (☰) next to the Search box.

Down the left side of the window is a Navigation tree—a list of the music, videos, pictures, recorded TV shows, and playlists in your collection. The flippy triangles next to the major headings make it easy to collapse sections of the list. Under the Library headings, you can click Artist, Album, Genre, or whatever, to see your entire music library sorted by that criterion (Figure 15-1).

Media Player's top edge, as you may have noticed, offers three horizontal strips:

- **The menu bar.** As in so many Windows 7 programs, this one has a very useful menu bar, but Microsoft has hidden it in hopes of making Media Player seem less complicated. Fine, but you *need* the menu bar. Make it appear by pressing Ctrl+M. The rest of this chapter assumes that you've done so, as shown in Figure 15-1.

- **Address bar.** This "bread crumbs trail" of Media Player places shows what you've clicked to get where you are: for example, Library▶Music▶Genre▶Classical. You can click any of these words to backtrack.

- **Toolbar.** Here are the one- or two-word commands you'll use most often.

The largest portion of the window is filled by the Details pane—basically, your list of music, videos, or photos. The wider you make the window, the more information you can see here.

Tip: The pop-up menu next to the Search box lets you change how the album covers, videos, and photos are displayed: in a list, as icons only, or as icons with details.

When you're in any kind of List view, don't forget that you can right-click the column headings to get the "Choose columns" command. It lets you change what kinds of detail columns appear here. You can get rid of Length and Rating, if you like, and replace those columns with Mood and Conductor. (If you're weird, that is.)

At the right side, you may see the Play, Burn, and Sync tabs; more on these in a moment.

Down at the bottom, there's a standard set of playback controls.

Note: It's true: There's no more Now Playing view. But you won't miss it; read on.

Custom Express

The first time you open Media Player, a welcome message appears. It offers you two choices:

Express Settings. This option is "Recommended" because it makes Media Player the main music and video player for your PC, sends Microsoft anonymous details about what you buy and listen to, and downloads track lists and other details from the Internet when you insert a CD or DVD.

Custom Settings. If you'd rather be a little less free with your private information, or If you'd like Media Player not to

do quite such a big land grab of your multimedia playback rights, then choose this option. You're walked through three settings screens where you can tone down Media Player's ambitions: Turn off its transmission or recording of your activities, opt out of the link to the Media Guide online music store, or specify which file types Media Player considers itself the "owner" of (that will open in Media Player when double-clicked).

Importing Music Files

When you first open Media Player, it automatically searches the usual folders on your hard drive—Music, Pictures, Videos, Recorded TV—for files that it can play. It leaves the files where they are, but in the Navigation pane, it *lists* everything it finds.

Actually, it's *monitoring* those folders. If any new music files (or video or pictures) arrive in those folders, they're automatically listed in Media Player.

But what if there's some music in a *different* folder? Fortunately, you can add that new folder to Media Player's awareness.

Choose Organize→"Manage libraries"→Music. Proceed as shown in Figure 15-2.

Note: Any song, video, or photo that you ever play in Media Player gets automatically added to its Library—*if* it's on your hard drive or the Internet. If it's on another PC on the network, or on a removable disk like a CD, Media Player doesn't bother adding it, because it probably won't be there the next time you want it.

Figure 15-2:
Here's Monitored Folder Central. It lists the folders that Media Player monitors for the arrival of new music files. Click Add to add a new folder; click a folder and click Remove to stop monitoring it. Click OK.

You can also drag sound or video files directly from your desktop or folder windows into the Media Player window.

Music Playback

You can sort your collection by performer, album, year released, or whatever, just by clicking the corresponding icons in the Navigation tree. Whenever you want to play back some music, just click your way to the song or album you want—there's no need to hunt around in your shoeboxes for the original CD the songs came from.

But that's just the beginning of Media Player's organizational tools; see Figure 15-3.

Figure 15-3:
On the Library tab, the Navigation tree (left) lists your playlists. Under the Music heading, you see various ways to sort your collection. The button that starts out looking like this ▦ (next to the Search box) changes the layout in the central window: List view, Icon view, and so on. Don't miss the Search box at the top, which searches all text related to your songs and videos as you type, hiding entries that don't match.

You can pick something to listen to in a couple of different ways:

• Under Music in the Navigation pane, click Artist, Album, or Genre. Double-click an album cover to see what songs are on that album. Double-click a song to start playing it.

• Use the Search command to find a song, composer, album, or band.

When you've found something worth listening to, double-click to start playback. You can use the space bar to start and stop playback.

Tip: If you point to a song without clicking, a little Preview bubble pops up. Click the ▶ button to hear a 15-second snippet of it; click the ▶▶ button to skip ahead.

How is this new Media Player 12 feature any better than just clicking the song and hitting the space bar? Microsoft only knows.

Fun with Media Player

When your everyday work leaves you uninspired, here are a few of the experiments you can conduct on the Media Player screen design:

- **Shrink the window to Now Playing size.** If the Media Player window is taking up too much screen space, making it harder for you to work on that crucial business plan as you listen to Eminem, no problem: You can shrink it down to a three-inch square, a little panel called the Now Playing window (Figure 15-4). You can park this window off to the side of your screen as you do other work. It shows the current album cover, and when you point at it, playback controls appear.

  To fire up the Now Playing screen, press Ctrl+3, or choose View→Now Playing, or click the ▚ icon in the lower-right corner of the window.

UP TO SPEED

Redesigning the Navigation Pane

The Navigation pane starts out looking a little baffling. Under the Music heading, it looks like you can sort by only Artist, Album, or Genre—why not rating or composer?

And what's the deal about the Pictures category? You've already got two photo-playback programs (Picture Viewer and Photo Gallery)—why would you use Media Player to play photos?

And why is there a Recorded TV folder here, even on the vast majority of PCs that cannot, in fact, record TV?

Fortunately, it's easy enough to hide the items you'll never use and add the ones you will.

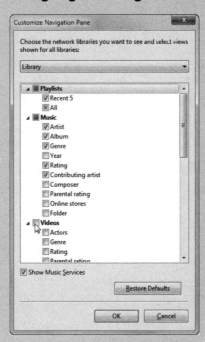

The key is to choose Organize→"Customize navigation pane." For Music, you're offered a long list of additional music-sorting categories, like Year, Rating, Composer, Folder, and so on. Turn on the checkboxes you want.

Meanwhile, the other Nav-pane headings have checkboxes here, too. Go ahead and turn off Recorded TV (you may have to click the checkbox twice to make it empty) or Pictures, if you like. If you don't plan to buy any music online, then turn off Show Music Services below the list, too.

Finally, click OK. You've finally made Media Player your player.

Press Ctrl+1 to return the Media Player window to its full-sized glory.

Tip: Of course, you can also just minimize Media Player, as you would any window. In fact, when you do that, Media Player's icon on the taskbar sprouts a jump list. In other words, you can right-click it to see a pop-up menu of handy commands, like "Resume previous list" and "Play all music." It also lists your most frequently played tunes.

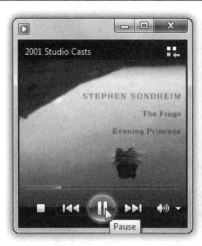

Figure 15-4:
Left: When the Now Playing window is on your screen, you get to see the album art and, when the mouse is in the window, a very tiny set of playback controls.

Right: Visualizations R Us.

- **Switch visualizations.** A *visualization* is a sort of laser light show, a screen saver that pulses in time to the music. It's available only in the Now Playing mode described above (Figure 15-4, right).

  To see it, right-click the Now Playing window. From the shortcut menu, choose Visualizations; from the submenu (and sub-submenus), choose a visualization style. Ctrl+click the window (to see the next style) or Shift+Ctrl+click (for the previous one).

  And if you tire of the displays built into Windows, simply download more of them from the Internet by choosing Visualizations→"Download visualizations" from the same shortcut menu.

- **Expand the window.** On the other hand, if your PC is briefly serving as a glorified stereo system at a cocktail party, double-click the visualization display itself (or press Alt+Enter). The screen-saver effect now fills the entire screen, hiding all text, buttons, and controls. If you have an available laptop and a coffee table to put it on, you've got yourself a great atmospheric effect. (When the party's over, just double-click again, or press Alt+Enter again, to make the standard controls reappear.)

- **Change the skin.** In hopes of riding the world's craze for MP3 files, Microsoft has helped itself to one of the old WinAmp program's most interesting features: *skins.* A skin is a design scheme that completely changes the look of Windows Media Player, as shown in Figure 15-5.

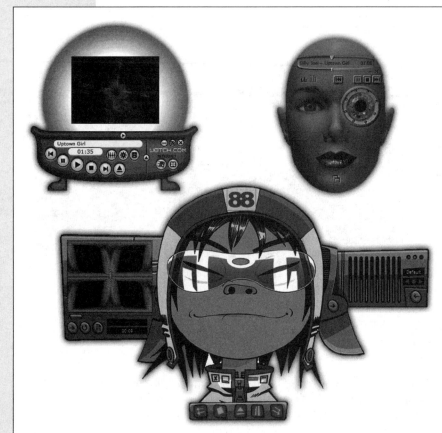

Figure 15-5:
To change the skin, choose View→Skin Chooser from the menu. A directory of available skins appears; it's empty at the outset. Click More Skins; Windows sends you online to Microsoft's grisly-sounding Skin Gallery.

Not all skins are, shall we say, masterpieces of intuitive design; it may take you several minutes just to find the Stop button. When you find a skin you like, click Apply Skin (above the list).

To choose a new skin, choose View→Skin Chooser. Then click each of the available skins, listed down the left side, to see a preview of its appearance. When you click the Apply Skin button (at the top-left corner of the window), your player takes on the look of the skin you chose *and* shrinks down into the compact Skin mode, as described in the previous tip.

- **Fool around with the sound.** Don't miss the graphic equalizer, a little row of sliders that lets you adjust the bass, treble, and other frequencies to suit your particular speakers and your particular ears. In the Now Playing window, right-click an empty spot. From the shortcut menu, choose Enhancements→Graphic Equalizer.

The same submenu offers a number of other audio effects, including Quiet Mode (smooths out the highs and the lows so that sudden blasts don't wake up the kids) and something called SRS WOW, which simulates a 3-D sound experience through nothing more than stereo speakers or headphones.

- **Fool around with the speed.** If you're in a hurry to get through an album, or just think the tempo's too slow, right-click an empty spot in the Now Playing window. From the shortcut menu, choose Enhancements→"Play speed settings." You're offered a new window containing a playback-speed slider for your music—a weird and wonderful feature.

Playing Music CDs

For its next trick, Media Player can simulate a $25 CD player. To fire it up, just insert an audio CD into your computer's CD or DVD drive.

If you insert a CD when you're at the desktop, and it's the first time you've ever taken this dramatic action, you see the dialog box shown in Figure 15-6. It asks how you want Windows to handle inserted CDs. Do you want it to *play* them? Or *rip* them (start copying their songs to your hard drive)? And if you said "play," do you want to use Media Player or Media *Center*, if you have it?

GEM IN THE ROUGH

Filling in Track Names

Weird though it may seem, precious few audio CDs come programmed to know their own names (and song titles). (Remember, CDs were invented before the MP3/iTunes era; nobody expected them to be played on computers.)

Every day, millions of people insert music CDs into their computers and see the songs listed as nothing more than "Track 1," "Track 2," and so on—and the album itself goes by the catchy name "Unknown Album."

Fix #1. If your PC is online when you insert a certain music CD, you'll bypass that entire situation. Windows takes a quick glance at your CD, sends a query to *www.allmusic.com* (a massive database on the Web containing information on over 15 million songs), and downloads the track list and a picture of the album cover for your particular disc.

Fix #2. If *allmusic.com* draws a blank, as it often does for classical recordings, no big deal. Media Player makes it easy to search the Web for this information at a later time. In the main Media Player window (Ctrl+1), click Album in the Nav pane. Right-click an album cover, and then, from the shortcut menu, choose "Find album info." (Alternatively, you can highlight the names of the *tracks* with missing information; right-click one and then choose "Find album info.")

Fix #3. You can type in the names of your songs manually. Begin on the Library tab. Select the tracks you want to edit. (By Shift+clicking or Ctrl+clicking, you can add information to multiple tracks simultaneously—for example, if they all came from the same album.)

Now click carefully in the *specific column* you want to edit—Artist, Album, or whatever. A little text box opens so that you can type in the track information manually.

Fix #4. This is pretty cool: In the Navigation tree, click the criterion that's missing, like Artist or Album. Now you can *drag* an incorrectly labeled track or album *onto* one with the correct labeling—and marvel as Media Player copies the correct info onto the dragged item.

(If an album is missing its cover art, you can paste in a graphic you've copied from, for example, the Web. Just right-click it and, from the shortcut menu, choose "Paste album art.")

No matter how the track names and album art get onto your PC, Windows saves this information in your music library. Therefore, the next time you insert this CD, the Media Player will recognize it and display the track names and album information automatically.

CHAPTER 15: WINDOWS MEDIA PLAYER   **529**

For now, click "Play audio CD using Windows Media Player."

If you're in Media Player, on the other hand, the CD's contents show up right away.

Either way, you can start playing the CD just as though the files were on your PC, using the playback controls at the bottom of the window. All of the usual tricks—Now Playing, visualizations, and so on—are available for the CD playback.

Figure 15-6:
Top: Windows may ask what you want it to do with a music CD. If you accept the "Play Audio CD using Windows Media Player" option by clicking OK or pressing Enter, Media Player opens automatically and begins to play the songs on your CD.

Ripping CDs to Your Hard Drive

You can copy an album, or selected tracks, to your hard drive in the form of standalone music files that play when double-clicked. The process is called *ripping,* much to the consternation of sleepless record executives who think that's short for *ripping off.*

Having CD songs on your hard drive is handy, though:

- You can listen to your songs without having to hunt for the CDs they came from.

- You can listen to music even if you're using the CD-ROM drive for something else (like a CD-based game).

- You can build your own *playlists* (sets of favorite songs) consisting of tracks from different albums.

- You can compress the file in the process, so that each song takes up much less disk space.

- You can transfer the songs to a portable player or burn them onto a homemade CD.

If you're sold on the idea, open the "Rip settings" pop-up menu on your toolbar. Inspect your settings. For example:

- **Format.** Microsoft has designed Windows Media Player to generate files in the company's own format, called Windows Media Audio (.wma) format. But many people prefer, and even require, MP3 files. For example, certain CD players and portable music players (including the iPod) can play back MP3 files—but won't know what to do with WMA files.

If you'd prefer the more universally compatible MP3 files, choose "Rip settings"→Format→MP3 (Figure 15-7).

- **Audio quality.** The "Audio quality" submenu controls the tradeoff, in the resulting sound files, between audio quality and file size. At 128 kbps, for example, a 3-minute MP3 file might consume about 2.8 megabytes. At 192 kbps, the same file sounds better, but it eats up about 4.2 MB. And at a full 320 kbps, the file's roughly 7 MB.

Figure 15-7:
How much compression do you want? If you don't need MP3 compatibility, Windows Media Audio (Variable Bit Rate) maximizes quality and minimizes size by continuously adjusting the data rate along the song's length.

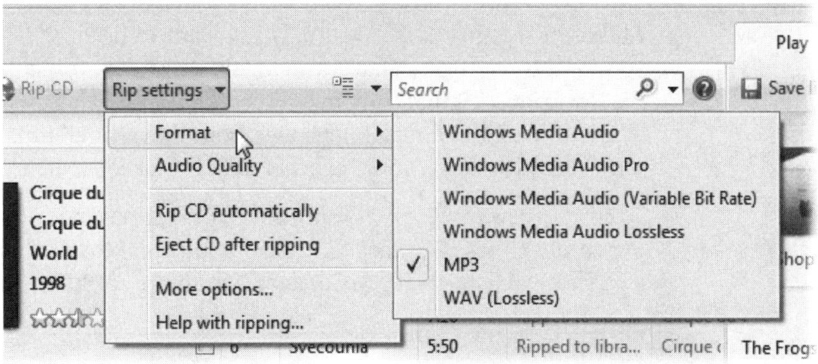

These are important considerations if you're ripping for an MP3 player. For instance, a 20-gigabyte music player can hold 142 hours of music you've ripped at 320 kbps, or 357 hours at 128 kbps.

For MP3 files, most people find the 192 kbps setting to produce great-sounding, relatively compact files. For WMA, 128 kbps might be a good starting point. Needless to say, let your ears (and the capacity of your portable music player) be your guide.

- **Storage location.** Windows likes to copy your song files into your Personal→Public→Music folder. If you'd prefer it to stash them somewhere else, choose "Rip settings"→"More options."

Tip: If you have a stack of CDs to rip, don't miss the two commands in the "Rip settings" menu: "Rip CD Automatically" and "Eject CD after ripping." Together, they turn your PC into an automated ripping machine, leaving nothing for you to do but feed it CDs and watch TV.

Here's how you rip:

1. **Insert the music CD.**

   The list of songs on the CD appears.

2. **Turn on the checkboxes of the tracks you want to copy.**

   You've waited all your life for this: At last, you have the power to eliminate any annoying songs and keep only the good ones.

3. On the toolbar, click Rip CD.

> Windows begins to copy the songs onto your hard drive. The Rip CD button changes to "Stop rip," which you can click to interrupt the process.

When it's all over, the CD's songs are now part of your library, nestled among whatever other files you had there.

Playlists

Microsoft recognizes that you may not want to listen to *all* your songs every time you need some tunes. That's why Media Player lets you create *playlists*—folders in the Navigation list that contain only certain songs. In effect, you can devise your own albums, mixing and matching songs from different albums for different purposes: one called "Downer Tunes," another called "Makeout Music," and so on.

To create a new playlist, make sure the Play tab is selected (right side). That pane starts out empty. (If it's not, click "Clear list" at the top.) It says, "Drag items here to create a playlist." Well, hey—it's worth a try. See Figure 15-8.

Figure 15-8:
To create a playlist, just start dragging tracks or whole albums to the Playlist pane. Switch views, or use the Search box, as necessary to find the tracks you want. Drag songs up and down in the Playlist pane to reorder them. Click where it now says "Untitled Playlist" to give your playlist a name. Use the upper-right pop-up menu to scramble or sort the playlist.

Tip: You can also right-click any album or song and, from the shortcut menu, choose "Add to"; the submenu lists all your existing playlists.

Once you've created a playlist, click "Save list" at the top of the pane. Thrill to the appearance of a new icon in the Playlists category of the Navigation tree.

Note: To create another playlist right away, close the first one by clicking the red ✖ beside its name.

Deleting things

Whenever you want to delete a selected song, playlist, or almost anything else, press the Delete key. Media Player generally asks if you want it deleted only from the library, or if you really want it gone from your computer.

GEM IN THE ROUGH

Auto Playlists

Auto playlists constantly rebuild themselves according to criteria you specify. You might tell one playlist to assemble 45 minutes' worth of songs you've rated higher than four stars but rarely listen to, and another to list your most-often-played songs from the '80s.

To make an auto playlist, choose "Create playlist"→"Create auto playlist" (on the toolbar). The dialog box shown here appears. The controls are designed to set up a search of your music database. Click "Click here to add criteria," click the first criterion (like Artist), and then click each underlined phrase ("is"/"is not") to build a sentence. For example, "Artist" "Is" "Beatles."

The example shown here illustrates how you'd find Beatles tunes released before the '70s—that you've rated three stars

or higher and that you've listened to exactly twice, and Billy Joel songs with at least four stars.

The last set of controls in this dialog box let you limit the playlist's total size, playback time, or song quantity.

When you click OK, your auto playlist is ready to show off; it appears in the Navigation tree like any other playlist. The difference, of course, is that it updates itself as you work with your music collection. This playlist gets updated as your collection changes, as you change your ratings, as your play count changes, and so on.

(To edit an auto playlist, right-click it; from the shortcut menu, choose Edit.)

Burning Your Own CDs

All Versions

The beauty of a CD burner is that it frees you from the stifling restrictions put on your musical tastes by the record companies. You can create your own "best of" CDs that play in any CD player—and that contain only your favorite songs in your favorite order. The procedure goes like this:

1. **Click the Burn tab. Insert a blank CD.**

   If you've inserted a rewriteable disc like a CD-RW, and you've burned it before, right-click its icon in the Navigation tree. Then, from the shortcut menu, choose "Erase disc" before you proceed.

2. **Specify which songs you want to burn by dragging them into the Burn List (where it says "Drag items here").**

   You can add music to your CD-to-be in just about any kind of chunk: individual songs, whole albums, playlists, random audio files on your hard drive, and so on; see Figure 15-9.

Figure 15-9:
Drag individual songs or albums directly into the Burn list. To add a whole playlist to the Burn List, drag its name right across the screen from the Navigation tree. To add a file that's not already in Media Player, drag it out of its Explorer window directly into the Burn List. Drag tracks up or down in the Burn list to change their sequence.

As you go, keep an eye on the time tally above your list of tracks. It lets you know how much you've put on your CD, measured in minutes:seconds. If you go over the limit (about an hour), Media Player will have to burn additional CDs. ("Next disc" markers will let you know where the breaks will come.)

Tip: Media Player adds 2 seconds of silence between each song, which might explain why you may not be able to fit that one last song onto the disc even though it seems like it should fit. It also applies volume leveling, which is great when you're mixing songs from various albums that would otherwise be at different volume levels. (You control both the gaps and the volume leveling by opening the Burn menu and choosing "More burn options.")

---

3. **Click "Start burn" above the list of songs.**

    It takes awhile to burn a CD. To wind up with the fewest "coasters" (mis-burned CDs that you have to throw away), allow your PC's full attention to focus on the task. Don't play music, for example.

Copying Music or Video to a Portable Player

If you have a pocket gizmo that's capable of playing music (like a SanDisk Sansa) or even videos (like an old Portable Media Center), then the process for loading your favorite material onto it is very similar to burning your own CD. The only difference in the procedure is that you do your work on the Sync tab instead of the Burn tab.

If you attach a player with a capacity greater than 4 gigabytes, Media Player automatically copies your entire collection onto it, if possible. If it's smaller, or if your whole library won't fit, Media Player switches into manual-sync mode, in which you handpick what gets copied.

Automatic sync

Connect the player. Media Player announces that it will perform an automatic sync. Click Finish. Smile. Wait.

POWER USERS' CLINIC

CD and DVD Format Fun

Most of the time, you'll probably want to burn a regular audio CD, of the type that plays in the world's 687 quintillion CD players. But you can also use the Burn tab to make a *data CD* or DVD—a disc designed to play in *computers*. That's a good way, for example, to make a backup of your tunes.

Actually, most recent CD players can also play *MP3 CDs,* which are basically data CDs filled with MP3 files. That's a great feature, because a single MP3 CD can hold 100 songs or more. (A few can even play *WMA CDs,* meaning CDs containing files in Microsoft's own audio format.)

You specify what kind of disc you intend to burn by choosing its name from the "Burn options" ☑▾ menu (upper-right).

If you're ever in doubt about how you burned a certain CD (audio or data?), here's a trick: Insert it into your PC, open its window, and examine its contents. If you see files with the suffix .cda, you've got yourself an audio CD; if it's full of other kinds of files, like .mp3, .wma, or even .jpg and .doc, it's a data CD.

From now on, just connecting the player to Media Player brings it up to date with whatever songs you've added or deleted on your PC. As your library grows, shrinks, or gets edited, you can sleep soundly, knowing that your portable gadget's contents will be updated automatically the next time you hook it up to your PC's USB port.

Manual sync

Connect the player. Read the dialog box. Click Finish.

In Media Player, click the Sync tab. Drag songs, videos, playlists, or albums into the List pane, exactly as you would when preparing to burn a CD (something like Figure 15-9). Click "Start sync."

Tip: If you'd like to surrender to the serendipity of Shuffle mode, you can let Media Player choose the songs you get. From the Sync options (⊡▾) menu, choose the name of your player; from the submenu, choose "Shuffle list." Each time you sync, you get a different random selection from your collection.

Sharing Music on the Network

When Microsoft called it "Windows Media Player," it wasn't kidding. This app can play music and video up, down, and sideways—and even across the network.

In a couple of ways, actually. For example:

- **Listen to other people's music.** If all the PCs in your house are part of the same network, you can sit at *your* PC and see what music and videos are on everyone *else's* PCs, right from within Media Player. Oh, yeah—see them and *play* them.

- **Send your music to another computer.** Using the new "Play to" command, you can use your PC as a glorified remote control that operates playback on a *different* PC, sending your music to it from across the network.

Note: And not just a different PC. This feature can also send music to a new generation of gear bearing the DLNA (Digital Living Network Alliance) logo—TV sets, video recorders, and so on. That's the theory, anyway.

- **Listen to your home music collection from across the Internet.** Yes, that's right: From any PC in the world, you can listen to the music that's on your PC back home—no charge.

Here are the step-by-steps.

Note: Amazingly, the record companies seem to be OK with all this music sharing. Microsoft has designed these features cleverly enough that it's always you (or your family) listening to your own collection. So the record companies, at least in principle, have nothing to worry about.

Browse One Another's Collections—Homegroup Method

If you've joined your home's Windows 7 computers together into a *homegroup* (Chapter 26), then you'll have a particularly effortless job of sharing one another's Media Player collections. You'll have to do—absolutely nothing.

As shown in Figure 15-10, your other computers' Media Player collections show up automatically at the bottom of the Navigation pane. Each shared *account* on each *PC* shows up here. Just click the flippy triangle to expand the name of an account or a PC.

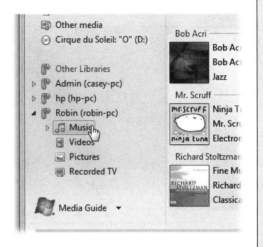

Figure 15-10:
As you sit here at the Casey PC, you can see two other computers on the network—"hp" and Robin—and one other account on your own PC—"Admin." Within, you see a duplicate of your own Media Player categories: Music, Videos, and so on. You can organize and play them exactly as though they're on your own PC.

Now, it's *possible* that you're on a homegroup and didn't turn on the "Stream my media" at the time you set it up, as suggested in Chapter 26. No problem.

If you're sitting at PC #1, and PC #2 isn't showing up in your copy of Media Player, go over to PC #2 and choose Stream→"Turn on home media streaming." (If you don't see that command, then it's already turned on.)

Now everything should work as described here.

Browse One Another's Collections—Manual Method

The homegroup method is great, because there aren't really any steps at all. But not every PC can be part of a homegroup, because not every PC on earth (or even in your home) is running Windows 7. And you can't be in a homegroup without Windows 7.

Fortunately, you're not out of luck. Even if there's no homegroup, even if some of the PCs aren't running Windows 7, you can still share one another's music.

The only difference is that each person must explicitly *turn on* sharing for his own PC.

To do that on your computer, in Media Player, choose Stream→"Turn on media sharing"; in the dialog box, click "Turn on media sharing." (You may be asked to authenticate [page 726].) Now everybody else can see and play your Media Player collection.

It's up to you to persuade *them* to turn on that feature on *their* machines (if you're not seeing them already in your copy of Media Player).

"Play to"

Everyone talks about this feature; it's one of the most interesting new Windows 7 tricks. In this scenario, you *send* music or video from your PC to another PC in the house.

Note: As noted above, you can also send your Media Player playback to any TV, stereo, or other gadget that bears the DLNA logo—and that you can figure out how to use.

FREQUENTLY ASKED QUESTION

Shutting Out Others From Your Music

I'm especially annoyed with my sister right now. I don't think she deserves the privilege of listening to my music. Can I block just her PC from listening to my stuff over the network?

But of course.

In Media Player, choose Stream→"More streaming options." (This option appears only after you've turned on streaming.) You see, in a scrolling list, the individual PCs on your network—and you can use the pop-up menu to its right to choose Blocked.

Now she can't get to your music—until she apologizes for her behavior and you change this setting back to Allowed.

If you want to stop everyone from listening to your stuff—we've all had days when we've felt like that—there's a much easier step you can take. Just choose Stream→"Automatically allow devices to play my media" so that the checkmark disappears. That's the master on/off switch for letting other people play with your stuff.

Finally, it's worth noting that you can also limit what other people are allowed to see of your collection. For example, you might want only the best stuff to be available (the highest star ratings) so your network doesn't bog down because your library is so huge. Or you might want to limit what's shared to music or movies with certain parental ratings, so you don't corrupt your kids' minds with filth.

To do that, choose Stream→"More streaming options." In the dialog box that appears, you can click either "Choose default settings" (meaning that you're going to limit what everyone shares) or "Customize" (next to the first computer in the list), to limit what you're sharing.

In the resulting dialog box, turn off "Use default settings," if necessary. Now you see the controls that let you limit what's shared to, for example, "3 stars or higher." Or, in the "Choose parental ratings" box, turn off the checkboxes of "Rated R" or whatever you don't want your impressionable young minds to see. Click OK.

Why? Because you probably keep *most* of your music on a single computer, and it can't be everywhere. Suppose you're planning to have a dinner party, but your music collection is on the PC in the attic office. Thanks to the "Play to" feature, you can line up enough background music for the whole evening, up there in the attic, and send it down to the laptop with the nice speakers in the kitchen. You won't have to keep running back upstairs to choose more music. You can stay downstairs and enjoy the whole party, uninterrupted.

There's one step of setup on the PC that will be *receiving* the playback (in this example, the laptop in the kitchen). Open Media Player. Choose Stream→"Allow remote control of my Player." In the resulting confirmation box, click—you guessed it—"Allow remote control on this network."

Note: This option doesn't work on networks you've designated as Public; see page 348.

Leave Media Player running (you can minimize it if you like).

Now go to the attic PC. In Media Player, on the Play tab, click the "Play to" icon (📭). Its pop-up menu lists all the PCs in your house that have been prepared for remote controlling, including the kitchen laptop. Choose its name.

If all has gone well, the Play To window appears. It's a waiting list of music that will play in sequence. Fill it up with albums, songs, and playlists, as shown in Figure 15-11.

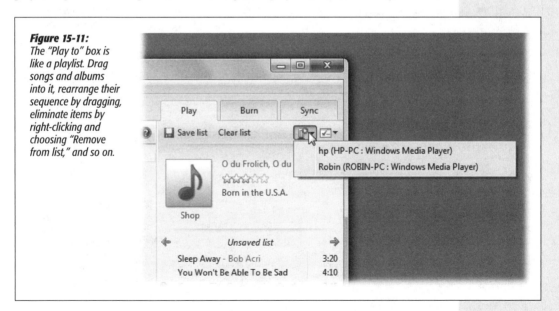

Figure 15-11:
The "Play to" box is like a playlist. Drag songs and albums into it, rearrange their sequence by dragging, eliminate items by right-clicking and choosing "Remove from list," and so on.

When you click the big ▶ button in the Play To window, the music, amazingly enough, begins to play on the kitchen laptop. Go downstairs and have some fun.

Play over the Internet

For its final stunt, Media Player lets you listen to your home music collection from *anywhere in the world*—across the Internet.

How does it know it's you, and not some teenage software pirate who just wants free music? Because you have to sign in with your Windows Live ID at both ends.

To set this up, open Media Player on your home computer. Choose Stream→"Allow Internet access to home media." Proceed as shown in Figure 15-12.

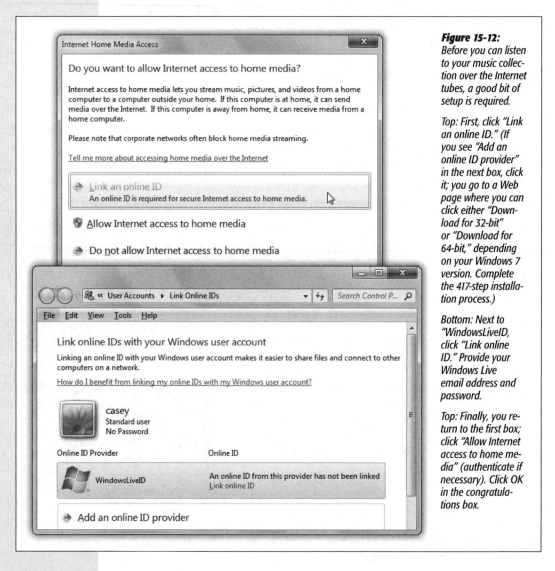

Figure 15-12:
Before you can listen to your music collection over the Internet tubes, a good bit of setup is required.

Top: First, click "Link an online ID." (If you see "Add an online ID provider" in the next box, click it; you go to a Web page where you can click either "Download for 32-bit" or "Download for 64-bit," depending on your Windows 7 version. Complete the 417-step installation process.)

Bottom: Next to "WindowsLiveID, click "Link online ID." Provide your Windows Live email address and password.

Top: Finally, you return to the first box; click "Allow Internet access to home media" (authenticate if necessary). Click OK in the congratulations box.

Now, on any other PC that's online and has Media Player 12 or later, repeat the steps shown in 15-12. And presto: In the Other Libraries category of your Navigation pane, your home music library shows up! It's ready to examine and play, across the Internet. If that ain't magic, what is?

Online Music Stores

All Versions

Right from within Media Player, you can search or browse for millions of pop songs, classical pieces, and even comedy excerpts—and then buy them or rent them. (You can pay about $1 per song to own it, or about $15 per month to download as many songs as you want, with the understanding that they'll all go *poof!* if you ever stop paying the fee.)

At first, the Online Store tab features Microsoft's own Media Guide store. But with a little effort, you can also access MixPlay, eMusic, or FaroLatino Music (what?).

Note: Two stores you *can't* get to from here are iTunes and Zune Marketplace. You have to get to those using the software that came with your iPod or Zune, as noted at the beginning of this chapter.

To look over your options, click the ▾ in the lower-left corner of the window. (The pop-up menu starts out saying Media Guide, but it may change if it's been fiddled with.)

Click "Browse all online stores." Now Media Player window ducks into a phone booth and becomes a Web browser, filled with company logos. Anything you buy gets gulped right into your Library, ready for burning to a CD or syncing with an audio player, if the store's copy-protection scheme allows it.

Internet Radio

The 21st century's twist on listening to the radio as you work is listening *without* a radio. Media Player itself can tune in to hundreds of Internet-based radio stations all over the world, which may turn out to be the most convenient music source of all. They're free, they play 24 hours a day, and their music collections make yours look like a drop in the bucket.

For radio, click that Media Guide button (lower-left corner). Media Guide is a window into *www.windowsmedia.com*. It's not just a store—it's also a promotional/news site that plugs new movies, songs, and videos; displays movie trailers and music videos; and so on.

And it lists radio stations. See Figure 15-13 for details.

Note: Unfortunately, there's no easy way to capture Internet broadcasts or save them onto your hard drive.

DVD Movies

All Versions

If your PC has a drive capable of playing DVDs, you're in for a treat. Media Player can play rented or purchased Hollywood movies on DVD as though it was born for the job. (If you have the Home Premium, Professional, Enterprise, or Ultimate editions of Windows 7, of course, you may prefer Windows Media *Center* for this task; see Chapter 16.)

Note: Media Player can't play Blu-ray DVDs. For that, you need the right kind of drive *and* accompanying software (drivers, decoder software, and player software).

Figure 15-13:
In the Media Guide toolbar, click Internet Radio. Click through the music genres to find what you're up for. Click a station that looks interesting, and then click Listen. Wait for your PC to connect to the Internet site, and then let the music begin!

Watching movies on your screen couldn't be simpler. Just insert the DVD. Media Player automatically detects that it's a video DVD—as opposed to, say, one that's just filled with files. (If the AutoPlay dialog box appears, just close it, or click "Play DVD Movie using Windows Media Player.")

Note: Actually, the first thing you see might be an insane little warning about your DVD system being set to the wrong region. You can Google "DVD regions" for the full scoop, but basically it's a copy-protection scheme to prevent you from buying a DVD in China and playing it in the U.S. You pretty much have no choice but to comply with the suggestion; change it to, for example, Region 1 (for the U.S.).

The movie begins playing. Most of the time, that means the DVD menu appears; click the Play button to get started.

If you're the interactive sort, you can also take actions like these:

- **Switch between full-screen mode and window mode** by pressing Alt+Enter. In the smaller view, the movie plays in Now Playing mode; as when you're playing music, you can right-click the screen for a pop-up menu of useful audio and visual controls, including control over subtitles.

Tip: For real fun, turn on *English* subtitles but switch the *soundtrack* to a foreign language. No matter how trashy the movie, you'll gain respect from your friends when you say you're watching a foreign film.

Figure 15-14:
Once the DVD is playing, you control the playback using the standard Media Player controls (bottom edge of the window). To switch to a different "chapter," click the ▶▶ button. To change language or parental-control options, right-click the screen; from the shortcut menu, choose Audio and Language Tracks. When you're playing the movie full-screen, the playback controls reappear when you move the mouse a bit.

- **Pause, skip, or adjust the volume** by wiggling your mouse. Playback controls appear for a few seconds at the bottom of the screen, permitting you to pause, adjust the volume, or skip backward or forward, and then fade away so as not to obscure Arnold Schwarzenegger's face.

- **Right-click the movie; from the shortcut menu, choose "Show list."** That's how you get to the list of DVD "chapters." (The same shortcut menu then says, "Hide list.")

- **Return to the DVD's main menu** by clicking the DVD pop-up menu at the left side of the playback controls; from the shortcut menu, choose "Title menu."

Ditching the remote control

When the remote control is hidden, you can always return it to the screen just by moving your mouse. But the true DVD master would never bother with such a sissy technique. The secret keystrokes of Media Player are all you really need to know:

Function	Keystroke
Play	Ctrl+P
Stop	Ctrl+S
Fast Forward, Rewind	Ctrl+Shift+F, Ctrl+Shift+B
Quieter, louder	F9, F10
Slower, faster	Ctrl+Shift+S, Ctrl+Shift+G
Normal speed	Ctrl+Shift+N
Mute	F8
Next/previous "chapter"	Ctrl+F, Ctrl+B
Full-screen mode	Alt+Enter
Eject	Ctrl+E

Of course, watching a movie while sitting in front of your PC is not exactly the great American movie-watching dream. To enhance your viewing experience, you can always connect the video-output jacks of your DVD-equipped PC (most models) to your TV. Details are in Chapter 16.

Pictures and Videos

Microsoft may like to think that music, photos, and videos are all equally important in Media Player; photos, recorded TV shows, and videos all get equal billing with music.

But that's just silly. Media Player is really all about music, and everyone knows it. If you want to play your photos and videos, Windows Photo Gallery is infinitely better suited to the task; for example, you can't edit photos or apply tags within Media Player.

Nevertheless, here's the rundown.

Start by clicking Pictures or Videos in the Navigation tree. The screen changes to something that closely resembles Photo Gallery (Figure 15-15). Here's what you can do in Pictures or Videos mode:

- **See a photo or video at full size** by double-clicking it. The video plays, or a slideshow begins automatically, showing that photo and the others in its group.

- **Rate a photo or video** by right-clicking it and, from the shortcut menu, choosing Rate→4 Stars (or whatever).

Tip: In Tiles view, it's easier to rate pictures and videos, because a row of stars appears next to each thumbnail. You just click the third star (for example). Use the View Options pop-up menu next to the Search box to choose Tiles view.

- **Create a playlist** by dragging thumbnails into the List pane at right (on the Library tab). In the context of photos or videos, a playlist basically means a slideshow or a sequence of self-playing videos. Click the big ▶ button at the bottom of the screen to see it.

- **Delete a photo or video** by clicking its thumbnail and then pressing the Delete key. Media Player asks if you want it removed only from the library, or from your computer altogether.

Figure 15-15:
In Pictures mode, you see thumbnails of your photo collection. The Navigation tree offers one-click grouping mechanisms like Keywords (tags), Rating, Date Taken, and Folder. Double-click a photo to open it and begin a slideshow of it and its neighbors.

Windows Media Center

Most of the time, you sit about three feet away from the computer screen. But the modern PC is a digital hub for your photos, music, and videos; the concept of the Media Center program, therefore, is to transform playback of these goodies into a *10-foot-away* experience. You can play them on your TV while you're sitting on the couch, or you can play them on your PC from across the room. Media Center uses jumbo fonts, buttons, and controls, so you can see them, and lets you operate them with a wireless mouse and keyboard, or a special Media Center remote control.

Better still, Media Center can turn your PC into a full-blown digital video recorder, like a TiVo. If your PC has a TV tuner card, you can watch TV, pause it, rewind and then fast-forward it, record it, and even burn the result to a DVD.

In fact, if you exploit Media Center to its extreme potential, you could ultimately sell every piece of entertainment hardware you own, including DVD players, televisions, and stereos, as well as your membership to the neighborhood movie rental store. With the right version of Windows 7, always-on Internet, and a well-endowed PC, you can simplify and organize your life and unclutter your home at the same time—all with a single piece of equipment.

You no longer need a special "Media Center Edition PC" to get all this multimedia power; any PC can do this stuff, as long as it's running the Home Premium or better versions of Windows 7. (The Starter and Home Basic editions don't include Media Center.)

Your Gear List

Home Premium • Professional • Enterprise • Ultimate

Media Center works on any Windows 7 PC. But it reserves its best tricks for people whose computers have these high-end luxuries:

- **A TV tuner and cable connection.** You'll need these extras if you want to watch and record live TV on your PC. If your PC didn't come with a TV tuner, you can add one, either in the form of an external USB box or as an expansion card, for under $100.

  All of Media Center's other features work fine even if you don't have a TV tuner (videos, photos, music, and so on)—in fact, it works beautifully in showing you TV shows played straight from the Internet.

- **A DVD burner.** It's really great to be able to burn your recorded or downloaded TV shows to a DVD so you can watch them away from home.

- **A connection to your TV.** You can always curl up at your desk to watch TV and movies, but a lot of people find that setup a bit too geeky for their tastes. In a perfect world, you'd connect the PC to your television.

  The easiest way to do that is to run an S-video cable from the PC to the TV, although there are various other ways to do the job.

- **A remote control.** If you're going to connect your PC to a TV, you don't want to have to scramble across the room every time you want to make an adjustment. That's why some computers come with remote controls, so you can run the whole show from your couch. (A wireless keyboard and mouse are useful, too.)

POWER USERS' CLINIC

The Dedicated Media Center PC

The ultimate Media Center setup, of course, is to have a PC dedicated to being a Media Center PC—that is, it sits in your home-entertainment system and never does anything else. Some companies sell PCs expressly for this purpose; for example, they're shaped like DVD players and sit on top of the rest of your set-top boxes, and come with a special remote controls.

If you'd like to recreate this effect with an ordinary PC, you'll want Media Center to open automatically whenever the PC is turned on. And you won't want to risk having regular Windows elements popping into the large-type world of Media Center.

On the Tasks list, choose Settings→General→"Startup and window behavior." Turn on "Start Windows Media Center when Windows starts" and "Always keep Windows Media Center on top."

On the far right end of the Tasks strip, turn on "Media only." That hides the usual window controls in the upper-right corner, so you won't risk dropping back into regular Windows land if someone clicks there by accident.

Wrap it up by making sure your account opens automatically when you turn on the PC, and doesn't stop to make you enter your password; page 726 has instructions.

Enjoy your new super-TiVo!

- A *lot* of **hard drive space.** Those recorded TV shows have an insatiable appetite for hard drive space.

Setup

Home Premium • Professional • Enterprise • Ultimate

Open Media Center by choosing its name from the Start→All Programs menu, or by typing *media cen* into the Start menu Search box, or by pressing the big green button on the TV-style remote control that may have come with your PC.

Tip: Thanks to its jump list—Windows Media Center's submenu in the Start menu—you can now open up Media Center directly to the module you want, like the TV guide or the list of new recordings.

The first time you run this program (and click Continue on the welcome screen), the Getting Started screen offers two setup options: Express and Custom.

Express

If you don't have a TV tuner and you're not worried about Microsoft's invasion of your privacy, click this button. You save a lot of time; you go straight to the main menu.

Tip: You can always walk through the fine-tuning steps of the Custom option later. Open Media Center. Then, from the main menu screen, choose Tasks→Settings→General→Windows Media Center Setup→Run Setup Again. It's as though you'd never run Media Center before.

POWER USERS' CLINIC

Media Center Extender

Q: What could possibly be better than running a cable from your PC to a TV, bringing all your Media Center videos and slideshows to the big screen?

A: *Not* running a cable.

That's right: You can connect the PC to the TV wirelessly—*if* you have a Windows Media Center Extender.

That's a gadget, or a feature of a gadget, that receives Media Center's playback signal from across the house, so that you can watch and listen on a real TV instead of your computer.

The Extender feature is built into certain DVD players or TVs—and, most famously, it's built into the XBox 360, Microsoft's game console. You can also buy dedicated Media Center

boxes from companies like HP and Linksys. They connect to your home network either wirelessly, using WiFi, or, um, *wirefully,* using Ethernet.

To add a Media Center Extender to your PC, open Media Center, scroll down to Tasks, then scroll across to Add Extender. The Extender Setup walks you through the process of setting up the Extender.

Along the way, you'll be asked to enter the Media Center Extender's eight-digit serial number on your PC. That's a security measure that ties *your* Extender to *your* PC. (You wouldn't want your next-door neighbor enjoying your pictures and TV shows without your knowledge, would you?)

Custom

If your PC does have a TV tuner, you can click this option to set it up—along with several thousand other options. The first screen lets you know that you'll be walked through two setup procedures: a Required one and an Optional one. Here's what they entail (Figure 16-1).

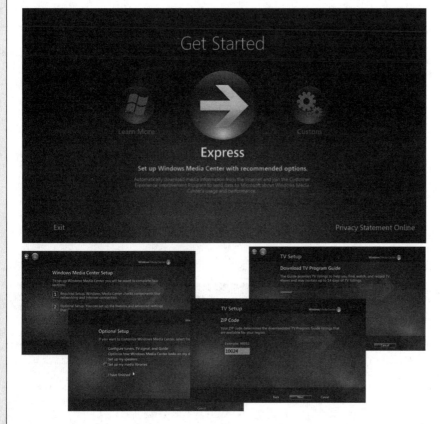

Figure 16-1:
The non-Express setup for Media Center entails two clumps of options: Required Setup and Optional Setup. The Optional choices vary depending on what hardware is installed. The first option, "Configure tuners, TV signal, and Guide," is displayed only if your Media Center has a working TV tuner card and is otherwise ready for television viewing. If you don't see this option, then your PC needs a little work in the hardware department.

Required Setup

The setup sequence walks you through two privacy-related options:

- **Help Improve Media Center.** Is it OK for Media Center to send Microsoft reports about what you do in the program, anonymously and in the background?

- **Get the Most from Windows Media Center.** Is it OK if Media Center downloads information automatically in the background—TV listings, cover art, stuff like that?

Optional Setup

After you've completed the setup for the TV tuner, signal, and Guide, the Optional Setup page appears. It offers additional branches to the setup labyrinth.

Tip: You don't have to do all this now. At any time, you can return to these options by going to the main screen and clicking Tasks→Settings.

- **Configure tuners, TV signal, and Guide.** You see this option only if your PC is, in fact, connected to a TV signal: a cable box, satellite box, CableCard, or antenna, for example. You're asked to specify where you live (in the world, and in what Zip code); when you click "Yes, configure TV with these results," Media Center auto-downloads the current TV listings for your neighborhood. Later, the Guide will show you everything that's going to be on TV in the next two weeks, making it simple for you to record stuff.

  You may also be prompted to select your TV signal provider—Time Warner Cable or Comcast, for example. If you have a remote control, you'll be asked to configure it as well.

  If you ever want to revisit this wizard, from the main screen, choose Settings→ General→Windows Media Center Setup→Set Up TV Signal.

Tip: Later, you'll want to cull the stations to hide the ones you never watch. From the main screen, choose TV→Guide→Edit Channels. Turn off the checkboxes for, you know, the Lithuanian Farming Channel and the Bermuda Curling Network.

- **Optimize how Windows Media Center looks on my display.** Answer the questions to adjust Media Center's brightness, contrast, aspect ratio (widescreen or not), and so on.

Tip: Path to get here later: Tasks→Settings→General→Windows Media Center Setup→Configure Your TV or Monitor.

- **Set up my speakers.** Use these controls to set up your surround-sound system, if any.

Tip: Path to get here later: Tasks→Settings→General→Windows Media Center Setup→Set Up Your Speakers.

- **Set up my media libraries.** Media Center automatically knows about the photos, movies, and music on your main hard drive. You have to intervene only if you want Media Center to catalog and "watch" *other* folders—folders you've created, folders on other drives, or data on other computers on your network.

Tip: If this business about importing your music and videos sounds familiar, it may be because you've already done this job using Windows Media *Player* (not the same thing as Windows Media *Center*), as described in Chapter 15. In that case, you can skip this section; your Library should already be in place, since Player and Center share the same Library folders.

In that situation, click "Add folder to watch," and then browse to the folders when prompted. (If you're adding a folder on another PC on the network, select "Add shared folders from another computer." Note that you'll be able to "see" only folders that you've explicitly *shared,* or that are part of a homegroup.)

Click the proper folder, and then click OK.

Tip: Path to get here later: Tasks→Settings→Library Setup.

When this setup adventure is over, click "I am finished" to start using your new digital hub.

The Main Menu

Home Premium • Professional • Enterprise • Ultimate

Once the setup is complete—or once you click the Express button—you land at the main menu (Figure 16-2). Already, you can see that the Media Center *looks* nothing like normal Windows programs. There are no standard windows or menus. And the fonts are *huge*—they look like they've been designed to be read by someone 10 feet away.

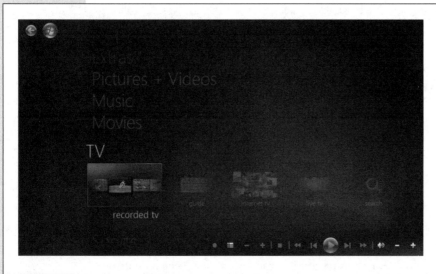

Figure 16-2:
If you're actually operating the PC from a chair right in front of it, working at your PC as usual, the whole thing might strike you as a little weird. But you'll remember the plight of the people who are sitting 10 feet away, and you'll thank Microsoft on their behalf.

The main menu is easy to get to: No matter what else you're doing in Media Center, you can always get back here by pressing the round, green button on your remote—or clicking the round, green button in the upper-right corner of the screen.

It's also easy to understand. The main screen presents a scrolling vertical list of playback categories: Extras, Pictures+Videos, Music, Movies, TV, Sports, Tasks. They're described in the following pages.

Use the ↑ and ↓ arrow keys or arrow buttons to walk through this list.

Once you've highlighted one of these categories, you can press the ← and → arrow keys or buttons to move *horizontally* among its suboptions, which are arrayed on what Microsoft calls a *strip*. For example, once you select Pictures+Videos, you can move the highlighting left or right to get to "picture library," "play all," and "video library."

Whenever you've highlighted the option you want, press the remote's OK button, or your keyboard's Enter key, to "click" it.

Tip: If all your PCs are part of a homegroup (Chapter 26), then all their pictures, music, and movies show up in Media Center. It also shares the same library with Windows Media Player, which means that all the work you've done in that program—rating your songs and shows, applying tags, creating playlists and so on—isn't wasted. Handy!

Here follows a tour of the main menu, item by item.

Extras

Home Premium • Professional • Enterprise • Ultimate

Microsoft intends for Media Center to be expandable. You'll be able to get to (and pay for) new services as they come along.

To start you off, you get these two options:

- **Extras library.** Here are the standard Windows games—Chess, Solitaire, and so on—ready to play on your TV set. The links at top let you sort the icons.

UP TO SPEED

The Golden Rules

It may look like Media Center offers a lot of features and a lot of modules—and it does—but really, you need to learn only a few basics to operate everything. Here they are: the golden rules of Media Center.

- Click something to see its details screen. Click an album to see what songs are on it. Click a movie to see who's in it. Click a TV show in the Guide listings to record it, or every episode of it. Nothing ever plays instantly; you have to open its details screen first. (Oh, all right—you can play something directly if you right-click it and choose Play from the shortcut menu. But that's a secret.)

- The More Info button on the remote = right-clicking. And right-clicking is a good habit; right-

clicking things often takes you directly to the functions you want.

- The playback controls appear when you wiggle the mouse. They're always in the lower-right corner of the screen when you're playing music or video.

- The round green button always takes you back to the main screen. If you have a remote, there's a round green button on it. If not, wiggle your mouse to make the round green button appear in the upper-left corner of the screen.

- Whatever's available in Windows Media Player is also available in Windows Media Center. Music, photos, videos, playlists, album information—both programs access the same libraries on your hard drive.

Tip: You can hide the ones you don't want by clicking the "manage extras" link at the top; then choose Extras Library and turn off the undesired checkboxes. You can also add items to the Extras library; that's a hacky maneuver that you can easily find with a quick Google search ("add to Media Center extras," for example).

- **Extras gallery.** Here's another pot of Media Center add-ons—this time, they're mostly things you have to subscribe to and pay for. They include movie services like Netflix and Cinema Now, satellite feeds from XM Satellite radio, NASCAR and boxing pay-per-view events, and so on.

Pictures+Videos

Home Premium • Professional • Enterprise • Ultimate

Ah, yes: Pictures+Videos. Here you'll find a list of all the digital photos and video clips that Media Center has found in all the likely folders on your hard drive. You're just a few clicks away from watching your high-res photos on your high-res TV or computer screen.

These are in the horizontal strip of options under Pictures+Videos:

- **picture library.** This panel (Figure 16-3) is one of the payoffs for getting to know the *libraries* concept (Chapter 2); it shows everything in your Pictures library. That includes photo files lying loose in there, as well as folders *within* the library.

Tip: To close the picture, click the Back button. (Don't click the ⊠ button at the top right of the screen—you'll shut down the entire Media Center!)

The links at the top let you sort the thumbnails by folders, tags, date taken, ratings, slide shows, or shared status. At the very top, the "play slide show" is a handy way to start an immediate playback of whatever batch of photos you're looking for.

UP TO SPEED

Videos

Media Center can also handle video clips, like the ones you've imported from your camcorder. A Videos category is also listed in the Pictures+Videos mode. As it turns out, you navigate your Videos and Pictures folders in exactly the same way:

Find a video by drilling down to it.

Sort the videos by clicking a heading above them: Folders, Date Taken, Tags, and so on. (Tags are keywords that you make up; see Chapter 14.)

Play a video by highlighting its icon and pressing Enter or Play.

Control playback using your remote control, if you have one. If not, use the buttons that appear when your mouse approaches the lower-right corner of the screen.

After a video plays, you're offered a Finished screen with three choices: Done, Restart (meaning play again), and Delete. The fourth option—Back—appears only when you mouse your way to the top-left corner of the screen.

- **play favorites.** With just a couple of clicks, you can start a crazy mosaic-like, screensaver-ish slideshow of your favorite photos. And which are your "favorites"? Whatever you've selected in advance; see Figure 16-4.

Figure 16-3:
Top: The thumbnails with names under them are the folders. Click a folder to open it.

Bottom: You now see the thumbnails of the photos within that folder. Click one to open it full-screen (and then wiggle the mouse to make slideshow controls appear). Drill down, baby, drill down.

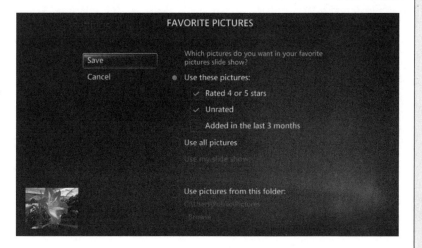

Figure 16-4:
On the Tasks→Settings→Pictures→Favorite Pictures screen, you can define your Favorites: photos with four stars or more; photos added in the past three months; unrated photos; or any combination of those. You can also define Favorites to be all your photos, or one of your predefined slideshows, or a certain folder of pictures.

- **video library.** This screen works just like "picture library": It shows you all your video clips and lets you click one to begin playback. Sort 'em by date or name, or click "play all" to view them one after another. (There's no way to specify a sequence, or to build a saved "video slideshow.")

Slideshows

For a magnificent full-screen display of just *some* of your pictures, consider creating a slideshow: a sequence of photos you've selected in advance.

To get started, click "slide shows" at the top of the screen, and then click Create Slide Show. You're guided through the process of creating a canned, ready-to-roll-anytime slideshow that incorporates only the pictures you choose. Type a name for it, click Picture Library, and then work through the folders and photos in your collection, turning on the checkboxes for the photos you want to include. On the Review and Edit screen, you can change your mind about certain shots (click the **✕**), or rearrange their slideshow sequence (click the up and down arrows). Finally, click Create.

Later, whenever you want to soak in the reminders of your past glory, click "slide shows" at the top of the picture library screen, then click the saved slideshow you want. You're shown a summary screen, and then when you click "play slide show," playback starts immediately, and—with its slow fades and pans—looks great.

You can control playback using your remote control buttons or, if you're using the mouse, move the cursor to the bottom-right corner of the screen to make the playback controls appear. You can also manually move from one image to another using the Fast Forward and Rewind buttons.

Tip: If you have a remote, use the channel up/down buttons to go forward/back through your photos.

Click the Back button in the top-left corner to close the slideshow.

Adding music

Of course, just about any slideshow is more compelling if there's music playing in the background. In Media Center, that's an easy effect:

1. **Start the music playing.**

   In Media Center, click Music→Music Library. Select an album, playlist, or other music grouping, and then click Play.

2. **Return to the Pictures+Videos screen.**

   To do that, click the Back button enough times to return to Media Center's main menu, and then select Pictures+Videos.

3. **Select "picture library," select a photos folder, and then hit Play Slideshow.**

   The music you started continues as the slideshow proceeds.

Slideshow settings

Unless you change the settings, the standard slideshow presents your pix in random order, a new photo every 12 seconds, with a standard crossfade (transition) effect.

Frankly, however, 12 seconds per photo is an *eternity* if you're anyone but the subject of the photo (or you're in love with that subject). Fortunately, you can change the settings easily enough. During the slideshow, right-click the screen; from the shortcut menu, choose Settings, and then Slideshows; use the "Show pictures for" controls. (Or, from the main screen, get there by choosing Tasks→Settings→Slideshows.)

Tip: And how do you right-click if you're using a TV-style remote? Press the More Info button. Same thing.

Editing Pictures

If you really want to edit your photos, of course, Microsoft has a specialized new tool just for you: Windows Live Photo Gallery (Chapter 14).

But sometimes you spot a misrotated photo, a picture that needs cropping, or some red eye in a portrait that you just want to fix quickly without exiting Media Center. Sure enough, you can actually perform basic photo editing from the comfort of your own living room couch.

Start at the thumbnails page. Right-click the problem photo; next, from the shortcut menu, choose Picture Details.

Now you arrive at a new screen that lists tasks like Rotate and Print. The real fun, though, awaits when you click Touch Up. On this new screen, these more powerful editing options beckon:

- **Red Eye** is a fully automatic tool. Click the words "Red Eye" to trigger the "Do your best to remove the reddish retinal reflection from the subject of this flash photo so my loved one doesn't look so much like the spawn of Satan" function.

- **Contrast** is another fully automated feature. One click makes Media Center attempt to improve the tonal range of the photo—the brights and darks.

- **Crop** places a smaller rectangle within the larger frame of your photo, indicating which part of the photo it plans to keep. Everything in the dimmed, foggy outer margins will shortly be hacked away. Click the directional arrow buttons to position the crop box, the magnifying glass buttons to shrink or enlarge the cropping rectangle, or the far-right button to rotate the cropping rectangle by 90 degrees. The actual crop doesn't take place until you click Save.

When you're finished, click Save. You're asked if you want to replace the original; click Yes. There is no other option for saving.

Tip: Click Next and Previous to edit additional pictures.

Burn a CD of Pictures or Videos

Burning photos or videos to a CD or DVD is a handy way to make a backup of them, and it's also a convenient way of taking them with you to a friend's house or a party.

> **Note:** You're not actually creating a music CD that will play in a CD player, or a video DVD that plays in a DVD player. You're basically creating backup discs that hold a lot of computer files—and that are designed to go into another *computer.*
>
> If you want to burn a music CD, see Chapter 15. To burn a video DVD, see the free PDF appendix, "Movie Maker & DVD Maker." You can download it from this book's "Missing CD" at *www.missingmanuals.com.*

Start on the Media Center main menu. Choose Tasks→Burn CD/DVD.

Windows asks you to insert a blank CD or DVD, if you haven't done so already. (What it *actually* says is, "Insert media," but it means a blank disc; nobody expects you to insert *CBS News* or *The New York Times.)*

Insert a blank disc and then click Retry; choose the CD or DVD type (Data CD or Audio CD); type a name; choose the photos folder or music album you want to back up (Figure 16-4); and then click Burn CD (or Burn DVD).

> **Tip:** During the Burn CD/DVD process, Windows invites you to click OK if you want to do other work while the disc is being burned. Light background work like typing or Web surfing should be no problem. Heavy work (Photoshop, video editing) can interfere with the burning, however, resulting in a half-burned, failed disc—yet another Frisbee for the yard!

Music: Your PC as Jukebox

Home Premium • Professional • Enterprise • Ultimate

Sooner or later, it will occur to you that your copy of Windows actually came with *two* massive music- and video-playing programs: Windows Media *Center* and Windows Media *Player*. And it's true: There's quite a bit of duplication.

Fortunately, your PC has only *one* video and music library, which serves up the same music and movies to *both* programs. In other words, if you've already added music to Media Player (Chapter 15), then it shows up in Media Center, too.

Using Media Center as your jukebox has its charms—for example, you can use a remote control.

> **Tip:** Media Center music—any music, actually—sounds best on good speakers. To get the most out of your sound system, though, you'll need to connect them correctly, take the room's size and layout into consideration, and consider equalization options. If you'd like some guidance, you can download a free bonus appendix to this chapter that describes how to set up a surround-sound system step by step. It's called Surround Sound Setup.pdf, and it's available on this book's "Missing CD" at *www.missingmanuals.com.*

Here's what you'll find on the horizontal Music strip.

- **music library.** The Music Library is, wildly enough, where Media Center displays the contents of your music collection. Use the buttons at the top (albums, artists, genres, and so on) to sort the display (Figure 16-5).

Figure 16-5:
Another game of "drill down." Click an album name or playlist name to see the "album actions" screen, where you can just start listening (click "play album"), highlight the name of a song within and start playing it, or click "add to now playing." (Now Playing is described later in this chapter.).

- **play favorites.** As with the Pictures Favorites, this option gives you a quick way to start music a-playin' without a lot of fussin'.

  You're supposed to define what "Favorites" means to you ahead of time, on the Tasks→Music pane. Here, you can specify that it means highly rated songs, a certain playlist, your most-played songs, and/or songs you've added in the past 30 days.

- **radio.** If your PC contains a radio-tuner card—most *TV* tuner cards include radio tuners, too—then Media Center's Music Library also offers an option called Radio. That's not Internet radio—we're talking genuine, bona fide, over-the-air FM radio.

  Use the Seek buttons to find the station you want. You can also select Save as Preset to save the station for easier access next time.

Tip: (If you *don't* have a radio tuner, you can still listen to hundreds of *Internet* radio stations—but not with Media Center; you need Windows Media Player for that. See Chapter 15.)

- **search.** Use this command to help you pluck a needle out of your music-collection haystack.

Playback Fun

While music is playing, a new album-art screensaver fills your screen; details on what's playing now bounce around. You can also click View Song List (for the same album), Visualize (for more traditional visual displays), Shuffle (scramble the sequence), Repeat (play the same song again once it's done), and, inevitably, Buy Music (go online to Microsoft's version of the iTunes Store).

Tip: When you've turned on one of the visualizations, you can click the **+** and **−** channel buttons on your remote (or your keyboard) to switch to other visualization styles.

Ripping CDs

To *rip* a CD means to copy its songs onto your computer. You now have two different programs that can do the ripping: Media Center and Media Player.

Truth is, Media Player is the better program to use for ripping CDs. For one thing, it lets you rip only *some* of the songs from a CD. For another, you can configure Media Player to start ripping automatically whenever you insert a CD into your drive. And you're not wasting any effort, since all CD music winds up in the same central PC music library, whether Media Player or Media Center does the work.

Still, Media Center *can* rip CDs if you're so inclined. Here's how it works:

1. **Open Media Center and insert a CD.**

   The CD starts playing. If you want to listen to the CD, that's fine; it can keep playing while you rip the tunes. If you don't want to listen to the CD, move the mouse to the lower right of the screen and click the Pause button.

Figure 16-6:
When you insert a CD while Media Center is on, the CD plays automatically. Several choices are then displayed on the left side: Rip CD, Eject CD, View Song List, Visualize, Resume Pictures, Shuffle, Repeat, and Buy Music. To rip the CD to your PC, select Rip CD.

In the meantime, the left side of the screen offers a list of useful tasks, like View Song List, Visualize, Shuffle, Repeat—and Rip CD (Figure 16-6).

2. **Click Rip CD. When asked if you're sure, click Yes.**

Ripping an entire CD (that is, copying it to your hard drive) takes about 5 minutes. Once the ripping process is done, nothing happens at all; you see only a little note that the ripping process is complete. To rip another CD, eject the first one and insert another.

To return to the Music Library, click Back *again*; select Music, and then Music Library. (Media Center remote controls usually have a Music button that shortens those steps.)

Tip: To edit the information for a song, album, or album artist, right-click it; from the shortcut menu, choose Edit. You can change the album title, artist name, and genre. This is particularly helpful for songs that are listed in the wrong genre or for a remake or live version of a song you already have on your hard drive.

Playlists

A *playlist* is a set of songs you've handpicked and hand-sequenced, even from different albums. You can read more about playlists in the Media Player chapter (Chapter 15)—because guess what? The same playlists show up in *both* programs. Any playlists you create in Media Player appear in Media Center, and vice versa.

Auto playlists are self-building, self-updating lists of songs that change as you listen, download, and change ratings. These, too, are described in Chapter 15—but unlike Media Player, Media *Center* comes pre-stocked with auto playlists. Here you'll find playlists of music you listen to the most, music you've listened to in the last month, music rated at four or five stars, and so on. As your preferences and playback habits change, so do the items in the playlists.

Note: Media Center has playlists for videos and pictures, too.

To view all your playlists—ones that you made, and auto playlists that Microsoft made—select Music→"music library"→playlists.

Click Play (or press Enter) to open the details screen for a highlighted playlist, where you can see the songs within it, start playing it, or add it to the Now Playing list. You can also delete a playlist by selecting Delete.

Tip: Once you've set up a playlist, you can immortalize it by burning it to a new, custom CD. Suddenly, you're a one-person record company. Any songs you've imported from your own CD collection or bought online are fair game. (You generally can't burn songs you've only "rented" using one of those online-music-store monthly subscription programs.)

Creating playlists

You can create playlists of your own in Media Center, but it's awkward; the only way to go about it is to add songs, albums, or other playlists to the Now Playing list—and then save *that* as a playlist, as described below.

All this explains why you'll probably be a lot happier building your playlists in Media *Player,* as described in Chapter 15. The playlists you build there also show up in Media Center.

Now Playing

Home Premium • Professional • Enterprise • Ultimate

Whenever music or video is playing, a new item appears on the Media Center main screen, nestled between the Music and Movies headings: Now Playing.

This is something like a special, on-the-fly playlist that holds the items in your music or video queue, and plays them one after another so you don't have to hand-feed your PC new music.

If you click Now Playing→View Song List, you open up a screen where you can examine the songs-in-waiting. Buttons at left let you edit the list, empty it out, shuffle it, repeat it, burn it to a CD, or save the whole thing as a playlist that you can enjoy again and again.

Movies

Home Premium • Professional • Enterprise • Ultimate

In Windows 7, Movies gets its own heading on the main Media Center screen. Here are your options:

- **Netflix.** If you're a member of Netflix's DVDs-by-mail program, you also have unlimited access to 15,000 *streaming* movies at no extra charge. That is, you can play them right now, from over the Internet, without having to wait by the mailbox. (They're not what you'd call new releases, but still—there are some gems in there.)

  The first time you select this item, Media Center downloads and installs an add-on software blob and then asks for your Netflix name and password. A few seconds later, your screen fills with the movie posters of your entire Netflix *online queue*—that is, movies you've asked to have available for instant watching on your computer.

  That's right: You can't actually browse the catalog from within Media Center. You have to do that beforehand, using your Web browser, at *Netflix.com.*

  Click a movie poster to view its details, and then click Play to start watching.

- **movie library.** This screen lists movies from whatever sources it can find: movies you've recorded from TV, movies you've ripped from DVDs, movies you've bought online. It works much like the pictures and music modules of Media Center.

In other words, use the links at top (title, genre, year, parental rating, type) to find a movie worth watching. Click a movie to see its Synopsis page; from there, you can view cast and production details, a list of similar movies, even reviews—or just start watching.

Tip: If you right-click a movie (or select it and then press More Info on your remote), you get options to play the movie, delete it, burn it to a DVD, or perform other housekeeping tasks.

- **play dvd.** Not much ambiguity here. This takes you to the controls for playing movie DVDs that you insert into your PC.

TV: Your PC as TiVo
Home Premium • Professional • Enterprise • Ultimate

There's nothing as cool as controlling TV: pausing it, rewinding to watch a football pass (or fumble) again, and fast-forwarding through commercials, all right there on your PC. Eat your heart out, TiVo owners!

(What's even more fun is taping *Jeopardy!,* watching it to learn the answers, and then playing it again "for the first time" when your spouse gets home.)

If your PC has a TV tuner card or a USB tuner box, that's exactly what Media Center offers. Once you've tasted life with a DVR (digital video recorder), you'll find the commercials, rehashes, and previews of *live* TV to be excruciating.

Tip: Don't miss the Media Center gadget. (See Chapter 6 for more on gadgets.) It displays recently recorded TV shows (click the program's name for a little panel showing details), news, sports, your music categories, and so on. Right from this little gadget you can play a recorded program, play an Internet program, or fire up some music, without having to open Media Center itself.

The TV category of Media Center is really its heart, and it's by far the most complicated. All of it except the Internet TV portion requires a computer with a TV tuner.

internet tv
Everyone else under the age of 25 is watching TV online, so why shouldn't Windows get with the program(s)?

Microsoft's free Internet TV service includes lots of brand-name TV series, sports, news, music channels, Web videos, and so on.

It's not quite as joyous as something like Hulu.com, the Internet's global center for legal, free, full-length TV episodes. You have to sit through ads on Media Center (and they're longer than on Hulu), the selection is much smaller, and the navigation is harder to figure out. Still, it's handy to make the Media Center window small and tuck it off to one side as you do other work, and it's all right in the Start menu.

The first time you click "internet tv," a setup screen asks you to click the "I have read the legalese" checkbox and click the Install button, so Media Center can download

---

the Internet TV module (a one-time deal). Later, when you click an actual show to watch, you may be asked to OK another installation (of Adobe Flash).

Thereafter, things are a lot more straightforward. The main Internet TV screen is a bit baffling, but here's the rundown:

- **Giant ads on the top row.** Each ad is actually for a TV series, each bearing a Watch Now button, so the marketing isn't especially offensive. Scroll horizontally to see more banners. When you click a Watch Now button, the banner is replaced by a row of episode buttons, so you can jump right to the Internet (Figure 16-7).

Figure 16-7:
Top: Click a banner to see its episodes, or scroll down through the horizontal rows of other TV options. There's no particular logic to their organiza-tion—one row might be called Full Episodes, another Top TV (most popular clips), but a lot of them are random promos ("Superspies" or "Oscar Winners from Netflix," for example).

- **Rows of TV buffet.** The strips of tiles farther down the screen—you can scroll through them—are a motley assortment of structured listings (like Channels or Headlines) and whatever Microsoft is promoting this week (like "Special Agents and Superspies").

Click your way to any show if you like—but if you're just confused by the layout, try the Guide instead (described next).

guide

If you click "guide" (on the main screen under TV) instead, you get a much more comprehensive look at what Internet shows are available. If your PC has a TV tuner, you find the Internet options way off at the right end of the regular TV guide; if it *doesn't* have a TV tuner, the Internet grid is the *only* guide you see (Figure 16-8).

Note: Alas, you can't record Internet TV shows.

Click a promising-looking TV show to read its Synopsis screen; click "play" to have a look.

recorded tv

Here's the list of shows you've told Media Center to record for you—that it has, in fact, recorded. Click to open a Synopsis screen; click "play" to play. Click a heading (like "date recorded" or "title") to sort your holdings.

Tip: Click "view scheduled" to see the shows you've requested that haven't been broadcast or recorded yet.

Figure 16-8:
Internet TV is organized by category. There's no timeline, of course (like 7:00 p.m., 8:00 p.m.), because Internet shows air whenever you want them. But you can still scroll horizontally; point to the right or left end of a row and wait for the large < or > button to appear. Click it to scroll.

While you're watching the show, you can use your remote, the keyboard, or the mouse to fast-forward through the commercials, to rewind to review a scene, or to pause to get a bite to eat. As usual, if you're using the mouse, point to the lower-right corner to make the controls appear. Otherwise, use the keys and buttons on the keyboard or remote; see Figure 16-9.

UP TO SPEED

Managing Recorded TV

Recorded shows can really suck up a lot of hard drive space. Recording your favorite series and *Star Trek* reruns can bleed even the biggest hard drive dry in a matter of months. The next thing you know, you're struggling to grasp why you can't install a game of Tetris for lack of space.

That's why you'll want to watch and then delete shows as often as you can. For the ones you'd like to keep for a while, like a good movie or the last season of *The Sopranos* on HBO, consider burning them to DVD and then deleting the hard drive copy.

If you stop the program before it's finished playing, you're offered a Resume command. If the program ends, or if you've had enough of it before it's over, you can choose Delete.

Save a show onto a DVD

If you've found something you really like and want to burn it to a DVD—to save forever, or maybe just to let the kids watch in the car—follow these directions:

1. **Open Media Center. Insert a blank DVD. Go to Tasks→Burn CD/DVD.**

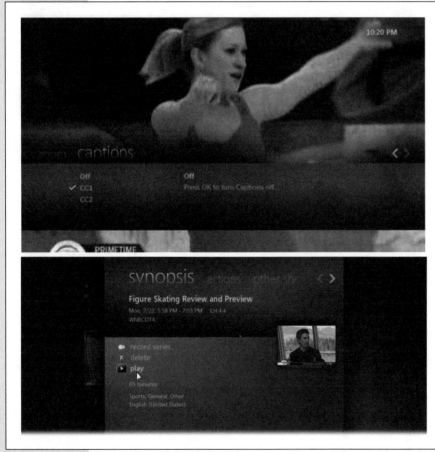

Figure 16-9:
Top: This info bar appears when you right-click the screen (or press More Info on your remote). The three "tabs" offer controls like Zoom (magnifies the picture in various ways to fill your window or monitor) and Captions (lets you turn on closed-caption subtitles, if they're available). Press Enter or click OK to get rid of this window.

Bottom: The Synopsis screens contain reams of information about the recorded show.

You're offered several DVD formats to burn, like Data DVD, Video DVD, or DVD Slide Show. To make a *backup* of your TV shows, for example (for use in a PC), you'd opt for the Data DVD. To save a TV show or movie onto a regular old DVD for playback in a DVD player, you want the regular Video DVD format.

2. **Select Video DVD. Click Next.**

Now you're asked to name the DVD. If you have a remote control that has only number keys, you can use the clever little cellphone-like dialing pad to tap out alphabet letters. For example, to enter *Shrek,* you'd tap 7777 (for the letter S), 44, 777, 33, 55.

3. **Type out a name, and then click Next.**

Now you're asked to choose *what* you want to burn onto your DVD. You can choose either Recorded TV or Video Library (which means any video file on your hard drive that *didn't* come from your TV tuner—your camcorder imports, for example).

4. **Click Recorded TV, and then click Next.**

Media Center displays what's in your Recorded TV Library. Each show appears as a giant thumbnail image, complete with a checkbox in the lower-right corner.

5. **Turn on the checkboxes of the shows you want to transfer to DVD.**

You can also use the Select All, Clear All, "by name," and "by date" controls for help in selecting or sorting the videos.

6. **Click Next.**

You're offered one final chance to review and edit the list of shows. Here, you can click the up or down arrow buttons to rearrange their sequence on the DVD, to rename a show, and so on.

7. **Click Burn DVD.**

The burning process can take quite a while, depending on how much data you've added and how fast your CD/DVD burner is. Once the burn is finished, eject the disc and reinsert it to make sure it works.

Overall, though, this is a great way to get that must-see television show from your computer to the living room—or even those scintillating vacation pictures of Mexico, if you don't have a Media Center Extender!

Tip: You can follow these same steps to burn a slideshow onto a DVD, except, of course, that you should choose DVD Slide Show in step 2.

In fact, you can also insert a regular blank *CD,* although your options in that case are limited to making data discs or burning music CDs.

---

guide

This is your master TV guide—and the place to schedule TV shows you want to record.

The listings here are for your Zip code, specific to your cable or satellite company. The Guide is downloaded automatically (if that's the way you configured it).

Tip: If a TV show is already playing, you see it playing in the background, faintly, behind the TV listings grid. That's intentional.

If your PC has a TV tuner, the Guide is a traditional time/channel grid (Figure 16-10, top). You can scroll it up, down, left, or right by pressing your arrow keys, or by pointing to the edge of the grid until an arrow button appears and then clicking it.

Tip: Some special Media Center remote controls and keyboards offer a button that lets you scroll a day at a time; with the mouse, you're pretty much stuck scrolling hour by hour.

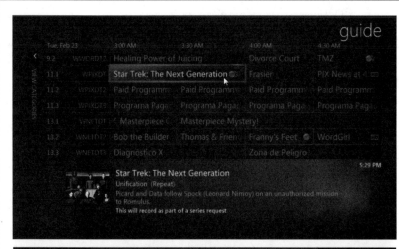

Figure 16-10:
Top: Type a number into the remote's keypad to change channels. Click Skip to move forward in the Guide. Point to a title to read a synopsis. Right-click a title (or use the remote's Info button) to get more program info, record the program, or record the series. Press Record on the remote once (one red dot) for, "record this episode"; twice (double dots) for, "record all episodes."

Bottom: Using the links at the top of the Synopsis page, you can see a list of upcoming episodes of the show (handy if there's a conflict with a show you wanted to record), a cast list, and so on. "Record series" makes your PC record every episode of the selected show.

Once you've found a show that looks interesting, click it once with the mouse, hit Enter on the keyboard, or click OK on the remote control. The Synopsis screen appears (Figure 16-10, bottom). Scroll horizontally to check out its tabs:

• **synopsis.** A plot and broadcast summary: date, time, channel, duration, language, category, and so on. Here, too, is where you can click either "record" (this episode) or "record series" (all episodes).

Note: If you have a Media Center remote, press the Record button once for "Record this episode," twice for "Record all episodes," or three times to turn recording off.

- **actions.** Pretty much the same thing as the "synopsis" page, except that now you get access to the Advanced Record button, which reveals some not-at-all advanced settings for recording. For example, you can specify the Frequency. (Just this show, or the whole series? And if you want the whole series, do you also want reruns, and do you want to limit the broadcasts to a certain channel?)

  You can also specify how long you want to Keep the show on the hard drive before it's auto-deleted (Until Space Needed, For One Week, Until I Watch, Until I Delete). Finally, you can change the Stop time (lets you end the recording between 5 minutes and 3 hours after it's scheduled to end, so that you don't miss the ends of football games that run long).

- **other showings.** Here you can see when the selected show will be aired again. This is a good option when a conflict arises between two shows you want to record at the same time. If you find out that one of the shows will be aired again in the next day or two, you can work through the conflict by recording the later airing.

Tip: Once a show is scheduled to record, you can right-click its name in the Guide to set options quickly. You can also right-click any program to record it on the fly, without having to wade through any options at all—a convenient option when you're trying to get out the door.

---

live tv

Your expensive PC can do more than just imitate a TiVo. It can also imitate a regular old TV set. This option simply shows whatever is on TV right now; you can use the **+/−** buttons on the playback controls, or the channel buttons on your remote, to change the channel.

Note: If you have a cable box connected to your PC, you should be able to get anything on Media Center that you can get when the box is plugged into a television. That includes premium channels and on-demand movies.

Plenty of people just plug the cable directly into the TV tuner, though. They don't get the premium channels but can still tune in to 30 or so standard cable stations. Doing without a cable box simplifies the setup and saves another monthly fee.

---

search

This tool helps you pluck one show out of your TV-guide haystack. For instance, from Search, select Title, type *South Park,* and find out instantly when the next *South Park* airs. Choose Categories→Educational to find something really boring for your kids to watch. Choose Movie Actor and type *Goldie Hawn* to see what movies or TV shows are coming up with her in the cast.

If you get any "hits," recording them is just a button-click away.

Tricks with Live TV

With Media Center, watching TV is anything but a passive activity. As Figure 16-11 shows, several buttons await.

OK, that all seems reasonable—except for the Rewind and Fast Forward buttons and, well, Pause. How is it possible to rewind a live TV broadcast? Or fast-forward it? Or pause it?

When live TV comes into the computer, Media Center saves *(caches)* the show that's playing. Even if you haven't explicitly asked for it to be recorded, it caches the most recent 60 minutes or so.

Once it's cached, you can rewind what you've already watched (or what has been cached), and fast-forward through what you don't want to see, like commercials. If you hit the Pause button, your PC freezes the frame. But behind the scenes, it's still recording, saving up what's coming in live, so that you can fast-forward again when you're back from the bathroom or from answering the door.

Figure 16-11:
If you're remoteless, move your mouse to the lower-right corner of the screen to summon these TV controls.

This snapshot comes from playback of an Internet show, not a TV broadcast. How do you know? Because the tick marks on the scroll bar show where the ad breaks occur. Mercifully, they're short, and there aren't many at each break.

TROUBLESHOOTING MOMENT

Figure Out What's Not Working

Every month or so, it's a good idea to take inventory, to see how the Media Center TV recording empire is going. Perhaps you thought *American Idol* was a good program to record, but it turns out that everyone in your family watches it live, and nobody deletes the recorded episodes. Perhaps you thought you'd watch *Survivor* but decided after a few shows that you just weren't into it. Every now and then, in other words, you should revisit your automatic recording schedule.

One way to take inventory is to see what's not being deleted (because it's not being watched). If you have 10 episodes of *Pimp My Ride,* for example, it may be because your kids are watching it at someone else's house; get it off of the Recorded TV list.

To cancel any recording, navigate to Recorded TV. Right-click the show you no longer want to record. Click Program Info, then Series Info, then Cancel Series

---

Note: You can't fast-forward into a live TV show until after you've paused or rewound it. Even Microsoft hasn't figured out a way to let you fast-forward into part of a TV show that hasn't yet been broadcast.

A typical Media Center maven learns to harness this caching business in order to skip the ads. For example, you might turn on *Judge Judy* at 4:00 p.m., pause it, and then come back around 4:12. Now you can start it from the beginning and fast-forward through all the commercials when they appear. You'll be done by 4:30, in time to watch something else.

Sports

Home Premium • Professional • Enterprise • Ultimate

Here's a new category in the Windows 7 version of Media Center; clearly, Microsoft knows a hot-button TV interest when it sees one. The Sports strip offers these options:

- **on now/on later.** Available only if you have a TV tuner. Shows you all sports shows that are on right now, or coming up.

- **scores.** A handy non-video scrolling list of today's final game scores (Figure 16-12).

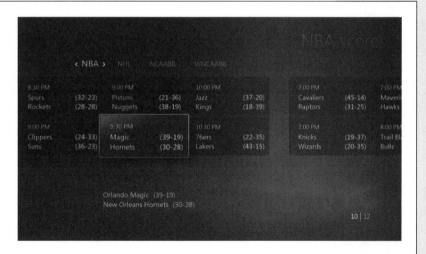

Figure 16-12:
The Sports option is available to all, TV tunerless or not. Use the links at top to specify what sports league you want (NBA, NHL, and so on).

- **players.** Click the league you love, and then click "add players." After a moment, your PC shows you a long list of current players in that league. Click "save."

  From now on, the Players screen will show you a tidy list of those players' current stats. It's got nothing to do with playing media (in terms of music, photos, or videos), but it's very cool.

- **leagues.** This is basically a settings screen for the *other* Sports options. For each league, you can specify whether you want its games to show up in "on now" and "on later"; its scores to show up in "scores"; alerts to pop up announcing its imminent games on TV; and its players to be available to the "players" feature.

Tasks

Home Premium • Professional • Enterprise • Ultimate

This row on the main menu offers a motley collection of administrative tools like these:

- **shut down.** Brings up icons for Close, Log Off, Restart, and Shut Down. They're provided here primarily for people who use the PC for *nothing* but running Media Center. There's no Start menu in that case, and no other way to turn the thing off.

- **settings.** An endless array of options, as described in the next section.

- **learn more.** Opens up a weird little ad for Media Center.

- **burn cd/dvd.** Lets you burn TV shows or photo slideshows to a CD or DVD, as described earlier in this chapter.

- **sync.** Auto-copies selected music or video files onto a pocket music player, exactly the way Windows Media Player does (but with fewer options and more awkwardness).

- **add extender.** A wizard that helps you set up a Media Center Extender, so that you can play back your PC's Media Center holdings to a TV somewhere else in the house. See page 549.

- **media only.** This mode hides the Minimize and Close buttons in the upper-right corner so that nobody can ever *leave* the Media Center program. That's what you'd want on a PC that's connected right to the TV and never does anything *but* run Media Center.

Settings

Home Premium • Professional • Enterprise • Ultimate

Once you've had a little experience with Media Center, the elaborate preferences screens (Tasks→Settings) will make a lot more sense. Here you find all sorts of ways to personalize Media Center. Most are self-explanatory, but here are a few items worthy of special note:

General

On the General options screen, you can change the following:

- **Startup and Windows Behavior.** Should Media Center always stay on top of other windows, start up automatically when Windows starts, or allow alert messages to appear?

- **Parental Controls.** You can set up a four-digit password that stands between your kids and TV, movies, and DVDs that you consider too violent or racy for them.

- **Optimization.** Schedule a time to run these hard drive tune-up tasks, and they'll run automatically. You should configure this for a time when you won't be using the Media Center, but when the computer is on and idle.

TV

From the TV options page, you can change things like these:

- **Set Up TV Signal.** Don't go here unless you need to make changes to your TV signal setup. You might have to add or remove a set-top box, change cable or satellite companies, or upgrade your television service, for example.

- **Closed Captioning.** "Closed captioning" refers to subtitles that appear at the bottom of the TV screen. Closed captioning is a free service (paid for by the TV networks) and is great for loud rec rooms, workout rooms, parties, and anyone who's hard of hearing or learning to read. (If you tune into the football game with closed captioning on, people can follow it while listening to music. Loudly.)

  Note that even if you turn on closed captioning, not all television shows or television channels offer it.

Tip: The Closed Captioning setting in TV Signal options doesn't affect DVDs.

To make captions appear on DVDs, visit Tasks→Settings→DVD→Closed Captioning. Even then, if your DVD doesn't show captions, you may have to open DVD Setup, described below, and turn on subtitles in your own language.

Pictures

In Tasks→Pictures, you find options like these:

- **Slide shows.** Controls how photos appear during slideshows: how long they stick around, whether they pan and zoom, whether photo and song information appears, and what the background screen color is.

- **Ratings.** If you turn on this option, then whenever a slideshow is playing, you can rate each photo by tapping the 0 through 5 keys on your keyboard or remote—a very handy way to rate them, indeed.

Tip: An identical option is available in the Music settings.

Music

From the Music options, you have choices like these:

- **Visualizations.** If you like to trip with the daisies while listening to music, then check all of the visualizations (music-driven screen savers) here.

- **Now Playing.** What's in the background of the Now Playing screen, and when does song information appear?

Start Menu and Extras

If you've added to the list of items on the main menu, use the Start Menu options to turn them off again. The Extras options govern which games show up in Extras.

DVD

From the DVD options, you can change the language, audio, and subtitle options here, just as you would on a real DVD player. You can also use the Remote Control Options to change the Skip and Replay buttons to skip chapters, to skip forward and back, or to change angles.

Extenders

Add, delete, or manage your Media Center Extenders (page 549).

Media Libraries

On this screen, you can tell Media Center to "watch" a new folder (that is, to add the video, photo, or music contents of a folder on your hard drive to its listings automatically) or to stop watching one.

Tip: For reams of additional tips, tricks, and conversation about Media Center, visit *www.thegreenbutton. com*, the Web's world headquarters for Media Center info.

Part Five:
Hardware & Peripherals

5

Print, Fax, & Scan

Technologists got pretty excited about "the paperless office" in the 1980s, but the PC explosion had exactly the opposite effect. Thanks to the proliferation of inexpensive, high-quality PC printers, the world generates far more printouts than ever. Fortunately, there's not much to printing from Windows 7.

Installing a Printer

All Versions

A printer is a peripheral device—something outside of the PC—and as such, it won't work without a piece of driver software explaining the new hardware to Windows. In general, getting this driver installed is a simple process. It's described in more detail in Chapter 18; here are a few notes on the process to get you started.

USB Printers

If the technology gods are smiling, then installing the driver for a typical inkjet USB printer works just as described in Chapter 18: You connect the printer, turn it on, and marvel as Windows autodetects it and autoinstalls the driver, thanks to its secret cache of hundreds of printer drivers (Figure 17-1).

If you have a really old printer, its drivers might not be compatible with Windows 7. Check the manufacturer's Web site, such as *www.epson.com* or *www.lexmark.com,* or a central driver repository like *www.windrivers.com,* to see if there's anything newer.

Network Printers

If you work in an office where people on the network share a single printer (usually a laser printer), the printer usually isn't connected directly to your computer. Instead, it's elsewhere on the network; your PC's Ethernet cable or wireless antenna connects you to it indirectly.

In general, there's very little involved in ensuring that your PC "sees" this printer. Its icon simply shows up in the Start→Devices and Printers folder. (If you don't see it, click "Add a printer" in the toolbar. On the wizard's second screen, you're offered the chance to "Add a network, wireless or Bluetooth printer." That's the one you want.)

Note: As you've probably guessed, that's also how you install a wireless or Bluetooth printer.

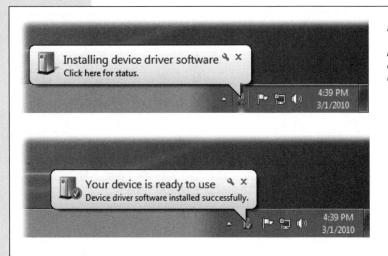

Figure 17-1:
You got lucky. Windows dug into its own bag of included drivers and installed the correct one. Let the printing begin.

Parallel, Serial, and Infrared Printers

Although USB printers are the world's most popular type today, there was, believe it or not, a time before USB. In those days, most home printers fell into one of these categories:

• **Parallel.** Before USB changed the world, most printers connected to PCs using a printer cable or *parallel cable.* The cable connects to your PC's parallel port, which Microsoft's help screens call the LPT1 port—a 25-pin, D-shaped jack. (This connector is marked with a printer-icon on the back panel of many PCs.)

• **Serial.** Other older printers use a cable connected to one of your computer's *serial* (or *COM*) ports, the connectors that often accommodate an external modem. The primary advantage of a serial connection is the extended cable length—parallel cables must be no more than nine feet long, while serial cables up to 50 feet long work fine.

Tip: To protect its innards, turn off the PC before connecting or disconnecting a parallel or serial cable.

- **Infrared.** Certain printers from HP, Canon, Citizen, and other companies print using *infrared* technology—that is, there's no cable at all. Instead, if your PC has an infrared lens (a few aging laptops may still have them), it can communicate with the printer's similar lens wirelessly, as long as the printer and PC are within sight of, and relatively close to, each other.

Sometimes you get lucky, and these printers work just like modern USB printers: You connect the printer, turn on your PC, and delight in the "Found new hardware" message that appears on your taskbar. You're ready to print.

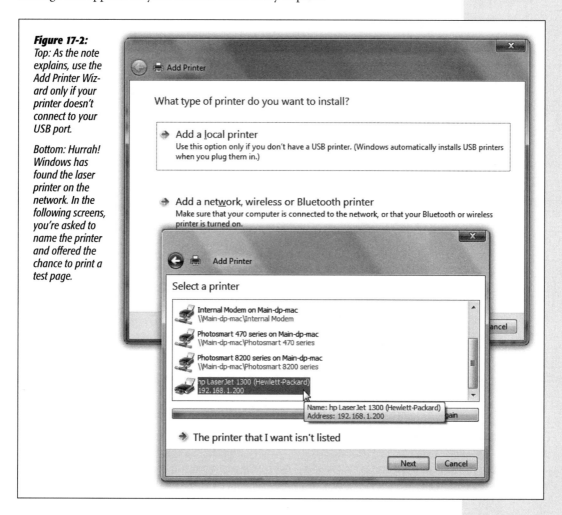

Figure 17-2:
Top: As the note explains, use the Add Printer Wizard only if your printer doesn't connect to your USB port.

Bottom: Hurrah! Windows has found the laser printer on the network. In the following screens, you're asked to name the printer and offered the chance to print a test page.

But if Windows doesn't recognize the printer model you've hooked up, it can't install its drivers automatically.

In that case, you'll have to call upon the mighty powers of the Add Printer Wizard (Figure 17-2). Choose Start→Devices and Printers, and then click "Add a printer" on the toolbar—if indeed the Add Printer wizard hasn't appeared automatically. Click Next to walk through the questions until you've correctly identified your printer (Figure 17-3), told Windows which computer it's connected to, and installed the appropriate software.

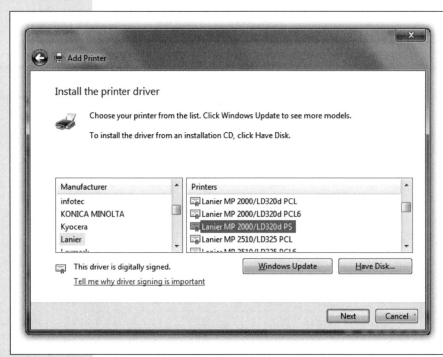

Figure 17-3:
The left pane lists every printer manufacturer Microsoft has ever heard of. Once you've selected your printer's manufacturer, a list of all the printer models from that manufacturer (that Windows knows about) appears in the right pane. Click the Have Disk button if your printer's driver is on a disc supplied by the manufacturer.

The Devices and Printers Window

If your driver-installation efforts are ultimately successful, you're rewarded by the appearance of an icon that represents your printer.

TROUBLESHOOTING MOMENT

If Your Printer Model Isn't Listed

If your printer model isn't in the list of printers (Figure 17-3), then Windows doesn't have a driver for it. Your printer model may be very new (more recent than Windows 7, that is) or very old. You have two choices for getting around this roadblock.

First, you can contact the manufacturer (or its Web site) to get the drivers. Then install the driver software as described in the previous section.

Second, you can use the *printer emulation* feature. As it turns out, many printers work with one of several standard drivers that come from other companies. For example, many laser printers work fine with the HP LaserJet driver. (These laser printers are not, in fact, HP LaserJets, but they *emulate* one.)

The instructions that came with your printer should have a section on emulation; the manufacturer's help line can also tell you which popular printer yours can impersonate.

This icon appears in the new *Devices and Printers* window—an important window that you'll be reading a lot about in this chapter. The Start menu includes a link to Devices and Printers, but you can also open the window in other ways, depending on how you've set up Windows 7:

- If you've set up your Start menu to display a submenu for the Control Panel (page 44), just choose Start→Control Panel→Devices and Printers.

- If you view your Control Panel in Category view, choose Start→Control Panel, and then click "View devices and printers" (in the Hardware and Sound category).

- If you view your Control Panel in the Small Icons or Large Icons view, choose Start→Control Panel, and then click the Devices and Printers icon.

In any case, the Devices and Printers window contains big, good-looking icons representing every gadget plugged into your PC—including the printers you've installed (Figure 17-4).

If you have a printer from a big-name company, double-clicking its icon here might open the Device Stage, a new Windows 7 feature: a mini-Web page full of details and useful links like what's printing now, ink levels, and so on. Other devices and printers may open a more generic preference pane or management program.

GEM IN THE ROUGH

Installing Fake Printers

If your printer has two paper trays, switching to the secondary one is something of a hassle. You must spend time making the changes in the Print dialog box, as described later in this chapter. Similarly, switching the printout resolution from, say, 300 dpi to 600 dpi when printing important graphic documents is a multistep procedure.

That's why you may find it useful to create several different icons for *the same printer.* The beauty of this stunt is that you can set up different settings for each of these icons. One might store canned settings for 600 dpi printouts from the top paper tray, another might represent 300 dpi printouts from the bottom one, and so on. When it comes time to print, you can switch between these virtual printers quickly and easily.

To create another icon, just run the Add Printer Wizard a second time, as described on the preceding pages. At the point in the installation where you name the printer, invent

a name that describes this printer's alternate settings, like *HP6-600 dpi* or *Lexmark-Legal Size.*

When the installation process is complete, you see both printer icons—the old and the new—in the Devices and Printers window. Right-click the new "printer" icon, choose "Printing preferences" from the shortcut menu, and change the settings to match its role.

To specify which one you want as your *default* printer—the one you use most of the time—right-click the appropriate icon and choose "Set as default printer" from the shortcut menu.

Thereafter, whenever you want to switch to the other set of printer settings—when you need better graphics, a different paper tray, or other special options for a document—just select the appropriate printer from the Select Printer list in the Print dialog box (Figure 17-5, top). You've just saved yourself a half-dozen additional mouse clicks and settings changes.

No matter which approach you take, printer icons come in handy in several different situations, as the rest of this chapter clarifies.

Note: When you're finished with a printer—when you sell it, for example—you can eliminate its icon from your Devices and Printers window. Right-click its icon; from the shortcut menu, choose "Remove device."

Figure 17-4:
At first, the toolbar in the Devices and Printers window offers few commands. But when you click a particular printer icon, other useful options appear, as shown here. Some of them duplicate the options that appear when you right-click a printer icon.

Printing
All versions

Fortunately, the setup described so far in this chapter is a one-time-only task. Once it's over, printing is little more than a one-click operation.

Printing from Programs

After you've created a document you want to see on paper, start the printout (choose File→Print, click the Print button on the toolbar, or press Ctrl+P. The Print dialog box appears, as shown at top in Figure 17-5.

This dialog box, too, changes depending on the program you're using—the Print dialog box in Microsoft Word looks a lot more intimidating than the WordPad version—but here are the basics:

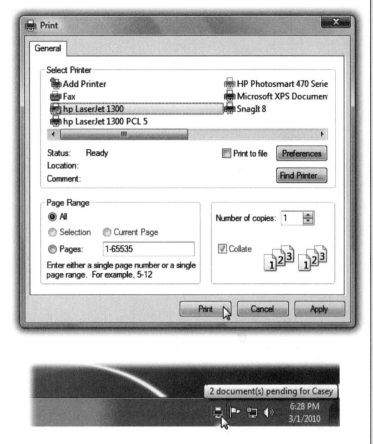

Figure 17-5:
Top: The options in the Print dialog box are different for each printer model and each application, so your Print dialog box may look slightly different. For example, here is the Print dialog box from WordPad in Windows 7. Most of the time, the factory settings shown here are what you want (one copy, print all pages). Just click OK or Print (or press Enter) to close this dialog box and send the document to the printer.

Bottom: During printing, the tiny icon of a printer appears in your notification area. Pointing to it without clicking produces a pop-up tooltip, like this one, that reveals the background printing activity.

- **Name.** If your PC is connected to several printers, or if you've created several differently configured icons for the same printer, choose the one you want from this list of printers.

- **Preferences/Properties.** Clicking this button opens a version of the printer's Properties dialog box, as shown in Figure 17-6.

- **Page range** controls which pages of the document you want to print. If you want to print only some of the pages, click the Pages option and type in the page numbers you want (with a hyphen, like *3-6* to print pages 3 through 6).

Tip: *You can also type in individual page numbers with commas, like 2, 4, 9, to print only those three pages–or even add hyphens to the mix, like this: 1-3, 5-6, 13-18.*

Click Current Page to print only the page where you've placed the blinking insertion point. Click Selection to print only the text you selected (highlighted) before opening the Print dialog box. (If this option button is dimmed, it's because you didn't highlight any text—or because you're using a program that doesn't offer this feature.)

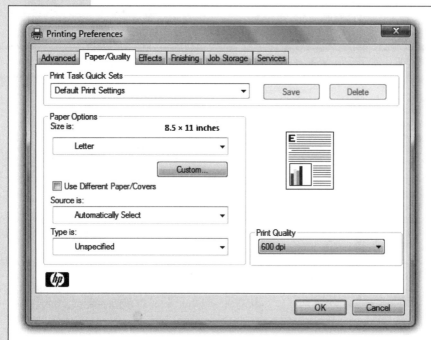

Figure 17-6:
When you open Properties from the Print dialog box, you can specify the paper size you're using, whether you want to print sideways on the page (landscape orientation), what kind of photo paper you're using, and so on. Here, you're making changes only for a particular printout; you're not changing any settings for the printer itself. (The specific features of this dialog box depend on the program you're using.)

- **Number of copies.** To print out several copies of the same thing, use this box to specify the exact number. You get several copies of page 1, then several copies of page 2, and so on, in sequence—*unless* you also turn on the Collate checkbox, which produces complete sets of pages, in order.

- **Print.** The Print drop-down list that might appear in the lower-left section of the dialog box offers three options: "All pages in range," "Odd pages," and "Even pages."

  Use the Odd and Even pages options when you have to print on both sides of the paper but your printer has no special feature for this purpose. You'll have to print all the odd pages, turn the stack of printouts over, and run the pages through the printer again to print even pages.

- **Application-specific options.** The particular program you're using may add a few extra options of its own to an Options tab in this dialog box. For example, Internet Explorer offers an Options tab (Figure 17-7).

When you've finished making changes to the print job, click OK or Print, or press Enter. Thanks to the miracle of *background printing* (also called spooling), you don't have to wait for the document to emerge from the printer before returning to work on your PC. In fact, you can even exit the application while the printout is still under way, generally speaking. (Just don't put your machine to sleep until it's finished printing.)

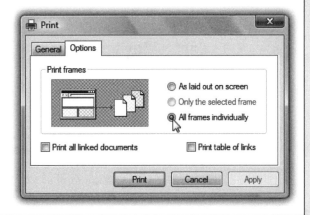

Figure 17-7:
Say you're printing something from Internet Explorer. The Web page about to be printed uses frames (individual, independent, rectangular sections). The Print dialog box in Internet Explorer recognizes frames and lets you specify exactly which frame or frames you want to print. If the page contains links to other Web pages (and these days, what Web page doesn't?), you can print those Web pages, too, or just print a table of the links (a list of the URLs).

Printing from the Desktop

You don't necessarily have to print a document while it's open in front of you. You can, if you wish, print it directly from the desktop or from an Explorer window in a couple of ways:

- Right-click the document icon, and then choose Print from the shortcut menu. Windows launches the program that created it—Word or Excel, for example. The document is then printed automatically to the default printer.

- If you've opened the printer's own print queue window (Figure 17-8) by right-clicking the Printers icon in your Devices and Printers window and choosing "See

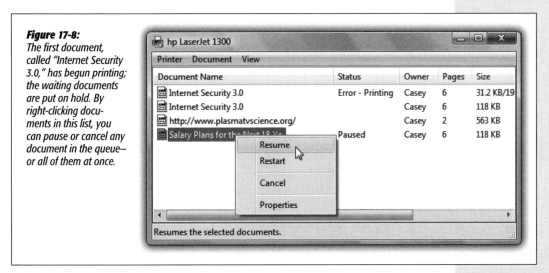

Figure 17-8:
The first document, called "Internet Security 3.0," has begun printing; the waiting documents are put on hold. By right-clicking documents in this list, you can pause or cancel any document in the queue—or all of them at once.

what's printing," then you can drag any document icon directly into the list of waiting printouts. Its name joins the others on the list.

These methods bypass the Print dialog box and therefore give you no way to specify which pages you want to print, or how many copies. You just get one copy of the entire document.

Controlling Printouts
All Versions

Between the moment you click OK in the Print dialog box and the arrival of the first page in the printer's tray, there's a delay. Usually, it's very brief, but when you're printing a complex document with lots of graphics, the delay can be considerable.

Fortunately, the waiting doesn't necessarily make you less productive, since you can return to work on your PC, or even quit the application and go watch TV. An invisible program called the *print spooler* supervises this background printing process. The spooler collects the document that's being sent to the printer, along with all the codes the printer expects to receive, and then sends this information, little by little, to the printer.

Note: The spooler program creates huge temporary printer files, so a hard drive that's nearly full can wreak havoc with background printing.

To see the list of documents waiting to be printed—the ones that have been stored by the spooler—open the Devices and Printers window, right-click your printer's icon (Figure 17-4), and then choose "See what's printing" to open its window.

Tip: While the printer is printing, a printer icon appears in the notification area. As a shortcut to opening the printer's window, just double-click that icon.

The printer's window lists the documents currently printing and waiting; this list is called the *print queue* (or just the *queue*), as shown in Figure 17-8. (Documents in the list print in top-to-bottom order.)

You can manipulate documents in a print queue in any of the following ways during printing:

- **Put one on hold.** To pause a document (put it on hold), right-click its name, and then choose Pause from the shortcut menu. When you're ready to let the paused document continue to print, right-click its listing and choose Resume (Figure 17-8).

- **Put them all on hold.** To pause the printer, choose Printer→Pause Printing from the window's menu bar. You might do this when, for example, you need to change the paper in the printer's tray. (Choose Printer→Pause Printing again when you want the printing to pick up from where it left off.)

- **Add another one.** As noted earlier, you can drag any document icon directly *from its disk or folder window* into the printer queue. Its name joins the list of printouts-in-waiting.

- **Cancel one.** To cancel a printout, click its name and then press the Delete key. If you click Yes in the confirmation box, the document disappears from the queue; it'll never print out.

- **Cancel all of them.** To cancel the printing of all the documents in the queue, choose Printer→Cancel All Documents.

Note: A page or so may still print after you've paused or canceled a printout. Your printer has its own memory (the *buffer*), which stores the printout as it's sent from your PC. If you pause or cancel printing, you're only stopping the spooler from sending *more* data to the printer.

- **Rearrange them.** If you're used to, say, Windows Me, it may take you a moment—or an afternoon—to figure out why you can't simply drag documents up or down in the list of waiting printouts to rearrange their printing order. In Windows 7, the procedure is slightly more involved.

  Start by right-clicking the name of one of the printouts-in-waiting; from the shortcut menu, choose Properties. On the General tab, drag the Priority slider left or right. Documents with higher priorities print first.

Fancy Printer Tricks

The masses of Windows users generally slog through life choosing File→Print, clicking OK, and then drumming their fingers as they wait for the paper to slide out of the printer. But your printer can do more than that—much more. Here are just a few of the stunts that await the savvy PC fan.

Printing at 39,000 Feet

Printing any document is really a two-step procedure. First, Windows converts the document into a seething mass of printer codes in the form of a *spool file* on your hard drive. Second, it feeds that mass of code to the printer.

When you're not connected to your printer—for example, when you're sitting in seat 23B several miles over Detroit—you can separate these two tasks. You can do the time-consuming part of the printing operation (creating the spool files) right there on the plane. Then, later, upon your happy reunion with the printer, you can simply unleash the flood of stored spool files, which then print very quickly.

To set this up, right-click the icon for your printer in the Devices and Printers window (Figure 17-4). From the shortcut menu, choose "See what's printing." Then, on the Printer menu, choose "Pause printing." That's all there is to it. Now you can merrily "print" your documents, 100 percent free of error messages. Windows quietly stores all the half-finished printouts as files on your hard drive.

When the printer is reconnected to your PC, right-click its icon once again, choose "See what's printing," and then click "Pause printing" again to clear this setting. The printer springs to life almost immediately, spewing forth your stored printouts with impressive speed.

Sharing a Printer

If you have more than one PC connected to a network, as described in Chapter 24, they all can use the same printer. In the old days, this convenience was restricted to expensive network printers like laser printers. But in Windows 7, you can share even the cheapest little inkjet connected to the USB port of one computer.

To begin, sit down at the computer to which the printer is attached. Choose Start→ Control Panel. Click Network and Internet, and then open Network and Sharing Center. In the left pane, click "Change advanced sharing settings." Proceed as described in Figure 17-9.

Once you've *shared* the printer, other people on the network can add it to their own Devices and Printers windows using these steps:

1. **Choose Start→Devices and Printers. In the Devices and Printers window, click "Add a printer."**

   The "What type of printer do you want to install" window appears.

2. **Click "Add a network, wireless or Bluetooth printer."**

   After a pause while your PC searches, you see a window populated by all the printers available to the other PC.

UP TO SPEED

Location-Aware Printing

Speaking of shared printers, if you're running the Professional or Ultimate edition of Windows 7 and working on a laptop computer, you can let Windows handle the printing chores that arise when you move from one network to another. Windows uses a feature called location-aware printing to do this.

When you're at home, for example, and printing to your family's homegroup printer, Windows uses that as your default printer. When you head back to the office the next day and log onto your company's network, Windows knows which printer you used the last time you printed at the office and switches to that printer as the default.

To associate printers with a particular network, choose Start→Devices and Printers, and then select one of the printers you've installed. On the toolbar, click "Manage default printers."

In the resulting dialog box, you can tell Windows to always use the same printer as your default (if that's your preference) or change default printers network to network. Use the Select Network and Select Printer lists to assign the printers you want to use.

---

3. Click the icon of the printer you want to use, and then click Next. On the "which driver" page, click Next again. Finally, type a name for the printer (as you want it to appear on your PC), and then click Next. On the final screen, click Finish.

Figure 17-9:
Top: Sharing a printer takes a couple of steps. First be sure that the network you're using has printer sharing turned on. (Home and Work networks have this setting turned on automatically.) Under the current network profile, check that "Turn on file and printer sharing" is selected. If it isn't turned on, select it, and then click Save Changes. (Authenticate yourself if necessary.)

Bottom: Open Devices and Printers from the Start menu. Right-click the printer you want to share, and then click Printer properties. Click the Sharing tab, and select the "Share this printer" checkbox.

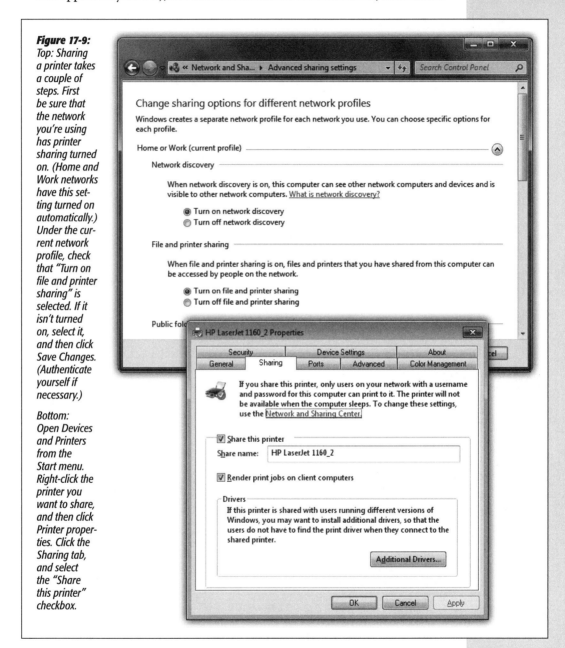

The shared printer appears in *your* Devices and Printers window, even though it's not directly connected to your machine. It's now available for any printing you want to do.

Printing to a File

When it comes to printing, most of the time you probably think of printing onto paper. In certain circumstances, however, you may not actually want a printout. Instead, you might want to create an electronic printer file on your hard drive, which can be printed later. You might want to do so, for example, when:

- You're working on a document at home, and you've got only a cheesy $49 inkjet printer. By creating a printer file, you can delay printing until tomorrow, in order to use the office's $4,000 color laser printer.

- You plan to send your finished work to a service bureau—that is, a professional typesetting shop. Sending a finished printer file avoids incompatibilities of applications, fonts, layout programs, and so on. (OK, these days, you'd just send a PDF. But let's just pretend.)

Creating a printer file

To create such a printer file, choose File→Print, just as you would print any document. The Print dialog box appears; now turn on the "Print to file" option. When you then click OK or Print, the Print to File dialog box opens.

Some programs let you choose *where* you want to save the file; others ask you only to name the file itself. In that case, your saved printout goes automatically into your Documents folder. The file extension for these printer files is .prn.

Printing a printer file

To print a printer file, type *cmd.exe* into the Start menu and press Enter. You've just started command-line session; your cursor is blinking on the command line.

Now type *copy c:\foldername\filename.prn lpt1: /b* and then press Enter.

Here's how this instruction breaks down:

- **Copy** is the name of the command you use to print the file—notice that it's followed by a space.

- **C:** is the letter of the drive that contains your printer file. You can omit this part if the printer file is on the current drive (usually C:).

- **\foldername** is the name of the folder into which you saved the printer file (Documents, for example).

- **\filename** is the name you gave the file.

- **.prn** is the filename extension (which Windows added to the file automatically when you saved the printer file).

- **lpt1:** is the port to which the printer is connected. Note the colon following the name, and also note that there's a space *before* this part of the command. If the printer is attached to LPT2, substitute that port name.

- **/b** tells the Copy command that the file is *binary* (containing formatting and other codes), not simply text.

Note: A printer file (a *.prn* file) can be printed only on the same printer model that was selected in the Print dialog box when the file was generated. If you want to create a printer file for that color printer at work, in other words, be sure to first install its driver on your computer.

Limiting Hours of Access

If it's just you, your Dell, and a color inkjet, then you're entitled to feel baffled by this feature, which lets you declare your printer off-limits during certain hours of the day. But if you're the manager of some office whose expensive color laser printer makes printouts that cost a dollar apiece, you may welcome a feature that prevents employees from hanging around after hours in order to print out 500 copies of their head shots.

To specify such an access schedule for a certain printer, follow the instructions in Figure 17-10.

Figure 17-10:
Right-click your printer's icon in the Printers window. From the shortcut menu, choose Properties, and then click the Advanced tab, shown here. Select "Available from," and use the time-setting controls to specify when your underlings are allowed to use this printer from across the network. Clicking OK renders the printer inoperable during off hours.

Add a Separator Page

If your PC is on a network whose other members bombard a single laser printer with printouts, you might find *separator pages* useful—the printer version of fax cover sheets. A separator page is generated before each printout, identifying the document and its owner.

This option, too, is accessible from the Advanced tab of the printer's Properties dialog box (Figure 17-10). Click the Separator Page button at the bottom of the dialog box. In the Separator Page dialog box, click the Browse button to choose a *.sep* (separator page) file.

Color Management

As you may have discovered through painful experience, computers aren't great with color. That's because each device you use to create and print digital images "sees" color a little bit differently, which explains why the deep amber captured by your scanner may be rendered as brownish on your monitor, but come out as a bit orangey on your Epson inkjet printer. Since every gadget defines and renders color in its own way, colors are often inconsistent as a print job moves from design to proof to press.

The Windows *color management system* (CMS) attempts to sort out this mess, serving as a translator among all the different pieces of hardware in your workflow. For this to work, each device (scanner, monitor, printer, copier, and so

on) must be calibrated with a unique *CMS profile*—a file that tells your PC exactly how your particular monitor (or scanner, or printer, or digital camera) defines colors. Armed with the knowledge contained within the profiles, the CMS software can make on-the-fly color corrections, compensating for the quirks of the various devices.

Most of the people who lose sleep over color fidelity do commercial color scanning and printing, where "off" colors

are a big deal—after all, a customer might return a product after discovering, for example, that the actual product color doesn't match the photo on a Web site. Furthermore, not every gadget comes with a CMS profile, and not every gadget can even accommodate one. (If yours does, you'll see a tab called Color Management in the Properties dialog box for your printer, as shown here.)

If you're interested in this topic, open the Color Management tab for your printer. (Opening the Color Management applet in the Control Panel gets you to the same place, shown here.) The Automatic setting usually means that Windows came with its own profile for your printer, which it has automatically assigned. If you click Manual, you can override this decision and apply a new color profile (that you downloaded from the printer company's Web site, for example).

Remember to follow the same procedure for the other pieces of your color chain—monitors, scanners, and so on. Look for the Color Management tab or dialog box, accessible from their respective Properties dialog boxes.

If you scroll to the very bottom of the resulting list of geeky Windows folder names, you'll find four of them:

- **Sysprint.sep** is the one you probably want. Not only does this page include the name, date, time, and so on, but it also automatically switches the laser printer to PostScript mode—if it's not already in that mode, and if it's a PostScript printer.

- **Pcl.sep** is the same idea, except that it switches the laser printer to PCL mode— commonly found on HP printers—before printing. (PostScript and PCL are the two most common languages understood by office laser printers.)

- **Pscript.sep** switches the printer to PostScript mode but doesn't print out a separator page.

- **Sysprtj.sep** prints a separator page, switches the printer to PostScript mode, and sets Japanese fonts, if they're available on your printer.

Printer Troubleshooting
All Versions

If you're having a problem printing, the first diagnosis you must make is whether the problem is related to *software* or *hardware.* A software problem means the driver files have become damaged. A hardware problem means there's something wrong with the printer, the port, the cable, the toner, the ink, or whatever.

Test the printer by sending it a generic text file from the command line. To perform such a test, locate a text file or create one in Notepad. Then open a command prompt (type *cmd.exe* into the Start menu ; press Enter). Send the file to the printer by typing *copy filename.txt prn* and then pressing Enter. (Of course, remember to type the file's actual name and three-letter extension instead of *filename.txt.*)

If the file prints, then the printing problem is software-related. If it doesn't, then the problem is hardware-related.

For software problems, reinstall the printer driver. Open the Devices and Printers window, right-click the printer's icon, and then choose Remove Device from the shortcut menu. Then reinstall the printer as described at the beginning of this chapter.

If the problem seems to be hardware-related, try these steps in sequence:

- Check the lights or the LED panel readout on the printer. If you see anything other than the normal "Ready" indicator, check the printer's manual to diagnose the problem.

- Turn the printer off and on to clear any memory problems.

- Check the printer's manual to learn how to print a test page.

- Check the cable to make sure both ends are firmly and securely plugged into the correct ports.

- Test the cable. Use another cable, or take your cable to another computer/printer combination.

Another way to check all these conditions is to use the built-in Windows *troubleshooter*—a wizard specifically designed to help you solve printing problems. To run, choose Start→Help and Support. Type *printing troubleshooting* into the Search box and press Enter. Click "Open the Printer troubleshooter" to open that article.

If none of these steps leads to an accurate diagnosis, you may have a problem with the port, which is more complicated. Or even worse, the problem may originate from your PC's motherboard (main circuit board), or the printer's. In that case, your computer (or printer) needs professional attention.

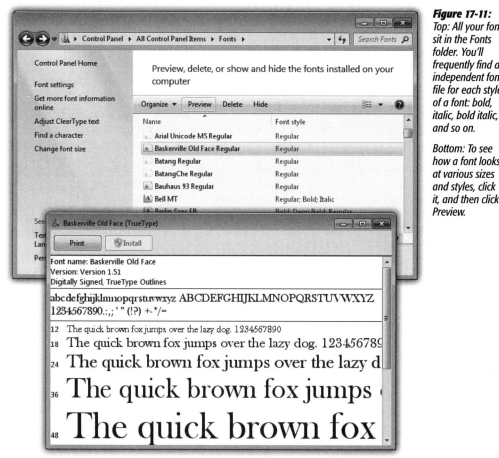

Figure 17-11:

Top: All your fonts sit in the Fonts folder. You'll frequently find an independent font file for each style of a font: bold, italic, bold italic, and so on.

Bottom: To see how a font looks at various sizes and styles, click it, and then click Preview.

Fonts
All Versions

Some extremely sophisticated programming has gone into the typefaces that are listed in the Fonts dialog boxes of your word processor and other programs. They use *OpenType* and *TrueType* technology, meaning that no matter what point size you select for these fonts, they look smooth and professional—both on the screen and when you print.

Managing Your Fonts

Windows comes with several dozen great-looking fonts: Arial, Book Antiqua, Helvetica, Times New Roman, and so on. But the world is filled with additional fonts. You may find them on Web sites or in the catalogs of commercial typeface companies. Sometimes you'll find new fonts on your system after installing a new program, courtesy of its installer.

To review the files that represent your typefaces, open the Fonts icon in the Control Panel. (Switch to Large Icons or Small Icons view to see the Fonts icon.) As Figure 17-11 illustrates, it's easy and enlightening to explore this folder.

Tip: The Fonts icon in your Control Panel window is only a shortcut to the *real* folder, which is in your Local Disk (C:)→Windows→Fonts folder.

To remove a font from your system, right-click it and then choose Delete from the shortcut menu, or highlight it and then click Delete on the toolbar. To install a new font, first download the font (from the Internet, for example) and then drag its file icon into this window (or right-click the font and then click Install). You can also choose to show or hide specific fonts in your programs. The Fonts window in Control Panel includes a column that shows the status of a font. Select a font, and then click Show or Hide to make this font available in the programs you use.

Whatever you do, you see the changes immediately reflected in your programs' Font dialog boxes; you don't even have to quit and re-open them.

Faxing
Professional • Enterprise • Ultimate

One of Windows 7's most spectacular features is its ability to turn your PC's built-in fax modem into a fax machine. This feature works like a charm, saves all kinds of money on paper and fax cartridges, and may even spare you the expense of buying a physical fax machine.

Faxing in Windows 7 is a much more official feature than it was in Windows XP, where it wasn't even installed automatically. Now there's a new program dedicated just to faxing: Windows Fax and Scan.

Sending a fax is even easier on a PC than on a real fax machine; you just use the regular File→Print command (Ctrl+P), exactly as though you're making a printout of the onscreen document. When faxes come *in,* you can opt to have them printed automatically, or you can simply read them on the screen.

Tip: The similarity with printing doesn't stop there. The Devices and Printers folder even contains a Fax icon that works just like a printer icon.

Sending a Fax from Any Program

Now, the one big limitation of PC-based faxing is that you can only transmit documents that are, in fact, *on the computer.* That pretty much rules out faxing notes scribbled on a legal pad, clippings from *People* magazine, and so on (unless you scan them first).

If you're still undaunted, the procedure for sending a fax is very easy:

1. **Open up whatever document you want to fax. Choose File→Print.**

   The Print dialog box appears.

2. **Click the Fax icon (or choose Fax from the Select Printer list, as shown in Figure 17-12), and then click OK or Print.**

   The very first time you try faxing, you encounter the Fax Setup Wizard. It first asks you to connect to a fax modem. Choose that option, and then type a name for your fax modem.

POWER USERS' CLINIC

Cover-Page Art Class

You don't have to be content with the handful of fax cover pages that Microsoft provides. The Fax and Scan program comes with its own little cover-page design studio. To get started, choose Tools→Cover Pages.

At this point, you could click the New button to call up a pure, empty, virginal cover page. But by far the easiest way to get going is to open one of the existing cover pages, make changes to it, and then save it under a different name.

To do so, click the Copy button now in front of you, and then open one of the four cover-page templates that Windows presents. Windows puts it into what's now a one-item list. Select the item and click Rename to give it a new name, if you like, and then click Open to begin work on your redesign.

The design program works like any standard drawing program. In order to type text that won't change—a confidentiality notice, for example—click the Text tool on the toolbar

(which looks like this: **ab|**), and then click the page. Use the commands in the Insert menu to plop placeholder text boxes onto the page—special rectangles that, on the actual cover sheet, will be filled by your name, fax number, the number of pages, and so on. You can transfer your own company logo onto the page just by pasting it there (Edit→Paste).

Every item you place on the page—a text block, a graphic, and so on—is a separate object that you can move around independently using the arrow tool. In fact, you can even move a selected object in front of, or behind, other objects, using the commands in the Layout menu.

When you're finished with your masterpiece, choose File→Save. It gets saved into your Documents→Fax→Personal CoverPages folder (meaning that only you have access to it—not other people who share the PC and log in with their own accounts).

Next, it wants you to specify what happens when someone sends a fax to *you* (that is, when the phone line your PC is connected to "rings"). Click "Answer automatically" if you want Windows to answer incoming calls after five rings, assuming that if you haven't picked up by that time, the incoming call is probably a fax.

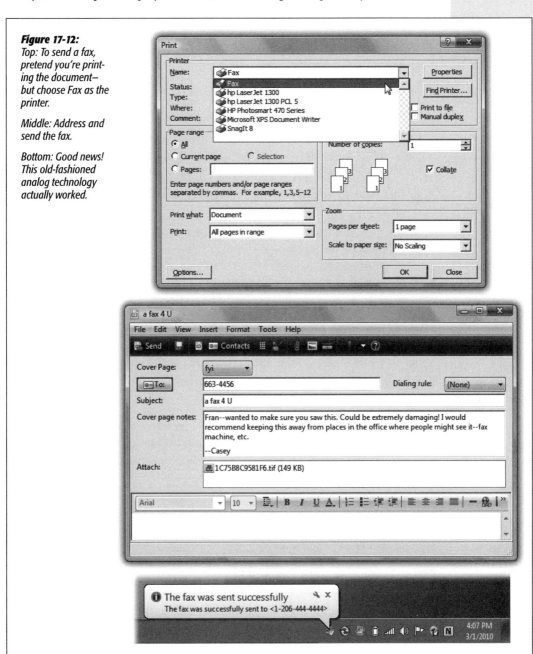

Figure 17-12:
Top: To send a fax, pretend you're printing the document—but choose Fax as the printer.

Middle: Address and send the fax.

Bottom: Good news! This old-fashioned analog technology actually worked.

If you choose "Notify me," then each incoming call triggers an onscreen message, asking you whether you want the PC to answer as a fax machine. And if you choose "I'll choose later," you can postpone the decision and get on with sending your first fax.

Note: At this point, the Windows Firewall, rather stupidly, may interrupt to ask if it's OK for Windows Fax and Scan to run. Click Unblock.

Finally, you arrive at a New Fax window (like a New Message window) (Figure 17-12, middle).

3. **Type the recipient's fax number into the "To:" box.**

Or click the tiny envelope next to "To:" to open up the Select Recipients list (where you can find people listed as your Windows Contacts and others). Double-click the name of the fax-equipped buddy you want.

4. **If you want a cover page, choose a cover-page design from the Cover Page drop-down menu.**

If you do, then a new text box opens up, where you can type a little note, which also appears on the cover page.

Note: You can ignore the main message box at the bottom of the window for now. It's intended for creating faxes from thin air, as described below, rather than faxes that began life as documents on your PC.

At this point, type a subject for your fax. You may also want to choose View→Preview (or click the tiny Preview icon on the toolbar) to give it a final inspection before it goes forth over the wires. When you're finished looking it over, your fax is ready to send.

5. **Click Send in the toolbar.**

Your modem dials, and the fax goes on its merry way. A status dialog box appears (although its progress bar doesn't actually indicate how much time remains). You can go do other work on the PC; when the fax goes through, a cheerful message appears in your notification area (Figure 17-12, bottom).

Your recipient is in for a real treat. Faxes you send straight from your PC's brain emerge at the receiving fax machine looking twice as crisp and clean as faxes sent from a standalone fax machine. After all, you never scanned them through a typical fax machine's crude scanner on your end.

Faxing Using Windows Fax and Scan

If you just have a few quick words to fax to somebody, you can use Fax and Scan by itself, without first opening a document on your PC. Open the Fax and Scan program from your Start→All Programs menu.

Click New Fax in the toolbar, fill in the fax number, and choose a cover page as described in the preceding steps. This time, however, you can use the broad message area at the bottom of the window to type the body of your text.

Tip: Cover pages automatically include your name, fax number, and so on. And how does it know all this? Because, in Fax and Scan, you chose Tools→Sender Information and filled it out.

Receiving Faxes

There are several reasons why you may *not* want your PC to receive faxes. Maybe you already have a standalone fax machine that you use for receiving them. Maybe your house has only one phone line, whose number you don't want to give out to people who might blast your ear with fax tones.

But receiving faxes on the PC has a number of advantages, too. You don't pay a cent for paper or ink cartridges, for example, and you have a handy, organized software program that helps you track every fax you've ever received.

Note: The discussion here applies to normal people who send faxes using a computer's built-in fax modem. If you work in a corporation where the network geeks have installed a *fax server,* life is even easier. Incoming faxes automatically arrive in the Inbox of the Fax and Scan program.

Exactly what happens when a fax comes in is up to you. Start by opening Windows Fax and Scan; then choose Tools→Fax Settings, and proceed as shown in Figure 17-13.

You have two options for receiving faxes:

- **Manually answer.** This option is an almost-perfect solution if your PC and telephone share the same phone line—that is, if you use the line mostly for talking, but occasionally receive a fax. From now on, every time the phone rings, a balloon in your notification area announces: "Incoming call from [the phone number]. Click here to answer this call as a fax call." (See Figure 17-13.)

  When you do so, your PC answers the phone and begins to receive the fax. To see it, open Fax and Scan.

- **Automatically answer after.** Use this option if your PC has a phone line all to itself. In this case, incoming faxes produce a telephone-ringing sound, but there's otherwise no activity on your screen until the fax has been safely received. Once again, received faxes secret themselves away in your Fax and Scan program.

While you're setting things up in the Fax Settings dialog box, don't miss the "More options" button. It's the gateway to two useful features:

- **Print a copy to.** If you like, Windows can print out each incoming fax, using the printer you specify here. Of course, doing so defeats the environmental and cost advantages of viewing your faxes onscreen, but at least you've got something you can hold in your hand.

- **Save a copy to.** Ordinarily, incoming faxes are transferred to your Fax and Scan program. If you turn on this option, however, you can direct Windows to place a *duplicate* copy of each one—stored as a graphics file—in a folder of your choice.

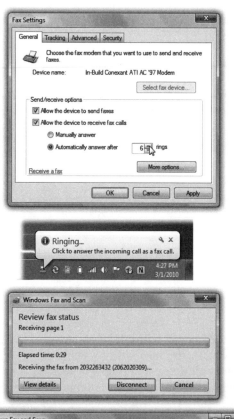

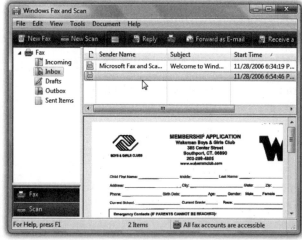

Figure 17-13:

Top: Click the General tab, and then turn on "Allow device to receive fax calls." If you choose "Automatically answer," you can also specify how many rings you want to go by before the PC answers; you don't want it answering regular incoming voice calls before you've had a chance to pick up.

Second from top: Uh-oh! You're getting a call! Click the balloon itself if you think it's a fax.

Third from top: Windows Fax and Scan takes over and begins to download the fax. This window is cleverly known as the Fax Status Monitor.

Bottom: The incoming fax winds up in your Inbox, just as though it's a particularly old-fashioned email message.

(Either way, it's handy to know that these are standard TIFF graphics files that you can email to somebody else—or even edit.)

To look at the faxes you've received, open Fax and Scan. Click the Inbox to see a list of faxes that have come in—and then double-click one to open it up (Figure 17-13, bottom).

Tip: Another great way to capitalize on the power of your PC for fax purposes is to sign up for J2 or eFax (*www.j2.com* and *www.efax.com*). These services issue you your own personal fax number. And here's the twist–all faxes sent to that number arrive at your PC as email attachments.

The brilliance of the system, of course, is that you don't need another phone line for this, and you can get these faxes anywhere in the world, even on the road. And here's the best part: As of this writing, both of these services are absolutely free. (You might consider reserving a separate email address just for your J2 or eFax account, however, since waves of junk mail are part of the "free" bargain.)

Scanning Documents
Professional • Enterprise • Ultimate

You already know that Windows Fax and Scan makes a great little fax center. But faxing is only one technology that turns paper into digital bits. Scanning is the other—and that, too, is a talent of Fax and Scan.

First, install your scanner (and its driver) as described in Chapter 18.

Load it up with the page you want to scan. In Fax and Scan, click New Scan. The New Scan dialog box appears. Click Preview to trigger a quick, temporary scan so that you can see how the document will look after the scan (Figure 17-14). If it all looks good, click Scan.

FREQUENTLY ASKED QUESTION

Scanning Text—and Then Editing It

I scanned an article from a magazine. How do I copy a couple of paragraphs from it into my word processor?

When you scan an article or a page of a book, you're not capturing text; you're just taking a *picture* of text. You can no more copy and paste a paragraph out of the resulting graphics file than you can copy text out of a photograph. Your PC sees everything on the scanned page as one gigantic graphic.

If you want to edit text that you've scanned, then you need

optical character recognition (OCR) software, which comes free with certain scanners. This kind of software analyzes the patterns of dots in each scanned graphics file and does a fairly good job of turning it into a word processor document that contains the original text. When businesses decide to convert old paper documents into computer files (insurance policies, research papers, and so on), OCR software is what they use.

Once the document has magically turned into a graphic in your Scan list, you can do all kinds of neat things with it: Forward it as a fax or an email attachment (click "Forward as Fax" or "Forward as E-mail" on the toolbar); export it as a JPEG, GIF, BMP, TIFF, or PNG document (click "Save as" on the toolbar); print it; or delete it.

Figure 17-14:
In this box, you have the chance to specify what sort of thing you want to scan—picture? document?—and specify its resolution and color settings.

Choose 300 to 600 dots per inch resolution (dpi) for professional scans; for everyday scanning, 150 to 200 dpi is plenty. The more dots, the bigger the resulting file.

Hardware

A PC contains several pounds of wires, slots, cards, and chips—enough hardware to open a True Value store. Fortunately, you don't have to worry about making all your PC's preinstalled components work together. In theory, at least, the PC maker did that part for you. (Unless you built the machine yourself, that is. In that case, best of luck.)

But adding *new* gear to your computer is another story. For the power user, hard drives, flash drives, cameras, printers, scanners, network cards, video cards, keyboards,

---

UP TO SPEED

The Master Compatibility List

Remember that Windows 7 is another leap ahead in the evolution of the operating system. Discovering that a piece of your existing equipment is now flaky or nonfunctional is par for the course.

If you'd like to eliminate every glitch and every shred of troubleshooting inconvenience, limit your add-on gear to products that pass the test—the one administered by the Windows 7 Upgrade Advisor. That's a little program you can download from this Web site:

www.microsoft.com/windows/windows-7/get/upgrade-advisor.aspx

Even if your computer uses Windows Vista—which means it's probably fine for Windows 7—running the Upgrade Advisor is a good idea. If you plan to upgrade to Windows 7 from Windows XP, you'll definitely want to test things out; you should know how many of your peripherals won't work *before* you install Windows 7. (The Upgrade Advisor takes the place of the old Hardware Compatibility List [HCL], an online list of every gadget and program on earth that had been shown to work with Windows XP.)

Plug in all your external gadgets—scanners, printers, hard drives, and so on—and then run the Advisor program you've downloaded.

---

monitors, game controllers, palmtop cradles, and other accessories all make life worth living. When you introduce a new piece of equipment to the PC, you must hook it up and install its *driver*, the software that lets a new gadget talk to the rest of the PC.

The driver issue is a chronic, nagging worry for the average Windows fan, however. Drivers conflict; drivers are missing; drivers go bad; drivers go out of date.

Fortunately, in Windows 7, Microsoft has made further strides in addressing the driver problem. Win7 comes with thousands upon thousands of drivers for common products already built in, and Microsoft deposits dozens more on your hard drive, behind the scenes, with every Windows Update (page 662). Chances are good that you'll live a long and happy life with Windows 7 without ever having to lose a Saturday manually configuring new gizmos, as your forefathers did.

This chapter guides you through installing accessory gadgets and their drivers—and counsels you on what to do when the built-in, auto-recognized drivers don't do the trick.

Note: Chapter 17 contains additional hardware-installation details specific to printers.

External Gadgets
All Versions

Over the years, various engineering organizations have devised an almost silly number of different connectors for printers, scanners, and other *peripherals* (Figure 18-1 shows a typical assortment). The back panel—or front, or even side panel—of your PC may include any of these connector varieties.

USB Jacks
Man, you gotta love USB (Universal Serial Bus). The more of these jacks your PC has, the better.

UP TO SPEED

Of Hubs and Power

If your PC doesn't have enough built-in USB jacks to handle all your USB devices, you can also attach a USB *hub* (with, for example, four or eight additional USB ports), in order to attach multiple USB devices simultaneously.

Whether the jacks are built in or on a hub, though, you have to be aware of whether or not they're *powered* or *unpowered* jacks.

Unpowered ones just transmit communication signals with the USB gadget. These kinds of USB gadgets work fine with unpowered jacks: mice, keyboards, flash drives, and anything with its own power cord (like printers).

Powered USB jacks also supply current to whatever's plugged in. You need that for scanners, Webcams, hard drives, and other gadgets that don't have their own power cords but transmit lots of data.

The bottom line? If a gadget isn't working, it may be because it requires a powered jack and you've given it an unpowered one.

The USB jack itself is a compact, thin, rectangular connector that's easy to plug and unplug. It often provides power to the gadget, saving you one more cord and one more bit of clutter. And it's hot-pluggable, so you don't have to turn off the gadget (or the PC) before connecting or disconnecting it.

Tip: Be careful, though, not to yank a USB flash drive or hard drive out of the PC when it might be in the middle of copying files.

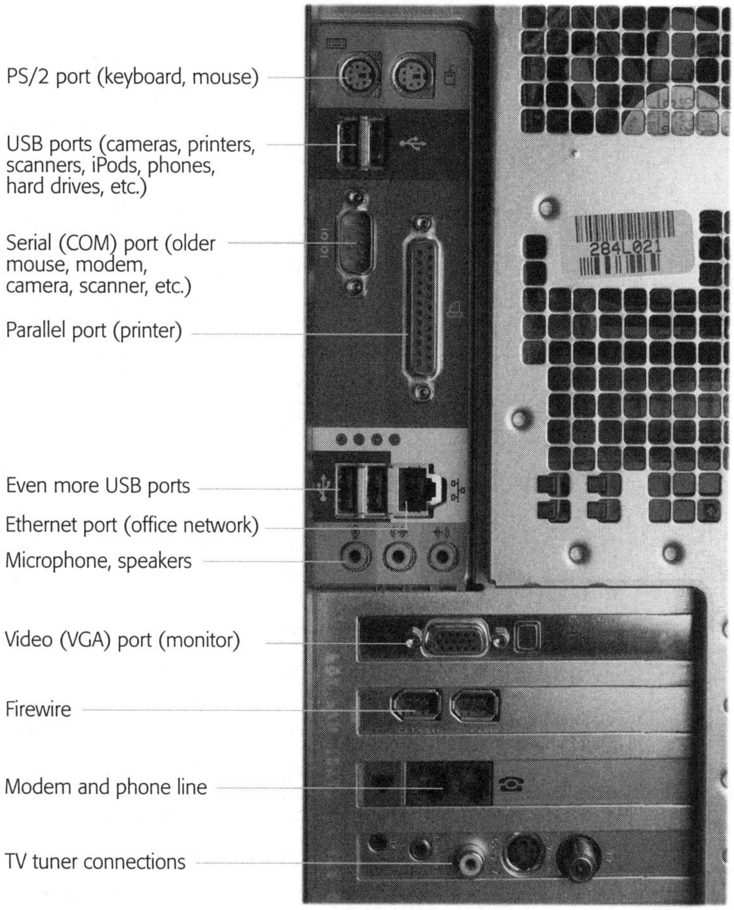

Figure 18-1:
The back panel of a typical PC. Not every computer has every kind of jack, and the standard assortment is evolving. But these days, you can generally count on a basic collection like the one shown here.

PS/2 port (keyboard, mouse)

USB ports (cameras, printers, scanners, iPods, phones, hard drives, etc.)

Serial (COM) port (older mouse, modem, camera, scanner, etc.)

Parallel port (printer)

Even more USB ports

Ethernet port (office network)

Microphone, speakers

Video (VGA) port (monitor)

Firewire

Modem and phone line

TV tuner connections

USB accommodates a huge variety of gadgets: USB hard drives, scanners, mice, phones, keyboards, printers, palmtop cradles, digital cameras, camcorders, and so on.

Most modern PCs come with two or more USB ports, often on both the front and back panels.

Note: Today's USB gadgets and PCs offer *USB 2.0* jacks—a faster, enhanced form of USB. You can still plug the older, slower USB 1.1 gadgets into USB 2.0 jacks, and vice versa—but you'll get the older, slower speed.

Other Jacks

At one time, the backs of PCs were pockmarked with all manner of crazy jacks: serial ports, PS/2 ports, SCSI ports, parallel ports, keyboard ports. Today, all these connectors are rapidly disappearing, thanks to the all-powerful superiority of the USB jack.

Here's what else you may find on the modern PC, though:

- **FireWire port.** Not all PCs come with this special jack (the faster FireWire 800 has a rectangular jack; the original, FireWire 400 jack is a rectangle-with-one-V-shaped-end), but it's a winner nevertheless. (Various companies may also call it IEEE 1394 or i.Link.) It's a hot-pluggable, extremely high-speed connector that's ideal for digital camcorders (for video editing) and external hard drives.

- **Bluetooth adapters.** Bluetooth is a fascinating short-range wireless technology. Don't think of it as a networking scheme—it's intended for the elimination of *cable clutter.* A Bluetooth-equipped PC can print to a Bluetooth printer, or "talk" to a Bluetooth headset, or sync with a Bluetooth phone, from up to 30 feet away.

- **PC card or ExpressCard slot.** These slots are found primarily on laptops. They accommodate miniature expansion cards, which look like metal Visa cards. Each card adds a useful feature to your laptop: additional USB jacks, a cellular high-speed modem, external eSATA adapters (for plugging in hard drives), and so on.

Tip: Hundreds of PC cards are available, for thousands of laptop models. The industry has moved to a narrower type of card, however, called ExpressCard, which fits into a narrower kind of slot. (Actually, there are *two* ExpressCard types—one narrow, and one *really* narrow.) Just make sure, before you buy any card, that it fits the kind of slot your laptop has.

- **Video (VGA) or DVI port.** The VGA connector is a narrow female port with 15 holes along three rows. Most monitors are designed to plug into either a VGA jack or the more modern DVI (digital visual interface) jack, which has 24 pins and is designed for modern digital LCD screens.

- **Game port.** This connector, which is usually part of a sound card, is a wide female port that accepts joysticks and steering wheels.

- **SD card reader.** Pop the SD memory card out of your camera and straight into this slot to import the photos. Sweet.

Connecting New Gadgets

In books, magazines, and online chatter about Windows, you'll frequently hear people talk about *installing* a new component. In many cases, they aren't talking about physically hooking it up to the PC—they're talking about installing its driver software.

The really good news is that Windows 7 comes equipped with thousands of drivers for gadgets, especially USB gadgets. When you plug the thing into the PC for the first time, Windows 7 autodetects its presence, digs into its trunk for the driver, and installs it automatically. Only a flurry of balloons in the notification area lets you know what's going on (Figure 18-2).

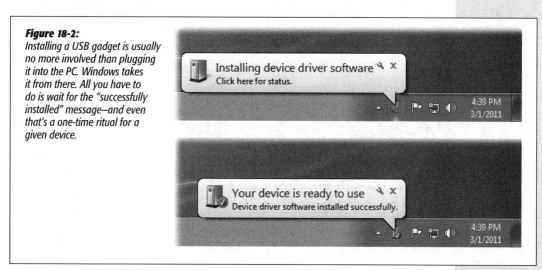

Figure 18-2:
Installing a USB gadget is usually no more involved than plugging it into the PC. Windows takes it from there. All you have to do is wait for the "successfully installed" message—and even that's a one-time ritual for a given device.

If Windows can't find the driver, a dialog box appears, suggesting that you insert whatever software-installation disc came with the gadget.

And now, the fine print:

- Usually the process shown in Figure 18-2 is all it takes—that is, you start by plugging the device in. Sometimes, though, you're supposed to install the driver before connecting the gizmo. (Check the manual.)

- Usually, the device should be turned on before you plug it in. Again, though, check the manual, because some devices are supposed to be switched on during the installation.

In either case, your gear is now completely installed—both its hardware and its software—and ready to use.

Device Stage

The *Device Stage* is a new Windows 7 feature that does wonders to demystify the sometimes baffling world of external gadgets. Its mission: to depict, in visual form, Windows's understanding of whatever gadgets you've connected to it.

Microsoft refers to Device Stage as a "home page" for the most popular kinds of gadgets: cellphones, music players, cameras, printers, scanners, multifunction printers, mice, and keyboards. They can be connected to your PC by a USB cable or even a wireless Bluetooth or WiFi connection.

For each gadget, the Device Stage window (Figure 18-3, bottom) is supposed to display highly specific information and links. For a camera, you might see a handsome photo of the camera model you've plugged in, the number of photos on it to be downloaded, how much space remains on the card, and the current battery level—and you're offered links to import the photos, read the manual, buy accessories, and so on.

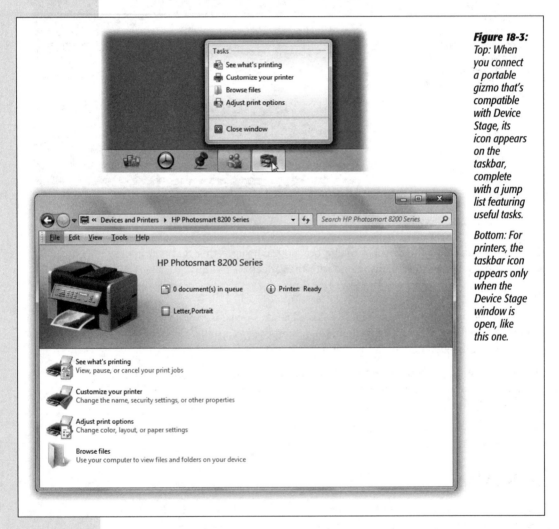

Figure 18-3:
Top: When you connect a portable gizmo that's compatible with Device Stage, its icon appears on the taskbar, complete with a jump list featuring useful tasks.

Bottom: For printers, the taskbar icon appears only when the Device Stage window is open, like this one.

For a printer, you might see ink-level details, options to buy paper and ink online, and so on; for a cellphone, you see options to edit or buy ringtones, sync with your Windows address book and calendar, and so on. For any kind of gadget, you probably get a link to the manufacturer's Web site, too.

There's usually a "Change how your device works with Windows" link, too, which brings up what looks like a glorified AutoPlay box: You specify what function you want to trigger the next time you plug this thing in (auto-downloading photos, for example).

Microsoft doesn't create these little model-specific pages; the gadget manufacturers are supposed to do it and submit them to Microsoft. When you attach the device to your PC, you see its own custom Device Stage page.

When you connect a portable gadget (cellphone, music player, camera), you get a handy related bonus feature: Your taskbar shows an actual *icon* for that model. Here's what you can do with it:

- Right-click that icon to see a jump list offering a handy set of options: "Import pictures and videos," "Read the manual," "Browse files," and so on.

- Point to the taskbar icon without clicking to see a thumbnail panel with key statistics: battery level, shots remaining, and so on.

- Click the taskbar icon to open the gadget's Device Stage page.

Note: No taskbar icon appears for permanently attached gadgets like printers until you open their Device Stage window yourself. To do that, choose Start→Devices and Printers, and then double-click the picture of your device.

When you disconnect your gadget, its icon disappears from the taskbar, and all Device Stage windows close automatically.

Device Stage is great for both Windows veterans, who should appreciate the nifty graphics and ease of use, and for novices, who'll appreciate knowing exactly where to do things and the simply stated commands, like "Set ringtones."

Now, the bad news: Very few gadgets *do* have Device Stage information built in. As Windows 7's master world-domination plan chugs along, more gadgets will presumably become Device Stage–compatible. But for now, a lot of gadgets—including most of the several trillion pre-Windows 7 models—produce either no Device Stage at all, or, sometimes a generic one. This "baseline" page may offer the basic tasks—import pictures from a camera, for example—but won't offer the photo and functions of your exact model.

Note: When the hardware makers get around to it, they'll update their Device Stage screens, or add them to gizmos that are currently showing you only the generic basic pages. You'll know when an updated Device Stage is available, because the top of the window will sprout a little banner inviting you to download it.

Installing Cards in Expansion Slots
All Versions

Modems and adapter cards for video, TV, sound, network cabling, disk drives, and tape drives generally take the form of circuit boards, or *cards,* that you install inside your PC's case. These slots are connected to your PC's *bus,* an electrical conduit that connects all the components of the machine to the brains of the outfit: the processor and memory.

The two common (and incompatible) kinds of slots are called *PCI* and *PCI Express (PCIe)*. The PCI slot (Peripheral Component Interconnect) has been around since the dawn of the PC in the early 1990s. PCI Express is newer and offers much better speed, but is typically used only for graphics cards. Most computers in use today have both kinds of slots.

Note: *There's a third type of slot in some computers, called AGP (Accelerated Graphics Port). This slot is almost always occupied by a graphics card. PCIe is the most popular slot type for graphics cards, but you may encounter AGP in older PCs.*

Knowing the characteristics of the different bus types isn't especially important. What *is* important is knowing what type of slots your computer has free, so you can purchase the correct type of expansion card. To do this, you'll have to open your PC's case to see which type of slots are empty:

The Add Hardware Wizard

Microsoft really, really hopes you'll never need the Add Hardware Wizard. This little program is a holdover from Windows past, designed for very old, pre-Plug-and-Play gadgets (what Microsoft calls "legacy hardware") that Windows doesn't autorecognize when you plug them in.

Begin by connecting the new gear; turn off the computer first, if necessary. Turn the machine on again, and then open the Add Hardware Wizard program, which takes a few steps. Open the Start menu; start typing *device manager* until you see its name in the results list; click it. Then right-click your PC at the top of the list and choose "Add legacy hardware" from the shortcut menu.

The wizard makes another attempt to detect the new equipment and install its driver. If a happy little "Found new hardware" balloon appears in your notification area, all is well; the wizard's work is done. If

not, you're walked through the process of specifying exactly *what* kind of gadget seems to have gone missing, choosing its manufacturer, inserting its driver disc, and so on.

If you choose "Install the hardware that I manually select from a list" and click Next (or if the previous option fails), the wizard displays a list of device types, as shown here. From that list, find and select the type of hardware you want to install—"Imaging devices" for a digital camera or a scanner, for example, "PCMCIA adapters" for a PC card, and so on. (Click Show All Devices if you can't figure out which category to choose.)

Click Next to forge on through the wizard pages. You may be asked to select a port or configure other settings. When you click the Finish button on the last screen, Windows transfers the drivers to your hard drive. As a final step, you may be asked to restart the PC.

- PCIe slots come in different lengths, depending on their speed (from x1, the slowest, to x16, the fastest and most common). The have metal pins or teeth in the center and a small crossbar partway down the slot. There's also a slot on one end that the card uses to lock into place.

- The plastic wall around a PCI slot is usually white or off-white, and shorter than an ISA slot. A PCI slot has a metal center and a crossbar about three-quarters of the way along its length.

Installing a card usually involves removing a narrow plate (the *slot cover*) from the back panel of your PC, which allows the card's connector to peek through to the outside world. After unplugging the PC and touching something metal to discharge static, unwrap the card, and then carefully push it into its slot until it's fully seated.

Note: Depending on the type of card, you may have to insert one end first, and then press the other end down with considerable force to get it into the slot. A friendly suggestion, however: Don't press so hard that you flex and crack the motherboard.

Troubleshooting Newly Installed Gear
All Versions

If, when you connect a new component, Windows doesn't display a "successfully installed" message like the one at the bottom of Figure 18-2, it probably can't "see" your new device.

- If you've installed an internal card, make sure that it's seated in the slot firmly (after shutting down your computer, of course).

- If you attached something external, make sure that it's turned on, has power (if it came with a power cord), and is correctly connected to the PC.

In either case, before panicking, try restarting the PC. If you still have no luck, try the Add New Hardware Wizard described in the box on the facing page. (And if even *that* doesn't work, call the manufacturer.)

FREQUENTLY ASKED QUESTION

Driver vs. Driver

Which is better: the drivers that come with Windows, or the drivers I've downloaded from the manufacturer's Web site?

In many cases, they're the same thing. The drivers included with Windows usually did come from the hardware's manufacturer, which gave them to Microsoft. However, you should still use the drivers that came from your gadget's manufacturer whenever possible, especially if you got them from the manufacturer's Web site. They're likely to be newer versions than the ones that came with Windows.

If your new gadget didn't come with a disc (or maybe just a disc with drivers, but no installer), then hooking it up may produce a "Found New Hardware" balloon in the notification area, but no message about happy success. In that case, click the balloon to make the New Hardware Wizard appear.

Proceed as shown in Figure 18-4.

Tip: As you work with newly installed gadgets, don't forget about their new informational headquarters: the Device Stage screen. Choose Start→Devices and Printers; you see a window that pictures and lists the devices connected to your machine. Right-click a device to change settings and properties, or double-click it to open its Properties dialog box or a Device Stage window. Details on page 607.

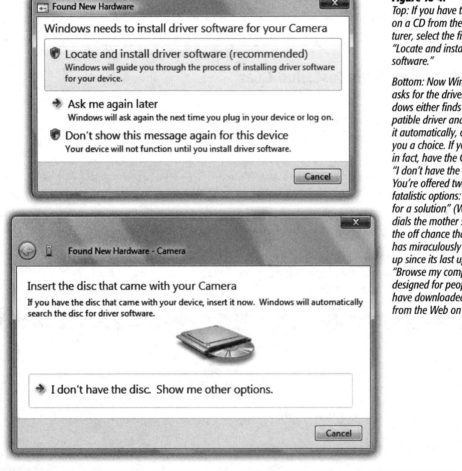

Figure 18-4:
Top: If you have the drivers on a CD from the manufacturer, select the first option, "Locate and install driver software."

Bottom: Now Windows asks for the driver CD. Windows either finds the compatible driver and installs it automatically, or it offers you a choice. If you do not, in fact, have the CD, click "I don't have the disc." You're offered two final, fatalistic options: "Check for a solution" (Windows dials the mother ship on the off chance that a driver has miraculously cropped up since its last update) or "Browse my computer," designed for people who have downloaded a driver from the Web on their own.

Driver Signing

All Versions

Every now and then, when you try to install the software for one new gadget or another, you'll see a warning box that says, "Windows can't verify the publisher of this driver software."

It's not really as scary as it sounds. It's just telling you that Microsoft has not tested this driver for Windows 7 compatibility and programming solidity. (Technically speaking, Microsoft has not put its digital signature on that driver; it's an *unsigned driver*.)

Note: In very rare circumstances, you may also see messages that say, "This driver software has been altered" or "Windows cannot install this driver software." In those cases, go directly to the hardware maker's Web site to download the official driver software; Windows is trying to warn you that hackers may have gotten their hands on the driver version you're trying to install.

In theory, you're supposed to drop everything and contact the manufacturer or its Web site to find out if a Windows 7–certified driver is now available.

In practice, just because a driver isn't signed doesn't mean it's no good; it may be that the manufacturer simply didn't pony up the testing fee required by Microsoft's Windows Hardware Quality Labs. After all, sometimes checking with the manufacturer isn't even possible—for example, it may have gone to that great dot-com in the sky.

So most people just plow ahead. If the installation winds up making your system slower or less stable, you can always uninstall the driver, or rewind your entire operating system to its condition before you installed the questionable driver. (Use System Restore, described on page 697, for that purpose. Windows automatically takes a snapshot of your working system just before you install any unsigned driver.)

Tip: There is no way to turn off the "unsigned driver" messages permanently in Windows 7, much to the dismay of Windows veterans who want to be left alone. (If you Google this problem, you'll find some hacks that purport to do the trick—but you'll also find reports that they don't actually work.) There *is* a way to turn off the messages, but you have to repeat it each time you turn on your PC. See page 704.

The Device Manager

All Versions

The Device Manager is an extremely powerful tool that lets you troubleshoot and update drivers for gear you've already installed. It's a master list of every component that makes up your PC: floppy drive, CD-ROM drive, keyboard, modem, and so on (Figure 18-5). It's also a status screen that lets you know which drivers are working properly and which ones need some attention.

The quickest way to open the Device Manager, as usual, is to open the Start menu. Start typing *device manager* until you see its name in the results list; click it.

Tip: Or type *devmgmt.msc* into the Start menu's Search box, and press Enter. That's the Device Manger's real name.

Authenticate yourself if necessary. You then arrive at the screen shown in Figure 18-5.

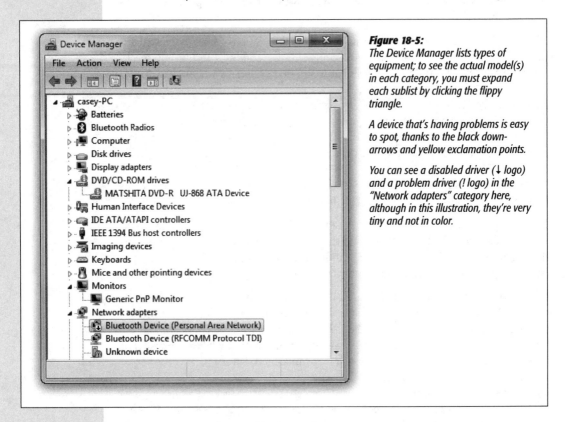

Figure 18-5:
The Device Manager lists types of equipment; to see the actual model(s) in each category, you must expand each sublist by clicking the flippy triangle.

A device that's having problems is easy to spot, thanks to the black down-arrows and yellow exclamation points.

You can see a disabled driver (↓ logo) and a problem driver (! logo) in the "Network adapters" category here, although in this illustration, they're very tiny and not in color.

The Curse of the Yellow ! Badge

A yellow circled exclamation point next to the name indicates a problem with the device's driver. It could mean that either you or Windows installed the *wrong* driver, or that the device is fighting for resources being used by another component. It could also mean that a driver can't find the equipment it's supposed to control. That's what happens to your Webcam driver, for example, if you've detached the Webcam.

The yellow badget may also be the result of a serious incompatibility between the component and your computer, or the component and Windows. In that case, a call to the manufacturer's help line is almost certainly in your future.

Tip: To find out which company actually created a certain driver, double-click the component's name in the Device Manager. In the resulting Properties dialog box, click the General tab, where you see the name of the company, and the Driver tab to see the date the driver was created, the version of the driver, and so on.

Duplicate devices

If the Device Manager displays icons for duplicate devices (for example, two modems), remove *both* of them. (To remove a device, click Uninstall in the dialog box shown in fi 18-7.) If you remove only one, Windows will find it again the next time the PC starts up, and you'll have duplicate devices again.

If Windows asks if you want to restart your computer after you remove the first icon, click No, and then delete the second one. Windows won't ask again after you remove the second incarnation; you have to restart your computer manually.

When the PC starts up again, Windows finds the hardware device and installs it (only once this time). Open the Device Manager and make sure there's only one of everything. If not, contact the manufacturer's help line.

Resolving resource conflicts

If the yellow-! problem isn't caused by a duplicate component, then double-click the component's name. Here you find an explanation of the problem (see Figure 18-6).

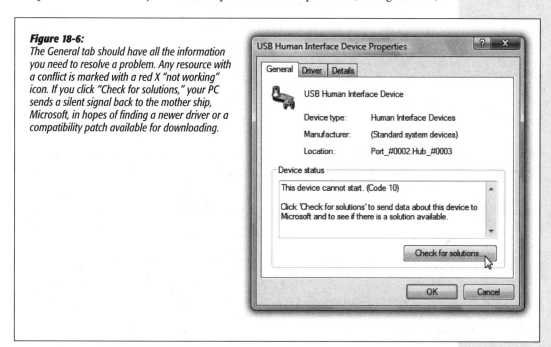

Figure 18-6:
The General tab should have all the information you need to resolve a problem. Any resource with a conflict is marked with a red X "not working" icon. If you click "Check for solutions," your PC sends a silent signal back to the mother ship, Microsoft, in hopes of finding a newer driver or a compatibility patch available for downloading.

Turning Components Off

The Driver tab shown in Figure 18-7 contains another useful tool: the Disable button. It makes your PC treat the component in question as though it's not even there.

You can use this function to test device conflicts. For example, if a yellow exclamation point indicates that there's a resource conflict, then you can disable one of the two gadgets, which may clear up a problem with its competitor.

When you disable a component, a circled ↓ appears next to the component's listing in the Device Manager. To undo your action, click the device's name and click the Enable button in the toolbar (formerly the Disable button).

Updating Drivers

If you get your hands on a new, more powerful (or more reliable) driver for a device, you can use the Device Manager to install it.

Tip: Newer isn't *always* better, however; in the world of Windows, the rule "If it ain't broke, don't fix it" contains a grain of truth the size of Texas.

Open the dialog box shown in Figure 18-7, and then click the Update Driver button. The Update Device Driver Wizard walks you through the process.

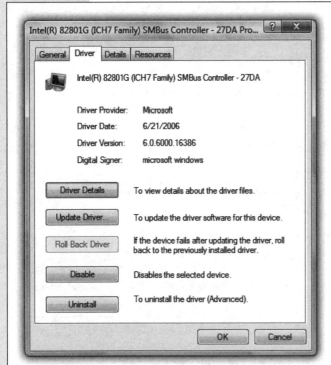

Figure 18-7:
To get here, double-click a component listed in your Device Manager and then click the Driver tab. Here, you find four buttons and a lot of information. The Driver Provider information, for example, lets you know who's responsible for your current driver—Microsoft or the maker of the component.

Click the Driver Details button to find out where on your hard drive the actual driver file is. Or click Update Driver to install a newer version, the Roll Back Driver button to reinstate the earlier version, the Disable button to hide this component from Windows until you change your mind, or the Uninstall button to remove the driver from your system entirely—a drastic decision.

(If the buttons here are dimmed, click the General tab, click "Change settings," shown in Figure 18-6, and then authenticate.)

Along the way, the wizard offers to search for a better driver, or to display a list of drivers in a certain folder so you can make your own selection. In either case, you may have to restart the PC to put the newly installed driver into service.

Driver Rollback

Suppose that you, the increasingly proficient PC user, have indeed downloaded a new driver for some component—your scanner, say—and successfully installed it using the instructions in the previous paragraphs. Life is sweet—until you discover that your scanner no longer scans in color.

In this situation, you'd probably give quite a bit for the chance to return to the previous driver, which, though older, seemed to work better. That's the beauty of Driver Rollback. To find it, open the dialog box shown in Figure 18-7, and click Roll Back Driver.

Windows 7, forgiving as always, instantly undoes the installation of the newer driver, and reinstates the previous driver.

Laptops, Tablets, & Touchscreens

Portability is today's reality in computing. Laptop sales are trouncing desktop PC sales. Netbooks are cheap and insanely popular. And for millions of people, the computing platform of choice isn't a computer at all—it's a cellphone.

That's why Windows 7 is crammed with special features for the peripatetic PC. On a laptop, for example, you can change your power-consumption configuration with a quick click on the battery icon in the notification area. All the important laptop settings, like network switching and projector settings, are clustered in a single place: the Windows Mobility Center.

Touchscreen computing is, in Microsoft's opinion, ready for prime time, despite the fact that only about six people ever bought those tablet PC machines that Bill Gates was once so excited about. To prove its point, Microsoft has built iPhone-like multi-touch gestures—pinching and spreading, swiping a finger, rotating two fingers—right into the operating system, ready for any touchscreen-equipped PC that comes along.

Those features join all the existing tablet PC features like pen control, digital ink text input, and handwriting recognition. (This stuff used to be available only in a special Tablet PC Edition of Windows; now it's part of the basic operating system.)

And finally, are you a fan of the old offline files feature, which keeps folders on your laptop synchronized with the master copies on the company network? If so, you're in luck; the Sync Center is still around. It's covered in this chapter, too.

Note: Are you in the market for a netbook? Microsoft's take is that any version of Windows 7 will run on these lightweight, low-cost machines. But be careful to check the hardware specs for a netbook to be sure they meet Microsoft's minimum requirements. If you own a netbook that runs Windows XP, you must upgrade to Windows 7. You can purchase a copy online at *http://store.microsoft.com/win7netbooks,* and you can find more information by Googling "Windows 7 on a netbook."

Laptops
All Versions

Windows 7 is full of special software features designed expressly for battery-powered computing. There's a whole control panel, for example, dedicated to managing battery power. You can control screen brightness, when your computer sleeps, and other features, all in the name of saving juice.

That's not the only gift to laptoppers in Windows 7, however. Read on for all the good stuff.

Battery Meter

The notification area (system tray) has always displayed a little battery meter that shows how your laptop's battery charge is doing. Its icon looks like a tiny battery—or a battery with a plug (⌧) when the laptop's charging.

If you point to this icon, a tooltip displays the status of your laptop's battery, including the current battery charge. Click this icon, and you see what power plan you're using. There's even more to it than that, though, as you can see in Figure 19-1.

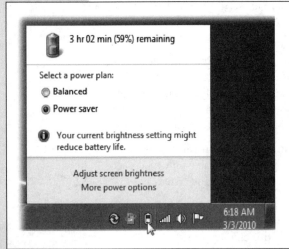

Figure 19-1:
To change the power configuration plan on the fly, click the Power icon once, and click again on the power plan you'd like to use. (A power plan is a set of settings like, "Put the laptop to sleep after ___ minutes of inactivity, to save power.")

Mobility Center

The Windows Mobility Center is a handy, centralized hub for managing everything that makes a laptop a laptop (Figure 19-2): battery, wireless networking, external projector connection, and so on. To find it, open the Start menu. Start typing *mobility* until you see its name in the results list; click it.

Or just press ⊞+X, which is quite a bit quicker. (On a desktop, ⊞+X does nothing.)

Tip: You can also open one of these icons entirely from the keyboard. See the underlined letter beneath each panel, such as Battery Status or Wireless Network? Tap that letter to highlight the icon, and then press Enter.

Figure 19-2:
Each setting in Mobility Center is illustrated with a cute little icon—but don't be fooled. This is so much more than an icon! It's also a button that, when double-clicked, opens up a Control Panel applet or configuration page.

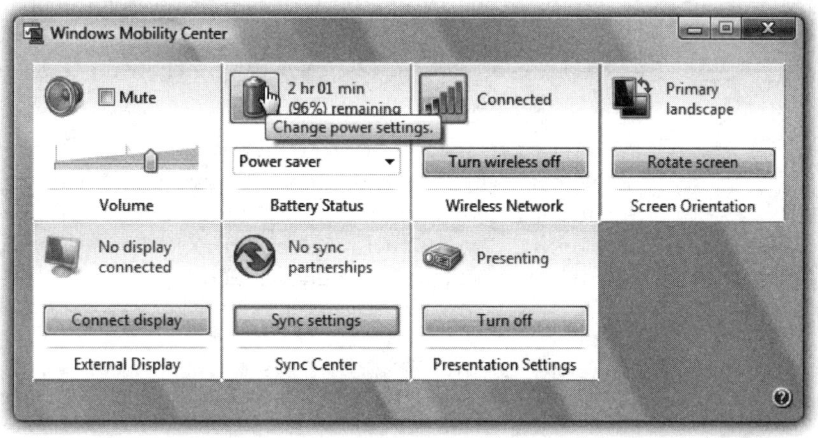

Here's the complete list of tiles that may appear in your Mobility Center. (You may not have all of them, depending on what kind of computer you're using and what components it has. And you may have more of them, if your computer company has installed its own options.)

- **Display brightness.** The slider dims your screen for this work session only, which can save enormous amounts of battery power. Click the icon to open the Power Options control panel, where you can make brightness changes that are always in effect.

- **Volume.** Change your speakers' volume, or mute them entirely. Click the icon to open the Sound control panel.

- **Battery Status.** This is your battery's fuel gauge. The drop-down menu lets you choose a canned setting like "High performance" (your PC doesn't go to sleep, but uses up battery power faster) or "Power saver" (the laptop goes to sleep sooner to conserve juice). Click the icon to open the Power Options control panel, where you can change the power-plan settings for good.

- **Wireless Network.** Turns your WiFi circuitry on or off (which saves power and makes flight attendants happy), and shows how many bars of signal you have. Click the icon to open the "Connect to a network" dialog box, which lists all wireless networks within your range.

- **Screen Orientation.** This one shows up mostly on tablet PCs. It lets you turn the screen image 90 degrees. Click the icon to open the Display Settings control panel for additional screen settings.

Tip: On some laptops and tablets, Ctrl+Alt+arrow key rotates the screen, which saves you a few steps.

- **External Display.** Have you hooked up a second monitor? If so, click "Connect display" to make Windows aware of its new responsibilities. This tile also reveals whether or not Windows "sees" the second screen. Click the icon to open the Display control panel, where you can configure the resolution and other settings of the second monitor.

- **Sync Center.** The Sync Center is the communications hub for *offline files*, the "sync my copies with the network copies" feature described on page 635. This tile shows you the status of a sync that's already under way. Click the icon (or "Sync settings") to open the Sync Center program, where you can set up new "sync partnerships" between your PC and other network PCs.

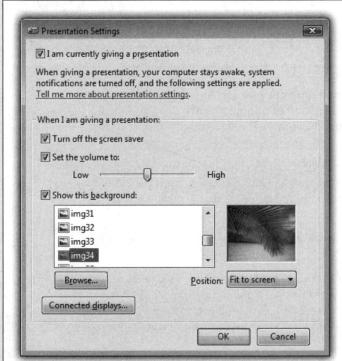

Figure 19-3:
When you're in Presentation mode, your screen saver and system notifications don't appear, and your laptop won't go to sleep. You might also want to specify a piece of uncontroversial artwork for your desktop wallpaper, so your bosses and potential employers won't accidentally spot the HotBikiniBabes.com JPEG you usually use.

• **Presentation Settings.** This feature is available only in the Professional, Enterprise, and Ultimate editions of Windows 7, but it's great; it's the answer to a million PowerPoint pitchers' prayers. It makes sure that your laptop won't do anything embarrassing while you're in the middle of your boardroom presentation.

On the Presentation Settings tile of Mobility Center, click "Turn on." When the tile says "Presenting," your laptop won't go to sleep. No alarms or reminder dialog boxes appear. The screen saver doesn't kick in. You're free to give your pitch in peace. Click the icon to open the Presentation Settings dialog box shown in Figure 19-3.

Note: You also enter Presentation mode when you hook up a network projector (page 273), or when you connect an external monitor.

Tablet PCs and Touchscreen PCs

Home Premium • Professional • Enterprise • Ultimate

A tablet PC is a laptop or a slate-shaped computer with a touchscreen that you operate with a stylus (pen). In theory, that design means a tablet PC can be thinner and lighter than a laptop, because it can do without a keyboard.

When Microsoft unveiled its concept for the tablet PC in 2002, it was convinced that the tablet was the future. "Within five years, I predict it will be the most popular form of PC sold in America," Bill Gates told the crowd at a keynote speech.

Clearly, that never happened. The tablet PC isn't exactly dead, but its popularity is concentrated in fairly rarefied circles: healthcare, insurance, and so on.

In the meantime, in the age of the Apple iPad, *finger*-touchscreen computers are coming on strong. Windows 7 was designed to handle, in fact, *multitouch* laptops and desktops, where you can touch the screen with two fingers to pinch, spread, or rotate objects, just as on the iPhone.

As a bonus, many of the existing Windows features for *pen*-based computers—digital ink, handwriting recognition, and so on—work very well on this newer breed of touch machines.

Handwriting Recognition

The accuracy and convenience of Window's handwriting recognition have come a very long way—which is fortunate indeed, since some tablet PCs don't have keyboards (or they have keyboards that you can detach). Hey, if tablet PCs can decipher doctors' handwriting, surely you can get your tablet PC to recognize yours.

Using a pop-up transcription window called the Input panel, you can enter text anywhere you can type: Microsoft Word, your email program, your Web browser, and so on. Windows 7 also comes with a special program called Windows Journal that's a note-taking module designed expressly for tablets.

Teaching Windows how you write

The first step in using the handwriting recognition feature is to *train* your PC to recognize your writing. You provide samples of your handwriting, and Windows studies your style.

To get started, open the Start menu. Start typing *handwriting* until you see "Personalize Handwriting Recognition" in the results list; click it. From the options, choose "Teach the recognizer your handwriting style." Proceed as shown in Figure 19-4.

After working through the exercises, you can start using handwriting recognition.

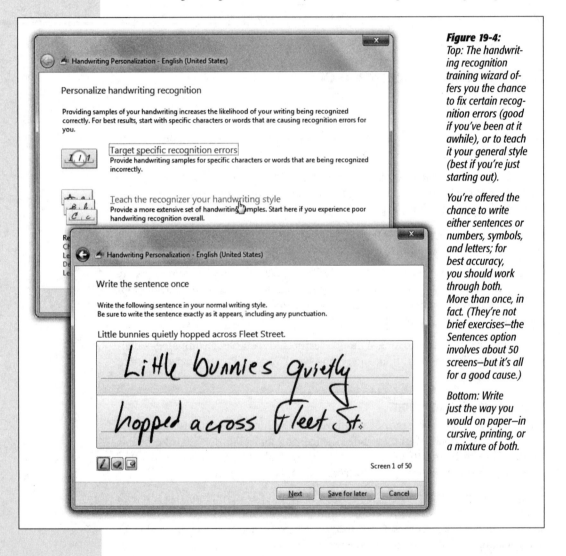

Figure 19-4:
Top: The handwriting recognition training wizard offers you the chance to fix certain recognition errors (good if you've been at it awhile), or to teach it your general style (best if you're just starting out).

You're offered the chance to write either sentences or numbers, symbols, and letters; for best accuracy, you should work through both. More than once, in fact. (They're not brief exercises—the Sentences option involves about 50 screens—but it's all for a good cause.)

Bottom: Write just the way you would on paper—in cursive, printing, or a mixture of both.

Handwriting anywhere

To make Windows recognize your handwriting, open any program where you would otherwise type—a word processor, for example.

Now open the Input panel, which is a floating handwriting window that automatically converts anything you write into typed text (Figure 19-5). You can summon the Input panel in a couple of ways:

- Tap to put the insertion point in a text-entry area—an empty word processor document or email message, for example, or the address bar of a Web browser. A tiny Input panel *icon* appears right by the insertion point (Figure 19-5, top); tap it.

Figure 19-5:
Top: You can open the Input panel by tapping the Input panel icon that appears next to any selected text box.

Middle: You can also tap the tiny tab that hugs the edge of the screen.

Bottom: Once the Input panel is open, you can use it to enter text into any program at all. If you make an error before hitting the Insert button, you can just scratch it out, with a right-to-left horizontal line, to make it disappear. (Hint: You can customize the heck out of the Input panel—ink thickness, tab appearance, and so on—by choosing Tools→Options within the panel.)

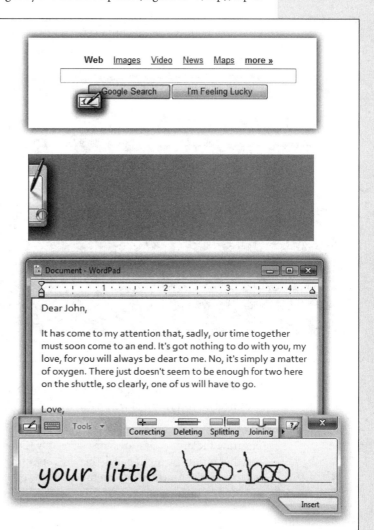

- Tap the Input panel *tab*, which peeks out from the left edge of the screen (Figure 19-5, middle).

- If you have a touchscreen PC that's not technically a tablet, the Input panel may not appear automatically. But you can summon it easily enough. Open the Start menu. Start typing *tablet* until you see "Tablet PC Input Panel" in the results list; click it.

Tip: If you're left-handed, you'll probably want to move the panel to the *right* side of the screen, which you can do by clicking Tools→Options in the Input panel, and then choosing "Right edge of the screen" on the Opening tab.

Once the Input panel is open, the buttons in the top-left corner offer a couple of ways to enter text. (Point without clicking to see their names, or consult Figure 19-6.)

Figure 19-6:
Top: If Windows is having trouble understanding, say, an Eastern European last name, you can open the Character pad by choosing "Write character by character" on the tools menu. Write letters one by one and wait as they're recognized.

Bottom: The On-Screen keyboard. Use your pen (or your fingers on a touchscreen) to tap letters.

The Writing pad is by far the most convenient method. To use it, just start writing on the line. Use your normal writing style.

The buttons at the top *right* (shown in Figure 19-5) trigger tiny, short animations that illustrate the proper gestures for Correcting, Deleting, Splitting, and Joining words together inside the Input panel, thereby correcting mistakes before they get committed to your document. (You can hide this row of "play video" buttons by clicking the ▸ button to their right.)

Tip: The little video shows a single straight line, right to left, as the "Delete text" gesture. And it works fine. But it's a lot more fun to use the old one: literally scribble out a word, scritch-scratching up and down a few times to make it disappear.

Now then: The "digital ink" doesn't just sit there where you wrote it. A split second after you finish each word, Windows transcribes that word into typed text within the Input panel, as shown at bottom in Figure 19-5. Cute how it uses a handwriting-style font to keep you in the mood, eh?

You can edit or correct this transcription while it's still in the panel, as described below.

But finally, when you tap the little Insert button, all of this writing and typing vanishes—and the converted, typed text appears in your document or dialog box. (If you'd rather simply point to the Insert button, open the Input panel's Tools menu and choose Options. On the Insertion tab, choose "Point to the Insert button.")

Gestures

In the pen-computing world, a *gesture* is a quick pen movement that lets you "type" a space (a long, quick line to the right), a Backspace (long and quick to the left), a press of the Enter key, or a Tab (Figure 19-7).

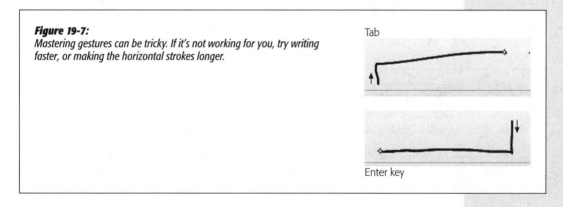

Figure 19-7:
Mastering gestures can be tricky. If it's not working for you, try writing faster, or making the horizontal strokes longer.

Tab

Enter key

To try out a gesture or two, make sure the Input panel is *completely empty*. You're going to draw one of these special shapes in the Input panel, but you'll see its *effect* in whatever Windows program you're using. You don't have to tap Insert or wait, as you do when writing; Windows recognizes the gestures instantly.

You can also scratch out text in the Writing pad *before* it gets transcribed. Scribble it out just as you'd scratch out handwriting on a real piece of paper. You can draw a straight line through what you've written, scribble out with an M or W motion, draw looping scribbles, and so on. The text disappears from the pad.

Fixing mistakes

Windows's handwriting recognition is amazingly accurate. It is not, however, perfect—in part because your handwriting isn't either.

Correcting a mistake is important for two reasons. First, it fixes the error in your document—and second, it *teaches* Windows so that it's less likely to make that mistake again. Figure 19-8 shows the steps. (This is where the Correcting, Deleting, Splitting, and Joining techniques illustrated by the videos at the top edge of the panel come in very handy.)

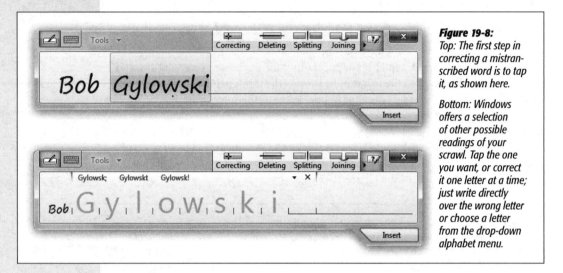

Figure 19-8:
Top: The first step in correcting a mistranscribed word is to tap it, as shown here.

Bottom: Windows offers a selection of other possible readings of your scrawl. Tap the one you want, or correct it one letter at a time; just write directly over the wrong letter or choose a letter from the drop-down alphabet menu.

The finer points of handwriting recognition

The handwriting recognition feature in Windows 7 is considerably better than it was on the old Windows XP Tablet Edition. Here are a few reasons why:

- **AutoComplete.** As you write items in the Input panel such as email addresses, filenames, or URLs, AutoComplete attempts to save you time by guessing what you're going for. If it's right, tap the guess and enjoy how Windows finishes your word.

- **Scratch-out gestures.** As mentioned earlier, scratch-out gestures let you use your pen to erase anything you've handwritten by scratching it out with the pen.

- **Back-of-pen erase.** Some tablet pens have an "eraser end" that lets you erase text you've written. To find out if your pen is so equipped, flip it upside-down and drag across something you've written. If an eraser icon appears—and your text disappears—then you're one of the lucky ones.

- **Web quick keys.** The Web button in the Input panel opens a panel filled with one-tap bits of Web addresses: http://, www., .com, and so on. It's a lifesaver when you're using your tablet with a Web browser.

Note: Anything you tap on the Num, Sym, or Web panels gets deposited directly into your document. It doesn't first appear in the Input panel, like your handwriting does. After all, Windows is already *sure* of what you intended to type; there's no need for you to approve or correct it.

Some of the old features, meanwhile, are still useful:

- **Numbers and symbols.** The Input panel displays buttons for Bksp (Backspace), Del (Delete), Tab, Enter, Space, and left and right arrow keys. For ease in entering numbers and symbols, special number and symbol pads are available, too (tap Num or Sym).

- **Add words to the Handwriting Dictionary.** To add a word to the Handwriting Dictionary, write the word neatly in the Writing pad, and correct it if necessary in the Character pad. In the Character pad, tap the tiny ▾ above the word; select "Add [this word] to the handwriting dictionary." Consider adding your own name, acronyms, and other information you use often.

- **Calibrating.** Calibration involves fine-tuning how accurately your tablet detects the pen's location. If you feel as though your tablet could benefit from calibration, choose Start→Control Panel. In the Search box, type *Tablet PC Settings*, and then choose this option in the list of results. (It's not available on non-touch PCs.) On the Display tab, under Display Options, click Calibrate.

Tip: Windows Help is full of tips and tricks for getting better handwriting recognition. You've just read some of them (add words to the dictionary, recalibrate your screen, use the pads of shortcuts for numbers, symbols, and Web address bits). Help also advises lefties to inform the machine by opening the Tablet PC Settings dialog box from Control Panel and choosing Left-Handed.

Windows Journal

Among programs that work well with handwriting, few can top Windows Journal. It's a program for taking notes, keeping a journal, or recording info-tidbits as you come across them during the work day. It's a great tool for students, since it does away with the usual note-taking tools (notebooks, pens, and paper).

When you open it (type *journal* into the Start menu), you're presented with a blank page of what looks like the lined paper of an old spiral notebook.

Note: The first time your start Windows Journal, click Install when Windows asks if you want to install the Journal Note Writer print driver.

So why not just make your scribbles, doodles, and math equations in a program like Word? Because Word doesn't accept handwriting—only typed text *converted* from handwriting. Windows Journal, on the other hand, stores the actual graphic representation of anything you write (Figure 19-9).

As you write along, keep in mind that your notes and sketches aren't locked in Journal forever. For example:

- **Mail it.** Choose File→Send to Mail Recipient to send a page by email. Be sure to choose Journal Note as the format for the message attachment if you want the recipient to be able to open and edit the note in Windows Journal.

  Of course, there are a couple of problems with this approach. Some people might not have Windows Journal on their computers, which means they can't open the

---

attachment. You can also send the attachment as a Web page or as a TIFF file. People who receive your message can see the image of the note, but they can't work with it in Windows Journal. If you're using a recent version of Outlook, you can search for and find text you've written in a Windows Journal note that's stored in email.

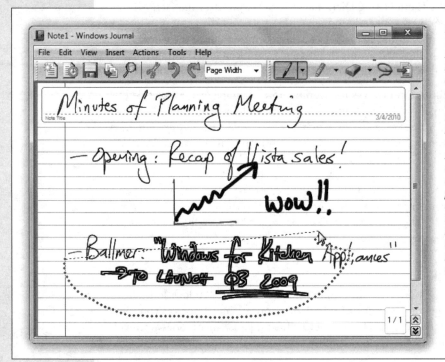

Figure 19-9:
Windows Journal stores your handwriting as digital ink, without attempting to convert everything to typed text. Still, it's not stupid. You can, for example, search your reams of notes for a certain word or phrase. You can also use the Selection tool (looks like a rope lasso) to select text to move, transcribe, or format.

You can also select a swath of handwriting and choose Action→Convert Selection to E-mail. Journal does its best to convert the handwriting to text, which it then pastes into an open outgoing email message.

- **Export it** to a Web archive or a TIFF graphics file (File→Export As).

- **Convert parts of it** to text. See Figure 19-10.

Tip: Pressing the button on the side of your stylus automatically puts it into Selection mode, saving you a trip to the toolbar or Edit menu.

- **Change your "pen."** Select some text, and then choose Edit→"Format ink" to change the thickness, color, and other attributes of the ink style.

Flicks

Pen flicks let you navigate documents and manipulate data using your stylus alone. With a flick of the wrist, you can scroll a page at a time, copy, paste, delete, undo, and so on. You have eight pen flicks available to you: up, down, left, right, and the four diagonals.

(So what's the difference between a *flick* and a *gesture?* Very little, except that to make a flick, you draw an invisible line across your *document,* rather than in the Input panel.)

To turn on this feature, open the Pen and Touch control panel (start typing *pen and touch* into the Start menu to find it). Once the dialog box opens, click the Flicks tab.

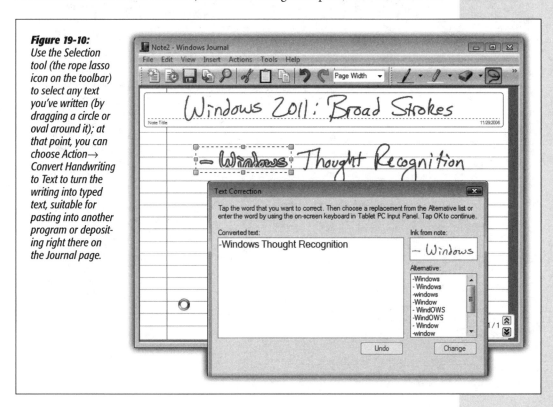

Figure 19-10:
Use the Selection tool (the rope lasso icon on the toolbar) to select any text you've written (by dragging a circle or oval around it); at that point, you can choose Action→ Convert Handwriting to Text to turn the writing into typed text, suitable for pasting into another program or depositing right there on the Journal page.

The Flicks tab opens. Turn on "Use flicks…" at the top of the dialog box. At this point, you get only four flicks: up and down (for scrolling) and left and right (for Back and Forward, as in a Web browser). If you turn on "Navigational flicks and editing flicks," however, you add the diagonal options, making flicks even more useful.

At the bottom, click "Practice using flicks." The Flicks Training dialog box opens, probably startling you with the sudden appearance of an actual *video* that shows someone scrolling with the pen.

When you click Next, you're offered the opportunity to practice the flicking technique. It suggests that you draw short lines "as though you were brushing something off the screen with the tip of the pen," which is well put.

Figure 19-11 shows the built-in flick movements for Page Up and Page Down, Back and Forward, Delete, Copy, Paste, and Undo. You can change these assignments if you'd prefer (click Customize on the Flicks tab), either by rearranging the flick directions or assigning entirely different functions to them: Save, Open, Print, press the Alt key (or Ctrl, Shift, or ⊞), and so on.

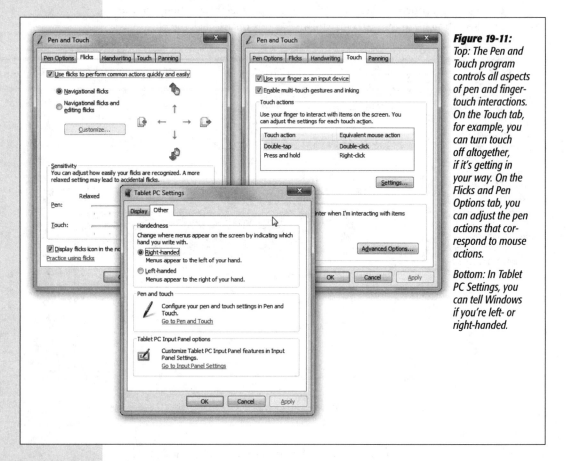

Figure 19-11:
Top: The Pen and Touch program controls all aspects of pen and finger-touch interactions. On the Touch tab, for example, you can turn touch off altogether, if it's getting in your way. On the Flicks and Pen Options tab, you can adjust the pen actions that correspond to mouse actions.

Bottom: In Tablet PC Settings, you can tell Windows if you're left- or right-handed.

Tablet and touch settings

If you get into flicking, you should know that, since Microsoft is Microsoft, you have a long list of customizations and tweaks available to you. Open the Pen and Touch control panel. (Fastest way to get there: Open the Start menu. Start typing *pen and* until you see "Pen and Touch" in the results list; click it.)

Tip: If you have a tablet, you can make life easier for yourself by adding the Pen and Touch control panel to the top of your Start menu, where it's easy to get to. Click Start→Control Panel. Click Hardware and Sound. Drag Pen and Touch—either the little pen icon or the words "Pen and Touch"—to the Start button. Without releasing the mouse, wait for the Start menu to open, and then drop the icon at the top-right corner of the Start menu. You can now get to the settings quickly.

Figure 19-11 shows both the Pen and Touch control panel and the Tablet PC Settings control panel. Each offers useful adjustments for touch computing. Neither makes clear why they're two separate programs.

Windows Touch

Home Premium • Professional • Enterprise • Ultimate

On a tablet PC, you navigate and operate your PC with gestures, flicks, and the touch of your pen. *Touchscreen* PCs, available as both laptops and desktops (usually all-in-one designs), take you one step further: You can scroll Web pages, select music and photos, zoom in and out, rotate things, or open documents by touching the screen with your *fingers*.

Windows 7 has *multitouch* features built in, meaning that—if your PC has a multitouch screen—you can use two fingers on the screen, iPhone style, to perform common commands. To imitate a right-click of the mouse, for example, you touch a file's icon with one finger and tap the screen with another.

All through Windows 7, you'll find indications that Microsoft designed Windows 7 with touch in mind. That's one reason icons on the taskbar are larger than before, making them more accessible to your touch. Jump lists are easily managed on a touchscreen. The onscreen keyboard, originally designed for tablets, has been upgraded for fingertip operation.

Touch Gestures

If your PC has a multitouch screen, here are the four basic built-in Windows 7 multitouch gestures that work at the desktop and in many programs:

- **Panning** is like scrolling with the mouse; it works anytime scroll bars are visible in a window. You can drag one or two fingers up, down, left, or right. (The problem with one-finger dragging is that you might accidentally select what's under your finger—a line of text, for example. Two-finger dragging is therefore usually safer.)

  The faster you drag, the faster you scroll.

- **Flicking** is a quick horizontal swipe with one finger. It's the same thing as clicking a Back or Forward button—in your Web browser or Windows Explorer, for example. When you've opened a photo (in, for example, Windows Live Photo Gallery), flicking means next/previous photo.

- **Zooming** works just as it does on an iPhone or iPod Touch. Place two fingers on the screen. Spreading them apart zooms in (enlarges a smaller area of a picture or a map); pinching them together zooms out for a larger view. This feature works in most basic Microsoft programs: Internet Explorer, Photo Viewer and Photo Gallery, Microsoft Office, and so on.

- **Rotating** a picture, a PDF page, or another object involves placing two fingers against the screen, then rotating them clockwise or counterclockwise.

• **Right-clicking,** to open something's shortcut menu, is done like this: While touching the object with one finger, tap another spot on the screen with a second finger.

Tip: You can use and customize flicks with a touchscreen PC in the same way you can use them with a tablet PC.

These gestures are supposed to work in all programs, even those that haven't been designed especially for touchscreens. Your mileage, however, may vary.

Minor Tweaks

Other nods to the new finger-driven generation are lurking everywhere in Windows 7. For example, on a touchscreen PC, you'll notice these changes:

• The Show Desktop button (far right of the taskbar) is twice as wide.

• Windows snap against the edge of the screen with more "magnetism," so you don't have to be as precise.

• When you open a jump list (page 51) by flicking upward from a taskbar icon, the commands in it are spaced more widely than usual, for easier targeting with a finger.

• In Paint, you can paint with two fingers at once (or as many as your computer's multitouch screen is designed to track simultaneously).

• In Windows Media Center, you can swipe up, down, left, or right from most screens.

• The Hearts and Solitaire games have been rewritten for touch control.

Note: You can turn multitouch input off, if you like, in the Pen and Touch control panel. (But why?) Here, you can also set up custom touch actions to match common mouse actions.

UP TO SPEED

Touch and Internet Explorer

Windows Touch and Internet Explorer go especially well together. There's something about the direct manipulation of Web links and buttons on the screen that makes this combination appealing.

All the usual two-finger gestures work here: panning (scrolling), zooming, and flicking (to go back or forward a page).

You can swipe downward from the address bar to see the list of recent Web sites and bookmarks, rather than having to aim for the tiny arrow next to it—and the resulting menu has extra-wide spacing, for greater finger comfort.

But links on traditional Web pages can be tiny—too tiny for fat fingers. There are, however, some workarounds.

For example, a two-finger tap zooms into that spot on any Web page, which is especially handy when you want to magnify the area of a link you want to tap, making a bigger target.

You can return the page to normal size with another two-finger tap. (Of course, you can also zoom in much more, and with much greater control, using the two-finger spreading gesture described above. Pinch to shrink the page back down.)

Remember, too, that you can flick right or left to simulate clicks on the Back or Forward buttons.

Finally, try this: To open a link in a new tab, don't just click it; drag it a short way in any direction. (It takes practice.)

Overall, you'll probably find that multitouch computing is better in theory than in practice. You never know which gestures a certain program is going to recognize. Worst, very few programs have been designed for touch—with big, finger-friendly buttons and controls. (That, at least, you can partly ameliorate by blowing up the size of Windows's on-screen elements; see page 194.)

Windows Mobile
All Versions

Windows Mobile isn't really Windows. It's a much smaller, simpler series of operating systems designed for cellphones, palmtops, ultra-mobile PCs, and portable media centers (handheld music/video/photo players).

All of them have certain Windows-esque interface elements—a Start menu is a common one—but they are not, in fact, all the same.

The Sync Center, described next, used to be responsible for keeping Windows Mobile gadgets up to date with the latest info on your PC, including your email, address book, and calendar. These days, though, Device Stage (page 607) has taken over that job.

Sync Center is now used for only one purpose: managing offline files.

Offline Files & Sync Center
Professional • Enterprise • Ultimate

The *offline files feature* is designed for laptop lovers. It lets you carry off files that generally live on your office network, so you can get some work done while you're away.

Then, when you return and connect your laptop to the office network, Windows automatically copies your edited, updated documents back to their original locations on the network, intelligently keeping straight which copies are the most recent. (And vice versa—if people changed the network copies while you were away, Windows copies them onto your laptop.)

Tip: If your purpose is to have the same files waiting for you at home that are on your PC at work, Windows Live Sync is a better choice. See page 474.

Offline Files is a great feature for corporate workers, which explains why it's not available in all versions of Windows 7. And it's been greatly simplified since the Windows XP version. For example, reconnecting to the network now triggers an automatic, seamless, invisible synchronization of the files you worked on while you were away—there's no more alert balloon, no need to shut down all programs and manually trigger the sync, and so on.

You can also command Windows to sync at more specific times: every time you connect to the network, for example, or at 3:00 a.m.

Preparing to Leave the Network

To tell Windows which files and folders you want to take away with you on the laptop, find them on the network. Proceed as shown in Figure 19-12.

Note: If you can't seem to make this work, it may be because the Offline Files master switch has been turned off. Open the Start menu. Start typing *offline* until you see "Manage offline files" in the results list; click it. On the General tab of the Offline Files dialog box, the Enable Offline Files button awaits. (Unless Offline Files is already turned on, in which case the button says "Disable offline files.")

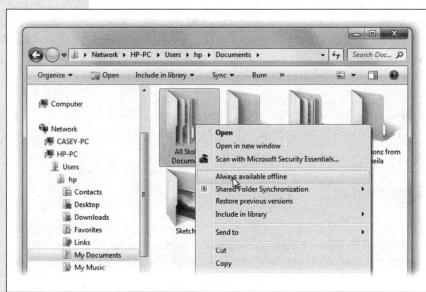

Figure 19-12:
Right-click the icon of a file or folder that's on another computer on the network. From the shortcut menu, choose "Always available offline." (A checkmark appears. To stop making this file or folder available offline, choose the same command again.) Your PC takes a quick moment to copy the files onto your own hard drive (that is, to the client machine—your laptop).

Windows now takes a moment—well, quite a few moments, actually—to copy the selected files and folders to your laptop. Fortunately, it works in the background, between your mouse clicks and keystrokes.

Note: If somebody on the network is actually using those files right now—has them open—you'll get an error message at this point. Wait until those documents are closed, and then try again.

It's an excellent idea to synchronize your folders manually every time you're about to leave the network, so the files on your laptop are up to date. (In fact, if you're away and you try to edit an out-of-date file, Windows won't even let you open it!)

To trigger the syncing, right-click the folder; from the shortcut menu, choose "Sync selected offline files." See "The Sync Schedule," below, for some other approaches.

Working Offline

Now suppose you're untethered from the network, and you have a moment to get some work done. You can find the synced folders in three different places:

- **In the ghost of the networked PC.** This might seem weird, but you can actually navigate to the network machine that originally stored those offline folders in the usual way—clicking its name in the Network folder in the Navigation pane, for example—even though you're no longer connected to it. Burrow into its folders far enough, and you'll eventually find the folder you "subscribed" to, just as though you were still connected.

(The files and folders you *haven't* subscribed to show up with Xs, as shown in Figure 19-13, indicating that you can't open them now.)

Tip: The folders you've subscribed to appear with a special green Offline Files logo. If you click it, the Details pane indicates that, indeed, this folder is "Always available."

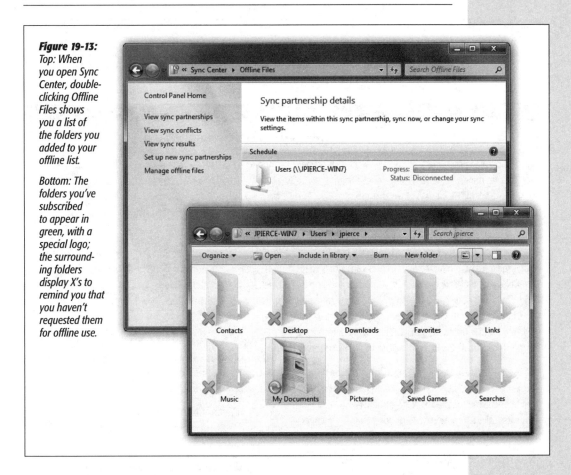

Figure 19-13:
Top: When you open Sync Center, double-clicking Offline Files shows you a list of the folders you added to your offline list.

Bottom: The folders you've subscribed to appear in green, with a special logo; the surrounding folders display X's to remind you that you haven't requested them for offline use.

- **In the Offline Files folder.** To see a complete list of all offline files from all PCs, open the Start menu and type *offline files*. Click "Manage offline files"; in the resulting dialog box, click "View your offline files."

- **In the Sync Center,** described below.

There, before you, is a list of all the files and folders to which you "subscribed" before you left the network. In fact, you also see icons for *all* the folders that were in that networked folder. Only the ones you explicitly requested are available, however; the rest display X's, as shown in Figure 19-13.

You're free to work with offline files and folders exactly as you would if you were still connected to the network. You can revise, edit, and duplicate files, and even create new documents inside offline folders. The permissions remain the same as when you connect to the network.

Tip: Sometimes, you want to work with your laptop copies (not than the network copies) even if you're still *on* the network—if, say, the network connection is not so much *absent* as *slow.* To do that, open the folder on the network that contains the offline files. On the toolbar, click "Work offline."

Reconnecting to the Network

Now suppose you return from your jaunt away from the office. You plop your laptop down on your desk and reconnect to the network.

NOSTALGIA CORNER

The Briefcase

The trouble with progress is that it entails change—and when you change things, somebody, somewhere is going to be upset. Just ask Microsoft's Windows division.

Anyway, Windows 7 may have the Sync Center, but it also still has the Briefcase, which is something like its predecessor. Microsoft plays it *way* down, to the point of invisibility. But it still does one thing the Sync Center can't do. It keeps your files straight between *two PCs* (as opposed to one PC and a network server). That's handy when you transport files from desktop to laptop, or from home to work. If you learn to use the Briefcase, you'll be less likely to lose track of which copies of your documents are the most current.

To use the Briefcase, start by adding a Briefcase icon on your desktop. To do so, right-click any spot on the desktop; from the shortcut menu, choose New→Briefcase. A new icon appears, called New Briefcase. (If you're feeling inspired, rename it as you would any folder.)

Now round up the icons of the documents you'll work on when away from your main PC. Drag them onto the Briefcase icon. Windows copies the files into this special temporary holding tank.

Connect your laptop to the desktop PC, if you haven't already. (See Chapter 24 for tips on connecting machines.) Or, if you plan to take your files with you on a USB flash drive, insert it. Drag the Briefcase icon onto the laptop or the flash drive.

You're ready to leave your office. When you get to wherever you're going, open and edit the documents in the copied Briefcase "folder" icon. Whatever you do, don't move those files. (For example, work on the documents right on the flash drive.)

If the copied Briefcase is actually on the laptop's hard drive (not a flash drive), Windows can keep track of changes made to the documents on *both* computers, the original and the copy.

When you return to your main PC, reconnect the laptop or reinsert the flash drive. All your careful step-following is about to pay off.

Right-click the briefcase icon; from the shortcut menu, choose Update All. Windows copies the edited files back to their original folders on your desktop-PC hard drive, automatically replacing the older, original copies.

Once Windows discovers that it's home again, it whirls into action, automatically comparing your set of offline files and folders with the master set on the network. (This process is much faster than it was in Windows XP, because Windows 7 copies only the changed *pieces* of each file—not the entire file.)

Along the way, Windows 7 attempts to handle discrepancies between the two sets of files as best it can. For example:

- If your copy and a network copy of a file don't match, Windows wipes out the older version with the newer version, so both locations have the latest edition.

- If you deleted your copy of a file, or if somebody on the network deleted the original, Windows deletes the corresponding file so that it no longer exists on either machine. (That's assuming that nobody edited the file in the meantime.)

- If somebody added a file to the network copy of a folder, you get a copy of it in your laptop's copy of the folder.

- If you've edited an offline file that somebody on the network has deleted in the meantime, Windows offers you the choice to save your version on the network or to delete it from your laptop.

- If you delete a file from your hard drive that somebody else on the network has edited in the meantime, Windows deletes the offline file from your hard drive but doesn't delete the network copy from the network.

- If both your copy and the network copy of a file were edited while you were away, a balloon in the notification area notifies you of the conflict. Click it to open the Sync Center, where you can decide which version "wins." (Until you do that, the file in question remains offline, on your laptop.)

The Sync Schedule

Ordinarily, Windows updates your offline files each time you connect to the network. (It also updates the folder a couple of times a day while you're still connected.)

GEM IN THE ROUGH

Windows SideShow

Device lovers, take note. SideShow, which was introduced in Windows Vista, is a feature built into a few—very few—portable computers and mobile phones. Microsoft had high hopes for it, but the feature has disappeared almost completely.

Still, for the record: SideShow-compatible devices use a tiny display screen to show you certain kinds of important information—your calendar, new email, the time or weather, your address book, a PowerPoint slide—even if the laptop is turned off or asleep.

With a SideShow machine, you can specify which gadget (mini-program) you want to see. You can download gadgets by clicking Start and typing *gadgets* into the Search box. Then click "Get more gadgets online." Check out Windows Help and Support to learn more about installing a device that's compatible with Windows SideShow. (You can run SideShow gadgets on your desktop to preview them; just right-click the desktop, and from the shortcut menu, choose Gadgets, just as you would for regular gadgets.)

If you're about to catch a flight, however, and you're nervous that you might not have the latest versions of all the network files you need, you can force Windows to do the entire copying job *right now*. The quickest way to do that is to open the offline folder and then click the Sync icon on its toolbar; from the shortcut menu, choose "Sync offline files in this folder." For even more control over the syncing schedule, see Figure 19-14.

Tip: You can even sync *one individual file* if you have to. Right-click it, and choose Sync from the shortcut menu. (The Sync buttons are available only while you are, in fact, connected to the network.)

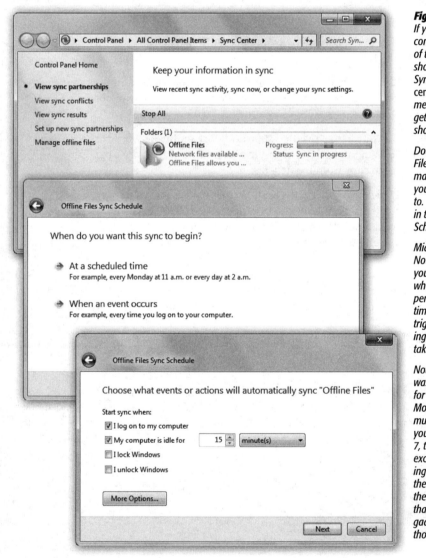

Figure 19-14:
If you'd like more control over the timing of the syncing, you should fire up the Sync Center (type sync center into the Start menu to find it). You get the special window shown here at top.

Double-click Offline Files to see a summary of all the folders you've "subscribed" to. Click Offline Files; in the toolbar, click Schedule.

Middle and bottom: Now a wizard walks you through setting when the syncing happens—not only at what time, but when certain triggers (like connecting or disconnecting) take place.

Note: Sync Center was once the hub for syncing Windows Mobile phones and music players with your PC. In Windows 7, the Sync Center is exclusively for managing offline files. Use the Device Stage, or the syncing software that came with your gadget, to handle those other gizmos.

Part Six: PC Health

6

Maintenance & Speed Tweaks

Your computer requires periodic checkups and preventive maintenance—pretty much like you, its human sidekick. Fortunately, Microsoft has put quite a bit of effort into equipping Windows 7 with special tools, all dedicated to keeping your system stable and fast. Here's a crash course in keeping your PC—and its hard drive—humming.

The Action Center
All Versions

If you're looking for the best place to go for at-a-glance information about the current state of your PC's maintenance and Internet security, open the new Action Center (it was called the Security Center in Windows Vista). To open it, click the tiny ▧ or ℙ on your system tray.

Here, all in one place, are all the security and maintenance messages that Windows wants you to see. Be grateful; they *used* to pop up as individual nag balloons on the system tray all day. Now they accumulate here.

Color coding lets you know what steps Windows thinks you should take. Messages marked with a *red* vertical bar are things you should fix right now, like not having a virus program installed. Items with a yellow bar are less urgent; they're maintenance recommendations, for example.

You can read the full scoop on the Action Center on page 361. For now, it's enough to remember that here's the place to check to see how your Windows Updates and PC backups are doing.

Disk Cleanup

All Versions

As you use your computer, Windows litters your hard drive with temporary files. Programs, utilities, and Web sites scatter disposable files everywhere. If you could see your hard drive's surface, it would eventually look like the floor of a minivan whose owners eat a lot of fast food.

To run Windows 7's built-in housekeeper program, the quickest route is to open the Start menu. Start typing *disk cleanup* until you see its name in the results list; click it. (Disk Cleanup is also available in the Control Panel.)

The Disk Cleanup program dives right in. If you have more than one drive, it lets you choose the one you want to work on; then it goes to work, inspecting your drive and reporting on files you can safely remove.

Left to its own devices, it will clean up only *your* files. But if you'd like to clean up all the files on the computer, including Microsoft's own detritus, click "Clean up system files." Authenticate if necessary.

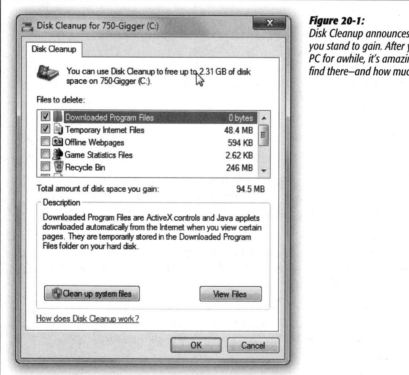

Figure 20-1:
Disk Cleanup announces how much free space you stand to gain. After you've been using your PC for awhile, it's amazing how much crud you'll find there—and how much space you can recover.

The Disk Cleanup dialog box shown in Figure 20-1 appears when the inspection is over. Turn on the checkboxes of the file categories you'd like to have cleaned out, and then click OK to send them to the digital landfill. It's like getting a bigger hard drive for free.

Disk Defragmenter
All Versions

When you save a new file, Windows records its information onto the hard drive in small pieces called *blocks*. On a new PC, Windows lays the blocks end-to-end on the hard drive's surface. Later, when you type more data into a document (thus enlarging it), the file no longer fits in the same space. Windows puts as much of the file in the original location as can fit, but it may have to store a few of its blocks in the next empty spot on the hard drive.

Ordinarily, you'll never even notice that your files are getting chopped up in this way, since they open promptly and seamlessly. Windows keeps track of where it has stored the various pieces, and reconstitutes them when necessary.

As your drive fills up, though, the free space that's left is made up of smaller and smaller groups of blocks. Eventually, a new file may not fit in a single "parking place" on the hard drive's surface, since there are no free spaces left large enough to hold it. Windows may have to store a file in several different areas of the disk, or even hundreds.

When you try to open such a *fragmented* file, the drive heads (which read the disk) must scamper all over the disk surface, rounding up each block in turn, which is slower than reading contiguous blocks one after the other. Over time, this *file fragmentation* gets worse and worse. Eventually, you wind up griping to your buddies or spouse that you need a new computer, because this one seems to have gotten *so slow*.

The solution: Disk Defragmenter, a program that puts together pieces of files that have become fragmented (split into pieces) on your drive. The "defragger" also rearranges the files on your drives to make the operating system and programs load more quickly. A freshly defragged PC feels faster and more responsive than a heavily fragmented one.

The big news in Windows 7 is that its disk-defragging software runs *automatically* at regular intervals, in the tiny moments when you're not actually typing or clicking. It's

---

POWER USERS' CLINIC

Beyond Disk Defragmenter

Disk Defragmenter isn't the only tool for the defrag job; the world is full of disk-defragmenting programs that offer additional features.

For example, some of them track how often you use the various files on your drive, so they can store the most frequently used files at the beginning of the disk for quicker access. In some programs, you can even *choose* which files go at the beginning of the disk.

Do these additional features actually produce a measurable improvement over Windows 7's built-in defragger? That's hard to say, especially when you remember the biggest advantage of Disk Defragmenter—it's free.

---

like having someone take out your garbage for you whenever the can is full. Slow-PC syndrome should, therefore, be a much less frequent occurrence.

Tip: Fragmentation doesn't become noticeable except on hard drives that have been very full for quite a while. Don't bother defragmenting your drive unless you've actually noticed it slowing down. The time you'll spend waiting for Disk Defragmenter to do its job is much longer than the fractions of seconds caused by a little bit of file fragmentation.

And if you're the lucky owner of a solid-state drive (SSD)—fast, quiet, super-expensive—you'll find that fragmentation has only a minimal hit on your computer's speed. In fact, if Windows 7 detects that you're using an SSD, it disables automatic defragmentation.

Defragging Settings

Even though Windows 7 defrags your hard drive automatically in the background, you can still exert some control. For example, you can change the schedule, and you can trigger a defragmentation manually when you're feeling like a control freak.

Start by opening the Disk Defragmenter main screen. You can get there via the Control Panel, but as usual, it's faster to type. Open the Start menu. Start typing *defragment* until you see Disk Defragmenter in the results list; click it.

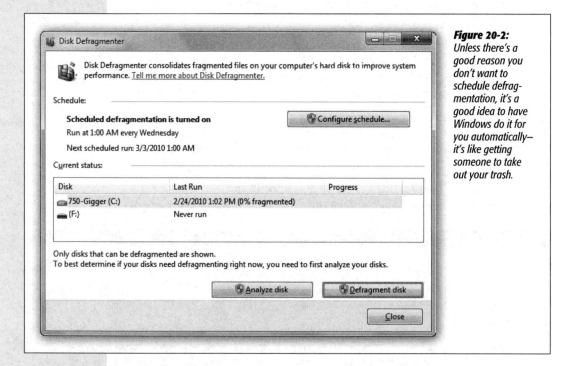

Figure 20-2:
Unless there's a good reason you don't want to schedule defragmentation, it's a good idea to have Windows do it for you automatically—it's like getting someone to take out your trash.

Tip: Throughout Windows, and throughout its book and magazine literature, disks are referred to as *volumes.* Usually, volume means disk. But technically, it refers to *anything with its own disk icon* in the Computer window—including disk *partitions* (page 651), DVDs, and so on.

The Disk Defragmenter window opens (Figure 20-2). From here, you can either adjust the schedule or trigger defragmentation manually.

- **Adjust the schedule.** Click "Configure schedule." Authenticate if necessary. A screen appears, showing that Windows 7 ordinarily defrags your disk late every Wednesday night (1:00 a.m., in fact). You can use the pop-up menus here to specify a Weekly, Daily, or Monthly schedule, complete with day-of-week and time-of-day options. Click OK, and then OK again.

- **Manually.** Click "Defragment disk"; the defragmenter does its work. Depending on the size of your hard disk, your processor speed, and the amount of fragmentation, it will take anywhere from several minutes to several hours.

Tip: During the defragmentation process, Windows picks up pieces of your files and temporarily sets them down in a different spot, like somebody trying to solve a jigsaw puzzle. If your hard drive is very full, defragmenting will take a lot longer than if you have some empty space available—and if there's not enough free disk space, Windows can't do the job completely. Before you run Disk Defragmenter, use Disk Cleanup and make as much free disk space as possible.

Hard Drive Checkups
All Versions

Every time you shut down the PC, Windows tidies up, ensuring that all files are saved properly on the drive. When all is well, Windows turns off the machine. (All Windows 7–compatible PCs can turn themselves off; the days of messages telling you, "It is now safe to turn off your computer" are over.) The time that elapses between your Turn Off Computer command and the actual power-down moment is the "tidying up" period.

But sometimes, thanks to a system crash, power outage, or toddler playing with your surge suppressor, your computer gets turned off without warning—and without the usual shutdown checks. In the olden days, way back even before Windows XP, restarting the PC after such a *dirty shutdown* automatically ran a program called ScanDisk, a utility designed to detect and, when possible, repair drive damage that may have occurred as a result of an improper shutdown.

ScanDisk doesn't exist in Windows 7, but its functions have been reincarnated. You get to this feature by right-clicking the icon of the hard drive you want to check (in the Computer window). From the shortcut menu, choose Properties; click the Tools tab, and click Check Now. Authenticate yourself if needed (page 726).

Note: Geeks fondly refer to the feature described here as *chkdsk* (apparently named by someone with no vowels on his keyboard). You get to the geek-friendly, text-only version of it by typing *chkdsk* in a Command Prompt window. But the method described here is much better-looking.

As shown in Figure 20-3, a box appears, offering two options:

- **Automatically fix file system errors.** Clearly, you want this option turned on, so that any problems Windows finds are taken care of automatically.

Figure 20-3:
Checking your disk for errors regularly will go a long way toward making sure your files won't get corrupted. If you use the "fix file errors" option, the check occurs at the next startup; the "scan" option goes into effect immediately.

FREQUENTLY ASKED QUESTION

When Good Drives Go Bad

I was surprised when the Check Disk dialog box found some problems with my hard drive. I don't understand what could have gone wrong. I treat my PC with respect, talk to it often, and never take it swimming. Why did my hard drive get flaky?

All kinds of things can cause problems with your hard drive, but the most common are low voltage, power outages, voltage spikes, and mechanical problems with the drive controller or the drive itself.

An inexpensive gadget called a *line conditioner* (sold at computer stores) can solve the low-voltage problem. A more expensive gizmo known as an *Uninterruptible Power Supply* (UPS) maintains enough backup battery power to keep your computer going when the power goes out completely—for a few minutes, anyway, so you can shut it down properly. The more expensive models have line conditioning built in. A UPS is also the answer to power outages, if they're common in your area.

Voltage spikes are the most dangerous to your PC. They frequently occur during the first seconds when the power comes back on after a power failure. A surge suppressor is the logical defense here. But remember that the very

cheap devices often sold as surge suppressors are actually little more than extension cords. Furthermore, some of the models that do provide adequate protection are designed to sacrifice themselves in battle. After a spike, you may have to replace them.

If you care about your computer (or the money you spent on it), buy a good surge suppressor, at the very least. The best ones come with a guarantee that the company will replace your equipment (up to a certain dollar value) if the unit fails to provide adequate protection.

On the other hand, insufficient power is just as dangerous as voltage spikes. If you own a desktop PC, chances are good that the built-in power supply is strong enough for whatever components your PC was born with. But if you've upgraded—adding a faster hard drive or a beefier video card, for example—you may be pushing your PC's power supply to its limits.

If you're doing a bunch of upgrades to convert an entry-level office PC into a gaming powerhouse, then make sure you're including a newer, stronger, power supply among those upgrades.

Note: Even though the button you clicked was called Check Now, Windows cannot, in fact, check for errors on the system disk (or a disk with open files) now; that'd be like a surgeon operating on herself. When you click Start, a message cheerfully informs you that Windows will be happy to run this error check the next time it starts up. And indeed it will. Click "Schedule disk check" to make it so.

- **Scan for and attempt recovery of bad sectors.** If you turn on this option, then whenever the scan finds a damaged section of a drive, it moves any files located there elsewhere on the drive. Then the program surrounds that hard-disk area with the digital equivalent of yellow "Police Line—Do Not Cross" tape so that Windows won't use the damaged area for storing files in the future.

When you've made your choice, click Start. If you selected only the "Scan" option, the procedure begins immediately; otherwise, the test is performed at the next startup.

Disk Management
All Versions

"Disk management" isn't just a cool, professional-sounding skill—it's the name of a built-in Windows maintenance program that lets you perform all kinds of operations on your hard disk.

To open this technical database of information about your disks and drives, you can use either of these two methods:

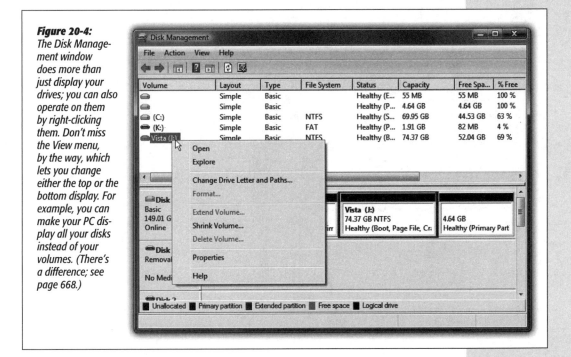

Figure 20-4:
The Disk Management window does more than just display your drives; you can also operate on them by right-clicking them. Don't miss the View menu, by the way, which lets you change either the top or the bottom display. For example, you can make your PC display all your disks instead of your volumes. (There's a difference; see page 668.)

• Choose Start→Control Panel. Click System and Security→"Create and format hard disk partitions." (It's at the very bottom of the window.)

• In the Start menu's Search box, type *diskmgmt.msc* and then press Enter.

In either case, you arrive at the window shown in Figure 20-4. At first glance, it appears to be nothing more than a table of every disk (and *partition* of every disk) currently connected to your PC. In truth, the Disk Management window is a software toolkit that lets you *operate* on these drives.

Change a Drive Letter

As you've probably noticed, Windows assigns a drive letter to each disk drive associated with your PC. In the age of floppy disks, the floppy drive was always A:. The primary internal hard drive is generally C:; your CD/DVD drive may be D: or E:; and so on. Among other places, you see these letters in parentheses following the names of your drives in the Start→Computer window.

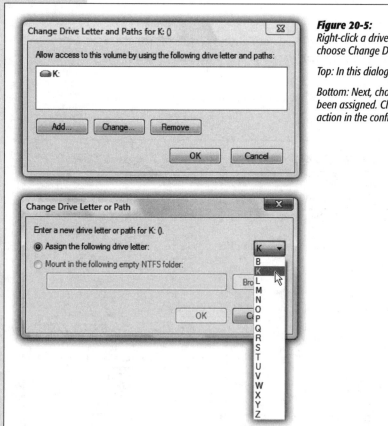

Figure 20-5:
Right-click a drive icon. From the shortcut menu, choose Change Drive Letter and Paths.

Top: In this dialog box, click Change.

Bottom: Next, choose a letter that hasn't already been assigned. Click OK, and then approve your action in the confirmation box.

Windows generally assigns these letters in the order that you install new drives to your system. You're not allowed to change the drive letter of the floppy drive or any startup hard drive (the C: drive and, if you're set up for dual booting, any other boot drives).

You can, however, override the *other* drives' unimaginative Windows letter assignments easily enough, as shown in Figure 20-5.

Note: If Windows 7 is currently using files on the disk whose drive letter you're trying to change, Disk Management might create the new drive letter assignment but leave the old one intact until the next time you restart the computer. This is an effort not to pull the rug out from under any open files.

Partition a New Drive

The vast majority of Windows PCs have only one hard drive, represented in the Computer window as a single icon.

Plenty of power users, however, delight in *partitioning* the hard drive—dividing its surface so that it appears on the screen as two different icons with two different names. At that point, you can live like a king, enjoying the following advantages (just like people who have two separate hard drives):

- You can keep Windows 7 on one of them and Windows XP (for example) on the other, so you can switch between the two at startup. (This feature, called *dual booting, is* described on page 821.)

- Two partitions make life much easier if you frequently install and reinstall the operating system, or different versions of it. Having the partitions allows you to keep all your files safely on one partition, confining all the installing/uninstalling activity to the other.

- You can use multiple partitions to keep your operating system(s) separate from folders and files. In this way, you can perform a *clean install* of Windows (page 820) onto one partition without having to worry about losing any of your important files or installation programs.

Now, in earlier Windows days, partitioning a hard drive using the tools built into Windows required first erasing the hard drive completely. Fortunately, Windows 7's Disk Management console (page 671) can save you from that hassle, although making a backup before you begin is still a smart idea. (The short version: Right-click the disk's icon in Disk Management; from the shortcut menu, choose Shrink Volume. In the Shrink dialog box, specify how much space you want to free up, and then click Shrink. Then turn the free space into a new volume, as described next.)

Creating a partition

In the Disk Management window, free space (suitable for turning into a partition of its own) shows up with a black bar and the label Unallocated.

To create a new partition, right-click one of these unallocated segments. From the shortcut menu, choose New Simple Volume (if this option isn't available, right-click the disk and choose Initialize Disk). A wizard appears; its screens ask you to make some decisions:

- **How big you want the volume to be.** If you're dividing up a 500 GB drive, for example, you might decide to make the first volume 300 GB and the second 200 GB. Begin by creating the 300 GB volume (right-clicking the big "Unallocated" bar in Figure 20-4). When that's done, you see a smaller "Unallocated" chunk still left in the Disk Management window. Right-click it and choose New Simple Volume *again,* this time accepting the size the wizard proposes (which is *all* the remaining free space).

- **What drive letter you want to assign to it.** Most of the alphabet is at your disposal.

- **What disk-formatting scheme you want to apply to it.** Windows 7 requires NTFS for the system drive. But if you're just using the drive to store data (and not to contain a copy of Windows 7), the old FAT32 format is fine. In fact, if you plan to dual-boot Windows 7 with Linux, Mac OS X, or an old version of Windows, then FAT32 might be the only file system all those OSes can recognize simultaneously.

When the wizard is through with you, it's safe to close the window. A quick look at your Computer window confirms that you now have new "disks" (actually partitions of the same disk), which you can use for different purposes.

Turn a Drive into a Folder

Talk about techie! Most people could go their entire lives without needing this feature, or even imagining that it exists. But it's there if you're a power user and you want it.

Using the Paths feature of Disk Management, you can actually turn a hard drive (or partition) into a *folder* on another hard drive (or partition). These disks-disguised-as-folders are technically known as *mounted drives, junction points,* or *drive paths.*

This arrangement affords the following possibilities:

- In effect, you can greatly expand the capacity of your main hard drive—by installing a second hard drive that masquerades as a folder on the first one.

- You can turn a burned CD or DVD into a folder on your main hard drive, too—a handy way to fool your programs into thinking the files they're looking for are still in the same old place on your hard drive. (You could pull this stunt in a crisis—when the "real" folder has become corrupted or has been thrown away.)

- If you're a *power* power user with lots of partitions, disks, and drives, you may feel hemmed in by the limitation of only 26 assignable letters (A through Z). Turning one of your disks into a mounted volume bypasses that limitation, because a mounted volume doesn't need a drive letter at all.

- A certain disk can be made to appear in more than one place at once. You could put all your MP3 files on a certain disk or partition—and then make it show up as a folder in the Music folder of everyone who uses the computer.

Note: You can create a mounted volume only on an *NTFS-formatted* hard drive.

To bring about this arrangement, visit the Disk Management window, and then right-click the icon of the disk or partition you want to turn into a mounted volume. From the shortcut menu, choose Change Drive Letter and Paths.

In the Change Drive Letter and Paths dialog box (Figure 20-8, top), click Add; in the next dialog box, click Browse. Navigate to and select an empty folder—the one that will represent the disk. (Click New Folder, shown at bottom in Figure 20-6, if you didn't create one in advance.) Finally, click OK.

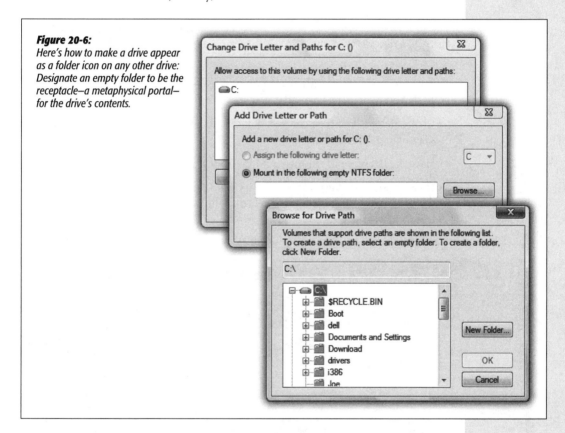

Figure 20-6:
Here's how to make a drive appear as a folder icon on any other drive: Designate an empty folder to be the receptacle—a metaphysical portal—for the drive's contents.

Once the deed is done, take time to note a few special characteristics of a mounted volume:

- The mounted volume may behave just like a folder, but its icon is a dead giveaway, since it still looks like a hard drive (or CD drive, or DVD drive, or whatever).

  Still, if you're in doubt about what it is, you can right-click it and choose Properties from the shortcut menu. You see that the Type information says "Mounted Volume," and the Target line identifies the disk from which it was made.

- Avoid circular references, in which you turn two drives into folders on *each other*. Otherwise, you risk throwing programs into a spasm of infinite-loop thrashing.

• To undo your mounted-drive effect, return to the Disk Management program and choose View→Drive Paths. You're shown a list of all the drives you've turned into folders; click one and then click Remove.

You've just turned that special, "I'm really a drive" folder into an ordinary folder.

Task Scheduler
All Versions

The Task Scheduler, another power-user trick for techies, lets you set up programs and tasks (like disk defragmentation) so they run automatically according to a schedule you specify.

This feature has been greatly beefed up and user-friendlified in Windows 7, to the point that both mere mortals and power geeks may actually find it useful. For example:

• Create an email message that gets sent to your boss each morning, with yesterday's sales figures attached automatically.

• Have the Recycle Bin emptied automatically once a month.

• Create a phony dialog box that appears every time the office know-it-all's PC starts up. Make it say: "The radiation shield on your PC has failed. Please keep back seven feet." You get the idea.

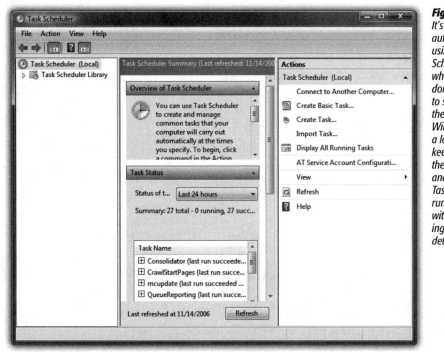

Figure 20-7:
It's easy to automate tasks using the Task Scheduler, but when you open it, don't be surprised to see many tasks there already. Windows 7 does a lot of house-keeping work in the background, and it uses the Task Scheduler to run a lot of tasks without your having to know the details.

Adding a Task

Here's how you add a new task:

1. **Open the Task Scheduler.**

   For example, open the Start menu. Start typing *scheduler* until you see Task Scheduler in the results list; click it. The Task Scheduler window appears (Figure 20-7).

2. **Click Create Basic Task.**

   This link appears on the right-hand pane of the Task Scheduler. A wizard appears.

3. **Type a name for the task and a description, and then click Next.**

   Now you're supposed to choose what Windows calls a "trigger"—in plain English, when to run the task (Figure 20-8). You can specify that it run daily, weekly, monthly, or just once; every time the computer starts or every time you log in; or when a specific event occurs—like when a program starts.

4. **Choose a trigger, and then click Next.**

   The next screen varies according to the trigger you chose. If you chose to run the task on a daily, weekly, or monthly basis, you're now asked to specify *when* during

Figure 20-8:
This screen lets you set a schedule for your task. Depending on the trigger you set, you may see a completely different screen here, because the options are determined by the trigger you choose.

that day, week, or month. Once that's done, click Next.

You now wind up at the Action screen. This is where you say *what* you want to happen at the appointed time. Your choices are "Start a program," "Send an e-mail," or "Display a message."

5. **Choose an action; click Next.**

   Now you're supposed to say *what* program, email, or message you want the PC to fire up.

If you chose the email option, you now fill out a form with the recipient's name, address, subject line, message body, and so on; you can even specify an attachment.

If you chose to run a program, you now browse to select the program. At this point, programmers can also add *arguments*, which are codes that customize how the program starts.

And if you opted to display a message, you get to type a name and text for the message. At the appointed time, an actual Windows dialog box will appear on the screen—except that it will contain text that *you* wrote.

6. **Complete the details about the email, program, or phony dialog box, and then click Next.**

   Finally, a screen appears, summarizing the task, when it will run, and so on. To edit it, click the Back button.

7. **To confirm the automated task, click Finish.**

   You return to the Task Scheduler window. Although you may have to scroll down to see it, your new task appears in the Active Tasks list at the bottom of the window. If all goes well, Windows will fire it up at the moment you specified.

Editing Scheduled Tasks

To change a scheduled task, you first need to find it in the Task Scheduler Library, which is on the left side of the window. Click Task Scheduler Library, and then look at the topmost pane in the middle part of your screen (Figure 20-9). You see a list of scheduled tasks. Highlight the one you want to change.

Delete the task by simply hitting the Delete key. To edit a task, click it and then click the Properties link at the right side of the screen. The tabs in the resulting dialog box (General, Triggers, and so on) may sound familiar, but they actually give you far more control over how each task runs than the basic controls you saw when you first set the task up.

Here are some examples of what you can do on each tab:

- **General.** Select which user account should run the task, and tell Windows whether or not to run when the user is logged in.

- **Triggers.** You can delay the task's execution by a few minutes or until a certain date; have it repeat automatically at regular intervals; stop it after a certain time period; and so on. The "Begin the task" pop-up menu offers a wealth of new triggers, like "On idle" and "On workstation unlock."

- **Actions.** Change the action.

- **Conditions.** Specify that the task will run only under certain conditions—for example, after the computer has been idle for a certain amount of time, when the computer is on AC power, or when it switches to battery power, and so on. You can even say you want to run the task if the PC is sleeping (by waking it first).

- **Settings.** Here's a miscellaneous batch of additional preferences: what actions to take if the task doesn't work, what to do if the computer was turned off at the appointed time, and so on.

- **History.** On this tab, you get to see the task's life story: when it ran and whether each attempt was successful.

Note: Lots of tasks are already present on your PC. Microsoft set them up to ensure the proper running of your computer. To see them all, expand the flippy triangle next to the words "Task Scheduler Library," and then expand Microsoft, and then Windows. You see dozens of tasks in many different categories. In other words, your PC is very busy even when you're not there.

Figure 20-9:
This screen lets you do more than just edit a task. Look at the right-hand pane; you see links that let you run the task right now, end the task if it's already started, and disable the task, among others.

Three Speed Tricks
All Versions

It's a fact of computing: Every PC seems to get slower the longer you own it.

There are plenty of reasons. When the PC is new, consider that:

- The hard drive has loads of free space and zero fragmentation.

- The boot process hasn't yet been cluttered up by startup code deposited by your programs.

- Few background programs are constantly running, eating up your memory.

- You haven't yet drained away horsepower with antivirus and automatic backup programs.

- Every year, the programs you buy or download are more demanding than the previous year's software.

Some of the usual advice about speeding up your PC applies here, of course: Install more memory or a faster hard drive.

But in Windows 7, here and there, nestled among the 50 million lines of code, you'll find some *free* tricks and tips for giving your PC a speed boost. For example:

SuperFetch

Your PC can grab data from RAM (memory) hundreds of times faster than from the hard drive. That's why it uses a *cache*, a portion of memory that holds bits of software code you've used recently. After all, if you've used some feature or command once, you may want to use it again soon—and this way, Windows is ready for you. It can deliver that bit of code nearly instantaneously the next time.

When you leave your PC for a while, however, background programs (virus checkers, backup programs, disk utilities) take advantage of the idle time. They run themselves when you're not around—and push out whatever was in the cache.

That's why, when you come back from lunch (or sit down first thing in the morning), your PC is especially sluggish. All the good stuff—*your* stuff—has been flushed from the cache and returned to the much slower hard drive, to make room for those background utilities.

SuperFetch attempts to reverse that cycle. It attempts to keep your most frequently used programs in the cache all the time. In fact, it actually *tracks you* and your cycle of work. If you generally fire up the computer at 9 a.m., for example, or return to it at 1:30 p.m., SuperFetch will anticipate you by restoring frequently used programs and documents to the cache.

There's no on/off switch for SuperFetch, and nothing for you to configure. It's on all the time, automatic, and very sweet.

ReadyBoost

Your PC can get to data in RAM (memory) hundreds of times faster than it can fetch something from the hard drive. That's why it uses a *cache*, a portion of memory that holds bits of software code you've used recently. (Does this paragraph sound familiar?)

The more memory your machine has, the more that's available for the cache, and the faster things should feel to you. Truth is, though, you may have a bunch of memory sitting around your desk at this moment that's *completely wasted*—namely, USB flash drives. That's perfectly good RAM that your PC can't even touch if it's sitting in a drawer.

Note: ReadyBoost can also work with memory cards, like SD and Compact Flash cards from digital cameras—but only *if* your PC has a built-in card slot. External card readers don't work. (All the descriptions below apply equally to these memory cards.)

PlaysForSure music players don't work, either—although Apple's iPod Shuffle does!

That's the whole point of ReadyBoost: to use a flash drive as described above as additional cache storage. You can achieve the same effect by installing more RAM, of course, but that job can be technical (especially on laptops), forbidden (by your corporate masters), or impossible (because you've used up all your PC's RAM slots already).

Note: You won't run into problems if you yank out the flash drive; ReadyBoost stores a *copy* of the hard drive's data on the card/flash drive.

You also don't have to worry that somebody can steal your flash drive and, by snooping around the cache files, read about your top-secret plans for world domination. Windows 7 encrypts the data using CIA-quality algorithms.

To take advantage of this speed-boosting feature, just plug a USB flash drive into your computer's USB jack.

Note: Both the flash drive *and* your PC must have USB 2.0 or later. USB 1.1 is too slow for this trick to work.

In any case, the AutoPlay dialog box now opens, as shown in Figure 20-10 (left).

Click "Speed up my system"; in the flash device's Properties dialog box (which opens automatically), turn on "Use this device." That box is shown in Figure 20-10 (right).

That's all there is to it. Your PC will now use the flash drive as an annex to its own built-in RAM, and you will, in theory, enjoy a tiny speed lift as a result.

And now, the fine print:

- Not all flash drives are equally fast, and therefore not all work with ReadyBoost. Look closely at the drive's packaging to see if there's a Windows ReadyBoost logo. (Technically speaking—very technically—its throughput must be capable of 2.5 MB per second for 4 KB random reads, and 1.75 MB per second for 512 KB random writes.)

- ReadyBoost works only with memory gadgets with capacities from 256 megabytes to 4 gigabytes.

- If Windows decides that your drive is fast enough *without* ReadyBoost, it disables ReadyBoost entirely. If you're the lucky owner of a computer with a solid state disk (SSD), for example, don't bother with ReadyBoost.

- Windows makes its own suggestions about how much of the drive's capacity to dedicate to ReadyBoost; but if you're the meddlesome type, you can return to the dialog box shown at bottom in Figure 20-10 and change how much of it is used for cache storage. Open Start→Computer and right-click the flash drive's icon. From the shortcut menu, choose Properties. Click the ReadyBoost tab, and configure away.

• Once you've set aside space on the flash drive for ReadyBoost, you can't use it for storing everyday files. (Unless, of course, you change the settings in its Properties dialog box or reformat it.)

• You can use one flash drive per PC, and one PC per flash drive.

• Ordinarily, saving files and then erasing them over and over again shortens a flash drive's life. Microsoft insists, however, that you can get 10 years out of one flash drive using ReadyBoost.

• The biggest speed gains appear when you have a 1-to-1 ratio between real PC memory and your flash drive. For example, if your PC has 1 gigabyte of RAM, adding a 1-gig flash drive should give you a noticeable speed boost.

The speed gains evaporate as you approach a 2.5-to-1 ratio. For example, suppose your PC has 1 gigabyte of RAM and you add a 256-megabyte flash drive. That's an 8-to-1 ratio, and you won't feel any acceleration at all.

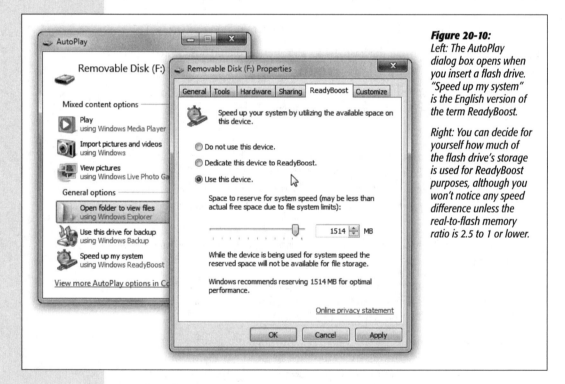

Figure 20-10:
Left: The AutoPlay dialog box opens when you insert a flash drive. "Speed up my system" is the English version of the term ReadyBoost.

Right: You can decide for yourself how much of the flash drive's storage is used for ReadyBoost purposes, although you won't notice any speed difference unless the real-to-flash memory ratio is 2.5 to 1 or lower.

Shutting Off Bells and Whistles

Windows, as you know, is all dressed up for "Where do you want to go today?" It's loaded with glitz, glamour, special effects, and animations. And every one of them saps away a little bit of speed.

With any luck, your PC is a mighty fortress of seething gigahertz that brushes off that kind of resource-sapping as though it were a mere cloud of gnats. But when things start to bog down, remember that you can turn off some of the bells and whistles—and recover the speed they were using.

Here's how.

Open the Start menu. Right-click Computer; from the shortcut menu, choose Properties. In the System control panel that appears, click "Advanced system settings" at left. Authenticate yourself if needed (page 726).

Now, on the Advanced tab (Figure 20-11, top), click the uppermost Settings button. You've just found, in the belly of the beast, the complete list of little animations that make up Windows's window dressing (Figure 20-11, bottom). For example, "Animate windows when minimizing and maximizing" makes Windows present a half-second animation showing your window actually shrinking down onto the taskbar when you

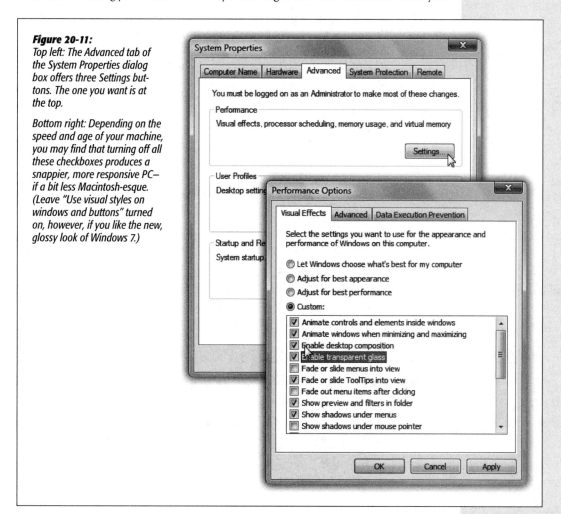

Figure 20-11:
Top left: The Advanced tab of the System Properties dialog box offers three Settings buttons. The one you want is at the top.

Bottom right: Depending on the speed and age of your machine, you may find that turning off all these checkboxes produces a snappier, more responsive PC—if a bit less Macintosh-esque. (Leave "Use visual styles on windows and buttons" turned on, however, if you like the new, glossy look of Windows 7.)

minimize it. "Show shadows under mouse pointer" produces a tiny shadow beneath your cursor, as though it were floating a quarter-inch above the surface of your screen.

With one click—on "Adjust for best performance"—you can turn off all these effects. Or, if there are some you can't live without—and let's face it, tooltips just aren't the same if they don't *fade* into view—click Custom, and then turn off the individual checkboxes for the features you don't need.

Windows Update
All Versions

Windows 7 is far more secure than previous versions of Windows, but you may have noticed that Microsoft isn't going so far as to say, "You don't need an antivirus program anymore." The hackers will have a *much* harder time of it, but with so many million lines of code to explore, they're sure to break in somehow.

Microsoft and other security researchers constantly find new security holes—and as soon as they're found, Microsoft rushes a patch out the door to fix it. But creating a patch is one thing; actually getting that patch installed on multiple millions of copies of Windows 7 around the world is another thing entirely.

Note: In fact, it's Microsoft's *patches* that usually alert hackers to the presence of the security hole in the first place! They exploit the fact that not everyone has the patch in place instantly. (Which brings up the question: Should Microsoft even be creating the patches? But that's another conversation.)

That's where Windows Update comes in. When Microsoft releases a security fix, it gets delivered straight to your PC and automatically installed. (If you want, you can first review the fix before installing it, although few people have enough knowledge to judge its value.)

Windows Update doesn't just deliver patches to Windows itself; it can also send you better drivers for your hardware and patches to other Microsoft products, notably Office.

If you bought a PC with Windows 7 already on it, Windows Update has already been turned on. And if you upgraded to Windows 7 or installed it from scratch, you were asked a series of questions about how you wanted Windows Update to work, although you may have forgotten by now.

DON'T PANIC

Whatever Happened to the Windows Update Sites?

In previous versions of Windows, you could forgo automatic updates entirely, and instead get your updates via Microsoft's Windows Update site. You'd get there via *http:// windowsupdate.microsoft.com,* or by choosing Start→All Programs→Windows Update.

But if you try these tactics in Windows 7, you just end up at the Windows Update screen on your PC. Updates via the Web site are a thing of the past; it's all done on your PC now.

Fiddling with Windows Update

To open Windows Update, open the Start menu. Start typing *update* until you see Windows Update in the results list; click it.

If there are any available updates that you haven't yet installed, you see them here (Figure 20-12).

If you click "Change settings," the screen pictured in Figure 20-13 appears. The four options here correspond to four levels of trust people have in Microsoft, the mother ship:

- **Install updates automatically (recommended).** Translation: "Download and install all patches automatically. We trust in thee, Microsoft, that thou knowest what thou do-est." (All of this will take place in the middle of the night—or according to whatever schedule you set on this screen—so as not to inconvenience you.)

- **Download updates but let me choose whether to install them.** The downloading takes place in the background and doesn't interfere with anything you're downloading for yourself. But instead of installing the newly downloaded patch, Windows asks your permission.

- **Check for updates but let me choose whether to download and install them.** When Windows detects that a patch has become available, a note pops up from your system tray, telling you an update is available. Click the icon in the system tray to indicate which updates to download and then install.

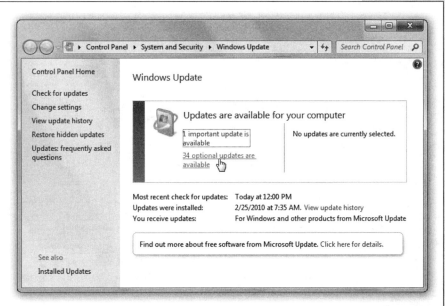

Figure 20-12:
If there are any available updates, you can install them by clicking "Install updates." To get details about an update, click "View available updates."

- **Never check for updates (Not recommended).** Microsoft will leave your copy of Windows completely alone—and completely vulnerable to attacks from the Internet.

Microsoft hates when people choose anything but the first option, because it leaves them potentially open to security holes. On the other hand, patches have sometimes been known to be a bit buggy, so some people like to do a Google search on any new patch before installing it.

Notice, at the bottom of Figure 20-13, that there are several sections, two of which affect which updates are downloaded: There's one for Recommended updates, and one for Microsoft Update. A *recommended update,* in Microsoft lingo, is an update that isn't required to keep your PC safe or to keep your operating system from blowing up, but that can solve "non-critical problems and help enhance your computing experience." That's usually an updated driver or a Windows bug fix or feature enhancement. Turn on Recommended updates if you want them to be included in Windows Update.

The *Microsoft Update* section delivers updates for other Microsoft software on your PC, notably Microsoft Office.

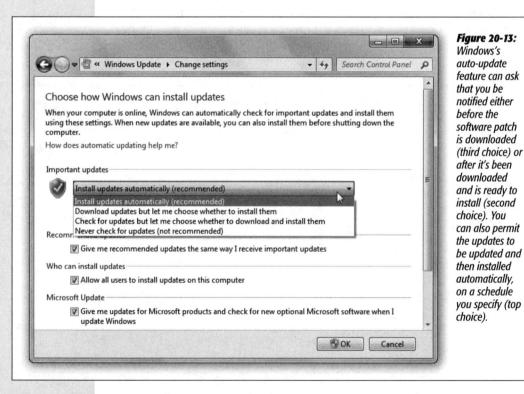

Figure 20-13:
Windows's auto-update feature can ask that you be notified either before the software patch is downloaded (third choice) or after it's been downloaded and is ready to install (second choice). You can also permit the updates to be updated and then installed automatically, on a schedule you specify (top choice).

Beyond the Basics

There's a lot more to Windows Update than these basics, though. You can take a look at all the updates installed on your PC, for example, and you can even uninstall an update. And you can also restore the mysterious-sounding "hidden updates."

To begin, get back to the screen shown in Figure 20-12. (Choose Control Panel→ System and Security→Windows Update to get there.) The left side of the screen includes these links:

- **Check for updates** checks for updates right now, and installs them, if you want.

- **Change settings** works as described earlier.

- **View update history** shows you a list of all the updates that have been downloaded and installed. You see the date of each update, whether it was successful, the type of update, and its purpose. Double-click one to get more details.

- **Restore hidden updates.** As noted below, you can *hide* an update to get it out of your hair. When you click "Restore hidden updates," they reappear so you can reinstall them.

FREQUENTLY ASKED QUESTION

Moving Virtual Memory

So how do you move the virtual memory swap file for more speed?

Well, you don't, really.

Virtual memory is a trick computers use to keep a lot of programs open at once—more, in fact, than they technically have enough memory (RAM) for. How do they manage keeping so many software balls in the air? Easy—they set some of them down on the hard drive.

When you bring Photoshop to the front, for example, Windows frees up the necessary memory for it by storing some of the *background* programs' code on the hard drive. When you switch back to, say, Microsoft Word, Windows swaps Photoshop for the Word code it needs from the hard drive, so that the frontmost program always has full command of your actual memory.

In the days of yore, power geeks argued that you could eke out a little extra speed by relocating this setting-down area—the *swap file*—to another hard drive. A clean, fast, dedicated drive, for example.

These days, though, that's a lot of effort for very little notice-

able speed boost, if any. Today's hard drives are a lot faster than they once were, and a lot better at handling multiple simultaneous requests for data.

Anyone who really wants to move the swap file to a different drive is probably the kind of power user who'd go whole hog, adding a RAID 0 or RAID 0+1 hard drive setup (and if you know what that is, you're enough of a techie to know how to set it up). That would speed up a lot of other aspects of the PC, too.

If you're still determined to move the swap file, though, you can do it. Open the System Properties dialog box. (Right-click Computer in the Start menu; choose Properties.) Click "Advanced system settings." Click the Advanced tab.

In the Performance section, click Settings. In the next dialog box, click the Advanced tab. (Are you getting the idea that this is an *advanced* technique?) Under "Virtual memory," click Change.

Turn off "Automatically manage paging size for all drives," highlight the new destination hard drive for the swap file, and then click OK.

Removing Updates

If an update winds up making life with your PC worse instead of better, you can remove it. Head to Control Panel→Programs→View Installed Updates, right-click an update, and then select Remove.

Note: You can't remove all updates, however. Security-related updates are usually nonremovable.

There's one problem with this action. The next time Windows Updates does its job, it will *re*install the update you just removed.

The workaround is to *hide* the update so that it doesn't get downloaded and installed again. Open Windows Update, and then click "Check for updates."

After Windows finds updates, click "View available updates." Right-click the update you don't want; select "Hide update." From now on, Windows Update ignores the update.

If, later, you change your mind, click "Restore hidden updates," select the update you want installed, and then click Restore.

FREQUENTLY ASKED QUESTION

Resource Monitor

This little app (type *resource* into the Start menu) is a dashboard for your PC's guts: its processor chip (CPU), memory, and disk space. It shows you how much of your PC's horsepower and capacity is being used up, and by what.

Even when you're only running a program or two, dozens of computational tasks *(processes)* are going on in the background. The top table of the Overview screen shows you all the different processes—visible and invisible—that your PC is handling at the moment.

Some are easily recognizable (such as *wmplayer.exe,* meaning Windows Media Player); others are background system-level operations you don't normally see. For each item, you can see the percentage of CPU being used, how much memory it's using, and other details.

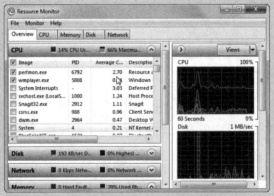

You can isolate one program (or one set of them) using the checkboxes down the left side of any Resource Monitor list; read the details of your selection in the lower half of the window. You can add or delete columns (right-click a column heading, choose Select Columns); you can also drag them to rearrange them or adjust their widths.

The tabs above the list let you drill down into the details of your CPU, memory use, disk space, and network activity.

Normal people living normal lives probably won't root around in Resource Monitor much. But in times of troubleshooting, either you or your designated tech guru may find its information very helpful indeed.

The Disk Chapter

Files and folders, as you've probably noticed, have a tendency to multiply. Creating new documents, installing new software, and downloading new files can fill up even the largest disk drives in no time—especially if, as Microsoft fervently hopes, you get heavily into music, pictures, and video.

Fortunately, Windows offers a number of ways to manage and expand the amount of space on your hard drives. You can subdivide your drives' storage into individual partitions (sections), save space using disk compression, encrypt the contents of your drives for security, and so on.

You can skip this entire chapter, if you wish, and get along quite well without using any of these features. They're strictly optional. But if you aspire to wear the "Power User" T-shirt, read on.

Note: Three of the features described in this chapter—dynamic disks, disk compression, and EFS (encryption file system)—all require the *NTFS file system* on your computer's disk drives. That's probably what you're using on your main hard drive, because Windows 7 requires it.

But other kinds of disks—memory cards, iPods, external USB disks, and so on—probably use the older FAT32 file system instead. You won't be able to use NTFS tricks on them.

Dynamic Disks
Professional • Enterprise • Ultimate

Suppose you've run out of space on the hard drive you use to store movies and music, and you've installed another one to collect the overflow. Thanks to a Windows 7 feature called *dynamic disks*, you don't have to move files to the new drive or reorganize your folder scheme. Instead, you can make the new drive fold its space seamlessly with the first drive's, so you suddenly have more disk space on your "one" combo drive.

If you're working with very large files (like those home movies you spend all your free time editing), you can do something similar; instead of folding one drive into another, you can tell Windows to treat a pair of disks as a single disk.

Windows can then save data onto them in an alternating pattern. This makes everything a lot faster, because Windows doesn't have to wait until the first disk finishes saving a chunk of a file to start saving the next chunk. Instead, it can save (or open) files two chunks at a time, on two disks simultaneously.

> **Note:** Unfortunately, you can't extend your startup drive (the C: drive that contains your Windows 7 installation). If you're running out of disk space on your C: drive, you can move your large documents and media files onto another drive you've installed. You can also save a lot of space by uninstalling large programs from the C: drive, and then reinstalling them on the other drive. (If you do this with a game, though, be sure to back up your saved games when you uninstall, and restore them when you reinstall; see the support forums or FAQ for the game before you proceed).

How Dynamic Disks Work

If this setup intrigues you, a bit more technical explanation is required.

When you (or your PC maker) first installed Windows, it configured each drive as a *basic disk*—a disk with its own drive letter. But before you can combine two actual drives into one volume, you must first convert them into a more flexible format that Microsoft calls a *dynamic disk*.

UP TO SPEED

Volumes Defined

You won't get far in this chapter, or at PC user group meetings, without understanding a key piece of Windows terminology: *volume.*

For most people, most of the time, volume means "disk." But technically, there's more to it than that—a distinction that becomes crucial if you explore the techniques described in this chapter.

If you open your Computer window, you see that each disk has its own icon and drive letter (C:, for example). But each icon isn't necessarily a separate disk. It's possible that you, or somebody in charge of your PC, has split a single drive into multiple *partitions* (Appendix A), each with a separate

icon and drive letter. Clearly, the world needs a term for "an icon/drive letter in the Computer window, whether it's a whole disk or not." That term is *volume.*

With Windows 7's dynamic disks, you can do more than partition one hard drive into multiple volumes—you can also do the reverse, as described in this chapter. If you've installed more than one hard drive, you can actually request that Windows represent them on the screen as *one* volume. This way, you can have as many hard disk drives in your computer as you want and combine their storage space into a unit, represented by one icon and drive letter.

The good news is that you can convert a basic disk into a dynamic disk without losing any data on the drive. The bad news is that you can't change a dynamic disk *back* to a basic disk unless you erase all the data stored there.

And why would you want to change it back? Because dynamic disks, for all their flexibility, also have some limitations. Before you proceed with converting basic disks to dynamic disks, assume a reclining position and read the following fine print:

- Once you've combined two physical disks into an über-disk (technically called a *spanned volume*), a fatal problem on *one* of the two hard drives will make you lose all the data on *both* drives—an event that can ruin your whole morning. Keeping regular backups of your spanned volume is critically important (see Chapter 22).

- Dynamic disks are a specialty of Windows 7 Professional, Enterprise, and Ultimate. No other version of Windows can read them (not even other Windows 7 versions).

- A dynamic disk can contain only one operating system. You can't *dual boot from another partition on a dynamic disk,* as you can with basic disks. (Dual booting means choosing which of two operating systems to use each time you turn on the PC.) Since you can't extend your boot drive, it's unlikely that you'd want to turn it into a dynamic disk, but you should keep this limitation in mind if you decide to install another operating system, such as Linux, onto the disks you want to convert to dynamic disks.

Note: You might have a dual-boot system and not even know it. Many manufacturers hide a bootable operating system on the hard drive whose sole purpose is to restore your computer to its original configuration when things go wrong.

For example, some manufacturers put a copy of DOS on a small partition. If you hold down F11 as the computer is starting up, it launches into DOS, loads disk-imaging software, and uses it to restore your hard drive using files from yet another partition—this time, a hidden *3.5 GB* partition.

If you convert your drive to a dynamic disk, you will lose the ability to invoke this rescue mode.

- To convert a hard drive to a dynamic disk, it must set aside an invisible storage area to hold a *dynamic disk database.* If you partitioned the drive using Windows, then it already reserved enough space for this purpose. But if the drive was partitioned with another operating system, you may have to erase it before converting it to a dynamic disk.

- Dynamic disks generally don't work on laptops, removable disks, disks connected by USB cables or IEEE 1394 (FireWire) cables, or disks connected to shared SCSI or Fibre Channel buses. If your disks fall into any of these categories, Windows 7 won't let you convert them to dynamic disks.

Extending onto Another Disk

If you've installed a new hard drive, Windows 7 treats it as *unallocated space*—disk space that doesn't belong to any volume yet. It's just sitting there, unaccounted for, unusable, waiting for you to make it part of one volume or another. And whenever you find yourself with unallocated space, you can savor the flexibility of dynamic disks.

If you haven't yet been scared off by the cautions in the previous section and are ready to extend one of your existing disks onto another, the procedure is simple. First, back up your computer. Tragedy isn't likely to befall you, but it's a good idea to back up before performing any kind of traumatic surgery to the disks in your computer.

Next, log onto the computer as a user with administrative privileges, and exit any programs that might be running on the disk you plan to convert.

You convert disks and manage the dynamic volumes on them using a special window called the Disk Management console. To open it, use either of these methods:

- Choose Start→Control Panel→System and Security and scroll down to the Administrative Tools section. Click the "Create and format hard disk partitions" link.

- Type *diskmgmt.msc* into the Start menu's Search box, and then press Enter.

Once this window is before you, you see a display of your drives and the partitions on them, as shown in Figure 21-1.

Note: If you've just installed an additional hard drive, Disk Management notices the next time you start it up. It prompts you to initialize the new disks; select the partition style you want to use. In most cases, you should choose the proposed format, MBR (Master Boot Record, which has been used by Windows and MS-DOS for years). The dialog box will tell you when the other choice, GPT (the newfangled GUID Partition Table, used by PCs that are designed around a replacement for the venerable PC BIOS called EFI), is appropriate. Click OK.

The top part of the window lists the partitions on your computer. The bottom part contains a horizontal box representing each drive on your computer, with smaller boxes inside indicating the partitions on each drive. Notice that the header box for each drive indicates the number of the drive in your system, its capacity, whether or not it's online, and the word "Basic" (indicating that it's currently a basic disk).

POWER USERS' CLINIC

Extending a Volume

One big advantage of dynamic disks is that you can extend an existing volume whenever you feel like it, just by allocating additional disk space to it. If, for example, you run out of space on a volume you've named Data, and you still have some unallocated space on some other disk, you can simply add it to the Data volume to make it bigger. The unallocated space you specify becomes a permanent part of the Data volume. (Note that this is a one-way trip. Once you've added free space to a dynamic volume, it becomes part of that volume permanently, or at least until you delete the volume—and its data—and recreate it.)

The disk space you use to extend the volume can come from either the same disk or another dynamic disk (in which case you create a *spanned* volume). Note, though, that you can't extend the *system* volume, nor any volume that was originally a partition created by another operating system.

Next, you need to decide how you want to expand the disk. You have a choice between *spanning* and *striping*. You can also choose to create a simple dynamic disk, but that won't let you combine two disks into one.

Tip: You can delete a dynamic volume as easily as you created it. Just right-click it in the Disk Management window and select Delete Volume from the shortcut menu. Doing so deletes the entire volume, erasing all the data on it and removing its space from any spanned or striped space on other disks.

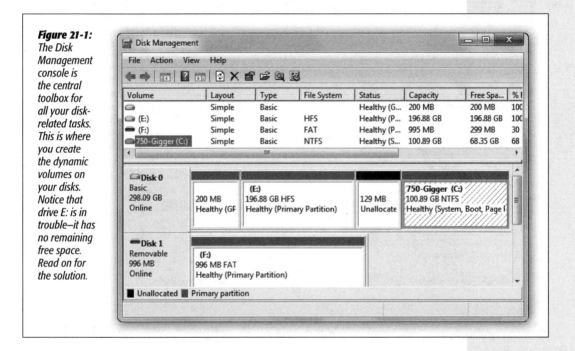

Figure 21-1:
The Disk Management console is the central toolbox for all your disk-related tasks. This is where you create the dynamic volumes on your disks. Notice that drive E: is in trouble—it has no remaining free space. Read on for the solution.

Here's a rundown of each:

Extending into a spanned volume

Suppose you've managed to shoehorn every byte of data you possibly can onto the hard drive you use for holding video files. You decide to install a second hard drive, to give you more space.

But then what? You don't want to spoil the carefully organized folder structure on your old hard drive by moving parts of it to the new drive; you just want to continue to build on your folders as they are.

The solution, as you know if you've read the beginning of this chapter, is to create a *spanned volume,* a single disk icon (and drive letter) that's actually composed of the space from both your old and new drives.

The first order of business (after restarting the computer) is to make sure Windows has recognized the new drive. When you launch the Disk Management console, a new drive appears in the list, with a great big block of unallocated space for you to fill, as shown in Figure 21-2.

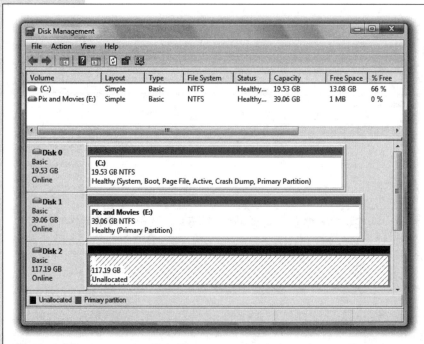

Figure 21-2:
When you install a new hard drive in your computer, it appears in the Disk Management console as a large block of unallocated space. Of course, you'll notice that the new drive is a basic drive; therefore, all you can do is create a basic partition on it.

GEM IN THE ROUGH

What About Extending Basic Disks?

Windows 7 allows you to extend (and shrink) basic disks as well as dynamic disks. Previously, you'd have to buy a program like Partition Magic to perform this kind of operation.

But why would you want to resize your basic disk? In most cases, your basic disk already takes up the entire physical disk drive. However, many computer manufacturers devote several gigabytes of precious disk space to storing *restore images* so you can quickly and easily restore your computer to its factory-fresh state (minus the new-computer smell).

You may not need these restore images. Maybe your PC manufacturer provided a utility program that can generate a set of installation discs, or will sell you a set for a small fee, or maybe you bought a full retail copy of Windows 7

(not an upgrade version). The point is, though, that if you're sure you'll never need the volume that contains your restore images, you may be able to delete it and extend your C: drive into the space you freed up.

To delete a partition, right-click it in the Disk Management window; from the shortcut menu, choose Delete Volume (this is a good time to pause and think about how fresh your backups are). Once you've done that, you can right-click your C: drive and select Extend Volume.

You can just as easily *shrink* your C: drive, perhaps to make room for dual-booting another operating system such as Linux.

To use the new drive to enlarge your existing volume, right-click your almost-full volume (drive E: in this example), and select Extend Volume from the shortcut menu. The Extend Volumes Wizard appears. Click Next to begin.

When the Select Disks screen appears (Figure 21-3), you see that the only available unallocated space in your computer is on your new drive. Select it in the Available column and click Add to add it to the Selected column. Specify how much of the new drive you want to add to the volume (or, to add *all* of it to your original drive, do nothing). Finally, click Next and then Finish.

Note: This operation doesn't erase any of your existing data. Still, this sort of major change is not without risk. So now is the time to ask yourself, "Do I feel lucky?" If not, make that backup before you do something we'll all regret.

Figure 21-3:
When extending a volume to another disk, click its name in the Available column before adding it to the Selected column.

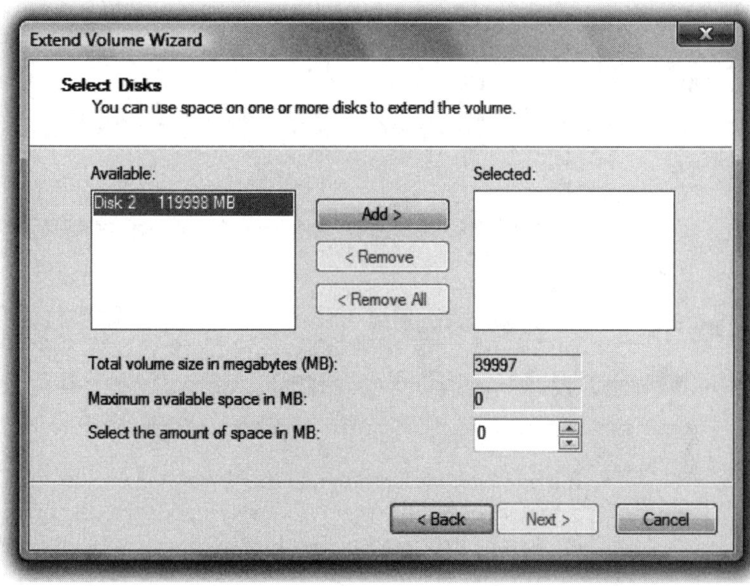

This process converts both disks into a dynamic disk and creates a spanned volume. You get a warning from Disk Management about the consequences of converting to a dynamic disk, as described earlier in this chapter. Click Yes to continue.

Notice now that your original volume and your new drive both have a purple header bar and use the same drive letter, as shown in Figure 21-4. You now have a spanned volume using space on both of your hard drives. Your hard drive is now effectively bigger (117 GB of free space out of a combined total of 156 GB), and you can continue to amass new files at your accustomed rate.

Creating a striped volume

As you now know, a *spanned volume* is like a virtual hard drive made up of storage space from more than one dynamic disk. When Windows saves data onto a spanned volume, it completely fills up the allotted space on one drive, then proceeds to the next drive in the volume, until the allotted space on all the drives is full.

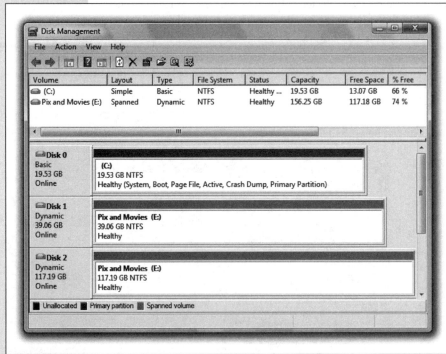

Figure 21-4:
A dynamic volume extended to another disk appears in the Disk Management console with the same color header bar and the same drive letter. Note, too, that the volume list in the top of this dialog box identifies this volume as "Spanned."

A *striped volume* is similar, in that it's a single volume made up of space from several actual disks, but the way Windows saves data to the drives is different. Instead of filling up one drive and proceeding to the next one, Windows saves pieces of each file on more than one disk. Because more than one hard drive is saving and reading data in parallel, a speed benefit can theoretically result.

The truth is, though, that for the sorts of small files most people work with, the differences are measured in milliseconds—thousandths of a second—so it's generally not worth creating striped volumes on everyday PC workstations. (On corporate file servers that handle hundreds or thousands of file access requests per minute, or on video-editing workstations, it's a different story. The cumulative savings in access times can be significant.)

If you're still tempted to create a striped-volume set, the process is nearly identical to creating a new *spanned* volume (see the box on the facing page), except that, when you right-click, you select New Striped Volume instead of New Spanned Volume. You must also use the same amount of space on each of the drives you select. For example, if you have 100 gigabytes of unallocated space on Disk 0 and 50 gigabytes of unallocated space on Disk 1, your striped volume can be no larger than 100 gigabytes—50 from each drive.

Compressing Files and Folders
All Versions

The hard drives made these days have greater capacities than ever, but programs and files are much bigger, too. Running out of disk space is still a common problem. Fortunately, Windows 7 is especially effective at compressing files and folders to take up less disk space.

Compressing files and folders can also be useful when you want to email files to someone without dooming them to an all-night modem-watching session. That's

---

UP TO SPEED

Data Compression

Data compression is the process of replacing repetitive material in a file with shorthand symbols. For example, if a speech you've written contains the phrase *going forward* 21 times, a compression scheme like the one in NTFS may replace each occurrence with a single symbol, making the file that much smaller. When you reopen the file later, the operating system almost instantaneously restores the original, expanded material.

The degree to which a file can be compressed depends on what kind of data the file contains and whether it's already been compressed by another program. For example, programs (executable files) often shrink by half when

compressed. Bitmapped graphics like TIFF files squish down to as little as one-seventh their original size, saving a great deal more space.

The PNG and JPEG graphics files so popular on the Web, however, are already compressed (which is why they're so popular—they take relatively little time to download). As a result, they don't get much smaller if you try to compress them manually. That's one of the main rules of data compression: Data can be compressed only once.

In short, there's no way to predict just how much disk space you'll save by using NTFS compression on your drives. It all depends on what you have stored there.

---

why Microsoft has endowed Windows 7 with two different schemes for compressing files and folders: *NTFS compression* for storing files on your hard drive, and *zipped folders* for files that might have to be transferred.

NTFS Compression

If Windows 7 was installed on your PC when you bought it, or if you upgraded your PC from Windows XP, or if you erased your hard drive before installing Windows 7, then your hard drive is probably formatted using a file system called *NTFS* (short for *NT file system*).

Most people can live a long and happy life without knowing anything about NTFS. If you work in a corporation, you might be grateful for the additional security it offers to Windows fans (Chapter 23), and leave it at that. Now and then, however, you'll read about features that are available *only* if your hard drive was prepared using NTFS—and this is one of those cases.

Tip: The hard drive that's running Windows 7 has the NTFS format; Windows 7 requires it. To find out what formatting some other drive uses (a flash drive or external hard drive, for example), choose Start→Computer. Right-click the hard drive icon; from the shortcut menu, choose Properties. In the resulting dialog box, you see either "File system: NTFS" or "File system: FAT 32." Unfortunately, special NTFS features like automatic compression aren't available to you unless you upgrade the drive formatting to NTFS. For instructions, download the free appendix to this chapter from this book's "Missing CD" page at *www.missingmanuals. com.* The file is called NTFS Upgrade (pdf). (Note, however, that if you convert a flash drive to NTFS, you may no longer be able to use it with non-Windows computers and devices like digital cameras and palmtops.)

The NTFS compression scheme is especially likable because it's completely invisible to you. Windows automatically compresses and decompresses your files, almost instantaneously. At some point, you may even forget you've turned it on. Consider:

- Whenever you open a compressed file, Windows quickly and invisibly expands it to its original form so you can read or edit it. When you close the file again, Windows instantly recompresses it.

- If you send compressed files via email or copy them to a PC whose hard drive doesn't use NTFS compression, Windows 7 once again decompresses them, quickly and invisibly.

- Any file you copy into a compressed folder or disk is compressed automatically. (If you only *move* it into such a folder from elsewhere on the disk, however, it stays compressed or uncompressed—whichever it was originally.)

Compressing files, folders, or disks

To turn on NTFS compression, right-click the icon for the file, folder, or disk whose contents you want to shrink. Choose Properties from the shortcut menu. Click the Advanced button, and in the resulting dialog box, turn on "Compress contents to save disk space" (Figure 21-5), click OK, and then click Apply or OK when you return to the Properties dialog box. If you have selected a folder for compression, you're prompted as to whether you also want to compress the files and subfolders within it.

Many Windows veterans wind up turning on compression for the entire hard drive. It can take Windows 7 several hours to perform the initial compression of every file on the drive.

Figure 21-5:
If you don't see the "Compress contents to save disk space" checkbox (highlighted here), then your hard drive probably doesn't use the NTFS formatting scheme.

If you do this, or even if you try to compress a large folder such as *C:\Program Files*, you will invariably run into a few files that can't be compressed because they're currently in use. Short of opening up the Task Manager and shutting down nearly every process on your system (not recommended), you won't be able to avoid a few of these. Your best bet is to select Ignore All the first time Windows 7 notifies you about this problem. Then you can safely walk away from your computer and let the compression continue.

When Windows is finished compressing, the compressed file and folder icons appear in a different color, a reminder that Windows is doing its part to maximize your disk space. (If they don't change color, then somebody—maybe you—must have turned off the "Show encrypted or compressed NTFS files in color" option described on page 100.)

When you look at the Properties dialog box for a compressed file (right-click the file and choose Properties from the shortcut menu), you see two file sizes. The Size value indicates the actual (uncompressed) size of the file, while the Size On Disk value is the compressed size of the file—that is, the amount of disk space it's occupying.

Zipped Folders

As noted above, NTFS compression is great for freeing up disk space while you're working at your PC. But when you email your files to somebody else or burn them to a CD, Windows 7 always decompresses them back to their original sizes first.

Fortunately, there's another way to compress files: Zip them. If you've ever used Windows before, you've probably encountered Zip files. Each one is a tiny little suitcase, an *archive*, whose contents have been tightly compressed to keep files together, to save space, and to transfer them online faster (see Figure 21-6). Use Zip files when you want to email something to someone, or when you want to pack up a completed project and remove it from your hard drive to free up space.

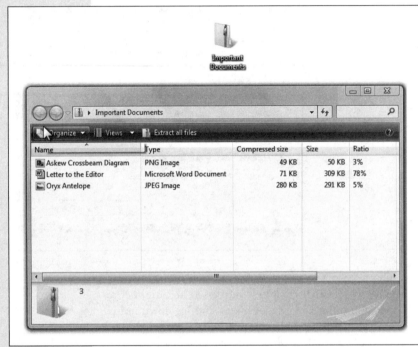

Figure 21-6:
Top: A Zip archive looks like an ordinary folder—except for the tiny zipper.

Bottom: Double-click one to open its window and see what's inside. Notice (in the Ratio column) that JPEG graphics and PNG graphics usually don't become much smaller than they were before zipping, since they're already compressed formats. But word processing files, program files, and other file types undergo quite a bit of shrinkage.

Creating zipped folders

In Windows 7, you don't even need a shareware program like PKZip or WinZip to create or open Zip files. You can create a Zip archive in either of two ways:

- Right-click any blank spot on the desktop or an open window. From the shortcut menu, choose New→Compressed (zipped) Folder. Type a name for your newly created, empty archive, and then press Enter.

HISTORY CLASS

PKZip

The Zip archive format was developed in the late 1980s by Phil Katz, a pioneer of PC compression technology. Katz's original product, PKZip, was a DOS-based archiving program that soon became an industry standard.

There have been many other archive compression standards over the years, but none of them became as ubiquitous as the Zip format. Every program today that creates or manipulates Zip files, including Windows 7, owes a debt of thanks—if not a free T-shirt or two—to Phil Katz.

Now, each time you drag a file or folder onto the archive's icon (or into its open window), Windows automatically stuffs a *copy* of it inside.

Of course, you haven't actually saved any disk space, since now you have two copies of the original material (one zipped, one untouched). If you'd rather *move* a file or folder into the archive—in the process deleting the full-size version and saving disk space—then right-drag the file or folder icon onto the *archive* icon. Now from the shortcut menu, choose Move Here.

- To turn an existing file or folder *into* a zipped archive, right-click its icon. (To zip up a handful of icons, select them first, then right-click any *one* of them.) Now, from the shortcut menu, choose Send To→Compressed (zipped) Folder. You've just created a new archive folder *and* copied the files or folders into it.

Tip: At this point, you can right-click the zipped folder's icon and choose Send To→Mail Recipient. Windows automatically whips open your email program, creates an outgoing message ready for you to address, and attaches the zipped file to it—which is now set for transport.

Working with zipped folders

In many respects, a zipped folder behaves just like any ordinary folder, in that you double-click it to see what's inside.

If you double-click one of the *files* you find inside, however, Windows 7 opens up a *read-only* copy of it—that is, a copy you can view, but not edit. To make changes to a read-only copy, you must use the File→Save As command and save it somewhere else on your hard drive first.

Note: Be sure to navigate to the desktop or the Documents folder, for example, before you save your edited document. Otherwise, Windows saves it into an invisible temporary folder, and you may never see it again.

To decompress only some of the icons in a zipped folder, just drag them out of the archive window; they instantly spring back to their original sizes. To decompress the entire archive, right-click its icon and choose Extract All from the shortcut menu (or, if its window is already open, click the "Extract all files" link on the toolbar). A wizard asks you to specify where you want the resulting files to wind up.

Encrypting Files and Folders

Professional • Enterprise • Ultimate

If your Documents folder contains nothing but laundry lists and letters to your mom, data security is probably not a major concern for you. But if there's some stuff on your hard drive that you'd rather keep private, Windows (Professional edition and higher) can help you out. The Encrypting File System (EFS) is an NTFS feature that stores your data in a coded format that only you can read.

The beauty of EFS is that it's effortless and invisible to you, the authorized owner. Windows 7 automatically encrypts your files before storing them on the drive, and decrypts them again when you want to read or modify them. Anyone else who logs onto your computer, however, will find these files locked and off-limits.

If you've read ahead to Chapter 23, of course, you might be frowning in confusion at this point. Isn't keeping private files private the whole point of Windows's *accounts* feature? Don't Windows's *NTFS permissions* (page 740) keep busybodies out already?

Yes, but encryption provides additional security. If, for example, you're a top-level agent assigned to protect your government's most closely guarded egg salad recipe, you can use NTFS permissions to deny all other users access to the file containing the information. Nobody but you can open the file in Windows 7.

However, a determined intruder from a foreign nation could conceivably boot the computer using *another* operating system—one that doesn't recognize the NTFS

POWER USERS' CLINIC

Disk Quotas

Does one of your account holders have a tendency to become overzealous about downloading stuff, threatening to overrun your drive with shareware junk and MP3 files? Fortunately, it's easy enough for you, the wise administrator, to curb such behavior among holders of Standard accounts.

Choose Start→Computer. Right-click the hard drive icon; from the shortcut menu, choose Properties. In the Properties dialog box, click the Quota tab. Click Show Quota Settings to bring up the Quota Settings dialog box, shown here, and then turn on Enable Quota Management.

You might start by turning on "Deny disk space to users exceeding quota limit." This, of course, is exactly the kind of muzzle you were hoping to place on out-of-control downloaders. The instant they try to save or download a file that pushes their stuff over the limit, an "Insufficient disk space" message appears.

Use the "Limit disk space to __" controls to specify the cap you want to put on each account holder. Using these controls, you can specify a certain number of kilobytes (KB),

megabytes (MB), gigabytes (GB)—or even terabytes (TB), petabytes (PB), or exabytes (EB). (Then write a letter to *PC World* and tell the editors where you bought a multiexabyte hard drive.)

You can also set up a disk-space limit ("Set warning level to ___") that will make a *warning* appear—not to the mad downloader, but to you, the administrator. By clicking the Quota Entries button, you get a report that shows how much disk space each account holder has used up. (This is where you see the warning as a written notation.)

If you just want to track your underlings' disk usage without actually limiting them, then set the warning level to the desired value, but set the Limit Disk Space value to something impossibly high, like several exabytes.

When you click OK, Windows warns you that it's about to take some time to calculate just how much disk space each account holder has used so far.

---

permissions—and access the hard drive using a special program that reads the raw data stored there. If, however, you had encrypted the file using EFS, that raw data would appear as gibberish, foiling your crafty nemesis.

Using EFS

You use EFS to encrypt your folders and files in much the same way that you use NTFS compression. To encrypt a file or a folder, open its Properties dialog box, click the Advanced button, turn on the "Encrypt contents to secure data" checkbox, and then click OK (see Figure 21-7). (For a quicker way, see page 839.)

Figure 21-7:
To encrypt a file or folder using EFS, turn on the "Encrypt contents to secure data" checkbox (at the bottom of its Properties dialog box). If you've selected a folder, a Confirm Attribute Changes dialog box appears, asking if you want to encrypt just that folder or everything inside it, too.

Depending on how much data you've selected, it may take some time for the encryption process to complete. Once the folders and files are encrypted, they appear in a different color from your compressed files (unless, once again, you've turned off the "Show encrypted or compressed NTFS files in color" option).

Note: You can't encrypt certain files and folders, such as system files, or any files in the system *root folder* (usually the Windows folder). You can't encrypt files and folders on FAT32 drives, either.

Finally, note that you can't both encrypt *and* compress the same file or folder. If you attempt to encrypt a compressed file or folder, Windows needs to decompress it first. You can, however, encrypt files that have been compressed using another technology, such as Zip files or compressed image files.

After your files have been encrypted, you may be surprised to see that, other than their color change, nothing seems to have changed. You can open them the same way you always did, change them, and save them as usual. Windows 7 is just doing its job: protecting these files with the minimum inconvenience to you.

Still, if you're having difficulty believing that your files are now protected by an invisible force field, try logging off and back on again with a different user name and password.

When you try to open an encrypted file now, a message cheerfully informs you that you don't have the proper permissions to access the file. (For more on Windows 7 security, see Chapter 10.)

EFS Rules

Any files or folders you move *into* an EFS-encrypted folder get encrypted, too. But dragging a file *out* of one doesn't unprotect it; it remains encrypted as long as it's on an NTFS drive. A protected file loses its encryption only in these circumstances:

- You manually decrypt the file (by turning off the corresponding checkbox in its Properties dialog box).

- You move it to a FAT32 drive.

- You transmit it via a network or email. When you attach the file to an email or send it across the network, Windows will decrypt the file before sending it on its way.

By the way, EFS doesn't protect files from being deleted. Even if passing evildoers can't *open* your private file, they can still *delete* it—unless you've protected it using Windows's permissions feature (Chapter 23). Here, again, truly protecting important material involves using several security mechanisms in combination.

BitLocker Drive Encryption

Enterprise • Ultimate

If you think EFS sounds like a great way to keep prying eyes out of your files, you ain't seen nothing yet!

GEM IN THE ROUGH

Recovering Encrypted Data

Every now and then, encrypted data becomes inaccessible. Maybe a hard drive crash nukes your password, and therefore your ability to open your own encrypted files. Or maybe a disgruntled employee quits, deliberately refusing to divulge his password or to decrypt his important files first.

The first time you encrypt a file, Windows puts a prompt in the notification area suggesting that you back up your encryption key. Click the prompt to start the process of backing up your key (that is, your password).

You can also back up your key by right-clicking an encrypted file and selecting Properties. In the Properties dialog box, click Advanced, and then click Details. You can then select your user name and click Back Up Keys to start the process.

Once you've backed it up to a CD or flash drive, keep it secret, keep it safe, and don't make multiple copies of it. If you lose your key, you can restore it by double-clicking on this file and then going through the Certificate Import Wizard. You'll need to provide the password you supplied when you backed up the key, so don't forget it!

If all else fails, Windows has a fallback mechanism—a back door. The local administrator account on a PC can be designated as a *recover agent* for users, which gives the administrator the ability to decrypt their files in case of an emergency. For instructions on setting up this feature, see *http://support.microsoft.com/kb/887414*.

Windows's standard protections—your account password, the encryption of certain files, and so on—are all very nice.

But when million-dollar corporate secrets are at stake, they're not going to stop a determined, knowledgeable thief. The guy could swipe your laptop or even steal the hard drive out of your desktop PC.

If security is that important for you, then you'll be happy to know about BitLocker Drive Encryption, a Windows 7 feature. When you turn on this feature, your PC automatically encrypts (scrambles) everything on your *entire system hard drive,* including all of Windows itself.

If the bad guy tries any industrial-strength tricks to get into the drive—trying to re-program the startup routines, for example, or starting up from a different hard drive—BitLocker presents a steel-reinforced password screen. No password, no decryption.

You won't notice much difference when BitLocker is turned on. You log in as usual, clicking your name and typing your password.

We're talking hard-core, corporate-level security—with hard-core, corporate-level requirements:

- The Enterprise or Ultimate edition of Windows 7.

- Two NTFS hard drives or drive partitions on your system: one that will be en-crypted, and one that Windows 7 will use to boot the system. (It won't move your Windows folder there, but it will use that drive to hold the files needed to boot up a PC whose C: drive is encrypted.)

    If you don't have this kind of setup, don't worry. BitLocker will do the partition-ing for you, even if you've already installed Windows 7 and lived in it for a while.

- You generally need a *Trusted Platform Module* (TPM), a special circuit that's built onto the system boards of BitLocker-compatible PCs. However, there's a sneaky workaround if your PC doesn't have this item. Read on.

To find out if the planets are aligned and all the components are installed for you to use BitLocker, choose Start→Control Panel→System and Security applet and click BitLocker Drive Encryption.

If you see an option there to "Turn on BitLocker" (Figure 21-8), well, great! You're ready to step up to the strongest encryption Windows 7 has to offer. Click that link, and wait while Windows 7 encrypts your hard drive. Oh, and don't forget the pass-word you provided.

You also have the option to print out a BitLocker Recovery Key, which gives you another way in. Keep this printout somewhere secret, somewhere safe.

Tweaking Windows 7 to Run BitLocker

If, on the other hand, you see a note there explaining why you can't use BitLocker (Figure 21-8), proceed like this:

- If you don't have a TPM, you need a USB flash drive. With some tweaks to Windows 7's configuration, you can use this as the "ignition key" to bootstrap BitLocker's strong encryption, eliminating the need for the TPM.

    The USB flash drive option works only on PCs whose BIOS can see flash drives in the "pre-OS environment"—that is, before Windows has actually loaded at startup.

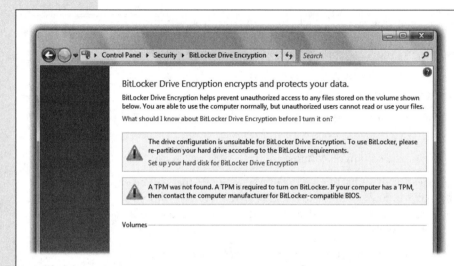

Figure 21-8:
Unfortunately, this computer doesn't have what it takes to run BitLocker. But with the right tweaks, you might be able to change Windows 7's mind about that.

The Flash-Drive Workaround

Of course, a TPM is a special circuit that you either have in your PC or you don't. Fortunately, there's a clever workaround that, believe it or not, lets you use an ordinary USB flash drive instead of a TPM:

1. **Open the Start menu. In the search box, type** *gpedit.msc.* **Press Enter.**

    You've just opened the Group Policy Object Editor, a program you can use to configure advanced settings on Windows.

GEM IN THE ROUGH

What About Encrypting Removable Drives?

Windows 7 brings a new feature, BitLocker To Go, which encrypts removable disks such as USB and flash memory. To use it, plug in your removable disk and visit the BitLocker Drive Encryption Control Panel. If you see an option to Turn

On BitLocker for your removable disk, you're all set. (Unlike your system disk, BitLocker To Go does not require a TPM to be encrypted.)

---

2. **Drill down to Local Computer Policy→Computer Configuration→Administrative Templates→Windows Components→BitLocker Drive Encryption→Operating System Drives.**

   Examine the right side of the window.

3. **Find "Require additional authentication at startup," and double-click it.**

   The Properties dialog box appears.

4. **Select Enabled. Make sure "Allow BitLocker without a compatible TPM (requires a startup key on a USB flash drive)" is turned on. Click OK.**

Reboot your computer.

Turning on BitLocker

Now reopen the Control Panel, and select Security→BitLocker Drive Encryption; the window should now look like Figure 21-9. Click Turn On BitLocker, follow the instructions, and let Windows encrypt your drive; this can take some time. You're now protected, even from the most determined and knowledgeable hard drive thieves.

Note: Along the way, BitLocker asks you to save your password somewhere. Be sure to keep it secret and safe. You're going to need it if you do something to make Windows think you're a hacker trying to get in, like installing a second operating system in a dual-boot configuration.

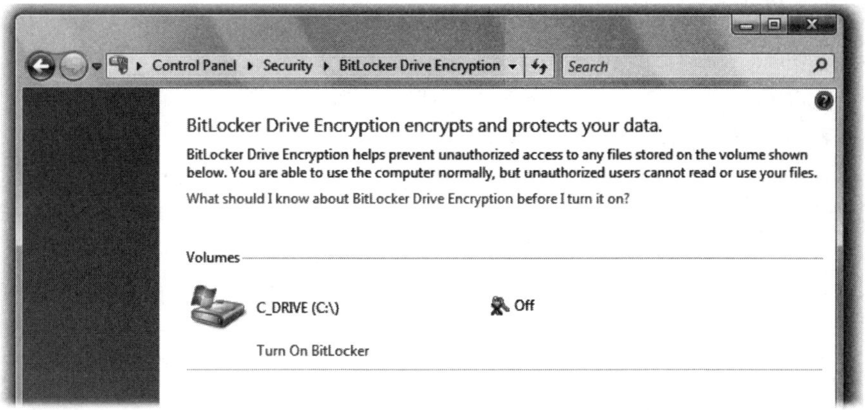
Control Panel ▸ Security ▸ BitLocker Drive Encryption
Search
BitLocker Drive Encryption encrypts and protects your data.
BitLocker Drive Encryption helps prevent unauthorized access to any files stored on the volume shown below. You are able to use the computer normally, but unauthorized users cannot read or use your files.
What should I know about BitLocker Drive Encryption before I turn it on?
Volumes
C_DRIVE (C:\)
Off
Turn On BitLocker

***Figure 21-9:** You're now ready to encrypt your drive to keep it safe from prying eyes.*

Backups, System Restore, & Troubleshooting

P C troubleshooting is among the most difficult propositions on earth, in part because your machine has so many cooks. Microsoft made the operating system, another company made the computer, and dozens of others contributed the programs you use every day. The number of conflicts that can arise and the number of problems you may encounter is nearly infinite. That's why, if you were lucky, you bought your PC from a company that offers a toll-free, 24-hour help line. You may need it.

In the meantime, Windows is crawling with special diagnostic modes, software tools, and workarounds designed to revive a gasping or dead PC. Some are clearly intended only for licensed geeks. Others, however, are available even to mere mortals armed with no more information than, "It's not working right."

Whether you get it working or not, however, there's one constant that applies to novices and programmers alike—you're always better off if you have a backup copy of your files. This chapter covers both the backing up—and the shooting of troubles.

Automatic Backups
All Versions

Consider that the proximity of your drive's spinning platters to the head that reads them is roughly the same proportion as the wheels of an airliner flying at 500 miles per hour, 12 inches off the ground. It's amazing that hard drives work as well, and as long, as they do.

Still, a hard drive is nothing more than a mass of moving parts in delicate alignment, so it should come as no surprise that every now and then, disaster strikes. That's why backing up your data (making a safety copy) on a regular basis is an essential part of using a PC. Even if computers aren't your career, there's probably a lot of valuable stuff on your hard drive: all your photos, the addresses and phone numbers you've spent hours typing in, a lifetime's worth of email, the Web sites in your Favorites folder, and so on.

If you use Windows in a corporation, you probably don't even have to think about backing up your stuff. A network administrator generally does the backing up for you and your coworkers.

But if you use Windows at home, or in a smaller company that doesn't have network nerds running around to ensure your files' safety, you'll be happy to know about the Windows 7 Backup program. It's much more flexible and powerful than the one that came with Vista, and light-years better than the Windows XP version (which couldn't even back up your stuff onto CDs or DVDs!).

Backup Hardware

If you have a home or small business network, backing up to a folder on another PC on your network is a wise idea. An inexpensive external hard drive makes a super-convenient backup disk, too.

The advantage of blank CDs and DVDs, though, is that you can store them some-where else: in a fireproof box, a safe deposit box at the bank, or the trunk of your car. Keep them anywhere except in your office, so your data is safe even in the case of fire or burglary.

Tip: You can't back up a laptop's files when it's running on battery power. The program won't let you—it's too worried about losing juice in the middle of the operation.

Your First Backup

Once you've decided to back up your PC and also figured out what you're going to back it up *onto,* proceed like this:

1. **Open the Backup and Restore program.**

   As usual, the quickest way is to use the Start menu. Open it and type *backup;* click "Backup and Restore." The Backup and Restore program opens (Figure 22-1).

2. **Click "Set up backup." Authenticate if necessary (page 726).**

   Now Windows looks through your system, locating hard disks and removable drives. The "Select where you want to save your backup" screen appears, offering you the chance to specify where you want to store the backup copies.

3. **Specify where you want to save the backup (Figure 22-2).**

   The best option is an external hard drive; it's safe, it's big, and it's fast.

You can also back up to CDs or DVDs, although not automatically on a schedule.

Tip: USB flash drives and memory cards show up in this list, too. Flash drives make particularly handy backup disks because they're small, inexpensive, and can store several gigabytes of data.

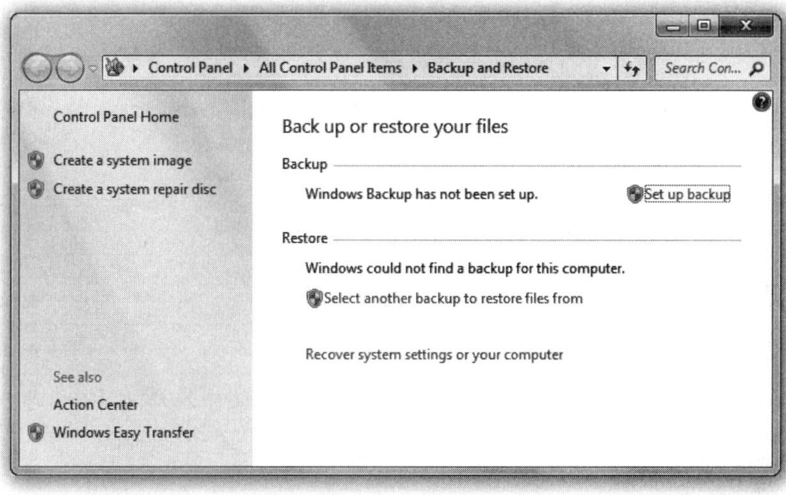

Figure 22-1:
The primary purpose of this screen is to back up and restore your PC. But on the left-hand side, you'll also find links for creating a system image (a perfect replica of your entire hard drive) and a system repair disc (a startup disc that can boot your PC when your hard drive can't).

Finally, you can back up to a folder that's shared on a networked PC; select "Save on a network," and then browse to the folder. (This option is available only in the Professional, Enterprise, and Ultimate editions of Windows 7.) You may have to type in a user name and password to use that folder, depending on how you've set up sharing on the PC.

4. **Click Next.**

   Now you meet the "What do you want to back up?" screen. Here, you get to choose which *kinds* of files to back up: Pictures, Music, Videos, E-mail, Documents, and several others.

5. **Click either "Let Windows choose" or "Let me choose."**

   If you click "Let Windows choose," then Windows will back up all account holders' libraries (Pictures, Music, Videos, Documents), plus the standard Windows folder (AppData, Contacts, Desktop, Downloads, Favorites, Links, Saved Games, and Searches). The AppData folder is especially important, because it's where prorams like Outlook and Windows Live Mail keep your email stash.

   Not included: your programs and Windows itself. Windows will also set up a schedule for this backup so that it repeats automatically every week.

If you click "Let me choose" instead, then you're shown the screen in Figure 22-3. Turn on the checkboxes for the things you want protected by a backup.

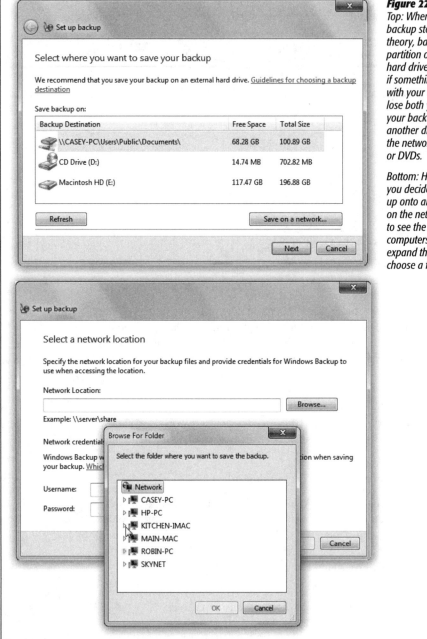

Figure 22-2:
Top: Where do you want the backup stored? You can, in theory, back up to another partition of your own main hard drive. It's risky, though; if something goes wrong with your drive, you could lose both your originals and your backup. Better to use another drive, another PC on the network, or a set of CDs or DVDs.

Bottom: Here's the cycle if you decide to back your stuff up onto another computer on the network. Click Browse to see the actual list of other computers on your network; expand the flippy triangles to choose a folder.

Tip: *Here's where your familiarity with Windows 7 libraries pays off. You can create a single library called Back Me Up. Fill it with folders, from all over your system, that might not otherwise get backed up, and designate Back Me Up to be backed up. (The original folders, of course, stay right where they are.)*

This is a great trick if you store important stuff outside of your Personal folder—on external drives, say—or if you don't feel the need for a full massive whole-system backup.

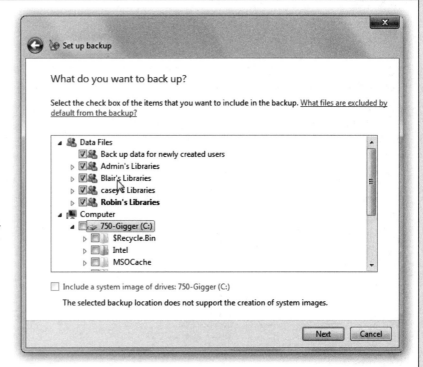

Figure 22-3:
Here, you get expandable checkboxes for everything in every account holder's libraries, plus another set for the entire computer. That lower "tree" lets you handpick what gets backed up, anywhere on your system, even on external drives. Note: The Backup program never backs up your programs, your copy of Windows, files in the Recycle Bin, or files on drives that have been formatted using the old FAT32 scheme.

6. **Click Next.**

Now, on the "Review your backup settings" dialog box, you see a summary of everything Windows intends to back up. Here, you can also see that Windows intends to perform this backup every Sunday at 7:00 p.m., presumably while you're watching "60 Minutes."

You can, of course, click "Change schedule" to choose a more opportune time. (For best results, choose times of day when you know the computer will be turned on.)

7. **Click "Save settings and start backup."**

Backup goes to work, copying your files to their new backup location (Figure 22-4).

From now on, your PC backs itself up, on the schedule you set for it (unless you set up a backup on CDs; it would be kind of hard for your PC to insert blank discs when you're not there). Each time, it backs up only new files or files that have changed since the last backup; it doesn't waste its time backing up files that haven't been touched.

If you want to change your backup settings—back up on a different schedule, say, or add or take away file types—return to the Backup and Restore Center, and click "Change backup settings." From here, you can change anything about your backup.

Tip: Windows stores the backup as a standard .zip file. That's great, because it means that in times of trouble, you can open and root through it to find a precious file or two even using a different computer that's not running Windows.

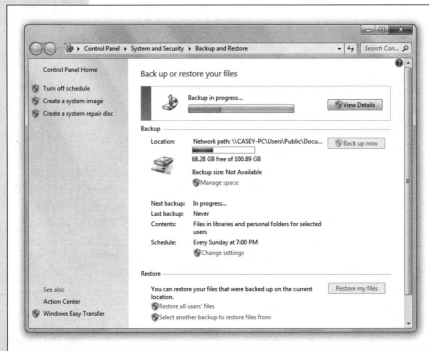

Figure 22-4:
The backing-up process may take several seconds or several hours, depending on how much you're copying. (If you specified backing up onto CDs or DVDs, you're prompted to insert a disc, erase it, and then replace it with a fresh one when the first one is full.) You can continue to work on your PC; copying takes place in the background. You'll be notified once the backup is complete.

Restoring Files from a Backup

When your good luck runs out, and you find yourself with a virus/drive crash/meddlesome toddler who threw out an important folder, you'll be glad indeed that you had a backup. This is the payoff.

Fortunately, Backup lets you restore individual files and folders—you don't have to restore all files in one fell swoop.

Tip: Perform regular test restores to make sure your data is retrievable from the backup disks. (Consider restoring your files to a test folder—not the folder where the files came from—so you don't wind up with duplicates.) There's no other way to be absolutely sure your backups are working properly.

Here are the steps. (These steps assume that your whole hard drive died, you replaced it with a new one, and that you reinstalled Windows.)

1. **Open the Backup and Restore program.**

   The quick way to find it: Type *backup* into the Start menu Search box.

2. **Click "Restore my files."**

   (You can also click "Restore all users' files"—which is what you want if you lost your entire hard drive.)

   Now you see the screen shown in Figure 22-5. This is where you indicate what you want restored.

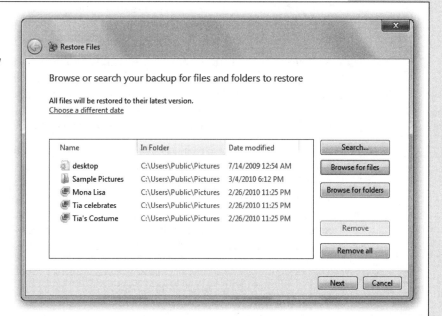

Figure 22-5:
At this point, although it may look like you're browsing through your hard disk, you're not. You're only browsing the backup you made.

3. **Fill the list with the names of the files and folders you want to resurrect.**

   Click "Browse for files" to restore individual files, or "Browse for folders" to restore individual folders.

   You can also *search* for files if you're not sure where a file is that you want to back up. Click Search, type what you're looking for, and then add the file or files.

4. **Click Next. Indicate where you want the restored files put.**

You can restore files to their original locations, or to a different folder on your PC.

5. **Click "Start restore."**

Backup now starts copying files and folders *back* from the backup to your hard drive.

If you've chosen to save files to their original locations, you may be asked what you want to happen if the original files are *still there.* Do you want the backup copies to "win," do you want to keep the originals, or do you want to keep both?

If you choose to keep both, the restored file gets a (2) after it. So the original file would be budget.doc, for instance, and the copy would be budget (2).doc.

System Images
All Versions

When your hard disk crashes, you lose more than just your personal files. You also lose your operating system—*and* all the programs you've installed, *and* all their updates and patches, *and* all your settings and options and tweaks. It can take you a very long time to restore your PC to that state.

A *system image* solves the problem easily. This feature, which was called Complete PC Backup in Windows Vista, creates a perfect snapshot of your *entire* hard drive at this moment: documents, email, pictures, and so on, *plus* Windows, *and* all your programs and settings. Someone could steal your *entire hard drive,* or your drive could die, and you'd be able to install a new, empty one and be back in business inside of an hour.

It's a good idea to make a fresh system image every few months, because you'll probably have installed new programs and changed your settings in the interim. (Then again, one of the options when you make a *regular* backup is to create a system image at the same time—so if you have the disk space, that's a convenient option.)

Note: For the techies scoring at home, the disk image created by Complete PC Backup is a .vhd file, the same kind that's created by Microsoft's Virtual PC software—and therefore, you can mount it using Virtual PC, if you like.

Make the Image
To make a system image, open the Backup and Restore program as described above. In the panel at left, click "Create a system image." Authenticate if necessary.

You're now asked where you want to store the backup image. Your options, once again: a hard drive (must be NTFS formatted), a stack of CDs or DVDs, or (if you have the Professional, Enterprise, or Ultimate editions of Windows 7) another computer on the network.

In each case, you'll need a *lot* of empty disk space. Not as much as your entire PC drive, because you won't be backing up empty space or temporary files. But a lot.

Note: You can keep multiple system images around—representing your PC's world at different times—if you back up to discs or hard drives. If you save to a network location, though, you can keep only the most recent system image.

After you make your selection, click Next. You're asked to choose your backup location—which hard drive or network folder, for example. If you're backing up to discs, you're told how many you'll need. (Hint: It's a *lot* of them.)

Click "Start backup"; the backup begins. You'll be prompted when you need to insert new DVDs or other discs.

Tip: At the end of the backing up, Windows asks if you'd like it to burn a system repair disc—a CD or DVD that can start up your PC when it won't start up from the hard drive. It's an excellent idea.

Restore the Image

Suppose the worst has come to pass: Your hard drive is trashed. Fortunately, restoring your entire system using a system image is very easy.

Start up your PC from the Windows 7 DVD; on the welcome screen, click "Repair your computer." (Alternatively, just boot up from the system repair disc you made when you created the system image.) In the System Recovery Options dialog box that appears, click "Restore your computer using a system image you created earlier," and click Next. When prompted, find that drive or disc; the rest, as they say, is history recreated.

Just be forewarned that this process *reformats your hard drive,* and in the process *wipes out* all your data and files. They'll be replaced with the Windows Complete PC Restore snapshot, and with the data from the most recent backup you've made. (Of course, you may well have a *regular* backup that's more recent; you can restore that as the final step.)

Note: If you were thinking of using a system image to turn a new PC into a replica of your old, crashed one, be warned: You can't restore a system image to a new PC's hard drive if it's smaller than the old one. (Yes, even if the data on the backup drive would easily fit on the target drive.)

System Restore
All Versions

As you get more proficient on a PC, pressing Ctrl+Z—the keyboard shortcut for Undo—eventually becomes an unconscious reflex. In fact, you can sometimes spot veteran Windows fans twitching their Ctrl+Z fingers even when they're not near the computer—after knocking over a cup of coffee, locking the car with the keys inside, or blurting out something inappropriate in a meeting.

Windows 7 offers the mother of all Undo commands: System Restore. This feature alone can be worth hours of your time and hundreds of dollars in consultant fees.

The pattern of things going wrong in Windows usually works like this: The PC works fine for a while, and then suddenly—maybe for no apparent reason, but most often following an installation or configuration change—it goes on the fritz. At that point, wouldn't it be pleasant to be able to tell the computer: "Go back to the way you were yesterday, please"?

System Restore does exactly that. It "rewinds" your copy of Windows back to the condition it was in before you, or something you tried to install, messed it up. Best of all, System Restore *doesn't change your files.* Your email, pictures, music, documents, and other files are left up to date.

Tip: If your PC manages to catch a virus, System Restore can even rewind it to a time before the infection–*if* the virus hasn't gotten into your documents in such a way that you reinfect yourself after the system restore. An up-to-date antivirus program is a much more effective security blanket.

In fact, if you don't like your PC after restoring it, you can always restore it to the way it was *before* you restored it. Back to the future!

POWER USERS' CLINIC

System Restore vs. Your Hard Drive

Ever wonder where Windows stashes all these backup copies of your operating system? They're in a folder called System Volume Information, which is in your Local Disk (C:) window. Inside *that* are individual files for each restore point. (System Volume Information is generally an invisible folder, but you can make it visible by following the instructions on page 99. You still won't be allowed to move, rename, or delete it, however–thank goodness. In fact, you won't even be able to look inside it.)

Now, in Windows XP, you could set a limit on how much disk space all these restore points consumed. But no longer. In Windows Vista, you could delete older restore points yourself. But no longer.

In Windows 7, you can turn off System Restore entirely, or you can limit it to eating up a certain percentage of your hard drive space.

Open the Start menu. Right-click Computer; from the shortcut menu, choose Properties.

In the resulting dialog box, click "System protection" in the left-side panel. Authenticate yourself if necessary. On the System Protection tab, click Configure. You get the dialog box shown here.

Use the Max Usage slider to put a cap on how much drive space all these restore points are allowed to eat up.

In times of strife, there's also a nuclear option here: the Delete button.

Note, however, that this button deletes not just all your restore points, but also the backups of all your *documents* (those created by the Shadow Copy feature described on page 700). So be careful out there.

Note: A new subfeature of System Restore also makes daily safety copies of your *documents.* See "Shadow Copies" on page 700.

In Windows 7, the System Restore feature has been polished and improved. Overall, it's one of the handiest tools in your kit.

About Restore Points

System Restore works by taking snapshots of your operating system. Your copy of Windows has been creating these memorized snapshots, called *restore points,* ever since you've been running it. When the worst comes to pass, and your PC starts acting up, you can use System Restore to rewind your machine to its configuration the last time you remember it working well.

Windows automatically creates landing points for your little PC time machine at the following times:

• Once a week.

• Every time you install a new program or install a new device driver for a piece of hardware.

• When you install a Windows Update.

• When you make a backup using Backup and Restore.

• Whenever you feel like it—for instance, just before you install some new component.

Note: When your hard drive is running low on space, System Restore turns off automatically, without notice. It turns itself back on when you free up some space.

To create one of these checkpoints *manually*, open the System Protection dialog box (follow the steps in the box on the facing page). At the bottom of that box, the Create button lets you create and name a new manual restore point. (Don't include the date and time in the name of the restore point; you'll see that when you get around to doing an actual restoration.)

As you can well imagine, storing all these copies of your Windows configuration consumes quite a bit of disk space. That's why Windows automatically begins *deleting* restore points when it's running out of disk space. That's also why the System Restore feature stops working if your hard drive is very full.

And that's *also* why you should run the System Restore feature promptly when your PC acts strangely.

Performing a System Restore

If something goes wrong with your PC, here's how to roll it back to the happy, bygone days of late last week—or this morning, for that matter:

1. Open the System Restore program.

The quickest way: Type *restore* into the Start menu. Click System Restore.

Authenticate if necessary; then the "Restore system files and settings" welcome screen appears.

2. **Click Next. Look over the restore points; click the one you want to rewind to (Figure 22-6, top).**

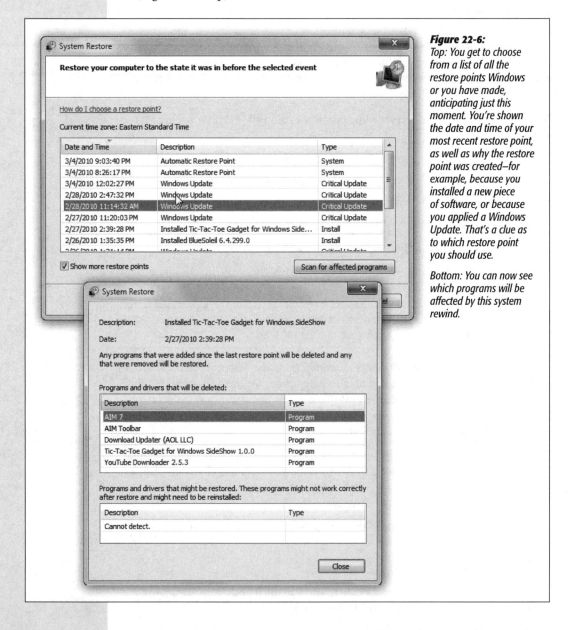

Figure 22-6:
Top: You get to choose from a list of all the restore points Windows or you have made, anticipating just this moment. You're shown the date and time of your most recent restore point, as well as why the restore point was created—for example, because you installed a new piece of software, or because you applied a Windows Update. That's a clue as to which restore point you should use.

Bottom: You can now see which programs will be affected by this system rewind.

As you survey the restore points, try to remember when, exactly, your system went wonky. Use the new "Scan for affected programs" button to help you figure out which apps and drivers will be affected if you go through with the restore. (It also lets you create a password-reset disk, which might be a lifesaver if, since the restore point was made, you've added or changed your account password.)

Tip: The list shows only the most recent five restore points; usually, one of those is what you want. But if you turn on "Show more restore points," you get to see the complete list, stretching back as far as Windows can remember.

---

3. **Click Next.**

   You have one more chance to back out: Windows displays the date and time of the restore point, shows you which drives will be affected, gives you another chance to create a password-reset disk, and asks if you *really* want to go back in time.

4. **Click Finish. In the confirmation box, click Yes.**

   Windows goes to town, reinstating your operating system to reflect its condition on the date you specified. Leave your PC alone while this occurs.

   When the process is complete, the computer restarts automatically. When you log back in, you're back to the past—and with any luck, your PC runs smoothly again. (None of your email or files are disturbed.)

If it didn't work—if you only made things worse—repeat step 1. At the top of the System Restore welcome screen, you'll see an option called Undo System Restore. It lets you *undo* your undoing.

Or, of course, you can click "Choose a different restore point" if you think that maybe you didn't rewind your PC far back *enough,* and want to try again with a different restore point.

Turning System Restore Off

You really shouldn't turn off System Restore. You really, really shouldn't. It's just so incredibly useful, when you're pressed for time and things start going wacky, to be able to hit rewind and grant yourself a perfectly smooth PC, even if you never do find out what the trouble was.

But if you're an advanced power user with no hard drive space to spare—is there such a person?—here's how you shut off this feature:

1. **Open the Start menu. While it's open, right-click Computer; from the shortcut menu, choose Properties.**

   The System Properties control panel appears.

2. **In the left-hand pane, click "System protection." Authenticate if necessary.**

   You arrive at the System Protection tab of the System Properties dialog box.

3. Click the hard drive in the Available Drives list, then click Configure, then click "Turn off system protection."

Or click "Only restore previous versions of files." It turns *off* System Restore, but leaves Previous Versions (described below) turned on.

4. Click OK. In the "Are you sure?" box, click Yes.

That's it. You're flying without a net now, baby.

Shadow Copies (Previous Versions)

Professional • Enterprise • Ultimate Edition

System Restore is an amazing, powerful, career-saving feature—but it's awfully self-interested. It cares only about protecting *Windows*.

How can you rewind your *documents* to their earlier, healthier, or pre-edited conditions?

The Shadow knows…*Shadow Copy,* that is.

Shadow Copy is a time machine for documents in the same way System Restore is a time machine for your system software. It's an incredible safety net against damage, accidental modification, or late-night bouts of ill-advised editing.

Making Shadow Copies

The beauty of Shadow Copy is that it's automatic and invisible. It's *part* of System Restore, actually, meaning that unless you've turned System Restore *off*, Shadow Copy is protecting your documents, too. To save time and disk space, Shadow Copy only bothers copying files that have changed since the last Restore Point was created.

Recovering Old Document Versions

If the worst should happen, and you realize that you really preferred the draft of your novel that you had three revisions ago, right-click the file or folder in question. From the shortcut menu, choose Restore Previous Version.

The Previous Versions tab of the Properties dialog box opens (Figure 22-7), complete with a list of all the shadow copies of the file. Select the file you want to restore.

UP TO SPEED

What Shadow Copies Aren't

The Shadow Copy feature isn't a substitute for backing up your computer. For example, this feature won't help you if you *deleted* a document, because it's designed only to give you previous versions of *existing* documents. It's also no protection against hard drive death, since shadow copies are usually stored on the same hard drive as the originals.

Shadow copies also aren't the same as an infinite Undo command. Copies are made only once a day, so you can't, for example, rewind a document to the state it was in three hours ago.

Now, you *could* just click Restore; that would certainly do the trick. Trouble is, this is a permanent maneuver, so once you restore a document to the Tuesday version, today's more recent draft is gone forever.

Figure 22-7:
Older versions of a file are listed on the Previous Versions tab. Before restoring a file, it's a good idea to open it first and preview it, to make sure you do want to use that version instead of the current one. For absolute safety, click Copy; the screen on the right appears, letting you save a copy of the file in a different folder.

Therefore, it's a good idea to play it safer using one of these techniques:

• Highlight the file; click Open. The document opens on the screen so you can make sure this is the version you wanted.

• Select the file and click Copy. A dialog box appears so you can peel off a copy of the older document instead of nuking the modern one.

Note: Here's a warning to anyone who *dual-boots* between Windows 7 and Windows XP: For some extremely technical and extremely unfortunate reasons, starting up in Windows XP *deletes* all your shadow copies *and* restore points.

The only workaround is to turn off the hard drive that contains these files before starting up in Windows XP. Microsoft is very sorry.

Safe Mode and the Startup Menu

All Versions

If the problems you're having are caused by drivers that load just as the computer is starting up, turning them all off can be helpful. At the very least, it allows you to get into your machine to begin your troubleshooting pursuit. That's precisely the purpose of the Startup menu screen—a menu most people never even know exists until they're initiated into its secret world by a technically savvy guru.

Making the Startup menu appear is a matter of delicate timing. First, restart the computer. Immediately after the BIOS startup messages disappear, press the F8 key (on the top row of most keyboards).

The BIOS startup messages—the usual crude-looking text on a black screen, filled with copyright notices and technical specs—are the first things you see after turning on the computer.

If you press the F8 key after the Windows logo makes its appearance, you're too late. But if all goes well, you see the Advanced Boot Options screen (Figure 22-8). Displayed against a black DOS screen, in rough lettering, is a long list of options that includes Safe Mode, Safe Mode with Networking, Safe Mode with Command Prompt, Enable Boot Logging, and so on. Use the arrow keys to "walk through" them.

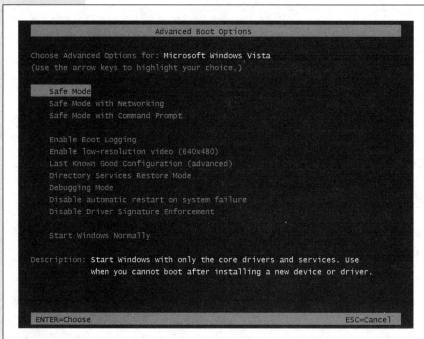

Figure 22-8:
Let's hope you never need to see this screen. It's the Advanced Boot Options screen—a graphically uninteresting but troubleshootingly critical starting point. To make a selection, press the ↑ or ↓ keys to walk through the list. Press Enter when you've highlighted the option you want.

Here's what the Startup menu commands do:

- **Safe Mode.** Safe Mode starts up Windows in a special, stripped-down, generic, somewhat frightening-looking startup mode—with the software for dozens of hardware and software features *turned off*. Only the very basic components work: your mouse, keyboard, screen, and disk drives. Everything else is shut down and cut off. In short, Safe Mode is the tactic to take if your PC *won't* start up normally, thanks to some recalcitrant driver.

  Once you select the Safe Mode option on the Startup menu, you see a list, filling your screen, of every driver Windows is loading. Eventually, you're asked to log in.

  Your screen now looks like it was designed by drunken cavemen, with jagged, awful graphics and text. That's because in Safe Mode, Windows doesn't load the driver for your video card. (It avoids that driver, on the assumption that it may be causing the very problem you're trying to troubleshoot.) Instead, Windows loads a crude, generic driver that works with *any* video card.

  The purpose of Safe Mode is to help you troubleshoot. If you discover that the problem you've been having is now gone, you've at least established that the culprit is one of the drivers Windows has now turned off. Safe Mode also gives you full access to the technical tools of Windows, including System Restore, the Device Manager, the Registry Editor, the Backup and Restore Center, and Help. You might use the Device Manager, for example, to roll back a driver you just updated, or System Restore to undo some other installation that seems to have thrown your PC into chaos.

  If this procedure doesn't solve the problem, contact a support technician.

- **Safe Mode with Networking.** This option is exactly the same as Safe Mode, except that it also lets you load the driver software needed to tap into a network, if you're on one, or onto the Internet—an arrangement that offers a few additional troubleshooting possibilities, like being able to access files and drivers on another PC or from the Internet. (If you have a laptop that uses a PC Card networking card, however, this option still may not help you, since the PC Card driver itself is still turned off.)

- **Safe Mode with Command Prompt.** Here's another variation of Safe Mode, this one intended for ultra–power users who are more comfortable typing out text commands at the command prompt than using icons, menus, and the mouse.

- **Enable Boot Logging.** This startup method is the same as Normal, except that Windows records every technical event that takes place during the startup in a log file named *ntbtlog.txt* (located on the startup drive, in the Windows folder).

  Most of the time, you'll use the Boot Logging option only at the request of a support technician you've phoned for help. After confirming the operating system startup, the technician may ask you to open ntbtlog.txt in your Notepad program and search for particular words or phrases—usually the word "fail."

- **Enable VGA Mode.** In this mode, your PC uses a standard VGA video driver that works with all graphics cards, instead of the hideously ugly generic one usually seen in Safe Mode. Use this option when you're troubleshooting video-display problems—problems that you're confident have less to do with drivers than with your settings in the Display control panel (which you're now ready to fiddle with).

  (Of course, VGA means 640 × 480 pixels, which looks huge and crude on today's big monitors. Do not adjust your set.)

- **Last Known Good Configuration.** Here's yet another method of resetting the clock to a time when your PC was working correctly, in effect undoing whatever configuration change you made that triggered your PC's current problems. It reinstates whichever set of drivers, and whichever Registry configuration, was in force the last time the PC was working right. (This option, however, isn't as effective as the System Restore option, which also restores operating-system files in the process.)

- **Directory Services Restore Mode.** This extremely technical option is useful only in corporations with specialized *domain controller* computers running Windows .NET Server or Windows 2000 Server.

- **Debugging Mode.** Here's another extremely obscure option, this one intended for very technical people who've connected one PC to another via a serial cable. They can then use the second computer to analyze the first, using specialized debugger software.

- **Disable automatic restart on system failure.** Under normal conditions, Windows will automatically reboot after a system crash. Choose this option if you don't want it to reboot.

- **Disable Driver Signature Enforcement.** As a way to protect your PC, Windows uses a technique called Driver Signature Enforcement, which is designed to load only drivers that are verified to be valid. Of course, there are plenty of times when drivers aren't verified but in fact are usable. If you suspect that to be the case, choose this option; Windows will load all your drivers.

- **Start Windows Normally.** This option starts the operating system in its usual fashion, exactly as though you never summoned the Startup menu to begin with. It lets you tell the PC, "Sorry to have interrupted you…go ahead."

Troubleshooting Tools
All Versions

These days, a first-time Windows user probably doesn't even know what you mean by the phrase "blue screen of death." PCs don't crash nearly as often as they used to.

But there are still a million things that can go wrong—and about a million troubleshooting tools to help you, or somebody you've begged to help you, solve them. Here's the, ahem, crash course.

Automatic Error Reporting

In the Windows XP days, every time a program crashed, a dialog box asked if you wanted to send details of the crash, anonymously, to Microsoft. Maybe, just maybe, the cumulative stream of these reports might lead some programmer somewhere to detect a pattern—and fix his darned bug.

In Windows 7, you can tell your PC to send those reports to Microsoft automatically—without interrupting or bothering you—or not to send them at all. You can also look over a running diary of all the crashes you've had.

To fiddle with these settings, open the Action center. (Click the ⚐ on your taskbar system tray, and click Open Action Center.) Expand the Maintenance section, if necessary, and then click Settings. Proceed as shown in Figure 22-9.

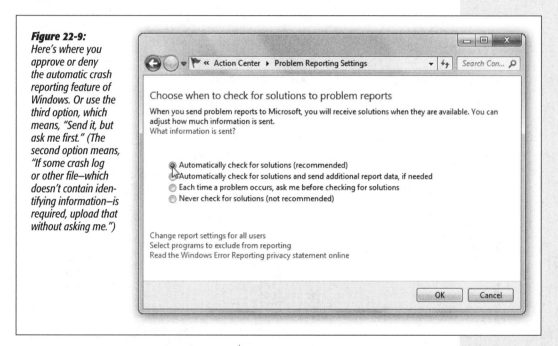

Figure 22-9:
Here's where you approve or deny the automatic crash reporting feature of Windows. Or use the third option, which means, "Send it, but ask me first." (The second option means, "If some crash log or other file—which doesn't contain identifying information—is required, upload that without asking me.")

Automatic Solution Reporting

It doesn't happen often, but it's conceivable that all those millions of crash reports that Microsoft collects might one day result in a patch that fixes the problem—maybe even a problem *you* reported. If Windows finds out that some bug-fix update is available for a crash you've had, a message in the Action Center will let you know and offer you the chance to download it.

The Diary of Windows Crashes

Windows 7 maintains a tidy list of all the problems you've been having with your machine. Needless to say, this little item isn't featured very prominently in Windows, but it's there.

To see it, type *reports* into the Start menu. Click "View all problem reports." You get the astonishing box shown in Figure 22-10 (top).

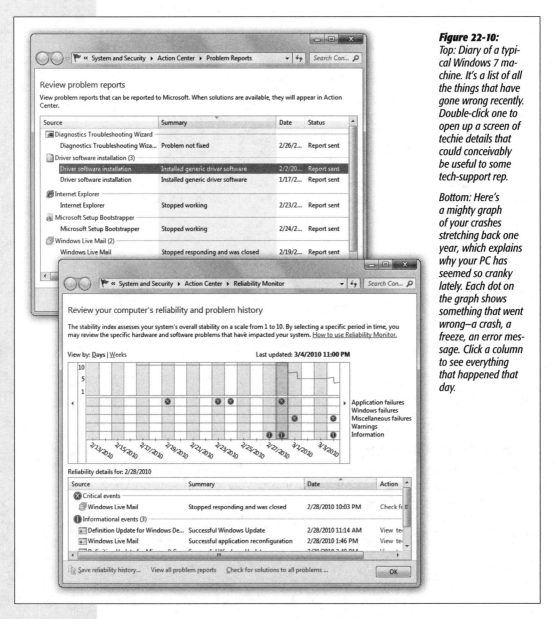

Figure 22-10:
Top: Diary of a typical Windows 7 machine. It's a list of all the things that have gone wrong recently. Double-click one to open up a screen of techie details that could conceivably be useful to some tech-support rep.

Bottom: Here's a mighty graph of your crashes stretching back one year, which explains why your PC has seemed so cranky lately. Each dot on the graph shows something that went wrong—a crash, a freeze, an error message. Click a column to see everything that happened that day.

Tip: For the even more technically inclined, Windows includes an older, even more technical list of the behind-the-scenes goings-on on your PC: the Event Viewer. Open it by typing *event viewer* into the Start menu. Enjoy looking over eye-glazing lists of every log that Windows keeps: lists of happenings concerning programs, setup, security, services, and more. You can sort, filter, and group these events—but if you can understand the significance of these obscure messages, you shouldn't be reading a Windows 7 book—you should be writing one.

Reliability Monitor

If you prefer to get the bad news in visual form, try opening the new Reliability Monitor (Figure 22-10, bottom). To see it, type *history* into the Start menu. Click "View reliability history."

If you see a lot of ❸ (crashes) following one of the little ❶'s (which represent installations and other changes to your system), you might have spotted yourself a cause-and-effect situation. You now have a clue to your PC's recent instability.

Startup Repair (Windows Recovery Environment)
All Versions

You might play by all the rules. You might make regular backups, keep your antivirus software up to date, and floss twice a day. And then one day, you get your reward: The PC won't even start up. You can't use any of Windows's software troubleshooting tools, because you can't even get to Windows.

In that most dire situation, Microsoft is pleased to introduce Startup Repair, known to techies as WinRE (Windows Recovery Environment). It's a special recovery mode, loaded with emergency tools. You can run it from the *Windows DVD*, so that it can fix whatever's damaged or missing on the hard drive's copy of Windows, or—new in Windows 7—it can run right from the hard drive.

Note: Depending on who sold you your PC, you might not have a traditional Windows DVD. Your PC company might even have replaced Startup Repair with a similar tool; check its Web site or manual.

To open Startup Repair, follow these steps:

- **From the hard drive.** If the hard drive is operational, you might save some time and steps by running WinRE right from your existing copy of Windows. To do that, hold down the F8 key as your PC is booting up; let go when you see the Advanced Boot Options screen (Figure 22-8). Repair Your Computer should be highlighted already; press Enter.

  After a moment of loading and waiting, you're asked to specify your keyboard input method (for example, U.S.). Click Next. Now log in with an administrator's name and password; click OK.

• **From the Windows DVD.** Insert the DVD. Then restart the PC—but as it's coming to life, press the F8 key. Your PC says something like, "Press a key to boot from CD or DVD." So do it—press a key.

After a moment, the Windows installation screen appears. But you're not going to install Windows—not yet. Instead, **click "Repair your computer."** Now you're asked which copy of Windows you want to repair. Chances are you've got only one; click it.

In either case, the Recovery Environment appears (Figure 22-11).

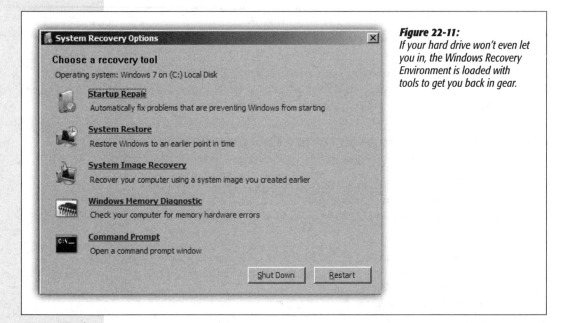

Figure 22-11:
If your hard drive won't even let you in, the Windows Recovery Environment is loaded with tools to get you back in gear.

At this point, you have some powerful tools available to help you out of your PC's mess. If you're running off the DVD, you can perform surgeries on the hard drive that you wouldn't be able to if the hard drive itself were in control. That'd be like trying to paint the floor under your own feet.

Your options are:

• **Startup Repair.** If there is indeed a missing or damaged file in your copy of Windows, click this link to trigger an automatic repair job. You're running off the original installation DVD, for heaven's sake, so it's extremely easy for Startup Repair to reach into its bag of spare parts if necessary.

• **System Restore.** Remember System Restore, described at the beginning of this chapter? When better to rewind your Windows installation to a healthier, happier time than right now? Click this link to choose a restore point. With any luck, the rewinding job will include restoring the undamaged startup files that your PC needs right about now.

- **System Image Recovery.** If you've taken advantage of the system image option (page 694), then you're in luck. You have at your disposal a complete disk image of your hard drive, presumably made when the disk was working fine. This mirror includes everything on it: your copy of Windows, all your programs, all your documents and settings, the works. It's like super System Restore. Click this link to copy the whole schmear back onto your hard drive. (Of course, you'll lose any documents or settings you've changed since the backup was made.)

- **Windows Memory Diagnostic.** Click this link if you suspect that it's your RAM (memory), not the hard drive, that's causing your problems. The software does a quick check to make sure your memory hardware is actually working right.

- **Command Prompt.** If you're lucky enough to know what you're doing at the command prompt (page 272), you're in luck. You can use it to issue commands, move and rename files, and generally perform repair surgery.

Thanks to these powerful tools, there's less reason than ever to pay $35 for the privilege of talking to some technician named "Mike" who's actually in India, following a tech-support script that instructs you to first erase your hard drive and reinstall Windows from scratch.

Part Seven:
Networking &
Homegroups

7

Accounts & Logging On

F or years, teachers, parents, tech directors, and computer lab instructors struggled to answer two difficult questions: How do you rig one PC so several different people can use it throughout the day, without interfering with one another's files and settings? And how do you protect a PC from getting fouled up by mischievous (or bumbling) students and employees?

Introducing User Accounts
All Versions

Windows 7 was designed from the ground up to be a multiple-user operating system. Anyone who uses the computer must *log on*—click (or type) your name and type in a password—when the computer turns on. Upon doing so, you discover the Windows universe just as you left it, including these elements:

- **Desktop.** Each person sees his own shortcut icons, folder icons, and other stuff left out on the desktop.

- **Start menu.** If you reorganize the Start menu, as described in Chapter 1, you won't confuse anybody else who uses the machine. No one else can even *see* the changes you make.

- **Documents folder.** Each person sees only her own stuff in the Documents folder.

- **Email.** Windows maintains a separate stash of email messages for each account holder—along with separate Web bookmarks, a Windows Messenger contact list, and other online details.

- **Favorites folder.** Any Web sites, folders, or other icons you've designated as Favorites appear in *your* Favorites menu, and nobody else's.

- **Internet cache.** This folder stores a copy of the Web pages you've visited recently for faster retrieval the next time you visit them.

- **History and cookies.** Windows maintains a list of recently visited Web sites independently for each person; likewise, it stores a personal collection of *cookies* (Web site preference files).

- **Control Panel settings.** Windows memorizes the preferences each person establishes using the Control Panel (see Chapter 8), including keyboard, sound, screen saver, and mouse settings.

Note: Not all Control Panel settings are available to everyone. Really important ones that affect the entire PC, like the date and time and network settings, can be changed only by the Lord of the PC–the *administrative* account holder, described in a moment.

- **Privileges.** Your user account also determines what you're allowed to do on the network and even on your own computer: which settings you can change in the Control Panel, and even which files and folders you can open.

Behind the scenes, Windows stores *all* these files and settings in a single folder—your Personal folder, the one that bears your name. You can open it easily enough; it's at the top right of the Start menu. (Technically, your Personal folder is in the Computer→ Local Disk (C:)→Users folder.)

This feature makes sharing the PC much more convenient, because you don't have to look at everybody else's files (and endure their desktop design schemes). It also adds a layer of security, making it less likely that a marauding 6-year-old will throw away your files.

Tip: Even if you don't share your PC with anyone and don't create any other accounts, you might still appreciate this feature because it effectively password-protects the entire computer. Your PC is protected from unauthorized casual fiddling when you're away from your desk (or if your laptop is stolen)–especially if you tell Windows to require your logon password after any time the screen saver has kicked in (page 185).

Since the day you installed Windows 7 or fired up a new Win7 machine, you may have made a number of changes to your desktop—fiddled with your Start menu, changed the desktop wallpaper, added some favorites to your Web browser, downloaded files onto your desktop, and so on—without realizing that you were actually making these changes only to *your account.*

Accordingly, if you create an account for a second person, then when she turns on the computer and signs in, she'll find the desktop exactly the way it was as factory-installed by Microsoft: basic Start menu, standard desktop picture, default Web browser home page, and so on. She can make the same kinds of changes to the PC that you've made, but nothing she does will affect your environment the next time *you* log on.

In other words, the multiple-accounts feature has two benefits: first, the convenience of hiding everyone else's junk; and second, security that protects both the PC's system software and everyone's work.

If you're content simply to *use* Windows, that's really all you need to know about accounts. If, on the other hand, you have shouldered some of the responsibility for *administering* Windows machines—if it's your job to add and remove accounts, for example—read on.

Windows 7: The OS with Two Faces
All Versions

Windows is designed to handle either of two different kinds of networks: *workgroups* (small, informal home or small-business networks) and *domains* (corporate networks, professionally and centrally administered).

This distinction becomes particularly important when it comes to user accounts.

- **Workgroup network.** In this smaller kind of network, each computer stores its own security settings, such as user accounts, passwords, and permissions. Clearly, setting up an account on every PC for every employee in a big company would get out of hand.

  If you're part of a workgroup network (or no network), you'll find that Windows gives you simplified access to user accounts and *permissions,* both of which are described in this chapter.

- **Domain network.** In a corporation, your files may not be sitting right there on your hard drive. They may, in fact, sit on a network server—a separate computer dedicated to dishing out files to employees from across the network. As you can probably imagine, protecting all this information is somebody's Job Number One.

  That's why, if your PC is part of a domain, you'll find Windows 7 more reminiscent of Windows 2000, with more business-oriented features and full access to the account-maintenance and permissions-management options. (Only the Professional, Enterprise, and Ultimate editions of 7 can speak to domain networks.)

This chapter tackles these two broad feature categories—the workgroup scenario and the domain scenario—one at a time.

Local Accounts
All Versions

This section is dedicated to computers in a workgroup network—or no network at all. Corporate networks (domains) are described later in this chapter.

To see what accounts are already on your PC, open the Start menu. Start typing *accounts* until you see User Accounts in the results list; click it. The User Accounts and Family Safety control panel opens (Figure 23-1).

Tip: The Start menu offers a big, fat shortcut to this dialog box: Just click your picture at the top of the open Start menu.

What you see here depends on which kind of account you have: *Administrator* or *Standard*. Read on.

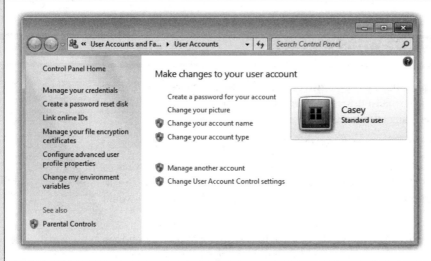

Figure 23-1:
The User Accounts and Family Safety control panel always opens up showing you only the details of your account. You can't even see who else has accounts on your PC—unless you click "Manage another account" and authenticate yourself.

Administrator vs. Standard Accounts

It's important to understand the phrase that appears just under your name in the panel shown in Figure 23-2. On your own personal PC, the word "Administrator" probably appears here.

Because you're the person who installed Windows 7, the PC assumes that you're one of its *administrators*—the technical wizards who will be in charge of it. You're the teacher, the parent, the resident guru. You're the one who will maintain this PC and who will be permitted to make system-wide changes to it.

You'll find settings all over Windows (and all over this book) that *only* people with Administrator accounts can change. For example, only an administrator is allowed to:

• **Create or delete accounts** and passwords on the PC.

• **Install new programs** (and certain hardware components).

• **Make changes** to certain Control Panel programs that are off-limits to non-administrators.

• **See and manipulate** *any* file on the machine.

There's another kind of account, too, for people who *don't* have to make those kinds of changes: the Standard account.

Now, for years, people doled out Administrator accounts pretty freely. You know: The parents got Administrator accounts, the kids got Standard ones.

The trouble is, an Administrator account *itself* is a kind of security hole. Any time you're logged in with this kind of account, any nasty software you may have caught from the Internet is *also,* in effect, logged in—and can make changes to important underlying settings on your PC, just the way a human administrator can.

Figure 23-2:
If you click "Manage another account" (in the box shown in Figure 23-1), you finally get to see, and make changes to, all the other accounts.

Choose the account you would like to change

Administrator
Administrator

Casey
Standard user

Robin
Administrator
Password protected

Guest
Guest account is off

Create a new account
What is a user account?

Additional things you can do

Set up Parental Controls
Go to the main User Accounts page

Put another way: A virus you've downloaded will have a much harder time infecting the rest of the machine if you were running a Standard account than an Administrator account.

Today, therefore, Microsoft recommends that *everyone* use Standard accounts—even you, the wise master and owner of the computer!

So how are you supposed to make important Control Panel changes, install new programs, and so on?

That's gotten a lot easier in Windows 7. Using a Standard account no longer means that you can't make important changes. In fact, you can do just about everything on the PC that an Administrator account can—*if* you know the *password* of a true Administrator account.

Note: Every Windows 7 PC can (and must) keep at least one Administrator account on hand, even if you rarely log in with that account.

Whenever you try to make a big change, you're asked to *authenticate yourself.* As described on page 726, that means supplying an Administrator account's password, even though you, the currently logged-in person, are a lowly Standard account holder.

If you have a Standard account because you're a student, a child, or an employee, you're supposed to call an administrator over to your PC to approve the change you're making. (If you're the PC's owner, but you're using a Standard account for security purposes, you know an administrator password, so it's no big deal.)

Now, making broad changes to a PC when you're an administrator *still* presents you with those "prove yourself worthy" authentication dialog boxes. The only difference is that you, the administrator, can click Continue to bypass them, rather than having to type in a password.

You'll have to weigh this security/convenience tradeoff. But you've been warned: The least vulnerable PC is one where everyone uses Standard accounts.

All of this is a long-winded way of explaining why, when you open User Accounts, you may see one of two different things.

Adding an Account

It's easy to create a new account in the User Accounts panel: Click "Manage another account." Authenticate yourself.

You arrive on the master list of accounts (Figure 23-2). If you're new at this, there's probably just one account listed here: yours. This is the account Windows created when you installed it.

If you see more than one account here—not just yours—then one of these situations probably applies:

• **You created them** when you installed Windows 7, as described in Appendix A.

• **You bought a new computer** with Windows 7 preinstalled and created several accounts when asked to do so the first time you turned on the machine.

• **You upgraded the machine** from an earlier version of Windows, and Windows 7 gracefully imported all your existing accounts.

To add another one, click "Create a new account." The next screen asks you to name the account and choose an account type: Administrator or Standard (Figure 23-3).

When you're finished with the settings, click Create Account (or press Enter). After a moment, you return to the User Accounts screen, where the new person's name joins whatever names were already there. You can continue adding new accounts forever or until your hard drive is full, whichever comes first.

Tip: If you never had the opportunity to set up a user account when installing Windows—if you bought a PC with Windows already on it, for example—you may see an account named Owner already in place. Nobody can use Windows at all unless there's at least *one* Administrator account on it, so Microsoft is doing you a favor here.

Just double-click it and click "Change the account name" to change the name Owner to one that suits you better. Make that account your own using the steps in the following paragraphs.

Figure 23-3:
If it's all in the family, the account's name could be Casey or Robin. If it's a corporation or school, you'll probably want to use both first and last names. Capitalization doesn't matter, but most punctuation is forbidden. This is also where you specify whether or not this unsuspecting computer user will be an administrator, as described above.

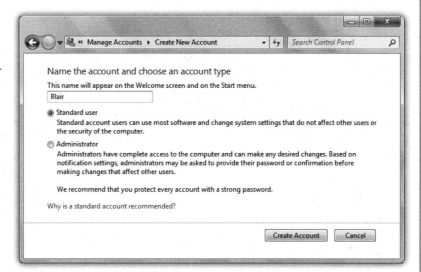

Editing an Account

Although the process of creating a new account is swift and simple, it doesn't offer you much in the way of flexibility. You don't even have a chance to specify the new person's password, let alone the tiny picture that appears next to the person's name and at the top of the Start menu (rubber ducky, flower, or whatever).

That's why the next step in creating an account is usually *editing* the one you just set up. To do so, once you've returned to the main User Accounts screen (Figure 23-2), click the name or icon of the freshly created account. You arrive at the screen shown at the top in Figure 23-4, where—if you are an administrator—you can choose from any of these options:

- **Change the account name.** You're offered the opportunity to type in a new name for this person and then click the Change Name button—just the ticket when one of your coworkers gets married or joins the Witness Protection Program.

- **Create a password.** Click this link if you'd like to require a password for access to this person's account (Figure 23-4, bottom). Capitalization counts.

The usual computer book takes this opportunity to stress the importance of having a long, complex password, such as a phrase that isn't in the dictionary, something made up of mixed letters and numbers—and *not, by the way,* the word "password." This is excellent advice if you create sensitive documents and work in a corporation.

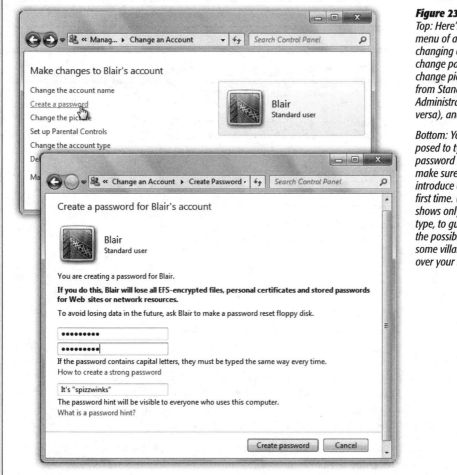

Figure 23-4:
Top: Here's the master menu of account-changing options. Add/ change password, change picture, change from Standard to Administrative (or vice versa), and so on.

Bottom: You're supposed to type your password twice to make sure you didn't introduce a typo the first time. (The PC shows only dots as you type, to guard against the possibility that some villain is snooping over your shoulder.)

But if you share the PC only with a spouse or a few trusted colleagues in a small office, you may have nothing to hide. You may see the multiple-users feature more as a convenience (for keeping your settings and files separate) than a way of protecting secrecy and security.

In these situations, there's no particular need to dream up a convoluted password. In fact, you may want to consider setting up *no* password—leaving both password blanks empty. Later, whenever you're asked for your password, just leave the

Password box blank. You'll be able to log on and authenticate yourself that much faster each day.

If you do decide to provide a password, you can also provide a *hint* (for yourself or whichever coworker's account you're operating on). This is a hint that anybody can see (including bad guys trying to log on as you), so choose something meaningful only to you. If your password is the first person who ever kissed you plus your junior-year phone number, for example, your hint might be "first person who ever kissed me plus my junior-year phone number."

Later, when you log in and can't remember your password, leave the Password box empty and hit Enter. You wind up back at the login screen to try again—but this time, your hint will appear just below the Password box to jog your memory.

Tip: This low-security, high-convenience attitude is precisely the idea behind homegroups (Chapter 26).

But homegroups work only if everybody in the house or the office is on Windows 7. If you're not, then you'll have to create accounts on each PC that each person might want to access over the network. A word of advice: On each PC, set them up with the same passwords they use when logging onto their own computers. You'll save them time and hassle. Once they've logged onto another machine on the network, they'll be able to connect to their own computer without having to type in another name and password.

- **Change the picture.** The usual sign-in screen displays each account holder's name, accompanied by a little picture. When you first create the account, however, it assigns a picture to you at random—and not all the pictures are necessarily appropriate for your personality. Not every extreme-sport headbanger, for example, is crazy about being represented by a kitten.

  If you like one of the selections Microsoft has provided, just click it to select it as the replacement graphic. If you'd rather use some other graphics file on the hard drive instead—a photo of your actual face, for example—see Figure 23-5.

- **Set up Parental Controls.** Whenever you edit a Standard account, this link is available, on the premise that this person is either a child or someone who acts like one. See page 390 for Parental Controls details.

- **Change the account type.** Change a Standard account into an Administrator account, or vice versa.

- **Delete the account.** See page 723

- **Manage another account.** You return to the accounts list.

You're free to make any of these changes to any account at any time; you don't have to do it immediately after creating the account.

The Forgotten Password Disk

As described above, Windows contains a handy *hint* mechanism for helping you recall your password if you've forgotten it.

But what if, having walked into a low-hanging branch, you've forgotten both your password *and* the correct interpretation of your hint? In that disastrous situation, your entire world of work and email would be locked inside the computer forever. (Yes, an administrator could issue you a new password—but as noted in the box on page 724, you'd lose all your secondary passwords in the process.)

Fortunately, Windows offers a clever solution-in-advance: the Password Reset Disk. It's a CD or USB flash drive (not a floppy, as in Windows XP) that you can use like a physical key to unlock your account in the event of a forgotten password. The catch: You have to make this disk *now*, while you still remember your password.

Figure 23-5:
Here's where you change your account picture. If you click "Browse for more pictures," then Windows shows you a list of the graphics files on your hard drive so you can choose one, which Windows then auto-matically scales down to postage-stamp size (48 pixels square).

To create this disk, insert a blank CD or a USB flash drive. Then open the Start menu and click your picture (top right). The "Make changes to your user account" window opens (Figure 23-1).

The second link in the task pane says, "Create a password reset disk." Click that to open the Forgotten Password Wizard shown in Figure 23-6. Click through it, supplying your current password when you're asked for it. When you click Finish, remove the CD or flash drive. Label it, and don't lose it!

Tip: Behind the scenes, Windows saves a file onto the CD or flash drive called *userkey.psw.* You can guess what that is.

When the day comes that you can't remember your password, leave the Password box empty and hit Enter. You wind up back at the login screen; this time, in addition to your password hint, you see a link called "Reset password." Insert your Password Reset CD or flash drive and then click that link.

A Password Reset Wizard now helps you create a new password (and a new hint to remind you of it). You're in.

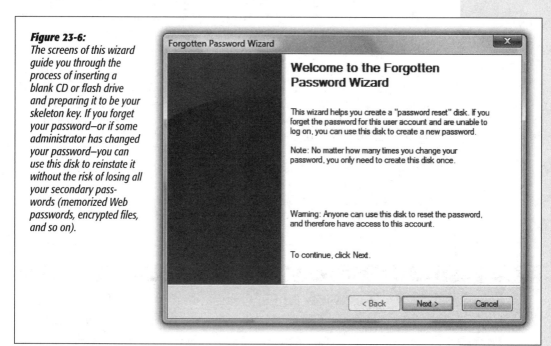

Figure 23-6:
The screens of this wizard guide you through the process of inserting a blank CD or flash drive and preparing it to be your skeleton key. If you forget your password—or if some administrator has changed your password—you can use this disk to reinstate it without the risk of losing all your secondary passwords (memorized Web passwords, encrypted files, and so on).

Even though you now have a new password, your existing Password Reset Disk is still good. Keep it in a drawer somewhere for use the next time you experience a temporarily blank brain.

Deleting User Accounts

It happens—somebody graduates, somebody gets fired, somebody dumps you. Sooner or later, you may need to delete an account from your PC.

To delete a user account, open User Accounts, click the appropriate account name, and then click "Delete the account."

Windows asks if you want to preserve the contents of this person's Documents folder. If you click the Keep Files button, you find a new folder, named for the dearly departed, on your desktop. (As noted in the dialog box, only the documents, the contents of the desktop, and the Documents folder are preserved—but *not* programs, email, or even Web favorites.) If that person ever returns to your life, you can create a new account for him and copy these files into the appropriate folder locations.

If you click the Delete Files button, though, the documents are gone forever.

A few more important points about deleting accounts:

- You can't delete the account you're logged into.

- You can't delete the last Administrator account. One must remain.

- You can create a new account with the same name and password as one you deleted earlier, but in Windows's head, it's still not the same account. As described in the box on this page, it won't have any of the original *secondary* passwords (for Web sites, encrypted files, and so on).

- Don't manipulate accounts manually (by fooling around in the Users folder). Create, delete, and rename them only using User Accounts in the Control Panel. Otherwise, you'll wind up with duplicate or triplicate folders in Users, with the PC name tacked onto the end of the original account name (Bob, Bob.DELL, and so on)—a sure recipe for confusion.

Tip: If you're an administrator, don't miss the Users tab of the Task Manager dialog box. (Press Ctrl+Shift+Esc to get to the Task Manager.) It offers a handy, centralized list of everybody who's logged into your machine and contains buttons that let you log them off, disconnect them, or even make a little message pop up on their screens. All of this can be handy whenever you need some information, a troubleshooting session, or a power trip.

UP TO SPEED

Passwords Within Passwords

The primary password that you or your administrator sets up in the User Accounts program has two functions. You already know that it lets you log on each day so you can enter your Windows world of desktop clutter, Start-menu tailoring, Web bookmarks, and so on.

But what you may not realize is that it's also the master key that unlocks all the *other* passwords associated with your account: the passwords that Internet Explorer memorizes for certain Web sites, the passwords that get you into shared disks and folders on the network, the password that protects your encrypted files, and so on. The simple act of logging onto your account also unlocks all these other secure areas of your PC life.

But remember that anyone with an Administrator account can *change* your password at any time. Does that mean that whoever has an Administrator account—your teacher, boss, or teenager, for example—has full access to your private stuff? After you leave the household, company, or school, what's

to stop an administrator from changing your password, thereby gaining access to your electronic-brokerage account (courtesy of its memorized Internet Explorer password), and so on?

Fortunately, Microsoft is way ahead of you on this one. The instant an administrator changes somebody else's password, Windows *wipes out* all secondary passwords associated with the account. That administrator can log onto your account and see your everyday files, but he can't see Web sites with memorized passwords and so on. (The bad news is that he'll also wipe out your stored passwords for EPS-encrypted files, if any; they're described on page 679.)

Note that if you change your *own* password—or if you use a Password Reset Disk, described in these pages—none of this applies. Your secondary passwords survive intact. It's only when *somebody else* changes your password that this little-known Windows security feature kicks in, sanitizing the account for your protection.

Disabling Accounts

If you *do* expect that your colleague may one day return to your life, you might consider *disabling* the account instead of deleting it. A disabled account doesn't show up on the login screen or in the User Accounts program, but it's still there on the hard drive, and you can bring it back when necessary.

There's no pretty Control Panel link for disabling an account; you'll have to get your hands greasy in the power-user underpinnings of Windows. See "Account is disabled" on page 732 for details.

The Guest Account

Believe it or not, Administrator and Standard aren't the only kinds of accounts you can set up on your PC.

A third kind, called the Guest account, is ideal for situations where somebody is just visiting you for the day. Rather than create an entire account for this person, complete with password, hint, little picture, and so on, you can just switch on the Guest account.

To find the on/off switch, open the Start menu and type guest; click "Turn guest account on or off" in the results list. Authenticate yourself if necessary.

In the Manage Accounts window, click Guest, and then click Turn On.

Now, when the visitor tries to log in, she can choose Guest as the account. She can use the computer but can't see anyone else's files or make any changes to your settings.

POWER USERS' CLINIC

The Other Administrator Account

This will sound confusing. But there's another kind of Administrator account—*the* Administrator account.

This is an emergency backup account with full administrator powers and *no password.* Even if you delete all your other accounts, this one still remains, if only to give you some way to get into your machine. It's called Administrator, and it's ordinarily hidden.

Most people see it only in times of troubleshooting, when they start up their PCs in Safe Mode. It's the ideal account to use in those situations. Not only does it come with no password assigned, but it's also not limited in any way. It gives you free powers over every file, which is just what you may need to troubleshoot your computer.

In Windows XP, the problem was, of course, that anyone who knew about it could get into Windows with full Administrator privileges—and no need to know a password. Your kid, for example, could blow right past your carefully established Parental Controls—and let's not even consider what a virus could do.

So in the more security-minded Windows 7, the secret Administrator account is still there. But it's ordinarily disabled. It comes to life *only* if (a) you're starting your PC in Safe Mode, and (b) there are no other, *real* Administrator accounts on the machine.

(That's on a standard home or small-office PC. On a corporate domain network, only a networking geek who's got a Domain Admins account can start up in Safe Mode. You know who you are.)

When the visitor to your office is finally out of your hair, healthy paranoia suggests that you turn off the Guest account once again. (To do so, follow precisely the same steps, except click "Turn off the guest account" in the final step.)

Authenticate Yourself: User Account Control

All Versions

You can't work in Windows 7 very long before encountering the dialog box shown in Figure 23-7. It appears any time you install a new program or try to change an important setting on your PC. (Throughout Windows, a colorful 🛡 icon next to a button or link indicates a change that will produce this message box.)

NOSTALGIA CORNER

The Secret, Fully Automatic Logon Trick

You're supposed to do most of your account-editing work in the User Accounts program of the Control Panel, which is basically a wizard that offers one option per screen. That requirement may not thrill veteran Windows 2000 fans, however, who are used to the much more direct—and more powerful—User Accounts screen.

Actually, it's still in Windows 7. To make it appear, press ⊞+R to open the Run dialog box, type out *control Userpasswords2*, authenticate yourself if necessary, and then press Enter. You see the program shown here.

Most of the functions are the same as what you'd find in the User Accounts program— it's just that you don't have to slog through several wizard screens to get things done. Here you can add, remove, or edit accounts, all in a single screen.

This older Control Panel program also offers a few features that you don't get at all in the new one. For example, you

can turn off the checkbox called, "Users must enter a user name and password to use this computer." When you do so, you get, when you click OK, a dialog box called Automatically Log On, where you can specify a user name and password of one special person. This lucky individual won't have to specify any name and password at logon time, and can instead turn on the PC and cruise directly to the desktop. (This feature works only at *startup time.* If you choose Start→Log Off, the standard Logon dialog box appears so that other people have the opportunity to sign in.)

This automatic-logon business is ordinarily a luxury enjoyed by solo operators whose PCs have only one account and no password. By using the secret User Accounts method, however, you can set up automatic logon even on a PC with several accounts, provided you recognize the security hole that it leaves open.

Clearly, Microsoft chose the name User Account Control (UAC) to put a positive spin on a fairly intrusive security feature; calling it the IYW (Interrupt Your Work) box probably wouldn't have sounded like so much fun.

Why do these boxes pop up? In the olden days, nasties like spyware and viruses could install themselves invisibly, behind your back. That's because Windows ran in *Admin-*

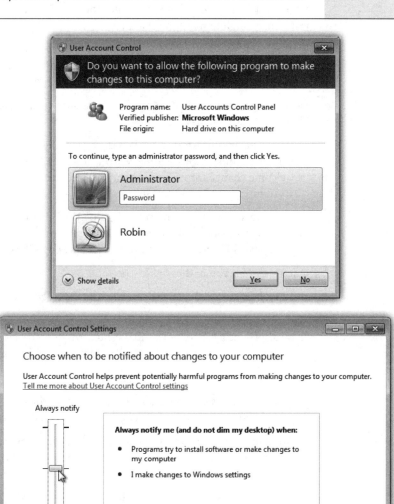

Figure 23-7:
Top: When you try to make a major change to Windows, like deleting an account or installing a new program, Windows wants to make absolutely sure that it's you and not some virus doing the changing. So it stops the show to ask for confirmation that it's you, an administrator, out there.

Bottom: This dialog box offers what amounts to a Nuisance slider; you control where Windows stands on the security/interruption continuum by dragging it up (more alarmist) or down (no interruptions at all).

istrative mode all the time, meaning it left the door open for anyone and anything to make important changes to your PC. Unfortunately, that included viruses.

Windows 7, on the other hand, runs in *Standard* mode all the time. Whenever somebody or some program wants to make a big change to your system—something that ought to have the permission of an *administrator* (page 716)—the UAC box alerts you. If you click Continue, Windows elevates (opens) the program's permissions settings just long enough to make the change.

Most of the time, *you* are the one making the changes, which can make the UAC box a bit annoying. But if that UAC dialog box ever appears by *itself*, you'll know something evil is afoot on your PC, and you'll have the chance to shut it down.

How you get past the UAC box—how you *authenticate yourself*—depends on the kind of account you have:

- **If you're an administrator,** the UAC box generally doesn't appear at all. Even when you click a link marked with a ♥ icon, you generally blow right past it. (That's a welcome change from Vista, when you'd see the UAC box for no good reason— you'd hit Enter to blow past it.)

- **If you're a Standard account holder,** the UAC dialog box requires the password of an administrator. You're supposed to call an administrator over to your desk to indicate his permission to proceed by entering his own name and password.

Questions? Yes, you in the back?

- **Why does the screen go dark around the dialog box?**

That's another security step. It's designed to prevent evil software from tricking you by displaying a *fake* Windows dialog box. Windows darkens and freezes everything on the screen except the one, true Windows dialog box: the UAC box.

- **Can I turn off the UAC interruptions?**

Well, yes. But listen: You should be grateful that they don't appear *nearly* as often as they did in Vista, where they became a profound nuisance.

All right then. If even the few remaining interruptions are too much for you, you can turn them off altogether. Open the Start menu. Type *uac;* click "Change User Account Control settings."

You get the dialog box shown at bottom in Figure 23-7. If you drag the slider all the way to the bottom, you won't be interrupted by UAC boxes at all.

This truly isn't a good idea, though. You're sending your PC right back to the days of Windows XP, when any sneaky old malware could install itself or change your system settings without your knowledge. Do this only on a PC that's not connected to a network or the Internet, for example, or maybe when you, the all-knowing system administrator, are trying to troubleshoot and the UAC interruptions are slowing you down.

Local Accounts on a Domain Computer
Professional • Enterprise • Ultimate

When your computer is a member of a corporate domain, the controls you use to create and manage user accounts are quite a bit different.

In this case, when you choose Start→Control Panel, you see a category called "User Accounts" instead of "User Accounts and Family Safety." And the option called "Add or remove user accounts" on a workgroup PC is now called "Give other users access to this computer."

When you click that option, you see the dialog box shown in Figure 23-8. The layout is different, but the idea is the same: You can see all the accounts on the computer.

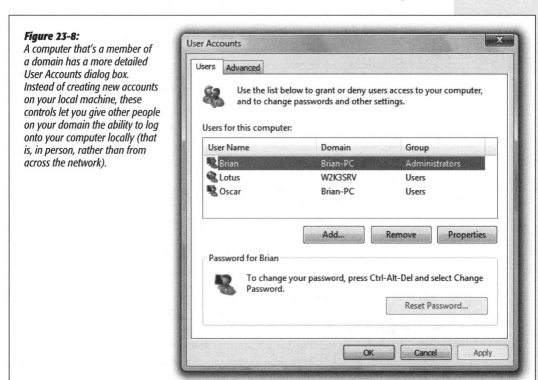

Figure 23-8:
A computer that's a member of a domain has a more detailed User Accounts dialog box. Instead of creating new accounts on your local machine, these controls let you give other people on your domain the ability to log onto your computer locally (that is, in person, rather than from across the network).

This dialog box lets you create *local* accounts—accounts stored only on your computer, and not on the corporate domain machine—for existing citizens of the domain.

Why would you need a local account, if all your files and settings are actually stored elsewhere on the network? Because certain tasks, like installing drivers for new hardware, require you to log on using a *local* Administrator account.

Note: This business of creating a local account that corresponds to an *existing domain account* isn't quite the same thing as creating a completely new account for a completely new person. For that purpose, see the following pages.

Creating a Local Account for a Domain Member

When you click the Add button (Figure 23-8), an Add New User Wizard appears. It lets you specify the person's name and the name of the domain that already stores his account. (You can also click the Browse button to search your domain for a specific person.)

When you click Next, the wizard prompts you to specify what level of access you want to grant this person. You have three choices:

- **Standard user.** This person will be allowed to change certain system settings and install programs that don't affect Windows settings for other users.

- **Administrator.** This person gets the same privileges as a local administrative user.

- **Other.** If you choose this option, you'll be allowed to specify what local *group* this person belongs to, as described later in this chapter.

Once the account you selected appears in the User Accounts list, that person is now ready to log into your PC using the local account.

Local Users and Groups

Professional • Enterprise • Ultimate

The control panels you've read about so far in this chapter are designed for simplicity and convenience, but not for power. Windows offers a second way to create, edit, and delete accounts: an alternative window that, depending on your taste for technical sophistication, is either intimidating and technical or liberating and flexible.

It's called the Local Users and Groups console.

Opening the Console

The quickest way to open up the Local Users and Groups window is to press ⊞+R to open the Run dialog box, type out *Lusrmgr.msc,* and authenticate yourself if necessary. (Microsoft swears that "Lusrmgr.msc" is *not* short for "loser manager," even though network administrators might hear that in their heads.)

The Local Users and Groups console appears, as shown in Figure 23-9.

In this console, you have complete control over the local accounts (and groups, as described in a moment) on your computer. This is the real, raw, unshielded command center, intended for power users who aren't easily frightened.

The truth is, you probably won't use these controls much on a domain computer. After all, most people's accounts live on the domain computer, not the local machine. You might occasionally have to log in using the local Administrator account to perform system maintenance and upgrade tasks, but you'll rarely have to create *new* accounts.

Workgroup computers (on a small network) are another story. Remember that you'll have to create a new account for each person who might want to use this computer—or even to access its files from across the network. If you use the Local Users and Groups console to create and edit these accounts, you have much more control over the new account holder's freedom than you do with the User Accounts control panel.

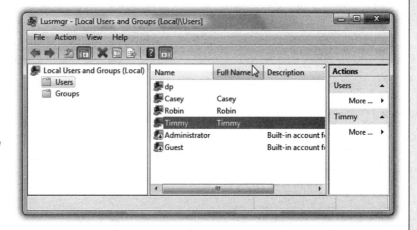

Figure 23-9:
Local Users and Groups is a Microsoft Management Console (MMC) snap-in. MMC is a shell program that lets you run most of Windows's system administration applications. An MMC snap-in typically has two panes. You select an item in the left (scope) pane to see information about it displayed in the right (detail) pane.

Creating a New Account

To create a new account in the Local Users and Groups console, start by double-clicking the Users folder in the middle of the window. It opens to show you a list of the accounts already on the machine. It includes not only the accounts you created during the Win7 installation (and thereafter), but also the Guest and secret Administrator accounts described earlier in this chapter.

To create a new account, choose Action→New User. In the New User dialog box (Figure 23-10), type a name for the account, the person's full name, and, if you like, a description. (The description can be anything you like, although Microsoft no doubt has in mind "Shipping manager" rather than "Short and balding.")

In the Password and Confirm Password text boxes, specify the password your new colleague will need to access the account. Its complexity and length are up to your innate sense of paranoia.

Tip: If you can't create a new account, it's probably because you don't have the proper privileges yourself. You must have an Administrator account (page 716) or belong to the Administrators *group* (page 733).

If you turn off the "User must change password at next logon" checkbox, then you can turn on options like these:

- **User cannot change password.** This person won't be allowed to change the password you've just made up. (Some system administrators like to maintain sole control over the account passwords on their computers.)

- **Password never expires.** Using software rules called *local security policies,* an administrator can make account passwords expire after a specific time, periodically forcing employees to make up new ones. It's a security measure designed to foil intruders who somehow get hold of the existing passwords. But if you turn on this option, the person whose account you're now creating will be able to use the same password indefinitely, no matter what the local security policy says.

Figure 23-10:
When you first create a new user, the "User must change password at next logon" checkbox is turned on. It's telling you that no matter what password you make up when creating the account, your colleague will be asked to make up a new one the first time he logs in. This way, you can assign a simple password (or no password at all) to all new accounts, but your underlings will still be free to devise passwords of their own choosing, and the accounts won't go unprotected.

- **Account is disabled.** When you turn on this box, this account holder won't be able to log on. You might use this option when, for example, somebody goes on sabbatical—it's not as drastic a step as deleting the account, because you can always reactivate the account by turning the checkbox off. You can also use this option to set up certain accounts in advance, which you then activate when the time comes by turning this checkbox off again.

Note: When an account is disabled, a circled ↓ badge appears on its icon in the Local Users and Groups console. (You may have noticed that the Guest account appears this way when you first install Windows.)

When you click the Create button, you add the new account to the console, and you make the dialog box blank again, ready for you to create another new account, if necessary. When you're finished creating accounts, click Close to return to the main console window.

Groups

As you may have guessed from its name, you can also use the Local Users and Groups window to create *groups*—named collections of account holders.

Suppose you work for a small company that uses a workgroup network. You want to be able to share various files on your computer with certain other people on the network. You'd like to be able to permit them to access some folders but not others. Smooth network operator that you are, you solve this problem by assigning *permissions* to the appropriate files and folders.

In fact, you can specify different access permissions to *each file for each person*. But if you had to set up these access privileges manually for every file on your hard drive, for every account holder on the network, you'd go out of your mind.

That's where groups come in. You can create one group—called Trusted Comrades, for example—and fill it with the names of every account holder who should be allowed to access your files. Thereafter, it's a piece of cake to give everybody in that group access to a certain folder, in one swift step. You end up having to create only one permission assignment for each file, instead of one for each *person* for each file.

Furthermore, if a new employee joins the company, you can simply add her to the group. Instantly, she has exactly the right access to the right files and folders, without your having to do any additional work.

Creating a group

To create a new group, click the Groups folder in the left side of the Local Users and Groups console (Figure 23-9). Choose Action→New Group. Into the appropriate boxes (Figure 23-11), type a name for the group, and a description, if you like. Then click Add.

Figure 23-11:
The New Group dialog box lets you specify the members of the group you're creating. A group can have any number of members, and a person can be a member of any number of groups.

A Select Users dialog box appears. Here you can specify who should be members of your new group. Type each account holder's name into the text box, separated by semicolons, and then click Check Names to make sure you spelled them right. (You can always add more members to the group, or remove them, later.)

Finally, click OK to close the dialog box, and then click Create to add the group to the list in the console. The box appears empty again, ready for you to create another group.

Built-in groups

You may have noticed that even the first time you opened the Users and Groups window, a few group names appeared there already. That's because Windows comes with a canned list of ready-made groups that Microsoft hopes will save you some time.

For example, when you use the User Accounts control panel program to set up a new account, Windows automatically places that person into the Standard or Administrators group, depending on whether or not you made him an administrator (page 716). In fact, that's how Windows knows what powers and freedom this person is supposed to have.

Here are some of the built-in groups on a Windows 7 computer:

- **Administrators.** Members of the Administrators group have complete control over every aspect of the computer. They can modify any setting, create or delete accounts and groups, install or remove any software, and modify or delete any file.

  But as Spider-Man's uncle might say, with great power comes great responsibility. Administrator powers make it possible to screw up your operating system in thousands of major and minor ways, either on purpose or by accident. That's why it's a good idea to keep the number of Administrator accounts to a minimum—and even to avoid using one for everyday purposes yourself.

Note: The Power Users group was a big deal in Windows XP. Power Users had fewer powers than Administrators, but still more than mere mortals in the Users group. But Microsoft felt that they added complexity and represented yet another potential security hole. In Win7, this group is essentially abandoned.

- **Users.** Standard account holders (page 716) are members of this group. They can access their own Start menu and desktop settings, their own Documents folder, the Shared Documents folder, and whatever folders they create themselves—but they can't change any computer-wide settings, Windows system files, or program files.

  If you're a member of this group, you can install new programs—but you'll be the only one who can use them. That's by design; any problems introduced by that program (viruses, for example) are limited to your files and not spread to the whole system.

  If you're the administrator, it's a good idea to put most new account holders into this group.

- **Guests.** If you're in this group, you have pretty much the same privileges as members of the Users group. You lose only a few nonessential perks, like the ability to read the computer's *system event log* (a record of behind-the-scenes technical happenings).

In addition to these basic groups, there are some special-purpose groups like Backup Operators, Replicator, Cryptographic Operators, Event Log Readers, and so on. These are all groups with specialized privileges, designed for high-end network administration. You can double-click one (or widen its Description column) to read all about it.

Note: You can add an individual account to as many groups as you like. That person will have the accumulated rights and privileges of all of those groups.

Modifying Users and Groups

To edit an account or group, just double-click its name in the Local Users and Groups window. A Properties dialog box appears, as shown in Figure 23-12.

Figure 23-12:
In the Properties dialog box for a user account, you can change the full name or description, modify the password options, and add this person to, or remove this person from, a group. The Properties dialog box for a group is simpler still, containing only a list of the group's members.

You can also change an account password by right-clicking the name and choosing Set Password from the shortcut menu. (But see page 724 for some cautions about this process.)

Fast User Switching

Home Premium • Professional • Enterprise • Ultimate

Suppose you're signed in and you've got things just the way you like them. You have 11 programs open in carefully arranged windows, your Web browser is downloading some gigantic file, and you're composing an important speech in Microsoft Word. Now Robin, a coworker/family member/fellow student, wants to duck in to do a quick email check.

In the old days, you might have rewarded Robin with eye-rolling and heavy sighs, or worse. If you chose to accommodate the request, you would have had to shut down your whole ecosystem—interrupting the download, closing your windows, saving your work, and exiting your programs. You would have had to log off completely.

Thanks to Fast User Switching, however, none of that is necessary. All you have to do is press the magic keystroke, ⊞+L (which locks the screen), and then click Switch User. (Maybe it's more direct to just choose Start→"Shut down"→"Switch user.")

Now the list of accounts appears (Figure 23-13), ready for the next person to sign in.

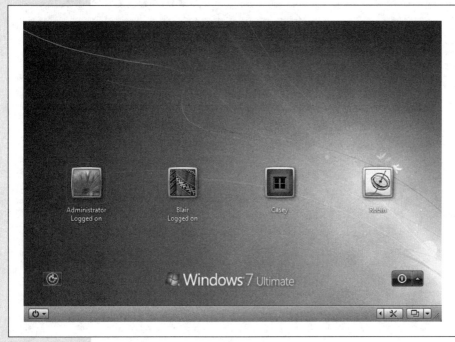

Figure 23-13:
At this moment, you have several alternatives. If you click the ⊙ button (lower-right corner of the screen), you can make the computer turn off, restart, sleep, and so on—maybe because you're in a sudden panic over the amount of work you have to do. Or you can just log in.

The words "Logged on" beneath your name indicate that you haven't actually logged off. Instead, Windows has *memorized* the state of affairs in your account—complete with all open windows, documents, and programs—and shoved it into the background.

Robin can now click the Robin button to sign in normally, do a little work, or look something up. When Robin logs out, the accounts screen comes back once again, at which point *you* can log on again. Without having to wait more than a couple of seconds, you find yourself exactly where you began, with all your programs and documents still open and running—an enormous timesaver.

Logging On
All Versions

When it comes to the screens you encounter when you log onto a Windows computer, your mileage may vary. What you see depends on how your PC has been set up. For example:

You Get the Accounts Screen

This is what people on standalone or workgroup computers see most of the time (Figure 23-13).

To sign in, click your account name in the list. If no password is required for your account, you proceed to your Windows desktop with no further interruption.

If there *is* a password associated with your account, you see a place for it. Type your password and then press Enter (or click the blue arrow button).

There's no limit to the number of times you can try to type in a password. With each incorrect guess, you're told, "The user name or password is incorrect," and an OK button appears to let you try again. The second time you try, your *password hint* appears, too (page 720).

Tip: If your Caps Lock key is pressed, another balloon lets you know. Otherwise, because you can't see anything on the screen as you type except dots, you might be trying to type a lowercase password with all capital letters.

You Zoom Straight to the Desktop

If you're the *only* account holder, and you've set up no password for yourself, you can cruise all the way to the desktop without any stops. The setup steps appear in the box on page 726

This password-free scenario, of course, is not very secure; any evildoer who walks by your machine when you're in the bathroom has complete access to all your files (and protected Web sites). But if you work in a home office, for example, where the threat of privacy invasion isn't very great, it's by far the most convenient arrangement.

You Get the "Press Ctrl-Alt-Delete to Begin" Dialog Box

You or your friendly network geek has added your PC to a domain while installing Windows 7 and activated the "Require Users to Press Ctrl-Alt-Delete" option. This is the most secure configuration, and also the least convenient.

Tip: Even when you're looking at the standard, friendly Accounts screen (Figure 23-13), you can switch to the older, Classic logon screen: Just press Ctrl+Alt+Delete. (If you're having trouble making it work, try pressing down the Alt key *before* the other ones.)

You may be used to using the Ctrl+Alt+Delete keystroke for summoning the box where you can open the Task Manager or lock your computer; but at the Accounts screen, it means something else entirely.

Profiles
All Versions

As you've read earlier in this chapter, every document, icon, and preference setting related to your account resides in a single folder: By default, it's the one bearing your name in the Local Disk (C:)→Users folder. This folder's friendly name is your Personal folder, but to network geeks, it's known as your *user profile*.

The Public Profile

Each account holder has a user profile. But your PC also has a couple of profiles that aren't linked to human beings' accounts.

Have you ever noticed, for example, that not everything you actually see in your Start menu and on your desktop is, in fact, in *your* user profile folder?

Part of the solution to this mystery is the Public profile, which also lurks in the Users folder (Figure 23-14). As you can probably tell by its name, this folder stores many of the same kinds of settings your profile folder does—except that anything in (C:) →Users→Public→Desktop appears on *everybody's* desktop.

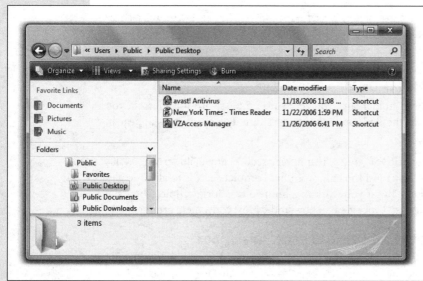

Figure 23-14:
Behind the scenes, Windows maintains another profile folder, whose subfolders closely parallel those in your own. What you see—the contents of the Desktop, Documents folder, Favorites list, and so on—is a combination of what's in your own user profile folder and what's in the Public folder.

All of this is a long-winded way of suggesting another way to make some icon available to everybody with an account on your machine. Drag it into the Desktop folder in the Public profile folder.

But if you're wondering where the common Start menu items are, you'll have to look somewhere else. If you're prowling around your hard drive, you'll find them in (C:)→ ProgramData→Microsoft→Windows→Start Menu. But the ProgramData folder is ordinarily hidden, so here's a faster way: Open the Start menu, right-click All Programs, and then choose Open All Users.

Whose software is it, anyway?

These locations also offer a handy solution to the "Whose software is it, anyway?" conundrum, the burning question of whose Start menu and desktop reflect new software that you've installed using your own account.

As noted in Chapter 6, some software installers ask if you'd like the new program to show up only in your Start menu, or in *everybody's* Start menu. But not every installer is this thoughtful. Some installers automatically deposit their new software into the ProgramData and Public folders, thereby making its Start menu and desktop icons available to everybody when they log on.

On the other hand, some installers may deposit a new software program only into *your* account (or that of whoever is logged in at the moment). In that case, other account holders won't be able to use the program at all, even if they know it's been installed, because their own Start Menu and Desktop folders won't reflect the installation. Worse, some people, not seeing the program's name on their Start menus, might not realize that you've already installed it—and may well install it *again*.

One possible solution is to open the Start Menu→Programs folder in your user profile folder (open the Start menu, right-click All Programs, and choose Open). Copy the newly installed icon, and then paste it into the "everybody" profile folder (open the Start menu, right-click All Programs, and then choose Open All Users.)

Repeat with the Desktop folder, if you'd like everyone to see a desktop icon for the new program. To open the shared desktop folder, open (C:)→Users→Public→Desktop. (You'll have to make the Desktop folder visible first—see "Show hidden files, folders, and drives" on page 99—and then make it invisible again afterward.) You've just made that software available and visible to everybody who logs onto the computer.

The Default User Profile

When you create a new account, who decides what the desktop picture will be—and the Start menu configuration, the assortment of desktop icons, and so on?

Well, Microsoft does, of course—but you can change all that. What a newly created account holder sees is only a reflection of the Default user profile. It's yet another folder—this one usually hidden—in your (C:)→Users folder, and it's the common starting point for all profiles.

If you'd like to make some changes to that starting point, turn on "Show hidden files, folders, and drives" (page 99). Then open the (C:)→Users→Default folder, and make whatever changes you like.

NTFS Permissions: Protecting Your Stuff
All Versions

There's one final aspect of user accounts that's worth mentioning: *NTFS permissions,* a technology that's a core part of Windows 7's security system. Using this feature, you can specify exactly which coworkers are allowed to open which files and folders on your machine. In fact, you can also specify *how much* access each person has. You can dictate, for example, that Gomez and Morticia aren't allowed to open your Fourth-Quarter Projections spreadsheet at all, that Fred and Ginger can open it but not make changes, and George and Gracie can both open it and make changes.

Your colleagues will encounter the permissions you've set up like this in two different situations: when tapping into your machine from across the network, or when sitting down at it and logging in using their own names and passwords. In either case, the NTFS permissions you set up protect your files and folders equally well.

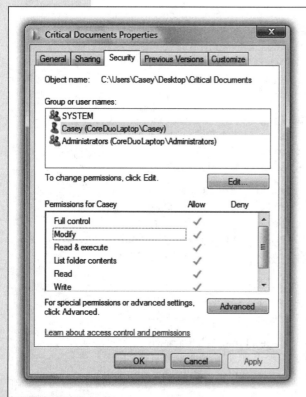

Figure 23-15:
The Security tab of an NTFS folder's Properties dialog box. If you have any aspirations to be a Windows power user, get used to this dialog box. You're going to see it a lot, because almost every icon on a Windows system—files, folders, disks, printers—has a Security tab like this one.

Tip: In Chapter 26, you can read about a very similar form of access privileges called *share permissions.* There's a big difference between share permissions and the NTFS permissions described here, though: Share permissions keep people out of your stuff only when they try to access your PC from *over the network.*

Actually, there are other differences, too. NTFS permissions offer more gradations of access. And using NTFS permissions, you can declare individual *files*—not just folders—accessible or inaccessible to specific coworkers. See page 740 for details.

Using NTFS permissions is most decidedly a power-user technique because of the added complexity it introduces. Entire books have been written on the topic of NTFS permissions alone.

You've been warned.

Setting Up NTFS Permissions

To change the permissions for an NTFS file or folder, you open its Properties dialog box by right-clicking its icon and then choosing Properties from the shortcut menu. Click the Security tab (Figure 23-15).

Step 1: Specify the person

The top of the Security tab lists the people and groups that have been granted or denied permissions to the selected file or folder. When you click a name in the list, the Permissions box at the bottom of the dialog box shows you how much access that person or group has.

The first step in assigning permissions, then, is to click Edit. You see an editable version of the dialog box shown in Figure 23-15.

If the person or group isn't listed, click the Add button to display the Select Users or Groups dialog box, where you can type them in (Figure 23-16).

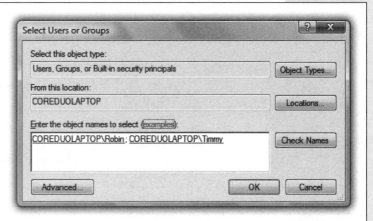

Figure 23-16:
Type the names of the people or groups in the "Enter the object names to select" box at the bottom, trying not to feel depersonalized by Microsoft's reference to you as an "object." If you're adding more than one name, separate them with semicolons. Because remembering exact spellings can be iffy, click Check Names to confirm that these are indeed legitimate account holders. Finally, click OK to insert them into the list on the Security tab.

Tip: Instead of typing in names one at a time, as shown in Figure 23-16, you can also choose them from a list, which lets you avoid spelling mistakes and having to guess at the variations. To do so, click the Advanced button to display an expanded version of the dialog box, and then click Find Now to search for all the accounts and groups on the computer. Finally, in the resulting list, click the names of the people and groups you want to add (Ctrl+click to select more than one at a time). Click OK to add them to the previous dialog box, and then click OK again to add the selected users and groups to the Security tab.

If you've used Windows 2000, you might wonder why this process is so much more convoluted in Windows 7. The answer is: Good question!

Step 2: Specify the permissions

Once you've added the users and groups you need to the list on the Security tab, you can highlight each one and set permissions for it. You do that by turning on the Allow or Deny checkboxes at the bottom half of the dialog box.

The different degrees of freedom break down as follows (they're listed here from least to most control, even though that's not how they're listed in the dialog box):

- **List folder contents,** available only for folders, means that the selected individuals can see (but not necessarily open) the files and folders inside. That may sound obvious—but believe it or not, if you *don't* turn on this option, the affected people won't even be able to see what's in this folder. The folder will just appear empty.

- **Read** lets people examine the contents of the file or folder, but not make changes. (They can also examine the permissions settings of these files and folders—the ones you're setting up right now.)

- **Read & Execute** is a lot like Read, except that it also lets people run any programs they find inside the affected folder. When applied to a folder, furthermore, this permission adds the ability to *traverse* folders. (Traversing means directly opening inner folders even when you're not allowed to open the outer folder. You might get

---

INFREQUENTLY ASKED QUESTION

Allow vs. Deny

Why do I see both Allow and Deny checkboxes in the Permissions dialog box? Isn't not allowing permission the same as denying it?

In this case, no. "Deny" permissions always take precedence over "Allow" permissions.

For example, if somebody has been granted access to a file or folder because he's a member of a group, you can explicitly revoke his permission by using the Deny checkboxes for his

account. You've just overridden the group permission, just for him, leaving the rest of the group's permissions intact.

You can also use the Deny checkboxes to override permissions granted by *inheritance* from a parent folder. For example, you can grant somebody access to the C: drive by sharing it and assigning her Allow permissions to it, but then prevent her from accessing the C:\Program Files folder by sharing that and *denying* her permission.

---

to an inner folder by double-clicking a shortcut icon, for example, or by typing the folder's path into the address bar of a window.)

- **Write** is like Read, but adds the freedom to make and save changes to the file. When applied to a folder, this permission means that people can create new files and folders inside it.

- **Modify** includes all the abilities of the Write and Read & Execute levels, plus the ability to *delete* the file or folder.

- **Full control** confers complete power over the file or folder. The selected person or group can do anything they like with it, including trashing it or its contents, changing its permissions, taking ownership of it (away from you, if they like), and so on.

Of course, turning on Allow grants that level of freedom to the specified user or group, and turning it off takes away that freedom. (For details on the Deny checkbox, see the box on the facing page.)

Note: If you're not careful, it's entirely possible to "orphan" a file or folder (or even your entire drive) by revoking everyone's permission to it, even your own, making it *completely* inaccessible by anyone. That's why, before you get too deeply into working with NTFS permissions, you might consider creating an extra user account on your system and granting it full control for all your drives, just in case something goes wrong.

Groups and Permissions

Once you understand the concept of permissions, and you've enjoyed a thorough shudder contemplating the complexity of a network administrator's job (six levels of permissions × thousands of files × thousands of employees = way too many permutations), one other mystery of Windows will fully snap into focus: the purpose of *groups*, introduced on page 733.

On those pages, you can read about groups as canned categories, complete with predefined powers over the PC, into which you can put different individuals to save yourself the time of adjusting their permissions and privileges individually. As it turns out, each of the ready-made groups also comes with predefined *permissions* over the files and folders on your hard drive.

Here, for example, is how the system grants permissions to the items in your Windows folder for the Users and Administrators groups:

	Users	Administrators
Full control		X
Modify		X
Read & Execute	X	X
List folder contents	X	X
Read	X	X
Write		X

If you belong to the Users group, you have the List Folder Contents permission, which means you can see what's in the Windows folder; the Read permission, which means you can open up anything you find inside; and the Read & Execute permission, which means you can run programs in that folder (which is essential for Windows itself to run). But people in the Users group aren't allowed to change or delete anything in the Windows folder, or to put anything else inside. Windows is protecting itself against the mischievous and the clueless.

Members of the Administrators group have all those abilities and more—they also have Modify and Write permissions, which let them add new files and folders to the Windows folder (so that, for example, they can install a new software program on the machine).

When Permissions Collide

If you successfully absorbed all this information about permissions, one thing should be clear: People in the Administrators group ought to be able to change or delete any file in your Windows folder. After all, they have the Modify permission, which ought to give them that power.

In fact, they can move or delete anything in any folder *in* the Windows folder, because the first cardinal rule of NTFS permissions is this:

NTFS permissions travel downstream, from outer folders to inner ones.
In other words, if you have the Modify and Write permissions to a folder, then you ought to have the same permissions for every file and folder inside it.

But in Windows XP, there was something called the Power Users group. It's been turned off in Windows 7, but for the sake of illustration, let's say you're part of it. You'd find that you can't, in fact, delete any files or folders in the Windows folder. That's because each of them comes with Modify and Write permissions turned *off* for Power Users, even though the folder that encloses them has those permissions turned on.

Why would Microsoft go to this trouble? Because it wanted to prevent people in this group from inadvertently changing or deleting important Windows files—and yet it wanted these people to be able to put *new* files into the Windows folder, so they can install new programs.

This is a perfect example of the second cardinal rule of NTFS permissions:

NTFS permissions that have been explicitly applied to a file or folder always override inherited permissions.
Here's another example: Suppose your sister, the technical whiz of the household, has given you Read, Write, Modify, Read & Execute, and List Folder Contents permissions to her own Documents folder. Now you can read, change, or delete any file there. But she can still protect an individual document or folder *inside* her Documents folder—the BirthdayPartyPlans.doc file, for example—by denying you all permissions to it. You'll be able to open anything else in there, but not that file.

Believe it or not, NTFS permissions get even more complicated, thanks to the third cardinal rule:

Permissions accumulate as you burrow downward through subfolders.

Now suppose your sister has given you the Read and List Folder Contents permissions to her Documents folder—a "look, but don't touch" policy. Thanks to the first cardinal rule, you automatically get the same permissions to every file and folder *inside* Documents.

Suppose one of these inner folders is called Grocery Lists. If she grants you the Modify and Write permissions to the Grocery Lists folder so you can add items to the shopping list, you end up having Read, Modify, *and* Write permissions for every file in that folder. Those files have *accumulated* permissions—they got the Read permission from Documents, and the Modify and Write permissions from the Grocery Lists folder.

Because these layers of inherited permissions can get dizzyingly complex, Microsoft has prepared for you a little cheat sheet, a dialog box that tells you the bottom line, the net result—the *effective* permissions. To see it, follow these steps:

1. **Click the Advanced button on the Security tab.**

   The Advanced Security Settings dialog box appears.

2. **Click the Effective Permissions tab; click Select.**

   Now you see the same Select User or Group dialog box you saw earlier when you were creating permissions.

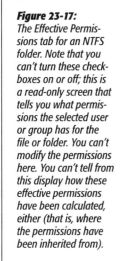

Figure 23-17:
The Effective Permissions tab for an NTFS folder. Note that you can't turn these checkboxes on or off; this is a read-only screen that tells you what permissions the selected user or group has for the file or folder. You can't modify the permissions here. You can't tell from this display how these effective permissions have been calculated, either (that is, where the permissions have been inherited from).

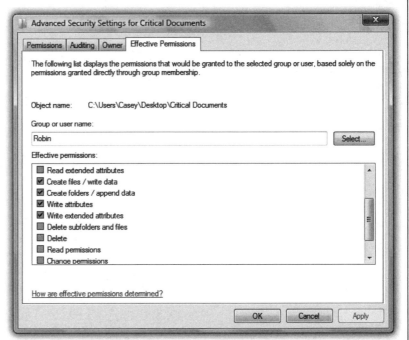

3. Click the user or group whose effective permissions you want to see, and then click OK.

You now see checkmarks next to the permissions that are in effect, taking into account folder-permission inheritance and all other factors, for the user or group of that particular file or folder (Figure 23-17).

Setting Up a Workgroup

I t's a rare Windows machine indeed that isn't connected, sooner or later, to some kind of network (known to nerds as a *local area network,* or *LAN*). And no wonder: The payoff is considerable. Once you've created a network, you can copy files from one machine to another just as you'd drag files between folders on your own PC. You can store your music or photo files on one computer and play them on any other. Everyone on the network can consult the same database, phone book, or calendar. When the workday's done, you can play games over the network.

Most importantly, you can share a single printer, cable modem or DSL Internet connection, fax modem, or phone line among all the PCs in the house.

If you work at a biggish company, you probably work on a *domain network,* which is described in Chapter 25. You, lucky thing, won't have to fool around with building or designing a network, because your job, and your PC, presumably came with a fully functioning network (and a fully functioning geek responsible for running it).

If you work at home, or if you're responsible for setting up a network in a smaller office, this chapter is for you. It guides you through the construction of a less formal *workgroup network,* which ordinary mortals can put together.

You'll soon discover that, when it comes to simplicity, setting up a network has a long way to go before it approaches, say, setting up a desk lamp. It involves buying equipment, hooking up (or even installing) network adapter cards, and configuring software.

But in Windows 7, there's some terrific news on this front. A new feature called *HomeGroups* makes the setup incredibly fast and easy—*if* all your PCs are running Windows 7, and *if* you have no particular need to keep your music, photo, and video collections private from the rest of your family members.

If not, you can still use the networking methods that were refined back in Windows Vista. They'll take you an afternoon to set up and understand—but they've come a long way since Windows XP.

Kinds of Networks
All Versions

You can connect your PCs using any of several different kinds of gear. Many of the world's offices are wired with *Ethernet cable,* but, as you probably know, wireless networks are very popular for small offices and homes. Here and there, a few renegades are even installing networking systems that rely on the phone or power lines already in the walls. Here's an overview of the most popular networking systems.

Note: Be sure that whatever networking gear you buy is compatible with Windows 7, either by checking logos on the package or by checking the maker's Web site. Networking is complicated enough without having to troubleshoot some gadget that's not designed for Win7.

Ethernet

Ethernet is the world's most popular networking protocol. It gives you fast, reliable, cheap, trouble-free communication. All you need are three components:

- **Network adapters.** An Ethernet jack is built into virtually every Windows 7-compatible PC ever made. That's your *network adapter*—the circuitry that provides the Ethernet jack (Figure 24-1). You may also hear a network adapter called a *network interface card* or NIC ("nick").

  In the freakish event that your desktop PC doesn't have an Ethernet jack, you can add one—as an internal card, an external USB attachment, or a laptop card.

- **A router.** If you have a cable modem or DSL connection to the Internet, a *router* (about $60) distributes that Internet signal to all the computers on your network. (The dialog boxes in Windows call these devices *gateways,* although almost no one else does.)

  Routers with five or eight ports (that is, Ethernet jacks where you can plug in computers) are popular in homes and small offices.

  It's worth noting that you can inexpensively expand your network by plugging a *hub* or *switch* into one of the router's jacks. Hubs and switches are similar-looking little boxes that offer *another* five or eight Ethernet jacks, connecting all your computers together. (A *switch* is more intelligent than a hub. It's more selective when sending data to the right PCs on your network; as a result, the bits and bytes move a little faster.)

Tip: There's also such a thing as a *wireless* router, which offers both physical Ethernet jacks and wireless antennas that broadcast the signal throughout your place.

To set up a router, plug it into your cable or DSL modem using an Ethernet cable. Restart the cable modem. Now use whatever software came with the router to set up its security features. Often, the software is actually built into the *router;* you're supposed to view it by opening up a special page in your Web browser, of all things.

The router then logs onto your Internet service and stands ready to transmit Internet data to and from all the computers on your network.

As a bonus, the router provides excellent security, serving as a firewall that isolates your network computers from the Internet and keeps out hackers. (See Chapter 10 for much more on firewalls.)

Figure 24-1:
Top: The Ethernet cable is connected to a computer at one end, and the router (shown here) at the other end. The computers communicate through the router; there's no direct connection between any two computers. The front of the router has little lights for each connector port, which light up only on the ports in use. You can watch the lights flash as the computers communicate with one another.

Bottom: Here's what a typical "I've got three PCs in the house, and I'd like them to share my cable modem" setup might look like.

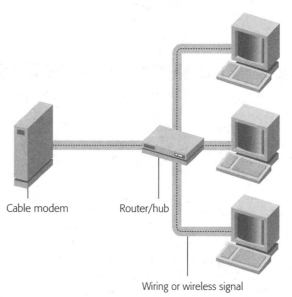

Cable modem   Router/hub

Wiring or wireless signal

- **Ethernet cables.** The cables used for most Ethernet networks look something like telephone cables, but they're not the same thing—and they're definitely not interchangeable! Both the cable itself (called *10BaseT, 100BaseT,* or *Cat 5*) and the little clips at each end (*RJ-45* connectors) are slightly fatter than those on a phone cable (Figure 24-1). You can buy Ethernet cables in a variety of lengths and colors. Each computer must be connected to the hub, switch, or router with a cable that's no longer than about 100 yards.

> **Tip:** If you've got a computer that sits in one place, like a desktop PC, you should use an Ethernet cable even if you have a wireless network.
>
> One reason is security (wired networks are harder for the baddies to "sniff"). Another is speed. Yes, wireless technologies like 802.11n promise speeds of 300 megabits per second, which is very, very fast. But first of all, the real-world speed is about a third of that; second, that speed is shared among all computers on the network. As a result, if you're copying a big file across the network, it will probably go twice as fast if it's going between one wireless and one wired PC than between two wireless PCs.

Ethernet gear can be shockingly inexpensive; a search at *www.buy.com*, for example, reveals five-port Ethernet hubs for $30 from no-name companies. If you're willing to pay slightly more—$20 for the card, $50 for the hub, for example—you can get brand-name gear (like D-Link, NETGEAR, 3Com, or Linksys) whose support with installation, phone help, and driver updates through the years may reward you many times over. Setting up an Ethernet network generally goes very smoothly, but in the few cases where trouble arises, cheapo equipment is often the problem.

Network hookups

On paper, the hardware part of setting up the network is simple: Just connect each computer to the router or hub using an Ethernet cable.

UP TO SPEED

Network Devices Have Speed Limits

Ethernet cards and hubs are available in different speeds. The most common are *10BaseT* (10 megabits per second, or Mbps) and *100BaseT* (100 Mbps, sometimes cleverly called *Fast Ethernet*).

Note, however, that the speed of the network has no effect on your computers' *Internet* speed—Web surfing, email downloading, and so on. The reason: Even the slowest network operates far faster than your Internet connection. Remember, the top speed of a typical broadband Internet connection is around 5 or 10 megabits per second—still five to 10 times slower than the *slowest* home network.

So why does a faster network matter? Primarily to save time when you're transferring big files between the PCs on the network. For example, you can play MP3 music files stored on another computer over a 10BaseT connection with no problems at all. However, if you plan to install video cameras all around your palatial estate and want to watch all the video feeds simultaneously, opt for Fast Ethernet—or even Gigabit Ethernet, the current Ethernet speed champ at 1,000 Mbps.

The bottom line? As you shop for gear, you may as well go for the higher speeds so you'll be ready for any high-bandwidth application that comes down the pike.

It's that "using an Ethernet cable" part that sometimes gets sticky. Depending on where your PCs are and how concerned you are about the network's appearance, this wiring process may involve drilling holes in floors or walls, stapling cables to baseboard trim, or calling in an electrician to do the job.

When all your computers are in the same room, you can run the cables along the walls and behind the furniture. (Buying cables that are the same color as your walls or floors can help hide the installation.) If you have to run cables between rooms, you can secure the cables to the floor or baseboards using staples—use the round kind that won't crush the cables—or plastic "raceways" with adhesive backing.

Of course, you might not be thrilled about having *any* exposed cables in your home or office. In that case, the installation process can be much more complicated. You should probably hire a professional cable installer to do the job—or don't use cables at all. Read on.

Wireless Networks (WiFi or 802.11)

So far, this discussion has focused on using wired Ethernet to hook up your computers. Millions of people, however, have embraced the flexibility of *WiFi* (802.11), a *wireless* networking system. (Your Macintosh friends probably call the same thing *AirPort*, because that's what Apple calls it.)

Every laptop sold today has a WiFi antenna built in. You can also add it to a desktop in the form of a wireless card or USB adapter. Once all your equipment is wireless, that's it: Your PCs can now communicate with one another.

To get onto an *existing* wireless network, follow the steps on page 346.

But if you want your *own* wireless network, right there in your own home or office, you also need a *wireless router* (about $50)—a box that connects to your router or hub and broadcasts the Internet signal to the whole building. The usual suspects— Linksys, NETGEAR, D-Link, and others—sell these routers. They're also called base stations or access points.

Now, 802.11 equipment has a range of about 150 feet, even through walls. In concept, this setup works much like a cordless phone, where the base station is plugged into the wall phone jack and a wireless handset can talk to it from anywhere in the house.

Wireless networking is not without its downsides, however. You may get intermittent service interruptions from 2.4-gigahertz cordless phones and other machinery, or even the weather. Furthermore, big metal things, or walls *containing* big metal things (like pipes) can interfere with communication among the PCs, much to the disappointment of people who work in subways and meat lockers.

A wireless network isn't as secure as a cabled network, either. It's theoretically possible for some hacker, sitting nearby, armed with "sniffing" software, to intercept the email you're sending or the Web page you're downloading. (Except secure Web sites, those marked by a little padlock in your Web browser.)

Still, nothing beats the freedom of wireless networking, particularly if you're a laptop lover; you can set up shop almost anywhere in the house or in the yard, slumped into any kind of rubbery posture. No matter where you go within your home, you're online at full speed, without hooking up a single wire.

Other Kinds of Networks

There are a couple of other network types that are worth looking into. Both are wired networks, but they use the wires you already have.

Phone line networks

Instead of going to the trouble of wiring your home with Ethernet cables, you might consider using the wiring that's already *in* your house—telephone wiring. That's the idea behind a kind of networking gear called HomePNA. With this system, you can use the network even when using the modem or talking on the phone, although you can't make a modem and a voice call simultaneously.

Unfortunately, the average American household has only two or three phone jacks in the *entire house*, meaning you don't have much flexibility in positioning your PCs.

UP TO SPEED

802.11 Networks: Regular or Supersized?

Wireless gear comes in several flavors, each offering different degrees of speed, distance, and compatibility. They have such appetizing-sounding names as 802.11b, 802.11a, 802.11g, and 802.11n.

So what's the difference? Equipment bearing the "b" label transfers data through the air at up to 11 megabits per second; the "g" system is almost five times as fast. (Traditionally, geeks measure network speeds in megabits, not megabytes. Here's a translation: The older "b" gear has a top speed of 1.4 megabytes per second, versus more than 6 megabytes per second for the "a" and "g" stuff. Remember, though, you'll usually get around half that speed. Your wireless network uses a lot of the bandwidth for such network housekeeping chores as correcting transmission errors.)

The beauty of 802.11g gear, though, is that it's backward-compatible with the older "b" gear. If your laptop has an 802.11b card, you can hop onto an 802.11g base station simultaneously with people using "g" cards. And if you have an 802.11g card, you can hop onto older base stations. You won't get better speed, of course, but at least you won't need a separate base station.

The current standard is 802.11n, which offers better speed *and* better range than its predecessors (thanks to multiple antennas). Remember, though, you won't get the better speed unless *both* your base station *and* your networking cards speak "n."

Faster equipment doesn't speed up your email and Web activity, though. A cable modem or DSL box delivers Internet information at a fraction of the speed of your home or office network. The bottleneck is the Internet connection, not your network.

Instead, the speed boost you get with "g" gear is useful only for transferring files among computers on your own network, streaming video or audio between computers (or PCs and your TV), and playing networked games.

Finally, the great thing about wireless networking is that it all works together, no matter what kind of computer you have. There's no such thing as an "Apple" wireless network or a "Windows" wireless network. All computers work with any kind of access point.

If you're trying to avoid the plaster-dust experience of installing additional wiring, consider WiFi or Powerline networking.

Power outlet networks

Here's another way to connect your computers without rewiring the building: Use the electrical wiring that's already in your walls. Unlike phone jacks, electrical outlets are usually available in every room in the house.

If you buy *Powerline adapters* (also called HomePlug adapters), you get very fast speeds (from 14 up to 100 Mbps), very good range (1,000 feet, although that includes the twists and turns your wiring takes within the walls), and the ultimate in installation simplicity. You just plug the Powerline adapter from your PC's Ethernet or USB jack into any wall power outlet. Presto—all the PCs are connected.

Powerline adapters are inexpensive (about $40 apiece) and extremely convenient.

Sharing an Internet Connection
All Versions

If you have high-speed Internet service, like a cable modem or DSL, you're a very lucky individual. Not only do you get spectacular speed when surfing the Web or doing email, but you also have a full-time connection. You never have to manually connect or disconnect.

But you'd be nuts to confine that glorious connection to *one* PC. Share it! Make it available to the whole house!

Your broadband company probably supplied you with a router (probably both wireless and wired) that shares the Internet connection with more than one computer. If not, there are two ways to do it yourself.

UP TO SPEED

PC-to-PC Micronetworks

If your network has modest ambitions—that is, if you have only two computers you want to connect—you can ignore all this business about hubs, routers, and wiring. Instead, you can create a tiny, two-computer wireless network between them.

These so-called ad hoc networks are great when you want to grab a folder full of files from a friend on a plane, for example. (You can't create a wired ad-hoc network anymore, using an Ethernet crossover cable—only wireless.)

To bring about this arrangement, open the Network and Sharing Center. (Quickest way: Click the ⊿ or 🖳 icon on your system tray; from the shortcut menu, choose Open Network and Sharing Center.)

Click "Set up a new connection or network." On the next screen, click "Set up a wireless ad hoc (computer-to-computer) network." Windows walks you through the steps to set up the connection.

Get a Broadband Router

As noted earlier, a router (a *gateway* in Microsoft lingo) is a little box, about $60, that connects directly to the cable modem or DSL box. It generally doubles as a hub, providing multiple Ethernet jacks to accommodate your wired PCs, plus WiFi antennas that broadcast to your wireless PCs. The Internet signal is automatically shared among all the PCs on your home network.

Use Internet Connection Sharing

Internet Connection Sharing (ICS) is a built-in Windows feature that *simulates* a router. Like a hardware router, ICS distributes a single Internet connection to every computer on the network—but unlike a router, it's free. You just fire it up on the *one* PC that's connected directly to your cable modem or DSL box—or, as networking geeks would say, the *gateway* or *host* PC.

But there's a downside: If the gateway PC is turned off or goes into Sleep mode, nobody else in the house can go online.

Also, the gateway PC requires *two* network connections: one that goes to the cable modem or DSL box, and another that connects it your network. It might be two Ethernet cards, two WiFi cards, or—most commonly of all, especially for laptops—one Ethernet and one WiFi card. One connects to the Internet (for example, via a cable modem, DSL box, or WiFi), and the other goes to the hub or the router to distribute the signal to the other computers.

If you decide to use Internet Connection Sharing, start by making sure the gateway PC can already get onto the Internet on its own.

Open the Network and Sharing Center (for example, click the ▂▃ or 💻 icon on your system tray, and choose "Open Network and Sharing Center.") At left, click "Manage network connections."

Right-click the icon of the network connection you want to share. From the shortcut menu, choose Properties. Authenticate yourself if necessary, and then click the Sharing tab. Finally, turn on "Allow other network users to connect through this computer's Internet connection," shown in Figure 24-2, and click OK.

Thereafter, other computers on the network can share the gateway PC's Internet connection, even if they're running earlier versions of Windows, or even Mac OS X and Linux. In fact, they don't need to be computers at all: You can use ICS to share your Internet connection with a video game console, palmtop, or smartphone.

Tip: If you've created a VPN (virtual private network) on the gateway machine (page 803), *all* the PCs sharing the Internet connection can get onto the corporate network!

And now the fine print:

- Internet Connection Sharing doesn't work with domain networks, DNS servers, gateways, or DHCP servers (you know who you are, network geeks).

- The "receiving" PCs (the ones that will share the connection) can't have static (fixed) IP addresses. (You'll know if you have one, because you're the one who set it up.)

Figure 24-2:
Internet Connection Sharing lets you broadcast your cable modem/DSL's signal to all the grateful, connectionless computers in the house. Your savings: the price of a hardware router.

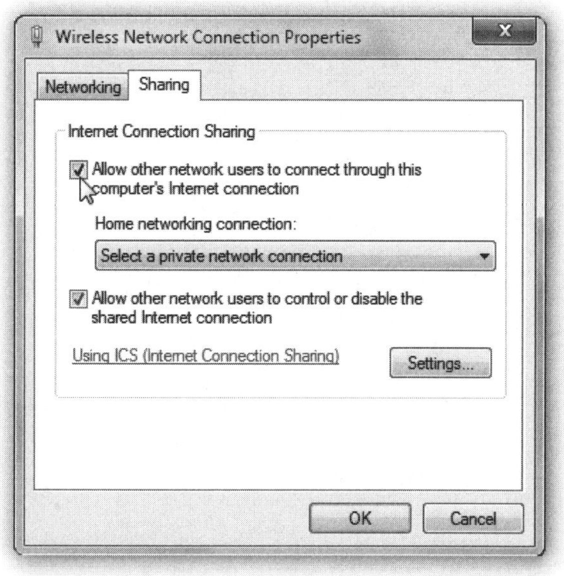

The Network and Sharing Center
All Versions

Once you've set up the networking equipment, Windows does a remarkable job of determining how to configure everything. To see how well it's doing, visit the Network and Sharing Center. This, by the way, is where you set up the sharing of files, folders, printers, and multimedia files over the network.

To open the center, click the Network icon in the system tray (⚞ or 🖳); from the shortcut menu, choose Open Network and Sharing Center (Figure 24-3). It gives you an excellent central status screen for your network.

To *do* anything with your network, however, you need to click one of the links in blue.

Links at the Left Side
The commands in the panel at the left side include these:

"Manage wireless networks"

This one shows up, of course, only if your PC has WiFi networking. It shows you a list of all the WiFi networks you've told your PC to memorize. The little table shows you

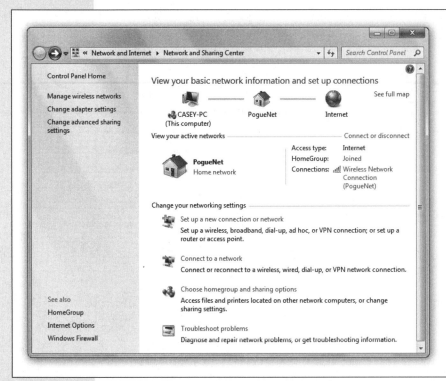

Figure 24-3:
The Network and Sharing Center is where you specify how Windows talks to the network. The network map at the top gives you, at a glance, reassurance that you're connected both to your network and to the Internet

---

GEM IN THE ROUGH

The Full Map

The map that appears when you first open the Network center has only three icons, representing your PC, your network, and the Internet.

But if you click "See full map," your PC sends out silent signals to all the other computers on your network. It then processes the responses so that it may draw you a far more detailed map, showing *all* the computers on the network.

All right, not *all.* The mapping feature relies on Windows's Link-Layer Topology Discovery (LLTD) technology, which, despite its fancy name, is actually pretty simple. It provides a way for computers and other devices to describe themselves to one another, announcing their presence to the other

machines on the network.

Unfortunately, computers that don't know about LLTD don't show up in the map. Windows Vista and Win7, of course, have LLTD, and there's a software add-on for Windows XP that adds LLTD to it. Older Windows computers (not to mention Macs and Linux machines), however, are out of luck.

If you're on a home or office network, clicking "See full map" makes Windows query the computers and devices on your network and draw a map of the results.

Note: On networks you've designated as public (such as wireless hot spots), no map appears, for security reasons.

what kind of password security is on each one, whether you've told the computer to autoconnect, and so on. You can add, remove, or change the settings for each.

You can drag and drop them to choose the priority of each network, too. That is, if Windows detects *two* wireless networks where you are, it will connect to the one closer to the top of the list.

You can double-click a network's name to open its Properties dialog box, where you can specify whether or not you want to connect to the network automatically.

"Change adapter settings"

Click this link to view a list of all your network adapters—Ethernet cards and WiFi adapters, mainly—as well as any VPNs or dial-up connections you've set up on your computer (Figure 24-4).

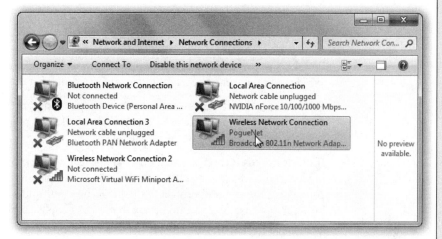

Figure 24-4:
The network connection status dialog box lets you view the details of a connection, disable (or enable) the adapter, or diagnose a problem with a network connection.

Double-click a listing to see its connection status, which leads to several other dialog boxes where you can reconfigure the connection or see more information. The toolbar offers buttons that let you rename, troubleshoot, disable, or connect to one of these network doodads.

Note: If you right-click one of these icons and then choose Properties, you get a list of protocols that your network connection uses. Double-click "Internet Protocol Version 4" to tell Windows whether to get its IP and DNS server addresses automatically, or whether to use addresses you've specified. Ninety-nine times out of 100, the right choice is to get those addresses automatically. Every once in a while, though, you'll come across a network that requires manually entered addresses.

"Change advanced sharing settings"

This section is the master control panel of on/off switches for Windows's *network sharing* features. (Most of these have on/off switches in other, more scattered places, too.) Here's a rundown.

Note: The options here are actually listed twice: once for networks you've designated as Home or Work networks, and one for Public networks. (Page 348 has details on these differences.)

- **Network discovery** makes your computer visible to others and allows your computer to see other computers on the network. (It's that LLTD feature in action.)

- **File and printer sharing** lets you share files and printers over the network. (See Chapter 26.)

- **Public folder sharing** lets you share whatever files you've put in the Users→Public folder. (See Chapter 26.)

- **Media streaming** is where you listen to one PC's music playing back over the network while seated at another. (See Chapter 15.)

- **File sharing connections** lets you turn off the super-strong security features of Windows file sharing, to accommodate older gadgets that don't recognize it.

- **Password protected sharing** requires other people to supply their account names and passwords before they can access the shared files, folders, and printers on your PC—including, by the way, the Public folder.

  If this feature is turned off, then other people can get at your stuff *without* having to sign in, which makes life easier if you're on a small network among trusted colleagues. You can still protect your shared files and folders using *permissions*, however. For instance, you might say that other people can see what files you've shared, but not view or edit them. (All this stuff is described in Chapter 26.)

- **HomeGroup connections.** Here's the master on/off switch for the delightful HomeGroup feature described in the next chapter.

Links in the Main Window

In the main part of the Network and Sharing Center window, the "Change your networking settings" heading offers a few more handy tools:

"Set up a new connection or network"

Most of the time, Windows does the right thing when it encounters a new network. For example, if you plug in an Ethernet cable, it assumes that you want to use the wired network and automatically hops on. If you come within range of a wireless network, Windows offers to connect to it.

Some kinds of networks, however, require special setup. They're listed here:

- **Connect to the Internet.** Use this option when Windows fails to figure out how to connect to the Internet on its own. You can set up a WiFi, PPPoE broadband connection (required by certain DSL services that require you to sign in with a user name and password), or a dial-up networking connection.

- **Set up a new network.** You can use this option to configure a new wireless router that's not set up yet, although only some routers can "speak" to Windows in this way. You're better off using the configuration software that came in the box with the router.

- **Manually connect to a wireless network.** Some wireless networks don't announce (broadcast) their presence. That is, you won't see a message popping up on the screen, inviting you to join the network, just by wandering into it. Instead, the very name and existence of such networks are kept secret to keep the riffraff out. If you're told the name of such a network, use this option to type it in and connect.

- **Connect to a workplace.** That is, set up a secure VPN connection to the corporation that employs you, as described on page 803.

- **Set up a wireless ad hoc (computer-to-computer) network.** Consult the box on page 753.

- **Set up a dial-up connection.** See page 345.

Connect to a network

This link does nothing more than open the palette of available networks—the same balloon you'd get if you clicked the ⏶ or ⏹ icon on your system tray. The list includes wireless networks, dial-up connections, and VPN (secure corporate) connections. Select a network and click Connect to establish a connection to it. You can disconnect from your current network by selecting it and clicking Disconnect.

Choose homegroup and sharing options

Opens the HomeGroup box, where you can create or join (or leave) a homegroup, as described in Chapter 25.

These options let you see all the shared files and folders (which are accessible to other users on your computer), as well as folders you've shared with other people on your network.

Troubleshoot problems

Very few problems are as annoying or difficult to troubleshoot as flaky network connections. You visit the Network and Sharing Center, and instead of seeing those reassuring double lines connecting your PC's icon to the network icon and the Internet icon, you see a broken line.

With this option, Microsoft is giving you a tiny head start. See Figure 24-5.

If the troubleshooter doesn't pinpoint the problem, check to see that:

• Your cables are properly seated in the network adapter card and hub jacks.

• Your router, Ethernet hub, or wireless access point is plugged into a working power outlet.

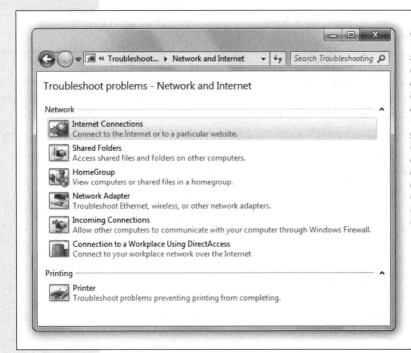

Figure 24-5:
When you click "Trouble-shoot problems," Windows asks what, exactly, you're having trouble with. Click the topic in question; invisibly and automatically, Windows performs several geek tweaks that were once the realm of highly paid networking professionals: It renews the DHCP address, reinitializes the connection, and, if nothing else works, turns the networking card off and on again.

• Your networking card is working. To check, open the Device Manager (type its name into the Start menu's Search box). Look for an error icon next to your networking card's name. See Chapter 18 for more on the Device Manager.

If that doesn't fix things, you'll have to call Microsoft, your PC, or your local teenage PC guru for help.

Network Domains

W indows 7 was designed to thrive in two very different kinds of network worlds: the *workgroup* (an informal, home or small-office network) and the *domain* (a hard-core, security-conscious corporate network of dozens or thousands of PCs). Depending on which kind of network your PC belongs to, the procedures and even dialog boxes you experience are quite a bit different.

Chapter 24 guides you through the process of setting up a workgroup network, but no single chapter could describe setting up a corporate domain. That's a job for Super Geek, otherwise known as the network administrator—somebody who has studied the complexities of corporate networking for years.

This chapter is designed to help you learn how to *use* a corporate domain. If your PC is connected to a workgroup network or no network at all, on the other hand, feel free to use these pages as scratch paper.

Note: In the context of this chapter, the term *domain* refers to a group of Windows computers on the same network. It's not the same as an *Internet* domain, which you may occasionally see mentioned. An Internet domain is still a group of computers, but they don't have to be connected to the same network, and they don't have to be running Windows. In addition, the domain name (like *amazon.com*) must be registered to ensure that there's no duplication on the Internet. Because Windows domains are private, they can be named any way the administrator chooses.

The Domain

Professional • Enterprise • Ultimate

As you may remember from Chapter 24, nobody else on a workgroup network can access the files on your PC unless you've created an account for them on your machine. Whenever somebody new joins the department, you have to create another new account; when people leave, you have to delete or disable their accounts. If something goes wrong with your hard drive, you have to recreate all of the accounts.

What's Wrong with Workgroups

You must have an account on each shared PC, too. If you're lucky, you have the same name and password on each machine—but that isn't always the case. You might have to remember that you're *pjenkins* on the front-desk computer, but *JenkinsP* on the administrative machine.

Similarly, suppose there's a network printer on one of the computers in your workgroup. If you want to use it, you have to find out whose computer the printer is connected to, call him to ask if he'll create an account for you, and hope that he knows how to do it. You either have to tell him your user name and password, or find out what user name and password he's assigned to you. In that case, every time you want to use that printer, you might have to log on by typing that user name and password.

If you multiply all of this hassle by the number of PCs on your small network, it's easy to see how you might suddenly find yourself spending more time managing accounts and permissions than getting any work done.

The Domain Concept

The solution to all of these problems is the network domain. In a domain, you only have a single name and password, which gets you into every shared PC and printer on the network. Everyone's account information resides on a central computer called a *domain controller*—a computer so important, it's usually locked away in a closet or a data-center room.

A domain controller keeps track of who is allowed to log on, who *is* logged on, and what each person is allowed to do on the network. When you log onto the domain with your PC, the domain controller verifies your credentials and permits (or denies) you access.

Most domain networks have at least two domain controllers with identical information, so if one computer dies, the other one can take over. (Some networks have many more than two.) This redundancy is a critical safety net, because without a happy, healthy domain controller, the entire network is dead.

Without budging from their chairs, network administrators can use a domain controller to create new accounts, manage existing ones, and assign permissions. The domain takes the equipment-management and security concerns of the network out of the hands of individuals and puts them into the hands of trained professionals. You may sometimes hear this kind of networking called *client/server networking*.

Each *workstation*—that is, each mere mortal PC like yours—relies on a central server machine for its network access.

If you use Windows in a medium- to large-sized company, you probably use a domain every day. You may not even have been aware of it, but that's no big deal; knowing what's been going on right under your nose isn't especially important to your ability to get work done. After all, it's not your job—it's the network administrator's. But understanding the domain system can help you take better advantage of a domain's features.

Active Directory

As you know, Microsoft sells several versions of Windows 7: Home Basic, Home Premium, Professional, Enterprise, and Ultimate. One key difference is that computers running the two Home editions can't join a domain.

There are other versions of Windows, however: the specialized ones that run on those domain-controller computers. To create a domain, at least one computer must be running either Windows Server 2003 or Windows 2000 Server. These are far more expensive operating systems (the price depends on the number of machines that they serve) and they run only on high-octane PCs. They also require high-octane expertise to install and maintain.

One key offering of these specialized Windows versions is an elaborate application called *Active Directory*. It's a single, centralized database that stores every scrap of information about the hardware, software, and people on the network. (The older operating system called Windows NT Server can create domains, but it doesn't include Active Directory.)

After creating a domain by installing Active Directory on a server computer, network administrators can set about filling the directory (database) with information about the network's resources. Every computer, printer, and person is represented by an *object* in the database and *attributes* (properties) that describe it. For example, a *user object's* attributes specify that person's name, location, telephone number, email address, and other, more technical, elements.

Active Directory lets network administrators maintain an enormous hierarchy of computers. A multinational corporation with tens of thousands of employees in offices worldwide can all be part of one Active Directory domain, with servers distributed in hundreds of locations, all connected by wide-area networking links. (A group of domains is known as a *tree*. Huge networks might even have more than one tree; if so, they're called—yes, you guessed it—a *forest*.)

The objects in an Active Directory domain are arranged in a hierarchy, something like the hierarchy of folders within folders on your hard drive. Some companies base their directory-tree designs on the organization of the company, using departments and divisions as the building blocks. Others use geographic locations as the basis for the design, or use a combination of both.

Unless you've decided to take up the rewarding career of network administration, you'll never have to install an Active Directory domain controller, design a directory tree, or create domain objects. However, you very well may encounter the Active Directory at your company. You can use it to search for the mailing address of somebody else on the network, for example, or locate a printer that can print on both sides of the page at once. Having some idea of the directory's structure can help in these cases.

Domain Security

Security is one of the primary reasons for Active Directory's existence. First off, all of the account names and passwords reside on a single machine (the domain controller), which can easily be locked away, protected, and backed up. The multiple domain controllers automatically *replicate* the changes to one another, so that each one has up-to-date information.

Active Directory is also a vital part of the network's other security mechanisms. When your computer is a member of a domain, the first thing you do is log on, just as in a workgroup. But when you log into a domain, Windows 7 transmits your name and password (in encrypted form) to the domain controller, which checks your credentials and grants or denies you access.

Joining a Domain

Professional • Enterprise • Ultimate

If you work in a corporation, the computer supplied to you generally has Windows already installed and joined to the domain, ready to go.

But if you ever have occasion to add a PC to a domain yourself, here's how you go about it. (You can make your PC join a domain either during the installation of Windows 7, or at any time afterward.)

1. **Log on using the local Administrator account.**

   See page 716 for details.

2. **Choose Start→Control Panel→System and Maintenance→System. In the page that comes up, click the Change Settings button under "Computer name, domain, and workgroup settings."**

   Authenticate yourself (page 726). You should now see the names of your computer and any workgroup or domain it belongs to (see Figure 25-1).

3. **Click the Network ID button.**

   The Join a Domain or a Workgroup Wizard appears.

4. **Click "This computer is part of a business network," and then click Next.**

   Now the wizard wants to know: "Is your company network on a domain?"

5. **Click "My company uses a network with a domain," and then click Next.**

   An information screen appears. It lets you know that, before you can join a domain, you need a domain user account, user name, and password. Your network administrator should create and give these to you in advance.

6. **Click Next.**

   The next page asks you to "Type your user name, password, and domain name."

7. **Enter the user account name and password supplied by your administrator, plus the name of the domain in which your account has been created.**

   Remember this domain name; you'll need it again later to log on.

8. **Click Next again.**

   If the wizard asks you whether you want to use the existing domain account for your computer, say Yes. Otherwise, you'll be prompted to specify the name of your computer and the domain the *computer object* is in. If you see this page, it means that your computer isn't listed in the Active Directory domain you specified on the previous wizard screen. Flag down your network administrator and point out the problem. Then click Next to proceed.

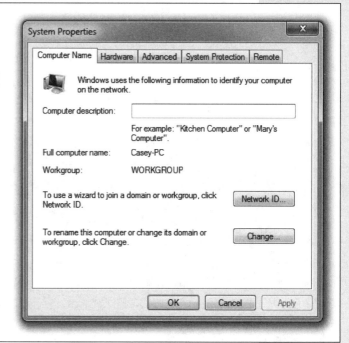

Figure 25-1:
The Computer Name tab of the System Properties dialog box displays the name of your computer and the workgroup or domain of which it is currently a member. From here, you can change the computer or workgroup name or join a new domain. The Network ID button launches a Network Identification Wizard, while the Change button displays a dialog box in which a more experienced person can perform the same tasks.

In any case, you should now arrive at a page where you're asked whether you want to enable the domain user account as a local account for your computer. Of course, if you're going to be logging onto a domain, you don't really need a local account on your PC.

9. Click "Do not add a domain user account." Click Next, and finally click Finish to complete the wizard.

You wind up back at the System Properties dialog box.

10. Click OK to dismiss the System Properties dialog box.

Restart the computer for your changes to take effect.

Four Ways Life Is Different on a Domain
Professional • Enterprise • Ultimate

The domain and workgroup personalities of Windows are quite different. Here are some of the most important differences.

Logging On
What you see when you log onto your PC is very different when you're part of a domain. Instead of the standard Welcome screen (which shows a list of people with accounts on your PC), you generally encounter a two-step sign-in process:

• First, you see a startup screen that instructs you to press Ctrl+Alt+Delete to log on. (As noted on page 771, this step is a security precaution.)

• When you select Switch User from the Logon screen, you'll have the opportunity to click "Other User" and then log into the domain you joined (see Figure 25-2).

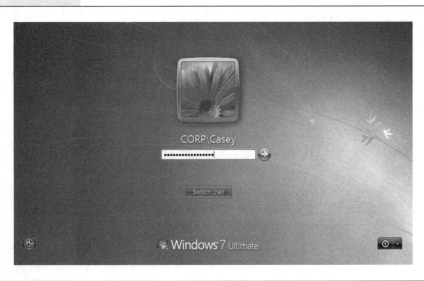

Figure 25-2:
Joining a domain lets you keep using the Windows 7 Welcome screen, but you can click Switch User and choose Other User to have the opportunity to log in as a domain user.

Tip: You can turn off the requirement to press Ctrl+Alt+Delete at each log on, if you like. Choose Start→ Control Panel; then click User Accounts→User Accounts. Next, click Manage User Accounts. (You may be prompted for a local administrator's password.) Now select the Advanced tab and turn off the "Require users to press Ctrl+Alt+Delete" checkbox.

As you see in Figure 25-2, the Log onto Windows dialog box provides a place for you to type your user name and password. To save you time, Windows fills in the User Name box with whatever name was used the last time somebody logged in.

Browsing the Domain

When your PC is part of the domain, all of its resources—printers, shared files, and so on—magically appear in your desktop windows, the Start→Network window, and so on (Figure 25-3).

Tip: If you open the Network window (Start→Network), a message might appear that says, "Network discovery and file sharing are turned off," which means you're cut off from the network. To rejoin the game, click this message (or click Network and Sharing Center in the toolbar) to turn on Network Discovery.

Figure 25-3:
When you choose Start→Network, you see an icon for each computer on the network. You can browse through the computers in a domain and access their shared folders (if you have the appropriate permissions) just as you would those of a workgroup. On a large network, you'll just see a lot more computers.

Searching the Domain

You can read all about the Search command in Chapter 3. But when you're on a domain, this tool becomes far more powerful—and more interesting.

Figure 25-4:
Top left: Searching for people in your network's Active Directory is like using a phone book. You supply the information you know about the person.

Lower right: When you find that person (technically, her user object), you can view the information stored in the user object's attributes. Of course, the usefulness of this feature depends on how much information your network administrators enter when creating the user objects.

Knowing What You're Logging Onto

You may remember from Chapter 23 that there are two kinds of accounts: *domain* accounts, maintained by a highly paid professional in your company, and *local* accounts—accounts that exist only on the PC itself. It's actually possible to find domain accounts and local accounts that have the same name—a perennial source of confusion for beginners (and occasionally experts).

For example, you know that every Windows computer has an Administrator account, which the Windows 7 installer creates automatically. The trouble is, so does the domain controller.

In other words, typing *Administrator* into the User Name text box might log you onto either the local machine or the domain, depending on what password you supply. (With luck, the two accounts won't have the same password, but you never know.)

To avoid this kind of confusion, Windows 7 lets you specify which domain to log onto. Just prefix the account name with the domain name, like this: *2K3DOMAIN\Administrator.*

And if you forget this secret code, you can always click the link marked "How do I log onto another domain?" at the logon screen.

When you choose Start→Network, the toolbar changes to include an option to Search Active Directory. Click it to open the dialog box shown at top left in Figure 25-4.

The name of this dialog box depends on what you're looking for. Your choices are:

- **Users, Contacts, and Groups.** Use this option to search the network for a particular person or network group (Figure 25-4). If your search is successful, you can, for example, find out someone's telephone number, email address, or mailing address, or see what users belong to a particular group.

- **Computers.** This option helps you find a certain PC in the domain. It's of interest primarily to network administrators, because it lets them open a Computer Management window for the computer they find. It also lets them manage many of the PC's functions by remote control.

- **Printers.** In a large office, it's entirely possible that you might not know where you can find a printer with certain features—tabloid-size paper, for example, or double-sided printing. That's where this option comes in handy (see Figure 25-5).

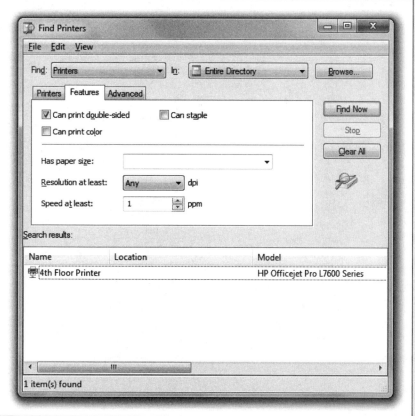

Figure 25-5:
Searching for a printer in Active Directory lets you find the printing features you need. Network administrators may also record the physical locations of the network printers. This way, when your search uncovers a printer that can handle executive paper and also print double-sided, you can simply look at its attributes to find out that it's located on the fourth floor of the building.

- **Shared Folders.** In theory, this option lets you search for shared folders on the domain's computers—but you'll quickly discover that searches for a certain shared folder generally come up empty-handed.

  That's because just sharing a folder on your computer doesn't "publish" it to Active Directory, which would make it available to this kind of search. Only network administrators can publish a shared folder in Active Directory.

- **Organizational Units.** You may not have heard of organizational units, but your network administrator lives and breathes them. (They're the building blocks of an Active Directory hierarchy.) You, the mere mortal, can safely ignore this search option.

Figure 25-6:
To perform a custom search, use the drop-down menus to select an object type and then a particular field in that object. You then specify a condition (such as whether you want to search for an exact value or just the beginning or end of the value) and the value you want to look for. When you click Find Now, a list of the objects matching your criteria appears.

Custom Searches

In addition to these predefined searches, you can also create a custom search of your own by looking for information in specific fields (that is, attributes) of Active Directory, as shown in Figure 25-6.

When used creatively, these custom searches can be powerful indeed, in ways you might not expect. For example, suppose your car won't start, and you need a ride home from the office. You can open this dialog box, click the Field button, and choose User→Home Phone. Change the Condition drop-down menu to Starts With, and then type your own area code and telephone exchange into the Value text box. When you click the Find Now button, you'll get a list of coworkers who live in your neighborhood (as indicated by the first three digits of their phone numbers).

Assigning Permissions to Domain Members

Chapter 26 describes the process of assigning permissions to certain files and folders, so that only designated people and groups can open them from across the network. When you're a member of a domain, the process is the same, except that you can select people and groups from the domain as well.

When you open the Properties dialog box for a file or folder, click the Security tab, then click Edit and then Add, you don't get the same dialog box that you'd see on a

---

NOSTALGIA CORNER

The Double-Thick Security Trick

If you use Windows Vista in a corporation, you may see the startup box shown here when you first turn on the machine. You don't proceed to the Classic logon box (Figure 23-12) until you first press Ctrl+Alt+Delete.

This somewhat inconvenient setup is intended as a security feature. By forcing you to press Ctrl+Alt+Delete to bypass the initial Welcome box, Windows rules out the possibility that some sneaky program (such as a Trojan-horse program), designed to *look* like the Classic logon box, is posing *as* the Classic logon box—in order to "capture" the name and password you type there.

Press CTRL + ALT + DELETE to log on

This two-layer logon system is what you get when you add your PC to a network domain during the Windows Vista installation. If you want to use it on a workgroup machine, you can, but you have to do a little digging to find it. Press ⊞+R to open the Run dialog box; type *control Userpasswords2*, and then press Enter. Authenticate yourself (page 191). You see the program shown on page 680—the old-style User Accounts box. Click the Advanced tab.

At the bottom of the Advanced tab, turn on "Require users to press Ctrl+Alt+Delete," and then click OK. From now on, turning on the PC greets you not with a logon screen, but with the unfakeable Welcome box shown here.

---

workgroup network. On a domain, it's called the Select Users, Computers, or Groups dialog box (Figure 25-7). You'll also see this dialog box if you right-click on a folder, click Share, and then select Find from the drop-down menu to the left of the Add button.

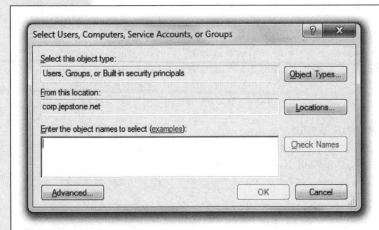

Figure 25-7:
Note that the standard location for the objects is your current domain. You can still click the Locations button and select your computer's name (to specify local user and group accounts), or even choose another domain on the network, if others are available.

Sharing Files on the Network

Whether you built the network yourself (Chapter 24) or work in an office where somebody has done that work for you, all kinds of fun can come from having a network. You're now ready to share all kinds of stuff among the various PCs on the network:

- **Files, folders, and disks.** No matter what PC you're using on the network, you can open the files and folders on any *other* networked PC, as long as the other PCs' owners have made these files available for public inspection. That's where *file sharing* comes in, and that's what this chapter is all about.

  The uses for file sharing are almost endless. It means you can finish writing a letter in the bedroom, even if you started it downstairs at the kitchen table—without having to carry a flash drive around. It means you can watch a slideshow drawn from photos on your spouse's PC somewhere else in the house. It means your underlings can turn in articles for your small-company newsletter by depositing them directly into a folder on your laptop.

Tip: File sharing also lets you access your files and folders from the road, using a laptop. See Chapter 27 for more information on this road-warrior trick.

- **Music and video playback.** Windows Media Center can *stream* music and videos from one PC to another one on the network—that is, play in real time across the network, without your having to copy any files. In a family situation, it's super-convenient to have Dad's Mondo Upstairs PC serve as the master holding tank for the family's entire music collection—and be able to play it using any PC in the house.

• **Printers.** You don't need a printer for every PC; all the PCs can share a much smaller number of printers. If several printers are on your network—say, a high-speed laser printer for one computer and a color printer on another—everyone on the network can use whichever printer is appropriate to a particular document. You'll find step-by-step instructions starting on page 588.

• **Your Internet connection.** Having a network means that all the PCs in your home or office can share a single connection (Chapter 24).

Note: Your network might include a Windows 7 PC, a couple of Windows XP or Vista machines, older PCs, and even Macs. That's perfectly OK; all of these computers can participate as equals in this party. This chapter points out whatever differences you may find in the procedures.

Three Ways to Share Files
All Versions

It's not easy to write *one* operating system that's supposed to please *everyone,* from a husband and wife at home, to a small business owner, to a network administrator for the federal government. Clearly, these people might have slightly different attitudes on the tradeoff between convenience and security.

That's why Windows 7 offers *three ways* to share files. Each is light-years more convenient, secure, and comprehensible than file sharing in the Windows XP days. And each falls at a different spot on the security/convenience spectrum:

• **Homegroups.** This is the big networking news in Windows 7. The HomeGroup feature was invented for families or small-business owners—places where people don't have a lot to hide from one another. This kind of network is *really* easy to set up and use; nobody has to enter names and passwords to use files on other PCs in the house.

Setup is a one-time deal: You type the same code into each computer, and presto: Everyone can see everyone else's Music, Photos, Videos, and Documents folders. Everyone can send printouts to everyone else's printers. Everyone can listen to everyone else's Windows Media Player music collections, too. (You can turn these shared items off individually, if you like.)

Downsides: A PC can join a homegroup only if it's running Windows 7. And homegroups don't offer the level of security, passwords, and networky red tape that bigger companies require. The idea is to give everyone in the house free access to everyone else's stuff with one click.

• **The Public folder.** There's a Public folder on every PC. It's free for anyone on the network to access, like a grocery store bulletin board. Super-convenient, super-easy.

Downsides: First, you have to move or copy files *into* the Public folder before anyone else can see them. Depending on how many files you wish to share, this can get tedious.

Second, this method isn't especially secure. If you worry about people rummaging through the files and deleting or vandalizing them, or if bad things could happen if the wrong person in your building gets a look at them, well, then, don't use this method (although you can still give the Public folder a password).

- **Any folder.** At the far end of the security/convenience spectrum, you have the "any folder" method. In this scheme, you can make any ordinary folder available for inspection by other people on the network.

  This method means you don't have to move files into the Public folder. It also gives you elaborate control over who's allowed to do what to your files. You might want to permit your company's executives to see and edit your documents but allow the peons in accounting only to see them. And Andy, that unreliable goofball in sales? You don't want him even seeing what's in your shared folder.

  Downsides: More complex and inconvenient than the other methods.

The following pages walk you through all three kinds of file sharing.

Tip: These networking types can coexist. So you can have a homegroup for the benefit of the other Windows 7 computers in your house, but still share with Windows Vista or XP machines using the other methods. Nobody said this was going to be simple.

Homegroups
All Versions

Let's suppose there are two PCs in your house. Setting up a homegroup is incredibly easy—especially compared to the complications of setting up "real" file sharing, as described later in this chapter. In fact, it's as easy as 1, 2, 3, 4, 5, 6, 7.

1. **On the first PC, open the HomeGroup program.**

   It doesn't matter which PC you start with, as long as it's running Windows 7 Home Premium, Professional, Enterprise, or Ultimate. (Other versions can *join* your homegroup—just can't create one.)

   The quickest way is to open the Start menu, then start typing *homegroup* until you see "HomeGroup" in the results list; click it. You see the dialog box shown in Figure 26-1, top.

2. **Click "Create a homegroup."**

   Now the middle dialog box shown in Figure 26-1 appears.

3. **Turn on the checkboxes for the stuff you want to share.**

   Windows proposes making your Photos, Music, and Videos libraries available for the other PCs in your house to use. If you like, you can also turn on the Documents library. (Microsoft starts out with that one turned off in case you keep private stuff in there.) And you can share whatever printer is connected to your PC—an inkjet, for example.

Tip: You can always change these settings later, as described below.

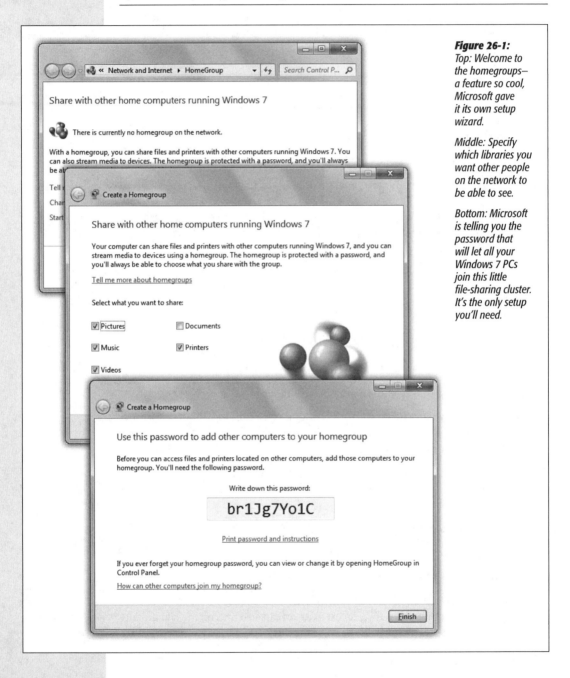

Figure 26-1:
Top: Welcome to the homegroups—a feature so cool, Microsoft gave it its own setup wizard.

Middle: Specify which libraries you want other people on the network to be able to see.

Bottom: Microsoft is telling you the password that will let all your Windows 7 PCs join this little file-sharing cluster. It's the only setup you'll need.

4. **Click Next.**

Now Windows displays a ridiculously unmemorable password, like E6fQ9UX3uR. Fortunately, you'll never have to memorize it.

Tip: Even more fortunately, you can *change* the password. When you see the dialog box shown in Figure 26-1, bottom, click Finish. You arrive at the "Change homegroup settings" page (Figure 26-3). Here, you can click "Change the password," authenticate if necessary, and make up any new password you like (eight characters or longer). ("Bluefish" is much easier to remember than E6fQ9UX3uR.)

---

5. **Walk over to the second PC. Open the HomeGroup program on this one.**

This time, the wording of the dialog box is slightly different. It sees the *first* PC already on the network, already with a homegroup initiative under way.

6. **Click "Join now." On the next screen (Figure 26-1, middle), choose which folders you'd like to share. Click Next.**

Now you're invited to type *that* password into *this* PC's box.

7. **Type the password from step 4. Click Next, and then Finish.**

If you have a third PC, or a fourth or a fifth, repeat steps 5–7. If you buy another PC a year from now, repeat steps 5–7.

And that's all there is to it. Your computers are now joined in blissful network harmony.

Note: Only your stuff is shared at the outset—only your pictures, music, video, and documents. Other account holders have to turn on sharing for their own stuff; Microsoft didn't think they'd appreciate having all their stuff shared on the network unawares.

Suppose you're one of the other family members. Log in and open the HomeGroup program. A message says "[Name of other person] has joined your computer to a homegroup. You haven't shared any libraries." You see a screen like the one shown in Figure 26-1, middle; turn on the libraries you want to share, and then click "Save changes."

How to Use Your Homegroup

Once a homegroup is set up, using it is a piece of cake.

- **Root through other people's libraries.** On PC #2, click Homegroup at the left side of any Explorer window. Voila! There are the icons for every PC—in fact, every *account* on every PC (Figure 26-2).

  And if you open one of them, you can see the pictures, music, videos, documents, and whatever else they've made available for sharing. See Figure 26-2. (You can click the HomeGroup heading and see icons for each account holder/PC, or you can open the flippy triangles in the Navigation pane.)

- **Share each other's printers.** When you go to print, you'll see that *all* the printers in the house are now available to *all* the PCs in the house. For example, if there's a color inkjet plugged into the USB jack of Computer #1, you can send printouts to it from the Print dialog box of Computer #2. (The other computers' shared printers even have their own icons in the Devices and Printers folder, as described in Chapter 24.)

Note: If the printer is a relatively recent, brand-name model, it should "just work"; Windows installs the printer automatically. If not, the HomeGroup feature notifies you that a printer is available, but you have to click Install to OK the driver installation.

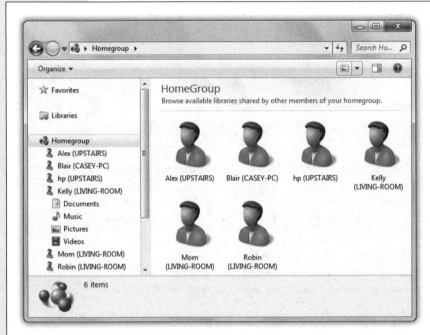

Figure 26-2:
Sitting at PC #1, any Explorer window lets you work with the contents of all the other PCs' libraries. Just expand the Homegroup triangle at the left side of any Explorer window. There they are: individual listings for each account on each PC. You're free to edit or even delete what's in Public folders and libraries; you can see and open, but not change, what's in other folders.

- **Play each other's music and video.** When you're in Windows Media Player or Media Center, same thing: You'll see the names of all the other computers listed for your browsing pleasure, and inside, all their music, photos, and videos, ready to play. (The other machines are listed in the Navigation pane at left, in a category called "Other libraries.")

Tip: For quicker access to your homegroup, list it in your Start menu. To do that, right-click the Start button; from the shortcut menu, choose Properties. Click Customize; in the long scrolling list, turn on Homegroup, and then click OK twice. Now Homegroup appears in the right side of the shortcut Start menu.

How to Share More Folders

Microsoft starts you off by sharing your main libraries, and anything you put in them becomes available immediately.

But that doesn't mean you're limited to sharing those folders. You can share any folder you like, making it available for ransacking by everyone else in the homegroup.

To do that, right-click the folder; from the shortcut menu, choose "Share with." (If the folder is already open, click "Share with" on the toolbar.)

The submenu offers you three choices:

• **Nobody.** This folder is invisible to other people on the network.

• **Homegroup (Read).** Other people on the network can see and read what's in this folder, but can't edit, add, or delete anything.

• **Homegroup (Read/Write).** Other people on the network can do anything to the stuff in this folder: edit, delete, whatever.

• **Specific people.** Here, you can assign *privileges* to manipulate this folder's contents individually to each account holder. See Figure 26-6, later in this chapter.

Leaving a Homegroup

If you're feeling a little private, you can remove your PC from the big happy network family, either temporarily or permanently.

Open the HomeGroup program (type *homegroup* into the Start menu), and click "Leave the homegroup." Confirm by clicking "Leave the homegroup." That wasn't so hard, was it?

You can rejoin at any time—you'll see a Join button in the HomeGroup program—but you'll need the password. (You can find out the password by opening the HomeGroup program on any *other* PC and clicking "View or print the homegroup password.")

Tip: If you're not using the HomeGroup feature at all, you can also disable it completely. The advantage is that the Homegroup heading won't take up space in your Navigation bar anymore.

To do that, switch your network to the Work type (instead of Home). Click the ◢ or ▧ icon in your system tray; click Open Network and Sharing Center. Under the name of your network, click "Home network." The Set Network Location dialog box opens; click "Work network." The next time you start the PC, Homegroup will have vanished from your Explorer windows.

Editing the Shared Homegroup Libraries

As you can see in Figure 26-1, Microsoft suggests starting you off by sharing your Music, Pictures, and Videos libraries, plus any USB printer you're connected to; one more click shares your Documents library as well.

If you ever decide to adjust that setup—to turn off your Music, turn on your Documents, or whatever—no biggie. Open the HomeGroup program (type *homegroup* into the Start menu). You find yourself at the "Change homegroup settings" screen shown in Figure 26-3.

Figure 26-3:
Here, you can decide which libraries you want to share with your network colleagues. Here's also where you turn printer sharing on or off, and Windows Media Player sharing (playback streaming) on or off. You can also remind yourself of the password, change the password, leave the homegroup, or view the master sharing control panel for your computer ("Advanced sharing settings.")

Sharing the Public Folders

Homegroups are incredibly easy to set up and easy to use. But they're limited to Windows 7 computers.

If you have older versions of Windows on hand, Microsoft's *previous* attempt at quick-setup, low-security file sharing is also available: the Public-folders method.

Inside each of your Windows 7 libraries, you'll see a Public folder. You know: Inside the Pictures library is a folder called Public Pictures; inside Music is the Public Music folder; and so on. (See Figure 26-4.) They start out empty, except for some sample files in the Music, Pictures, and Videos folders.

Note: Behind the scenes, these folders are all inside the master Public folder (there's one per PC). It sits in the Local Disk (C:)→Users folder.

When you want to share some of your *own* stuff with fellow network denizens, Job One is to drag your files and folders *into* one of these Public folders.

Before you go live with your Public folder, though, you have a few more options to look over:

- **Set up accounts.** Ordinarily, each person who wants to get into your PC from the network requires an account (Chapter 23). They already have accounts on their own machines, of course, but you need to create corresponding ones on your machine.

Figure 26-4:
Each Public folder is like a central public square, a shared meeting point for all PCs on the network. Anything in one of these folders is available to anyone on the network—free and clear. You can find the Public folders listed inside each of your standard libraries.

So if, on your own Dell, your name is Casey and your password is *fishsandwich*, then you should see to it that the Toshiba downstairs also has a user account called Casey with the same password.

Tip: When you try to access a shared folder, you can enter any account name and password on that computer. But the beauty of having an account of your own on that machine (with exactly the same name and password) is that you'll breeze right in. You'll connect instantly, without having to encounter the "Connect to" login box every time you connect.

- **Turn off the password requirement (optional).** Anyone who *doesn't* have an account will still be able to see the files that are in the Public folders, open them, and make their own copies of them—but not make changes to them. Such people can't add files, delete anything, or edit anything. (Technically, they'll be using the Guest account feature of every Windows PC.)

To set up password-free access, open the Start menu and type *sharing;* in the results menu, click "Manage advanced sharing settings."

As shown in Figure 26-5, "Public folder sharing" comes turned on. Out of the box, it requires your guests to type their names and passwords when connecting. But

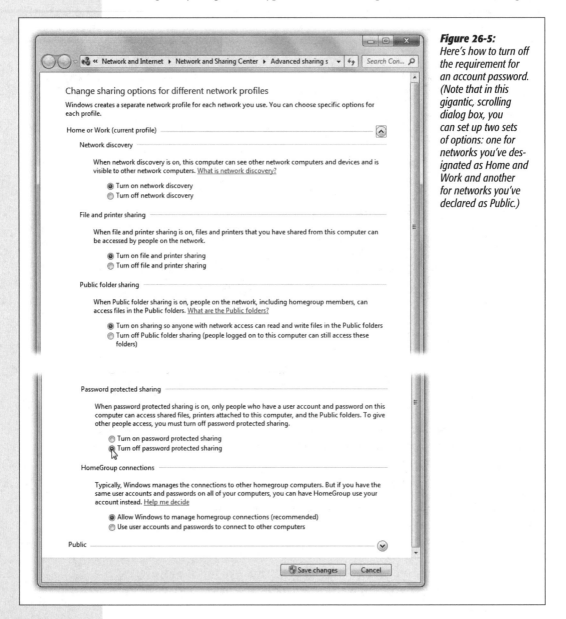

Figure 26-5:
Here's how to turn off the requirement for an account password. (Note that in this gigantic, scrolling dialog box, you can set up two sets of options: one for networks you've designated as Home and Work and another for networks you've declared as Public.)

if you also click "Turn off password protected sharing," then anyone will be able to see what's in your Public folder, even without an account on your machine.

To make your changes stick, click "Save changes," and then authenticate yourself if necessary.

• **Turn off Public folder sharing altogether (definitely optional).** Proceed as described above, but click "Turn off Public folder sharing" (shown in Figure 26-5). Now your Public folder is completely invisible on the network.

So now that you've set up Public folder sharing, how are other people supposed to access your Public folder? See page 789.

Sharing Any Folder

If the Public folder method seems too simple, restrictive, and insecure to you, then you can graduate to what Microsoft cleverly calls the "share any folder" method. In this scheme, you can make *any* folder available to other people on the network.

This time, you don't have to move your files anywhere; they sit right where you left them. And this time, you can set up elaborate *sharing permissions* that grant individuals different amount of access over your files.

Better yet, files you share this way are available to other people on the network *and* other account holders on the *same computer*.

Here's how to share a file or folder disk on your PC:

1. **In an Explorer window, highlight the files or folders you want to share. On the toolbar, choose "Share with"→"Specific people."**

   The "Choose people to share with" dialog box appears (Figure 26-6). You wanted individual control over each account holder's access? You got it.

Note: The steps for sharing a *disk* are different. See the box below.

GEM IN THE ROUGH

Sharing Disks

You can share files and folders, of course, but also *disks.*

Sharing an entire disk means that every folder on it, and therefore every file, is available to everyone on the network. If security isn't a big deal at your place (because it's just you and a couple of family members, for example), this feature can be a timesaving convenience that spares you the trouble of sharing every new folder you create.

On the other hand, people with privacy concerns generally prefer to share individual *folders.* By sharing only a folder or two, you can keep *most* of the stuff on your hard drive private, out of view of curious network comrades. For that matter, sharing only a folder or two does *them* a favor, too, by making it easier for them to find the files you've made available. This way, they don't have to root through your entire drive looking for the folder they actually need.

2. Choose a person's name from the upper pop-up menu, and then click Add.

This is the list of account holders (Chapter 23)—or account-holder *groups,* if someone has created them (page 730).

If the person who'll be connecting across the network doesn't yet have an account on your machine, choose "Create a new user" from this pop-up menu. (This option is available if the PC is *not* part of a homegroup. Also, "Create a new user" isn't some kind of sci-fi breakthrough. You are not, in fact, going to create a human being—only an account for an *existing* person.)

The name appears in the list.

Now your job is to work through this list of people, specify *how much* control each person has over the file or folder you're sharing.

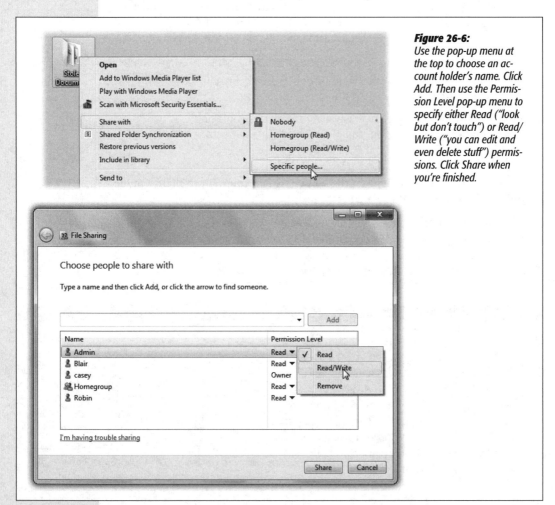

Figure 26-6:
Use the pop-up menu at the top to choose an account holder's name. Click Add. Then use the Permission Level pop-up menu to specify either Read ("look but don't touch") or Read/Write ("you can edit and even delete stuff") permissions. Click Share when you're finished.

3. **Click a name in the list. Click the ▾ in the Permission Level column and choose Read or Read/Write.**

   Read is that "look, but don't touch" business. This person can see what's in the folder (or file) and can copy it, but can't delete or change the original.

   Contributors (available for folders only—not files) have much broader access. These people can add, change, or delete files in the shared folder—but only files *that they put there.* Stuff placed there by other people (Owners or Co-owners) appears as "look, but don't touch" to a Contributor.

   Read/Write means that this person, like you, can add, change, or delete any file in the shared folder.

Note: Your name shows up here as Owner. You have the most power of all—after all, it's your stuff.

   This stuff may sound technical and confusing, but you have no idea how much simpler it is than it was before Windows 7 came along.

4. **Click Share.**

   The "Your folder [or file] is shared" dialog box appears. This is more than a simple message, however; it contains the *network address* of the files or folders you shared. Without this address, your colleagues won't know that you've shared stuff and will have a tough time finding it.

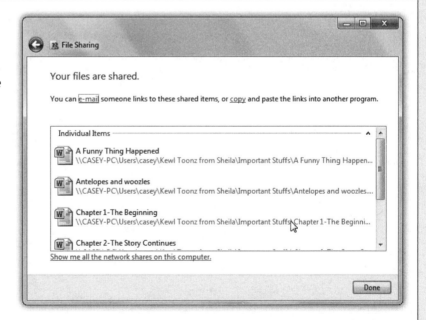

Figure 26-7:
Windows wants to make absolutely sure that you know what you've done. Wouldn't want the wrong people sniffing around the wrong personal files, now.

Note: If you've shared some files, you may see an interim message that appears before the "Your files are shared" box, warning you that Windows is about to adjust the access permissions to the folder that encloses them. That's normal.

5. **Click "e-mail" or "copy" (Figure 26-7).**

The "e-mail" link opens a new, outgoing message in your email program, letting the gang know that you've shared something and offering them a link to it. The "copy" link copies the address to the Clipboard so you can paste it into another program—which is your best bet if Mail isn't your email program of choice.

Tip: To stop sharing a folder or file, click it. Then, from the toolbar of whatever window contains it, choose "Share with"→Nobody.

GEM IN THE ROUGH

Accessing Macs Across the Network

When it comes to networking, Macs are people, too.

Windows is perfectly capable of letting you rifle through a Mac's contents from across the network. Here's how to set that up (these instructions cover Mac OS X 10.6, called Snow Leopard.)

On the Mac, choose → System Preferences. Click Sharing, and then turn on File Sharing. Click Options.

Now you see the dialog box shown here. Turn on "Share files and folders using SMB (Windows)." Then specify *which* Mac user accounts you want to be able to access; enter their passwords as necessary, and then click Done.

(Before you close System Preferences, you might notice that the line in the middle of the dialog box says: "Windows users can access your computer at smb://192.168.1.203."

Those numbers are the Mac's IP address. You'd need it

only if you decided to access the Mac by typing its UNC code [page 792] into your Windows address bar, like this: *102.168.1.203.*)

On the PC, proceed exactly as though you were trying to connect to another Windows PC. The Mac's name shows up in the Network section of the Navigation pane (left side of any Explorer window).

When you click the Mac's name, you see the dialog box shown in Figure 26-9. Enter your Mac account name and password, and turn on "Remember my credentials" (so you won't be bothered for a name or password the next time you perform this amazing act of détente). Click OK.

Now your Mac home folder opens on the screen before you. Feel free to work with those files exactly as though they were in a folder on your PC. Détente has never been so easy.

Advanced Folder Sharing—and Disk Sharing

Microsoft made a noble step forward in simplicity with the "share any folder" wizard described in the previous pages. But the older, more complicated—yet more flexible—method is still available. Here's a quick review of this alternate route (which is, by the way, the *only* route for sharing entire *disks):*

1. **Right-click the folder or disk you want to share. If it's a folder, choose Properties from the shortcut menu; if it's a disk, choose "Share with"→"Advanced sharing." In the dialog box, click the Sharing tab.**

   At this point, you *could* click the Share button (if you're operating on a folder, anyway). You'd arrive at the dialog box shown in Figure 26-6, where you could specify the account holders and permission levels, just as described earlier. But don't.

2. **Click Advanced Sharing. Authenticate, if necessary (page 726).**

   The Advanced Sharing dialog box appears.

3. **Turn on "Share this folder." (See Figure 26-8, top.) Next, set up the power-user sharing options.**

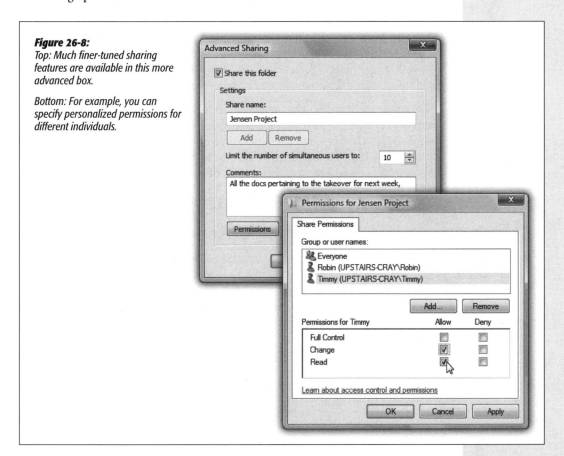

Figure 26-8:
Top: Much finer-tuned sharing features are available in this more advanced box.

Bottom: For example, you can specify personalized permissions for different individuals.

For example, you can limit the number of people who are browsing this folder at once. You can click Permissions to fine-tune who can do what (Figure 26-8, bottom). And you can edit the "Share name"—in fact, you can create *more than one* name for the same shared folder—to make it more recognizable on the network when people are browsing your PC.

Tip: For more on Allow, Deny, and other sharing privileges, see page 740.

Notes on File Sharing

And now, the fine print on sharing files:

- Sharing a folder also shares all the folders inside it, including new ones you create later.

  On the other hand, it's OK to *change* the sharing settings of a subfolder. For example, if you've shared a folder called America, you can make the Minnesota folder inside it off-limits by making it private.

  To do this, right-click the inner folder, choose Properties→Sharing, click Advanced Sharing, and use the dialog box shown in Figure 26-8.

- Be careful with nested folders. Suppose, for example, that you share your Documents folder, and you permit other people to change the files inside it. Now suppose that you share a folder that's *inside* Documents—called Spreadsheets, for example—but you turn *off* the ability for other people to change its files.

  You wind up with a strange situation. Both folders—Documents and Spreadsheets—show up in other people's Network windows, as described below. If they double-click the Spreadsheets folder directly, they won't be able to change anything inside it. But if they double-click the Documents folder and then open the Spreadsheets folder inside *it,* they *can* modify the files.

POWER USERS' CLINIC

Unhiding Hidden Folders

As sneaky and delightful as the hidden-folder trick is, it has a distinct drawback—*you* can't see your hidden folder from across the network, either. Suppose you want to use another computer on the network—the one in the upstairs office, for example—to open something in your hidden My Novel folder (which is downstairs in the kitchen). Fortunately, you can do so—if you know the secret.

On the office computer, choose Start→Run. In the Run dialog box, type the path of the hidden folder, using the format *\\Computer Name\Folder Name.*

For example, enter *\\kitchen\my novel$* to get to the hidden folder called "My Novel$" on the PC called "Kitchen." (Capitalization doesn't matter, but don't forget the $ sign.) Then click OK to open a window showing the contents of your hidden folder. (See page 792 for more on the Universal Naming Convention system.)

Hiding Folders

If a certain folder on your hard drive is really private, you can hide the folder so that other people on the network can't even *see* it. The secret is to type a $ symbol at the end of the *share name* (see step 3 on page 787).

For example, if you name a certain folder My Novel, anyone else on the network can see it (even if they can't read the contents). But if you name the folder *My Novel$*, it won't show up in anybody's Network window. They won't even know it exists.

Accessing Shared Folders

All Versions

Now suppose you're not you. You're your coworker, spouse, or employee. You're using your laptop downstairs, and you want access to the stuff that's in a shared folder on the Beefy Main Dell computer upstairs. Here's what to do (the steps are the same whether the Public folder or *any* folder was shared):

1. **Open any Explorer window.**

   The Navigation pane at left shows a Network heading. Click its flippy triangle, if necessary, to see icons for all the computers on the network (Figure 26-9, bottom). The same Navigation pane is available in the Save and Open dialog boxes of your programs, too, making the entire network available to you for opening and saving files.

Tip: Alternatively, type *network* into the Start menu; click Network in the results list.

   If you *don't* see a certain computer's icon here, it might be turned off, or off the network. It also might have *network discovery* turned off; that's the feature that lets a PC announce its presence to the network. (Its on/off switch is one of the buttons shown in Figure 26-5.)

   And if you don't see any computers at *all* in the Network window, then network discovery might be turned off on *your* computer.

2. **Double-click the computer whose files you want to open.**

   If you're on a corporate domain, you may first have to double-click your way through some other icons, representing the networks in other buildings or floors, before you get to the actual PC icons.

   If you *don't* have an account on the PC you're invading—an account with the same name and password as you have on your own PC—then the Connect To box now appears (Figure 26-9, top).

   Obviously, you have to fill the name and password of an account on the *other* **computer.** This, of course, is a real drag, especially if you access other people's files frequently. Fortunately, you have two timesaving tricks available to you here.

First, if you turn on "Remember my credentials," then you'll never see this box again. The next time you want to visit the other PC, you'll be able to double-click its icon for instant access.

Finally, if you're trying to get to someone's Public folder, and you don't need to modify the files, but just read or copy them, you don't need a password, ever. Just type *guest* into the "User name" box and click OK. You'll have full read-only access. And here again, next time, you won't be bothered for a name or password.

Figure 26-9:
Top: Supply your account name and password as it exists on the distant PC, the one you're trying to access.

Bottom: The computers on your network are arrayed before you! Double-click the one you want to visit.

Tip: In the unlikely event that you want Windows to *stop* memorizing your password, open the Start menu; start typing *Credential Manager* until you can click its name in the results. You see a list of every name/password Windows has memorized for you. You can use the options here to add a new memorized name/password, or expand one of the existing items in the list to remove it ("Remove from vault") or edit it.

3. **Click OK.**

If all went well, the other computer's window opens, presenting you with the icons of its shared folders and disks.

FREQUENTLY ASKED QUESTION

Accessing Windows 7 from XP, Vista, Mac...

How do I access my Windows 7 PC from my non-Win7 machines?

Piece of cake. Turns out all versions of Windows use the same networking scheme, so you can share files freely among PCs using different Windows versions.

Once some files are shared (on any PC), here's how to find them:

In Windows Vista: Choose Start→Network.

In Windows XP or Windows Me: Choose Start→My Network Places.

In earlier versions: Double-click the desktop icon called Network Neighborhood or My Network Places.

On the Mac: Just look in the Sidebar of any Finder window in the Shared category. Open the Workgroup icon, if you see it, and then double-click the name of the computer you want. Enter your PC account's name and password. (You'll probably have trouble if your PC account doesn't have a password.) The whole thing looks exactly like Figure 26-9.

Now you see icons that correspond to the computers on

your network (including your own machine), much as shown in Figure 26-9.

If you don't see the Windows 7 computers, it may because all the machines don't have the same *workgroup* name. (A workgroup is a cluster of networked machines. See Chapter 24 for details.) To change your Windows XP computer's workgroup name to match, choose Start→Control Panel, click "Performance and Maintenance," and then open System. Click the Computer Name tab, and then select Change.

To change a Vista PC's workgroup name, choose Start→Control Panel; click System and Maintenance; open System. Under the "Computer Name, Domain, and Workgroup Settings" heading, click Change Settings.

To change a Mac's workgroup name, open ☀️→System Preferences→Network. Click Advanced→WINS, and type right into the Workgroup box.

And to change your Windows 7 machine's name, type *rename* into the Start menu; click "Change workgroup name." Authenticate if necessary, and enjoy the box shown here.

Tip: Working with the same shared folders often? Save yourself a lot of time and burrowing—make a desktop shortcut of it right now!

Once you've opened the window that contains the shared folder, grab your mouse. Right-click the shared item and drag it to the desktop. When you release the mouse, choose "Create shortcuts here" from the shortcut menu. From now on, you can double-click that shortcut to open the shared item directly.

Once you've brought a networked folder onto your screen, you can double-click icons to open them, drag them to the Recycle Bin, make copies of them, and otherwise manipulate them exactly as though they were icons on your own hard drive. (Of course, if you weren't given permission to change the contents of the shared folder, you have less freedom.)

Tip: There's one significant difference between working with "local" icons and working with those that sit elsewhere on the network. When you delete a file from another computer on the network (if you're allowed to do so), either by pressing the Delete key or by dragging it to the Recycle Bin, it disappears instantly and permanently, without ever appearing in the Recycle Bin.

You can even use Windows's Search feature to find files elsewhere on the network. This kind of searching can be very slow, however; see page 133 for details on how Search handles networked disks.

Extra Credit: Universal Naming Convention (UNC)

For hard-core nerds, that business of double-clicking icons in the Network folder is for sissies. When they want to call up a shared folder from the network, or even a particular document *in* a shared folder, they just type a special address into the address bar of any folder window, or even Internet Explorer—and then press the Enter key. You can also type such addresses into the Start→Run dialog box.

It might look like this: *laptop**shared documents**salaries 2012.doc*.

Tip: Actually, you don't have to type nearly that much. The AutoComplete feature may propose the full expression as soon as you type just a few letters of it.

This path format (including the double-backslash before the PC name and a single backslash before a folder name) is called the *Universal Naming Convention (UNC)*. It was devised to create a method of denoting the exact location of a particular file or folder on a network. It also lets network geeks open various folders and files on networked machines without having to use the Network window.

You can use this system in all kinds of interesting ways:

- Open a particular folder like this: *computer name**folder name*.

- You can also substitute the IP address for the computer instead of using its name, like this: *192.1681.44**my documents*.

- You can even substitute the name of a shared *printer* for the folder name.

- As described later in this chapter, Windows can even access shared folders that sit elsewhere on the Internet (offline backup services, for example). You can call these items onto your screen (once you're online) just by adding *http:* before the UNC code and using regular forward slashes instead of backward slashes, like this: *http://Computer Name/Folder Name.*

Tip: A great place to type UNC addresses is in the address bar at the top of any desktop window.

Mapping Shares to Drive Letters
All Versions

If you access network shares on a regular basis, you may want to consider another access technique, called *mapping shares*. Using this trick, you can assign a *letter* to a particular shared disk or folder on the network. Just as your hard drive is called C: and your floppy drive is A:, you can give your Family Stuff folder the letter F: and the backup drive in the kitchen the letter J:.

Doing so confers several benefits. First, these disks and folders now appear directly in the Computer window. Getting to them this way can be faster than navigating to the Network window.

Second, when you choose File→Open from within one of your applications, you'll be able to jump directly to a particular shared folder instead of having to double-click, ever deeper, through the icons in the Open File dialog box. You can also use the mapped drive letter in pathnames anywhere you would use a path on a local drive, such as the Run dialog box, a File→Save As dialog box, or the Command Line.

WORKAROUND WORKSHOP

Automatic Reconnections Can Be Tricky

If you select "Reconnect at logon" when mapping a shared disk or folder to a letter, the order in which you start your computers becomes important. The PC containing the shared disk or folder should start up before the computer that refers to it as, say, drive K:. That way, when the second computer searches for "drive K:" on the network, its quest will be successful.

On the other hand, this guideline presents a seemingly insurmountable problem if you have two computers on the network and each of them maps drive letters to folders or disks on the other.

In that situation, you get an error message to the effect that the permanent connection is not available. It asks if you want to reconnect the next time you start the computer. Click Yes.

Then, after all the computers have started up, open your Computer window or an Explorer window. You can see the mapped drive, but there's a red X under the icon. Ignore the X. Just double-click the icon. The shared folder or disk opens normally (because the other machine is now available), and the red X goes away.

To map a drive letter to a disk or folder, open any folder or disk window. Then:

1. **In any Explorer window, press Alt (or F10) to make the old menu bar appear. Choose Tools→"Map network drive."**

   The Map Network Drive dialog box appears, as shown in Figure 26-10.

2. **Using the drop-down list, choose a drive letter.**

   You can select any unused letter you like (except B, which is still reserved for the second floppy disk drive that PCs don't have anymore).

3. **Indicate which folder or disk you want this letter to represent.**

   You can type its UNC code into the Folder box, choose from the drop-down list of recently accessed folders, or click Browse.

FREQUENTLY ASKED QUESTION

FTP Sites and Other Online Disks

How do I bring an FTP server, or one of those Web-based backup drives, onto my PC?

The trick to bringing these servers online is the "Add a network place" link—but you won't find it in the task pane of the Network window, as it was in Windows XP.

The trick is to right-click a blank spot in the *Computer* window. From the shortcut menu, choose "Add a network location."

When the wizard appears, click Next. Then, on the second screen, click "Choose a custom network location." Click Next.

Finally you arrive at the critical screen, where you can type in the address of the Web site, FTP site, or other network location that you want your new shortcut to open.

Into the first text box, you can type any of these network addresses:

The UNC code. As described earlier in this chapter, a UNC code pinpoints a particular shared folder on the network. For example, if you want to open the shared folder named FamilyBiz on the computer named Dad, enter *dad\family-biz*. Capitalization doesn't matter. Or, to open a specific file, you could enter something like *dad\finances\budget.xls*.

http://website/folder. To see what's in a folder called

Customers on a company Web site called BigBiz.com, enter *http://bigbiz.com/customers.* (You can't just type in any old Web address. It has to be a Web site that's been specifically designed to serve as a "folder" containing files.)

ftp://ftp.website/folder. This is the address format for FTP sites. For example, if you want to use a file in a folder named Bids on a company site named WeBuyStuff.com, enter *ftp://ftp.webuystuff.com/bids.*

What happens when you click Next depends on the kind of address you specified. If it was an FTP site, you're offered the chance to specify your user name. (Access to every FTP site requires a user name and password. You won't be asked for the password until you actually try to open the newly created folder shortcut.)

Click Finish to complete the creation of your network short-cut, which now appears in the Network Location area in the Computer window. To save you a step, the wizard also offers to connect to and open the corresponding folder.

You can work with these remote folders exactly as though they were sitting on your own hard drive. The only difference is that because you're actually communicating with a hard drive via the Internet, the slower speed may make it feel as if your PC has been drugged.

Tip: Most people use the mapping function for disks and drives elsewhere on the network, but there's nothing to stop you from mapping a folder that's sitting right there on your own PC.

4. **To make this letter assignment stick, turn on "Reconnect at logon."**

   If you don't use this option, Windows forgets this assignment the next time you turn on the computer. (Use the "Connect using different credentials" option if your account name on the shared folder's machine isn't the same as it is on this one.)

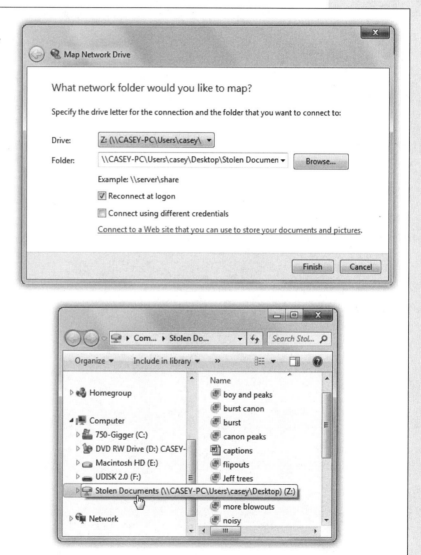

Figure 26-10:
Top: Choose a letter, any letter. Then choose a folder, any folder.

Bottom: You've just turned a folder into a drive, complete with its own drive letter—and instant access to the Navigation pane.

5. **Click Finish.**

   A window opens to display the contents of the folder or disk. If you don't want to work with any files at the moment, just close the window.

From now on (depending on your setting in step 4), that shared disk or folder shows up in your Navigation pane along with the disks that are actually in your PC, as shown at bottom in Figure 26-9.

Tip: If you see a red X on one of these mapped icons, it means that the PC on which one of the shared folders or disks resides is either off the network or is turned off completely.

Windows by Remote Control

Windows provides many avenues for accessing one PC from another across the Internet. If you're a road warrior armed with a laptop, you may be delighted by these features. If you're a corporate employee who used to think you could escape the office by going home, you may not.

In any case, each of these *remote access* features requires a good deal of setup and some scavenging through the technical underbrush, and each offers slightly different benefits and drawbacks. But when you're in Tulsa and a spreadsheet you need is on your PC in Tallahassee, you may be grateful to have at least one of these systems in place.

And besides—if you're connecting to PCs at your corporate office, your corporate IT people have probably already done all the hard work of getting the computers at work set up for you to connect to them from home or the road.

Remote Access Basics
All Versions

The two most common scenarios for using these remote access features are: (a) controlling your home PC remotely using a laptop, and (b) connecting to your office network from your PC at home. To help you keep the roles of these various computers straight, the computer industry has done you the favor of introducing specialized terminology:

- The *host computer* is the home-base computer—the unattended one that's waiting for you to connect.

- The *remote computer* is the one you'll be using: your laptop on the road, for example, or your home machine (or laptop) when you tap into the office network.

This chapter covers three systems of connecting:

- **Dialing direct.** The remote computer can dial the host PC directly, modem to modem, becoming part of the network at the host location. At that point, you can access shared folders exactly as described in the previous chapter.

  The downside? The host PC must have its own phone line that only it answers. Otherwise, its modem answers every incoming phone call, occasionally blasting the ears of hapless human callers. No wonder this is becoming a less common connection method.

- **Virtual private networking (VPN).** Using this system, you don't have to make a direct connection from the remote PC to the host. Instead, you use the Internet as an intermediary. You avoid long-distance charges, and the host PC doesn't have to have its own phone line. Once again, the remote computer behaves exactly as though it has joined the network of the system you're dialing into.

- **Remote Desktop.** This feature doesn't just make the remote PC join the network of the host; it actually turns your computer *into* the faraway host PC, filling your screen with its screen image. When you touch the trackpad on your laptop, you're actually moving the cursor on the home-base PC's screen, and so forth.

Tip: For added protection against snoopers, you should use Remote Desktop *with* a VPN connection.

To make Remote Desktop work, you have to connect *to* a computer running Windows 7 (Professional and above), Vista (Business and above), XP Pro, or Windows Server. But the machine you're connecting *from* can be any relatively recent Windows PC, a Macintosh (to get a free copy of Remote Desktop Connection for Mac, visit *www.microsoft.com/mac/*), or even a computer running Linux (you'll need the free *rdesktop client*, available from *www.rdesktop.org*).

Tip: The world is filled with more powerful, more flexible products that let you accomplish the same things as these Windows features, from software programs like LapLink, Carbon Copy, and PC Anywhere to Web sites like *www.gotomypc.com*.

On the other hand, Remote Desktop is free.

Note, by the way, that these are all methods of connecting to an *unattended* machine. If somebody is sitting at the PC back home, you might find it far more convenient to connect using Remote Assistance, described in Chapter 5. It's easier to set up and offers the same kind of "screen sharing" as Remote Desktop.

Dialing Direct
All Versions

Here, then, is Method 1, dialing in from the road, modem to modem. To set up the host to make it ready for access from afar, you first must prepare it to answer calls. Then you need to set up the remote computer to dial in.

Setting Up the Host PC

Professional • Enterprise • Ultimate

If your host PC has its own private phone line—the lucky thing—here's how to prepare it for remote access:

1. **Choose Start→Control Panel→Network and Internet→Network and Sharing Center.**

   The Network and Sharing Center appears.

2. **Click the "Change adapter settings" link on the left side.**

   The Network Connections window appears. Icons now appear, representing your various network connections. (See Chapter 9.)

3. **Press the Alt or F10 key to make the menu bar appear. Choose File→New Incoming Connection.**

   The Allow Connections to this Computer wizard appears (Figure 27-1, top). You're now looking at a list of every account holder on your PC (Chapter 23).

4. **Choose the names of the users who are allowed to dial in.**

   If you highlight a name, turn on its checkbox, and then click Account Properties, you can turn on the *callback* feature—a security feature that, after you've dialed in, makes your host PC hang up and call you back at a specific number. You can either (a) specify a callback number at the host machine in advance, so that outsiders won't be able to connect, or (b) let the remote user *specify* the callback number, which puts most of the telephone charges on the host computer's bill (so that you can bypass obscene hotel long-distance surcharges). Click OK to close the dialog box.

5. **Click Next.**

   Now you can choose *how* remote users will connect (Figure 27-1, bottom).

6. **Select "Through a dial-up modem." Select your modem in the list, and then click Next.**

   Now you're prompted to choose which networking capabilities to offer over the dial-up connection. Ensure that the "Internet Protocol Version 4" and "File and Printer Sharing for Microsoft Networks" options are selected.

7. **Click "Allow access."**

   The final screen says, "The people you chose can now connect to this computer. To connect, they will need the following information:"—and then you see your computer's official name.

   Truth is, though, if you plan to dial in, you don't even need to know that; all you need is your phone number!

A new icon in your Network Connections window, called Incoming Connections, is born.

Your home-base PC is ready for connections. When the phone rings, the modem answers it. (Of course, you shouldn't use this feature with the same phone line as your answering machine or your fax machine.)

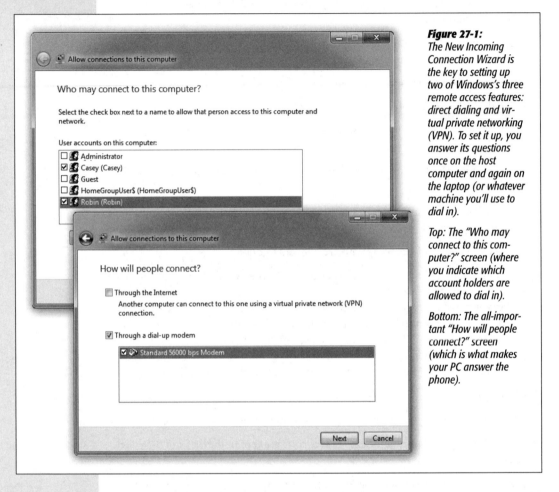

Figure 27-1:
The New Incoming Connection Wizard is the key to setting up two of Windows's three remote access features: direct dialing and virtual private networking (VPN). To set it up, you answer its questions once on the host computer and again on the laptop (or whatever machine you'll use to dial in).

Top: The "Who may connect to this computer?" screen (where you indicate which account holders are allowed to dial in).

Bottom: The all-important "How will people connect?" screen (which is what makes your PC answer the phone).

You might want to make a few changes to the configuration now. Right-click on the incoming connection's icon; from the shortcut menu, choose Properties.

In the Incoming Connections Properties dialog box, you can open your *modem's* Properties to turn on "Disconnect a call if idle for more than __ minutes." Doing so makes sure that your home-base PC won't tie up the line after your laptop in the hotel room is finished going about its business.

Setting Up the Remote PC
All Versions

Next, go to the remote computer and get it ready to phone home. Here's what to do:

1. Choose Start→Control Panel→Network and Internet→Network and Sharing Center. In the Tasks pane on the left, click "Set up a new connection or network."

   The "Set up a connection or network" wizard appears.

2. Scroll down, if necessary, and double-click "Connect to a workplace."

   If you already have a dial-up connection, Windows asks if you want to use the connection you already have. "No, create a new connection" is already selected.

3. Click Next.

   Now Windows wants to know if you'll be connecting via modem ("Dial directly") or via Internet ("Use my Internet connection (VPN)").

4. Click "Dial directly."

   Now you're asked to type in the phone number you'll want your laptop to call.

5. Type in the phone number and a name for your connection (like "Phone home"). Click "Don't connect now; just set it up so I can connect later" and then click Next.

   Another screen, another form to fill out.

6. Type in your user name and password, and if a network administrator so dictates, specify a domain name. Then click Create.

   Windows tells you, "The connection is ready to use."

7. Click Close.

You're now ready to establish a connection between the two computers.

Making the Call

Once you've configured both computers, make sure both the host and remote systems are running. To connect from the remote system to the host, follow these steps on your laptop:

1. **Click the Network icon in the notification area of the taskbar.**

   A list of connections appears.

2. **Click the connection you created; click Connect.**

   The Connect dialog box shown in Figure 27-2 appears.

Note: If you're using a laptop while traveling, you might have to tell Windows where you are before you attempt to connect. If you're in a different area code, for example, open Control Panel→Hardware and Sound→Phone and Modem Options. Make sure you've specified your current location, complete with whatever fancy dialing numbers it requires. Click the current location and then click OK. Now Windows knows what area code and prefixes to use.

---

3. **Check your name, password, and phone number.**

This is the same name and password you'd use to log in at the Welcome screen if you were sitting in front of the host PC (Chapter 23).

Don't blow off this step. Typing the wrong name and password is the number-one source of problems.

Figure 27-2:
You're ready to phone home. If you click the Properties button, you can invoke a dialing rule, if you created one, which can save you a bit of fiddling with area codes and access numbers.

To set that up, download the free PDF appendix called "Details on Dial-Up." You'll find it on this book's "Missing CD" page at www.missingmanuals.com.

4. Click Dial.

Windows dials into your home or office PC, makes the connection, and—if the phone number, name, and password are all correct—puts an icon for this connection into the list of connections you see when you click the network icon in the notification area (Figure 27-3, top).

You're free to open up any shared folders, even use shared printers, on your network back home. And although it may make your brain hurt to contemplate it, you can even surf the Internet if your home PC has, say, a cable modem.

Note: Don't try to run any *programs* that reside on your host PC, however; you'll be old and gray by the time they even finish opening.

When you're finished with your email check, address lookup, document transfer, or whatever, click the little network icon in your notification area, choose "Connect or disconnect" and choose Disconnect from the dialog that appears (Figure 27-3, bottom).

Figure 27-3:
Congratulations—you're in. Disconnect by clicking the notification area icon and choosing "Connect or disconnect."

Virtual Private Networking
All Versions

If you're a frequent traveler who regularly connects to a distant home or office by dialing direct, you must be the toast of your long-distance phone company.

Fortunately, there's a more economical solution. Virtual private networking (VPN) is a fancy way of saying, "Your remote computer can become part of your host network by using the Internet instead of a long-distance phone connection."

It's a lot like the direct-dialing feature described above—except this time, you don't pay any long-distance bills, your host PC doesn't require its own phone line, and (if the computers on both ends have fast connections) you're not limited to the sluglike speeds of dial-up modems.

With a VPN connection, both the host and the remote computers connect to the Internet the usual way: WiFi, DSL, cable modem, *or* good old dial-up. If you travel with a laptop, that's a good argument for signing up with a cellular data plan (see "Cellular Modems" in Chapter 9) or using a national or international dial-up ISP that has local access numbers wherever you plan to be.

Note: To make VPN work, both computers require Internet connections; that much is obvious.

The one at home (or at the office) is probably all set. You should, however, put some thought into getting the *laptop* online. You'll have to find wireless hot spots, for example, or, if you do this a lot, you can sign up for a cellular modem plan (page 351) or even a dial-up account.

Not only can VPN save the frequent traveler quite a bit of money in phone calls, but it's also extremely secure. When you connect using VPN, the information traveling between the two connected computers is encoded (encrypted) using a technology called *tunneling.* Your connection is like a reinforced steel pipe wending its way through the Internet to connect the two computers.

To create a VPN connection, the host computer has two important requirements. If you're VPNing into a corporation or school, it's probably all set already. Otherwise:

- It must be on the Internet at the moment you try to connect. Usually, that means it needs a full-time Internet connection, like cable modem or DSL. But in a pinch—if it has only a dial-up modem, for example—you could phone a family member or coworker just before you need to connect and beg her to go online with your home PC.

- It needs a fixed *IP address.* (See the Note below.)

On the other hand, the remote computer—your laptop—doesn't have any such requirements. It just needs an Internet connection.

Note: Several of the remote-connection methods described in this chapter require that your home-base PC have a *fixed, public* IP address. (An IP address is a unique number that identifies a particular computer on the Internet. It's made up of four numbers separated by periods.)

If you're not immediately nodding in understanding, murmuring, "Aaaaah, right," then download the bonus document available on this book's "Missing CD" at *www.missingmanuals.com.* The free PDF supplement you'll find there is called "Getting a Fixed, Public IP Address."

Setting Up the Host Machine

To set up the host PC for the VPN connection, do exactly as you would for direct-dial connections (page 801)—but in step 5, choose "Through the Internet" instead of "Through a dial-up modem." When the wizard finishes its work, the host machine is ready for action. Instead of setting up the modem to answer incoming calls, Windows now listens for incoming VPN connection requests from the Internet.

Making the Connection

Now move to the laptop, or whatever machine you'll be using when you're away from the main office. These steps, too, should seem familiar—they start out just like those that began on page 801. But in step 4, instead of clicking "Dial directly," you should choose "Use my Internet connection (VPN)."

Now you arrive at a screen that says, "Type the Internet address to connect to." Proceed like this:

1. **Type the host name or registered IP address of the VPN host—that is, the computer you'll be tunneling into. Click "Don't connect now; just set it up so I can connect later," and then click Next.**

   If you're connecting to a server at work or school, your system administrator can tell you what to type here. If you're connecting to a computer you set up yourself, specify its public IP address. (See the Note above.)

   This is *not* the private IP address on your home network, and definitely not its computer name (despite the fact that the New Incoming Connection Wizard told you that you would need to use that name); neither of these work when you're logged into another network.

2. **Type your user name, password, and, if required by the network administrator, the domain name. Then click Create.**

   Windows tells you, "The connection is ready to use."

3. **Click Connect Now or, if you plan to connect later, Close.**

   The result is a new entry in the "Connect to a network" dialog box shown in Figure 27-3; click the network icon in the taskbar's notification area to see it.

When you make the VPN connection, you've once again joined your home or office network. Exactly as with the direct-dial connection described earlier, you should feel free to transfer files, make printouts, and so on. Unless both computers are using high-speed Internet connections, avoid actually running programs on the distant PC.

When you want to disconnect, click the ▄ icon in your notification area, click the VPN Connection from the list that pops up, and then choose Disconnect.

(You can also disconnect using the Network and Sharing Center.)

Remote Desktop

Professional • Enterprise • Ultimate • (Home Premium and Starter are limited)

The third remote-access option, Remote Desktop, offers some spectacular advantages. When you use Remote Desktop, you're not just tapping into your home computer's network—you're actually bringing its screen onto your screen. You can run its programs, print on its printers, "type" on its keyboard, move its cursor, manage its files, and so on, all by remote control.

Remote Desktop isn't useful only when you're trying to connect to the office or reach your home computer from the road; it even works over an office network. You can actually take control of another computer in the office—to troubleshoot a novice's PC without having to run up or down a flight of stairs, perhaps, or just to run a program that isn't on your own machine.

If you do decide to use Remote Desktop over the Internet, consider setting up a VPN connection first; using Remote Desktop *over* a VPN connection adds a nice layer of security to the connection. It also means that you become part of your home or office network—and you can therefore connect to the distant computer using its private network address or even its computer name.

Tip: The computers on the *receiving* end of the connections require the Professional, Enterprise, or Ultimate editions of Windows 7. The laptop you're using can be running any edition.

In fact, it can be running any version of Windows all the way back to 95, and even Mac OS X or Linux. To install the Remote Desktop Connection client on Mac OS X or an older version of Windows, visit the Microsoft Download Center (*www.microsoft.com/downloads/*) and search for "Remote Desktop Connection." For Linux, get the free rdesktop program at *www.rdesktop.org*.

Setting Up the Host Machine

To get a PC ready for invasion—that is, to turn it into a host—proceed like this:

1. **Choose Start→Control Panel→System and Security→System. Click the "Remote settings" link.**

   Authenticate yourself if needed (page 726). The System Properties dialog opens to the Remote tab, as shown in Figure 27-4.

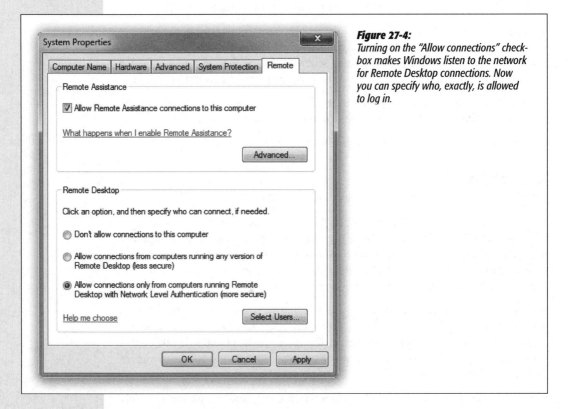

Figure 27-4:
Turning on the "Allow connections" checkbox makes Windows listen to the network for Remote Desktop connections. Now you can specify who, exactly, is allowed to log in.

2. Turn on "Allow connections only from computers running Remote Desktop with Network Level Authentication (more secure)."

You've just turned on the master switch that lets outsiders connect to your machine and take it over.

Tip: If this "more secure" option doesn't work, you can return here and try the "less secure" option. That should be necessary only when you're connecting from a much older version of Windows.

---

3. Click Select Users.

The Remote Desktop Users dialog box appears. You certainly don't want teenage hackers to visit your precious PC from across the Internet, playing your games and reading your personal info. Fortunately, the Remote Desktop feature requires you to specify precisely who is allowed to connect.

4. **(Optional) Click Add. In the resulting dialog box, type the names of the people who are allowed to access your PC using Remote Desktop.**

This dialog box might seem familiar—it's exactly the same idea as the Select Users, Computers, or Groups dialog box shown on page 740.

By default, local users with administrative privileges are automatically given access.

Choose your comrades carefully; remember that they'll be able to do anything to your system, by remote control, that you could do while sitting in front of it. (To ensure security, Windows insists that the accounts you're selecting here have passwords. Although you can add them to this list, password-free accounts can't connect.) Click OK.

5. **Click OK twice to close the dialog boxes you opened.**

The host computer is now ready for invasion. It's listening to the network for incoming connections from Remote Desktop clients.

Making the Connection

When you're ready to try Remote Desktop, fire up your laptop, or whatever computer will be doing the remote connecting. Then:

1. **Connect to the VPN of the distant host computer (page 803).**

If the host computer is elsewhere on your local network—in the same building, that is—you can skip this step.

2. **Choose Start→All Programs→Accessories→Remote Desktop Connection.**

The Remote Desktop Connection dialog box appears.

3. **Click Options to expand the dialog box (if necessary). Fill it out as shown in Figure 27-5.**

The idea is to specify the IP address or DNS name of the computer you're trying to reach. If it's on the same network, or if you're connected via a VPN, you can use its computer name instead.

Figure 27-5:
Type in the IP address, registered DNS name, or local computer name of your host computer. When prompted, fill in your name and password (and domain, if necessary), exactly the way you would if you were logging onto it in person.

4. **Click Connect.**

Now a freaky thing happens: After a moment of pitch-blackness, the host computer's screen fills your own (Figure 27-6). Don't be confused by the fact that all the open windows on the computer you're using have now *disappeared*. (Actually,

Figure 27-6:
The strange little bar at the top of your screen lets you minimize the distant computer's screen or turn it into a floating window. To hide this title bar, click the pushpin icon so that it turns horizontal. It slides into the top of the screen, out of your way, until you move the cursor to the top edge of the screen.

they won't if you click the Display tab and choose a smaller-than-full-screen remote desktop size before you connect.)

You can now operate the distant PC as though you were there in the flesh, using your own keyboard (or trackpad) and mouse. You can answer your email, make long-distance printouts, and so on. All the action—running programs, changing settings, and so on—is actually taking place on the faraway host computer.

Tip: You can even shut down or restart the faraway machine by remote control. Open a Command Prompt and run the command *shutdown /s*. The computer will shut down in less than a minute.

Keep in mind a few other points:

- You don't need to feel completely blocked out of your own machine. The little title bar at the top of the screen offers you the chance to put the remote computer's screen into a floating window of its own, permitting you to see both your own screen and the home-base computer's screen simultaneously (Figure 27-7). You can return to full-screen mode by pressing Ctrl+Alt+Break.

Figure 27-7:
By putting the other computer's screen into a window of its own, you save yourself a little bit of confusion. You can even minimize the remote computer's screen entirely, reducing it to a tab on your taskbar until you need it again.

- You can copy and paste highlighted text or graphics between the two machines (using regular Copy and Paste), and even transfer entire documents back and forth (using Copy and Paste on the desktop icons). Of course, if you've made both desktops visible simultaneously (Figure 27-7), you can move more quickly between local and remote.

- Even Windows can't keep its mind focused on two people at once. If somebody is trying to use the host machine in person, you'll see a message to the effect that you're about to bump that person off the PC.

  Similarly, if somebody tries to log on at the host computer while you're connected from the remote, *you* get unceremoniously dumped off. (You just get a message that tells you "Another user connected to the remote computer.") Fortunately, you don't lose work this way—your account remains logged on behind the scenes, just as in fast user switching. When you connect again later (after the interloper has signed off), you'll find all your programs and documents open exactly as you (or your interloper) left them.

- Back at the host computer, nobody can see what you're doing. The standard Welcome screen appears on the remote PC, masking your activities.

Keyboard Shortcuts for the Hopelessly Confused

When the Remote Desktop Connection window is maximized (that is, it fills your entire screen), all the standard Windows keyboard shortcuts operate on the *host* computer, not the one you're actually using. When you press the ⊞ key, for example, you see the host computer's Start menu.

Note: There's one exception. When you press Ctrl+Alt+Delete, *your* computer processes the keystroke.

But when you turn the Remote Desktop Connection into a floating window that doesn't fill your entire screen, it's a different story. Now your current computer "hears" your keystrokes. Now, pressing ⊞ opens *your* Start menu. So how, with the remote PC's screen in a window, are you supposed to operate it by remote control?

UP TO SPEED

For the Paranoid

If you see an error message indicating that "the identity of the remote computer cannot be verified," it means that you (or your network administrator) haven't obtained a security certificate from a trusted authority. This means you can't be absolutely, positively, 100 percent certain you're connecting to the computer you think you're connecting to.

But if you're super paranoid, you can click View Certificate, click the Details tab, and scroll down to look at the thumbprint.

Then, go over to the host machine, click Start, type *mmc* into the Search box, and click the icon that appears in the results. This brings up the Microsoft Management Console. Click File→Add/Remove Snap-In and add the Certificates

snap-in (choose Computer Account when prompted); click Finish, and then click OK.

Now, double-click the Remote Desktop folder on the left pane of the Console window, and then click Certificates. You should see one certificate appear in the middle pane. Double-click it, and examine the details to make sure they're identical to what you're seeing on the remote machine you're connecting from. When you close the Console, click No when it asks you if you want to save changes.

Now you're 100 percent certain, and can confidently click the box labeled "Don't ask me again for connections to this computer" when you make a Remote Desktop Connection to the host!

Microsoft has thought of everything. It's even given you alternatives for the key combinations you're accustomed to using. For example, suppose you've connected to your office PC using your laptop. When the Remote Desktop window isn't full-screen, pressing Alt+Tab switches to the next open program on the laptop—but pressing Alt+Page Up switches to the next program on the host computer.

Here's a summary of the special keys that operate the distant host computer—a table that can be useful if you're either an extreme power user or somebody who likes to win bar bets:

Standard Windows Key Combination	Remote Desktop Key Combination	Function
Alt+Tab	Alt+Page Up	Switches to the next open program
Alt+Shift+Tab	Alt+Page Down	Switches to the previous open program
Alt+Esc	Alt+Insert	Cycles through programs in the order in which you open them
Ctrl+Esc (or 🔳)	Alt+Home	Opens the Start menu
Ctrl+Alt+Delete	Ctrl+Alt+End	Displays the Windows Security dialog box

(Actually, you should use the alternative key combination for the Security dialog box whether the Remote Desktop window is maximized or not, because Ctrl+Alt+Delete is always interpreted by the computer you're currently using.)

Disconnecting

To get out of Remote Desktop full-screen mode, click the Close box in the strange little title bar at the top of your screen, as shown in Figure 27-6 (if you're using the floating window, you can click the usual ✖ in the upper-right of the window). Or, from the Start menu, choose X. (Yes, X. This special button means "Disconnect," and when you're using Remote Desktop, it replaces the ⏻ symbol at the bottom of the Start menu.)

Note, however, that this method leaves all your programs running and your documents open on the distant machine, exactly as though you had used fast user switching. If you log on again, either from the road or in person, you'll find all those programs and documents still on the screen, just as you left them.

If you'd rather log off in a more permanent way, closing all your distant documents and programs, choose Start→Log Off (from the other computer's Start menu, not yours).

Fine-tuning Remote Desktop Connections

Windows offers all kinds of settings for tailoring the way this bizarre, schizophrenic connection method works. The trick is, however, that you have to change them *before* you connect, using the tabs on the dialog box shown in Figure 27-8.

Here's what you find:

- **General tab.** Here's where you can tell Windows to edit or delete credentials (user name and password) from your last login, or to save all the current settings as a shortcut icon, which makes it faster to reconnect later. (If you connect to a number of different distant computers, saving a setup for each one in this way can be a huge timesaver.)

- **Display tab.** Use these options to specify the *size* (resolution) of the host computer's display (see Figure 27-8).

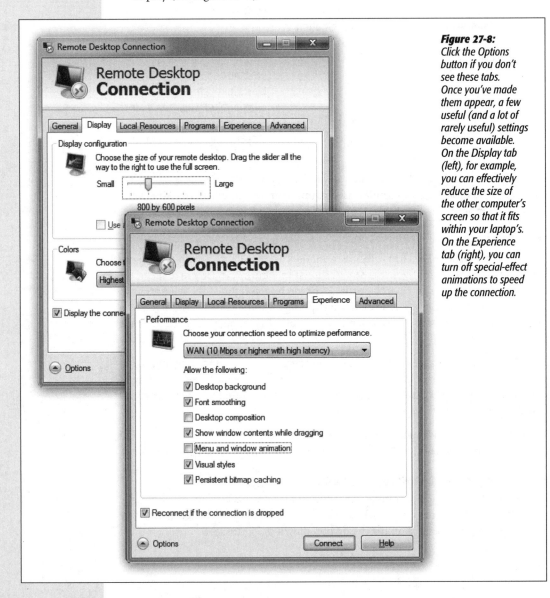

Figure 27-8:
Click the Options button if you don't see these tabs. Once you've made them appear, a few useful (and a lot of rarely useful) settings become available. On the Display tab (left), for example, you can effectively reduce the size of the other computer's screen so that it fits within your laptop's. On the Experience tab (right), you can turn off special-effect animations to speed up the connection.

- **Local Resources tab.** Using these controls, you can set up local peripherals and add-ons so they behave as though they were connected to the computer you're using. This is also where you tell Windows which PC should "hear" keystrokes like Alt+Tab, and whether or not you want to hear sound effects played by the distant machine.

- **Programs tab.** You can set up a certain program to run automatically as soon as you connect to the host machine.

- **Experience tab.** Tell Windows the speed of your connection, so it can limit fancy visual effects like menu animation, the desktop wallpaper, and so on, to avoid slowing down the connection. The Desktop Composition option controls whether Remote Desktop uses Windows's Aero glass effects (if, in fact, your computer has the horsepower).

- **Advanced.** You can control whether Remote Desktop Connection warns you if it can't verify the identity of a computer, and also whether to connect through a special gateway server (if you need to use one of these, your system administrator will tell you.)

UP TO SPEED

Remote Networking vs. Remote Control

When you connect to a PC using direct dial or virtual private networking (VPN), you're simply joining the host's network from far away. When you try to open a Word document that's actually sitting on the distant PC, your *laptop's* copy of Word opens and loads the file. Your laptop is doing the actual word processing; the host just sends and receives files as needed.

Windows's Remote Desktop feature is a different animal. In this case, you're using your laptop to *control* the host computer. If you double-click that Word file on the host computer, you open the copy of Word *on the host computer.* All the word processing takes place on the distant machine; all that passes over the connection between the two computers is a series of keystrokes, mouse movements, and screen displays. The host is doing all the work. Your laptop is just peeking at the results.

Once you understand the differences between these technologies, you can make a more informed decision about which to use when. For example, suppose your PC at the office has a folder containing 100 megabytes of images you

need to incorporate into a PowerPoint document. Using a remote networking connection means you'll have to wait for the files to be transmitted to your laptop before you can begin working—and if you've connected to the office machine using a dial-up modem, you'll be waiting, literally, for several *days*.

If you use a Remote Desktop connection, on the other hand, the files remain right where they are: on the host computer, which does all the processing. You see on your screen exactly what you would see if you were sitting at the office. When you drag and drop one of those images into your PowerPoint document, all the action is taking place on the PC at the other end.

Of course, if the computer doing the dialing is a brand-new Pentium 7 zillion-megahertz screamer, and the host system is a 5-year-old rustbucket on its last legs, you might actually *prefer* a remote network connection, so the faster machine can do most of the heavy work.

Part Eight: Appendixes

8

Installing & Upgrading to Windows 7

I f your computer came with Windows 7 already installed on it, you can skip this appendix—for now. But if you're running an earlier version of Windows and want to savor the Win7 experience, this appendix describes how to install the new operating system on your computer.

Before You Begin

Believe it or not, most of the work involved in installing Windows 7 takes place well before the installation DVD even approaches your computer. You have a lot of research and planning to do, especially if you want to avoid spending a five-day weekend in Upgrade Hell.

For example, you must ensure that your PC is beefy enough to handle Windows 7—not a sure thing at all. You also have to decide which of two types of installation you want to perform: an *upgrade* or a *clean install*. (More on this in a moment.)

If you opt for the clean install (a process that begins with *erasing your hard drive completely*), you must back up your data. Finally, you have to gather all the software bits and pieces you need in order to perform the installation.

Hardware Requirements

Before you even buy a copy of Windows, your first order of business should be to check your computer against the list of hardware requirements for Windows, as published by Microsoft. Windows 7, as it turns out, requires some fairly decent memory, speed, disk space, and, above all, graphics-card horsepower. Most 2004-era computers (and earlier ones) aren't up to the challenge.

A lower-powered computer can *run* Windows 7. It may feel slow, and you don't see the Aero Glass look (transparent window edges, taskbar thumbnails, and so on; see Chapter 1). It does, however, offer all the other security and feature enhancements.

Here's what such a computer requires:

- **Processor:** 1 gigahertz or faster.

- **Memory:** 1 gigabyte or more.

- **Hard-disk space:** At least 16 gigabytes free.

- **Graphics card:** DirectX 9 support with WDDM 1.0 driver (check the packaging or, for laptops, the manufacturer's Web site).

Tip: A DVD drive is a good idea, but it's not essential. Most netbooks don't have one. If you want to install Windows 7 on such a computer, you can either buy an external USB DVD drive ($50 or less) or use Microsoft's Windows 7 USB/DVD Download Tool to install Windows 7 from a USB memory stick. For more information, see *http://store.microsoft.com/Help/ISO-Tool.*

The tool requires access to a computer with a DVD drive that's running Windows XP Service Pack 2 or later.

If your computer doesn't meet these requirements, then consider a hardware upgrade—especially a memory upgrade. With memory prices what they are today (read: dirt cheap), you'll thank yourself later for adding as much RAM as you can afford.

Adding more hard-disk space is also a reasonably easy and inexpensive upgrade, and there are inexpensive graphics adapters that will handle Windows's visual effects (that Aero business described in Chapter 1).

The one place where you may be stuck, though, is on the processor issue. The state of the art in processor speeds seems to advance almost weekly, but it's safe to say that a PC running at 1 GHz or less is certifiably geriatric. It may be time to think about passing the old girl on to the kids or donating it to a worthy cause and getting yourself a newer, faster computer. As a bonus, it will come with Windows 7 preinstalled.

The Compatibility Issue

Once you've had a conversation with yourself about your equipment, it's time to investigate the suitability of your existing software and add-on gear for use with Windows.

- **Hardware.** In general, products released since October 2006 are Windows 7–compatible, but you should still proceed with caution before using them with Windows 7. You should by all means check the Web sites of these components' manufacturers in hopes of finding updated driver software.

- **Software.** *Most* programs and drivers that work with Windows XP work fine in Windows 7, but not all. And programs designed for Windows 95, 98, and Me may well cause you problems.

Unless you're that lucky individual who's starting fresh with a brand new PC and software suite, you'd be wise to run the Windows 7 Upgrade Advisor program *before* you move into Windows 7 World.

If you haven't yet bought Windows 7, you can download this important program from Microsoft's Web site at *windows.microsoft.com/upgradeadvisor*. It runs only on Windows XP and Vista (and, pointlessly, Windows 7), and it scans your system to produce a report on the Windows 7 compatibility of your hardware and software.

If you have a Windows 7 DVD, insert it. On its welcome screen (Figure A-2, top), click "Check compatibility online," and then download the Windows 7 Upgrade Advisor.

Tip: A compatibility checker also runs automatically during the installation process itself.

The Upgrade Advisor first offers to download updates from Microsoft's Web site. If you can get online, it's an excellent idea to take it up on this offer. You'll get all the patches, updates, and bug fixes Microsoft has released since the debut of Windows 7.

Next, the advisor shows you a report that identifies potential problems. Almost everybody finds some incompatibilities reported here, because Microsoft is particularly conservative about which programs will work with Windows 7.

But if the report lists a serious incompatibility, it's not worth proceeding with the installation until you've updated or uninstalled the offending program.

Note: Utilities like hard-drive formatting software, virus checkers, firewall programs, and so on are especially troublesome. Do not use them in Windows 7 unless they're specifically advertised for Windows 7 compatibility.

Upgrade vs. Clean Install

If your PC currently runs Vista, the next big question is whether or not you should *upgrade* it to Windows 7, or *erase* it and perform a clean install of Windows 7. (If if you have Windows XP now, you have no choice; you must perform a clean install.)

Upgrading the operating system retains all your existing settings and data files. Your Favorites list and the files in your Documents folder will all be there after the upgrade.

Sounds great, right? Who wouldn't want to avoid having to redo all those settings?

Unfortunately, in past version of Windows, upgrading from an older copy of Windows often brought along unwelcome baggage: outdated drivers, fragmented disk drives, and a clutter of unneeded registry settings. If all this artery-clogging gunk had already begun to slow down your computer, upgrading to a newer version of Windows only made things worse.

Microsoft says it's drastically improved the upgrade process. Rather than merging the old operating system in with the new, Windows 7's Setup program pushes all the old stuff (programs, settings, and documents) aside, and then wipes the old OS clean. After that, Setup installs the new OS and then brings over your settings, documents, and programs. All of this leads to a cleaner upgrade that should be more stable than previous Windows upgrades.

Even so, some caution is still justified. The upgrade of the operating system itself may go smoothly, but there's no telling what glitches this procedure may introduce in your non-Microsoft programs. In general, such programs prefer to be installed fresh on the new operating system.

Your Windows 7 upgrade options depend on which *version* of Vista you have now:

- **Home Basic or Home Premium.** You can upgrade to the Home Premium or Ultimate versions of Windows 7.

- **Business.** You can upgrade only to Windows 7 Professional or Ultimate.

- **Ultimate.** You can upgrade only to Windows 7 Ultimate.

What's more, you can't upgrade a 32-bit version to a 64-bit version or vice versa. However, if you've got 4 GB or more of RAM in your computer, you need a 64-bit version of Windows 7 to use all of it. So if you think you've got an abundance of RAM in your future but you're running a 32-bit version of Vista, you may want to do a clean install of a 64-bit version of Windows 7.

Note: The Enterprise edition of Windows 7 isn't for sale to mere mortals. It's available only to corporations, whose system administrators will handle all the upgrading hassles without your involvement.

Buying Windows 7

If you do decide to upgrade from Windows Vista, you'll save some money, because the Upgrade version of Windows is less expensive than a Full version.

If you're not sure whether the Upgrade version will work on your machine, check this Microsoft Web page: *http://bit.ly/3YKvs*.

And remember: If your computer is currently running anything but Windows Vista, you *have* to buy the Full version of Windows 7 and perform a clean install.

Tip: As you shop, remember, too, that you can start now with one of the less expensive editions—and later, if you find your style cramped, upgrade your installed copy to a more powerful edition quickly and easily. Read about the Anytime Upgrade on page 268.

About the Clean Install

The alternative to an upgrade is the *clean install* of Windows 7. During a clean install, you reformat your hard disk, wiping out everything on it. The overwhelming advantage of a clean install is that you wind up with a fresh system, 100 percent free of all those creepy little glitches and inconsistencies that have been building up over the years. Ask any Windows veteran: The best way to boost the speed of a system that has grown sluggish is to perform a clean install of the operating system and start afresh.

Backing up

The drawback of a clean install, however, is the work it will take you to back up all your files and settings before you begin. If your computer has a tape drive, DVD burner, or external hard drive, that's not much of a problem. Just perform a full backup (or simply drag and drop every last file that's important to you), test it to make sure that everything you need has been copied and is restorable, and you're ready to install Windows 7.

Tip: One of the most convenient solutions is to install a new hard drive before you upgrade and put your current hard drive in an external enclosure that you've bought off the Web. You can put it on a shelf for safe keeping, and plug it in every time you need to grab a file from your old installation.

You can even do this with some laptops whose hard drives are user-replaceable: inexpensive USB or FireWire enclosures are available in both 2.5" (laptop hard drive) and 3.5" (desktop hard drive) size, and installation takes only a few minutes. Just be sure you know what kind of hard drive you have (Serial ATA or Parallel ATA, and in some cases, SCSI) before you choose either your new internal hard drive or your enclosure, because both of these must be compatible with whatever you're currently using.

If you have a second computer, you can also consider backing up your stuff onto it, via a network (Chapter 26). In any of these cases, you'll probably want to use Windows Easy Transfer to perform the backup (page 830).

Even having a full backup, however, doesn't mean a clean install will be a walk in the park. After the installation, you still have to reinstall all your programs, reconfigure all your personalized settings, recreate your network connections, and so on.

Tip: It's a good idea to spend a few days writing down the information you need as you're working on your computer. For example, if you're using dial-up Internet, copy down the phone number, user name, and password you use to connect to your Internet service provider (ISP), and the user names and passwords you need for various Web sites you frequent.

Performing a clean install also means buying the Full version of Windows 7. It's more expensive than the Upgrade version, but at least you can install it on a blank hard disk without having to install an old Windows version first or have your original installation CDs available. Each of the sold-in-stores Windows 7 editions (Home Premium, Professional, Ultimate) is available in Full or Upgrade versions.

Overall, a clean install is preferable to an upgrade. But if you don't have the time or the heart to back up your hard drive, wipe it clean, and re-establish all your settings, the upgrade option is always there for you.

Dual Booting

Here's yet another decision you have to make before you install Windows 7: whether or not you'll want to be able to *dual boot*.

In this advanced scenario, you install Windows 7 onto the same PC that contains an older version of Windows, maintaining both of them side by side. Then, each time you turn on the PC, it *asks you* which operating system you want to run for this computing session (see Figure A-1).

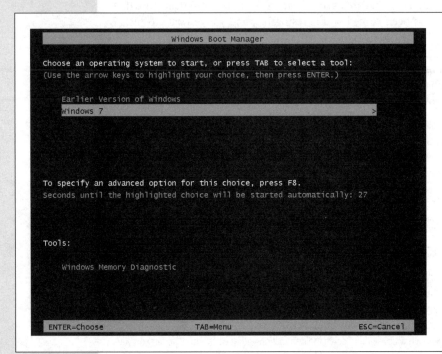

```
                    Windows Boot Manager

Choose an operating system to start, or press TAB to select a tool:
(Use the arrow keys to highlight your choice, then press ENTER.)


    Earlier Version of Windows
    Windows 7                                                   >




To specify an advanced option for this choice, press F8.
Seconds until the highlighted choice will be started automatically: 27




Tools:

    Windows Memory Diagnostic




 ENTER=Choose                TAB=Menu                   ESC=Cancel
```

Figure A-1:
When you dual boot, this menu appears each time you turn on your PC, offering you a choice of OS. (If you don't choose in 30 seconds, the PC chooses for you.)

Dual booting comes in handy when you have some program or hardware gadget that works with one operating system but not the other. For example, if you have a scanner with software that runs on Windows XP but not Windows 7, you can start up in XP only when you want to use the scanner.

If you intend to dual boot, keep this in mind: *You can't install both operating systems onto the same hard drive partition.* If you did, your programs would become horribly confused.

Instead, keep your two Windows versions separate using one of these avenues:

- Buy a second hard drive. Use it for one of the two operating systems.

- Back up your hard drive, erase it completely, and then *partition* it, which means dividing it so that each chunk shows up in the Disk Management window (Chapter 21) with its own icon, name, and drive letter. Then install each operating system on a separate disk partition.

- If you're less technically inclined, you might prefer to buy a program like Partition-Magic (*www.partitionmagic.com*). Not only does it let you create a new partition on your hard drive without erasing it first, but it's flexible and easy.

There's just one wrinkle with dual booting. If you install Windows 7 onto a separate partition (or a different drive), as you must, you won't find any of your existing programs listed in the Start menu, and your desktop won't be configured the way it is in your original operating system. You'll generally wind up having to reinstall every program into your new Windows 7 world, and to re-establish all your settings, exactly as though the Windows 7 "side" were a brand-new PC.

Installing Windows 7

Once you've decided to take the plunge and install Windows, you can begin the countdown.

Preparing for the Installation

If you've made all the plans and done all the thinking described so far in this chapter, you have only a short checklist left to follow:

- Update your virus program and scan for viruses. Then, if you're updating an existing copy of Windows, *turn off* your virus checker, along with other auto-loading programs like non-Microsoft firewall software and Web ad blockers.

- Confirm that your computer's BIOS—its basic startup circuitry—is compatible with Windows 7. To find out, contact the manufacturer of the computer or the BIOS.

  Don't skip this step. You may well need to upgrade your BIOS if the computer was made before mid-2006.

- Gather updated, Windows 7–compatible drivers for all your computer's components. Graphics and audio cards are particularly likely to need updates, so be sure to check the manufacturers' Web sites—and driver-information sites like *www.windrivers.com* and *www.driverguide.com*—and download any new drivers you find there.

- Disconnect any gear that's not absolutely necessary for using your computer. You'll have better luck if you reconnect devices *after* Windows 7 is in place. This includes scanners, game controllers, printers, and even that USB-powered lava lamp you like so much.

If you've gone to all this trouble and preparation, the Windows installation process can be surprisingly smooth. The Windows 7 installer is much less painful than the ones for previous versions of Windows. You won't see the old DOS-style startup screens, the installation requires fewer restarts, and if you're doing a clean install, it's amazingly fast (often 15 minutes or less).

Performing an Upgrade Installation

Here's how you upgrade your existing version of Windows to full Windows 7 status. (If you prefer to perform a clean install, skip these instructions.)

1. **Start your computer and log in. Insert the Windows 7 DVD into the drive.**

   The Setup program generally opens automatically (Figure A-2, top). If it doesn't, open Computer, double-click the DVD-ROM icon, and double-click the Setup.exe program in the DVD's root folder.

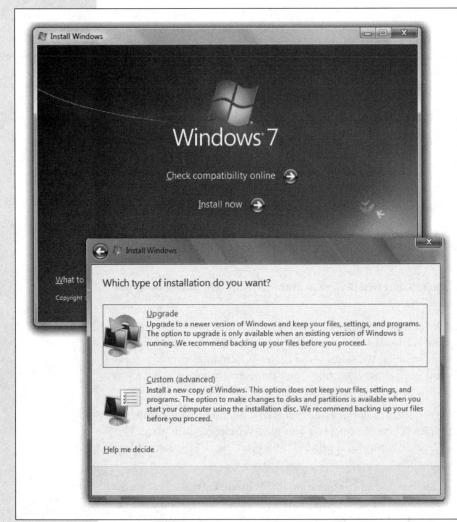

Figure A-2:
Top: The Setup program is ready for action. Close the doors, take the phone off the hook, and cancel your appointments. The installer will take at least an hour to go about its business—not including the time it will take you to iron out any post-installation glitches.

Bottom: Use the buttons on this screen to indicate whether you want a clean installation or an upgrade installation.

2. **Click Install Now.**

   The "Get important updates for installation" screen appears. Clearly, Microsoft thinks it's a good idea to download any software updates that have appeared since you bought your copy of Windows 7.

3. **Click "Go online to get the latest updates for installation."**

The installer searches the Web for updates and then downloads them for you. Then the "Type your product key" screen presents itself.

4. **Click Next.**

A screen full of legalese appears.

5. **Review the work of Microsoft's lawyers, and then click "I accept the license terms." Click Next.**

Now you're asked to choose between an upgrade and a clean install (Figure A-2, bottom).

6. **Click Upgrade.**

Now the installer checks to see if any of your PC's components are incompatible with Windows 7. If so, the Compatibility Report screen appears, shown in Figure A-3. There's not much you can do about it at this point, of course, other than to make a note of it and vow to investigate Windows 7–compatible updates later.

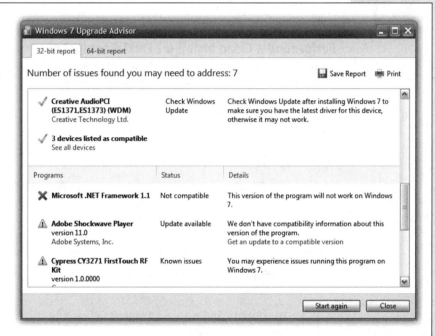

Figure A-3:
This screen lists any programs and drivers that Microsoft considers incompatible with Windows 7.

7. **Click Next.**

The installation program begins copying files and restarting the computer several times.

Unfortunately, this part can take a *lot* longer than 15 minutes.

8. **Type in your 25-character serial number (product key).**

The product key comes in the Windows 7 box or on the DVD case. If you bought Windows 7 from Microsoft and chose the download delivery method, you should have received it online.

If you turn on "Automatically activate Windows when I'm online," then Windows will try to activate itself after three days.

Note: You can leave the product key blank for now. You'll be offered the chance to enter it when you activate Windows 7.

After you type in your product key and press Enter, you're almost there. Before you can log in for the first time, you're asked to choose how to configure Windows's protection features. Select "Use recommended settings." After that, you're asked to confirm your date and time settings and, finally, tell Windows whether your network is at home, work, or a public location. (For more information on the implications of these choices, see page 348.)

After you log in, the Windows desktop appears at last.

Performing a Clean Install (or Dual-Boot Install)

To perform a clean installation of Windows 7, or to install it onto an empty partition for the purpose of dual booting, the steps are slightly different.

Tip: If you're upgrading a Windows XP machine to Windows 7, take advantage of the tips, tricks, and video tutorials on Microsoft's Web site here: *http://bit.ly/RyeCI.*

1. **Start up your PC from your Windows 7 DVD.**

Every Windows 7–compatible computer can start up from a DVD instead of from its hard drive. Sometimes, if you start up the computer with a DVD in the drive, instructions for booting from it appear right on the screen (you may be directed to hold down a certain key, or any key at all). If you don't see such an instruction, you might have to check with the computer's maker for instructions on this point.

At the beginning of the setup process, you just wait for a moment while the installer loads ups.

2. **When the Install Windows screen appears, click Next to bypass the Regional and Language Options screen.**

Bypass it, that is, unless you don't speak English or don't live in the United States.

3. **At the next screen, click Install Now.**

The usual legal notice pops up.

4. **Review the licensing agreement if you like, click "I accept the license terms," and then click Next to continue.**

Since you booted from the DVD, you don't have the option of performing an upgrade installation.

5. **Click "Custom (advanced)" to proceed with a clean install.**

Now Windows shows you a list of the *partitions* on your hard drive. Unless you've set up your hard drive for *dual booting* as described on page 821, you probably have only one.

6. **Click to highlight the name of the partition (or choose some unallocated space) on which you want to install Windows 7, and then click Next.**

Use the Drive Options at the bottom of this window to delete, create, or format partitions.

After the formatting process is complete, the Setup program begins copying files to the partition you selected and eventually restarts the computer a time or two.

7. **Choose a name for your main account and a computer name.**

Either accept the proposed computer name (your name followed by "-PC"), or type one that's short and punctuation-free (hyphens are OK).

You can always change the computer name later; see page 336.)

8. **Choose a password and password hint.**

You can read more about *accounts* in Chapter 23. This very first account, the one you're creating here, is very important; it's going to be an Administrator account (page 716). Once you log in using *this* account, you can create accounts for other people.

Tip: If it's just you and your laptop, you can leave the password blank; you'll be able to log in, wake the computer from sleep, and otherwise get to your stuff that much faster. Note, however, that if your account password is blank, some Windows features won't work (including Remote Desktop, described in Chapter 27).

---

9. **On the "Type your Windows product key" screen, enter the 25-character product key and click Next.**

The product key is the serial number that came with your Windows 7 DVD. If you turn on "Automatically activate Windows when I'm online," then Windows will try to activate itself in the next three days.

10. **Click Next.**

Now you can choose how to configure Windows's protection features.

11. **Select "Use recommended settings."**

The date and time settings screen appears.

12. **Set the date, time, and time zone, and then click Next.**

Now Windows tries to connect to your network, if you have one. If it succeeds, it asks whether your network is at home, at work, or in a public location. (For more information on the implications of these choices, see page 348.)

When it's all over, the Windows desktop appears. If you need a little help getting oriented, click Start→Getting Started, which is described next.

Getting Started

From this program, you can perform a number of post-installation tasks, including these:

• Transfer files from your old computer (see "Windows Easy Transfer").

• Find out what's new, learn about the basics of Windows, and see some demos.

• Add users to Windows. That means adding *accounts* to a PC that will be used by more than one person, as described in Chapter 23.

• Install Windows Live Essentials (page 265), which includes a lot of the applications that used to come with Windows, including an email program, an instant messenger, and a photo gallery.

Tip: While you're thinking about it, you may as well go download Microsoft's free—yes, free—antivirus and antispyware programs, called Microsoft Security Essentials. Google it; it'll come right up.

If you ever want to visit Getting Started when you *haven't* just started up, you can find it in Start→All Programs→Accessories.

Activation

After 30 days, Windows will insist that you *activate* it, as shown in Figure A-4. You'll see several reminders that grow increasingly stern before Windows forces you to activate.

Activation is copy protection. In some countries, a huge percentage of all copies of Windows are illegal duplicates; activation, introduced in Windows XP, is designed to stop such piracy in its tracks. Unfortunately, it also prevents you from installing one copy of Windows on even *two* computers. That's right: If you have a desktop PC as well as a laptop, you have to buy Windows twice.

How does it know you're being naughty? When you install Windows, the operating system inspects 10 crucial components inside your PC: the hard drive, motherboard, video card, memory, and so on. All this information is transmitted, along with the 25-character serial number that came with Windows (the product key), to Microsoft's database via your Internet account. The process takes about 2 seconds and involves little more than clicking an OK button. You have just *activated* Windows 7.

Note: If you don't have an Internet connection, activation is a much more grueling procedure. You have to call a toll-free number, read a 50-digit identification number to the Microsoft agent, and then type a 42-digit confirmation number into your software. Do whatever it takes to avoid having to endure this fingertip-numbing ritual.

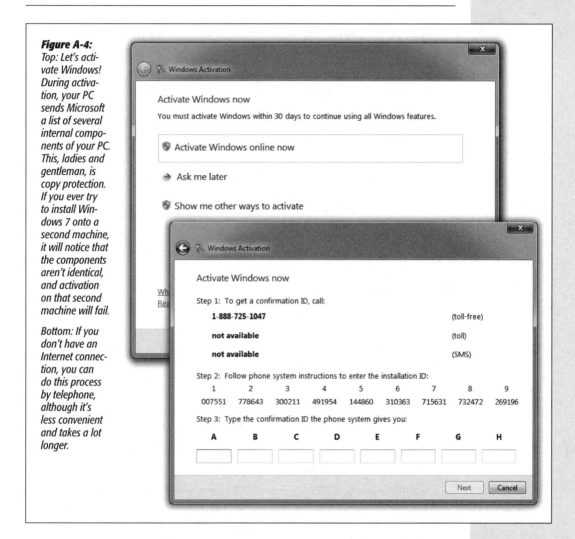

Figure A-4:
Top: Let's activate Windows! During activation, your PC sends Microsoft a list of several internal components of your PC. This, ladies and gentlemen, is copy protection. If you ever try to install Windows 7 onto a second machine, it will notice that the components aren't identical, and activation on that second machine will fail.

Bottom: If you don't have an Internet connection, you can do this process by telephone, although it's less convenient and takes a lot longer.

Later, if you try to install the same copy of Windows onto a different computer, it will check in with Microsoft and discover that the new machine's components aren't the same. It will conclude that you have tried to install the same copy of the operating system onto a different machine—and it will lock you out.

This aspect of Windows 7 has frightened or enraged many a computer fan. In truth, though, it isn't quite as bad as it seems. Here's why:

- If you buy a new PC with Windows 7 already installed, you don't have to activate anything; it's already been done.

- Copies of Windows that are distributed within corporations don't require this activation business, either.

- No information about *you* is transferred to Microsoft during this activation process—only a list of the components in your PC make the trip.

- Don't believe the Internet Chicken Littles who claim that activation will shut down your PC if you try to upgrade the memory or another component. In fact, you would have to replace four of the 10 key components within a period of four months—your basic hardware-upgrade frenzy—before Windows stopped recognizing your computer. And even then, you can just call Microsoft and explain what happened; in most cases, the company will cheerfully provide a new activation number.

If, during installation, you turned on "Automatically activate Windows when I'm online" (on the same screen where you enter your product key), Windows tries to activate itself for the first three days of installation by sending signals back to Microsoft.

If you don't activate it in time, Windows 7 switches into what's tactfully called Reduced Functionality Mode, in which many features become time-limited or stop working.

Windows Easy Transfer

Windows Easy Transfer is a program available for download from Microsoft. It's designed to round up the files and preference settings from one computer—and copy them into the proper places on a new one. For millions of upgrading Windows fans, this little piece of software is worth its weight in gold.

You can use Windows Easy Transfer in several ways:

- If you have two computers, you can run Windows Easy Transfer on the old computer, package its files and settings, and then transfer them to the new computer.

  You can make the transfer over a network connection, a direct cable connection, or via a flash drive or hard drive

- If you have only one computer, you can run Windows Easy Transfer before you install, saving the files and settings to a flash drive or a second hard drive. Then, after performing a clean install of Windows 7, you can run the wizard again, neatly importing and reinstating your saved files and settings.

Note: Easy Transfer doesn't bring over your programs—just your files and settings.

Phase 1: Backing up the Files

To save the files and settings on your old computer (or your old operating system), download Windows Easy Transfer from Microsoft's Web site at *http://bit.ly/9rt8eg*, and then proceed like this:

1. **Double-click the file you downloaded.**

   It has a name like "wet7xp_x86.exe." The Setup program opens. Install Windows Easy Transfer.

2. **Open the Start Menu, click All Programs, and choose Windows Easy Transfer for Windows 7.**

   Windows Easy Transfer opens up (Figure A-5, top).

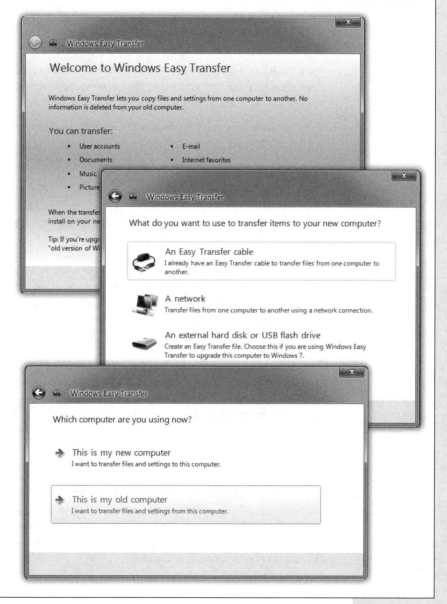

Figure A-5:
Top: Windows Easy Transfer can be a sanity-saving convenience.

Middle: It lets you transfer all your files and settings across a network or transfer cable, or onto a disk. (The Easy Transfer Cable mentioned here is a modified USB cable sold online for $40, or one may even have come with your new PC.)

Bottom: After you've installed Windows 7 or bought a new Windows 7 computer, you can reinstate all your old files and settings using the same wizard. Just locate the folder it saved originally.

3. Click Next. On the "What Do You Want to Use" screen, specify how you want to transfer the files and settings (Figure A-5, middle).

You can choose from a link to another computer using a direct cable or network connection, or to a flash drive or external hard disk. The last option also lets you use a network location, which could be a file server or another computer on your network.

4. Click the option you want to use, and click Next.

The "Which computer are you using now?" screen appears (Figure A-5, bottom).

5. Click "This is my old computer."

The "What do you want to transfer?" screen appears. If you're transferring across the network or a transfer cable, go over to your new computer and run Windows Easy Transfer there. If you're using the network method, you also have to provide the key that appears on this screen.

6. Specify which information you want to transfer to the other computer.

You can elect to transfer all the user accounts on the computer, complete with their files and settings, or just *your* account, files, and settings. (See Chapter 23 for details on accounts.) You can also transfer Shared Items.

You can also use the Customize button (under each user name and under Shared Items) to build a customized list of the *specific* files and settings you want to transfer.

7. Click Next.

If you're saving to a disk, the "Save your files and settings for transfer" screen appears. If you want to password-protect your saved files and settings, type a password twice. Click Save, and then choose a location to save your files and settings (a hard disk, a flash drive, or even a network location).

8. Click Next.

The progress screen appears. The wizard proceeds to search your drives for the necessary information and send it to the location you specified. If you saved your files and settings to an external disk, flash drive, or network location, Windows Easy Transfer tells you where it saved it; click Next.

9. Click Close.

Phase 2: Restoring the Files

To transfer the settings and files, use the following procedure.

If you're doing a clean install, make sure you've put the Windows Easy Transfer file somewhere safe. For maximum peace of mind, you should also have a separate backup of all your files somewhere, because the clean install deletes everything on your computer before installing Windows.

If you're moving files to a second computer and are using the transfer cable or network method, you'll have been instructed to start this procedure on your new computer in step 5 of Phase 1.

1. **Click Start→All Programs→Accessories→System Tools→Windows Easy Transfer.**

   Windows Easy Transfer appears.

2. **Click Next. On the "What Do You Want to Use" screen, specify how you want to transfer the files and settings.**

   You can choose from a link to another computer using a direct cable or network connection, or to a flash drive or external hard disk (or network location).

3. **Click the option you want to use, and click Next.**

   The "Which computer are you using now?" screen appears.

4. **Click "This is my new computer."**

   If you're using the network method or transfer cable, the "Do you need to install Windows Easy Transfer" screen appears. Click "I already installed it on my old computer." Click Next and (if you're using the network) enter the key from step 5 of Phase 1.

   If you're using a flash drive, external disk, or network location, you're asked whether Windows Easy Transfer has already saved your old files. Click Yes and choose the location where you saved the files. The location you specify could be a path to a hard drive or flash driver folder, or a network location. (See page 58 for details on paths.) Click Open.

WORKAROUND WORKSHOP

When No Windows DVD Comes With Your PC

It's becoming increasingly common for computer manufacturers to sell you a new PC without including an operating system CD-ROM. (Every 11 cents counts, right?) The machine has Windows installed on it—but if there's no installation CD or DVD, what are you supposed to do in case of emergency?

Instead of a physical Windows disc, the manufacturer provides something called a *restore image*—a CD-ROM or DVD (or more than one) containing a complete copy of the operating system *and* other software that was installed on the computer at the factory. If the contents of the computer's hard disk are ever lost or damaged, you can, in theory, restore the computer to its factory configuration by running a program on the restore image.

Of course, this image is a bit-by-bit facsimile of the computer's hard disk drive, and therefore, restoring it to your computer *completely erases* whatever files are already on the drive. You can't restore your computer from an image disk without losing all the data you saved since you got the computer from the manufacturer. (Talk about a good argument for keeping regular backups!)

Furthermore, some manufacturers install a copy of these installation files right on the hard drive, so you won't even have to hunt for your CDs.

---

5. **Click Next.**

Now verify the names of the accounts you're transferring to the new computer. You can either transfer the files and settings into existing people's accounts, or create new accounts (click Advanced Options to change the defaults). If you let it transfer the settings into existing accounts, you'll *replace* their current files and settings. Of course, if this is a fresh install of Windows, those people probably don't have many settings or files yet.

6. **Click Transfer.**

The wizard copies the files and applies the saved settings on the new computer.

7. **Click Finish to close the wizard.**

Windows Easy Transfer now reports how the transfer went. If Windows 7 couldn't restore some of your settings, you'll have to recreate these settings manually. You can also see a list of what was transferred and a list of suggested programs you might want to install. Depending on the settings you saved, you may have to log off and log on again before the transferred settings take effect.

Fun with the Registry

Occasionally, in books, articles, and conversations, you'll hear hushed references to something called the Windows Registry—usually accompanied by either knowing or bewildered glances.

The Registry is your PC's master database of preference settings. For example, most of the programs in the Control Panel are nothing more than graphic front ends that, behind the scenes, modify settings in the Registry.

The Registry also keeps track of almost every program you install, every peripheral device you add, every account you create, your networking configuration, and much more. If you've noticed that shortcut menus and Properties dialog boxes look different depending on what you're clicking, you have the Registry to thank. It knows what you're clicking and what options should appear as a result. In all, there are thousands and thousands of individual settings in your Registry.

As you can well imagine, therefore, the Registry is an extremely important cog in the Windows machine. That's why Windows marks most of your Registry files as hidden and non-deletable, and why it makes a Registry backup every single time you shut down the PC. If the Registry gets randomly edited, a grisly plague of problems may descend upon your machine. Granted, the System Restore feature (described in this appendix) can extract you from such a mess, but now you know why the Registry is rarely even mentioned to novices.

In fact, Microsoft would just as soon you not even know about the Registry. There's not a word about it in the basic user guides, and about the only information you'll find about it in the Help and Support center is a page that says, "Ordinarily, you do not need to make changes to the registry. The registry contains complex system information that is vital to your computer, and an incorrect change to your registry could render your computer inoperable."

Still, the Registry is worth learning about. You shouldn't edit it arbitrarily, but if you follow a step-by-step "recipe" from a book, magazine, Web site, or technical-help agent, you shouldn't fear opening the Registry to make a few changes.

Why would you want to? Because there are lots of Windows settings that you can't change in any other way, as you'll see in the following pages.

Meet Regedit

Windows comes with a built-in program for editing Registry entries, a little something called (what else?) the Registry editor. (There are dozens of other Registry-editing, Registry-fixing, and Registry-maintenance programs, too—both commercial and shareware—but this one is already on your PC.)

As an advanced tool that Microsoft doesn't want falling into the wrong hands, the Registry editor has no Start-menu icon. You must fire it up by typing its name into the Start menu's search box. Type *regedit* to find the program; select it in the results list.

Authenticate yourself if necessary. After a moment, you see a window like Figure B-1.

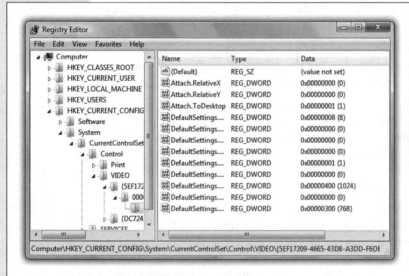

Figure B-1:
The Registry's settings are organized hierarchically; in fact, the Registry editor looks a lot like Windows Explorer. But there's no easy way to figure out which part of the Registry holds a particular setting or performs a particular function. It's like flying a plane that has no windows

The Big Five Categories

It turns out that Microsoft has arranged all those software settings into five broad categories. Microsoft calls them *root keys,* but they look and act like folders in a Windows Explorer window. You expand one of these folders (root keys) just as you would in Explorer, too, by clicking the little flippy triangle button beside its name.

The names of these five categories are not especially user-friendly:

- **HKEY_CLASSES_ROOT.** This root key stores all kinds of information about files: filename extensions, file types, shortcut menus, and so on.

Note: A number of Registry entries appear in more than one place, as live mirrors of each other, for convenience and clarity. Edit one, and you make a change in both places.

This root key, for example, is a pointer to the key at HKEY_LOCAL_MACHINE\SOFTWARE\Classes. (More on this slash notation below.)

- **HKEY_CURRENT_USER.** As you'd guess, here's where you'll find the settings pertaining to your account: your desktop arrangement, your wallpaper setting, and so on, plus information about connections to printers, cameras, and so on. (This key, too, is a live mirror—of the identical one in HKEY_USERS, described below.)

- **HKEY_LOCAL_MACHINE.** All about your PC and its copy of Windows. Drivers, security settings, hardware info, the works.

- **HKEY_USERS.** Here's where Windows stores the information about all the account holders (user profiles) on your PC, including the "Current_User's." You'll rarely be asked to edit this root key, since the good stuff—what applies to your own account—is in the CURRENT_USER key.

- **HKEY_CURRENT_CONFIG.** Most of this root key is made up of pointers to other places in the Registry. You'll rarely be asked to edit this one.

Keys and Values

If you expand one of these categories by clicking its flippy triangle, you see a long list of inner "folders," called *keys*. These are the actual settings that the Registry tracks, and that you can edit.

Some keys contain other keys, in fact. Keep clicking the flippy triangles until you find the subkey you're looking for.

In books, magazines, and tutorials on the Web, you'll often encounter references to particular Registry subkeys written out as a Registry path, like this:

HKEY_CURRENT_USER→Control Panel→Mouse

(You may see backslashes used instead of the arrows.) That instruction tells you to expand the HKEY_CURRENT_USER root key, expand Control Panel within it, and finally click the Mouse "folder." It works just like a folder path, like C:→Users→Chris→Desktop.

If you actually try this maneuver, you'll find, in the right half of the window, a bunch of keys named DoubleClickSpeed, MouseSpeed, MouseTrails, and so on. These should sound familiar, as they correspond to the options in the Mouse program of your Control Panel. (Figure B-2 clarifies this relationship.)

Each value usually contains either a number or a block of text. DoubleClickSpeed, for example, comes set at 500. In this case, that means 500 milliseconds between clicks, but each Registry value may refer to a different kind of unit.

Tip: Many of the Windows Explorer keyboard shortcuts also work in regedit. For example, once you've clicked a key, you can press the right or left arrow to reveal and hide its subkeys. You can also type the first letter of a subkey's name to highlight it in the left pane—same with a value's name in the right pane. And you can press the Backspace key to jump to the "parent" key, the one that contains the subkey.

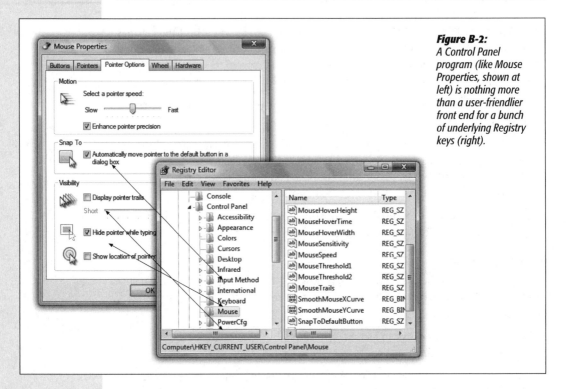

Figure B-2:
A Control Panel program (like Mouse Properties, shown at left) is nothing more than a user-friendlier front end for a bunch of underlying Registry keys (right).

Backing Up Key Values

In general, you won't go into the Registry unless you truly want to make a change. That's why the program is called regedit, not regviewer.

As you know, though, making the wrong change can botch up your copy of Windows—and regedit has no Undo command and no "Save change before closing?" message.

That's why it's essential to *back up* a Registry key—or even its entire root key—before you change it. Later, if the change you made doesn't work the way you'd hoped, you can restore the original.

To back up a key (including all its values and subkeys), just select it and then choose File→Export. Save the resulting key somewhere safe, like your desktop. Later, you can reinstate the key by double-clicking the .reg file you exported. (Or, if you're paid by the hour, open regedit, choose File→Import, and manually open the .reg file.)

Note: Importing a .reg file merges it with the data already in the Registry. Any values you edited will go back to their original versions, provided you haven't renamed them.

This means, for instance, that if you export a key, rename one of the values in that key, and then reimport the .reg file, the value you renamed will still be there, along with the value by its original name. In other words, a .reg file is a very good idea, but it's not a "get out of jail free card" that undoes all types of changes.

The only way to get a true Registry backup is to back up the Registry files themselves. Only the Backup and Restore program described on page 688 can do this for you. System Restore, described on page 695, can also restore your registry to a previous time.

Regedit Examples

Here are three typical regedit tweaks, spelled out for you step by step.

Encrypt/Decrypt from the Shortcut Menu

As you know from page 679, one of the perks of using Windows 7 (Professional, Enterprise, or Ultimate) is that you can encrypt files and folders, protecting them from people who try to open them from across the network or using a different account.

If you use this feature quite a bit, however, you'll quickly grow tired of opening the Properties box every time you want to encrypt something. Wouldn't it be much more convenient if the Encrypt and Decrypt commands were right there in the shortcut menu that appears when you right-click an icon?

Of course it would. To make it so, do this:

• **Navigate to:** HKEY_CURRENT_USER→Software→Microsoft→Windows→ CurrentVersion→Explorer→Advanced.

Now, for this trick, you're going to need a key that doesn't actually exist yet. Fortunately, it's very easy to create a new key. In this case, just right-click the Advanced "folder," and then, from the shortcut menu, choose New→DWORD (32-bit) Value. You see "New Value #1" appear in the right side of the window, ready to be renamed; type *EncryptionContextMenu*, and then press Enter.

Tip: The birth of a new Registry entry is a good opportunity to name it, but you can rename any value or key at any time, just the way you'd rename a file icon. That is, you can open the renaming rectangle by right-clicking or by pressing F2.

• **Double-click this value on the right side:** EncryptionContextMenu.

• **Make this change:** In the "Value data" box, type *1*.

- **Wrap up:** Click OK and quit regedit. When you right-click any file or folder icon, you'll see the new Encrypt command in the shortcut menu. (Or, if it's already encrypted, you'll see a Decrypt command.)

A Really, Really Clean Desktop

Windows XP used to nag you every now and then to get unused icons off your desktop. (Mercifully, the Desktop Cleanup Wizard isn't part of Windows 7.)

But why stop there? If you've got the world's most beautiful desktop wallpaper set up, you might not want any icons marring its majesty.

If you think about it, you can get by just fine without a single icon on the desktop. The Computer and similar icons are waiting in your Start menu. You can put things into the Recycle Bin without dragging them to its icon. (Just highlight icons and then press the Delete key, for instance.)

The following regedit hack doesn't actually remove anything from your desktop. It just hides them. You can still work with the icons on your desktop by using Windows Explorer to view the contents of your Desktop folder, for example.

- **Navigate to:** HKEY_CURRENT_USER→Software→Microsoft→Windows→CurrentVersion→Policies.

- **Right-click the Policies folder:** From the shortcut menu, choose New→Key, and rename it to Explorer.

- **Right-click the Explorer folder:** Choose New→Binary Value, and name the new value NoDesktop. Double-click this value.

- **Make this change:** In the "Value data" box, type *01 00 00 00*. (Regedit puts the spaces in automatically.) Click OK.

- **Wrap up:** Click OK, quit regedit, and then log out and log in. (To reverse the procedure, just delete the NoDesktop value you created, and then log out and log in.)

Tip: If you find your pulse racing with the illicit thrill of making tweaks to your system, why stop here? You can find hundreds more regedit "recipes" in books, computer magazines, and Web sites. A quick search of *"regedit hacks"* in Google will unearth plenty of them.

Slow Down the Animations

Windows 7's window animations and other eye candy are very cool. But they happen fast; Microsoft didn't want them to get in your way. That's a shame if you want to study the visual-FX majesty of these animations in more detail.

If you make this regedit tweak, though, you can make the window animation slow down on command—specifically, whenever you're pressing the Shift key.

- **Navigate to:** HKEY_CURRENT_USER→Software→Microsoft→Windows→DWM.

- **Right-click** the DWM folder. From the shortcut menu, choose New→DWORD (32-bit) Value. Name the new value *AnimationsShiftKey*.

- **Double-click this value on the right side:** In the "Value data" box for the Animations ShiftKey entry you just made, type *1*. Click OK.

- **Wrap up:** Quit regedit and then log out and log in. (To reverse the procedure, just delete the AnimationsShiftKey value you created, and then log out and log in.)

To see the effects in slow motion, press the Shift key just before they start to occur. For example, Shift-click a window's Close box—and watch in amazement as it *slowwwwly* fades into total transparency, like a ghost returning to the world beyond.

Or summon the Flip 3D effect (page 70) by pressing ⊞+Tab. Then, once the "deck of cards" window effect appears, hold down Shift as you tap your arrow keys, or click windows, to shuffle through them.

Where'd It Go?

A s the saying goes, you can't make an omelette without breaking a few eggs. And on the road to Windows 7, Microsoft broke enough eggs to make a Texan soufflé. Features got moved, renamed, and ripped out completely.

If you're fresh from Windows Vista, Windows XP, or even earlier versions of Windows, you might spend your first few days with Windows 7 wondering where things went. Here's a handy cheat sheet: features that aren't in Windows 7 (or aren't where you think they should be).

- **"Add or Remove Programs" control panel.** The Control Panel applet called Programs and Features performs the software-removal function (Start→Control Panel→Programs→Programs and Features). No Control Panel applet remains to *add* software, because all software these days comes with its *own* installer.

- **Calendar.** Windows Calendar, part of Vista, is gone now. The only calendars now are the one built into Windows Live Mail (Chapter 12) and the online Windows Live Calendar site (Chapter 13).

- **CDF protocol.** Gone.

- **Classic Start menu is gone.** You can make the Start menu *look* like the ugly old squared-off one, but a lot of the old features of it are gone for good (expanding folders by pointing without clicking, opening folders by double-clicking, and opening multiple programs by Shift-clicking, for example).

- **Clipbook Viewer.** This handy multi-Clipboard feature is no longer in Win7.

- **Complete PC Backups** (from Vista) have been renamed "system images," and they're alive and well in Windows 7.

- **Contacts.** This Vista address-book entity is gone. Now the only address book is the one in Windows Live Mail (Chapter 12).

- **Contacts gadget.** This one's gone, too.

- **Desktop cleanup wizard has gone away.** You can't actually pretend that you'll miss it, can you?

- **DirectAnimation.** This technology has been removed from Windows 7.

- **Discuss pane.** This Windows XP panel did nothing unless some technically proficient administrator set up something called a SharePoint Portal Server—a corporate software kit that permits chat sessions among employees. Anyway, it's no longer in Windows.

- **Documents & Settings folder.** Now called Users.

- **DVD Maker.** Its full name is Windows Live DVD Maker, and it's now part of the downloadable Windows Live Essentials (Chapter 7).

- **Explorer bar.** Gone.

- **Favorites folder.** Favorites are still around, in the sense of bookmarks from Internet Explorer. But the Favorites *toolbar* at the desktop is gone. But no grieving is necessary; you can create exactly the same effect with the Links toolbar or one you create yourself (page 116).

- **File types.** In Windows XP, you could define new file types and associate them with programs yourself, using the File Types tab in the Folder Options dialog box. In Windows 7, the File Types tab is gone. There's a similar dialog box now (page 243), but it doesn't let you make up your own file types and associations. It doesn't let you define custom secondary actions, either, or ask Explorer to reveal filename extensions only for specific file types.

- **Files & Settings Transfer Wizard.** Renamed Windows Easy Transfer (Appendix A).

- **Filmstrip view (Explorer windows).** Replaced by the any-size-you-like icon view feature.

- **Find Target.** This function, in a file shortcut's Properties dialog box, has been renamed Open File Location.

- **Gopher.** Removed.

- **Hardware profiles.** Removed. Nobody uses laptop docking stations anymore!

- **High performance power plan, for laptops, is no longer listed in the Power icon on the taskbar. It's available, though, if you open the Power control panel.**

- **HyperTerminal.** This old-time, text-only terminal program is gone, along with the BBS systems that were once its *raison d'être*.

- **Image toolbar (Internet Explorer).** Removed. Most of the commands that were on this auto-appearing IE 6 toolbar, though—Save Picture, E-mail Picture, Set as

Background, and so on—are now in the shortcut menu that appears when you right-click any picture on the Web.

- **Indexing Service.** This technical, generally ignored search option has been reborn in the glorious form of Windows Search (Chapter 3).

- **Inkball.** There are some good Windows 7 games, but Inkball is gone.

- **IP over FireWire.** Removed.

- **Macintosh services.** The software that offered file and print sharing via the Apple-Talk protocol (which even Apple has abandoned) is gone.

- **Media toolbar.** The Windows Media Player toolbar is the same idea: It lets you control your music playback right from the taskbar.

- **Meeting Space.** This was Vista's replacement for NetMeeting, but now Meeting Space is gone, too. If you want to share someone's screen, use Remote Assistance or Remote Desktop. If you want to have audio or video calls, use Windows Live Messenger.

- **Movie Maker.** Its full name is Windows Live Movie Maker, and it's now part of the downloadable Windows Live Essentials (page 265).

- **My Network Places.** You no longer have to open a special window to see the other computers on your network in Windows 7. They're listed right there in the Navigation pane at the left side of every Explorer window.

- **NetMeeting.** Removed. Well, there's always Skype.

- **Notes gadget** has been reborn as the Sticky Notes program.

- **Offline browsing/Offline favorites (Internet Explorer).** In Windows XP, you could right-click a Web page's name in your Favorites menu and store it for later perusal when you were no longer online—complete with whatever pages were linked to it. Internet Explorer would even update such pages automatically each time you got back online. This feature is gone from Internet Explorer 8.

- **Outlook Express.** Now called Windows Live Mail, and described in Chapter 12.

- **"Parent folder" button.** In Windows XP, you could click this button to go up one folder (that is, to see the folder that enclosed the current one). It's gone in Windows 7, although you can perform the same function by pressing Alt+↑ (or by clicking one of the folder names in the Address bar's "bread-crumb trail").

- **Parental controls.** There are some, but the Web filtering and activity reporting are no longer built into Windows. They're now part of a Windows Live Essentials service called Windows Live Family Safety (page 393).

- **Password protecting a .zip archive.** Removed. In the window of any open .zip file, there's still a column that indicates whether or not each file is password-protected—but there's no way to add such a password yourself.

- **Phishing filter,** the Internet Explorer feature that shields you from phony banking sites, has been renamed SmartScreen filter.

- **Photo Gallery.** Its full name is Windows Live Photo Gallery. It doesn't come built into Windows 7, but it's an easy download as part of Windows Live Essentials (page 265).

- **Pinball.** Gone, although there are several good new games that come with Windows 7.

- **Pointer themes.** You can make your cursor bigger or smaller in Windows 7, but the fun cursor designs like 3D-Bronze, 3D-White, Conductor, Dinosaur, Hands 1, Hands 2, Variations, and Windows Animated have been killed off by the No-Fun Committee.

- **PowerToys.** Microsoft seems to have lost its enthusiasm for these freebie software goody-bag items; they disappeared back in Windows Vista.

- **Quick Launch toolbar.** Since the entire *taskbar* is pretty much a giant Quick Launch toolbar now, Microsoft took out all visible evidence of the Quick Launch toolbar. But you can resurrect it with a quick hack. See page 118.

- **Reversi.** No longer part of the Windows game suite.

- **Run command.** It may seem to be missing from the Start menu, but you can put it right back (page 43). Or you can just press ⊞+R to call it up.

- **Search assistant (Internet Explorer).** Replaced by the new Search bar at the upper-right corner of the Internet Explorer window.

- **Search pane.** Gone. But the new Start menu Search box (Chapter 3) is infinitely superior.

- **SerialKeys.** This feature for specialized gadgets for the disabled is no longer supported.

- **Sidebar.** In Vista, the small, floating, single-purpose apps known as *gadgets* hung out in a panel called the Sidebar. Well, the Sidebar is gone, but the gadgets live on (right-click the desktop; choose Gadgets).

- **Sortable column headings** in Explorer windows have gone away, except for Details view. That is, there's no longer a row of column headings (Name, Date, Size, Kind...) across the top of every window that you can click to sort the window—except, as noted, in Details view.

- **Spades.** This XP card game is gone—but Hearts is here. Close enough, right?

- **Stacking,** as an activity for organizing similar files in any Explorer window, arrived in Vista and then departed in Windows 7. (You can clump the contents of library windows only, and only by a few criteria.)

- **Startup Hardware Profiles.** Removed.

- **Stocks gadget.** Removed, although plenty of similar gadgets are available in the Gadgets gallery online.

- **Taskbar dragging.** You can no longer drag the taskbar's top edge off the screen to hide it manually. You can't drag the taskbar to the middle of screen anymore, either. And you can't drag a folder to edge of screen to turn it into a toolbar. (One guess: Too many people were doing this stuff *accidentally* and then getting frustrated.)

- **Telnet.** Removed—or so it seems. Fortunately, you can restore it using the "Turn Windows Features on and Off" feature described on page 253; select Telnet Client.

- **Tip of the Day.** No longer part of Windows. Microsoft must expect you to get your tips from computer books now.

- **TweakUI.** Not available for Windows 7. But there are several billion freeware and shareware programs available to take on the task of making tweaky little changes to the look of Windows.

- **Wallpaper.** Now called Desktop Background. (Right-click the desktop; from the shortcut menu, choose Personalize.)

- **Web Publishing Wizard.** Gone.

- **What's This? button in dialog boxes.** This little link is gone from Windows dialog boxes, probably because it didn't work in most of them. Now, if help is available in a dialog box, it lurks behind the ? button.

- **Windows Address Book.** Gone. The only address book left in Windows now is the one that's built into Windows Live Mail—and even that doesn't come with Windows. It's a free download, though (Chapter 12).

- **Windows Calendar.** This Vista program is gone now. The only calendars now are the one built into Windows Live Mail (Chapter 12) and the online Windows Live Calendar site (Chapter 13).

- **Windows Components Wizard.** Now called the Windows Features dialog box (page 253).

- **Windows DVD Maker.** Its full name is Windows Live DVD Maker, and it's now part of the downloadable Windows Live Essentials (page 265).

- **Windows Mail.** Reborn as Windows Live Mail (Chapter 12).

- **Windows Media Player toolbar** is gone. Now Media Player's taskbar icon sprouts basic commands (although it lacks the old volume slider).

- **Windows Messenger.** Microsoft's chat program no longer comes preinstalled in Windows, thanks to antitrust legal trouble the company encountered. It's an easy download, though, as part of the Windows Live Essentials suite described at the beginning of Chapter 7.

- **Windows Movie Maker.** Its full name is Windows Live Movie Maker, and it's now part of the downloadable Windows Live Essentials (page 265).

- **Windows Picture and Fax Viewer.** This old program's functions have been split. Now you view pictures in Windows Photo Viewer (or, better yet, the free Windows Live Photo Gallery), and faxes in Windows Fax and Scan.

- **Windows Ultimate Extras.** You no longer get special bonus apps as Ultimate-edition exclusives.

- **XBM images.** Gone.

The Master Keyboard Shortcut List

H ere it is, by popular, frustrated demand: The master list of every secret (or not-so-secret) keystroke in Windows 7. Clip and post to your monitor (unless, of course, you got this book from the library).

Windows Explorer keyboard shortcuts

To do this	Press this key
Open a new window	Ctrl+N
Close the current window	Ctrl+W
Create a new folder	Ctrl+Shift+N
Display the bottom/top of the active window	End/Home
Maximize or minimize the active window	F11
Rotate a picture clockwise	Ctrl+period (.)
Rotate a picture counterclockwise	Ctrl+comma (,)
Display all subfolders under the selected folder	Num Lock+* on numeric keypad
Display the contents of the selected folder	Num Lock+plus (+) on numeric keypad
Collapse the selected folder	Num Lock+minus (-) on numeric keypad
Collapse the current selection (if expanded), or select parent folder	←
Open the Properties dialog box for selected item	Alt+Enter
Display the preview pane	Alt+P

Back to the previous folder	Alt+← or Backspace
Display the current selection (if it's collapsed), or select the first subfolder	→
Next folder	Alt+→
Open the parent folder	Alt+↑
Display all folders above the selected folder	Ctrl+Shift+E
Enlarge/shrink file and folder icons	Ctrl+mouse scroll wheel
Select the address bar	Alt+D
Select the Search box	Ctrl+E, Ctrl+F

General keyboard shortcuts

Open the Start menu	⊞ or Ctrl+Esc
Help	F1
Copy the selected item	Ctrl+C (or Ctrl+Insert)
Cut the selected item	Ctrl+X
Paste the selected item	Ctrl+V (or Shift+Insert)
Undo an action	Ctrl+Z
Redo an action	Ctrl+Y
Delete the selected item and move it to the Recycle Bin	Delete (or Ctrl+D)
Delete the selected item without moving it to the Recycle Bin first	Shift+Delete
Rename the selected item	F2
Move the cursor to the beginning of the next word	Ctrl+→
Move the cursor to the beginning of the previous word	Ctrl+←
Move the cursor to the beginning of the next paragraph	Ctrl+↓
Move the cursor to the beginning of the previous paragraph	Ctrl+↑
Select a block of text	Ctrl+Shift with an arrow key
Select more than one item in a window, or select text within a document	Shift+any arrow key
Select multiple individual items in a window or on the desktop	Ctrl + any arrow key + space bar
Select all items in a document or window	Ctrl+A
Search for a file or folder	F3
Display properties for the selected item	Alt+Enter

Open a menu	Alt+underlined letter
"Click" a menu command (or other underlined command)	Alt+underlined letter
Make the menu bar appear	F10
Open the next menu to the right, or open a submenu	→
Open the next menu to the left, or close a submenu	←
View the folder one level up in Windows Explorer	Alt+↑
Cancel the current task	Esc
Open Task Manager	Ctrl+Shift+Esc
Prevent the CD from automatically playing	Shift when you insert a CD
Switch the input language when multiple input languages are enabled	Left Alt+Shift
Switch the keyboard layout when multiple keyboard layouts are enabled	Ctrl+Shift
Change the reading direction of text in right-to-left reading languages	Ctrl+right Shift or Ctrl+left Shift

Window and Program-Switching Keyboard Shortcuts

Close the window	Alt+F4
Open the shortcut menu for the active window	Alt+space bar
Close the document (in apps that let you have multiple documents open)	Ctrl+F4
Switch between open programs	Alt+Tab
Use the arrow keys to switch between open programs	Ctrl+Alt+Tab
Cycle through programs on the taskbar by using Flip 3D	⊞+Tab
Use the arrow keys to cycle through programs by using Flip 3D	Ctrl+⊞+Tab
Cycle through programs in the order in which they were opened	Alt+Esc
Cycle through screen elements in a window or on the desktop	F6
Display the address bar list in Windows Explorer	F4
Display the shortcut menu for the selected item	Shift+F10
Refresh the active window	F5 (or Ctrl+R)

⊞-Key Shortcuts

Open or close the Start menu	⊞
Open System Properties dialog box	⊞+Pause
Display the desktop	⊞+D
Minimize all windows	⊞+M
Restore minimized windows to the desktop	⊞+Shift+M
Open Computer window	⊞+E
Search for a file or folder	⊞+F
Search for computers (if you're on a network)	Ctrl+⊞+F
Lock your computer or switch users	⊞+L
Open the Run dialog box	⊞+R
Cycle through programs on the taskbar	⊞+T
Open the first, second (etc.) program pinned to the taskbar	⊞+1, ⊞+2, etc.
Open another window in the first, second (etc.) pinned taskbar program	Shift+⊞+1, Shift+⊞+2, etc.
Switch to the last window in first, second (etc.) program pinned to the taskbar	Ctrl+⊞+1, Ctrl+⊞+2, etc.
Open a jump list for the first, second (etc.) program pinned to the taskbar	Alt+⊞+1, Alt+⊞+2, etc.
Cycle through open programs using Flip 3D	⊞+Tab
Use arrow keys to cycle through open programs using Flip 3D	Ctrl+⊞+Tab
Switch to the program that displayed a message in the notification area	Ctrl+⊞+B
Preview the desktop	⊞+space bar
Maximize the window	⊞+↑
Maximize the window to the left side of the screen	⊞+←
Maximize the window to the right side of the screen	⊞+→
Minimize the window	⊞+
Minimize all but the active window	⊞+Home
Stretch the window to the top and bottom of the screen	⊞+Shift+↑
Move a window from one monitor to another	⊞+Shift+← or →
Choose an external-monitor/projector mode (like mirroring)	⊞+P
Cycle through gadgets	⊞+G

Open Ease of Access Center	■+U
Open Windows Mobility Center	■+X

Taskbar keyboard shortcuts

Open a program or another window in a program	Shift+click a taskbar button
Open a program as an administrator	Ctrl+Shift+click a taskbar button
Show the window menu for the program	Shift+right-click a taskbar button
Show the window menu for the group	Shift+right-click a grouped taskbar button
Cycle through the windows of the group	Ctrl+click a grouped taskbar button

Ease of Access keyboard shortcuts

Turn Filter Keys on and off	Right Shift for 8 seconds
Turn High Contrast on or off	Left Alt+Left Shift+PrtScn (or PrtScn)
Turn Mouse Keys on or off	Left Alt+Left Shift+Num Lock
Turn Sticky Keys on or off	Shift five times
Turn Toggle Keys on or off	Num Lock for 5 seconds
Open the Ease of Access Center	■+U

Dialog Box keyboard shortcuts

Move forward through tabs	Ctrl+Tab
Move back through tabs	Ctrl+Shift+Tab
Move forward through options	Tab
Move back through options	Shift+Tab
Perform the command (or select the option) that goes with that letter	Alt+underlined letter
Replaces clicking the mouse for many selected commands	Enter

Magnifier keyboard shortcuts

Zoom in or out	■+plus (+) or minus (-)
Preview the desktop in full-screen mode	Ctrl+Alt+space bar
Switch to full-screen mode	Ctrl+Alt+F
Switch to lens mode	Ctrl+Alt+L
Switch to docked mode	Ctrl+Alt+D
Invert colors	Ctrl+Alt+I
Pan in the direction of the arrow keys	Ctrl+Alt+arrow keys
Resize the lens	Ctrl+Alt+R
Exit Magnifier	■+Esc

Remote Desktop Connection keyboard shortcuts

Move between programs, left to right	Alt+Page Up
Move between programs, right to left	Alt+Page Down
Cycle through programs in the order they were started in	Alt+Insert
Open Start menu	Alt+Home
Switch between a window and full screen	Ctrl+Alt+Break
Display the Windows Security dialog box	Ctrl+Alt+End
Display the system menu	Alt+Delete
Place a copy of the active window, within the client, on the Terminal server clipboard (same as pressing Alt+PrtScn on a local computer)	Ctrl+Alt+minus (-) on the numeric keypad
Place a copy of the entire client window area on the Terminal server clipboard (same as pressing PrtScn on a local computer)	Ctrl+Alt+plus (+) on the numeric keypad
"Tab" out of the Remote Desktop controls to a control in the host program (for example, a button or a text box)	Ctrl+Alt+→ or ←

Index

Index

WINDOWS 7: THE MISSING MANUAL

B

Colophon

The book was written and edited in Microsoft Word, whose revision-tracking feature made life far easier as drafts were circulated from author to technical and copy editors. The steps in thie book were tested on machines from Dell, HP, Toshiba, and Apple. (Yes, Apple: Windows 7 runs amazingly fast under Boot Camp, or even Parallels, on a Mac laptop.)

SnagIt (*www.techsmith.com*) captured the illustrations; Adobe Photoshop CS4 and Macromedia Freehand MX were called in as required for touching them up.

The book was designed and laid out in Adobe InDesign CS4 on a MacBook Pro, and Mac Pro. The fonts used include Formata (as the sans-serif family) and Minion (as the serif body face). To provide symbols like ⊞ and ⏻, custom fonts were created using Macromedia Fontographer.

The book was generated as an Adobe Acrobat PDF file for proofreading and indexing, and final transmission to the printing plant.

Get even more for your money.

Join the O'Reilly Community, and register the O'Reilly books you own. It's free, and you'll get:

- 40% upgrade offer on O'Reilly books
- Membership discounts on books and events
- Free lifetime updates to electronic formats of books
- Multiple ebook formats, DRM FREE
- Participation in the O'Reilly community
- Newsletters
- Account management
- 100% Satisfaction Guarantee

Signing up is easy:

1. **Go to: oreilly.com/go/register**
2. **Create an O'Reilly login.**
3. **Provide your address.**
4. **Register your books.**

Note: English-language books only

To order books online:

oreilly.com/order_new

For questions about products or an order:

orders@oreilly.com

To sign up to get topic-specific email announcements and/or news about upcoming books, conferences, special offers, and new technologies:

elists@oreilly.com

For technical questions about book content:

booktech@oreilly.com

To submit new book proposals to our editors:

proposals@oreilly.com

Many O'Reilly books are available in PDF and several ebook formats. For more information:

oreilly.com/ebooks

O'REILLY®

Spreading the knowledge of innovators   www.oreilly.com

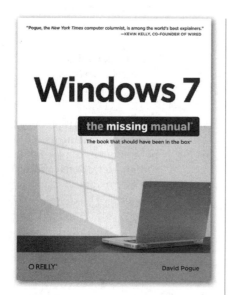